Understanding the Environment

KENNETH E. F. WATT

University of California, Davis

Allyn and Bacon, Inc.
Boston · London · Sydney · Toronto

Library of Congress Cataloging in Publication Data

Watt, Kenneth E. F., 1929–
   Understanding the environment.

   Includes bibliographies and index.

   1. Environmental policy. 2. Human ecology. 3. International economic relations. I. Title
HC79.E5W38   333.7   81–8050
ISBN 0–205–07265–8   AACR2

Printed in the United States of America
10 9 8 7 6 5 4 3 2 1   87 86 85 84 83 82

This book is dedicated to
George David,
who has drawn upon his training in ecology,
economics, and psychiatry to develop an
integrated systems philosophy that links
resources, capital, money, and human
behavior.

CONTENTS

FOREWORD

by Paul R. Ehrlich, Bing Professor of Population Studies, Stanford University

A basic characteristic of environmental problems is that they are cross-disciplinary; and it is this characteristic that so often makes them difficult to solve. In many cases their "scientific" content is relatively trivial. For example, most high school students readily grasp the notion that continued human population growth is sure to exceed the carrying capacity of our planet and result in environmental disasters. But there is an awesome gap between grasping the essence of the population problem and finding a way to solve it. To understand the reasons that the human birth rate is greater than the human death rate one must venture into such areas as economics, anthropology, sociology, political science, psychology, human physiology, and the history of medicine.

If students are to be properly prepared to deal with the escalating series of crises that are now upon us, they must be freed of the notion that proper environmental problem solving can be undertaken within the narrow confines of a single discipline. They must be trained to look for multiple causes and connections and to sort them out, defining major paths of influence and disregarding the trivial.

Understanding the Environment is a book with which to start that preparation. Its author, Kenneth E. F. Watt, is a brilliant ecologist, a man with an international reputation for his work on animal populations. But Professor Watt has gone far beyond the borders of his own discipline in his attack on the problems that bedevil our planet; he has, for example, published an exciting book on economics and has done distinguished work on resource management. Students using this book will benefit greatly from Watt's imaginative and rigorous approach, which so distinguishes *Understanding the Environment* from many texts in this area.

PREFACE

This book reflects the increasingly holistic perspective of environmental literature in the last decade. This literature is no longer largely restricted to discussion of resource, pollution, and population problems. More and more, it seeks fundamental explanations for environmental problems in economics, government and politics, our culture, and inadequacies of our information collection and dissemination system. I also address the issue raised in some writing, that environmental problems are traceable to inherent biological limitations of the human sensory system.

Accordingly, the first two parts of the book, which outline the causes of environmental problems, present a considerably wider array of topics than would have been expected as recently as 1972. While the problems of the physical environment, nonrenewable and renewable resources, and human population are treated at some length, there are additional chapters on economics, politics and government, culture, and information.

Part 3 and a number of other chapters in the book are motivated by another idea that is as old as civilization, but has only become popular again in the last decade. Fundamental explanations for environmental problems are not to be discovered within any traditional discipline but rather in the interstices and linkages between disciplines.

Also, explanations necessarily involve an international (as opposed to an intranational) perspective. The availability of energy at a particular price in the United States now depends on economic analysis by Saudi Arabia and agricultural policy in the Soviet Union, which determines how much grain they will buy from us. That, in turn determines the foreign exchange we have with which to purchase crude oil. The price of houses in the United States is affected by U.S. national energy policy via multiple causal pathways.

Part 4, which deals with the consequences of environmental systems dysfunction, includes chapters on social, economic, and political problems and history, as well as pollution and environmental degradation. Some reviewers have identified the historical chapter as the most important innovation in this book.

Part 5, on methods of solution, deals not only with economic and legal approaches, but also with a variety of institutional innovations. It is becoming widely recognized that we must have major changes in policy-making, conflict resolution, and the design of regulatory procedures. Part 5 deals with new ideas coming into the literature about these issues.

Part 6 deals with the future and demonstrates that major changes in the approach of our country to environmental matters are inevitable.

I argue that environmental problems can and probably will be dealt with by major changes in the economy, government, and most importantly, the cultural belief system. A drastic reorganization of American society in the next two decades is inevitable, incredible as that may seem. The one impossible future scenario is continued development of the pattern of social organization of the last two centuries. This has resulted in extraordinarily high rates of resource consumption per capita. More recently, with depletion of some of our cheap resources, it meant increasingly large movements of American money to other countries to compensate for a growing disparity between American consumption and production.

Environmental studies have been bedeviled by a multiplicity of facts and theories, some of which contradict each other. Also, much of the literature of environmental studies treats issues that are tangential or peripheral to the central issues. Therefore, this book attempts to be comprehensive yet digestible by concentrating on hard facts—only those theories unarguably true—and central, basic issues, rather than the cosmetics of the environment.

The material is designed for second-year college students, and is intended as either a survey course on the environment, or the introductory course to an environmental studies sequence. At Davis, the students enrolled in this course range from sophomores to seniors, and come from departments as diverse as botany, zoology, agricultural economics, economics, civil, electrical, mechanical and agricultural engineering, environmental policy analysis and planning, architecture and urban planning, landscape horticulture, environmental planning and management, international agricultural development, renewable natural resources, wildlife and fisheries biology, and economic history. The material is presented in sixty hours of lectures over two quarters, and is supplemented with hundreds of slides.

The manuscript has been carefully edited by a number of the author's students at Davis as well as by reviewers at other institutions, to ensure that the level of conceptual and verbal sophistication matches the level of comprehension of the intended audience. No prerequisites in other college-level subjects are assumed. However, the student editors do feel that a reader would be aided by the intellectual maturity developed in the freshman year, and by attention to environmental issues and related matters in newspapers and magazines.

Many people have read all or part of the manuscript and offered useful suggestions. I am also extremely indebted to all the scholars who went out of their way to introduce me to new developments in their fields. Certainly, no human being working alone could have begun to monitor the range of subjects treated in this text; that fact alone underscores the magnitude of my indebtedness to others. The following were particularly important in suggesting improvements, or bringing papers or books to my attention: David Deamer, Theodore Foin, William J. Hamilton III, Thomas Powell, and Arthur Shapiro (all of the University of California at Davis); Walter Auburn (California Conservation Corps); Richard Bellman (University of Southern California); Arthur Borror (University of New Hampshire); Reid Bryson (University of Wisconsin, Madison); James Conkey (Western Nevada Community College); Camille Courtney, George David, and Paul Ehrlich (Stanford); Kenneth Hammond (University of Colorado); Garrett Hardin (University of California at Santa Barbara); C. S. Holling (University of British Columbia); Stirling Keeley; Nathan Keyfitz (Harvard); Paul Nowak (University of Michigan); Jeremy Sabloff (University of Utah); and Lawrence Slobodkin (New York State University at Stoney Brook).

Also, many people have put in a great deal of effort to make this book attractive and to increase its usefulness as a tool for study. I am particularly indebted to Joseph E. Burns, Gary Folven and Wendy Ritger of Allyn and Bacon, Inc.; Nancy Farrell, a developmental editor; and Sarah Doyle and Judith Gimple of Bywater Production Services, for editing, design, production and photo research.

However, the universal caveat applies: all errors are the responsibility of the author alone.

I Introduction

Part I examines the nature of environmental problems using a number of case studies as illustrations. The first chapter introduces the basic outlines of the book; the second describes and explains some of the reasons people have difficulty understanding the problems.

Chapter 1 demonstrates that environmental problems typically originate in areas that may seem remote and unrelated: culture, the political system, and the economy. Chapters on these topics are included in Part II, on the components of environmental systems.

The first chapter also proves that understanding environmental problems requires us to work with mental models showing how many different types of factors affect each other. Part III describes such models. Chapter 1 shows that our view of environmental issues is affected by the availability, accuracy, and completeness of information, and the way in which the human mind perceives information detected by the sense organs. Chapter 2 expands on this theme. If there are defects with our information or perceptions of the environment, our approach to dealing with it and solving its problems may be inappropriate.

The first two chapters show that environmental problems are thoroughly interdisciplinary and multidisciplinary, and consequently the book, of necessity, weaves a tapestry out of skeins from many fields. This reflects state-of-the-art thinking in geophysics, climatology, energy policy, ecology, demography, economics, political science, cultural anthropology, history, strategic judgement theory (from psychology), decision analysis, futures research, and national and global computer systems analysis. In addition, some older bodies of literature have important implications for modern environmental studies. It is particularly important to incorporate classical cultural history, philosophy, and soil science into this integrated approach.

The first two chapters present such environmental problems as systemic phenomena made up of elements usually treated separately as physical, biological, social, cultural, and historical phenomena. This sets the tone for the book, which communicates a systems view using a formal conceptual model of environmental problems in harmony with the most modern thinking about systems theory. This model not only links many different types of factors, such as the physical environment and culture, but also specifically views the real world as being organized into hierarchical levels; city, country, the international trading and monetary system. This model is particularly useful for tracking the impacts of national environmental policies through that international system.

1 THE NATURE OF ENVIRONMENTAL PROBLEMS

All appearances are verily one's own concepts, self-contained in the mind, like reflections in a mirror.

Padma Sambhava, founder of Tantric Yoga (eighth century) quoted
in The Medium, the Mystic and the Physicist, *by Lawrence Leshan*
(New York: Viking Press, 1974).

MAIN THEMES OF THIS CHAPTER

Over the last several decades, an increasing number of environmental scientists and others have been attempting to communicate to the American public a sense of the perils of unwise environmental management policies. The success of this communication effort has been limited, and it has become apparent that there are serious impediments to public comprehension of the full nature of the environmental dilemma. What are these impediments?

Both the causes and the effects of environmental problems are different than generally recognized. Four characteristics of environmental problems have contributed to this confusion and have frustrated attempts at comprehension or solution.

1. Few people perceive the complete system of relationships by which economic policies affect environmental problems, and environmental phenomena affect the economy. Specifically, it is not widely understood that constant growth in use of resources inhibits, rather than promotes, growth in the economy and standard of living. Therefore, the political constituency for rational economic and environmental policies has been too small to be politically effective, because few people have grasped the full cost of bad policies.

2. The government's environmental policies have been unwise, because the constituency for wise policies was too small. Further, government has gone beyond the role of being a mediator between constituencies in environmental matters. Government often takes an active role itself and either distributes inaccurate information or suppresses accurate information.

3. Peoples' views on environmental matters are typically based on information rather than direct observation. This has made it possible for special interest groups to spread distorted views of environmental issues by manipulation of the availability or content of information.

4. The human brain has evolved not only to use information from the sense organs, but also to act as a filter. Otherwise, the sheer volume of incoming information would overwhelm us, and make it difficult to act in the interests of day-to-day survival. Information about problems developing slowly and irregularly, such as the Irish potato famine of 1845–1846 and the United States energy problem of the 1980s, tends to get filtered out of the conscious world-view of most people.

The effects of defective environmental policies in the United States have been very far-reaching. They included a decline in the purchasing power of our currency, an end to real growth in the standard of living after 1972, and a dangerous dependence on credit to maintain the illusion of economic health. Rather than allowing an adequate increase in the price of energy so as to encourage efficient use and domestic production, the country switched to dependence on importation of cheap crude oil from politically unstable foreign sources.

Political options are open to the society at large to deal effectively with our problems. Even if these options are not selected, individuals are not powerless: many of the most important choices concerning environmental strategies are choices made by individuals that impinge directly on their personal destinies.

THE PHILOSOPHY UNDERLYING THIS BOOK

Students in courses using this book realize quickly that the material is based on some kind of socio-economic-political philosophy. They are often tempted to make learning easier by trying to relate the book's content to some political viewpoint they know already, such as Democratic, Republican, Libertarian, Marxist, Liberal, Conservative, or Socialist. Since the beliefs underlying this book have a different origin than any of these political philosophies, any such attempt by students only introduces confusion rather than clarification.

Accordingly, it seems a good strategy to explain the origin and structure of my philosophy at the outset. Since the philosophy is based on conceptual models of systems, the book begins with explanations of "models" and "systems."

MODELS AND SYSTEMS

This book shows how environmental problems can be understood and solved using conceptual models of the practical world. Throughout, the meaning and significance of these conceptual models will be explained through description and example.

To illustrate the connection between the real environment and the conceptual models, consider how the notions of "model," "system," and "system component" develop from observations on carrots growing in the garden.

If we plant carrot seeds, the likely result is a crop of carrots. A perfectly reasonable question to ask is, "Why not plant twice as many seeds in the same-size plot, and get twice as many carrots?" If we conduct the experiment, we find that there are more carrots than in the previous season, but that the carrots are now on average much smaller. We then realize that an increase in the number of carrots per unit of ground area (that is, the carrot density) decreases the growth rate of individual carrot plants. The total weight of carrots does not double when the weight of seeds doubles, because of the compensatory decrease in the size of individual carrots.

We can make a more rigorous statement of these ideas in a little diagram, as in the top panel of Figure 1.1. In this diagram, an arrow from one box to another represents a causal pathway by which an influence travels from one box representing a cause to another representing an effect. The items in the boxes are variables, or quantities that can vary over a numerical range from low to high. If an increase in one variable causes an increase in another, the arrow is labeled with a positive sign. If an increase in one variable causes a decrease in another, the arrow is labeled with a negative sign.

The diagram constitutes our mental model of the set of causal pathways connecting the three variables. "System" describes the structure of the set of cause-effect pathways in the diagram. The four boxes in the diagram enclose the four components in the system. The system, as defined by the diagram, is affected by three things: the actual structure of the system in the real world, an arbitrary decision we make as to how much of the real world system we want to include in our mental model, and our knowledge of the real-world system. As our knowledge of the set of cause-effect relations in the real world increases, and we become aware of more system components, our mental model

of the system will become more complex (and more realistic). How much of the real world we include in our mental model of the system depends on the size and complexity of the real-world system we are trying to understand and manage. It is important to remember that the word "system" does not refer simply to a list of all the arrows in our mental model, but rather to the structure of the diagram.

To illustrate how systems models increase with further knowledge, we return to the carrot patch. Continued observation often reveals a large black, yellow, blue, and red butterfly with tails trailing from the hind wings flying around the carrot tops. This is the black swallowtail butterfly; on the carrot tops, it lays eggs that hatch into caterpillars that eat the carrot tops. It is clear that the greater the number of carrot plants we grow per square foot of garden, the greater will be the availability of food for the caterpillars, and hence, the greater will be the number of caterpillars. This increase in our knowledge of the real-world system can be expressed in a new, slightly larger system diagram, as in Panel 2 of Figure 1.1.

Finally, we might decide to observe all stages of the black swallowtail development by putting obviously mature caterpillars into little cages. They will make chrysalises, and after a time, butterflies will hatch from some of these. However not all of the chrysalises produce a butterfly: large orange wasps emerge from some of them. These are Ichneumonid parasites, whose larvae had completed eating up the butterfly larvae after the latter had formed their chrysalises.

We now have a new, enlarged mental model of the carrot system, which can be expressed as in the third panel of Figure 1.1.

This little example makes an important point about models of systems: they are critically dependent on our knowledge and our understanding of the real system. As our knowledge and understanding increase and

FIGURE 1.1
Different mental models of the carrot system: Panel 1, the system with carrots alone; Panel 2, the system with carrots and black swallowtail butterfly caterpillars; Panel 3, the system with carrots, black swallowtail butterfly caterpillars, and Ichneumonid parasites.

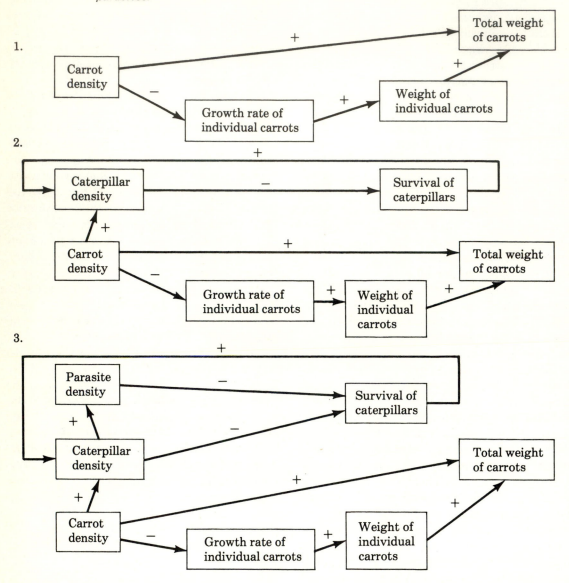

improve, we will add boxes (systems components) and arrrows (causal pathways) to our mental model of the system. We may even discover that we must eliminate some arrows, or connect them to a different cause, or a different effect. In other words, our mental model of the system describes something in our heads, not something in the real world. Hopefully, the two will correspond. As our knowledge grows, we change the way we bound the system: more components are enclosed by the system boundary. We could say that the system boundary has enlarged.

CHARACTERISTICS OF NATURAL SYSTEMS

Scientists and engineers who study natural systems notice certain characteristics that are almost invariably discovered. We can illustrate these by further consideration of the carrot patch. Why doesn't the volume of carrots in the soil increase until the soil has been replaced by a solid mass of carrot tissue? Why don't carrots spread out until they cover the earth? Why don't the black swallowtails eat up all the carrots? Why don't the parasites eat up all the black swallowtails? The answer to these questions for the carrots, as for all other natural systems, is that the system has mechanisms that maintain the stability of the system. That is, the natural world is regulated by laws of supply and demand, which function to balance the system. (20, 28).

To illustrate, if the number of black swallowtail caterpillars becomes unusually large, this will gradually lead to an increase in the number of parasites (this may take a few years). The increase in parasite numbers in turn leads to a decrease in the proportion of black swallowtail caterpillars that survive from one year to another. That is, if 3 percent survive at low swallowtail densities, only 1 percent of the swallowtails survive at high swallowtail densities, and this low percent survival (survival, for short) brings down the swallowtail density. This regulating mechanism by the parasites is indicated by the minus sign on the arrow from parasite density to survival of black swallowtails in the third panel of Figure 1.1.

Scientists have discovered stabilizing mechanisms of many different types throughout natural systems. In general,

whenever a component in a natural system grows until it reaches a limit on its growth imposed by the availability of resources (carrot tops, in this case), one or more stabilizing mechanisms come into operation. Those mechanisms operate to adjust the component, to bring it into balance with the supplies available to it.

Since various mechanisms are constantly operating to bring demand into balance with supply, natural systems not only tend to maintain stability but also tend to be efficient. That is, since demand is able to grow to meet supply, supply is typically not wasted. To illustrate, if the mass of green tissue on plants in a forest is able to grow to the greatest amount that can be supported by the sunlight coming into the forest, not only do we have the largest possible mass per unit of energy, we also have the smallest possible energy flow per unit of mass. Thus, we can say the system is efficient.

Natural systems have one more interesting feature: if we tamper with them, they act in ways that surprise us. Since this "surprising" behavior implies responses that violate our expectations from our intuitive understanding of the systems, it has been labeled "counterintuitive" (15). To illustrate, if we cut all the trees off a watershed, subsequent rain washes the minerals off the watershed into the rivers that drain it. Mineral accumulation in those rivers leads to nutrient enrichment of the rivers ("eutrophication") and a surprising dense growth of algae.

A POLITICAL PHILOSOPHY BASED ON NATURAL SYSTEMS

This book is based on a particular point of view, which has developed out of observations and analysis of many natural systems. In short, a scientist who has noticed the operation of stabilizing mechanisms, efficiency, and counterintuitive responses in many natural systems infers that an ideal socio-economic-political system devised by humans would have certain characteristics. Specifically, the system would be designed to promote stability and efficiency in use of resources. This is specifically not an anti-growth argument. Rather, this position holds that growth is perfectly natural so long as the number of organisms of a particular type has not begun to press against the limits to further growth set by the resources available. However, when those limits to growth are reached, a human system should have available stabilizing mechanisms analogous to those found in natural systems. In fact, many such mechanisms

are available, one of which is the price mechanism. (Other mechanisms that could be used to maintain stability in resource use are government and the law.)

Figure 1.2 shows the relationship between an ideal human system and the typical natural system. In the human system, when the resources available for each individual decline, the price of resources generally increases, and this stabilizes the system in three ways: birth rates decline, resource utilization declines (becomes more efficient), and the search for new resources increases. As will be explained in Chapter 7, this book does not argue against economic growth. Rather, it argues that the way to achieve economic growth is by use of the price

FIGURE 1.2

A conceptual systems model of a typical natural system, contrasted with a conceptual systems model of an ideal human socio-economic system.

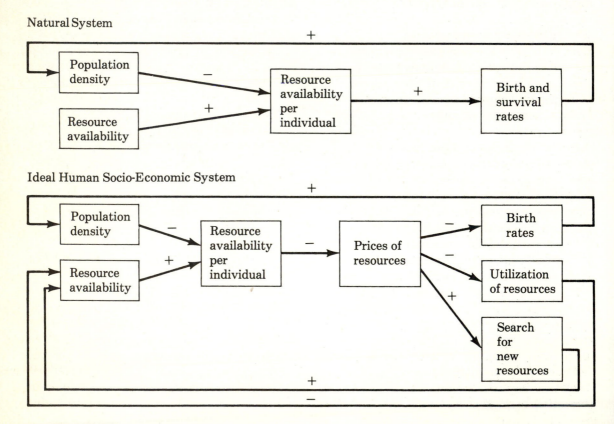

mechanism to discourage waste and excessive birth rates and stimulate efficiency and technological innovation. In short, it argues that observation of natural systems that have survived for very long times is a legitimate source of ideas on how to operate the socio-economic system so that it, too, can survive for a very long time.

The logical basis for seeking to copy the regulating mechanisms found in natural systems is that without them, particular types of animals and plants would be becoming extinct, or having their food supplies wiped out and then becoming extinct because of starvation. The student of natural systems carries away from them a strong emotional commitment to the value of allowing such mechanisms to operate without interference.

THE CONTRAST BETWEEN IDEAL AND ACTUAL HUMAN SYSTEMS

Now, against this background, what do students of natural systems see when they turn to the human socio-economic-political system that surrounds them? Certainly, many stabilizing mechanisms are available: if a commodity becomes scarce, the price goes up, supply increases, and demand decreases; if one group of people (polluters) violate the rights of others, the law can be used, and if the development of solar energy appears to be too slow, government may be called on to provide tax incentives to speed up development. Also, common sense suggests that the particular stabilizing mechanism operating in socio-economic-environmental systems that is most like the mechanisms in nature and operates most efficiently, with minimum cost and effort, is the price mechanism. It seems evident that it costs more in money and human time and effort to call in government, the law, or any other available stabilizing mechanism. Therefore, it appears that the price mechanism should be used on a routine basis to achieve stability, and the

government, the law, and other mechanisms should be regarded as backup mechanisms to be used in emergencies or other unusual circumstances.

What we observe in modern America is the socio-economic-environmental system operating in a fashion far from what our observations of nature would have suggested was ideal. Most of the population lives in cities where all resources are readily available at low prices. For this and other reasons we have developed a cultural belief system that attaches a very low value to all resources, relative to money. "Making money" is taken by most people to be an overridingly important life goal; ensuring the continued productivity of the resource base and the health of the environment is assigned a much lower priority. A very basic American expectation is that supplies of clean air and water, cheap fuel, food, clothing, housing, and transportation will always be available if we simply have enough money to buy them.

Instead of the price mechanism being used routinely to operate as a stabilizing mechanism, with government being used only as an emergency backup mechanism to achieve stability, we find that society fights the use of the price mechanism, and uses government to prevent it from operating. The most important example is energy: instead of letting prices rise as oil and gas become scarce, so that energy will be conserved, and new sources will be developed, government regulation has been used to keep energy prices much lower than they are in all other countries. In short, our society does not perceive the value in rising prices operating as a stabilizing mechanism, and tries to block this from happening.

The scientist observing this contempt for the value of stabilizing mechanisms becomes concerned that our society will meet the fate of a natural group of plants or animals that were no longer regulated by stabilizing mechanisms: extinction. In general, modern America is characterized by underpricing of resources relative to average wages, so that people can use up resources inefficiently, and the price mechanism is no longer a means of ensuring long-term stability in our society.

A remarkable variety of problems found in modern America result from this failure of the price mechanism to ensure efficient use of resources. Rapid resource depletion, soil degradation, and pollution are obvious results. This book will show how many other problems have the same cause: traffic congestion; species extinction; high rates of unemployment and crime, resulting from substitution of cheap resources for expensive labor; inflation; and high rates of interest on house mortgages are examples.

One can only conclude that the price we are paying for fighting the price mechanism as a means of wise resource use is too high. We must get back to use of the various mechanisms for ensuring a stable society.

Once we let these stabilizing mechanisms operate, increase in the price of resources relative to the cost of labor will allow a great variety of new technologies to become economically feasible. We will then see all kinds of novel means of generating and using energy. Our cities will be more compact and attractive, housing will be more attractive and efficient, and we will see wiser land use and resource management. The fundamental character of society will change, as for example when information and communication become substituted for wasteful use of matter and energy. Many of the key characteristics of our society, such as planned obsolescence, urban sprawl, traffic congestion, and lifeless streams will be regarded as hallmarks of a brief period in our history when we operated from a mistaken, blind socioeconomic-environmental policy.

In short, the reason why the belief system underlying this book will appear foreign to many readers is that it has an unusual origin. Rather than growing out of a more usual source, such as economics, political science, philosophy, or ethics, the book is based on a philosophical system that originated in ecology, the branch of biology that deals with the relationship between organisms and their environments.

Even so, the beliefs in this book do not violate common sense, and it is reasonable to ask why they have not been apparent to more people. The answer is that few people have been able to understand the real nature of environmental problems, because they have four characteristics that make them inherently difficult to understand and breed confusion. We now turn to consideration of those characteristics.

FOUR SOURCES OF CONFUSION ABOUT ENVIRONMENTAL SYSTEMS

We now consider six environmental case studies, in boxes, to see what they reveal in the way of common characteristics that tend to confuse the observer. Specifically, we are looking for evidence of the following four characteristics:

1. Long sequences of components connected by cause-effect pathways, such that it will not be apparent to most observers where the causes originate or the effects terminate.
2. Activities by government that go beyond being a mediator to being a constituency that spreads erroneous information or suppresses correct information.
3. Misunderstandings created by shortage of information, inaccurate information, or propaganda.
4. Very slowly changing, irregularly changing, or subtle environmental phenomena that are not perceived by the brains of most people.

BOX 1.1
**The counterintuitive effects of low energy prices
on inflation**

The United States has used up more than half of its domestic reserves of crude oil, and the remainder will be quite expensive to exploit, because of its depth and inaccessibility (Chapter 4). The federal government could have shown a number of different responses to this situation. One would have been to allow retail prices of energy to increase significantly, so as to stimulate search for and production of various forms of energy, and also to stimulate conservation. This is what has happened in most other countries. Instead, government policy has been to hold energy prices down, on the grounds that high energy prices create an increase in the price of all goods and services that would be accompanied by an increase in the money supply (inflation), decreasing the value of a unit of money, the purchasing power of consumers, and the standard of living of Americans.

In fact, holding the price of energy down has produced the effect that letting the price of energy increase was supposed to produce. By keeping the price of energy down, the government stimulated energy use and discouraged domestic energy production. The result has been a massive increase in imports of energy into this country (Panel 1 of Figure 1.3).

One important means of paying for this imported crude oil has been for this country to increase exports of a wide variety of other commodities enormously, particularly corn and wheat (Panel 2 of Figure 1.3). However, this massive export of commodities has had a variety of effects on the U.S. economy. For a wide variety of commodities (food, wood, textiles, and metal), domestic stocks dropped to low levels because so much was being exported. The third panel shows the drop in corn and wheat stocks between 1973 and 1976. Prices of commodities in the United States are very sensitive to the sizes of domestic stocks of those commodities. Wholesale commodity price increases are passed on to the consumer as retail price increases. To illustrate, as Panel 4 of the figure shows, decrease in U.S. stocks of corn and wheat resulted in higher food costs as a percentage of spendable earnings for American families. This in turn has been accompanied by an increase in the money supply (inflation). Consequently, by keeping the price of energy down, which most people would have expected to combat inflation, the government has had the surprising effect of increasing the rate of inflation. This surprising counterintuitive effect of cheap energy occurs principally because of the gigantic scale of the export of other goods to pay for imported energy. To illustrate, over the period 1972 to 1977, inclusive, 58.2 percent of all wheat grown in this country was exported.

If the United States cannot export other commodities fast enough to pay for imported crude oil, this results in an export of U.S. currency that does not return, and that in turn results in a drop in the value of our money relative to

FIGURE 1.3 (BOX 1.1 Cont.)

The impact of low energy prices on the purchasing power of a typical American family. As petroleum imports increase, food commodity exports increase and their stocks drop, so U.S. retail food prices take a higher percentage of the typical family budget. Note: all the data used to construct this figure are readily available; students are encouraged to become familiar with this data source, so they can explore issues such as this on their own. All data came from the Statistical Abstract of the United States, 1979 (100th edition), U.S. Bureau of the Census, Washington, D.C. Specific sources: Table 1516: value of petroleum and products imports; Tables 1234 and 1236: quantities of corn and wheat exported, and stocks on hand; Table 688: spendable weekly earnings of average worker in private nonagricultural establishment, with three dependents and in current dollars; Table 802: weekly food cost for couple with two children 12 to 19 years old; and Table 791: check on data in Table 802: consumer price indexes for total food at home.

VALUE OF CRUDE PETROLEUM AND PETROLEUM PRODUCTS IMPORTED INTO THE UNITED STATES (BILLIONS OF DOLLARS)

QUANTITY OF CORN AND WHEAT EXPORTED FROM THE UNITED STATES (MILLIONS OF BUSHELS)

STOCKS OF CORN AND WHEAT ON HAND IN THE UNITED STATES (MILLIONS OF BUSHELS)

AVERAGE FOOD COST AS A PERCENTAGE OF AVERAGE SPENDABLE EARNINGS FOR AMERICAN FAMILIES

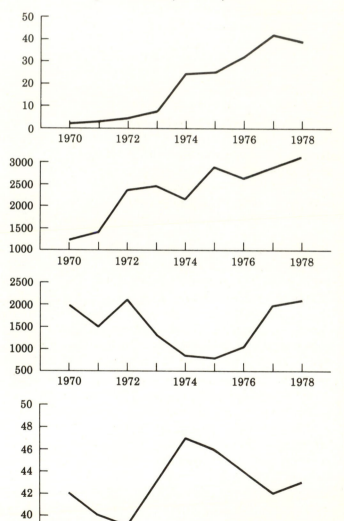

BOX 1.1 **(Cont.)**

the value of other country's currencies, as our money piles up unwanted in the banks of other countries. That, in turn, causes increases in the prices of foreign manufactured goods imported into this country.

In short, a cause operating at the national level (national energy policy) has an effect at a different level: the international economic, trade, and monetary level.

There is also an effect at the level of the individual city, which impacts on the individual home-buyer. Massive exports of food commodities cause increased demand for farmland in this country, implying less conversion of farmland to homesites at the city edge. There is less land for homebuilding than there otherwise would have been. The result has been that by far the most rapidly increasing component of the cost of new houses has been land: land was only 11 percent of house cost in 1949, and by 1978 was 25 percent (6).

Case Study 1. The Effect of Energy Prices on Inflation

Box 1.1. reveals the curious, counterintuitive effect of low energy prices on inflation (32, 33, 34, 35, 36, 37). Since the cost of energy is an input to the costs of all goods and services, it is reasonable to expect that keeping the price of energy down would combat inflation. Yet precisely the opposite happens, because energy prices have pervasive effects that radiate throughout a very complex system. This system includes weather (which affects the amount of food we can grow), the nonrenewable resource being imported (crude oil), the renewable resources being exported (wheat and corn), population (because total use of any resource is use per person multiplied by population size), economic variables (the costs and prices of the various commodities, and the money flowing out of the United States), political and governmental factors (such as the decision to keep energy prices down), and cultural variables, such as the perception that low energy prices are good for the economy and consumers. All together there are seven types of system components.

This example also illustrates causal pathways that pass between levels, or hierarchies. A hierarchical level is a level of organization: city and country are example levels. Domestic energy prices affect not only the nation, but the international trade and monetary systems, which in turn act on the U.S. economy and ultimately the interest rate charged for mortgages or car loans.

In this example government has a profound effect, and perceptual inadequacies are also central and crucial: the vast majority of the population believes that low energy prices imply the highest possible standard of living; there is no widespread comprehension of the significance of international trade and money flows for the domestic economy. Few people have given much thought to the notion that if this country buys more than it sells, the value of our currency drops relative to the value of other currencies (such as Swiss, Japanese, or West German money). Still fewer would perceive that in that case, interest rates on borrowed money would be very high to prevent a net outflow of capital to other countries where the value of money was dropping more slowly. This, in turn, would impact directly on Americans in the form of the interest rate they would have to pay on car loans, or house mortgages.

Information affects the energy problem in many ways. Several kinds of information that would have a profound impact on public understanding of the problem are not widely available. Two examples will make the point. Many politicians argue that corporations are making vast profits from crude oil, and hence, that there should be "windfall profits taxes." These politicians never seem to mention that the capital costs of oil exploration and drilling are staggering, and that the government is already bleeding most of the capital out of the oil industry, not only through taxation, but also through bonuses, royalties, and leases. All American corporations, from 1954 to 1978, paid the federal government 26.5 billion dollars simply for the right to explore offshore, and by March 1978, had not yet made that much from offshore activities. Thus, they made nothing to cover exploration and development costs, and no offshore profit whatever (31). Politicians have been very quiet about the fact that offshore oil and gas leasing has been one of the federal government's biggest sources of revenue outside the tax system.

A second example of an information problem in the energy area concerns the widespread notion that high and increasing energy consumption per capita is a prerequisite for a high economic growth rate. In fact, the relation between energy consumption per capita and economic growth rate is as most scientists would expect: economic growth rate rises to a peak, then falls, as the suffocating impacts of high energy consumption on the economy become inhibiting (Figure 7.5).

BOX 1.2
The surprising facts about "sending food to poor countries"

Soil scientists leave us with no doubt that the great pressure now being exerted on the United States agricultural system to grow food for export to pay for imported crude oil is degrading our agricultural land (4). So why do we grow and export so much food, besides the argument that we think we need the imported energy? Four arguments might be put forth: it is the ethical thing to do, because the poor countries need the food; the additional food will improve the standard of living in the countries to which we send it; the larger amounts of food being sold will make more money for our farmers; and, our food exports will have a useful effect on the economies of the nations to which we export the food. In fact, every one of these arguments becomes suspect on close scrutiny.

At least half of all the food we export goes to countries that already have a more than adequate diet. Countries on the verge of starvation receive a small fraction of all the food the U.S. exports (Table 1.1). There is a voluminous, long-standing, and completely convincing scientific literature arguing that too much food of animal origin causes arteriosclerotic and degenerative heart disease (13, 17). Much of the food the United States exports to countries that already have an adequate diet is not for direct human consumption, but is for feed to farm animals, and ultimate consumption by humans as meat, poultry, eggs, or milk. Any per capita intake of meat per year above that found in

TABLE 1.1

Amounts of wheat exported June 1977 to May 1978 from United States to other countries, classified by amount of meat in diet.

	Rich diet countries			Poor diet countries	
Country	Grams of meat supply per person per day	Millions of bushels of wheat from United States	Country	Grams of meat supply per person per day	Millions of bushels of wheat from United States
U.S.S.R.	106	125.4	India	4	6.4
Brazil	84	81.8	Indonesia	10	14.0
The Netherlands	163	38.5	Pakistan	11	21.3
Poland	138	28.0	Zaire	31	3.9
Venezuela	99	25.8	Bangladesh	?	23.3
Portugal	95	22.6	Algeria	22	25.9
			Nigeria	28	30.3
Chile	108	19.9	Morocco	37	32.5
Italy	136	19.6	Egypt	31	54.9
Columbia	91	17.5	Korea, Rep.	22	66.1
		379.1			278.6

Sources of data: Net food supplies per person from Table 162, *Statistical Yearbook 1972*, of the Statistical Office of the United Nations, New York; Copyright, United Nations (1973). Reproduced by permission; Annual summaries for wheat from *Grain Market News* Vol. 26, No. 27 (July 7, 1978).

Sweden appears to shorten life (Figure 1.4). It would appear that the United States could drop food exports to between 50 and 75 percent of the present level without having a serious effect on world health, if the exports were redirected.

It is simply not true that net income to farmers increases as they sell larger quantities of food. The income to U.S. farmers drops, rather than rises, when they increase production to very high levels. To illustrate, the 1977 U.S. wheat crop of 2.026 billion bushels had a value of 4.677 billion dollars; the smaller 1974 crop of 1.782 billion bushels had a larger value of 7.287 billion dollars. The price per unit of U.S. farm commodities is totally determined by stocks on hand, and projection of next year's stock after harvest. The stock, and hence the unit price, would be the same if 1.7 billion bushels were grown and 1.4 sold as if 2.5 billion were grown and 2.2 sold. Thus, there is no gain to U.S. farmers from massive amounts of commodities in storage, in the hope of huge sales abroad.

Finally, it is not at all clear that our food exports have the expected useful impacts on the countries that import our food; freeing up agricultural workers to migrate to the city and take up manufacturing or other urban occupations. Our country perceives itself as having a shortage of labor and a surplus of capital, and therefore tends to perceive other countries as if they were the same.

FIGURE 1.4 (BOX 1.2 Cont.)

The relationship between average national life expectancy for males and the meat supply per person. The line was drawn through the data points for all the countries for which such data were available. The data points for only eight of those countries have been entered, to suggest the type of life style represented by different positions along the line. Note that the countries with the highest life expectancies are not those with the highest meat supply, but those with an intermediate meat supply (about 40 to 70 kilograms per year). This graph makes a profoundly important point, which will reappear in various contexts throughout the book: all kinds of systems perform best at an intermediate level of resource availability, rather than the highest level of resource availability. Compare with Figures 5.6 and 7.5 (Copyright, United Nations, 1973. Reproduced by permission. All data from the 1972 Statistical Yearbook of the United Nations, New York. Meat supply per person computed by dividing meat supply data on pages 511–523 by population data on pp. 67–73. Data on life expectancies from pp. 89–93.

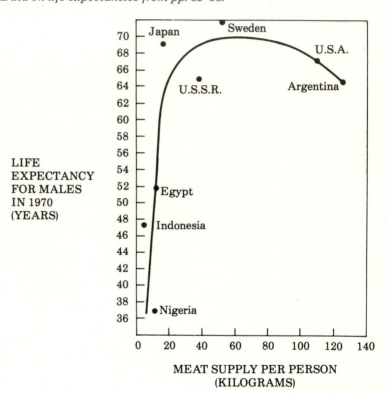

But many of the countries we send food to have a shortage of capital and a surplus of labor. They need jobs on the farm, and lack the capital needed to create a manufacturing sector rapidly. Massive food imports from us merely lead to mass migration off farms to the cities by people who no longer have jobs in the country, but have no jobs awaiting them in the city.

Case Study 2. Exporting Food to "Poor Countries"

Box 1.2 summarizes the information on a very different environmental problem. Given the impact of a massive annual production of corn, wheat, and soybeans on our agricultural soil, it seems reasonable to reconsider our motives for growing so much. Surprisingly, those motives turn out to be invalid on close inspection. Again, this exposes the role of certain basic attributes of environmental problems.

Our intuition suggests that we can only be doing good in the world by sending food to people in countries that have less food than we have. This example is particularly useful for exposing the role of perceptual problems and information inadequacy in environmental matters, because common sense leads us so far astray.

It is a basic human instinct to think that if you are giving someone something, you must be helping. However, if you give food to a nation with a rich diet, you might decrease life expectancy in the nation by four years, on average. If you give food to a poor nation, you might further weaken an already defective social fabric, because the real need of the society is for jobs to use their excess labor pool and generate capital assets. Our culture leads us to think that more production is always better, when more production may only lead to much lower net profit. Finally, since much of our population is urbanized and has lost touch with the soil, it would occur to few people besides farmers and soil scientists that sharply higher food production rates might be inimical to the structure and chemical composition of the soil.

Government figures prominently in this environmental problem, also. The terms under which food is sent to other countries are regulated to some degree by government, and the U.S. Department of Agriculture has consciously advocated grain sales to other countries as a means of paying for imported crude oil.

Our preoccupation with growth in use of resources has led us to overlook various policy options. What about deriving national energy policy from national agricultural policy, rather than basing national agricultural policy on the need to export food to pay for imported crude oil?

This case, and the next, clearly reveal an element in the cultural belief system implicated in many environmental problems: the blind faith in agricultural production systems as horns of plenty with no limit, no matter how hard they are pushed.

BOX 1.3
The Irish potato famine

The population in Ireland increased an average of 1.93 percent per year from 1779 to 1821, .99 percent from 1821 to 1841, and .36 percent from 1841 to 1845, the year the great famine began. Thus over the whole period the population only grew at 1.55 percent per year, well below the rate of growth of the world population over the last several decades. However, even modest growth rates can set the stage for disaster if continued long enough. From 1779 to 1821, the population increased from 3.0 million to 8.3 million, or 255 per square mile (roughly the density of modern France or China).

However, this population in 1845 was extremely poor, and extraordinarily dependent on one crop: the potato. To illustrate the standard of living, one

BOX 1.3 (Cont.)

town of 9000 people had 10 beds, 93 chairs and 243 stools. Nearly half of the national rural population lived in windowless mud huts with one room. The potato was easy to grow using the most primitive methods and did well in poor soil. One and a half acres of potatoes would feed five or six people for a year. However, potatoes cannot be stored under primitive conditions.

Prior to the great famine of 1845–1846, there had been eight milder famines, all associated with unusually cold or wet weather. In 1845, two environmental hazards occurred together. August was one of the three coldest in 260 years of weather records (21), presumably because a low level of solar radiation from the sun (10) coincided with the volcanic eruption that ejected more dust to block incoming radiation than any other in the previous 300 years: Coseguina, in 1835 (19). The second hazard was the fungus *Phytophthora infestans*, or potato blight, first noticed in North America in 1844 and then in Ireland in 1845.

The blight ruined a great deal of the potato crop in the fall of 1845, and an estimated 60 percent of the crop in 1846. Starvation was followed by an epidemic of relapsing fever and typhus in 1846–1847, which killed up to 750,000 people. By 1851, the population had dropped to 6.5 million, 2.1 million less than the 8.6 million to be expected in 1851, given the prevailing growth rate. Of the 2.1 million who disappeared from Ireland, an enormous number emigrated to Boston or New York. A great many died in transit or shortly after arrival. (For further details, see references 11, 25, and 40.)

Ireland never regained the lost population: Eire and Northern Ireland now only have a combined population of about 4.65 million.

Case Study 3. The Irish Potato Famine

The Irish potato famine (Box 1.3) is particularly useful for exposing the way our biological makeup and culture affect our perceptions of environmental risks. Humans do not perceive impending threat to security in a gradually changing situation, nor in events that occur with rather low probability. Consequently, in this instance, the Irish population gradually drifted into a state of extreme vulnerability to not just one, but two different kinds of environmental disasters. The population gradually increased to a density that, given the existing food production system, could only be supported by the food supply in years of good weather. It is particularly revealing that weather as bad as or worse than that which caused the potato crop failure in 1845 occurred every fourteen or fifteen years over 260 years of English temperature records (21). Even this frequency was not adequate to create a widespread perception that it was urgently necessary to diversify the crop mix to include more grains that could be stored over the winter. (The brain acts as an information filter as well as an information gatherer; one basis for the filtration is exclusion of sensory input unless it reveals large differences from expected conditions.) In addition to exceeding the carrying capacity of the environment, the Irish population made itself very vulnerable by being so dependent on the potato. This is a violation of the adage "not to put all the eggs in one basket," which in the literature of ecology translates, "diversity promotes stability."

The Irish potato famine case illustrates the systemic character of typical environmental problems. Factors included the effect of solar radiation and volcanic eruptions on the weather, soil fertility, the biology of the potato-blight system, the density of the human population, the lack of capital to produce a diversified economy, the lack of concern for Ireland by the government in England, and a culture unwittingly committed to sustained growth, not perceptive of environmental limits, and oblivious to catastrophic risks resulting from unwise collective behavior.

The Irish potato famine case, as with so many environmental problems, points up another problem in perception: at any time, a multiplicity of choices are available to a society. However, because we are creatures of habit, and because a culture leads us to be unaware that any path but the one we are on is the right one, most options are simply not perceived as being available. Thus, all through the period 1780 to 1845 the Irish could have practiced strict birth control, so as to stabilize the population, and could have worked hard to improve and diversify their agricultural system. Yet those options were not perceived, just as all through history, most nations have not perceived most of the options available to them. The potato famine shows startling parallels to the impending energy crisis in America.

BOX 1.4
The decline of the plain of Antioch

In the extreme south of Turkey, at the Syrian border, is a small town, Antakya, of about 58,000 people. In the second century A.D. this was Antioch, one of the richest and greatest cities of ancient Syria, with a population of about 500,000. What happened?

The Plain of Antioch, adjacent to Antakya, contains the ruins of about 175 different towns and villages, where now there are only seven inhabited towns. About a quarter of the plain is now a marshy swamp, in which the ruins of about twenty-five of the ancient towns are submerged; the rest of the plain is covered by silt, with erosion debris from the highlands surrounding the plain. Deforestation of the highlands resulted in soil erosion when it rained; the soil then washed off the highlands into the plain below. When this leached out, eroded soil occupied streams, and blocked their flow, creating the marsh. Where it accumulated on dry land, it covered the towns. So much silt has accumulated over the Plain of Antioch that the floors of some of the earliest towns are now below the ground water table. One of the richest areas on earth has been ruined by unwise land management: Syria's carrying capacity for people is now about a third what it was 2000 years ago (7).

Case Study 4. The Decline of the Plain of Antioch

Box 1.4 concerns the decline of the Plain of Antioch, formerly in Syria, now in Syria and the extreme southern corner of Turkey. The environmental problem here is deforestation, lack of wise soil management, and resultant soil erosion. Again, we have a complex system with many types of elements: rain, wind, the physics and chemistry of soil, hydrology, agricultural and forest management practices, population density, the relationships between governments (including Rome, Syria, Persia, and Palmyra), and a cultural belief system that perceived the maximization of production as an appropriate goal, rather than the maintenance of stability.

Perception plays an important role in this kind of environmental problem (16, 26). The environmental disintegration occurred very gradually. How would a person alive at any time be aware of what the place looked like several centuries or millenia before, or what it would look like thousands of years later?

Also, the lack of necessary information would be critical. No civilization has ever thought it worthwhile to fence off check areas indefinitely, to be kept in their pristine state. Consequently, if anyone did happen to perceive that the environment was changing, it could always be argued that this change was the consequence of a climatic shift, or war. It has always been easy to deny the real explanation of long-term degradation of forest or farmland: unwise management practices.

BOX 1.5
The manipulation of information concerning nuclear power

During the period up to about 1978, when electrical utilities placed orders for or had already constructed 201 nuclear plants in the United States, nuclear advocates created the impression that nuclear power would be cheaper than coal, and some enthusiasts went so far as to claim that nuclear power would be "too cheap to meter" (29). As more data have become available, it has become clear that early low estimates of the cost of nuclear power were based on incomplete understanding of the economics of the complete fuel cycle (24, 30). However, enthusiastic overselling is rather innocent; much more serious, deliberate information manipulation occurred, and federal government agencies were major offenders.

The Office of the Comptroller General of the United States was asked to determine if the Federal Energy Research and Development Administration had broken any laws by release of 78,600 copies of a document titled "Shedding Light on Facts About Nuclear Energy," which was released in California from February to April 1976 prior to a vote on the California Nuclear Safeguards Initiative. The Comptroller General's Report to the Congress concluded that the document "was not objective, is propaganda, and was not a proper document for release to the public . . ." and "was used by some recipients to influence California voters" (9).

The Central Intelligence Agency had a large number of documents pertaining to a major nuclear accident in Russia which they did not release to the U.S.

BOX 1.5 (Cont.)

public until forced to do so through use of the Freedom of Information Act (22).

The only possible way to interpret these two activities is that agencies of the federal government were trying to manipulate public opinion about nuclear energy, in the one case by releasing propaganda, and in the other case, by suppressing the truth.

Case Study 5. Government Distribution of Pronuclear Propaganda

Our fifth example illustrates the clearcut significance of information. More and more writers are pointing out that the favorable attitude of government and the public toward nuclear power has been very much the result of information manipulation by nuclear advocates prior to about 1975 (Box 1.5). The widespread perception that nuclear power would be very cheap and absolutely safe was clearly the product of information manipulation by individuals and institutions who advocated the use of nuclear power.

This environmental problem (use of nuclear power) has a complex systems aspect. As is now being pointed out, you can no more buy a complex piece of technology like a generating plant in isolation than you could buy a jumbo jet in isolation. In both cases, you must buy a system, including an operator's training program, a maintenance procedure, a system for educating maintenance staff, and the cost of nuclear waste disposal. The failure to understand the full implications of this systemic aspect of high technology was principally responsible for unrealistically low early cost estimates of nuclear power.

BOX 1.6
The matter of options: Is there really another way?

The dominant paradigm (belief system) has remarkably pervasive effects within any culture, that make possible alternate paradigms difficult to perceive. The United States has been on a particular evolutionary track for at least two centuries, with a pattern of social organization dictated by our cultural paradigm, and our paradigm in turn being reinforced by our success in its application. This track has been characterized by constant increase in the cost of labor relative to the cost of resources, stimulating constant increase in resource consumption per capita. While paying lip service to the need to get out of this trend, government has not yet done anything meaningful to alter it. The track we are on also involves centralization of government and economic power, and concentration of energy-generating facilities at a small number of very large installations. Our society is more and more characterized by very large, low density cities utterly dependent on the car.

Two other options are to be proconsumer, and place resource costs even lower relative to the cost of labor, or to be proconservation, and raise energy and other resource costs significantly relative to the cost of labor. We can't try

BOX 1.6 (Cont.)

all possible tracks simultaneously, because our capital is limited. Trying some of the tracks may use up so much capital that it excludes the possibility of trying other tracks at any time in the forseeable future. Consequently, there is a compelling reason to try to discover the consequences of various tracks before we make critical choices. Happily, there is an odd way to do this: some other countries have already tried some of the choices so we can see how they turned out. Table 1.2 compares patterns of social organization in the United States, Norway, Sweden, and Switzerland. The other three countries are all more affluent than the United States, yet use about a third to a half as much energy per capita. Sweden and Switzerland actually had a drop in energy use per capita from 1971 to 1976. How do we explain the high level of affluence obtained with so little energy use in the other three countries? Three other statistics provide much of the explanation, in addition to the fact that energy costs two to three times as much in these countries as in the United States. A far higher proportion of the energy comes from electricity in the other countries, a pattern associated with far greater use of electric rail systems than cars. Finally, the cities are much more compact, thus requiring less transportation energy.

TABLE 1.2

A comparison of two different patterns of social organization.

Descriptor		U.S.A.	Norway	Sweden	Switzerland
Gross National Product Per Capita (1978)		9644	9709	10387	14057
Consumption of all forms of energy per capita, in kilograms of coal equivalents	1971	11244	5189	6089	3575
	1976	11554	5263	6046	3340
Electrical energy production as a percentage of all energy consumed, 1976		10.5	47.6	21.4	20.9
Passenger-kilometers of rail traffic per motor vehicle in use, 1976		116	1707	1823	4276
Number of people per square mile in large city, around 1976		319 Houston	8017 Oslo	18653 Stockholm	5484 Geneva

Sources of data: G.N.P. from Table 1556, *Statistical Abstracts of the United States for 1979*, U.S. Department of Commerce; energy and transportation from *Statistical Yearbooks* of the Statistical Office of the United Nations, New York; Copyright, United Nations (1973, 1977, 1979). Reproduced by permission. (1972 *Yearbook* pp. 353–356; 1976 *Yearbook* pp. 372–375, 386–395; 1978 *Yearbook* pp. 390–392, 541–551).

Case Study 6. Energy Strategies of Different Nations

Our last sample environment problem (Box 1.6) involves energy pricing policy (18). A basic theme running through the previous five case studies has been the inability of most people or most societies to perceive that there are alternatives to the course of action they are currently following. But what good would it do them if they were more perceptive, and had an expanded consciousness? Are there other tracks to be followed than the ones leading to environmental deterioration? To get the answer, we do not need to invoke theory: all we need to do is look at the examples being set by various countries (36).

As with our other environmental case studies, the issue of national choices is a complex systemic phenomenon, with many types of components (8, 12, 18). Norway, Sweden, and Switzerland all followed a different evolutionary path than the United States because their physical environment contained a higher proportion of high mountains with fast-flowing rivers useful for hydroelectric power. Also, the United States had more crude oil reserves than the others. The three European countries have less agricultural land than the United States. The land shortage and the greater ease of perceiving exactly where the limit is with hydroelectric power than with crude oil have produced a cultural paradigm more sensitive to environmental limits than characterizes the United States belief system.

The pattern of governmental organization is quite different in the four countries. The contrast between the United States and Switzerland is particularly instructive. Local government in Switzerland is much more powerful relative to federal government than in the United States. Also, in Switzerland, decision-making is far more under the control of the electorate and less under the control of government; voting on particular issues occurs many times a year.

Perceptions of the environment are very different in Europe than in America. Since the countries have a far longer history and are much smaller, the people have a sense of the finiteness of the country they live in, which is only a very recent phenomenon in America.

Also, since the countries are smaller, the system is simpler and easier to comprehend; the mass of available information is not so overwhelming.

Generalizations from the Six Case Studies

The six case studies we have just considered allow us to draw some general conclusions about the characteristics of environmental problems, which are summarized in Table 1.3.

Each of the six cases involved deep-rooted dysfunction of a complex system with many components of several different types, and the system typically involved several hierarchical levels. Except for the degradation of the Plain of Antioch, where we do not have adequate information, government was involved in the problems. The inability of the human mind to perceive environmental threat is an important thread running through all of these cases; the normal experience of one lifetime prepares us poorly to deal with major, but infrequent discontinuities resulting from gradual, imperceptible changes sustained for long periods. Our perception of the relative severity of various risks is highly irrational.

One example brings out vividly the inappropriate way most people rank the relative severity of environmental threats. In a period of a few days in 1979, there were three serious environmental threats worldwide. The first was the Three Mile Island nuclear power plant accident at Harrisburg,

TABLE 1.3
The difference between typical simple problems and typical environmental problems.

Problem characteristic	Simple problems	Environmental problems
The nature of the problem system	Small number of components of one or few types in one hierarchical level; problem typically caused by accident, or short-term deviation from equilibrium state.	Large number of components of seven different types, and two to four or more hierarchical levels; problem typically caused by sustained, deep-rooted dysfunction of one or more system components; equilibrium itself may be drifting or undergoing traumatic discontinuity.
Role of politics and government	Clear consensus concerning appropriate action to solve problem; consequently, no need for government involvement.	Stalemated conflict of interests as to most appropriate problem solution because of competition for limited resources or defective perception of the nature of the problem; government brought in as mediator between constituencies and system regulator, but also acts as constituency with its own, unique goals.
Role of perception and consciousness	Normal human experience allows for appropriate perception of nature of problem; cultural paradigm does not distort perception of problem; most people are able to bound problem correctly; therefore problem responds as expected to attempts at solution.	Normal human experience in one lifetime and small number of places does not allow for appropriate perception of problem, because consciousness is built by perceiving frequent local changes, not infrequent changes, or changes remote in time and space. Few people are able to bound problem correctly; therefore problem shows surprising and counterintuitive responses to attempts at solution.
Role of information, and response to it	Accurate, revealing information is available on time, and is responded to appropriately.	Information is incomplete, inaccurate, may arrive too late to be useful, and may be propaganda. Response may be inappropriate for biological reasons (the filtration of sensory input by the sense organs and brain) or for cultural or political reasons.

Pennsylvania. This incident received an enormous amount of media attention. Yet not one person died and not one was injured. The second was a tornado in north central Texas and south central Oklahoma. About a hundred people died, a thousand were injured, and there were millions of dollars of property damage. This received a small amount of media coverage. The third was a volcanic eruption in the Caribbean, which received virtually no media attention at all: network television news programs devoted a few seconds to it for two days. Yet on May 8, 1902, when one of the volcanic islands in this group, Martinique, erupted, 30,000 people died almost instantly (5). Thus, the media perceived the threats in the opposite order to the order of their actual severity. This example reinforces the theme concerning the importance of information manipulation running through the six case studies: the public did not perceive the volcano as a serious threat, in part because network newscasters did not present it as a serious threat.

Now we have some understanding of the nature of environmental problems, we can proceed to design an approach to solution.

OPTIONS AVAILABLE FOR SOLVING ENVIRONMENTAL PROBLEMS

Obviously the first tool we need for solving environmental problems is a systems approach that matches the character of the problems. This tool has to provide us with two things: appropriate conceptual models for dealing with complex systems, which can help us perceive multiple interrelationships and their impacts and deal with many different types of variables, organized hierarchically; and specific techniques for performing computations to determine the best way to manage complex environmental systems. Happily, such a systems approach is avail-able, and well-developed (1, 2, 3, 14, 15, 18, 23, 27, 37, 38).

The remainder of this book is devoted to an elementary exposition of the insights obtained when we analyze environmental problems with tools which match their character. Chapter 2 explores the information-perception theme; Part II introduces the components of environmental systems problems; and Part III shows how all the components of environmental systems function together.

Given that society at large has tools available for understanding and dealing with environmental problems, is it reasonable to expect that humanity will use these tools appropriately, and take the options required to deal with the situation?

We have seen that one cause of environmental problems is the limits to perception in the human brain. Thus, our fate depends a lot on the ability of our species to change rapidly in response to environmental challenges. Could we? Human change can come about for two reasons: changes in the genetic makeup of the population (changes in inherited biological characteristics), and changes in our culture (the system of beliefs taught by each generation to its offspring). Much scientific work has been done on the factors that determine the speed of genetic change, and it is reasonable to believe that the speed of cultural change will be determined by analogous phenomena.

Modern evolutionary theory holds that the speed of genetic change is determined by (1) the speed with which the environment is changing with respect to factors that are critical for the survival of the organism; (2) the variability of the population with respect to genetic characteristics that can be selected for by changes in the environment; (3) the proportion of the population subjected to the selection process; and (4) the intensity with which selection operates on each individual.

Now suppose that culture follows the same rules as genetic evolution. As E. O. Wilson (39) has noted, it is a reasonable proposition that "the rate of change in a particular set of cultural behaviors reflects the rate of change in the environmental features to which the behaviors are keyed." Since the human environment is likely to change very rapidly in the future, it is reasonable to expect that the human culture will respond by also changing very rapidly. This rapid change is an entirely reasonable expectation further, because if one thing characterizes modern humanity, it is the extraordinary diversity of beliefs in the human population, a prerequisite for rapid cultural change. No matter what belief system will best allow us to make the transition to the future, we are unlikely to have to wait for it to develop: the diversity of beliefs already present is so great that it is probably already amongst us.

We can also expect rapid cultural change because the proportion of the population subjected to intense selection will be extremely high. Few individuals will have the financial resources to buffer themselves from major changes coming in the next few years, such as great increases in the prices of fossil fuels and other minerals. Also promoting rapid cultural change will be the great exposure of new ideas by advertising and the media.

The intensity of the selection process for good new ideas will be very great. Evolution of human thinking is likely to be rapid when there are important rewards for doing the right thing, and significant punishments for doing the wrong thing. New insights and information indicating what "right" and "wrong" are will become available very rapidly. Further, intense competition will operate at many levels, from that of the individual and city to that of the nation. To illustrate the form this competition will take, as fossil fuels become more expensive, there will be great competitive advantage to metropolitan areas which have highly energy-efficient public transportation systems, in contradistinction to metropolitan areas with an almost total commitment to gigantic freeway systems as the means of passenger transportation. Other factors being equal, people will tend to migrate away from the car-freeway cities to the transit-oriented cities, because the cost of living will be significantly lower in the latter.

The next twenty years will be a time of intense competition between various ideas, programs, and ideologies. Some of those will be bad. It will be important to resist the predictable great pressure for "quick fixes" that turn out to be expensive, elusive, and impermanent. It will also be important to oppose arguments that we all ought to adhere to old, comfortable dogmas. On balance, there is every reason to believe that as changes in the environment demand changes in humanity's thinking, humanity will be entirely capable of appropriate response. However, not every individual will. I hope this book will show some people how they can be sure that their response to the new condition is appropriate, so that they can be among the group that comes through a time of great changes with minimum personal difficulty.

Some people might wonder why they should be concerned about taking rational options with respect to the environment, on the grounds that their personal destiny is totally at the mercy of large-scale forces beyond their control and decisions made by society at large. In fact, the personal economic fortunes of each of us is remarkably sensitive to personal decisions on environmental matters.

To illustrate, consider two young couples. In the first case, they only have one child, and they both can work. They chose to live in a small town, so they can walk to work, and the family needs to have only one car.

The second couple has four children, and one of them chooses to stay home with the children. They selected a job in a very large urban area, and they live in a ranch bungalow thirty miles from the center of town, two miles from the nearest store, and fifty miles from the job. The family uses three cars, a camper, a boat trailer, and a boat.

It is a revealing exercise to work up hypothetical family budgets for these two families, using government statistics to obtain such items as national average costs for operating vehicles and vehicle depreciation. The economic situation of the two families is dramatically different, and the difference is directly traceable to personal decisions they made on issues related to the environment.

This book will suggest many ideas about the relationships between personal decisions and the environment.

A SYMBOLIC LANGUAGE FOR ENVIRONMENTAL SYSTEMS

The remainder of this book will deal with the roles played by seven categories of variables in environmental systems. In order to clarify the flow charts, seven symbols will be used throughout to represent each of these categories (Figure 1.5).

FIGURE 1.5
The seven symbols used to represent the seven categories of variables operating in environmental systems throughout this book.

Explanation:

Category of Variable	Meaning of the Symbol	
Physical enviornmental variables	the sun, the major determinant of our physical environment	
Nonrenewable natural resource variables	a barrel of crude oil, our most important present nonrenewable resource	
Renewable natural resources	a wheat plant	
Demographic factors	a person	
Economic factors	the symbol for a dollar	
Political-governmental factors	the Capitol, in Washington	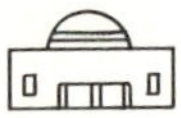
Socio-cultural variables	the cathedral of Notre Dame at Chartres, the single architectural masterpiece that most faithfully represents the value system on which modern Western civilization is based: a fascination and preoccupation with infinite time and space, out of which has grown the belief in infinite resources	

SUMMARY

Environmental problems are problems of systems. A system is the structure of the set of cause-effect relationships linking components in our mental model of a complex phenomenon.

Scientists have noticed that efficiency, stability, and surprising (counterintuitive) responses to human tampering characterize natural systems. It seems reasonable to suppose that an ideal society would show these same characteristics. In fact, it has been difficult for most people to perceive the value in allowing available mechanisms to operate so that society would be efficient and stable. Modern America is neither.

Why has it been so difficult for most people to see the real cost of unwise environmental management? Four sources of confusion have interfered with widespread understanding of relations between environment and the economy. The linkages between environment and the economy involve long sequences of causal pathways, and most people are not experienced in thinking about such pathways. The role of government has created confusion, because government has not always acted as a mediator between other constituencies, but rather has sometimes acted as a constituency in its own right. Inadequate information, inaccurate information, and outright propaganda have created misunderstandings. Finally, environmental phenomena are often subtle and slowly changing; these are not the types of things readily perceived by our brains, which have evolved to allow us to cope with our immediate surroundings on a daily basis.

Since environmental problems have their ultimate origins in such apparently unrelated sources as culture, politics, and economics, this book will deal with those areas.

SUGGESTED ACTIVITIES

Watch vegetables and fruit growing in your garden, or a friend's garden. Do you see any insects or other small animals eating the plants? If so, make careful observations, and try to raise some of the animals in small cages to see if you discover any parasites. Do you see any predators eating the animals that feed on the plants? Now combine the information from your observations and cage results into flow charts such as Figure 1.1. Write an essay suggesting the mechanisms that promote stability in the particular organisms you have been observing. What would happen if these mechanisms were absent?

Analyze some other environmental and nonenvironmental problems with respect to the set of characteristics in Table 1.3. Is there a consistent difference between environmental and nonenvironmental problems? Some particularly revealing problems to consider: overfishing on the high seas, inflation, whaling by the Russians and Japanese, infant mortality rates in the United States, the lung cancer death rate, suicide rates among adolescent Native Americans, the automobile accident fatality rate, the controversy between sheep ranchers and conservationists over the coyote, the causes of the decline of Spain in 1600, Mesopotamia around 500 B.C., and the pre-Columbian Indian civilizations. Stage a debate between two teams on the following theme: the "law and order" (crime in the streets) is, or is not really an environmental issue in disguise. The two debate teams should try and trace back to the root causes of crime.

Having considered the crime example, the class might now be ready for a debate on a more general and basic issue: complex but apparently "nonenvironmental" problems do (or do not) always turn out to be environmental problems on closer inspection. Use the debate format to explore the root causes of a variety of complex problems. Each team member should use this format as a stimulus to get practice in thinking through the steps in the cause-effect sequences that lead to an ultimate effect.

This chapter has suggested that the price mechanism actually regulates use of resources per person. Use government statistics to obtain data on the price of various resources, and the use per individual; then plot use against price to see if there really is such a relationship. Examine the data for gasoline, natural gas, electricity, wood, and various metals. Use per individual should decline as price rises. Have your professor show you how to use the consumer price index to correct for change in the value of money from year to year.

REFERENCES

1. Ashby, W. R. *An Introduction to Cybernetics.* London: Chapman and Hall, 1956.
2. Beer, S. *Platform for Change.* London: John Wiley and Sons, 1975.
3. Berlinski, David. *On Systems Analysis: An Essay Concerning the Limitations of Some Mathematical Methods in the Social, Political, and Biological Sciences.* Cambridge, Mass.: The MIT Press, 1976.
4. Brink, R. A., J. W. Densmore, and G. A. Hill. "Soil deterioration and the growing world demand for food," *Science,* 197, 625 (1977).
5. Bullard, F. M. *Volcanoes of the Earth,* rev. ed. Austin: University of Texas Press, 1976.
6. Carberry, J., "Land plays rising role, labor a reduced one in the long, steep climb in cost of new homes," *The Wall Street Journal,* Oct. 11, 1978.
7. Carter, V. G., and T. Dale. *Topsoil and Civilization,* rev. ed. Norman, Okla.: University of Oklahoma Press, 1974.
8. Commoner, B. *The Poverty of Power.* New York: Knopf, 1976.
9. Comptroller General of the United States, Report to Congress on evaluation of the publication and distribution of "Shedding light on facts about nuclear energy." EMD-76-12, 1976. Washington, D.C.: U.S. General Accounting Office, 1976.
10. Eddy, J. A., "The case of the missing sunspots," *Scientific American,* 236, No. 5 (1977), p. 80.
11. Edwards, R. D., and T. D. Williams (eds.), *The Great Famine,* New York: New York University Press, 1957.
12. Ehrlich, P. R., A. H. Ehrlich, and J. P. Holdren. *Ecoscience: Population, Resources, Environment.* San Francisco: W. H. Freeman, 1977.
13. Enselme, J. *Unsaturated fatty acids in atherosclerosis,* 2d ed., trans. R. D. Plummer. Oxford, England: Pergamon Press, 1962.
14. Forrester, J. W. *World Dynamics.* Cambridge, Mass.: Wright-Allen Press, 1971.
15. Forrester, J. W., "Counterintuitive behavior of social systems." In *Toward Global Equilibrium: Collected papers,* D. L. Meadows and D. H. Meadows (eds). Cambridge, Mass.: Wright-Allen Press, 1973, pp. 3–30.
16. Hayek, F. A. *The Sensory Order.* Chicago: The University of Chicago Press, 1952.
17. Katz, L. N., J. Stamler, and R. Pick, *Nutrition and atherosclerosis.* Philadelphia: Lea and Febiger, 1958.
18. Kannan, N. P., *Energy, Economic Growth and Equity in the U.S.* New York: Praeger, 1979.
19. Lamb, H. H., *Climate: Present, Past and Future.* Vol. 1, *Fundamentals and Climate Now.* London: Methuen, 1972.
20. Lindeman, R. L. "The trophic-dynamic aspect of ecology," *Ecology,* 23, 399 (1942).
21. Manley, G., "Temperature trends in England, 1698–1957," *Archiv für Meteorologie, Geophysik und Bioklimatologie.* Ser. B, Allgemeine und Biologische Klimatologie, 9, No. 3/4, 413 (1959).
22. Medvedev, Z. A., *Nuclear Disaster in the Urals.* New York: W. W. Norton, 1979.
23. Mesarovic, M., and E. Pestel. *Mankind at the Turning Point: The Second Report to the*

Club of Rome. New York: E. P. Dutton, 1974.

24. Miller, S., *The Economics of Nuclear and Coal Power.* New York: Praeger, 1976.

25. O'Brien, W. B., *The Great Famine in Ireland.* London: Downey, 1896.

26. Ornstein, R. E., *The Psychology of Consciousness.* New York: The Viking Press, 1972.

27. Patten, B. C., ed. *Systems Analysis and Simulation in Ecology,* vols. 1–4. New York: Academic Press, 1971, 1972, 1975, 1976.

28. Pierce, W. D., R. A. Cushman and C. E. Hood. *The Insect Enemies of the Cotton Boll Weevil.* Washington, D.C.: U.S. Department of Agriculture, Bur. Entom. Bull., 100:1–99 (1912).

29. Steinhart, J. S., "The impact of technical advice on the choice for nuclear power," in *Perspectives on Energy,* 2d ed., L. C. Ruedisili and M. W. Firebaugh (eds.). New York: Oxford University Press, 1978, pp. 239–248.

30. Stobaugh, R., and D. Yergin, eds. *Energy Future.* New York: Random House, 1979.

31. Stuart, A., "That very interesting dance in the Baltimore Canyon," *Fortune,* Sept. 11, 1978, p. 66.

32. United Nations. *Statistical Yearbook, 1972,* 24th ed., Table 21, Vital statistics rates, natural increase rates, and expectation of life at birth. New York, 1973.

33. United Nations, *Statistical Yearbook, 1972,* 24th ed., Table 162, Net food supplies per person. New York, 1973.

34. U.S. Department of Agriculture, *Grain Market News,* Vol. 26, No. 27 (July 7, 1978), pp. 12–20 (Annual summaries for wheat).

35. U.S. Department of Commerce. *Statistical Abstract of the United States,* 99th ed. Tables 422 and 1324. Washington, D.C., 1978.

36. U.S. Department of Commerce. Comparative international statistics," in *Statistical Abstract of the United States* (annual statistical yearbook).

37. Watt, K. E. F., J. W. Young, J. L. Mitchiner, and J. W. Brewer. "A simulation of the use of energy and land at the national level," *Simulation,* 24, 129 (1975).

38. Wiener, N. *Cybernetics or Control and Communication in the Animal and the Machine,* 2d ed. Cambridge, Mass.: The MIT Press, 1961.

39. Wilson, E. O. *Sociobiology: the New Synthesis.* Cambridge, Mass.: Harvard University Press, 1975.

40. Woodham-Smith, C. *The Great Hunger: Ireland 1845–1849.* New York: Harper and Row, 1962.

2 INFORMATION, THE MIND, AND ENVIRONMENTAL PROBLEMS

And as intellect is to opinion, so is science to belief, and understanding to the perception of shadows.

Plato (c. 428–348 B.C.), The Republic, *Book VII*

MAIN THEMES OF THIS CHAPTER

This chapter expands on the theme introduced in Chapter 1 that perceptions of the environment are shaped by information and by the functioning of connections between the sensory system and the brain as well as by the real world.

We may have a defective perception of the environment because information is not collected or disseminated, is defective or available too late to be useful. Information may be inappropriate or too complex to be widely understood. Human beings may not respond appropriately to information for cultural reasons or reasons related to the biology of brain function.

The positions people hold on a controversial environmental matter such as the coyote-sheep issue depend on their knowledge about different causal pathways.

A major concern of society from now on will be getting raw information and analyses of information more readily and more promptly. Either the public or private sectors can do this with new, cheap computer facilities.

THE AVAILABILITY OF INFORMATION

It may seem odd to some readers to discuss information and the mind in a text on environment; however, the process by which information gets into the mind is central and crucial to our perception of the state of the environment. Inadequacies of this process have been important contributors to environmental problems. Therefore, it is important that we understand and deal with these inadequacies.

Information Not Collected

Information necessary for an assessment of the nature and severity of an environmental problem may not even be collected. No one may have realized that some imbalance exists; no one may have a legislative mandate to collect the necessary data; it may be too politically embarrassing to gather information, or it may be too technically difficult or expensive to collect. Two important recent examples are illegal immigration into the United States and demographic statistics useful for demonstrating the exact impact of air pollution on mortality rates.

In the case of illegal immigrants, various estimates are published ranging from about 600,000 to 1,200,000 net illegal immigrants a year (the net number that stay after some have been caught and deported). The exact number, which is clearly of immense importance for public policy, is simply not known. The unavailability of this number obviously is important in minimizing public alarm about the problem.

It is impossible to demonstrate the impact of air pollution concentration on the health of the people in a county unless we know the migration history of the people in that county. Some diseases caused by air pollution, such as lung cancer, develop over very long periods (perhaps fifteen to thirty years). Therefore, the full significance of an individual in a particular county developing lung cancer is not clear unless we know whether that individual has lived in the county one year, ten years, or 30 years. In the few instances where government agencies have collected statistics on migration history, the histories of the people in different counties appeared to be very different. Some counties consist almost entirely of people who have always lived there; some counties have had large influxes of young women from major midwestern and northeastern cities; and some counties have had major influxes of elderly people from the northwest. Unless one had a migration history of each person, therefore, to correlate with a health history, it would be impossible to develop a completely satisfactory picture of the statistical relationship between air pollution concentrations in each county, and the resultant impact on pollution-caused disease and death rates in that county.

Information Not Disseminated

Sometimes the critical information has been collected, but is not available for use in political debate. For example, government agencies have a great deal of information on present and likely future threat from terrorist groups. However, this information is not widely disseminated, and this is one of a number of factors that prevent balanced public debate on nuclear power. A great deal of information that would be critical for informed political debate about energy is available only in data sources that are not widely known, even though they are readily available. For example, it is possible to argue that United States retail energy prices are outrageously high, because few people know where to obtain figures on retail energy prices in other countries. In fact, some agencies collect and publish these figures, such as the International Road Federation (63, rue de Lausanne, Geneva, Switzerland) but it would take some research to discover this.

The argument that increased energy consumption per capita leads to constant increase in the rate of growth in gross national product per capita can be shown to be false, but to do so, one must collect statistics from the World Bank, the London *Economist*, the United Nations, or the U.S. Department of Commerce, and none of these figures is well known to the general public, since this type of analysis rarely appears in newspapers or popular magazines. There would probably be much more aggressive political pressure to deal with air pollution if the public were better informed about the relation between pollution levels and mortality rates. However, it takes some research to get the statistics from the Vital Statistics Bureaus of State Public Health Departments, and the data have not been publicized.

Information Defective or Biased

In some cases, the necessary information may have been collected and it may be available, but it is defective for some reason. In some cases, an environmental problem occurs because something inherent in the phenomenon masks the truth of a situation.

The purchase of real estate by speculators, who have no long-term interest in living on it, may veil the fact that the market is supersaturated and that resources should be spent elsewhere. Also, speculation in real estate creates a temporary demand for space, simply to house the families of the construction workers. As soon as there is a lull in construction, it becomes apparent that the demand was illusory. The history of the United States is replete with instances of real estate bubbles produced by speculation, with important recent examples being in the Orlando, Florida, area, the area surrounding the Dallas-Fort Worth airport, and beach areas in Hawaii and California.

There may be systematic bias in survey responses or measurements. In polls designed to find the proportion of the public that is satisfied with their state of health, 63 percent of Americans report satisfaction compared with 51 percent in Europe. Yet the life expectancy of American men at birth is 67.4 years as opposed to 72.1 in Sweden, 70.8 in Denmark, and 70.2 in Switzerland. So Americans have a view of the state of their health that is biased and renders it difficult to develop a political constituency to press for improved diet, air, water, and health care delivery systems. Other areas of systematic measurement biases include underestimating the cost of developing new fossil-fuel energy sources, such as shale oil. This has contributed to our failure to recognize the acute need to increase energy prices.

The public and government may get a biased view about an environmental problem because a particular group of people takes it on itself to ensure that information that is favorable to their case is widely disseminated, whereas information not favorable to their case is not disseminated at all. Several people have written about this matter as it relates to nuclear power. John Steinhart has pointed out that between the origin of the President's Scientific Advisory Committee in 1951 and 1966, there were sixty-five members of whom forty-five had some ties to the nuclear energy field (10). He noted that there has never been a geologist or a resource expert on that committee. It is startling to realize that the views of the world's leading authority on the stocks of fossil fuels, Dr. M. King Hubbert, who worked in Washington in the U.S. Geological survey, were throughout the 1960s and early 1970s much better known to college students worldwide than to the U.S. Senate, House, or president, who worked down the street from him. The government was being bombarded with the message that nuclear electric power would be too cheap to meter.

Recent analysis by physicists such as Amory Lovins, outside the nuclear "club," suggest that nuclear power will be very expensive relative to other forms of energy, not very cheap. Only around 1976 did Congress become aware of the argument in Table 4.9, that the entire U.S. population of nuclear plants might be a net consumer, rather than a net producer, of energy. As Steinhart has pointed out, not only was the government science advisory apparatus dominated by physicists, but these were an unusual subset of the entire national population of physicists, who did not represent a national viewpoint among physicists.

Students should be alerted to the fact that various vested interest groups in society are constantly trying to promulgate viewpoints in newspapers and newsmagazines as if they were fact, when they have no basis in fact. Newsmagazines slip in the point almost as an aside that high rate of population growth is a prerequisite for a high rate of economic growth, and that high rates of energy consumption and military expenditures stimulate economic growth. While complex statistical analyzes show all these propositions are the opposite of the truth, common sense shows the same thing. Otherwise, how would we explain the very high rates of economic growth in Japan, which had low rates of population growth, low levels of energy consumption per capita, and a low rate of investment in military preparedness?

Information Available Too Late

In some cases, the critical problem with environmentally relevant information is that it becomes available too late. To illustrate, the July 1973 volume of the Statistical Abstract of the United States (which became generally available between November 1973 and February 1974) had a figure for 1968 as its most up-to-date measurement of birth rates for 20- to 24-year-old women. In this case, a very rapidly dropping U.S. birth rate, which had the most profound implications for planning by electrical utilities, hospitals, educational institutions, water systems, and many other institutions, was simply unknown. Now we know that from 1968 to 1974, the birth rate of 20- to 24-year-old women dropped 29 percent. The consequences for planning are clear when we compare the projections for the U.S. population of under-five-year-olds for 1980, published in the 1973 Statistical Abstract, with those published in the 1976 Abstract. In just three years, the high and low projections of this population estimate had dropped by 15 percent and 11 percent, respectively.

Clearly, it is very much in the national interest to arrange for timely availability of population or environmental information necessary for planning by all agencies. A lot of expensive overbuilding and overinvestment, which unnecessarily wastes resources and pollutes, could thereby be avoided.

Information Inappropriate

An information problem occurs when politicians and others focus on inappropriate measures of systems performance to describe the behavior of the economy and the society. For example, gross national product (in "current" dollars; that is, without correcting for inflation) is an inappropriate measure of economic health. It does not take into account inflation, population increase, and decreased standard of living brought about by environmental degradation or social dysfunction, as measured in tax costs and social security benefit payments and insurance premium costs. By focusing on gross national product, which ignores all these complications, politicians and others make it appear as if there is a conflict between economic and environmental goals, when in fact there is not. Those strategies that make for a healthy environment also make for a healthy economy, as Sweden, Denmark, Switzerland, and Norway are demonstrating.

Information may contribute to an environmental problem if it is too complex to be understood without a major, high-technology research effort that is highly interdisciplinary in character. In such cases, even though the information is collected and available, complete interpretation requires a large computer and methods of analysis or thought that are not possessed by most people. Further, because of the institutional fragmentation mentioned in Chapter 9, few organizations may be structured to support such an activity. Particularly, working with systemic data from many sources, as illustrated by the data in Chapter 10 and the flow charts of Chapter 11, may require advanced methodologies in statistics, computing, and mathematics. There are a number of areas in which political debate is blunted simply because of this inherent problem complexity. Two concern the effect of air pollution on public health, and the effect of national energy policies on the rate of economic growth, inflation, unemployment, crime, and the tax burden.

Indeed, a systemic problem of modern society is that while government collects a great deal of data, it does not analyze this information in a fashion that fully reveals its implications for government policy. Indeed, many of the best-known private citizens of the last several decades have become well-known precisely because they filled the niche that should have been filled by government, of explaining to society the significance of certain data, Ralph Nader, Rachel Carson, and Barry Commoner are examples.

One of the most complex and difficult environmental problems in the United States in recent years concerns the issue of nuclear safety. It is extremely difficult for the lay person to obtain information about this issue that is objective, rather than the interpretation of facts by people representing a particular interest. This point is made dramatically clear by contrasting versions of what actually happened at Kyshtym, in Southern Russia, in the fall of 1957 (or spring of 1958). All versions of the incident agree that a wide area was contaminated by radioactivity. However, there is complete disagreement as to what caused the contamination, and the severity of the consequences. It is instructive to read the two views of the situation in Box 2.1, trying to imagine how one's attitude toward the safety of nuclear waste disposal technology would have been affected, if one had been exposed only to information source A (and had been ignorant of B), or had been exposed only to B (and had been ignorant of A).

Students wishing to write papers on the treatment of information about this incident will also wish to consult a news story in the New Scientist, Vol. 85 (Jan. 10, 1980), p. 61, and the book review in the American Scientist, Vol. 68 (1980), p. 203. Both these sources dismiss as impossible or incredible the notion that the contamination resulted from a Novaya Zemlya weapons test. The New Scientist story mentioned that maps of the Kyshtym region in the Urals for the period after the accident were missing names of more than 30 small communities. At least 2000 people died or emigrated. The most definitive treatment of this incident is "Analysis of the 1957–1958 Soviet Nuclear Accident," by J. R. Trabalka, L. D. Eyman, and S. I. Auerbach, Science, Vol. 209 (1980), pp. 345–353.

Given an example such as this, it is clear that the particular way in which information about an incident is presented to the readers has a very large impact on their perceptions of reality. Clearly, one's attitudes about environmental matters are not only shaped by the facts: they are also shaped by the way in which the facts are interpreted and reported.

BOX 2.1
What Actually Happened? A typical environmental controversy illustrating the role of information in forming public perceptions of a situation.

Information source A: "sanitized" and declassified sections of C.I.A. files on Kyshtym nuclear accident in autumn of 1957, published in major U.S. daily newspapers, Nov. 26, 1977; Zhores A. Medvedev, *Nuclear Disaster in the Urals.* New York: W.W. Norton, 1979.
Information source B: W. Stratton, D. Stillman, S. Barr, and H. Agnew, "Are portions of the Urals really contaminated?" *Science* 206 (1979), p. 423.

What happened?
Source A: "Various Soviet employees and visitors to the Brussels fair have stated independently but consistently that the occurrence of an accidental atomic explosion during the spring of 1958 was widely known throughout the U.S.S.R." (C.I.A. file dated May 23, 1958).
Source B: "Another possibility, more plausible than Medvedev's, is that the contaminated area is simply the result of localized fallout of radioactive material from a Soviet atmospheric nuclear weapons test at Novaya Zemlya."

How serious was the incident?
Source A: "I lived with my parents in a village called Kopaesk, outside Chelyabinsk, in 1948 . . . Around the end of 1957, we began to hear rumours that a terrible accident had occurred at Chelyabinsk 40, that there had been a terrible nuclear explosion, an accident caused by the storage of the radioactive waste from the plant. Soon after the routes between Sverdlovsk and Kopaesk were closed. I could not see my parents for about a year.

"Also during that year, I spoke with friends who were doctors. I went once to a hospital in Sverdlovsk for the removal of a wart, and one of my friends, a doctor, told me that the entire hospital was crammed with victims of the Kyshtym catastrophe. He said that all the hospitals in the entire area were crammed full, not only in Sverdlovsk but also in Chelyabinsk. These are huge hospitals with many hundreds of beds. The doctors all told me that the victims were suffering from radioactive contamination. It was a tremendous number of people, I believe thousands. I was told that most of them died." (Account by witness who had lived in the southern Urals, broadcast on British television company Granada, November 1977.)

Source B: "In 1958 rumors surfaced in Western Europe that a radiation release accident had occurred in the Soviet Union. . .

"We find that the physical problems associated with widespread dispersal of large amounts of strontium-90 and cesium-137 from a plutonium ground-storage criticality event are so monumentally difficult that this postulate cannot be considered seriously."

PROBLEMS CONCERNING THE RESPONSE TO INFORMATION

Even if all the information problems just mentioned have been dealt with, there remains a further group of problems related to the response of people to information about the environment. The response may be inappropriate for cultural reasons or for reasons related to the biological makeup of the brain and sensory system.

Cultural Responses

For example, it is characteristic of people in our civilization at present to be strongly oriented toward an optimistic (as opposed to realistic) world view. Thus, the electorate is culturally biased toward believing optimistic forecasts of the rate of economic growth, the availability of energy, the state of public health, future resource depletion, agriculture, climate, and the omnipotence of technology, and to put alternative forecasts out of mind as "doomsaying."

A culture strongly programmed to believe that technology and the state can solve any problem, no matter how large, will tend not to perceive that there are limits to the carrying capacity of the nation for people. Consequently, a tidal wave of illegal immigrants will not be perceived as an imminent threat to national security. Thus, there will be political risks involved in politicians or newspapers attempting to promote open public discussion or debate about the need to take vigorous action, even when national unemployment rates are consistently high.

Indeed, culture responds slowly to changed conditions of life. Increasingly, we must deal with systems, and not things, yet the whole history of humanity until recently has been principally concerned with land, resources, and food. Merely stating this problem gives us a hint as to the indicated solution: we need to devise schemes for rapidly evolving new cultural patterns of appropriate response to new situations, in which the problems concern systems, not things. Happily, a newly available tool will facilitate this: the explosively growing new institutional approaches to adult reeducation.

A most important means by which the culture can affect our response to the environment is by means of advertising. As Wilson Bryan Key has pointed out, the most important messages being transmitted to us by advertising are not the ones of which we are aware. The subliminal messages are almost certainly more important in motivating our behavior. Thus, we may think that the real reason we buy large, energy-inefficient cars is to get from one place to another; the photographs used in automobile advertising suggest in many instances that the subliminal theme being implanted is the importance of the car as an aid in sexual success.

Two groups of facts suggest that Americans are very confused about the appropriate role of the car. Statistics on U.S. car use reveal that a surprisingly high proportion of all trips in cars are over very short distances, for which it would have been just as easy to walk. Also, careful exploration with classes of the motives for car driving suggests that transportation is only one of a wide array of functions. Protection against rape and assault, enforced isolation from other people, control over the rate at which information is bombarding the nervous system, and the desire to identify with a symbol of personal power and status are also important reasons for car-driving. The problem is that these kinds of needs could be better dealt with in other ways than by extraordinarily inefficient use of energy. Comparison of the texts and pictures in car advertising suggests that the ultimate cause for much of our strange use of the car may be the advertising.

Similarly, the tremendous amount of advertising of the ranch-bungalow, single-family life style in the suburbs has had a great impact on the virtually unique spatial layout of U.S. cities, which in extreme cases might occupy almost 5000 square miles. A functional unit of this much area maintains integrity only at a tremendous cost in energy overhead on all passenger and goods transportation. The situation would be very different if there had been equally aggressive and voluminous advertising for multi-family structures.

Biological Responses

Another class of phenomena affecting our response to information about the environment originates not in our culture, but in the biological structure and functioning of our brain-mind system. Richard Meier (7) and James Miller (8) pointed out that a characteristic of all systems is to malfunction if the rate of message receipt becomes too high. That applies to the individual human mind, or the organization, as well as other types of systems. The lack of response by most people to information about the state of the world may simply mean that while they don't have enough useful information, the total amount of information they have is more than they can cope with. One approach the individual can adopt is to deliberately screen out information of little or no value. Stafford Beer has suggested that organizations be restructured so that instead of having many hierarchical layers, they have only two (1). In the top layer, a few people would formulate broad policy on the basis of minimal (but carefully selected) information about the detailed working of the system for which they were responsible. The single lower layer of the organization would consist of a large number of teams that looked only at parts of the system relevant for

them, making up rules as they go along to keep the system performing properly. Most of the system information management and monitoring would be handled by computers.

Another feature of brain biology may result in an inappropriate response to environmental information. Arthur Koestler (5) has pointed out that lower levels of the cortex respond to information by integrating data from the sense organs with "data" from the viscera, which reflect our feelings, as well as an objective view of the world. Further, our response to information may not merely reflect a rational response to incoming environmental information by the highest level of our brain, the neocortex, but rather, this response may be altered or overridden by the lower levels of the cortex (the "limbic system"). It takes alertness and a sophisticated, trained awareness of our own biological nature to ensure that our response to environmental and other information is the product of our reason, rather than our emotions, but it can be done. Otherwise, we believe what our feelings make us want to believe, or what habit leads us to believe, rather than the truth, as revealed by a critical examination of the evidence.

Some simple exercises suggest the way in which lower levels of the nervous system interfere with the receipt of messages from the nervous system to the higher brain centers. If a subject is blindfolded in an active urban area, and asked to report everything he or she can infer about the environment from what he or she hears, the results can be most revealing. The subject will report surprise at the amount of traffic noise heard, and probably will also express irritation at this noise. This irritation may act as a filter interfering with the ability to "hear" other sounds in the environment. When asked if any other sound can be heard, the response may be no, even when the subject is pointed at a sound source a few score yards away, such as wind whistling through the leaves of a tree.

When the blindfold is removed, the subject immediately recognizes that there is another sound source close by. In general, feelings about an issue may serve as a filter impairing our ability to perceive information coming from the sense organs. The phenomenon is striking in the case of political confrontations that arise in connection with environmental issues.

Thus many different types of filters operate on the system by which information is transmitted from the sense organs to the brain. All operate on both our intellectual tools and our sense organs. The sense organs in turn operate on the conscious mind directly, but also indirectly via the subconscious mind. The main point is that each of us is only consciously aware of part of the pathway by which we form our perceptions of reality. When we look at an advertisement, our eyes are quickly scanning the page for information; some of that passes through the system of which we are immediately aware. Part of the information gleaned by the eye passes into our nervous system, unkown to the higher levels of our mind. This other information can be powerfully important in shaping our subsequent behavior. It is this "other" pathway on which skilled advertisers and politicians operate. The best available psychiatric information would suggest that Hitler was a master at exploitation of these "other" pathways in mass public meetings (6). Modern advertising, which makes sophisticated use of these pathways, is based on the notion of "imbedding" hidden messages that will be "read" by the subconscious but not the conscious mind (3, 4).

A SUMMARY OF THE ARGUMENT

Thus, political decisions are made, not necessarily on the basis of the realities of a situation, but on the basis of human response to the available information. Decisions are more likely to be influenced by early data than late data, even though the early data may be extremely misleading; by inexpensive and widely available data, even if it is wrong; and by simple rather than complex information and interpretations, even though the simple view of the phenomenon is wrong. In complex systems, the simple view will almost always be wrong. Further, people interested in personal power quickly discover the power that comes from control of information (Chapter 8). To illustrate the systemic effects of this situation, the United States has become strongly committed to a life style based on the assumption that there is unlimited availability of cheap energy because of the following reasons, all related to information and the response by the mind to information:

1. Correct information on remaining fossil fuel reserves and on the cost of nuclear power is difficult and expensive to obtain.
2. Powerful vested interests spread misinformation, and withhold some critically important components of the information.
3. Many aspects of the net energy problem and the world energy situation are simply too complex for many people and organizations to analyze and comprehend. Sophisticated computer techniques are used to assess mineral fuel reserves. The few organizations that have the resources to analyze the energy dilemma thoroughly and accurately may not have a vested interest in doing this, or in reporting the results to the public.
4. Our culture has programmed us to have an optimistic, rather than realistic view of the energy situation.
5. Our brains program us to take a particular view of the energy situation. Lower levels of the brain probably function by

keeping us functioning efficiently, and one way of doing this is to keep us happy. In turn, a way of doing this is to exclude from the conscious level of the mind disturbing, provoking, or ominous data. Thus, it would be reasonable to expect most people to put the energy problem "out of mind."

A COMPLEX EXAMPLE

To this point, our discussion of the role of information and the mind in environmental problems has been rather general. We can get a much better feeling for the way in which these phenomena affect an environmental problem if we consider a complex, real-world problem in some detail. A richly detailed example concerns one of the most politically difficult problems in America today: that of the sheep rancher versus conservationist controversy over coyote depredation of sheep. This example will be dealt with elsewhere in the book in analyzing the structure of political conflicts, and devising ways of conflict resolution; here, our only purpose is to analyze the problem from an information standpoint. Figure 2.1 is a flow chart of the causal pathways between the main elements in the coyote-sheep system. In order to make rational decisions about management of this system, one would need information about all the causal pathways indicated by the arrows. However, information is available only on the causal pathways indicated by the thickened arrows. Thus, for example, we have reasonably accurate estimates of the numbers of coyotes and other predators killed by humans in area-wide coyote control programs. Examples of causal pathways about which we have very little information are the effects of densities of other predators on the densities of herbivores that compete with sheep, and the effects of those, in turn, on range plants.

A little thought about this flow chart will point out innumerable ways in which our perception of the problem and our selection of control strategies are totally influenced by the fact that we know about the thick lines, but do not know about the thin lines. For example, consider the following line of reasoning. We notice that some sheep and lambs we find dead have coyote teeth marks on them, so we conclude that coyotes kill sheep. We also know that many coyotes die as a result of our control. Therefore, we control coyotes. But what if we were, in fact, successful in removing all the coyotes, and all other large predators from sheep-ranching country? The possibility does not alarm us, because we have virtually no knowledge of the extent to which the densities of herbivores competing with sheep are controlled by the entire ensemble of predatory species. Suppose, however, that the coyotes and other predators are very important in controlling densities of hares, rabbits, mice, voles, grasshoppers, and other herbivores that compete with the sheep. What we would win by total area-wide control of all predators would be an explosive growth in the populations of all these competitors of sheep. Given the extraordinarily great difficulty humans have had trying to eradicate the coyote and other large predators, all of which have relatively low reproductive potential, imagine the difficulty we would have eradicating from all sheep ranges hares, rabbits, voles, mice, grasshoppers, and so on. Clearly, the task would be impossible, and these competitors of sheep would shortly drive sheep from the range because some of them can crop range more completely than sheep. This is a clear instance in which our preoccupation with the causal pathways we did know about would blind us to the consequences of interfering with causal pathways we did not know about. Of course, this is only one way in which humanity's manipulation of this system is defective. The more

FIGURE 2.1

A flow chart of the causal pathways involved in the coyote-sheep system, which gener-
ates the sheep rancher-conservationist controversy. The thin lines represent causal
pathways on which the information developed by research to this point is inadequate.
The thick lines represent causal pathways on which the available information is ade-
quate, or approximately adequate.

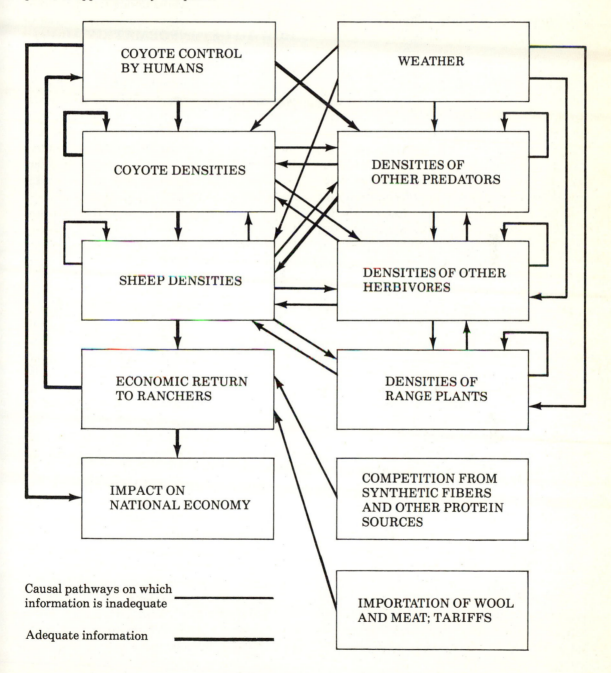

serious problem is that killing coyotes increases the rate of production of coyotes, as we would expect from Chapter 5. Any killing rate that has been attained to date has been far below that required to annhilate coyotes, and in fact has only been successful in increasing their densities (Chapter 14).

IMPROVING THE SYSTEM

The information problems described in this chapter could be solved if a number of steps were taken. There needs to be sufficient political pressure on government to guarantee that all necessary information about environmental problems will be collected, subjected to revealing and useful analysis, and distributed quickly. Government should stop being satisfied with simply distributing raw data. There should be political pressure to build more interdisciplinary data analysis capability into government.

However, we can't expect government to solve all our problems, and it may not solve very many unless pressured into it by the embarassment of outside competition. Fortunately, it is quickly becoming cheap, easy, and entertaining to do this. Advances in the manufacturing of microchip circuits are now making it possible to get significant computer installations into private homes for $500. This means that many individuals will be able to make hobbies out of analyzing government data, and inventing progressively more and more revealing ways of doing this.

Also, one of the most rapidly growing industries in this country (besides manufacture of home computers) is adult education and retraining. The cultural and biological problems mentioned will gradually be exposed and dealt with in these programs. If each individual can become sensitized to the extent that information availability shapes his or her thinking, the likelihood of inappropriate responses to environmental problems is lessened. Also, spread of the new educational programs will speed up the development of appropriate cultural responses to these problems.

HOW TO GET INFORMATION ABOUT ENVIRONMENTAL MATTERS

The literature in all fields is becoming overwhelming; this is particularly true in environmental studies, because it cuts across so many other disciplines. How can one find any given piece of information, or get an overview of any particular topic? A number of tools are available to facilitate such efforts.

Comprehensive textbooks often contain exhaustive references to other literature, and serve as useful places to begin a search. Two books with particularly large lists of references are:

1. Paul R. Ehrlich, Anne H. Ehrlich, and John P. Holdren. *Ecoscience.* San Francisco: W.H. Freeman, 1977.
2. G. Tyler Miller, Jr. *Living in the Environment,* 3rd ed. Belmont, Calif.: Wadsworth, 1981.

Experience suggests that these periodicals are particularly useful for keeping informed about environmental matters:

1. *Not Man Apart.* Available from Friends of the Earth, 124 Spear St., San Francisco, CA 94105. Semimonthly newsmagazine.
2. *Audubon.* Available from the National Audubon Society, 950 Third Ave., New York, NY 10022. Six issues a year.
3. *Environmental Action.* Available from Environmental Action, Inc., 1346 Connecticut Ave., NW, Washington, D.C. 20036. Eleven issues a year.

4. Zero Population Growth, Inc., 1346 Connecticut Ave., NW, Washington, D.C. 20036. Regular newsletters, and irregularly issued leaflets, which are most informative.

5. *Environmental Defense Fund Letter.* The Environmental Defense Fund, 475 Park Avenue South, New York, NY 10016. Bimonthly. Very useful information about the current status of legal actions taken on by EDF.

The following are particularly useful sources of raw data concerning environmental matters:

1. *Statistical Abstract of the United States.* Bureau of the Census, U.S. Dept. of Commerce. Annual, with vast mass of information on the United States, and thirty-four pages of tables comparing nations.

2. *Statistical Yearbook.* Statistical Office of the United Nations, New York.

3. *State and Metropolitan Area Data Book.* Bureau of the Census, U.S. Dept. of Commerce. Biennial.

Students conducting projects on transportation energy consumption will find the *Census of Retail Trade (Gasoline)* useful; for international comparisons, the yearbooks of the International Road Federation are excellent. Many states have an agency with a title such as Air Resources Board that publishes monthly or annual reports on air pollution concentrations. Agricultural and fisheries data are summarized in the *Production Yearbook,* and the *Fisheries Yearbook,* respectively, of the Food and Agriculture Organization of the United Nations.

Suppose you have absolutely no idea where to start. What then? Three most useful ways to get started are (1) the card catalogue of any major library, (2) journals that publish abstracts of scientific and technical literature, such as *Biological Abstracts,* and (3) the large volume, *Books in Print,* which is found in most libraries or bookstores. Most large libraries have Government Documents departments, staffed by specialists on finding obscure data sources for you.

Many large libraries now have experts at the reference desk who can introduce you to new computer systems for searching master information banks. By this means, or by going to the Interlibrary Loan Desk, you can locate and borrow materials from other institutions.

SUMMARY

Our perceptions of environmental issues are shaped by information, and the way our sensory systems and brains function, as well as by the real world.

Many political controversies over environmental issues are really information problems: solve the information problem and the controversy evaporates.

The roles of economics, government and politics, and culture in environmental problems can only be understood in terms of information and perception.

SUGGESTIONS FOR INDIVIDUAL AND GROUP PROJECTS

Select a complex, controversial environmental problem in your locality, and subject it to an analysis analogous to that applied to the coyote (e.g. reference 9). How will policy selection for solving the problem be affected by the availability of information? Are there some ways in which the problem could turn out badly because of bad decisions made on the basis of inadequate information? Don't forget the "boomerang" phenomenon (to be discussed in Chapter 5).

Write an essay in which you assess the role that information suppression or distortion has played in public perceptions concerning the safety of nuclear energy plants and waste disposal sites (2). Evaluate the detective work used to determine the magnitude of the damage in the 1957 Russian accident (see Zhores A. Medvedev, Appendix II of "The Ural nuclear disaster of 1957," in *Soviet Science*. New York: W.W. Norton, 1978, pp. 232–244), and the effect of suppression of twenty-nine documents on the incident for twenty years by the C.I.A. (San Francisco *Chronicle*, Nov. 26, 1977, p. 10 and other major newspapers for the same date). Assess the impact on the media of the document by Herbert Inhaber concerning the relative risks from nuclear and other energy sources. (Herbert Inhaber, "Risk with energy from conventional and nonconventional sources," *Science*, 203 (1979): 718–723; Rein Lemberg, letter to *Science*, 204 (1979): 454; J. P. Holdren, K. R. Smith, and G. Morris, letter to *Science*, 204 (1979): 564–567; *Wall Street Journal*, "Coming to grips with risk," 100 (50):20 (March 13, 1979).

Do you think that this manipulation with the process of information dissemination has any effect on public attitudes? What do friends and classmates tell you about how they formulated their attitudes towards the safety of nuclear power? Do their attitudes change if you explain to them the manipulation of information concerning the Russian incident, or the circumstances of the Inhaber document and the aftermath?

Organize the class into two debate teams, and debate the correctness of the proposition advanced by Julian Simon that there has been an oversupply of false bad news about the environment (*Science* 208, pp. 1431–1437). Pay particular attention to his handling of data and statistics.

REFERENCES

1. Beer, S. *Platform for Change*. London: John Wiley and Sons, 1975.
2. Comptroller General of the United States. Evaluation of the publication and distribution of "Shedding light on facts about nuclear energy." U.S. General Accounting Office, Washington, D.C. 1976.
3. Key, W. B. *Subliminal Seduction*. Englewood Cliffs, N.J.: Prentice-Hall, 1973.
4. Key, W. B. *Media Sexploitation*. Englewood Cliffs, N.J.: Prentice-Hall, 1976.
5. Koestler, A. *The Ghost in the Machine*. London: Hutchinson, 1967.
6. Langer, W. C. *The Mind of Adolf Hitler*. New York: Basic Books, 1972.
7. Meier, R. L. "Communications stress." *Annual Review of Ecology and Systematics*, 3 (1972): 289–314.
8. Miller, J. G. *Living Systems*. New York: McGraw-Hill, 1978.
9. Sanders, H. L. "The West Falmouth Saga. How an oil expert twisted the facts about a landmark oil spill study." *New Engineer*, May 1974, pp. 32–38.
10. Steinhart, J. S. "The impact of technical advice on the choice for nuclear power," in *Perspectives on Energy*, by L. C. Ruedisili and M. W. Firebaugh. New York: Oxford University Press, 1974, pp. 504–513.

II The Components of Environmental Systems

In Chapter 1 I introduced the notion that seven different types of components play a role in complex environmental systems. This part explains each of these seven types in turn, as preparation for explanation of their function together in Part 3.

Chapter 1 pointed out the significance of food exports as a means of paying for crude oil imports. Therefore, fluctuations in climate (average weather) are important in determining our ability to grow enough food to pay for fuel. Even more important, fluctuations in crop-growing climate in other countries determine their need to import our food. Chapter 3 considers the factors affecting climate and the links between climate and food production.

Chapters 4 and 5 explore the factors that determine the production of nonrenewable and renewable resources. The status of any nation is determined by the balance between the supply of these resources and the demand for them, which is partly determined by population size (considered in Chapter 6).

The balance between supply and demand for resources is reflected by the price. Price also determines the rate at which resources are used and the rate at which resources are substituted for each other. These substitutions in turn determine the efficiency with which various resources are used, and that in turn affects the rate of growth in the economy. Such linkages between the economic and environmental system are dealt with in Chapter 7.

Increasingly, the economic policies that determine patterns of resource utilization are imposed by government. Chapter 8 explores the way government operates and the reasons for its environmental policies.

Government policies on the environment are, in part, the result of public pressure, which depends on public perceptions of environmental issues. These perceptions are influenced by the prevailing cultural belief system. Accordingly, Chapter 9 examines the forces shaping our cultural beliefs on the environment.

3 THE PHYSICAL ENVIRONMENT: WEATHER AND CLIMATE

... fires breathe forth at times through the gorges of Mount Aetna with such hurricane-like fury; for with a destroying force of no ordinary kind the flame-storm gathered itself up and lording it over the lands of the Sicilians drew on itself the gaze of neighboring nations, when seeing all the quarters of heaven smoke and sparkle men were filled in heart with awe-struck apprehension, not knowing what strange change nature was travailing to work.

Titus Lucretius Carus (c. 98–c. 55 B.C.) On the Nature of Things,
Book VI

MAIN THEMES OF THIS CHAPTER

Over the last two centuries, the most important factor causing one-to-three-year temperature depressions extending over tens of millions of square miles has been the dust and gas from volcanic eruptions. Fluctuations in climate (average weather) have been surprisingly large and completely unpredictable. World climate from 1920 to 1960 was milder than it has been any time since 1600; lack of any major volcanic eruptions from 1913 to 1962 was a major cause.

Weather fluctuations and shifts in climate have large effects on all living systems and therefore on economic and political events. Variations in climate from place to place produce profound differences between places in the amount and type of plant growth.

The preceding facts have three important implications. (1) The great increase in world human population since 1900 has been made possible by an unusually mild climate, which allowed for high crop yields. It is not prudent for humanity to assume indefinite continuation of such climate. (2) The economy should be managed so as to minimize the impact of inevitable weather fluctuations on starvation and economic hardship. (3) Very large time-to-time differences in food production at any place are a natural consequence of climate. It would be wise, therefore, for human population at any given place to be determined by long-term average (rather than highest possible) food production, if mass suffering is to be avoided.

THE DETERMINANTS OF WEATHER AND CLIMATE

Chapter 1 mentioned that the United States paid for imported crude oil by exporting large quantities of wheat, corn, and soybeans. This implies that our economic health is dependent on crop-growing weather conditions. Consequently, our curiosity is aroused as to how much weather and climate (average weather) might vary from time to time. Indeed, for all nations throughout history, weather and climate have been critical determinants of the power of a country, because they determine not only the supply of food for the population, but also the surplus of agricultural commodities that could be sold to other nations in exchange for other goods. Further, the question as to how much climate might alter through time has an implication for the entire world human population.

Some people argue that the great increase in world human population from about 1.6 billion in 1900 to roughly 4.4 billion in 1980 was made possible almost entirely by a tre-

mendous improvement in agricultural technology (farm machinery innovations, fertilizer, irrigation, new strains of plants and livestock, and pesticides). Others argue, however, that much of the increased farm productivity during that period was due to an improvement in weather for crop growth. A number of very important questions are suggested by this controversy.

What is "normal" weather? If the weather from 1900 to 1980 was typical with respect to the long-term history of the planet, then argiculture did not get an unusual assist from the weather in that period, and it is reasonable to expect that on average, crop-growing conditions from now on will be equally favorable. If world weather from 1900 to 1980 was not typical, but was unusually favorable for crop growth, the implications would be very far-reaching. It would suggest that the human population of the planet had increased to a level that required not only a very high level of technological input to agriculture but also an indefinite continuation of weather unusually favorable for crop growth.

What determines favorable weather for crop growth? Three causes might be operating: (1) extraterrestrial factors, such as fluctuations in emission of energy by the sun; (2) terrestrial factors beyond human control, and (3) human-caused terrestrial factors. If we want to predict or partially to regulate weather on earth, then we must understand at the outset the types of effects due to these three groups of factors and their relative magnitudes.

There are several competing theories as to how climate is regulated (15); accordingly, we adopt a completely pragmatic, as opposed to theoretical, approach and examine the data. Long-term weather records can be a useful tool in separating effects due to the different factors. These records are useful in discovering trends in weather and also in

FIGURE 3.1

Long term changes in "normal" weather in the Northern Hemisphere. For each place, the average annual temperature for a ten-year period is expressed as a departure from the average for the period 1801–1950 (in degrees Celsius). In the bottom panel, the departure for each decade is the average of the other four departures for that decade. (Central England data from Gordon Manley in Archiv für Meterorologie, Geophysik und Bioklimatologie, *Ser. B,9, 1959; Copenhagen and Berlin data by permission of the Smithsonian Institution Press, from Smithsonian Miscellaneous Collections, Vol. 205, "World Weather Records," by H. Helm and Frances L. Clayton; New Haven data from* Historical Statistics of The United States, Colonial Times to 1970, *U.S. Department of Commerce.)*

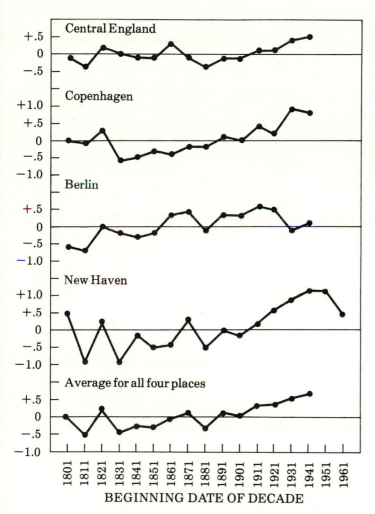

identifying the most likely causes of those trends.

Many books and articles report on changes that have occurred in world climate over extended periods, using various techniques for averaging weather records from many different places (3, 8, 13, 16, 17, 21, 23). However, a much simpler analysis reveals the same pattern. New Haven, Connecticut is the U.S. weather station for which temperature readings are available for the longest time. The fourth panel of Figure 3.1 is a graph of the mean New Haven temperatures over ten-year periods, beginning with 1801, all expressed as deviations from the 1801 to 1950 New Haven average annual temperature.

Climate at New Haven fluctuated a great deal from 1801 to 1920, but always around a lower average than characteristic of more recent decades. Then from 1920 to the decade beginning 1941, there was a steady increase in temperature. Finally, there has been a pronounced cooling since 1951.

The magnitude of the changes in climate at New Haven have been quite startling. The ten-year averages for the decades beginning 1811 and 1831 were a remarkable 2.1 degrees Celsius below the ten-year average for the decade beginning 1941. Those two cold nineteenth century decades in New Haven were completely outside the range of experience of anyone now alive (21). Which of the three causes previously mentioned might account for a climatic alteration this large? One way of answering this question is to compare very long sequences of weather records from several widely separated locations.

Unfortunately, there are very few places for which instrumental records are available for periods of up to two centuries. Four of the best are from New Haven, Connecticut; Copenhagen, Denmark; Berlin, Germany; and central England. In Figure 3.1 the average temperatures for a ten-year period are plotted against time for each decade from 1801 to 1950, for each of these four places. In each case, the temperatures for each decade are expressed in terms of the departure from the 150-year average temperature for that place. In the bottom panel, the average of the four departures for each decade is plotted against time.

The first thing we notice about this chart is a slight upward trend in each of the four places over the 150-year period. Since the places are spread over about a 4000-mile distance, this suggests that some global change in climate occurred during the interval. Examining the five trend lines in more detail, we notice something very striking. There are three decades in which the world temperature took a sharp drop: the decades beginning 1811, 1831, and 1881; and the first two drops were more serious than the last drop. A further fascinating fact is that for each of the three unusually cold decades, the drops occurred at each of the four places. Some factor operates to regulate weather over very large areas. What might that factor be?

To explore this matter, we can calculate the year-by-year change in weather for the four places, in each case expressed as a departure from the 150-year mean temperature for the place, for critical decades. The decades of most interest begin in 1811 and 1831, to try to isolate the causes of the temperature drops in those decades, and in 1941, to bring out the contrast between those cold decades and a recent decade we think of as "normal" weather.

When we do this calculation we find that the low average temperatures for the decades beginning 1811 and 1831 were not due to cold temperatures every year throughout those two decades, but to extremely cold temperatures that occurred everywhere in certain years. In the first decade, there were obviously very cold years in 1812, 1814, and 1816, and the entire period 1836 to 1840 was very cold, with 1838 being a particularly cold year. Clearly, these short, extremely cold periods drag down the average temperatures for the decade. In the warm decade beginning in 1941, there was never a particularly cold year. Now what produces a particularly cold year?

Benjamin Franklin's Explanation

Perhaps Benjamin Franklin, in 1784, was the first person to guess that tremendous changes in the temperature of the earth might be due not only to changes in the amount of energy coming from the sun, but also to changes in the extent to which that energy could penetrate the earth's atmosphere (11, 18). He noticed a dry fog covering much of the world in 1783 that might account for the cold autumn and winter of 1783 to 1784 and guessed that this fog might have been produced either by particles from volcanic eruptions or a comet.

Since his time, there has been a great development of the science of geophysics. It is now known that the material ejected into the atmosphere in a volcanic eruption can lower the temperature of the earth by at least 2 to 4 degrees Celsius (11). The most recent versions of this theory (18, 22) argue that there can be a time delay of at least two years from the time of the eruption to the time of maximum impact on temperature depression. There are two reasons for this delay.

The first is slow transport in the atmosphere of dust from the latitude where the eruption took place to the latitude where the temperature depression is observed.

The second is that a principal cause of the temperature depression is sulfuric acid aerosols, and these are formed only slowly, under

TABLE 3.1

Magnitudes of the largest natural explosions in the nineteenth and twentieth centuries relative to each other, to Mt. St. Helens (1980), and to a hydrogen (thermonuclear) bomb explosion.

Explosion	Total energy of explosion in ergs	Volume of material ejected into the atmosphere (cu. km.)	Dust veil index
Tambora, Sumbawa, 1815	8.4×10^{26}	100	3000
Coseguina, Nicaragua, 1835	4.8×10^{26}	50	4000
Katmai, Alaska, 1912	2.0×10^{26}	—	150
Krakatoa, Indonesia, 1883	1.0×10^{25}	18	1000
Agung, Bali, 1963	4.5×10^{24}	—	800
Bikini atoll hydrogen bomb, March 1, 1954	6.3×10^{23} (15 megatons)	—	—
Mount St. Helens, May 18, 1980	4×10^{23} (10 megatons)	—	—

Data on energies of explosion and volume of ejecta from Tables 9 and 10 in *Volcanoes of the Earth,* by Fred M. Bullard (University of Texas Press). Copyright © 1976 by Fred M. Bullard. All rights reserved. Data on dust veil indices from Table 10.3 in *Climate, Present, Past and Future, Volume 1,* by H. H. Lamb (Methuen and Co. Ltd.) and data on magnitude of explosion from "Observation on the Mount St. Helens' eruption," *American Scientist,* 68 (1980): 494–509.

the influence of sunlight, from the sulfur gases vented during a volcanic explosion.

With this knowledge, we examine historical data on major volcanic eruptions to see if they account for the trends in weather of Figure 3.1 (4). The data on the largest volcanic eruptions since 1800 are collated in Table 3.1 together with data on the Bikini atoll hydrogen bomb explosion and the 1980 Mount St. Helens eruption. Clearly, the largest volcanic eruptions involve an enormous amount of energy (about a thousand times that of a hydrogen bomb), and eject very large amounts of material into the upper atmosphere. Also, we note that the three largest volcanoes on which we have reasonably certain information would have had their maximum impact on world weather about 1816 to 1817 (Tambora), 1836 to 1837 (Coseguina), and 1884 to 1885 (Krakatoa). These dates account for the three major temperature depressions in Figure 3.1, and the particularly severe depressions in 1816 and 1837 to 1838, previously mentioned. It is noteworthy that Tambora and Coseguina had roughly 2000 and 1200 times the explosive force of Mount St. Helens in 1980 (19).

The only complication is the additional temperature depressions of 1812 and 1814, and these are due to a series of minor volcanic eruptions after 1811. In short, it appears that volcanic eruptions have been by far the most important determinant of climatic change in that part of the historical record for which we have reliable data. The technical literature arrives at the same conclusion (3, 13, 16, 18, 23).

Significance of Effect of Volcanoes

The implications of this finding are very important. Beginning with ancient times, there has been an immense interest in observational astronomy in virtually all high cul-

FIGURE 3.2

Plume of volcanic dust and vapors streaming out of Mt. Aetna, Sicily. Satellite photograph supplied by Professor Peter E. Baylis, Department of Electrical Engineering and Electronics, The University, Dundee. Copyright, The University, Dundee.

tures and civilizations, presumably because extraterrestrial phenomena were assumed to have an overriding importance for planting times, harvest times, and crop growth in between. Modern discoveries concerning volcanic eruptions indicate that events on this planet may also have a very large impact on changes in weather. The other implication is that if volcanic ejecta, a form of atmospheric pollution, have such a large impact on climate, then perhaps human-caused air pollution could also.

Some people may find it difficult to believe that a volcano, a mere point on the planet, might eject enough material into the atmosphere to affect weather over the entire globe. Unfortunately, from the standpoint of making the argument completely convincing, no very large volcano has erupted during the period when the planet was under constant surveillance by satellites. However, there are several excellent satellite photographs of the effect on the atmosphere of small volcanoes, with dust veil indices one percent or less that of Tambora and Coseguina. One particularly clear photograph shows volcanic ash and steam being emitted from Mt. Aetna on the island of Sicily (Fig. 3.2).

After viewing this photograph, it seems less surprising that an eruption one hundred to several hundred times as great could give rise to a plume that would gradually spread over the entire planet, diminishing incoming solar radiation by as much as 20 percent.

Our Effects on Climate

As it became more widely recognized that world climate could be strongly influenced by the characteristics of the atmosphere, scientists have become more and more concerned about a variety of possible mechanisms by which we could affect the atmosphere and the global energy system. Five of these mechanisms have attracted particular attention. We will explain each of these briefly, then evaluate their likely future impacts.

1. Our worldwide increase in combustion of fuels in industry and transportation leads to increase in atmospheric concentration of a product of combustion: carbon dioxide. This gas is a strong absorber of infrared radiation that would otherwise radiate back out into space. Since the infrared end of the light energy spectrum transmits heat, keeping this energy inside an atmospheric shell of carbon dioxide tends to heat the air at the surface of the planet. Because this phenomenon is analogous to that in greenhouses, in which the greenhouse glass allows light energy to enter but holds in heat energy, it is often called "the greenhouse effect."

2. All industrial, home, and transportation use of energy is inefficient, with waste heat ending up in the environment. As the worldwide tempo of our activities increases, the total release of this heat could warm the surface of the planet. Since most human activities are concentrated in cities, this heating effect is concentrated there, and is named the "urban heat island effect" (5, 7).

   Another phenomenon that exacerbates urban overheating is the cutting down of vegetation in cities. Trees, parks, and fountains all convert water to water vapor. In this change of state from a liquid to a gas, heat is used up, the "latent heat of vaporization," using essentially the same principle employed in refrigerators.

3. Tiny particles introduced into the atmosphere by industry, transportation, and agriculture decrease the transparency of the atmosphere to incoming solar radiation, the same phenomenon we have already noticed resulting from volcanic eruptions. When higher proportions of incoming solar radiation are bounced off the atmosphere because of this decreased transparency, we say there has been an increase in the reflectance or albedo of the atmosphere.

4. There is another way in which the albedo can be altered. In general, albedo refers to the proportion of incoming solar radiation reflected out into space by land and sea cover, as well as the atmosphere. Thus any large-scale changes in the surface of the planet cause changes in

albedo. Contributors to this effect are deforestation, large water impoundments, and large cement and asphalt surfaces.

5. Oil films on the ocean surface affect the transfer of heat between the water of the ocean and the air above. This changes global heat distributing mechanisms, which in turn are the driving forces behind world weather patterns.

It is one thing to itemize these processes; it is quite another to demonstrate that they have significant effects on weather or climate. Many things ameliorate these effects.

In the first place, in combination, some of the effects may be canceled. The carbon dioxide accumulation causes heating of the planet, but the increase in albedo cools it. Therefore, unless one of these effects increases much more rapidly than the other, they represent no threat to maintenance of present world temperature regime.

We also need to estimate the magnitude of the various effects relative to normal, natural phenomena. The likely rate of increase of the effects is important: at numerous times in history there have been environmental threats that would have been overwhelming if they had continued to grow, such as the accumulation of horse manure in cities. If likely future worldwide fuel price increases lead to lowered use of each fuel to an equal extent, the result will be less pollution; if there is a shift from oil and gas to coal with no lowering of total use, there will be more pollution, and government action will be necessary.

J. Murray Mitchell Jr. (16) estimated the world-wide atmospheric particulate load by volcanic activity and by human activity over the period 1850 to 1970. By 1970, the effect due to humans was roughly half of the average annual effect due to volcanoes. If the effect due to human activity were to continue to increase at the same rate as in the past, then within a very few decades, we would have a larger impact on the atmosphere than that of natural sources.

One way of making this point is to remember that human impact on the atmosphere is strongly correlated with the rate of increase in world use of crude oil, which has been at roughly 7 percent per year for many decades. As this effect continues year after year, the magnitude of the impact increases each decade by 1.07^{10}, or approximately doubles. So a continuation of such rates for forty years would involve an increased impact of about 2^4, or sixteen times.

However, as we shall see in subsequent chapters, continuation of a 7 percent per annum growth in world use of crude oil (or other fuels) is dependent on continuing low prices of fuels relative to average wages. As we further deplete world stocks of fossil fuels, prices will rise relative to wages, and the rate of increase in fuel use will decline, or even become negative. Since sharp worldwide increases in fuel prices have already begun, this will restrict human impact on climate relative to the impact of natural forces, unless there is a sharp shift to coal. Indeed, there is some reason to think that much of our apparent impact on the global climate in the twentieth century has not been real.

In the first place, major weather stations tend to be in or at the edges of large cities. Consequently, the local heating effects associated with large cities may have led us to believe that widespread planetary heating had occurred, when much of the effect was merely local. Also, the period from 1910 to 1981 was unusually free of major volcanic eruptions, and that was the major reason for gradual warming.

Actually, during the twentieth century, the average northern hemisphere temperature appears to have first warmed (to about 1950), then cooled. This would certainly invalidate the argument that the accumulation of carbon dioxide leaves the planet in imminent danger of overheating and melting of polar icecaps so as to flood coastal cities.

Place-to-Place Differences in Climate

To this point, we have only considered the forces producing unusual changes in weather through time. The dynamics of complex environmental systems also depend on the forces producing place-to-place differences in both average weather and weather variability. Our principal concern here is with global wind circulation patterns, because these distribute heat and moisture necessary for crop growth. Three types of wind motion are involved in prevailing wind systems: movement of air masses from east to west or west to east, from the surface of the globe to high altitudes and back, and from equator to pole and back.

While many factors determine the behavior of winds in particular places (such as the location of mountain ranges), the broad features of the prevailing wind systems are the product of three interacting factors: (1) pressure gradient forces from high to low pressure air masses, (2) the apparent motion of air masses due to the rotation of the earth about its axis (the Coriolis force), and (3) centrifugal acceleration (the net of the first two factors).

Prevailing winds are strongest where the pressure gradients in air are greatest, and this in turn occurs where the greatest temperature gradients occur between the equator and the poles. Therefore, the strongest prevailing winds occur at middle-latitudes (30 to 60 degrees from the equator in each hemisphere): the westerlies. The band extending from about 30 degrees north of the equator to 30 degrees south encloses the trade winds. These move with much less average velocity than the westerlies; since they are slower than the speed of rotation of the earth on its axis, we perceive them as winds from east to west.

Many of the world's major crop-growing countries and those that export the largest amounts of agricultural commodities occur in the two belts 30 to 60 degrees from the equator. Thus, wind systems moving heat and moisture from west to east are critically important determinants of the planetary food situation. Sea water has a high specific heat: it takes 4.7 times as much heat to raise the temperature of a gram of water one degree as it does for rock. Conversely, a gram of water can give off 4.7 times as much heat as a gram of rock before its temperature drops one degree. Therefore, the weather of any place on earth will tend to be more moderate if the winds bringing it passed over ocean than if they passed over vast stretches of continent. This notion is expressed in the popular wisdom as the differences between a marine or maritime climate (stable), as opposed to a continental climate (highly unstable). The winds bringing heat and moisture to Russia and China have passed over vast land masses so their weather is highly unstable; the weather of San Francisco or Lisbon is highly stable.

Deserts are found where the winds pass over land on the lee side of mountains, where the rain in clouds carried by prevailing winds has mostly fallen on the windward side of high mountains and where there has been excessive deforestation or grazing. It now appears that people can affect the location and aridity of deserts (Box 3.1).

This brief survey indicates that natural forces on this planet can produce unpredictable weather fluctuations of very large magnitude, that have very great impacts on biological, economic, and political phenomena. One way we can cope with these uncertain-

BOX 3.1
Case study: A hypothesis as to how humans affect the location of deserts

From 1960 to 1976, average shifts in the distribution of world precipitation (9) caused the devastating African Sahel condition, in which the parched area of the Sahara desert moved southward to the sub-Saharan belt of countries including Mali, Niger, Chad, Sudan, and Ethiopia (Fig. 3.3). England and California became much drier, as did important grain states such as South Dakota.

FIGURE 3.3
An illustration of the utter environmental destruction resulting from the southward movement of hot, desert-producing winds in the countries below the Sahara desert. Courtesy of Oxfam, America.

BOX 3.1 (Cont.)

Given that important grain-producing areas were simultaneously affected in many countries, such shifts in the distribution of rainfall and snow could have a calamitous effect on the world food production.

One hypothesis suggests how human activities could have produced this shift in the distribution of rain and snow (1). The hypothesis postulates that two different phenomena acting together were the cause. First, an increase in the concentration of carbon dioxide in the atmosphere, due to greater combustion of fossil fuels, would tend to increase the temperature at the surface of the earth. Putting it differently, there would be an increased difference between the high temperature at the earth's surface, and the low temperatures three and more kilometers above the surface of the earth. Second, an increase in the concentration of fine particles suspended in the atmosphere, due to increased industrial and agricultural activity, would create an increased difference between low temperatures at high latitudes and high temperatures at the equator, because most of the world's industry is concentrated in the north temperate zone. Putting these two phenomena together, we see that there would be stronger differences between the temperatures from low altitudes to high, and from low latitudes to high. Experiments have shown that such an increase in temperature differences would make desert-producing wind systems move southward toward the equator. Or we would expect a failure of the summer monsoon rains around the world, for example in Mexico, the Sahel, and Northern India.

While humans could have an impact on regional climate, as just indicated, to this date the human impact on the planetary climate has been minor relative to the impact of natural forces. People have not yet produced an ice age, and nothing people have done can compare to the cooling effects of one or more very large volcanoes.

---

ties is to make sure that we do not inadvertently design our economic systems so as to be unduly sensitive to the impact of weather fluctuations (Chapters 10 and 11).

Weather and the Economy

An example will illustrate the curious, roundabout way that weather can affect the economic system. Chapter 1 mentioned that the United States is now dependent on exports of agricultural commodities to other countries to raise the money needed to pay for imported crude oil. This means that our economy is now influenced, not only by the effect of crop-growing weather on our ability to export crops, but also by the effect of crop-growing weather elsewhere on the need for other countries to import our crops. The Soviet Union is a particularly important customer for our wheat and corn. Therefore, our wheat and corn exports are influenced by crop-growing weather in Russia. Fluctuations in precipitation have been the preeminent determinant of recent year-to-year fluctuations in wheat production in Russia, as has been the case here. Consequently, it is of interest to see just how important precipitation fluctuations are in important wheat-growing areas of the United States and Russia. Wheat-growing areas in both countries experience great year-to-year fluctuation in precipitation, but these occur around a lower average level in Russia, causing violent year-to-year fluctuations in their wheat production.

Unlike the United States, Russia does not produce enough wheat relative to domestic demand so that carryover of stocks from previous years can compensate for lowered production in a bad year. Thus, Russia frequently enters the international market seeking to purchase enough to make up for their own production shortfall. Since Russia normally produces far more wheat than the United States, her shortfall in a particular year might be equal to our entire production for one year. Thus, if the United States economy is dependent on selling vast amounts of wheat to Russia to pay for imported crude oil, we expose ourselves to violent perturbations that have large-scale internal impacts on our economy. In short, year-to-year fluctuations in precipitation in the wheat-growing regions of Russia have become a major determinant of the behavior of the U.S. economy.

FIGURE 3.4

The relation between the rate of photosynthesis (plant tissue formation) and leaf temperature in red kidney beans. The experiment was carefully designed so that no other factors (such as light intensity or carbon dioxide concentration) would be limiting. Figure redrawn from Figure 5 in J. D. Tenhunen, J. A. Weber, C. S. Yocum and D. M. Gates, Oecologia, *26:113 (1976). Heidelberg: Springer-Verlag.*

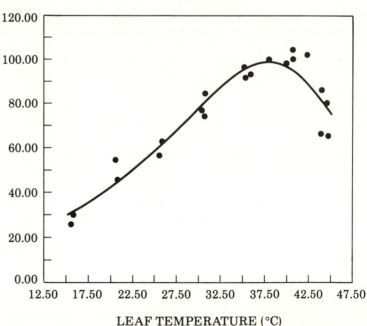

RATE OF PLANT TISSUE FORMATION (AS A PERCENT OF RATE AT OPTIMUM TEMPERATURE)

LEAF TEMPERATURE (°C)

THE EFFECTS OF FLUCTUATIONS IN WEATHER ON LIVING SYSTEMS

All farmers, hunters, trappers, and fishers are aware of great year-to-year fluctuations in numbers of living organisms. In many cases, these fluctuations are widely understood to be caused by the weather, as when poor crops occur in a year of late frosts or drought (6, 14). However, in many other cases, the relation between weather fluctuations and fluctuations in production of plants or animals is obscured, because there is a lag between the time of the cause (weather) and the effect (production of plant or animal material).

One simple example illustrates how lags can make it difficult to perceive the relation between cause and effect. A sport fishery in which there is great fluctuation in numbers caught from one year to another is the small-mouth bass fishery of South Bay, Manitoulin Island, in Lake Huron. The age of fish can be determined by reading rings in their scales with a microscope or a scale-reading machine; therefore, the fish caught in any year can be separated into year classes, just as we can separate trees into year classes by reading the rings in their trunks when they are cut down. The estimated number of four-year-old smallmouth bass in that fishery fluctated over the brief period 1949 to 1956 from 12, to 2100. Such fluctuations were truly startling. In the very poor years of 1954 and 1955 fishers wondered what had happened: had the resource been overfished to the point of extinction or devastated by disease, a predator, or a pollutant? Many people will have had a similar experience with one or more animal or plant resources.

Scientists know that young fish are very delicate and highly sensitive to water temperature changes in the first few months of their lives. Consequently, it is reasonable to hypothesize that year-to-year fluctuations in the number of four-year olds in this fishery can be explained in terms of water temperatures in the summer they were spawned. Since we have discovered that temperature drops can be widespread (Figure 3.1), the hypothesis can be tested using summer air temperature data from North Bay, the closest weather station, 140 miles away. When this is done, it appears that the number of four-year-olds caught each year is largely determined by summer temperature in the year they were spawned.

Weather Fluctuations and Crop Production

Since weather fluctuations seem to be implicated in fluctuations in this bass fishery, can they explain a variety of other similar phenomena such as fluctuations in production of crop plants? Very careful laboratory research has been conducted to determine the effect of temperature on the rate of photosynthesis (plant tissue production) in the red kidney bean (Figure 3.4). Given this striking effect of temperature under carefully controlled laboratory conditions, we can now determine if temperature has a similar effect on the U.S. annual production of wheat.

Since we have already seen that major temperature depressions can be remarkably widespread, we can plot total U.S. wheat production against average annual temperature at the one weather station for which we have weather records extending back to 1780: New Haven. From Figure 3.5 we see that when the average annual temperature at New Haven drops below 49°F, U.S. wheat production is lowered; further, production drops more steeply with lower temperatures. The New Haven temperature records extend over enough years so that we can discover the range of average annual temperatures, and the probability of occurrence of extreme values, with some con-

FIGURE 3.5

*The effect of major cooling spells on total U.S. production of wheat. This graph is based
on wheat production statistics for all years from 1880 to 1970, inclusive. The production
statistics were adjusted to correct for year number, in order to remove the effect of
acreage planted and technology inputs, and expose the effect of major, widespread
temperature changes. Also, since production gradually increased from year to year, production for each year has been expressed as a proportion of what would have been
expected under best growing conditions (which occur when the average annual
temperature at New Haven is 51°F). Each dot represents the average production (as a
proportion of best production) for all those years with the same average annual
temperature at New Haven. The numbers above each data point represent the number
of years included in the average represented by the point. The line is calculated from a
logistic equation fitted to these data. The lines at the lower right of the graph indicate
the ranges of average annual temperatures at New Haven encountered in particular sequences of years. Thus, over the whole range 1927 to 1970, the average annual temperature at New Haven never dropped below 49°F. One has to go back to 1838 to encounter
a New Haven annual average temperature as cold as 47°F. Yet once in the last two centuries, the New Haven average annual temperature dropped to 45°F. This graph indicates vividly how grossly we can err by assuming that conditions will always be like
those we have experienced recently. (Wheat production data and New Haven average
annual temperature data from series K-507 and J-254, in* Historical Statistics of the
United States, *U.S. Department of Commerce, Bureau of the Census, 1975.)*

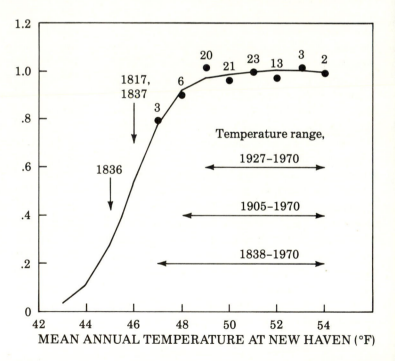

TOTAL U.S. WHEAT PRODUCTION AS A PROPORTION OF PRODUCTION EXPECTED AT 51°F

fidence in the statistical reliability of our estimates. Over the entire 190 years, average annual temperatures at New Haven were 47°F or colder sixteen years, or 8.4 percent of all years. From the equation fitted to the available years of U.S. wheat production statistics in Figure 3.5, we see that such low temperatures would be likely to lead to U.S. wheat production between 28 and 77 percent of that experienced in average years since 1927.

The graph exposes the false sense of security we get by assuming that the only crop-growing conditions we are likely to experience are those experienced in our own lifetimes. How many planners would examine such "ancient history" to discover the full range of temperatures and wheat production that might reasonably be expected in the future? Obviously, almost all planning is based on the assumption that "normal" temperature and wheat production are those encountered since 1927. The implications of making such an assumption about "normal" go surprisingly far, as we shall see in later chapters.

To indicate the apparently unrelated issues on which this matter has a bearing, consider the availability of crude oil in the United States. Now that domestic supplies of cheap petroleum in the United States are declining, our demand for gasoline, fuel oil, jet fuel, and diesel fuel is increasingly met by imports of petroleum from other countries. Our ability to pay for those imports depends on our ability to sell adequate quantities of such commodities as wheat to other countries. In turn, our ability to export wheat depends on our ability to grow it, which we now see depends on the average national temperature. Consequently, if there should be a new volcanic eruption that depressed our average annual temperature about 5 to 8 degrees Fahrenheit below recent "normal" levels, we would not be able to grow enough food for export to pay for imported energy. (Mt. St. Helens in 1980 was very small relative to such eruptions.) A volcanic eruption, therefore, would worsen the U.S. energy problem. At the very least, there would likely be very significant increases in U.S. national energy prices.

This example illustrates a point introduced in Chapter 1: the mechanisms by which human beings build a conscious world view are important components of environmental problems. We see now that the length of time over which experience is averaged is critical in determining the character of the conscious world view, and one lifetime may not be long enough to yield an accurate picture.

SOCIAL, ECONOMIC, AND POLITICAL IMPLICATIONS OF WEATHER FLUCTUATIONS

Common sense leads us to expect that when stocks of a valuable commodity decline, demand will drive prices up, and when stocks increase relative to demand, prices will fall. Since weather affects supply of many commodities, we would expect it to affect prices also. To illustrate this relation, a particularly useful period in American history is 1815 to 1852. This time was free of major internal political upheavals that can mask the effect of weather: it fell between the end of the War of 1812 and the Civil War. We have already seen that it was a period of great climatic instability.

A complication is that the prices of agricultural commodities do not depend just on the weather in a particular year, because most nations keep large stocks of cereal grain in storage as insurance against bad harvests. Consequently, the price of wheat in any given year depends on the weather that year and in the two previous years. Sta-

FIGURE 3.6

A flow chart for the effect of weather fluctuations on agricultural systems, now including economic effects. Note that a self-regulatory loop has now been included: increased acreage planted in response to sharply increased wholesale prices. Also note that traditional disciplinary and organizational boundaries in educational and governmental institutions make it difficult to deal with the whole problem.

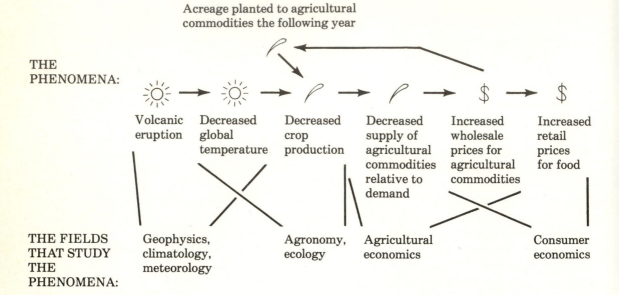

tistical analysis reveals a striking relationship in the United States between the price of a bushel of wheat and the average annual temperatures for that year and the two previous years, from 1815 and 1852: a seven-degree drop in average annual temperature results in wholesale wheat prices increasing by almost three times. We can calculate the wheat wholesale prices that would have been expected every year from 1815 to 1852, if no other factors had been operating. When we do this, we see that while temperature at New Haven does not account for all the year-to-year variation in average U.S. wholesale wheat prices, it does account for the very large price increases associated with major volcanic eruptions.

We also discover an interesting pattern. Following cold periods, actual prices fall more than we would expect from the equation relating prices to temperatures. Why might that be? After cold spells, national stocks of wheat drop, prices increase, and this encourages farmers to take advantage of the high wheat prices by planting increased wheat acreage. As a result, supply rises rapidly to meet demand, and the price drops. This is an example of a class of phenomena we will see repeatedly in this book: self-regulatory, stabilizing, or homeostatic mechanisms at work.

Now we can express our perception of the causal system regulating wheat prices by the flow chart in Figure 3.6. Decreased crop production leads to higher wholesale prices, which in turn produce higher retail prices. The higher wholesale prices also lead, with a one-year lag, to increased acreage planted out by farmers. This response by farmers to higher commodity prices illustrates how stability is maintained in systems. A departure away from "normal" or "steady state" conditions results in a return to "normal" or "steady state" conditions.

Figure 3.6 reveals another interesting point. Once we begin to sketch in all the components, we see that the entire causal pathway cuts across lines between subjects or disciplines as taught in most educational institutions. Different parts of this causal pathway would be dealt with by climatology, meteorology, agronomy, agricultural economics, or general or consumer economics. The significance of fields such as environmental studies is that they consider all aspects of such causal pathways, because interdisciplinary fields, by design, are problem-oriented or causal-pathway-oriented, not discipline-oriented.

Now that we have the idea that causal pathways can cut across fields, from climatology through biology into economics, it is worthwhile to ask, "Just how far might such causal pathways extend?" Might the economic consequences of weather go even further, into social and political phenomena? In fact, the whole sweep of history takes on a very different appearance, now that we have the idea about long-chain causal pathways (2, 12, 14, 21, 23). Consider, for example, the Irish potato famine of 1846 to 1851, which resulted in a million deaths due to starvation and disease and two million emigrants, largely to the United States. Referring back to Figure 3.1, we see that the period 1831 to 1861 was very cold throughout Europe (and the entire Northern Hemisphere). Consequently, Ireland's support capacity dropped, and the surplus population died or emigrated. Even this did not solve the political problems created by the weather in Ireland. The remaining Irish fought a continual battle with absentee landlords, as well as with poverty. Tenants who were unable to pay their rent were evicted by the police, leading to mob violence and attacks against authority.

Indeed, a detailed reading of European newspapers published between 1800 and 1850, a period of violently fluctuating weather conditions, reveals a series of political, economic, and social problems, many of which we now know were produced by volcanic eruptions. Amazingly, even though the newspapers sometimes contained letters from other continents pointing out that conditions were the same there, there is no evidence that people at the time had the remotest idea as to the ultimate origin of their problems. Indeed, it is difficult for people nowadays to imagine the severity of the hardships experienced in the first half of the nineteenth century because of fluctuations in weather.

One way to minimize our vulnerability to risk of such hardships in the future is to stop growth in world energy use. If past trends in this growth continue, by 2040 the resultant air pollution will chill the earth permanently as it was chilled temporarily after major volcanic eruptions, decreasing crop and livestock production in regions more than 35° north or south of the equator. A chilling that serious would produce frosts in Pennsylvania every month of the year.

PLACE-TO-PLACE DIFFERENCES IN THE PHYSICAL ENVIRONMENT

Temperature and precipitation not only produce occasional changes at a particular place on the earth's surface; they also produce great differences from place to place. Indeed, if we know enough about the average conditions of a particular site, we can predict the type of plant and animal life that would typically be expected there; con-

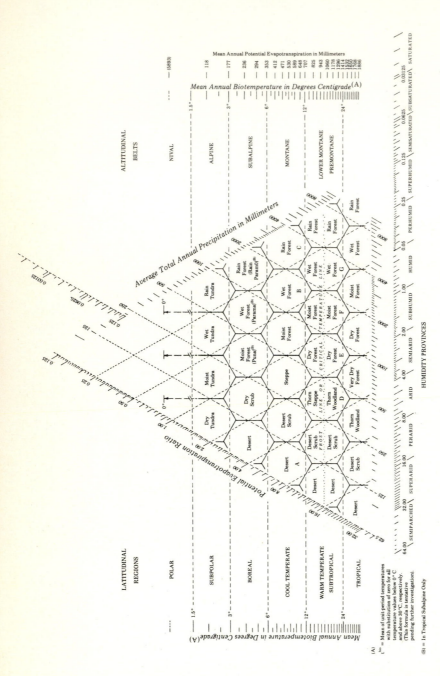

FIGURE 3.7

The relationship between the types of plant communities that occur in a particular climatic zone and the mean annual biotemperature, average total annual precipitation, and potential evapotranspiration ratio within the climatic zone. The biotemperature is the average temperature throughout the year, with zero being substituted for all temperatures either below 0°C or above 30°C. Potential evapotranspiration is the opposite of rain: it measures the rate at which moisture leaves the surface of living tissue in the zone, and depends on air temperature and precipitation. Evapotranspiration is greater at higher temperatures, and lower rates of humidity. Letters on the chart correspond to the photographs of Figures 3.8 to 3.15. (Chart invented by L. R. Holdridge, Tropical Science Center, San Jose, Costa Rica, and published in Life Zone Ecology, available from the Center.)

versely, if we know enough about the plant and animal life that normally occupies a certain site under natural conditions, we know the average weather there. Scientists such as Holdridge (10) have developed charts that express these relationships (Figure 3.7). The chart also expresses the effect of evapotranspiration, the combined effect of evaporation from the soil and transpiration from vegetation. Figures 3.8 to 3.15 illustrate the types of vegetation characteristic of par-

ticular average annual temperatures and amounts of precipitation.

The oceans, like the land, show great differences in place-to-place productivity brought about by differences in the physical

FIGURE 3.9

A cool temperate environment, with 1000 to 2000 mm total precipitation per year. The vegetation is dense, with thick grass cover and broad-leaved plants interspersed with conifers. However, the trees are only about 60 feet high. Similar plant communities are found in the eastern United States and southern Ontario. (Corresponds to B in Figure 3.7.) Photograph by Harold M. Lambert.

FIGURE 3.8

A cool temperate (6 to 12 degrees Celsius biotemperature), very dry environment at the top of the island of Mauai, above the clouds. Because of the slight precipitation and very high evapotranspiration, only plants adapted to very dry conditions can survive. As with all the other pictures in this series, similar associations of plant species would be found anywhere in the world where this average annual temperature occurred in combination with extreme drought. (Corresponds to A in Figure 3.7.) Photograph courtesy of Camera Hawaii, Inc.

TABLE 3.2
The relative productivity of different parts of the earth

Ecosystem	Area (10⁶ km²)	Proportion of earth	Langleys per year gross primary production
Planet	509.6		
Open ocean	326.0	.64	100
Coastal zones	34.0	.07	200
Upwelling zones	.4	.0008	600
Estuaries and reefs	2.0	.0039	2000
All land	148.0	.29	
Deserts and tundras	40.0	.08	20
Grasslands	42.0	.08	250
Dry forests	9.4	.02	250
Boreal coniferous forests	10.0	.02	300
Cultivated land (unmechanized)	10.0	.02	300
Moist temperate forests	4.9	.01	800
Mechanized agriculture	4.0	.01	1200
Wet tropical and subtropical forests	14.7	.03	2000

From *Fundamentals of Ecology,* Third Edition, by Eugene P. Odum. Copyright © 1971 by W. B. Saunders Company. Copyright 1953 and 1959 by W. B. Saunders Company. Adapted by permission of Holt, Rinehart and Winston.

SOME IMPORTANT GENERALIZATIONS:

1. Very large proportions of the earth's surface have very low productivities. Note particularly that the open ocean is not a munificent cornucopia, but has only five times the productivity per unit area of a desert.
2. A remarkably high proportion of the gross primary productivity of the planet occurs in a very small area and proportion of the total. Further, those areas are very vulnerable to destruction through stupidity, and already are being destroyed (estuaries, reefs, rain forests).
3. Wet systems on land are more productive than dry (look out the airplane window and spot the river valleys).
4. Warm systems are more productive than cold.
5. Mechanization increases agricultural production over all areas by a factor of four, but in small areas can increase it by ten or more (at a price in energy and related costs).
6. The most productive situations all have an input from outside, either a natural input (upwelling from below, river sediment, or rain) or an input from human activity (such as fertilizer and farm machinery).

OVERALL CONCLUSIONS ABOUT ECOLOGICAL ENERGETICS:

1. There is no "free lunch." It always costs energy to get energy, and because all energy conversion is inefficient, you always put in more than you get. So "synthetic food from algae" etc. will always cost more energy than it yields.
2. Many processes that have made sense up to now will no longer make sense when we run out of cheap energy. (High-seas whaling at low whale densities.)
3. Life is full of tradeoffs. High human population densities come at many prices, one of which is loss of the option of eating predators, such as tuna and salmon, that make very inefficient use of organisms lower down in the food pyramid (Chapter 5).

Production estimates from E. P. Odum, *Fundamentals of Ecology,* 3rd ed. Philadelphia: W. B. Saunders, 1971.

FIGURE 3.10

A cool temperate environment with 2000 to 4000 mm precipitation per year. This is a rain forest at the 3500-foot level on the island of Hawaii, on the windward east face where precipitation is adequate to support tree growth to 120 feet in height. (Corresponds to C on Figure 3.7.) Photograph courtesy of Camera Hawaii, Inc.

THE "GENESIS STRATEGY"

Stephen Schneider has argued, very wisely in my view, that only one type of national strategy is sensible, given what we know about past weather fluctuations. It is simply not prudent to assume that because a few recent years have had favorable weather, future years will have equally favorable weather. Therefore, all nations should take out a variety of types of insurance against the possibility of bad weather in the future. A simple, ancient, but immensely important first step is to ensure that enough agricultural commodities are in storage at any time so that the population will not starve if the next harvest is surprisingly bad. This idea is as old as the warning of Joseph to Pharaoh reported in the Book of Genesis. A more general application of this principle suggests the need for new planning institutions that try to foresee possible consequences of various present actions and policies and try to provide the overview across disciplinary boundaries that modern real-world problems require (20).

THE IMPLICATIONS OF A PRELIMINARY SURVEY OF PHYSICAL ENVIRONMENTAL FACTORS

We can now bring together the main themes of this chapter.

environment. In much of the ocean, the great stores of nutrient minerals are too far below to be brought back to the surface by upward movement of warm water. Consequently, much of the ocean is relatively barren, contrary to the view of many optimists. Table 3.2 summarizes information on the productivity of various parts of the earth's surface, expressed in langleys (calories per square centimeter). Many people need to develop a more realistic appreciation of the actual productivity of the earth.

1. *The carrying capacity argument.* The ability of the planet to support life (the "carrying capacity" of the planet) depends on a number of factors, including the physical environment. However, the physical environment is by no means constant: it changes markedly from time to time at a given place, and from place to place at any time. We must make sure

FIGURE 3.11

A warm temperate environment (12 to 16 degrees Celsius biotemperature) in a perarid humidity province (250 to 500 mm average annual precipitation). This environment is on the boundary between a thorn steppe and thorn woodland; it appears to us as the familiar oak woodland, separated by extensive tracts of dry grass, that characterizes the "Mediterranean" landscape. The example in the picture is not from Spain, but rather San Benito County, California. (Location D in Figure 3.7.) Photograph by H. Armstrong Roberts.

that plans for our future are not unwittingly based on extrapolations from unusually good times at a particular place to "average" future times at that place, or from unusually fortunate places, to all other places. Such extrapolations are grossly unrealistic, and can create great mischief by raising other peoples' expectations to levels that no one can ever satisfy. This only creates frustrations that lead to ultimate political upheaval.

2. *The relative position of nations.* At any point in history, some nations are unusually blessed by favorable physical environmental conditions. However, we should respond to that situation with some humility and foresight. Changes in the latitudinal distribution of rainfall, for example, could make rich nations poor and poor nations rich.

3. *Weather fluctuations can result in changes of immense human significance, even over the very short term.* However,

FIGURE 3.12

A warm temperate environment in a moist sub-humid province. View of typical prairie of the "Flint Hills" around Manhattan, Kansas. This area is still subject to frequent burning. Photograph courtesy of Kansas Farmer, Topeka, Kansas. (Location E in Figure 3.7.)

we are often ignorant of the role of weather in important phenomena, because effects are revealed after a lag of up to several years.

catches, trap returns, crop, orchard or vegetable production, or wine quality, try to explain these fluctuations in terms of weather fluctuations.

Develop an essay describing all the consequences of any major volcanic eruption.

Try to find out if weather changes can be used to explain any major historical event. For example, use long-run weather records for Germany and Russia (such as World Weather Records) to explain the campaigns of Napoleon and Hitler in Russia.*

Use encyclopedias or other sources to determine if outbreaks of infectious disease or pests of plants, animals, or humans coincided with major changes in weather or with volcanic eruptions.

Does fashion, art or music respond to changes in climate resulting from volcanic eruptions? (See, for example, John R. Hale, *Renaissance*, pp. 99–100. New York: Time Inc. Books, 1965; or Millia Davenport, *The Book of Costume*, p. 630. New York: Crown Publishers, 1948.)

Collect and interpret all the information you can obtain on any recent volcanic eruption, such as that of Mt. St. Helens in Washington state in the first week of April 1980. Obtain satellite photographs of the dust plume from the National Aeronautics and Space Administration.

SUGGESTIONS FOR INDIVIDUAL AND GROUP PROJECTS

Do library research to discover the effects on the area where you live of major climatic changes in the past, such as the chilling of 1816, 1838, or 1884, or the drought of 1936. How serious were the effects relative to the effects of more recent climate changes?

If you are aware of any phenomena that fluctuate violently year to year, such as fish

*World Weather Records are available from the United States government and can be obtained from the following sources: Smithsonian Institution Miscellaneous Collections, Washington, D.C. (1944, Vol. 79, Publication 2913. Vol. 90, Publication 3218.) U.S. Department of Commerce Weather Bureau. Washington, D.C. (1941–1950. 1959.) U.S. Department of Commerce Environmental Science Services Administration. Environmental Data Services. Washington D.C. (1966. 6 volumes.) U.S. Department of Commerce National Oceanic and Atmospheric Administration, National Climatic Center, Asheville, North Carolina. (1979.)

FIGURE 3.13
This picture was taken where environmental conditions were similar to those in the previous picture (warm temperate, dry). Here we see the distinct boundaries produced between different plant communities that arise because high up on the mountain it is cool and dry, whereas lower down, where the trees start, it is warmer and wetter. This obvious "banding" or "striping" of the environment occurs all over the world, particularly up the slopes of mountains in the tropics, and represents the effect of different temperature and precipitation regimes in producing different plant communities. Photograph by Harold M. Lambert.

FIGURE 3.14
A warm temperate environment with 1000 to 2000 mm total annual precipitation produces this moist forest at the Kalalau Lookout on the island of Kauai. This scene is typical of moist warm temperate forests, in that some plants ("epiphytes") hang on other plants, creating a tangled, web-like appearance. (Location F in Figure 3.7.)

FIGURE 3.15
A subtropical environment, with an average annual biotemperature of 16 to 24 degrees Celsius and rainfall of about 3800 mm per year. This plant community is a wet forest, close to a rain forest. The vegetation is extremely dense, and a great variety of plant species are found in the community. The leaves are broad, thin, and delicate, since no adaptations to withstand drying at any time in the annual cycle are necessary. This picture was taken at about sea level on the windward northeast slope of the island of Hawaii. Where the rainfall is greater, and we have a rain forest, the vegetation appears as a tall, almost impenetrable mass of green, made up of a very large number of different species of trees, shrubs, and herbs. (Location G on Figure 3.7.)

REFERENCES

1. Bryson, R., "Drought in Sahelia: who or what is to blame?" *The Ecologist*, 3, (1973), pp. 366–371.

2. Bryson, Reid A., and Thomas J. Murray, *Climates of Hunger*. Madison, Wis.: University of Wisconsin Press, 1977.

3. Bryson, Reid A., and Wayne M. Wendland, "Climatic effects of atmospheric pollution," in *Global Effects of Environmental Pollution*, ed. by S. Fred Singer, pp. 130–138. Dordrecht, Holland: D. Reidel, 1970.

4. Bullard, F. M., *Volcanoes of the Earth*. Austin, Tex.: University of Texas Press, 1976.

5. Cech, L., R. Weisberg, C. Hacker, and R. Lane, "Relative contribution of land uses to the urban heat problem in the coastal subtropics," *International Journal of Biometeorology*, 20, (1976), pp. 9–15.

6. Chang, Jen-Hu, *Climate and Agriculture.* Chicago: Aldine, 1968.

7. Damon, P. E., and S. M. Kunen, "Global cooling?" *Science*, 193, (1976), pp. 447–453.

8. Eddy, J. A., "The case of the missing sunspots," *Scientific American*, 236, (May 1977), pp. 80–92.

9. Gribbin, J., "Climatic change and food production," *Food Policy*, 1, (1976), pp. 301–310.

10. Holdridge, L. R., *Life Zone Ecology.* San Jose, Costa Rica: Life Zone Science Center, 1967.

11. Humphreys, W. J. "Volcanic dust and other factors in the production of climatic change, and their possible relation to ice ages," *Journal of the Franklin Institute*, 176, (1913).

12. Ladurie, E. L. R., *Times of Feast, Times of Famine.* Garden City, N.Y.: Doubleday, 1971.

13. Lamb, H. H., *Climate: Present, Past and Future. Volume 1. Fundamentals and Climate Now.* London: Methuen, 1972. *Volume 2: Climatic History and the Future.* London: Methuen, 1977.

14. Lockeretz, W., "The lessons of the dust bowl," *American Scientist*, 66, (1978), pp. 560–569.

15. Mitchell, J. Murray, ed., "Causes of climatic change," *Meteorological Monographs,* 8, No. 20 (Feb. 1968), pp. 1–159.

16. Mitchell, J. Murray Jr., "A preliminary evaluation of atmospheric pollution as a cause of the global temperature fluctuation of the past century," in *Global Effects of Environmental Pollution*, ed. by S. Fred Singer, pp. 139–155. Dordrecht, Holland: D. Reidel, 1970.

17. Newell, R. E., "Climate and the ocean," *American Scientist*, 67, (1979), pp. 405–416.

18. Pollack, James B., Owen B. Toon, Carl Sagan, Audrey Summers, Betty Baldwin, and Warren Van Camp, "Volcanic explosions and climatic change: a theoretical assessment," *Journal of Geophysical Research*, 81, (1976), pp. 1071–1083.

19. Rosenfeld, C. L., "Observations on the Mount St. Helens eruption," *American Scientist*, 68, (1980), pp. 494–509.

20. Schneider, Stephen, and Lynne E. Mesirow, *The Genesis Strategy.* New York: Plenum Press, 1976.

21. Stommel, H., and Elizabeth Stommel, "The year without a summer," *Scientific American*, 240, 176 (June 1979), pp. 176–186.

22. Toon, O. B., and J. B. Pollack, "Atmospheric aerosols and climate," *American Scientist*, 68, (1980), pp. 268–278.

23. Winkless, Nels III, and Iben Browning, *Climate and the Affairs of Men.* New York: Harper's Magazine Press, 1975.

4 NONRENEWABLE RESOURCES

> . . . the U.S. petroleum industry, exclusive of Alaska, is now [1969] in the region
> of its all-time maximum rate of production, but it will probably not be possible to
> assign an accurate date to this event until about five years after it has happened.
> *M. King Hubbert, Chapter 8 "Energy resources," in* Resources and
> Man, *ed. by the Committee on Resources and Man, National
> Academy of Sciences-National Research Council. San Francisco:
> W. H. Freeman, 1969.*

MAIN THEMES FOR THIS CHAPTER

This chapter introduces the notion of a non-renewable resource which in the process of being used is converted to a less useful form (a rusting, deserted automobile), or a useless form (heat and exhaust gases from combustion of gasoline).

We could reach the end of available supply of a nonrenewable resource with surprising suddenness, if national or world use rate had been very high and constantly increasing. Also, the additional supply per unit effort spent in drilling or mining drops remarkably rapidly as ultimate depletion of the stock is approached.

The United States is running out of cheap energy and several minerals very rapidly, because use per person is much higher here than in other countries. This is making us critically dependent on imports.

The "net energy principle" states that no activity to obtain energy is profitable unless the energy obtained exceeds the energy spent in obtaining it; it means that "crash programs" to increase the number of nuclear, solar, or wind power plants rapidly would consume more energy than they would produce. Therefore, we could not compensate for rapidly declining availability of oil and gas by rapidly increasing the number of power generating plants.

THE TYPES OF RESOURCES

All resources available to us are of two kinds: renewable and nonrenewable.

A renewable resource cannot be used up; either it comes from a source that is in effect permanent, such as the sun, or it constantly cycles through the planetary system, such as fresh water. However, renewable resources may become useless because of pollution (for example, water) or may be unavailable over the short term because of prior overuse (for example, firewood). Examples of renewable resources, besides solar radiation and water, are wind energy, hydroelectric power, tidal energy, and the energy gathered by green plants through photosynthesis. This last-named renewable resource is available to us either through burning, as in the case of fuel wood, or by obtaining synthetic gasoline or gas from plant material. Since renewable resources if unperturbed are available continuously, they are also known as flow resources.

Nonrenewable resources, on the other hand, are available to us as a stock of material or energy that can ultimately be depleted totally. Once such resources are depleted, they are converted to other forms of matter or energy that are less useful (as when combustion of gasoline ultimately leads to useless exhaust fumes and heat). Because nonrenewable resources are not available indefinitely, but are gradually depleted totally, they are also known as stock resources. Examples are: the fossil fuels—gasoline (which comes from crude oil),

natural gas, and coal; uranium ore, one of the raw materials for nuclear power; metals, such as iron, aluminum, tungsten, copper, silver, nickel, and titanium; and the nonmetallic minerals such as phosphate and potassium (both used in fertilizers), and diamonds. However, some nonrenewable resources are, in part, renewable in principle because energy could be used to obtain and recycle materials that had drifted to the bottom of the sea or been scrapped.

In addition, there are many resources that some people would not think of as being nonrenewable: top-quality agricultural soil is a very slowly renewable resource. It is true that such soil is created over a very long period of time by geological and biological forces; however, humans use it up quickly by bad management leading to erosion or by paving it over with asphalt or concrete, and it is extremely unlikely that we will replace it at the rate at which it has been lost through our activities. In effect, therefore, since the loss rate is much higher than the formation rate in the presence of human activity, top-quality agricultural soil is a nonrenewable resource.

There are three other important types of nonrenewable resources that will come as surprises to most people. The first is time. While there always will be time, there will not always be particular times. Certain things must be done during particular periods of time if they are to be most useful. If we do not take the appropriate actions during the most suitable periods of time, the chance will be lost permanently.

Space also can be a stock resource. While space is infinite, there are particular spaces that are peculiarly appropriate for a certain activity or use. When those spaces are used up, further increase in the activity is rendered difficult, impossible, or uneconomic. For example, there are many regions in the world that are largely mountainous, but have small flat areas useful for cities or growing food. Once those areas are used up, a significant limitation has been reached. Many of the world's great cities are in small flat plains adjacent to water but surrounded by mountains: Vancouver, Rio de Janeiro, Geneva, Hong Kong, San Francisco. Mountains clearly limit city expansion in such cases. A deeper problem is that the city and the land on which vegetables and other food for the city are grown compete for space. If the city expands on to the land that had been used to grow its food, the city will have to import its food from a distance with the transportation overhead cost now added to the price of food. Further, if all cities in the world use up their food-growing land, this can significantly diminish the worldwide production of certain kinds of food relative to demand. The significance of this point becomes clear when we realize that many cities begin as small agricultural villages situated in the heart of the best agricultural soil in an entire area, and gradually spread so as to totally cover that soil. A country has a limited amount of soil on which any particular crop, such as wheat or corn, can be grown. We can upgrade marginal soil to increase the national acreage available for growing any crop, but this comes at a price in irrigation, energy, fertilizer, and the like.

Variety is a valuable resource that can be nonrenewable. For example, wild stocks of plant populations may contain a great deal of genetic (inheritable) variety, from one plant to another. This genetic variety is a critically important resource for plant breeders, who constantly need it to develop new strains of commercial plants. This genetic diversity in wild strains of plants may be used to develop new strains of wheat, resistant to the latest strains of rust (a wheat fungal disease); new strains of berries that are plumper or juicier; or new strains of tomatoes that are less likely to be bruised or cut by modern harvesting and processing equipment. But if we are constantly cutting down the woodlots or paving over the fields where wild plant relatives of our commercial plants grow, then the valuable genetic diversity can be lost forever. Diversity in the plant and animal

TABLE 4.1

Examples of different types of resources.

Always nonrenewable	Oil, gas, coal, uranium oxide ore, phosphate, potassium, diamonds. Particular times and spaces.
Nonrenewable in effect, because of slow rates of formation and rapid rates of human-caused destruction	Top-quality agricultural soil. Variety (diversity) in the number of species of plants and animals.
Renewable unless environment destroyed	Grass, trees.
Renewable only if energy used to recycle	Mineral fertilizers or nutrients that drift to bottom of ocean or very deep lake. Scrap iron, aluminum, tungsten, copper, silver, gold, nickel, titanium.

world is a resource worth preserving, because we never know when or how we will need it in the future. Wild plants and animals may be totally unexpected sources of medicinal chemicals, biological control agents to combat pests, or research subjects to teach us new insights about ourselves. For these and many other reasons, wild plants and animals are an important resource that we can eliminate through ignorance or a lack of thought.

The distinction between different types of resources is illustrated by Table 4.1.

THE SIGNIFICANCE OF EXPONENTIAL GROWTH AND THE FORM OF PRODUCTION CYCLES

Since renewable resources cannot be used up, it is meaningless to speak of their complete production cycles: production continues indefinitely. However, the way in which we spread use of a nonrenewable resource over time is of great concern for a variety of reasons. The complete production cycle for a nonrenewable resource, from the time we begin using it to the time it is all used up, can take many different forms. Figure 4.1. illustrates three of these forms, using a simple hypothetical resource with an initial stock of one hundred units of matter or energy available for us to exploit. Thus, in the complete production cycle, we can use up a maximum, or ultimate cumulative production of 100 units. (By cumulative production we mean the total production for all years up to the end of a particular year; the ultimate cumulative production is the total production for all years up to the end of the last year in which there was any production at all.)

In each of the three cases illustrated in Figure 4.1. we begin by using one unit in the first year.

FIGURE 4.1

Three different cases of complete historical production cycles for a nonrenewable resource for which there were 100 units at the outset of production. In each case, one unit was produced in the first year of the production cycle.

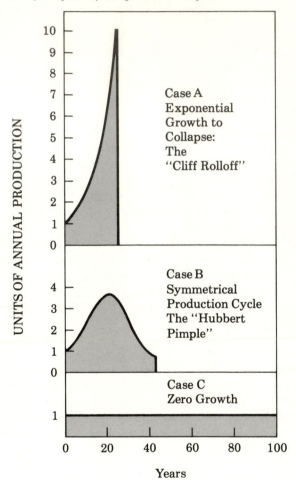

Exponential Production Cycle

In the first case, human production of the resource increases by exactly 10 percent every year after the first year. Thus, production in the second year is 110 percent of production in the first year, or 1.10 units. In the third year, production is 110 percent of production in the second year, or $1.10 \times 1.10 = 1.21$ units. When production increases by a constant percentage every year like this, the annual production shortly becomes very great. After production has been increasing by 10 percent a year for just 7.27 years, it has doubled; after an additional 7.27 years it has doubled again and is now four times as great as the original one unit of production a year. This type of growth pattern is called "exponential growth." It produces the type of historical production cycle observed in Figure 4.1, Case A. Annual production has surpassed 10 units per year by the twenty-sixth year, but by then the original 100 units are all used up. If the country, region, or company exploiting such a resource did not have an alternate resource, there would now be a catastrophic collapse in production. This cycle of production might be called, therefore, exponential growth to collapse. Because collapse is so sudden, the production cycle could be called a "cliff rolloff" because there is no gradual descent from the high level of production. To indicate that this "cliff rolloff" is not hypothetical: there were about 80 million buffalo in the United States in 1800; 200,000 hides were shipped East from the northern plains states in 1882, 40,000 in 1883, and 300 in 1884. By 1884 the resource of 80 million animals had been reduced to less than 300 in the entire United States, and a major industry had collapsed.

Symmetrical Production Cycle

A second possible type of production cycle is illustrated by Case B. Here, exploitation again grows exponentially to year 12. But the industry (or country) realizes that the resource will run out very quickly unless there is an attempt at conservation. So in order to "buy time" in which to seek an alternate source of supply after this resource is depleted, conservation efforts are intensified each year to produce a symmetrical production cycle in which the descending limb of the annual production curve is the mirror-image of the ascending limb. This is the curve for the complete cycle of production of nonrenewable resources postulated by M. King Hubbert, one of the world's most highly regarded experts on the stocks of fossil fuels. Hubbert assumes that as it becomes clear that fossil fuel stocks are being depleted worldwide and as it becomes more expensive to discover progressively less accessible stocks, prices will rise, thus intensifying efforts at conservation. Since prices should be expected to rise faster and faster as total depletion is reached, this could be expected to produce exponentially growing efforts at conservation, which will produce the type of curve in Case B. Because Hubbert has popularized the notion of production curves with this shape, they have become known as the "Hubbert Pimple." The word pimple describes the tiny width of such curves when plotted on a graph for a long sweep of human history, such as 10,000 years. The complete production cycle for fossil fuel will appear very brief, looked at a thousand years from now.

Conservation-Oriented Production Cycle

A third possible type of nonrenewable resource production cycle appears in Case C. Here, it was recognized at the outset of production that the resource was limited, and use was planned at exactly one percent of the resource each year for 100 years. This case presupposes that it would be possible to make a very precise estimate of the size of the resource as soon as production began, and this would be most difficult. This type of production cycle also implies an attitude toward conservation and an ability to plan and organize production that the world has not yet seen. However, we could develop this attitude. The payoff from conservation is time: Case B extends the lifetime of the resource from 26 years to 42, and Case C to 100. The significance of the additional 14 or 74 years will be very clear shortly.

The Surprising Consequence of Exponential Growth

Another feature of exponential growth is brought out by considering the world stock of crude oil. Suppose we accept 2100 billion barrels as the maximum and 1350 as the minimum estimate for the ultimate cumulative worldwide production of crude oil. If we extrapolate trends for annual world production and cumulative world production that occurred to 1973 (the time of the Arab oil embargo), the latter reaches the minimum estimate in 1996 and the maximum estimate in 2002.

The main surprise is how large annual production is in any year, relative to previous cumulative production, under the growth rate in production encountered to 1973 (long term average of 6.92 percent per year). For example, by 1973, annual production of crude oil worldwide was equal to worldwide production for all years up to and including 1936. If exponential growth were to continue at 6.92 percent per year, by 1990 production in a single year would be equal to the production for all years up to 1953. Thus we see that a 6.92 percent annual growth in use means that production in any year will be equal to cumulative production for all years up to 37 years ago.

Exponential growth catches people by surprise: they are always astounded at how suddenly drastic problems appear. If any population growing in a lake were to double in size every day, how many days' warning would you get after it half filled the lake before it would completely fill it, no matter how long it had been growing? The answer: one day.

It would take a long period of exponential growth before most problems surpassed a threshold at which they were just perceived by most people. By that time, there would be precious little time to take remedial action. Obviously, a characteristic of exponentially growing problems is that we must spot them early and take remedial action fast, before they overwhelm us with their surprising growth. Exponentially growing problems make planning extraordinarily valuable.

As might be expected, nonrenewable resources and the policies used in managing them generate storms of controversy. Some people argue for conservation, and others argue that a sufficient increase in the price of crude oil and gasoline would stimulate the search for new supplies, so we would never be in danger of running out. This argument is rendered murky for two reasons. First, there are not two positions with respect to this controversy but several. For example, one might advocate higher prices in the interests of conservation, but might not believe that this would thereby increase the ultimate cumulative production. Indeed, near the end of production cycles, price changes may extend the life of a resource by only a very few years.

A second source of confusion surrounding discussion of nonrenewable resources stems from use of the term "proved reserves." Proved reserves refers to the remaining volume of a resource that geological and engineering information indicate, beyond reasonable doubt, to be recoverable in the future under existing economic and operating conditions. For a long time during the initial years of a production cycle for any resource, "proved reserves" keep increasing, and in some peoples' minds, this creates the impression that ultimate recoverable production can also keep increasing, or has no limit, which of course is a contradiction.

The Conceptual Model of M. King Hubbert

Is there any way to resolve controversy about the limits to a nonrenewable resource? Hubbert (4) has proposed such a conceptual model, which is illustrated by Figure 4.2. The term "cumulative discoveries" is defined as the cumulative production plus the proved reserves. According to Hubbert's model, cumulative discoveries and cumulative production both begin at zero, and increase, first slowly, then rapidly. Cumulative production reaches its maximum rate of increase at about the halfway point in the complete cycle, then rises more and more slowly until the ultimate cumulative production has been reached. The curve for proved reserves also starts at zero, rises to a maximum at about the halfway point in the cycle, then falls to zero again at the completion of

FIGURE 4.2

M. King Hubbert's figure showing the relationship between cumulative discoveries, cumulative production, and proved reserves. In any year, "cumulative discoveries" is the sum of cumulative production plus proved reserves. Reproduced from Resources and Man, 1962, *with the permission of the National Academy of Sciences, Washington, D.C.*

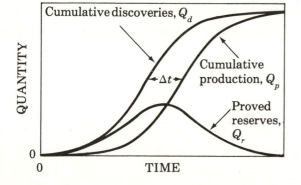

the production cycle. Since cumulative discoveries are the sum of cumulative production and proved reserves, that curve leads the curve for cumulative production.

The relationships between these variables suggest an interesting approach toward clarifying controversy about nonrenewable resources. One could use an estimate of ultimate cumulative production and the historical trend in cumulative discoveries to produce a theoretical trend line for future cumulative discoveries. The difficulty in doing this for the U.S. stock of crude oil is that for a long time Alaska crude oil was not part of the U.S. stock, but suddenly became an important component of national supply in the late 1970s. To deal with this problem, Hubbert made separate estimates for the coterminous United States, including continental shelves, of 165 billion barrels, and for Alaska of 25 billion barrels. Knowing that the cumulative discoveries curve will most likely stop growing at the sum of these two estimates, 190 billion barrels, and knowing an equation to describe the historical trend in cumulative discoveries of U.S. crude oil, we can project the likely future trend in cumulative discoveries for all fifty states. If we do this, we notice that as we get closer to the present, and crude oil from Alaska becomes an increasingly important component of the national total of cumulative discoveries, the observed data points move up closer to the projected line. Also, we notice that the trend in observed data points begins to bend toward the right, as we would expect from Hubbert's conceptual model. This suggests that the estimate of 190 billion barrels is a credible estimate of the ultimate cumulative production of crude oil from all fifty states and their adjacent continental shelves.

There is a provocative and revealing way in which this figure of 190 can be used. Hubbert postulated that the curve for proved reserves plotted against year would peak

FIGURE 4.3

Proved reserves of U.S. crude oil (for all fifty states plus adjacent continental shelves), and percentage of ultimate cumulative production, both plotted against year.

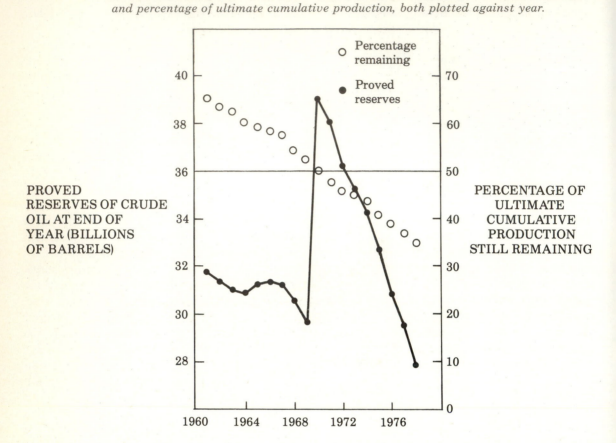

about halfway through the production cycle, then fall. If we accept the 190 figure, we know exactly where in the cycle of production we are each year. For each year, we can subtract from 190 the cumulative production to that year, then divide by 190 to obtain the proportion (or multiplying by 100, the percentage) of the resource still remaining. When we plot proved reserves against year and percentage of the resource remaining against year, both on the same graph, we should observe that proved reserves begin to drop at about the year when the percentage of the resource remaining crosses the 50 percent line. This is done in Figure 4.3, and we see that proved reserves

do indeed begin to drop very rapidly in 1971, the year that the percentage of the resource remaining dropped below the 50 percent line for the first time. The curious behavior of the line for proved reserves is caused by the sudden addition of Alaskan discoveries to reserves in 1970. The coincidence between the crossing of the 50 percent line and the dropping of the proved reserves line suggests that both the Hubbert conceptual model and the estimate of 190 billion barrels are credible. Figure 4.3 provides a very difficult counter-argument for anyone suggesting that the United States has a long way to go before it totally depletes its supply of crude oil. In short, a very sharp increase in the price of domestic crude oil might increase proved reserves for a few years by stimulating the search for new discoveries, but it would not and could not increase ultimate cumulative production. Since we are already so close to the ultimate in any case, no price change could have other than a marginal effect. We must initiate an extremely aggressive search for new sources of energy immediately.

THE LAW OF DIMINISHING RETURNS

Another topic of controversy concerns the "fair" price for nonrenewable resources. For a long time in the early stages of a production cycle, the resource is sold at a low retail price. However, well into the production cycle, the producers attempt to increase the price, and finally they attempt to increase it very sharply. To explain these price increases we need to consider the law of diminishing returns.

When a nonrenewable resource is first exploited, the most readily accessible part of the resource will be exploited first. Crude oil and natural gas reserves on land and in the shallowest, largest pools will be exploited first (9). In the case of metallic minerals, the first deposits to be exploited are the shallowest and have the highest ore grade (concentration of valuable mineral per unit volume of rock). As the fossil fuels are more and more exploited (cumulative production passes the halfway mark), the industry must turn to deeper and deeper pools, the outer continental shelves, and smaller pools. In the case of metallic minerals, the industry must turn to deeper and lower-grade deposits.

In short, the nonrenewable resources that are exploited first in the production cycle are those for which the real extractive costs are lowest, on average. Greater cumulative production of a nonrenewable resource will cause higher average productive (extractive) costs, because the cheapest portion of the resource has already been produced. Box 4.1 explains the law of diminishing returns with two examples.

If the law of diminishing returns is realistic, we would expect to find it reflected in

---

BOX 4.1
The law of diminishing returns: Two examples

The law of diminishing returns can be clarified with two hypothetical illustrations.

In case A, there is no improvement in resource-extraction technology (such as drilling or exploration equipment or methods) through the production cycle, whereas in Case B there is. In Case A, more effort already expended to produce the resource lowers the amount of resource produced per incremental (marginal) unit of additional effort expended. Thus, for each of three equal units of effort (first E1, then E2, and finally E3) the corresponding resultant amounts of production are P1, P2 (which is smaller than P1), and P3 (which is smaller than P2). The situation is a bit more complicated in Case B, because as we progress through the production cycle, there is an improvement in the techniques of exploration for the resource and the methods of resource production. For a while the total number of units of resource obtained per unit of effort expended actually increases because of economies of scale also. That is, as in manufac-

BOX 4.1 (Cont.)

turing, the greater the number of units being produced, the lower the cost to produce one unit (the driving force behind modern assembly-line techniques). Thus, in Case B, the curve for resource obtained (or produced) as a function of effort is flat for a time, before dropping. This case is more like the situation encountered in the real world than Case A. Resource extraction cost per unit of resource is inversely proportional to resource obtained per unit effort. Thus, in Case A, the price rises, first slowly, then rapidly, as the resource is more and more completely exploited. In Case B, the price actually drops at first, because of technological improvements and economies of scale. However, after a while, price has dropped as far as it is going to, and then begins to rise very rapidly.

FIGURE 4.4

Change in the real cost of drilling for gas and oil in the United States as cumulative production increases and the most accessible, cheap-to-produce wells have already been exploited.

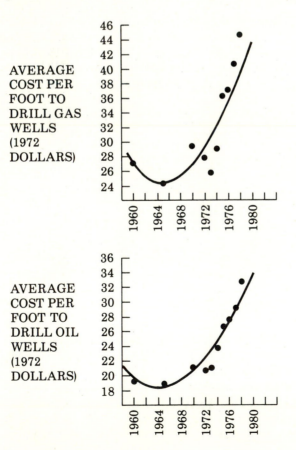

the real cost of extraction as cumulative production increases. That is, with increasing cumulative production, or with an increasing number of years that a resource has been exploited, we would expect to find that the cost per unit of obtaining the resource rose, not just because of inflation, but even faster than inflation. To test this notion, we convert the average cost of drilling one foot of gas and oil wells in the United States in each year, to the cost in 1972 dollars, thus correcting for change from year to year in the value of money. When this is done, as in Figure 4.4, we see that there has been a tremendous real dollar increase in the cost of drilling for gas and oil. Further, the trend in prices per unit matches the pattern described in Case B, Box 4.1, because cumulative production is correlated with year number. Table 4.2 expresses the law of diminishing returns differently: here we see the year-to-year trend in barrels discovered per foot drilled. This makes the case for a rapidly vanishing resource as convincingly as it can be made. Evidently, the drilling

required to discover one new barrel of oil was about 2.78 times as high in 1978 as in 1973 (89/32). When this is reflected in consumer prices, it will lead to a diminution in demand, as we shall see in later chapters, and that will tend to produce curves for the complete cycle of production like those postulated by Hubbert.

Another way of displaying the present energy situation in the United States is to ask this question: "If all energy imports into the United States were to be cut off for political reasons, how long could this country supply oil to its refineries using only its own reserves?" To answer this question, we divide, for each year, U.S. proved crude oil reserves at the end of the year by the consumption of crude oil during the year. The resulting ratio is the number of years U.S. consumption of crude oil could be maintained using only domestic proved reserves. This ratio is displayed for the years 1970 to 1978 in Table 4.3. We see that the ratio has dropped regularly from 1970 to 1978. We can use statistics to find an equation that

TABLE 4.2

The trend in the number of new barrels of crude oil discovered per well drilled in the United States.

Year	Thousands of completed wells drilled[1]	New crude oil discoveries, billions of barrels[2]	Thousands of barrels of new oil discovered per well drilled[3]
1973	26	2.32	89
1974	31	2.15	69
1975	37	1.49	40
1976	41	1.24	30
1977	45	1.55	34
1978	47	1.50	32

[1]*Statistical Abstract of the United States for 1979*, Table 1328.
[2]*Statistical Abstract of the United States for 1979*, Table 1329, and use of the formula:

$$\text{Discoveries}_t = \text{Reserves}_t - \text{Reserves}_{t-1} + \text{Production}_t$$

which is derived from the more obvious relationship:

$$\text{Reserves}_t = \text{Reserves}_{t-1} - \text{Production}_t + \text{Discoveries}_t$$

where t is year number.
[3]Third column number divided by second column number.

TABLE 4.3
The trend in U.S. crude oil proved reserves relative to consumption.

Year	U.S. proved reserves of crude oil as of Dec. 31 (billions of barrels)[1]	U.S. consumption of crude oil (billions of barrels)[2]	Number of years U.S. consumption of crude oil could be maintained using only domestic proved reserves	
			(Column 2/Column 3)	Computed from equation[3]
1970	39.0	5.4	7.3	7.1
1971	38.1	5.5	6.9	6.7
1972	36.3	6.0	6.1	6.4
1973	35.3	6.3	5.6	6.0
1974	34.3	6.1	5.6	5.6
1975	32.7	6.0	5.5	5.2
1976	30.9	6.4	4.8	4.8
1977	29.5	6.7	4.4	4.4
1978	27.8	6.9	4.1	4.1
1979	27.1	6.7	4.0	3.7
1986				1.0
1988				.2
1989				−.2

[1]*Statistical Abstract of the United States for 1979*, Table 1329.
[2]*Statistical Abstract of the United States for 1979*, Table 1325.
[3]Years remaining = 33.91 − .3828 (year − 1900); r^2 = .961.

describes the way the ratio drops through time, then use that equation to project ahead in order to determine a likely time at which the country would no longer be able to survive, without imports of crude oil. Barring imports, we would evidently run out early in 1989.

THE HISTORY AND GEOGRAPHY OF NONRENEWABLE RESOURCE USE

Figure 4.5 illustrates some of the most important facts about the history and geography of resource use in the world, using fuels as an example. Perhaps the most startling feature of this chart is that since the earliest days of the United States, when the principal fuel source (and almost the only source other than human and animal labor) was fuel wood, *total per capita energy consumption has been higher than the world average energy consumption in 1970.* Indeed, only a handful of countries have ever exceeded the level of per capita energy consumption experienced in the United States at the time of its development by European settlers.

What accounts for this great disparity between countries? The explanation cannot lie in international differences in technological sophistication: other countries sell us cameras, jet airliners, cars, color television sets, tankships, computers, and a wide variety of very high-technology products at competitive prices. A large number of countries are obviously capable of building and operating train systems that are faster, safer, and more punctual than ours. Also, the level of economic activity cannot account for the enormously high level of resource consumption in the United States:

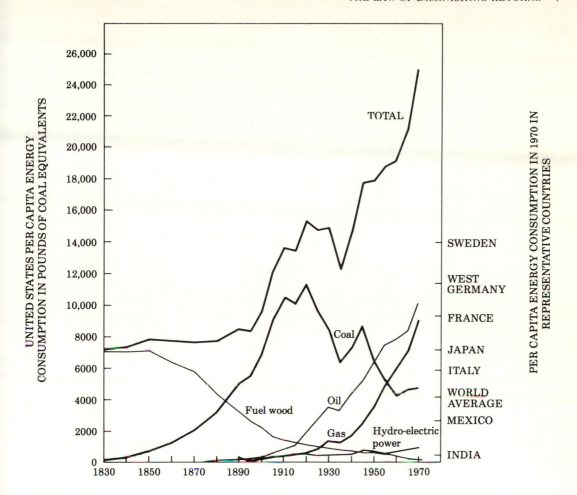

FIGURE 4.5

United States per capita energy consumption by type, through history, relative to energy consumption per capita in representative countries in 1970. U.S. historical data from Historical Statistics of the United States, Colonial Times to 1970. Washington, D.C.: U.S. Department of Commerce, Bureau of the Census, 1976. *Data on energy in other countries calculated from data in* Statistical Yearbook of the United Nations, 1971. Copyright, United Nations (1972). Reproduced by permission.

Denmark, Norway, Switzerland, Sweden, and West Germany all have Gross National Product per capita equal to or higher than that of the United States, yet have rates of energy consumption per capita between a quarter and two-thirds that encountered here.

The explanation, amazingly, is pure luck. A fundamental principle of human behavior appears to be that people do what they are able to do, when it is possible. The first settlers to the United States discovered an awesome superabundance of trees, so they were used. Long before the supply of fuel wood was exhausted, luckily, coal was discovered. Long before coal was depleted, oil was discovered. Long before oil was depleted, natural gas became an important substitute source of energy. There were a number of stimulants to the enormous U.S. increase in energy consumption after 1880. The great development of the railroads, combined with the use of coal in home heating and industry, explains the increase in coal use from 1850 to 1910. The expansion in the number of cars, from 8,000 in 1900 to 27.5 million in 1940, explains the increase in the use of crude oil to 1940.

Since the United States has always had a superabundance of cheap energy, there has been no reason to be efficient in energy use until very recently. Another factor is the vast area of the United States: all activities have a tremendous transportation energy overhead not found in compact, high density areas such as West Europe and Japan.

Limits on Substitution Between Energy Sources

One very profound message in Figure 4.5 is that great increases in total energy consumption per capita are made possible by the discovery of new energy sources: coal made possible the total increase from 1890 to 1910, oil made possible the further increase to 1945, and natural gas made possible the great increase after 1945. In general, this figure is a history of substitution of one resource for another: coal for wood, oil for coal, and gas for oil. This leads very naturally to an important question: might this substitution process be constrained by any important limitations?

That question is answered by Figure 4.6, which expresses the data of the previous figure in a different fashion. Now, we focus not on the amount of energy from each source, but the proportion of the total. We ask the question, how long does it take for a new energy source to provide 10 or 30 percent of all the energy used? Figure 4.6 shows that this substitution process takes a surprisingly long time and repeatedly demonstrates the same pattern. It took fifty years for coal, replacing wood, to supply 10 percent of the nation's energy, fifty-six years for oil, replacing coal, to supply 10 percent of the total, and forty-four years for gas to supply 10 percent of the total. It has taken about fifty years, plus or minus six, for a new energy source to supply 10 percent of U.S. total energy consumption (the discrepancy of plus or minus 6 might merely reflect inaccuracies in the statistics). The corresponding interval for a new energy source to supply 30 percent of U.S. total consumption is about seventy-four years. These figures are particularly significant when we realize that the U.S. will shortly run out of two energy sources, oil and gas, that between them now supply not 30 percent of national total energy consumption, but about 80 percent. Even under conditions of wartime emergency and national mobilization of resources, workers, and technological capability, it would probably take at least thirty years to get a new source or combination of sources to the point where they could supply the energy now coming from oil and gas; and this may be a wildly optimistic estimate.

FIGURE 4.6

The length of time that new U.S. energy sources took to supply 10 percent and 30 percent of national energy consumption, dating from the time when use began.

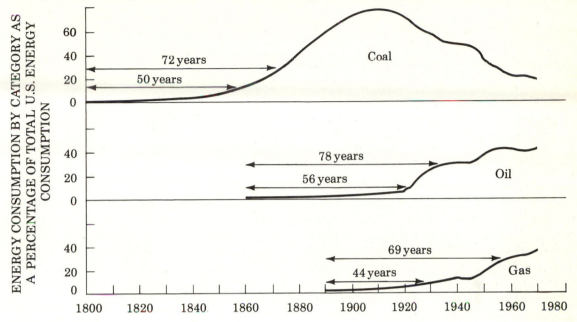

Two conclusions seem inescapable: we must plan on a nationwide basis, and time can be a critical limiting, nonrenewable resource.

Buying Time through Conservation

How much time can we buy through conservation efforts? If world crude oil production grew at only 2 percent after 1973, instead of almost 7 percent, the lifetime of the resource would be extended by between twelve and twenty-two years, depending on whether we assume low or high estimates of the ultimate recoverable total. As we decrease the rate of increase in production, we buy more time. Halting production growth after 1973 could have bought us thirty to sixty years. Making production decline each year by one percent after 1973 could have bought us at least fifty years, and perhaps a century. Clearly, sufficiently aggressive efforts at conservation will buy us all the time we need

to get substitute energy sources in place. Decades being required to substitute one energy source for another emphasizes the critical limiting role of time in attempted future repetition of substitution for old energy technologies. It will be difficult to achieve rapid buildup in the number of nuclear or solar energy-generating systems.

To this point, our discussion has largely centered on crude oil. How long will other fossil fuels last? Estimates of resource lifetimes are clearly very sensitive to the shape of the complete production cycle, as illustrated in Figure 4.1. However, if we assume that all complete production cycles will have the approximate shape of Hubbert pimples, then the resource lifetimes will be approximately as follows. World crude oil will last to about 2120 A.D., U.S. natural gas will last to about 2060, and world coal will last to about 2850. Also, compared to the world at large, the United States is in an unfavorable competitive position with respect to oil and

TABLE 4.4

Proven reserves of oil and gas by region, Jan. 1, 1978.

	Oil reserves (billions of barrels)	Gas reserves (Trillions of cubic feet)
North America	36	268
Latin America	40	109
Western Europe	27	138
Communist world	98	955
Africa	59	208
Middle East	366	720
Asia and the Pacific	20	123

Data from *Oil and Gas Journal,* Dec. 26, 1977.

gas (it will run out here about 2060, before it runs out elsewhere), but a favorable competitive position with respect to coal (it will last here as long as it lasts any place). The particular distribution of oil and gas will have a major impact on the relative competitive position of various nations over the intermediate term (between 1990 and 2020). Table 4.4 itemizes proven reserves of oil and gas by groups of countries. Clearly, the Middle East is very favorably situated with respect to oil, and the communist block countries have a very favorable competitive position with respect to gas.

Clearly, also, the United States is shifting from a pattern of being largely self-reliant for fuel to being increasingly dependent on importation from other countries. Over half of U.S. crude oil consumption is now supplied by foreign importation, largely from the Middle East.

This same pattern of dependence on foreign supplies shows up when we examine the national situation with respect to minerals. There is a wide variety of minerals for which the United States is no longer self-sufficient. But perhaps more meaningful than simply listing these would be to indicate what some of the most important of these deficiencies cost us. Table 4.5. gathers data on the cost of some of our most critical shortages and on the rate of increase in those costs. There are

TABLE 4.5

Cost of importing some of the more important minerals into the United States.

Category	Cost of imports, in millions of dollars		1975 import cost
	1960	1975	1960 import cost
Pig iron and ferroalloys	55	557	10.1
Iron and steelmill products	431	4138	9.6
Manufactured fertilizers	77	557	7.2
Nickel	89	464	5.2
Aluminum	107	411	3.8
Platinum group metals	13	243	18.7

two responses a nation can make to these cost data: to minimize import cost by conserving, or simply to meet the costs by exporting other commodities to pay for the imports. But the pattern of exporting massive quantities of commodities to pay for massive imports of other commodities comes at a very steep price, as we shall see in subsequent chapters.

ENERGY USE AND THE PATTERN OF SOCIAL ORGANIZATION IN DIFFERENT COUNTRIES

Anyone who travels in a variety of countries will gradually come to realize that they have a very different overall appearance, and pattern of social organization (Figures 4.7 and 4.8). A major determinant of these differences is the relative availability of different resources, particularly energy. One of the most important resource differences between countries is in the type of available energy. The countries that have managed to reach high levels of economic development fall into two very different categories: crude oil societies and electricity societies. As Table 4.6 brings out, countries in which electricity is very important tend to be electric-train-oriented societies, whereas countries in which crude oil is more important tend to be car-oriented societies. But the differences go much further than this, because car-oriented societies will be organized around freeways, with the resultant implications for patterns

FIGURE 4.7
An aerial view of a typical American city, showing the relative absence of trains, the enormously complex system of freeways, the great urban sprawl, and the high proportion of the downtown area devoted to parking lots for cars. Photograph by Owen Franken. Courtesy of Stock, Boston, Inc.

TABLE 4.6
Different patterns of energy generation in different countries, and relation to mix of national transportation systems.

Country	Kilowatt hours of electricity produced per metric ton of coal equivalents of total energy consumed in 1974	Passenger kilometers travelled in trains per passenger car in use in 1974
CRUDE OIL SOCIETIES		
U.S.A.	808	159
Venezuela	991	70
ELECTRICITY SOCIETIES		
Norway	3902	2117
Switzerland	1616	4805
New Zealand	1759	456
Sweden	1586	2020

FIGURE 4.8
An aerial view of a typical European city, showing the train tracks leading to a central point, the relatively small number of freeways, the lack of urban sprawl, and the small proportion of the downtown area devoted to parking lots. Photograph courtesy of the Swiss National Tourist Office.

of urban development; train-oriented societies will be organized around rail lines and train stations. Freeway societies exhibit "leapfrog" development patterns with sprawl, if land is cheap enough; train societies have compact city development, particularly if land values are high. In subsequent chapters, we will see how the interacting systems of energy and land availability operate as a powerful shaping force on the character of society.

THE EFFICIENCY OF ENERGY USE

Two very important scientific principles are basic to any discussion of energy use in society: the first and second laws of thermodynamics. The first law states that energy is never created or destroyed, but can only be transformed from one state to another (as in the transformation from light to biochemical energy by green plants, heat to kinetic energy in steam engines, or light to electricity in solar-electric systems). The second law is that none of these transformations are 100 percent efficient: energy is always being transformed from more useful to less useful forms. Thus when we drive a car, using gasoline, much of the energy generated is not used for propulsion but is wasted as heat (the steaming car radiator on a hot day reflects a situation in which this waste heat cannot be dissipated fast enough to keep the radiator fluid cool).

Efficiency in Transportation Systems

Since efficiency is a basic property of all systems, animate and inanimate, and since the world is clearly using up fossil fuel resources stored over millions of years, it is of great interest to discover what determines efficiency, and how it might be increased. Table 4.7 collates some data that suggest some of the factors involved. Clearly, different types of equipment have different inherent fuel efficiencies: railroads are more efficient than airplanes, because they are slower, and need not expend fuel to counteract gravity. Buses are more efficient than cars. However, many other factors come into the picture: different models of cars have different efficiencies, and different models of airplanes have dif-

ferent efficiencies. Cars in the United States are significantly less fuel-efficient than cars in other countries, and, more startling yet, the average efficiency of U.S. cars has decreased: they obtained 14.95 miles a gallon in 1950, and only 14.26 miles a gallon in 1978. On the other hand, because of the switch to newer models of jets, the fuel cost per passenger mile in jets declined 40 percent from 1970 to 1979. However, there are two explanations for this: passenger load factor (proportion of the seats filled) was higher, as a consequence of reduced frequency of service on some routes, as well as the new plane models being more efficient. This suggests another important cluster of factors bearing on efficiency, which are suggested by Table 4.7. The average number of passengers who travel in any type of vehicle is lower than the maximum number the vehicle could carry in comfort and safety. Thus, any policy measure that would increase the number of passengers per vehicle would increase societal fuel efficiency. Toll charges that are highest for one-occupant cars and

TABLE 4.7

The energy efficiency and percentage of the total traffic volume handled by different types of intercity passenger vehicles in the United States in 1973.

Type of vehicle	Average mileage per gallon of fuel	Average number of passengers per vehicle	Average passenger mileage per gallon of fuel	Percentage of total traffic
Railroads	.66	153	100	.7
Buses	5.86	8.97	52	2.0
Private cars	13.29	2.64	35	86.5
Airlines	.25	61.37	15	10.6

Fuel consumption statistics for cars and buses from U.S. Federal Highway Administration; average number of passengers per vehicle obtained by dividing passenger-mile statistics of U.S. Interstate Commerce Commission by vehicle-mile statistics of Federal Highway Administration; percentage of total traffic data from I.C.C.; airline statistics calculated from statistics of U.S. Federal Aviation Administration, by dividing revenue passenger miles by fuel consumption, and revenue-miles by fuel consumption (domestic flights only); average number of rail passengers per train from I.C.C.; railroad fuel consumption from I.C.C., prorating fuel use over passenger and freight trains following allocation computed by E. Hirst.

zero for four-occupant cars are an example. It also will be noticed that the two least fuel-efficient types of vehicles carry most of the intercity traffic volume, while buses and trains carry almost none of it. There are two reasons for this, in turn: very low fuel prices, which discourage use of public transportation; and a pattern of land use (urban sprawl) in which densities are too low to allow economically efficient use of public transportation. Cars are most fuel-efficient at about 500 passengers per foot width of right of way per hour, buses at about 1100, and mass transit trains at about 3000 passengers per foot width of right of way per hour. Therefore, urban land use must be organized so that population densities allow for fuel-efficient vehicles, if society is to be energy-efficient.

The way vehicles are used also has an impact on energy efficiency. In the United States, cars are often used for very short trips, with a high proportion of all the trip energy going into warming up the motor rather than propulsion. In other countries, people are much more likely to walk for very short trips. Also, continuous driving is much more fuel-efficient, than stop-and-start driving created by traffic congestion. Traffic congestion should be interpreted as a signal that society is malfunctioning: the problem arises because the wrong type of vehicle is being used, but can also be dealt with through use of staggered working hours. The "wrong type of vehicle" is the car; congestion arises from using too much highway space per passenger. Buses or trains use far less right of way space per passenger. Stalled traffic because of congestion flashes us a message that a limit on transportation space has been reached, and warns us that energy as well as space are being misused.

Efficiency of energy use in transportation is affected by a number of other factors that express our patterns of social organization and our life styles. All intraurban trips are shorter, on average, when cities are more compact and less sprawling. The degree of urbanization (percentage of the population living in large cities) has a considerable effect on overall social efficiency of energy use. Some of the effects are positive, but others are negative, because of the large average distances between farmers and their consumers. Where a high proportion of a nation's inhabitants live in small towns, no one is too far away from the place where his or her food is produced, and the transportation energy overhead on all food items is minimal. One particularly remarkable misuse of energy in the United States is the practice of towing campers and boats great distances from the home to a recreational area many times a summer, instead of renting boats and other recreational equipment at the site where they are to be used. This practice makes inefficient use of energy and material in another sense: a great deal of energy and material go into making a pleasure boat that will have a low number of hours of use over its lifetime.

Efficiency in Other Systems

Most of the preceding remarks about efficiency of transportation systems also apply to other aspects of our lives: offices, homes, industry, and city organization. Different kinds of refrigerators, stoves, air-conditioners and elevators have different energy efficiencies. A pattern of social organization in which people shop for groceries by going to the first floor of a city-in-a-building in an elevator is about seven times as efficient as driving from a suburban home to a shopping center. The city-in-a-building experiment, as at Lignon on the outskirts of Geneva, Switzerland, offers a much more pleasant life style than suburban sprawl, if organized to have the population adjacent to the countryside, and if adequate services are adjacent to the building.

J. G. Moyers has discovered that for a typical New York residence, the fuel required to heat the home could be approximately cut in half by use of appropriate insulation. One reason the United States uses so much more energy per capita than other countries is that our building codes are not designed to achieve energy efficiency in our houses.

A very basic concept central to arguments about energy use efficiency is that of social centralization versus decentralization. For example, do we want most of our energy to come from a small number of sites that then distribute the energy to consumers, or do we want to have energy produced at a very large number of sites, at the places where it is used? In the former case, most of our energy will come from a relatively few coal mines, oil and gas wells, refineries, or electricity generating plants. In the latter case, a high proportion of all the energy used by society will come from solar and wind collectors in the gardens or on the rooftops of family residences or apartment buildings. Centralization produces "economies of scale," efficiency of the entire national energy system because bulk handling allows for more energy and money efficiency per unit handled. Also, the energy sources represent very concentrated energy; a lot of energy is stored per unit volume of coal, oil, or gas. However, centralization comes at a price: a great deal of energy is used up in the process of transmitting or distributing the energy to ultimate consumers. M. L. Baughman and D. J. Bottaro (cited in reference 5) have discovered that almost 70 percent of the costs of power to residential and small light and power customers are related to transmission and distribution. If customers could generate electricity in their gardens or on their rooftops at 100/30 the cost per unit of a utility company, the ultimate cost would be the same, because transmission and distribution overhead would have been eliminated from the system.

THE NET ENERGY PRINCIPLE

Many people and institutions argue that it does not matter that the world has already used up a lot of fossil fuel and minerals, and that we are approaching the limits to "cumulative production." They argue that in fact, cumulative production ultimate totals only have meaning in a particular economic context: increasing the price of any energy or mineral in effect increases the amount available, by making it possible to exploit lower and lower grades of minerals, and more and more inaccessible oil, gas, and coal. This is an extremely important controversy, because the entire argument for conservation rests on the assumption that the availability of resources is limited. If the limit can be increased by increasing the price, so that in effect there is no limit, then the only argument for conservation is economic: as we use more of any nonrenewable resource the remaining quantity will rise in price. Further, if government decides that the price of a resource should be determined by governmental decree, rather than by supply and demand, or geological cost of extraction, or the capital costs of getting more energy, then the argument for conservation is eroded even more.

However, Howard Odum, Amory Lovins, Peter Chapman, Nigel Mortimer, and John H. Price (5, 6, 8) have added an entirely new dimension to this issue by introducing the concept of "net energy," which renders it meaningless to speak only of the energy we get out of any energy-extraction or generation program; we must also figure in the energy spent to get energy. Thus, no matter what the economics of the process, any system for obtaining energy that uses more energy than it obtains is worthless. This concept is important because for many processes designed to generate energy, the energy spent to that end may be far greater than we have realized, simply because the overall bookkeeping on the system has been incomplete or defective. For example, the energy cost to produce energy from a generating plant includes: the energy cost of travel by the designers, engineers, and architects for the plant; the energy cost of site preparation (bulldozing, excavation, laying the foundation); manufacture of the equipment, the machine tools that made the equipment, and the vehicles that hauled it; and the energy cost of maintenance and administration (such as driving by employees and lighting and heating their offices).

This type of analysis must be applied to every kind of energy generating system, solar and wind systems as well as fossil fuel and nuclear systems. The results are surprising. Exotic systems, such as solar-electric and wind-electric, are not as efficient as one would expect, because against the energy they obtain, we must charge off the overhead energy required to manufacture them. Particularly if the manufacture involved components with a great energy cost per unit, such as solar-electric cells, the lifetime system net energy may be surprisingly low.

Two important systems features of net energy computations are particularly noteworthy. First, because energy conversion inefficiency occurs at each step in a sequence of conversions, systems with the smallest possible number of conversions are more efficient than systems with a larger number of conversions, all other things being equal. Second, the overall national energy efficiency for an energy-production system of a particular type is dependent on the rate at which plants of that type are being built. To illustrate: if the number of plants is being increased very slowly, then at any point in

time, most of the plants have already been completed and are producing energy. The national level of inefficiency because some of the plants are not yet completed represents a small proportion of the total system. But if the total national population of plants of a particuar type is being increased very rapidly, then at any point in time during this high growth period, a high proportion of all the plants will be incomplete (under construction). Clearly, it is logically possible for the population of plants to grow so fast that the net energy output from the entire population, including complete and incomplete plants, is negative! This means that the entire national system of energy-generating plants of a certain type could be a net consumer of energy, rather than a net producer, with the entire system being supported by an energy subsidy from some other type of energy-generating system that was already largely complete.

Examples of Net Energy Calculations

Two examples illustrate net energy principles. Table 4.8 compares two different means of using natural gas to heat a home hot water tank. At first glance, using electricity to heat water seems very efficient, with about 100 percent efficiency at that step. But because this includes one more conversion step than direct use of natural gas, the high efficiency within the home is illusory: using electricity from natural gas to heat home water tanks is only half as efficient as using gas directly when we consider the efficiency of the entire system (2). The significance of examining the overall efficiency of entire systems is clear when we bear in mind that energy conversion systems in modern society can include as many as eight steps, not two.

TABLE 4.8
Two ways of using natural gas to heat fifty gallons of water from 32°F to 312°F.

	Efficiency of energy conversion, percent		
	First step	Second step	Overall system
First alternative: convert natural gas to electricity, at generating plant, then use electricity in home to heat hot water tank	32	100	32
Second alternative: heat home hot water tank with natural gas directly	62		62

Adapted from Earl Cook, *Scientific American* vol. 224 [Sept. 1971], pp. 134–144.

The effect of rate of increase in the number of energy-generating plants on overall system efficiency is particularly important in the case of nuclear plants, where it is clearly intended to use nuclear energy as an important substitute for other types of energy, in a very short time (twenty to thirty years). Peter Chapman, Nigel Mortimer, and John H. Price have developed calculations showing that the net energy output from a rapidly growing population of nuclear plants could be negative. The following discussion, and Table 4.9, presents a condensed and modified version of their argument. All the numbers are based on their analyses of nuclear construction and operation programs. We assume, first, that a nuclear plant does not begin generating electricity until the seventh year after the year in which construction began. In the seventh year, and for twenty-four following years, it delivers an average of 4613 million kilowatt hours of electricity each year. However, for five years while the plant is under construction, it uses up an average of 1784 million kilowatt hours of energy each year (the figures 4613 and 1784 were averages for six kinds of nuclear plants). Table 4.9 presents the national energy statistics for a population of plants in which construction of a new plant is started

each year. Column 1 shows that the energy cost of such a program does not stabilize until the fifth year. Column 2 indicates that gross energy output rises by 4613 each year, beginning with the seventh year. Column 3 is the cumulative sum of the energy investment figures in column 1, and column 4 is the cumulative sum of the energy generation figures in column 2. Column 5, the cumulative net energy, is simply the difference between columns 3 and 4. Amazingly, there is no cumulative net energy until the twelfth year of such a program. The final column computes the percentage per annum growth rate in gross energy output, by dividing the column 2 figure by the column 2 figure for the preceding year.

The results of this calculation are startling, to say the least. After this program has been in effect for sixteen years, the percentage growth rate in gross output has still not stopped dropping, and it has dropped to 11 percent per year. At this growth rate, it would take 6.3 years for gross energy production to double. The point is that the countries interested in developing nuclear power programs are not interested in doubling times this long; in the United States, for example, nuclear power production to 1976 increased about 36 per-

TABLE 4.9

Net energy calculations on populations of nuclear plants, assuming one new plant started each year. [1]
All figures in millions of kilowatt hours per year.

Year	(1) Energy invested this year	(2) Energy output this year	Cumulative energy to and including this year			(6) Percent growth in gross output since last year
			(3) investment	(4) output	(5) net	
1	1784	0	1784	0	−1784	—
2	3568	0	5352	0	−5352	—
3	5352	0	10704	0	−10704	—
4	7136	0	17840	0	−17840	—
5	8920	0	26760	0	−26760	—
6	8920	0	35680	0	−35680	—
7	8920	4613	44600	4613	−39987	—
8	8920	9226	53520	13839	−39681	100
9	8920	13839	62440	27678	−34762	50
10	8920	18452	71360	46130	−25230	33
11	8920	23065	80280	69195	−11085	25
12	8920	27678	89200	96873	7673	20
13	8920	32291	98120	129164	31044	17
14	8920	36904	107040	166068	59028	14
15	8920	41517	115960	207585	91625	13
16	8920	46130	124880	253715	128835	11

[1]Derived from tables by John H. Price in *Non-Nuclear Futures,* Copyright 1975, Friends of the Earth. Reprinted with permission from Ballinger Publishing Company.

cent. But as Table 4.9. indicates, at that high a growth rate in the production of gross energy from the entire population of plants, the systemic net energy contribution is negative.

Now we understand why it took so long for a new energy source to supply 30 percent of national needs (Figure 4.6.). If the number of plants had been increased more rapidly, there would have been no net energy return, and the shareholders would have made no return on their investment. The gross output of energy from the national population of nuclear plants was allowed to grow very rapidly, because the complete nuclear fuel cycle contained hidden subsidies from the public to the private sector. That is, much of the cost of this new energy source was covered

in connection with the development and manufacturing of nuclear weapons.

This calculation has an interesting general implication we will encounter repeatedly in this book: the systemic properties of a system are often quite different than those we would expect from the most careful examination of individual components of the system. In this case, the energy output/input ratio for a single plant is entirely reasonable: $(4613 \times 25)/(1784 \times 5)$. However, when we consider the complete time trend in the statistics for an entire population of plants, we get a very different picture.

The net energy principle means that many things that superficially appear feasible are not worth doing: they do not pay for themselves. For example, some technological optimists argue that humanity will never be short of energy as long as there is bare granite rock, because all rock contains some fissionable heavy elements that could be used to power nuclear reactors. This argument is spurious, because it ignores the energy cost of mining and separating the fissionable material (a tiny proportion of the total volume) from the rest of the rock.

All kinds of schemes proposed as the salvation of humanity are infeasible because of the net energy argument. For example, there are claims that humanity could be supported with synthetic food. The problem is that the factories that would produce the synthetic food consume more energy than is contained in the food. It would be nice to raise lobsters (or crabs, shrimp, or salmon) in factories. The problem is that vast amounts of energy would be required to flush rotting food remnants, wastes, toxins, and diseases out of the system; the reason why these lucrative-appearing systems are not already running is that daring pioneers soon ran into the net energy problem. Profitable culture of marine organisms will probably require solar or tidal energy for flushing.

We may be able to surmount the net energy problem with tremendously ingenious design or planning, as by taking less time to construct nuclear plants and by making them more efficient, or by innovations in the manufacture of solar energy cells to lower the energy requirements of the process. But as the world runs out of cheap fossil fuel energy, the net energy principle is something we will all hear more and more about.

THE GEOGRAPHY OF MINERAL AVAILABILITY

The likely future availability of minerals is a subject of extreme controversy. One position is that we will never run out of needed minerals, because increased scarcity will cause a rise in prices, which in turn will stimulate the development of new technology, make lower grade ores accessible, and lead to the search for or synthesis of substitutes. The contrary position is that by the year 2000, the United States will run out of the following minerals: nickel, tungsten, aluminum, gold, chromium, copper, platinum, lead, zinc, mercury, cobalt, and tin. Of these, tungsten, gold, copper, zinc, lead, and tin are expected to be depleted worldwide by the year 2000. How can there be so much disagreement about simple matters of fact?

Much of this controversy hinges on a technical argument. Some people hold that as the grade of an ore declines, as in the case of copper ore, the tonnage of the ore worldwide increases in a compensatory fashion, so that, for example, a decrease in the copper content of an ore to one-fourth the previous level will imply an increase in the availability of the ore by a factor of four. Preston Cloud (1) has presented up-to-date evidence to show that this relationship does not hold. A decrease in the metal content of most ore to one-fifth does not imply a five-fold increase in the amount of ore at the lower level of metal content, but much less than a 5 times increase. Therefore, with decreasing valuable metal content in rock per unit weight of rock, the energy cost of extraction rises very rapidly with decreasing availability of high-grade ores. The increased energy cost of extracting the valuable minerals from low-grade ores was not an insurmountable problem when energy was itself cheap. But now that energy is rising in price rapidly, the extraction of ores will be limited by the net energy problem. As more and more mineral resources of the developed countries are depleted, the remaining ores in various countries will increase in value, just as declining U.S. oil reserves have strengthened the relative international position of O.P.E.C. (Organization of Petroleum Ex-

TABLE 4.10

Countries with mineral surpluses benefiting from depletion of domestic reserves in United States.

Mineral	Countries exporting to the United States	Value of net exports to the United States in 1977 (millions of dollars)
Iron ore	Canada, Venezuela, Brazil, Liberia	957
Copper	Canada, Peru, Chile, Zaire	430
Nickel	Canada, Norway, New Caledonia, Dominican Republic	716
Silver	Canada, Mexico, Peru, United Kingdom	359
Bauxite	Jamaica, Australia, Surinam, Guinea	339
Tin	Malaysia, Thailand, Bolivia, Indonesia	523
Zinc	Canada, Mexico, Australia, Peru	363
Platinum group	South Africa, Soviet Union, United Kingdom	272
Asbestos	Canada, South Africa	141
Aluminum	Canada	101

From Tables 1313, 1314, 1520, and 1521, *Statistical Abstracts of the United States, 1978.*

porting Countries). Table 4.10 shows how, for a few selected minerals, shortages developing in the United States are creating an important source of income for other countries.

These mineral shortages affect the United States in a variety of ways. Exotic elements such as gallium, beryllium, germanium, and tantalum are important in electronics, as is sheet mica. Titanium is important as a constituent of alloys used in very high-performance aircraft. Silver is important in photographic film, and copper is important as a conductor of electricity. Nickel, chromium, and vanadium are all constituents of steel alloys with great strength, durability, or other high-performance characteristics.

One important means of dealing with all such shortages is to sharply increase retail prices, so as to encourage both conservation and recycling.

ARE THE OCEANS A PANACEA OR AN INFINITE CORNUCOPIA?

Some people adopt the attitude that none of these impending mineral shortages is worthy of discussion, because the oceans are a limitless source for all of them. How valid is this position? Again, the argument hinges on energy costs. Minerals could, in principle, be recovered from the ocean in three ways: by extraction from seawater, from deposits or sediments on or underneath the surface of the sea bottom, or from the crystalline rock of the sea floor. At first glance, seawater does seem like an inexhaustible source of minerals, because there are 1.3 billion cubic kilometers of it, containing sixty-four of the ninety naturally occurring elements. The problem is that many of the elements occur in seawater at very low concentrations. Magnesium, bromine, sodium, chlorine, sulfur, calcium, potassium, lithium, and rubidium occur in seawater at concentrations of 1.8 kilograms per million liters or more, and economic extraction is feasible. However, energy would have to be virtually costless to make extraction of gold from sea water feasible since it only occurs at .0013 troy ounces per million liters. The same applies to about fifty two of the sixty four elements in the sea.

Many materials are found on the sea bed. However, there are two major problems. To illustrate, the cost of recovering diamonds from the sea bed can be in excess of the value of the diamonds. Something is a resource only if someone will volunteer to obtain the resource and sell it at a price some buyer is prepared to pay. The price of extracting crude oil from the ocean is far in excess of well-drilling prices on land. The second problem about mineral recovery from the sea bed is that beyond the continental shelves, the ocean bottom sediments and rock are different than those surrounding the continents and do not seem to have the variety of elements or concentration of economically valuable minerals that would justify enormously expensive extraction procedures. In short, while the oceans will be an important future source of oil, gas, and some other elements, they are by no means a limitless cornucopia waiting to be harvested.

SOIL AND AGRICULTURAL LAND

Four processes resulting from human activities lead effectively to permanent loss of agricultural soil, since we have not yet learned how to make top-quality soil rapidly on a meaningful scale. Deforestation (3), salinization, desertification, and land lost to highways and urbanization all decrease the ultimate agricultural productivity of the earth (7).

The roots of a forest function as a giant sponge, so that a high proportion of the water in a rainfall does not run off the land immediately, but soaks in. A river fed by a forest upstream tends to flow at a more even rate than a river flowing out of hill- or mountainsides that have lost their trees. When we remove all or most of the trees from a watershed, most of the water in a rainfall rushes off the land, generating such enormous force that it carries away great quantities of topsoil and may even generate dangerous flash floods, which create agriculturally useless gullies. The lost topsoil does not become a useful material someplace downstream; it is more likely to create marshes and silted-up stream beds and irrigation systems. As we shall see in Chapter 15, slash-cutting forests has been a key step in the downfall of many civilizations.

Salinization occurs when a semiarid area under intense cultivation does not have a system of drainage pipes to carry away the salt-rich agricultural waste water caused by evaporation. (Fertilizer use would increase the mineral content of waste water.) Yields per acre declined to about one-third their previous level in the Sumerian civilization after the irrigation system was no longer properly maintained. The present population of Iraq is perhaps as low as 40 percent of the population supported in Mesopotamia before salinity sharply lowered the carrying capacity of the area for people.

Desertification is a serious problem in many countries, but particularly the twelve African countries south and southeast of the Sahara desert. These countries experienced a terrible drought from about 1965 to 1973, partly because of a shift in climate, but partly also because ecologically fragile semidesert lands with a very low carrying capacity were forced to support more people and animals than they could on a sustained basis. Excessive grazing, cropping, and tree-cutting in marginal arid lands leads to destruction of the soil structure and erosion due to wind. A similar phenomenon was extremely severe in the United States in the "dust bowl" era that climaxed in 1934. Many people simply gave up trying to farm the ravaged land in states such as Oklahoma and headed west to California. The terrible effects of soil erosion on the lives of these "Okies" are described in Steinbeck's *The Grapes of Wrath.*

In subsequent chapters we shall bring out some of the basic reasons these things have happened and point out the various institutional and other changes that could halt and reverse these processes in the future.

SUMMARY

Exponential growth in the use of a nonrenewable resource results in startlingly sudden depletion and price increases at the end of the production cycle. The United States is now roughly 65 percent through its complete production cycle for crude oil. The effort and cost per unit to discover new oil and gas in the United States will rise sharply from now on.

The United States uses energy much less efficiently than other countries. One cause of this inefficiency is heavy dependence on vehicles that are very fuel-inefficient (cars and airplanes instead of buses and trains).

The net energy principle implies that the rate at which new energy-generating systems can be added to the national population of generating plants is limited. The limit is imposed because there is no money earned for stockholders or net energy generated, if the number of plants increases too rapidly.

Energy could be conserved by decentralization if the local systems were at least one-fourth as efficient as central systems for many customers. This is because of the great cost of transmission-distribution systems. Energy efficiency can be achieved by examining various prospective systems step-by-step, from energy generation to end use.

While the United States is running out of many minerals, other countries still have exportable surpluses of these. Consequently, the United States is now critically dependent on purchasing minerals abroad, including mineral fuels.

SUGGESTIONS FOR INDIVIDUAL AND GROUP PROJECTS

Collect articles by newspaper or magazine columnists discussing whether or not there is a developing crisis in nonrenewable resources; analyze their position for technical accuracy.

To illustrate, the following passage is designed to express ideas that sometimes appear in print, and is similar to published columnist's opinions that have actually appeared.

> We usually assume that manufacturing processes are inefficient, so that some of the raw material is lost during production. However, in nuclear technology it has been shown that the supply of fissionable material we began with can be increased (the "breeder" reaction). With further advances in technology we can expect to see this defiance of the laws of thermodynamics and conservation of matter show up throughout the manufacturing sector.

Find out about the physics and economics of the nuclear fuel enrichment and breeder processes. What are the facts about the energy efficiency of this procedure? Could it be generalized to other materials, such as copper, iron, or aluminum?

Also find out about attempts to feed the world's population with synthetic food, or algae, shrimp, or lobsters reared in factories. Given that nuclear fuel enrichment, or the production of synthetic food, or algae, fish, lobsters, or shrimp in factories ought to be highly profitable activities, why is no one making a great deal of profit from them?

Collect the most up-to-date figures you can find on nuclear fuel plants in the United States and see if any energy (net) has ever come out of the U.S. atomic "energy" program. Update the graphs and charts in this chapter, on nuclear and fossil fuel energy. Do you think an increase in prices would result in an increase in discoveries? Why?

Collect data on the energy efficiency of various types of vehicles in your state or region. How does load factor effect the efficiency of mass transportation in buses or trains? Using government statistics, see if the efficiency of new models of cars, buses, jet transports, and trains is higher than, the same as, or lower than older models.

Analyze the flow of energy into and out of your house. Where is there waste? Where could large savings be effected?

Collect data on the history of land use in your area. Has a lot of land been lost to agriculture? Will any more be lost to agriculture? Where will the food for your area come from in the future? Are your prospective food supplying areas going to set up agricultural land banks that will be more secure than the agricultural land near where you live?

REFERENCES

1. Cloud, P., "Mineral resources today and tomorrow." Chapter 4 in *Environment, Resources, Pollution, and Society*. W. W. Murdoch, ed. Sunderland, Mass.: Sinauer Associates, 1975.
2. Cook, E., "The flow of energy in an industrial society," 224 (1971), pp. 134–144.
3. Eckholm, E. P., *Losing Ground*. New York: W. W. Norton, 1976.
4. Hubbert, M. K. "Energy resources." Chapter 2 in *Energy Crisis: Danger and Opportunity*. V. J. Yannacone, Jr., ed. St. Paul: West Pub. Co., 1974.
5. Lovins, A. B., *Soft Energy Paths*. Cambridge, Mass.: Ballinger, 1977.
6. Odum, H. T., and E. C. Odum. *Energy Basis for Man and Nature*. New York: McGraw-Hill, 1976.
7. Pimentel, D., and eight others. "Land degradation: effects on food and energy resources," *Science*, 194 (1976), pp. 149–155.
8. Price, J. H. *Dynamic Energy Analysis and Nuclear Power*. Part 2 in *Non-Nuclear Futures*, by A. B. Lovins and J. H. Price. Cambridge, Mass.: Ballinger, 1975.
9. Root, D. H., and L. J. Drew, "The pattern of petroleum discovery rates," *Americn Scientist*, 67 (1979), pp. 648–652.
10. *Science*, 20 February 1976, special issue on "Materials." Hirst, E. "Energy intensiveness of passenger and freight transportation modes: 1950-1970," Report ORNL-NSF-EP-44. Oak Ridge, Tenn.: Oak Ridge National Laboratory, 1973. This technical document was of great help in the preparation of this chapter.

5 RENEWABLE RESOURCES

Variety in animal life may be produced by variety of locality: thus in one place an animal will not be found at all, in another it will be small, or short-lived, or will not thrive . . . The difference, where it exists, is attributed to the food, as being abundant in one case and insufficient in another . . . In many places the climate will account for peculiarities . . . Locality will differentiate habitats also: for instance, rugged highlands will not produce the same results as the soft lowlands.
Aristotle (384-322 B.C.), History of Animals, *Book VIII, Chapters 28 and 29.*

MAIN THEMES OF THIS CHAPTER

This chapter outlines the scientific principles that can be used to maximize the sustained yield of renewable natural resources. These principles describe the dynamic behavior of exploited groups of plants and animals. We discover that while sound management strategies can often increase yields, limits are set by birth and growth rates of organisms, resource availability, the efficiency of food use by living systems, and the tolerance of living organisms to increased availability of nutrients. At excessive concentra-

tions, nutrients become poisons. Thus the ability of the planet to produce living tissue is limited. This in turn means that the carrying capacity of the planet to support human beings is also limited.

INTRODUCTION AND OVERVIEW

Unlike the stock resources of the previous chapter, renewable or flow resources are produced or recycled constantly. They include the animals and plants that give us food, clothing, housing, paper, and packaging materials, as well as flow energy sources (sun, wind, and the ocean) and water.

As we saw in Chapter 1, we as a nation are dependent on renewable resources not only directly but also indirectly, because the United States sells food, textiles, and wood products to other countries to obtain some of the foreign currency we need to purchase foreign resources such as crude oil. Therefore, we must understand the factors that can be manipulated to maximize the sustained production of renewable resources. Also, we want to stabilize the economy by ensuring that production does not fluctuate wildly from year to year.

To this end, we need to understand the forces that determine production and stability in crops, livestock, game, fish stocks, and forests.

THE CONCEPT OF A HIERARCHY OF LEVELS OF ORGANIZATION

We can think of the world as being organized in hierarchical fashion. Reality can be perceived as layers of increasingly complex levels of organization, from the simplest to the very complex (16). To illustrate, our bodies may be thought about at the level of cells, tissues (such as the retina), organs (kidneys), or as a whole organism that swims and can fly aeroplanes. Very large numbers of people organize themselves into cities, and cities are organized into nations. All nations are now organized into a global economic system linked by flows of trade and money.

There are two important points about this hierarchical perspective of the real world.

First, each of the levels has rules of organization and functioning that are not ob-

vious consequences of the rules for lower levels; the global economic system has properties that are not obvious consequences of the characteristics of national economies. A population of animals has properties that would not be obvious even after a great deal of study of the individual animals in the population. As we go from simple to more complex levels of organization, new and often unsuspected "emergent properties" of the system appear (22). These characteristics are not simply the sum of the characteristics of the elements in the next lower level, but are in addition to that sum. Thus, the metropolitan region has mechanisms for internal information communication that would never be expected from any amount of study of individual people (16). Also, when metropolitan regions have excessive numbers of people, types of phenomena show up that could not be predicted from limitless study of individuals: crime, increasing cost per capita for bureaucracies, and fire-fighting.

A second point about hierarchically organized systems is that understanding and managing the complexity at any level can completely absorb the mental capacity of any human being. Thus, most people try to maximize their personal effectiveness by concentrating on one or a few layers of organization. Therefore, most human beings have their view of reality strongly affected by the properties of the layer or layers of reality on which they focus most of their time. We can scarcely expect a biologist studying a particular fish population (say, sardines or tuna) to view the world from the same perspective as a U.S. senator. The limitation of each person's focus only on certain levels implies person-to-person differences in mindset that become an important barrier to communication.

Purely in the interests of clarity of exposition, in this chapter we will focus on just three levels: the species population, the multispecies community, and the ecosystem.

The population is the assemblage of individuals within one species that inhabits a particular place at a particular time; the species is defined as a population within which all individuals are free to interbreed. The process by which a species splits into two or more species has begun when geographic or other barriers prevent interbreeding.

At a higher level of organization, the multispecies community is more than simply a collection of different species populations, because the various species interact with each other in many ways. Some species in a community prey on or parasitize other species, and two or more species eating the same food or requiring the same space compete with each other. This competition can affect birth, death, growth, and migration rates of the individuals in each of the competing species (1, 2).

The ecosystem is a still higher level of organization, which includes not only the community of species in a habitat, but the energy (originating in the sun) that cascades through the community, from plants to herbivores to carnivores, and the matter that cycles through the system. The matter begins as minerals in soil or water, then becomes plant tissue, animal tissue, and finally waste and decomposed material incorporated into the soil.

POPULATION DYNAMICS

When any species population first immigrates into a new environment, if the population can adjust to the environment, there is a long, slow period of growth while the population increases to the level that can be supported by the resources in the environment: this level is the "carrying capacity" of that environment for that population. The typical pattern of population growth seen in

such situations is depicted in Figure 5.1. While this figure has been generated from an equation, the equation (and hence the figure) are of approximately the same form that has been found in many laboratory, natural, and human populations (1). The pattern has come to be known as the logistic, or sigmoid growth curve (because it is reminiscent of a stretched-out letter S).

In this growth form, the rate of growth is first slow, then very rapid, then slow again. After the first growth phase is complete, the population typically declines, then rises again, repeatedly, as it seems to hunt for some equilibrium value about which it fluctuates for a long time.

Why do populations appear to fluctuate about some equilibrium value? Why don't they become extinct, or grow endlessly, until they cause their food to go extinct? What determines the equilibrium population density? Mechanisms for regulating population numbers and weight have been studied in a great many laboratory and field populations (9, 18, 19, 21). These mechanisms have been found to operate on the birth rate, survival rate, and rate of growth in weight. (Birth rate means the number of young born per female per unit time; survival rate means the proportion of the population surviving through a designated period, such as one year; growth rate refers to the percentage increase in weight over a designated period.) Wherever these mechanisms have been studied, in plants and animals, field and laboratory populations, the results have taken the approximate form of the three lines in Figure 5.2. The term "density" used in this figure simply means the number of individuals per unit area. In all three cases, when density is much higher than "equilibrium density," the rates drop. This tends to make population numbers and average weight drop to the equilibrium level. When densities are lower than the "equilibrium density," the rates increase, and population

FIGURE 5.1

The logistic or sigmoid population growth pattern, which assumes that the population can thrive in a new environment it has just entered, and that the number of immigrants was small compared to the number the environment could support. This curve was generated from the equation

$$N_t = \frac{10,000}{1 + e^{4 - .02t}}$$

where t *represents the time in years,* N_t *is the number present in year* t, *and* e *represents the base of natural logarithms. This equation is obtained by integrating the differential equation of form*

$$\frac{dN_t}{dt} = r \; N_t (N_{max} - N)$$

where

$\dfrac{dN_t}{dt}$ = *the instantaneous rate of population increase*

r = *the instantaneous per capita rate of natural popuation increase in a limitless environment (the instantaneous birth rate minus the instantanteous death rate)*

N_{max} = *the carrying capacity of this environment for this population (the maximum N that can be supported with the resources in the environment)*

$(N_{max} - N)$ = *the depressing impact of environmental limits on population growth rate*

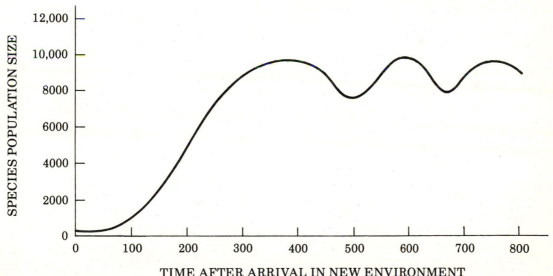

SPECIES POPULATION SIZE

TIME AFTER ARRIVAL IN NEW ENVIRONMENT
(Years)

FIGURE 5.2
The roles of birth and survival rates as regulators of population numbers, and of growth rate as a regulator of population biomass. When densities depart from equilibrium, these rates tend to restore numbers and biomass to equilibrium values. These curves are not based on any one species, but are composites based on examination of data for several species. The actual shape of the curves varies from species to species: the slopes of the lines increase as the sensitivity of the species to changes in its own density increases.

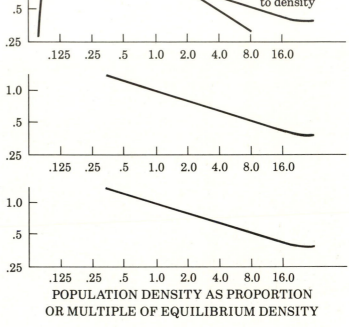

BIRTH RATE PER FEMALE AS PROPORTION OR MULTIPLE OF BIRTH RATE AT EQUILIBRIUM DENSITY

AVERAGE SURVIVAL RATE AS PROPORTION OR MULTIPLE OF SURVIVAL RATE AT EQUILIBRIUM DENSITY

AVERAGE GROWTH RATE OF INDIVIDUALS AS PROPORTION OR MULTIPLE OF GROWTH RATE AT EQUILIBRIUM DENSITY

POPULATION DENSITY AS PROPORTION OR MULTIPLE OF EQUILIBRIUM DENSITY

numbers and average weight rise, making the population tend to return to equilibrium. One complication is that at very low densities, birth rates may collapse because prospective mates simply cannot find each other: they are too scarce. There was concern that this might be the case for blue whales in recent years, when some estimates of the entire population in all oceans of the world ran as low as 640 animals.

Thus there are mechanisms tending to hold population numbers and total weight at

about those values that can be supported by a given environment: the carrying capacity. What determines this carrying capacity? Is it a fixed quantity, dependent on the space in the environment, or is it variable, depending at any moment on the resources available within the environment?

These questions are easy to answer. Consider a cattle feedlot. We all realize that the very high-density cattle populations supported in these small areas are much greater than those that could be supported on natural range land (Figures 5.3 and 5.4). The great quantities of food added to the feedlot each day allow the high density. Therefore, the ability of an area to support life, the carrying capacity, is not constant, but depends on resource availability in the area. However, food is not the only determinant of carrying capacity. Divers and snorkelers notice that coral reef fish populations they see in tanks in pet stores are at much lower densities than they often see in the ocean. The difference is that in the ocean, very high density fish populations can survive for short periods close to the coast in any given volume of water, because of the great amount of kinetic energy in wave action. This kinetic energy whips in a rich supply of oxygen, washes in nutrients, and flushes out wastes. These phenomena jointly make the high densities possible, although even so, the highest densities of all are seen in large schools of migratory species, which do not stay in any one volume of water for very long.

FIGURE 5.3

A cattle feedlot. Notice the very high densities of cattle made possible when there is a constant resource addition in the form of hay and grain. The carrying capacity is artificially elevated over that of natural pasture. Photograph by Owen Franken. Courtesy of Stock, Boston, Inc.

FIGURE 5.4
Cattle on natural pasture. Notice how much lower the cattle densities are than in the previous picture. In this case, the carrying capacity of the pasture for cattle is set by the natural growth of grass. Photograph by Read D. Brugger. The Picture Cube.

An Illustration from Nature: Sardines

One example from nature will suffice to show how the population regulating mechanisms operate. We will consider the stock of sardines in the ocean off the coast of California between 1934 and 1942 (19). In the top panel of Figure 5.5, an index of food per individual in each offspring generation of sardines is plotted against the food per individual in each parent generation of sardines. In each case, "food per individual" was calculated as the reciprocal of population size. The same self-regulating principle depicted in Figure 5.2 is shown in this figure, although it is expressed in different terms.

In the top panel, we see that where food availability was low for the parent generation, it tended to be high for the offspring. Where it was high for the parents, it tended to be low for the offspring. This comes about because low food availability for the parents (the result of excessive densities) results in low birth rates. This, in turn, means that the offspring from these parents will be low in numbers, and therefore will have high food availability per capita. In other words, the system operates so as to be compensatory,

FIGURE 5.5

Effect of resources on population trend in Pacific Ocean Sardine populations off coast of California. Top panel: the effect of resource availability per sardine in parent genera-tion on resource availability per sardine in offspring generation. Data from J. Rado-vich, "Effects of sardine spawning stock size and environment on year-class produc-tion," California Department Fishery Game Bulletin 48 (1962), pp. 123–140. Years after 1942 eliminated because of impact of fishery on stock. (Fitted equation:
$Y = .79 - 2.70X$). *Bottom panel: the effect of water temperatures in the year of spawn-ing on subsequent year class strength in populations of sardines. Data from J. C. Marr, "The causes of major variations in the catch of Pacific sardines,"* Proceedings of the World Scientific Meeting on the Biology of Sardines and Related Species, *Vol. 3, pp. 667–791. Rome: Food and Agriculture Organization of the United Nations, 1960.*

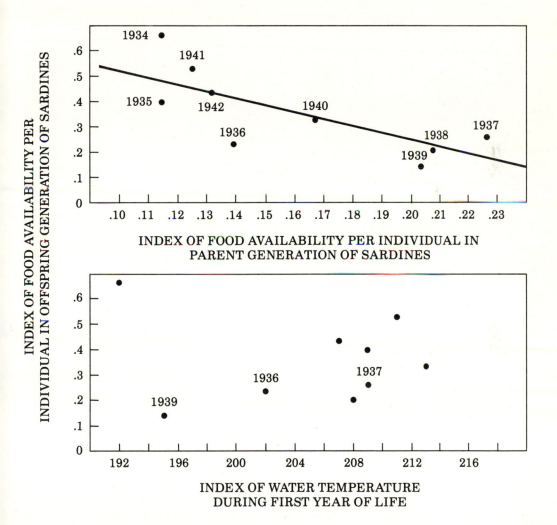

from generation to generation. Dense generations produce scarce generations; scarce generations produce dense generations.

However, as the second panel of Figure 5.5 brings out, there is a complication. Not only does food affect sardine reproduction and maturation, but so also does water temperature. This panel means that when the water temperature is high, the resource availability per capita for offspring generations is higher than it otherwise would be. To illustrate, in the top panel of the figure, the data point for 1937 lies above the line fitted statistically through the nine points; the point for 1939 lies below the line. The second panel explains this discrepancy: 1937 was warmer than 1939. In this case as in most others in nature, two or more factors interact to produce the observed results.

To summarize, population sizes are regulated through the effect of resource availability on birth and death rates in the equation:

$$\text{rate of population change} = \text{birth rate} - \text{death rate}$$

Note that this formula only applies where there is no immigration or emigration. Where migration occurs, the appropriate formula is:

$$\text{rate of population change} = \text{birth rate} - \text{death rate} + \text{net immigration rate}$$

When resource availability per individual is low, a compensatory mechanism comes into play in which birth rate is decreased and death rate is increased (survival rate is decreased). This results in a decrease in population size in the next generation. Or putting it differently, the result is an increase in resource availability per capita.

Thus we have a homeostatic or self-regulatory mechanism of the type that engineers build into systems such as aircraft and rockets, so that they maintain stability. The input to the system is food and other resources (such as heat). The availability of resources per capita affects the controlling system (birth and death rates). This in turn affects the controlled system (change in population density). The change is added to or subtracted from the previous population density, giving the density of the next generation. The system "senses" the new density, by adjusting resource availability per individual up or down. The phrase "negative feedback loop" is used to describe such system control, because if the population is too high, growth rate goes down, and if it is too low, growth rate goes up; that is, the key to self-regulation is a change in sign from positive to negative or negative to positive.

This regulatory mechanism is affected by all resources: if density goes too low because a change in the physical environment (cold weather or a typhoon, for example) caused an unusually high death rate, the result is the same subsequent increase in population that would have been produced by excessive predation, disease, starvation, or human harvesting. In short, populations can compensate for changes in their numbers, up to a point.

The underlying important principle running through this discussion is illustrated by Figure 5.6. We can think of the population as a system that converts input resources to outputs. As we increase the availability of resource inputs to the system, resource output increases. This increase continues up until some optimal level of resource availability has been reached. Beyond that level of availability, further increase in the available resource makes system output fall again, either because the system cannot use the excessive resource, or because the resource has now become toxic, as in the case of excessive heat, or concentrations of salt or fluorides in soil or water. We can illustrate the operation of this principle with the effect of flour availability on the reproduction of flour beetles. At very

FIGURE 5.6

The population stabilization mechanism: resource availability per parent regulates off-spring per parent. More generally, system output for any living system tends to be greatest at intermediate levels of output.

A: *population excessively large: production suppressed by competition.*
B: *population at optimum size for maximum sustained production.*
C: *population too small to adequately exploit habitat.*

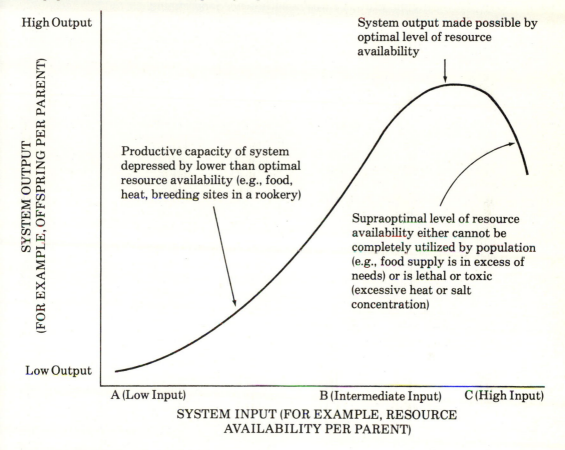

high levels of flour availability per beetle (low beetle densities), male beetles and female beetles simply have trouble finding each other to copulate, and this depresses the reproductive rate. This assertion is not based on conjecture: the relation between density and copulation rate has been studied repeatedly, with the expected findings. But not only is it true that very high levels of flour availability per beetle depress repro-

duction, many experiments have shown that very low levels of flour availability per beetle depress reproduction, and also survival.

In general, rate of population increase amongst beetles is highest at intermediate levels of flour availability per beetle. More generally, the principle illustrated by Figure 5.6 is one of the most important central ideas to come out of environmental science. This principle operates in a wide variety of contexts. All kinds of systems perform best at some optimal level of resource availability, intermediate between very low and very high levels of availability. To illustrate, when the population of a nation or a civilization becomes excessive, given the carrying capacity of the resource base, birth and survival rates decline. Or, when a nation uses too much energy, the economic growth rate declines (Figure 7.5). Or, when people eat too much meat, survival declines (Figure 1.4).

Some species normally occupy environments with rapidly changing physical conditions; they have evolved for explosive growth in numbers when favorable conditions occur. This is a strategy of success through high growth (high r); such species are called r-strategists. Other species normally occupy stable environments; they are adapted to maintain numerical stability in the face of competition, predation, and parasitism by many different species. This is a strategy of success through maintenance of stability; such species are called K-strategists, because ecologists have come to speak of N_{max} as K (r and N_{max} are explained in the legend to Figure 5.1).

The basic theory of population dynamics just presented has implications for how we manage farming, forestry, fisheries, wildlife management, and human population densities. However, before we turn to these applications, we will consider some simple theory of communities and ecosystems.

THE ORGANIZATION AND DYNAMICS OF COMMUNITIES

Our outdoor experience teaches us that some animals (the herbivores) eat plants, and other animals (the carnivores) eat herbivores. Also, sometimes higher carnivores eat lower carnivores, as when a pike eats a perch that has eaten bluegill sunfish eggs. We can assemble such information about food habits into sequences of species in which the higher member of each pair eats the lower member. These sequences are called food chains. Occasionally, and particularly in the ocean which can support populations of some very large predators, these food chains may be seven or even eight species long. Food chains often share species with other food chains.

This suggests that we might construct food webs, as in Figure 5.7. For a long time, some scientists have speculated about the inner significance of the structure of these webs (10, 14, 24). Figure 5.8 indicates the various types of food web structure that might be found. Observations in nature and, more recently, some statistical analyses of very large sets of data have suggested that certain types of structural patterns promote the stability of the community, whereas other types of structure work against stability. This is an issue of great practical significance, because farming practice has an effect on the structure of food webs, as do fishing and whaling strategy, wildlife management, and, surprisingly, even the way we manage the economies of our cities.

Community Stability

Two kinds of arguments support the notion that there might be some causal relationship between the structure of these food webs and the stability of the community.

The first argument is based on the same principle that encourages insurance companies to sell as many policies as possible (20). The argument might be expressed as "decreasing vulnerability by spreading the risk." The argument is that the larger the number of kinds of things vulnerable to various types of risk, the lower the proportion of the total number will be likely to succumb to any one type of risk (14). For example, if a community consists of a very large number

FIGURE 5.7
A simplified and idealized food web for a large North American lake.

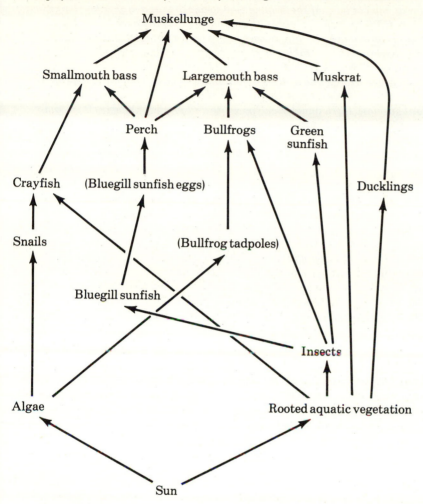

of different species, with a great variety of susceptibilities to disease, then it is highly unlikely that an outbreak of any particular disease will decimate more than a small proportion of all species. On the other hand, if there were only three species, then a major disease might wipe out a third of the individuals in the community. A special case of this argument applies to the number of food species eaten by a particular carnivore (or herbivore). The larger the number of food species

eaten, the lower is the probability that any given disaster will eliminate all of them.

Figure 5.9 gives a graphic example of how this "safety in numbers" works, using two hypothetical examples (14). The two columns of graphs compare a low species-diversity community and a high species-diversity community. Each community is subjected to a wide variation in soil moisture over a forty-eight-year period, although the time trend in the change is the same for both

FIGURE 5.8

Examples of the different types of structural relationships found in community food webs. Each circle represents a species which is a source of and destination for food; the lines represent paths between species along which food energy flows. That is, a line from one species at a lower level of the trophic web to another at a higher level means that the latter eats the former (for example, the carnivore eats the herbivore). First panel: Euryphagous (broad diet) herbivore eats many species of plant foods. Second panel: Competing herbivores; several herbivore species compete for the chance to eat one food plant species. Third panel: Many species of parasites and predators, in competition with each other, attack one species of herbivore. Fourth panel: Each herbivore species is in competition with other species of herbivores, all of which have broad diets (eat several plant species). Fifth panel: Each parasite and predator species is in competition with others for the same herbivore species; all have broad diets (parasites and predators are carnivores). Sixth panel: Both the herbivores and the carnivores have broad diets; thus the trophic web chart is replete with cross-linkages. In many real-world situations, species have broad diets, giving rise to the cross-linkages depicted in the last three panels. On the other hand, some species are monophagous, rather than euryphagous (have one food species rather than many). A well-known example is the Monarch butterfly, whose larva (caterpillar) eats only the milkweed plant. Note that these situations differ with respect to the trophic level on which competition occurs. Since the impact of species diversity on the trophic level and on the entire community depends on the trophic level at which the diversity occurs, this is an important distinction. High species diversity at one trophic level tends to increase stability of all species together at that level, but decrease stability in the next trophic level up, and the next trophic level down (see text discussion). Reproduced with permission from Figure 3.2 in Principles of Environmental Science, *K. E. F. Watt, McGraw-Hill Book Co., 1973.*

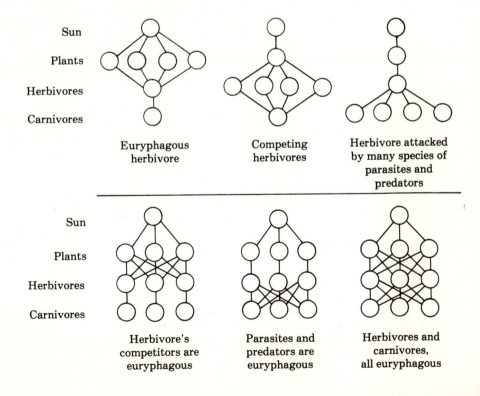

FIGURE 5.9

A simple illustration of how increased species diversity in a community may increase the stability of the functional properties of the entire community (in this case, community biomass production). The low diversity community has only two species, A and D, only one of which occurs at any time, because they have nonoverlapping soil moisture requirements. The high diversity community has the same two species, plus two others. The four species overlap considerably with respect to soil moisture requirements. Each community is subject to the same sequence of soil moisture conditions, over a forty-eight-year period, as illustrated in the top panel. Adapted from Figure 1 by S. J. McNaughton, "Diversity and stability of ecological communities: a comment on the role of empiricism in ecology." The American Naturalist, *111 (1977), pp. 515–525. Reprinted by permission of the University of Chicago Press.*

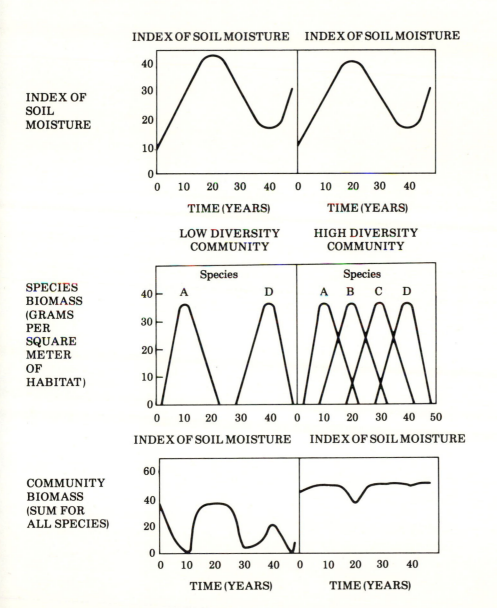

communities. The low diversity community has only two species: A and D. The high species diversity community has four species: the same A and D, and two additional species with response to soil moisture in between that of A and D. To simplify the argument, we assume that each species has a curve for the effect of moisture on species biomass (live weight) that is the same shape; but that the four curves differ with respect to the moisture level that produces the maximum biomass. Thus, if the soil moisture drops very low, species A is favored, and D can no longer survive in the area; if it becomes very moist, D is favored and A can no longer survive in the area.

The bottom panels show the response of the entire community to the forty-eight-year history of soil moisture changes for the two communities. Where there are only two species with no overlap in moisture requirements, there are violent year-to-year fluctuations in the biomass of the two-species community. Where there are four species representing an overlapping gradation of responses to soil moisture, the sum of the species biomasses for the entire community shows very little fluctuation. In the four-species case, whenever one species is doing badly because of adverse moisture conditions, some other species is doing well. Of course, in a real community, these curves would overlap more than in this diagram. Also, soil moisture would not be the only factor fluctuating through time. Note, also, that the shape of these curves has been over-simplified.

A second argument for the relationship between species diversity in communities and communities stability comes from the theory of interspecies competition. Swimming through a coral reef, for example, we are struck by the perfection of adaptation of the structure and function of each species to its particular role in the reef. Some fish have

short, powerful jaws and chisel-like teeth for crunching pieces of coral from the reef, so that the algae on the coral may be digested (the parrotfish). Other fish have long, needle-like mouths for picking fragments out of coral heads (the bird wrasses and long-snouted butterfly fish). Some are obviously adapted for eating fish (the morays, jacks, tuna, and sharks). Others are obviously adapted for sieving plankton out of the water (the manta rays). With this great variety of highly co-evolved specific structures and functions, each species is obviously fine-tuned to exploit its niche better than it could be exploited by many of the other species in the area. This, in turn, implies that no particular species is likely to become super-abundant at the expense of the rest: it is only fine-tuned to one group of functions. Other species will always be able to out-compete it at other functions.

In general, a force operating against a species becoming too abundant is competition (and predation and parasitism) by other species, all of which will be very well adapted to their function. One way this intense specialization shows itself even to the casual observer is in territorialism. That is, for each type of potential home area (territory), there will be some species unusually fitted to make very good use of that home and defend it effectively against invasion by a potential competitor. A particularly amusing example of this fine-tuned adaptation occurs in the hermit crab, which has one front claw designed to act as a perfectly fitted door for the opening to its snail home. Being attacked by a large fish or shark whose territory one has invaded is less amusing but makes the point more memorable.

Data to test these notions have not been collected frequently; however, the few sets of data that do bear on these hypotheses suggest they are correct (24). Table 5.1 com-

TABLE 5.1

The impact of grazing by African buffalo on diversity and green biomass of grasslands in Serengeti National Park, Tanzania.

Property	High-diversity stand	Low-diversity stand
Index of diversity without grazing	1.783	1.069
Index of diversity after grazing	1.302	1.357
Percentage of green biomass eaten	66.9	75.9
Green biomass reduction, as a percentage of ungrazed stand	11.3	69.3

Modified from Table 2 in S. J. McNaughton, "Diversity and stability of ecological communities: a comment on the role of empiricism in ecology," *The American Naturalist*, 111 (1977), pp. 515–525, by permission of the University of Chicago Press.

pares the impact of grazing by buffalo on the diversity (variety of species) and green biomass of grasslands in Africa, on high- and low-diversity plant communities. In plant communities with high species diversity, grazing reduced the diversity, presumably by sharply reducing the abundance of the most palatable food species. Where there was low diversity prior to grazing, grazing increased the diversity, presumably by making more palatable foods less abundant relative to the less palatable foods (evening out the relative abundance of all species is one way of increasing the species diversity per individual organism). While the percentage of green biomass eaten was similar in the low and high diversity communities, the green biomass reduction was far less in the high diversity stand. The significance is that where there are many species, any factor (such as grazing) that reduces the biomass of some species will elicit a compensatory mechanism: increased growth of other species. Thus, high species diversity within a community operates as a stabilizing mechanism. We have discovered a new important principle: there can be different stabilizing mechanisms operating on different

levels of organization (an "emergent property").

Is it true that high species diversity implies interspecific competition which will tend to stabilize species populations? (Interspecific competition occurs when two or more species in a locality have a common need for a limited resource, and the result is decreased birth, survival, or growth rates in at least one of the species.) We can test this proposition using the results of a massive program of data collection and analysis, the Canadian Forest Insect Survey. This is a survey of all the major forest insects in Canada that has been conducted each year for several decades. The data can be analyzed so as to reveal the relationship between the number of insect species that eat a particular plant host species and the average amount of year-to-year variation in the insect species populations feeding on the plant. We find that as the diversity of insect species feeding on a plant increases, those insect species will fluctuate less in number from one year to another. This is not the same point tested in Table 5.1, which measures the collective behavior of all the species in the community. If increasing the species diversity of the herbivores feeding on a particular plant increases the average stability of those species, then it follows that this also implies an increase in the stability of the entire herbivore trophic level.

But Figure 5.8 pointed out that there are different ways in which the species diversity of a community might be increased: the increase might occur at the plant level, the herbivore level, or the carnivore level. Does it make any difference at which level the increase in species diversity occurs? To explore that issue, the same body of data was used to test the effect on community stability, not of species diversity amongst the feeder species, but amongst the food species (the forest trees). In this case, as the species diversity of food species increases, the stability of the feeding species decreases. This result is another phenomenon: as a greater proportion of the environment of a feeding species is filled with its food, it is more likely to increase rapidly when conditions (such as weather) allow for that increase.

Community Structure and Resource Management

Now what are the practical implications of these principles of community structure and dynamics? In general, we simplify systems at our peril. Whenever we concentrate our resources on one or a small number of species or activities, we run the risk of being wiped out by a disaster. Our culture recognizes this danger, which is often expressed in the admonition, "Don't put all your eggs in one basket." Thus, if enormous tracts of land are planted out to one crop (the "monoculture" approach to agriculture), we run the risk of losing the crop in the entire area to weather, blight, wheat rust, or some analogous disaster. Also, we should be careful not to fill up an area with plant species that are vulnerable to a particular herbivore (insect, rabbit, or deer, for example). We

make our land too vulnerable to a pest outbreak by that species.

These community principles do not apply just to biological or resource management systems. A city is undesirably vulnerable to economic disaster when its industrial base is excessively concentrated on one product (textiles, cars, or aerospace, for example).

The reason why we find monoculture over vast areas in modern society (wheat in Kansas, corn in Iowa), and cities in which one industry dominates the economy (aerospace in Seattle, cars in Detroit) is economies of scale (lowering the cost of working with one unit by increasing the number of units). This brings out an essential feature of modern life: the need to make tradeoffs between two conflicting objectives (economies of scale and stability, in this instance).

Succession

For a long time, environmental scientists have been interested in another community phenomenon called succession (8, 26). This refers to the process in which groups of species replace each other through time because of a change in the environment. However, succession refers to a phenomenon in which much of the environment change is not due to some physical factor, but results from the effects of the species themselves on the community. Three typical instances of succession are those due to colonization of sand dunes, the filling of glacial lakes, and the recolonization of areas in which all life has been destroyed by lava flow.

In each case the principle is the same. A new environment is created by some geophysical force. A few very hardy species invade this new environment and start creating soil, or sediment, in the case of deep lakes. Gradually, the action of these initial invader species alters the environment so that it is hospitable to further invaders. However, gradually these new invaders alter the environment still more so that it is now hospitable to a third wave of invaders, and so on. Each wave of these invaders not only make the environment more suitable for future waves of invaders, they also make it less suitable for previous waves. Thus, we have a process of succession, in which one wave succeeds another, with later waves replacing earlier waves. The phenomenon is illustrated by the photograph in Figure 5.10.

In the early stages of succession, a high proportion of the energy captured as sunlight by plants goes into production of living

FIGURE 5.10

Succession, as illustrated by recolonization of bare rock resulting from cooling of lava flows on the island of Hawaii. The molten rock that flows out of a volcano and down the mountainside kills all life. The first invaders to establish a foothold on the flat rock surface are the lichens (a flat, primitive symbiotic system involving an algal species living together with a fungus). These lichens are tough and highly resistant to drying out; they appear in the figure as the light areas on the flat rock faces. After lichens have initiated the process of soil formation, grasses and other drought-resistant herbs can put down roots. This, in turn, creates more soil so that shrubs can become established. Then large shrubs and finally trees can become established. As the total volume of plant life on the rock increases, the evaporation of moisture from all the leaves increases the relative humidity of the environment, and this, together with the shade created by the leaves, allows less drought-resistant species to get established. As each wave of invaders moves in, it gradually replaces early waves. Thus, after the process of succession is well along in this lava flow habitat, we no longer find lichens, the first wave of invaders.

After many years, tall trees return, and the area originally made desolate by the lava flow appears as it did before the flow. All stages in this process of succession can be seen by hiking around the big island of Hawaii. Parallel successional processes are involved in colonization of sand dunes, or by terrestrial plants after a lake fills in with sediment and becomes a swamp.

plant tissue. We say the "net primary productivity" is high, and therefore the total biomass of the community increases. In terrestrial succession, this increase in biomass accompanies change in the community from a grass-dominated stage, through a meadow stage, to a shrub stage, and finally through a series of tree stages. Finally, because of all the biomass accumulated at the late tree stages, the rate of tissue formation reaches an asymptote, or upper limit, because all the leaves now represent a multistoried canopy of tissue, the highest layers of which block sunlight from lower layers at least part of each day.

In the early stages of succession, there is a small amount of biomass relative to the rate at which energy is being captured and converted to new plant tissue. In short, the ratio of biomass to productivity is low. We can perceive the deeper meaning in this if we think of productivity as that portion of the energy flux used to make new living stuff. At a later stage, because of all the prior biomass accumulation, there is a large amount of biomass relative to the rate at which energy is being converted to tissue.

The change in the biomass/productivity ratio through succession would occur, for instance, in a sequence from annual plants on abandoned farm fields or burned over land, to oak-pine forest.

The increase in the ratio of biomass to productivity through succession means that the amount of energy required per unit of biomass present declines. Or, putting it differently: communities change through succession so that energy is used more efficiently in biomass production; it takes less energy to support a given biomass in late successional stages than was required in early stages.

At the community level of organization, therefore, natural systems tend to develop in the direction of making greatest possible use of available energy. This is in noteworthy contrast to the present U.S. economy, as pointed out in Chapter 4, in which energy is used very inefficiently. This same point will come up in different form in Chapters 8, 9, and 10.

Clearly, humanity is constantly surrounded by large-scale, yet slow-changing and subtle phenomena occurring at the level of natural plant-animal communities (3). Some of these phenomena can be very inimical to us, without our being aware of them. To illustrate, we could slowly and gradually decrease the number of species (the community diversity) so as to make the community highly unstable. This could facilitate the rapid development of a pest species, such as an insect pest, which could wipe out the remaining species. An illustration of the way in which community simplification leads to vulnerability to instability occurs when large tracts of land planted only to corn are afflicted with corn blight over the whole area (the Irish potato famine of 1845–1846 mentioned in Chapter 1 was a spectacular example). One way to monitor these important community-level changes is to set aside certain check plots as natural areas, to be totally undisturbed except for periodic measurement. Our understanding of the real reasons for the decline of the Roman Empire today would be far greater if anyone had had the foresight to set aside such plots then and leave us the records on them. It is widely believed in much of the world that the diminution of the species diversity of plants and animals there is almost entirely due to climate. Setting aside a fenced check plot with a completely natural community might allow us to make the surprising observation that the real reason for reduction in species diversity was killing off all the large predators of sheep and goats, then allowing sheep and goat populations to increase unchecked, thus preventing many plant species from regenerating. In one instance where such a check plot was set aside, this was the finding. Plants which no one thought could perform well in the area became important, almost miraculously, when sheep and goats were excluded (5).

Succession is particularly useful for illustrating the role of human perception and awareness as root causes of environmental problems. The process is slow and subtle, and would be particularly unlikely to be perceived by our largely urban civilization (Chapter 8). Therefore, because of our ignorance of slow, subtle, but extremely powerful and almost irreversible processes, we are vulnerable to making catastrophic errors on a gigantic scale, such as decreasing species diversity, and maintaining early, unstable successional stages in natural communities.

THE ECOSYSTEM

The entire community of plants and animals that occupy an area, together with the matter and the energy they use, constitute a new, higher level of organization: the ecosystem (6). However, there is a fundamental difference between the roles matter and energy play in the ecosystem: each unit of matter can pass through the ecosystem many times, but each unit of energy only passes through once. Matter cycles through ecosystems; energy cascades through, as the light from a fireworks display cascades once only through the night sky. The reason for this distinction can be seen in two very different ways in which matter and energy relate to the ecosystem.

Plants take minerals from the soil and by means of the photosynthetic process, with light as the energy source, produce plant tissue. However, plant tissue ultimately gives up the minerals to the soil again, although there are many pathways by which this might occur. If the plant is never eaten, but dies, it will decompose and become soil. Alternatively, the plant might be eaten by an animal that dies, returning the minerals to the soil. Or the animal may be eaten by another animal that ultimately dies, returning the minerals to the system. The element common to all these circumstances is that the minerals are not lost from the system. Having originated in the soil, they ultimately return to the soil, where they will be available to be used by the ecosystem again and again. This is why it is accurate to say that matter cycles through ecosystems.

Energy, on the other hand, behaves in accord with the two laws of thermodynamics. The first of these laws states that energy is never lost or created, but can only be converted from one form to another. The second law states that these conversion processes are never completely efficient. Whenever energy is used in any process, a considerable proportion of the source energy does not get converted into useful activity, but is lost as heat. This heat loss is simply a consequence of the inefficiency inherent in all processes, described in the second law of thermodynamics.

Because energy conversion processes are inefficient, and because food chains may be three or more steps long, the inefficiency characteristic of each step adds up to a tremendous inefficiency for the entire ecosystem. So much of the energy originally entering the system is lost as heat in passing through the system that very little is left for the highest trophic level of the ecosystem, the top carnivores. Because of the energy loss at each stage, in fact, the total amount of biomass decreases as we follow the energy from plant to herbivore, herbivore to carnivore, and carnivore to top carnivore. The relation between inefficiency of energy use by the ecosystem and the structure of the resultant trophic pyramid is brought out in Table 5.2. This table shows the energy flow through the different levels of a typical trophic pyramid. Particularly when we notice that the numbers vary by several orders

TABLE 5.2

Energy flow through a typical trophic pyramid. All measures of energy flow are in kilo-calories per hectare per year. The data are from a southern Michigan food chain consisting of old-field vegetation, the meadow mouse, and the least weasel.

Level i	Gross photosynthetic production by plants or consumption by animal levels C_i	Respiration R_i	$\dfrac{C_i}{C_{i-1}}$	$\dfrac{R_i}{C_i}$
Sunlight	1.6 $\times 10^{10}$			
Plants	5.83 $\times 10^7$	8.76 $\times 10^6$	.00364	.15
Field (meadow) mouse (herbivore)	2.5 $\times 10^5$	1.7 $\times 10^5$	.00426	.68
Least weasel (carnivore)	5.824 $\times 10^3$	5.434 $\times 10^3$	.02330	.93

Data from F. B. Golley, "Energy dynamics of a food chain of an old-field community," *Ecological Monographs,* 30 (1960), pp. 187–206. Copyright 1960 by the Ecological Society of America.

of magnitude, we realize that the energy loss down through the pyramid is staggering. Since the amount of matter that can be supported at each level is determined by the amount of energy flowing through the level, a chart for the relative biomass at the different levels has a pyramidal shape, like those for energy at each level.

Given this great energy loss down through the trophic pyramid, our curiosity is aroused as to where all the energy went to at each step. Table 5.2 reveals some aspects of the loss. The third column of numbers (C_i/C_{i-1}) reveals one cause for the great ecosystem inefficiency: of the total amount of energy flow at each level, only a tiny proportion shows up in the next level. One reason for this, in turn, is that a high proportion of the food available at each level is simply not eaten by the organisms at the next level. Another is metabolic inefficiency: some of the food eaten is excreted, unused. The fourth column of numbers reveals a third reason for system inefficiency: much of the energy flowing into each level is unavailable for higher levels, because it is burned up in metabolic activity (and measured as respira-

tion) rather than being incorporated into tissue. Note that in the last column, there is an increase in the proportion lost to respiration at each step, from plants to carnivores. This reflects the greater amount of energy that must be spent by carnivores in high-speed pursuit of active food (in contradistinction to plants, which do not move).

Unlike energy, which only cascades through an ecosystem once, matter cycles through repeatedly, and we gain further insight into the dynamics of ecosystems when we explore the mechanisms that make this continual recycling possible (6). Since these cycles of matter through ecosystems involve inorganic as well as organic elements, they are referred to as biogeochemical cycles.

An idealized, simplified composite biogeochemical cycle for a typical nutrient is sketched in the flow chart of Figure 5.11. Of course, the details for particular minerals vary considerably: for example, sulfur is unimportant in the atmosphere, but an important constituent of rock, whereas carbon is an important constituent of the atmosphere, but not of igneous rock. A key element in all these mineral cycles is the

FIGURE 5.11
An idealized, simplified composite biogeochemical cycle for most chemical elements.
This is a composite drawing based on several sources, but principally Figure 6 by F. B.
Golley, "Productivity and mineral cycling in tropical forests," reproduced from
Productivity of World Ecosystems, *1975, with the permission of the National Academy*
of Sciences, Washington, D.C.

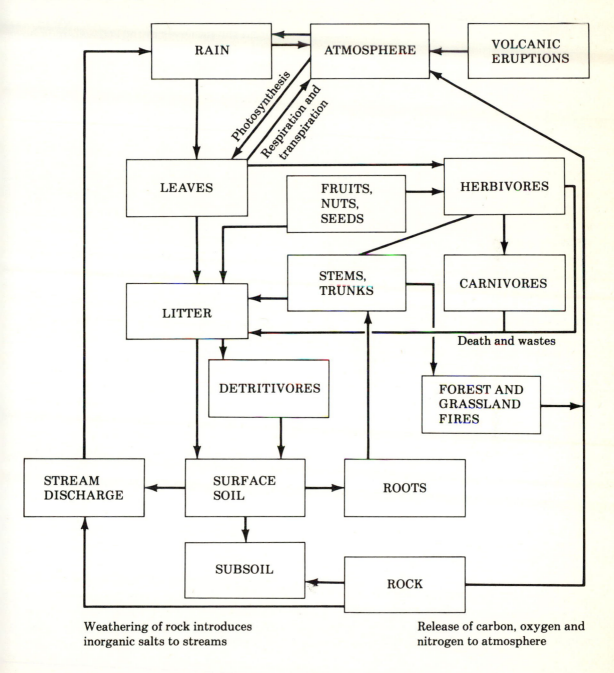

feeders on detritus or litter, the detritivores. The organisms that break down dead organic material range from fungi and bacteria to carrion beetles, blowfly larvae, and a wide variety of other types. The critical role they fill is returning matter to the soil, so that it again occurs in a form accessible to the roots of plants, for incorporation into new plant tissue.

The detritivores, or decomposers, are relatively efficient, because it is easier to break down an ordered structure than to build one. The presence of detritivores in natural systems has an important philosophical implication for people. Nature, over very long time periods, evolves in the direction of making efficient use of all available resources. Detritivores show that recycling is a necessary ecosystem function, if the whole ecosystem is to be as efficient as possible: reusing materials already partly ordered is more efficient then starting from scratch to make order out of raw inorganic chemicals and rock. Similarly, a highly evolved society with realistically priced raw resources would attach great value to recycling.

The elements in boxes in Figure 5.11 can be thought of as mineral or chemical pools; the arrows represent rates of transfer between pools. Many scientists in many countries and ecosystems have measured both pools and transfer rates, and some important generalizations about these cycles are now becoming apparent (17).

1. Different types of ecosystems are quite different with respect to the speed with which mineral elements are cycled by the ecosystem. In turn, this difference is related to the tons of litter accumulated per hectare. Where a forest has a very small amount of accumulated litter on the soil, the ecosystem cycles mineral elements very rapidly. However, where there is a vast amount of litter on the soil, as in forests with swampy soil and a great deal of moss, the ecosystem cycles mineral elements very slowly.

2. In tropical forests a higher proportion of all the minerals in the ecosystem is in the stems of plants than is the case in temperate forests.

3. In temperate forests a higher proportion of all the minerals in the ecosystem is in soil surface litter than is the case in tropical forests. That is, the illusion of great productivity given by the vast luxuriance of the plant material in the tropical forest can be deceiving. If the forest is cut down and the area is planted out to maize (a common practice), it is quickly discovered that the minerals needed by the maize are not present in the quantities that one might have thought: they were in the plants, not the soil. In the temperate forest, on the other hand, removing the trees does not remove nearly so high a proportion of the nutrients in the ecosystem as in the tropical forest. In short, national planners viewing the vast Amazon jungle as a potential home for tens of millions of maize-growing farmers could be in for a terrible surprise.

4. The "clear-cutting" forest strategy, particularly when conducted on slopes, disturbs the ecosystem by leaving the soil exposed to the immediate force of raindrops. Torrential rainstorms leach the minerals out of the soil so that they run off the surface and into the rivers. This has two bad effects: the productivity of the forest soil is seriously lowered, and the productivity of the streams is excessively elevated. This leads to eutrophication (overenrichment) of the stream water, which can lead to algal blooms, lowering of the oxygen content of the water, and destruction of the stream environment for fish species that require high oxygen content in the water (salmon and trout).

5. The overall conclusion from research on biogeochemical cycles is that we will soon have the knowledge to provide the highest-efficiency use of solar energy for the production of plant communities. It will be possible to optimize the use of the sun's energy, fertilizers, and the inherent productivity of the soil by selecting ecosystem types that perform best under given environmental conditions.

STRATEGIES FOR MANAGING RENEWABLE RESOURCES

All renewable resources used by humans need to be managed, to keep their productivity high. We begin by introducing the simple, "classical" theory of resource management (1). Then we will consider how this theory needs some modification in the light of two recent discoveries.

At the population level, all problems in management of renewable resources can be viewed in terms of Figure 5.6. Suppose we wish to maximize the production of some economically important resources (trees, crops, cattle, fish, or wildlife). The secret of good harvesting is to drive resource availability per capita from A to B (by cropping excess individuals), so as to get production to the highest possible sustainable level. However, we do not want to overharvest, and drive resource availability per capita to C.

How do we manage the resource availability per capita? In agriculture, we avoid such high stocking levels for livestock, or such high seed densities for crops, that the production by the population will be suppressed by excessive competition. In forestry, we manage the stock size of the trees in the forest by selection of the appropriate rotation age, or age of a generation of trees at which they will be cut. If the rotation age is too long, the biomass of trees on the land will be excessive, and the trees will be too old to give us the fastest tree growth rate per acre. If the rotation age is too short, the trees cannot adequately exploit the resources available to them in the habitat. In the case of fisheries, we can select both the age at which we harvest the fish stocks, and the proportion of the stock that is harvested (11). The age of harvest is selected by selecting the mesh size of nets (or some other attribute of the gear that determines the size and age of the fish caught). The proportion of the stock caught can be selected by the government through a system of quotas. When the quota for the season is reached, fishing should stop.

In the case of pest control, whether the pests be insects, rabbits, rats, or deer, the object is to drive resource availability per individual in the pest population down from A to C, without getting stuck at B or boomeranging back to A (the most common response by a pest population to control). There are two criteria for good pest control: the control measure should kill a very high proportion of the pests, and a few successive applications of the control measure should gradually decrease the need for equally intense control in the future. Unfortunately, a characteristic of many types of pest control is that they only create a perpetual need for more pest control. Certain pest control measures are used repeatedly when they have built-in defects because of cultural, information, and political problems, all of which will be explained in subsequent chapters. Use of pest control measures year after year that in fact increase, rather than decrease, the number of pests reveals that the "environmental problem" has many components, which often have little to do with the classical theories of resource management.

Two recent developments in the theory of resource management suggest that the view embodied in Figure 5.6 is too simplistic. A new field has developed called bioeconomics, which argues that it may not be wise to harvest a population hard enough to drive the stock remaining to *B*, the level that results in maximum production (7). The reason is that in order for fishers, for example, to fish that hard, they may have to run into the law of "diminishing returns." The extra effort expended per fish caught in order to get the resource availability per capita up to *B* may not be economically justifiable; the economically optimal intensity of harvest effort may be lower than the biologically optimal intensity of harvest effort. More recently, a new objection to the classical theory of maximum sustainable yield has been put forth. The argument is that if we fish a mixed-species group of fishes hard enough to produce the maximum sustainable yield for some of them, we will have driven some of the less productive species to the brink of extinction (13). We do not want to do this, because as explained in this chapter, high levels of species diversity are an "insurance policy" against community instability.

The bottom panel of Figure 5.9 suggested that when there is a high level of species diversity in a community, not only is the stability of the community greater, but the average production is higher than in the case of low-diversity communities. A large number of species are better able to exploit a wide variety of conditions. As the number of species present increases, therefore, it will be more likely that for any opportunity that arises in the environment of the community, there will be at least one species present able to exploit that opportunity ("niche") effectively. This leads us to suspect that there might be an immensely important practical application of community theory; maximizing species diversity should maximize community-level production. Two important bodies of data suggest that this is the case.

One of these comes from game ranching in Africa, where it appears to be more profitable to produce meat in the form of mixed-species harvests of wild game than by traditional cattle ranching on the same land. The other comes from experience with reservoirs, where the pounds of fish that can be supported per acre are higher where the species diversity of the reservoir fish community is greater. Since the standing crop (the biomass of fish present) is usually strongly correlated with the productivity, this suggests that the productivity of fish would also be greater in the reservoirs with more diverse communities.

We have seen that the energy flow through ecosystems decreases drastically as we follow the progression from plants to herbivores to carnivores (Table 5.2). But at present, we often harvest ecosystems by exploiting populations at the end of very long chains, such as tuna, salmon, and swordfish. Clearly, this luxury would be appropriate only if there were fewer people on earth. If we believe that people ought to be allowed the luxury of exploiting food chains at their ends, rather than near their beginnings, then we ought to work vigorously for reduced human population sizes.

THE HISTORY AND PRESENT STATUS OF RENEWABLE RESOURCES

Having had a brief introduction to the theory of managing renewable natural resources, it is interesting to see how resources have in fact been managed in the past. Two points are noteworthy. In Chapter 4, Hubbert's theory was presented, arguing that as resources become half depleted, economic forces would operate sharply to slow down the approach to depletion. In effect, the last half of the curve of production versus time would be the mirror image of the first part of the curve. Also, we have discovered that there are theories that allow us to compute how much we should harvest

FIGURE 5.12

Harvest curves for fin whales (top panel) and the buffalo (bottom panel). Top curve based on tables of the Bureau of International Whaling Statistics, Oslo. The estimate of maximum sustainable yield is from D. G. Chapman, "Status of Antarctic rorqual stocks," in The Whale Problem, *W. E. Schevill, ed. Cambridge, Mass.: Harvard University Press, 1974. Data used to construct the bottom curve were obtained principally from F. G. Roe,* The North American Buffalo. *Toronto: University of Toronto Press, 1951. Estimate of maximum sustained yield from* Ecology and Resource Management *by K. E. F. Watt. Copyright © 1968. Used with the permission of the McGraw-Hill Book Company.*

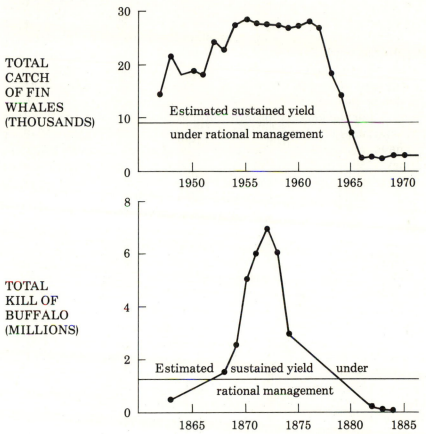

each year. Figure 5.12 shows graphs of the production curves for two famous examples to see how they were in fact managed. The top production curve is for the fin whale, an open ocean "common property resource" (belonging to no one) from 1946 to 1971. Far from being managed rationally, the resource was exploited much more intensively than it should have been for about twenty years,

and as a consequence there was a collapse in production after 1962 (23).

The bottom curve is for the buffalo of the American west. There was a very sharp increase in production after 1867, and for about ten years, the numbers killed each year were up to five times as great as they should have been under rational management.

The curious feature of these two curves is that while they have the same final outcome (collapse of the resource), the circumstances were very different. In the buffalo case, there was no scientific effort to find out how many should be killed each year. There was no organization to manage the buffalo. In the whale case, there was a management organization, the International Whaling Commission, and there was extremely sophisticated scientific advice coming from an international panel of scientific advisors expert on the analysis of catch statistics, all in agreement. Yet the result was the same. This type of example suggests that the "environmental problem" is far more complex than a problem in estimating the long-term sustained yield from statistics on the resource. In fact we are dealing here with a highly complex problem, with many aspects, extending into such domains as our cultural belief system and our political organizations.

Some people feel that it will be possible to increase the production of commodities from the oceans indefinitely. Even prominent politicians assert that because the oceans are essentially infinite in volume, they should be an essentially infinite source of resources. It introduces some realism into discussions about renewable resources, therefore, to note that catches of fish from the oceans over the last several years, by all countries, have apparently reached a limit at about 80 million metric tons, in spite of an enormous increase in the sophistication of fishing techniques and intensity of effort.

One highly important feature of the present world situation in renewable resources is that whereas in the period 1934 to 1938, all parts of the world except Western Europe had a surplus of grain, by the mid-1970s, only four countries had significant quantities of grain for export. Note, however, that all four of these countries (the United States, Canada, Australia, and Argentina) are in high latitudes and could be susceptible to significant crop reductions because of drought or frost. More alarming, the world supply of wheat for export came largely from two countries: 57 percent from the United States and 24 percent from Canada. As explained previously in this chapter, there is safety in numbers, or diversity of origins for a critically important resource. The world would be less vulnerable to a climatic disaster if many countries, in different climate zones, contributed to the world stock of exportable food surpluses.

SUMMARY

Any growing population reaches a limit in a particular environment; therefore, there must be forces restricting production. These forces are the decreases in birth, survival, and growth rates that result when population size increases so as to produce a per capita decline in availability of resources (food, space, and the like). These rates function as population stabilizing mechanisms. Each environment has a limited capacity to support a particular species population (the "carrying capacity" for that population), set by the availability of resources in the environment. However, the carrying capacity of an environment can be increased to some extent by increasing the availability of resources (such as mineral nutrients) that had been limiting population size. But as we increase resource availability so as to increase population productivity, we run into the law of diminishing returns. Ultimately, excessive availability of any resource becomes poisonous (as when too much fertilizer decreases crop growth).

Shifting our attention to the community level of organization, we discover new principles governing production and stability. Increasing the diversity of species in a community, up to an optimal level, increases both the productivity and the stability of the entire community. Also, communities undergo succession, in which the number of species and the total mass of living material (biomass) in an environment increases. Since the energy input from the sun remains approximately constant, this implies that communities gradually undergo increase in their biomass/energy flow ratio, or, the biomass/productivity ratio.

At the level of the ecosystem, the second law of thermodynamics implies great loss of energy flow from trophic level to trophic level, from plants to herbivores to carnivores. Also, the productivity of ecosystems may be limited by inadequate availability of certain materials, by waterlogging, or some other system limit.

From these principles we can discern a number of strategies for maximizing and stabilizing sustained yield of renewable resources. Restricting the harvesting rate will stimulate production if the population density is suboptimal; thinning the population will stimulate production if the population is at supraoptimal density. Increasing species diversity to an optimal level will increase production and stability of whole communities. Draining swamps, fertilizing, or stimulating upwelling in the ocean increases production. Also, the yield from ecosystems is increased by harvesting trophic levels closer to the input (solar radiation).

However, in spite of all these possible steps, we will reach the limits of the food production capability of the planet within a few decades (Chapter 6). A number of important resources already show clear signs of overharvesting, such as oceanic fish stocks and the great whales. Very few countries have food for export, whereas many were food exporters just a few decades ago.

Natural systems develop in the direction of making very efficient use of energy, as reflected in a high biomass/productivity ratio at the end of the successional process in communities. This is in striking contrast to human systems, in which maximization of energy production appears to have been a goal, not maximization of efficiency in use of energy.

Natural systems are also stable, on balance, after succession has resulted in large numbers of species in each community. Humans, on the other hand, tend to simplify systems, as when a tropical forest is replaced by a single crop over very large tracts of land (pineapple, corn, sugar cane, tea, oil palms, bananas, and the like). Such monocultures are very vulnerable to an insect pest or plant pathogen that would rapidly ravage immense tracts of crops.

The issues considered in this chapter are part of a larger picture. The physical environment determines the amount of crop growth, and inputs of nonrenewable resources affect the productivity of farms, lakes, and the oceans. Population size determines the total demand for renewable resources, and the relative costs of various resources determine whether farming and fishing will be labor-intensive, or energy and capital-intensive. Political considerations determine how much food can be grown by determining how much land should be planted out, and by setting quotas for oceanic catches. Finally, culture determines what steps the political system will take.

SUGGESTIONS FOR INDIVIDUAL AND GROUP PROJECTS

Select a renewable resource (such as forests in Sweden, Canada, or the United States; the Peruvian anchovies; the Pacific ocean tunas; or Russian wheat) and collect statistics on production. Also try to determine the sustainable long-term yield for the resource. Now try to project trends in demand. How long can the resource continue to meet demand? What could be done to increase production?

Many resource management problems involve difficult policy options. Look for such options shaping up in a resource you know about, and try to reason out an argument in support of the choice you believe to be correct. For example, Japan and Russia have a choice: wipe out all the whales in the oceans in ten years, or sixty years, or make them last indefinitely. Which is the optimal strategy and why? This is a difficult question, because you get different answers depending on your approach to answering the question. For example, if you consider purely the economics of the depreciation on the fishing or whaling fleets, fast annihilation of the oceanic resources might be the best strategy.

Try to analyze what really went wrong in a post-mortem analysis of some resources that have been overused, such as buffalo, Peruvian anchovies, the cedars of Lebanon, the forest of southern Italy, Carthage, the Greek city-states, or the Indio-Gangetic plain. Libraries and encyclopedias have a great deal of information on such matters.

Do forest or agricultural practices affect the weather? Find out how agricultural practices affect erosion.

Devise a management plan for a local sport fishery.

REFERENCES

1. Allee, W. C., A. E. Emerson, O. Park, T. Park, and K. P. Schmidt, *Principles of animal ecology.* Philadelphia: Saunders, 1949.
2. Andrewartha, H. G., and L. C. Birch, *The distribution and abundance of animals.* Chicago: University of Chicago Press, 1954.
3. Bormann, F. H., and G. E. Likens, "Catastrophic disturbance and the steady state in northern hardwood forests," *Amer. Scientist,* 67, 660 (1979).
4. Brown, L. R., *In the human interest.* New York: Norton, 1974.
5. Bryson, R. A., and T. J. Murray. *Climates of hunger.* Madison: University of Wisconsin Press, 1976.
6. Clapham, W. B. Jr., *Natural ecosystems.* New York: Macmillan, 1973.
7. Clark, C. W., *Mathematical bioeconomics.* New York: Wiley-Interscience, 1976.
8. Connell, J. H., and R. O. Slatyer, "Mechanisms of succession in natural communities and their role in community stability and organization," *Amer. Nat.* 111, 1119 (1977).
9. Crombie, A. C., "The effect of crowding upon the oviposition of grain-infesting insects," *The Journal of Experimental Biology,* 19 (1942), pp. 311–340.
10. Force, D. C., "Ecology of insect host-parasitoid communities," *Science* 184 (1974), pp. 624–632.
11. Gulland, J. A., "Ecological aspects of fishery research," Vol. 7 *Advances in Ecological Research,* J. B. Cragg, ed. London: Academic Press, 1971.
12. Krebs, C. J., *Ecology.* New York: Harper and Row, 1972.
13. Larkin, P. A., "An epitaph for the concept of maximum sustained yield," *Transactions of the American Fisheries Society,* 106 (1977), pp. 1–11.
14. McNaughton, S. J., "Diversity and stability of ecological communities: a comment on the role of empiricism in ecology," *The American Naturalist,* 111 (1977), pp. 515–525.
15. McNaughton, S. J., and L. L. Wolf, *General ecology.* New York: Holt, Rinehart and Winston, 1973.
16. Miller, J. G., *Living systems.* New York: McGraw-Hill, 1978.
17. National Academy of Sciences. *Productivity of world ecosystems.* Washington, D.C.: National Academy of Sciences, 1975.
18. Park, T., "Studies in population physiology: the relation of numbers to initial population growth in the flour beetle Tribolium confusum Duval," *Ecology,* 13 (1932), pp. 172–181.

19. Radovich, J., "Effects of sardine spawning stock size and environment on year class production," *California Fish and Game,* 48 (1962), pp. 123–140.

20. Reddingius, J., and P. J. den Boer, "Simulation experiments illustrating stabilization of animal numbers by spreading of risk," *Oceologia,* 5 (1970), pp. 240–284.

21. Rich, E. R., "Egg cannibalism and fecundity in Tribolium," *Ecology,* 37 (1956), pp. 109–120.

22. Salt, G. W., "A comment on the use of the term emergent properties," *American Naturalist,* 113 (1979), pp. 145–148.

23. Schevill, W. E., ed., *The whale problem.* Cambridge, Mass.: Harvard University Press, 1974.

24. Watt, K. E. F., "Community stability and the strategy of biological control," *The Canadian Entomologist,* 97 (1965), pp. 887–895.

25. van den Bosch, R., *The pesticide conspiracy.* Garden City, N.Y.: Doubleday, 1978.

26. Whittaker, R. H., *Communities and ecosystems.* New York: Macmillan, 1975.

6 HUMAN POPULATION AND THE ENVIRONMENT

The primary or fundamental check to the continued increase of man is the difficulty of gaining subsistence, and of living in comfort. We may infer that this is the case from what we see, for instance, in the United States, where subsistence is easy, and there is plenty of room.

Charles Darwin, The Descent of Man, *Chapter II, 1871.*

One would have thought that it was even more necessary to limit population than property; and that the limit should be fixed by calculating the chances of mortality in the children, and of sterility in married persons. The neglect of this subject, which in existing states is so common, is a never-failing cause of poverty among the citizens; and poverty is the parent of revolution and crime.

Aristotle (384–322 B.C.), Politics, *Book II, Chapter 6.*

MAIN THEMES OF THIS CHAPTER

When we examine the history of human population growth in the world, great increases in population size appear to have followed increases in the carrying capacity of the planet for people. The latter were the result of technological advances, such as the invention of agriculture, and the subsequent introduction of farm mechanization and fertilizer.

This observation suggests that it would be revealing to compute the carrying capacity of the planet for people, under different assumptions about life style. The world could support about one-eighth the present population, living rather well, or nine times the present population, living horribly and precariously.

The character of social existence is profoundly affected by the relative numbers of people of different ages, as well as the total population size. Rapidly growing populations have a large proportion of young people; in a developed nation such a population will create great costs for education and have a high crime rate.

OVERVIEW OF THE ARGUMENT

The previous chapter described natural forces operating on birth and death rates of wild populations. Similar forces operate on people; however, peculiarly human phenomena also operate on the human population: in postindustrial societies the balance between the availability of resources and population density and the relative prices of labor and resources are expressed in terms of job opportunities, and unemployment rates among young people; that is, if the number of young people trying to enter the labor force for the first time (at about age twenty-two) is too great, there simply aren't enough jobs. Since human beings adjust their birth rates somewhat to their economic opportunities, lowered job availability translates into lower birth rates, which in turn translate into fewer job applicants relative to the available supply of jobs twenty-three or so years later. Thus, the system of jobs and job applicants is self-regulatory.

The problem for the whole human population is that such voluntary reduction in birth rates tends to occur many years after death rates have dropped in a country. Human population growth increase has inertia: it takes many years before forces operat-

ing to depress rate of population increase are fully effective. As a result, humanity has spread and increased inordinately over the face of the planet because of the long lag in the self-regulatory mechanisms. Now we have become, in effect, a planetary pest with the power to disturb temporarily the planetary equilibria of many other systems.

THE HISTORY OF HUMAN POPULATION GROWTH

The first thing we notice in the pattern of world human population growth is that a long period of very slow growth was followed by a period of extremely rapid growth after 1800. However, this pattern by itself is not too revealing. There are many questions we might ask. What makes population growth possible, and what will limit it? Is population growth occurring equally in all places, and among all groups of people? How do various kinds of factors interact to regulate the rate of population growth? Are there any parallels between population dynamics in humans and those in animals?

Most graphs of long-term human population size versus time are not plotted on a scale appropriate for revealing details about the nature of population growth when it has occurred over a very long time and population size has grown by an enormous amount. Accordingly, Figure 6.1 uses scales much more appropriate to the nature of the human population growth phenomenon. In this figure, time is expressed as the number of years prior to the year 2000 A.D., and these intervals are expressed as logarithms rather than the raw intervals (3). This technique is appropriate because recently things have been changing very rapidly, whereas long ago they changed very slowly. By using logarithms, we space the record of growth on the page, so that a small amount of space

FIGURE 6.1

A more detailed look at the history of human population growth plotted on logarithmic graph paper. Data from "The human population" by E. S. Deevey. Scientific American, *1960; "Population growth and land control" by Colin Clark.* Introduction to Environmental Studies: An Integrated Systems Approach, *1967, St. Martin's Press, Inc. J. D. Durand "The modern expansion of world population," Proceedings of the American Philosophical Society 111 (1967), pp. 136–159; The United Nations Demographic Yearbooks; and the Statistical Office of the United Nations. Copyright, United Nations. Reproduced by permission.*

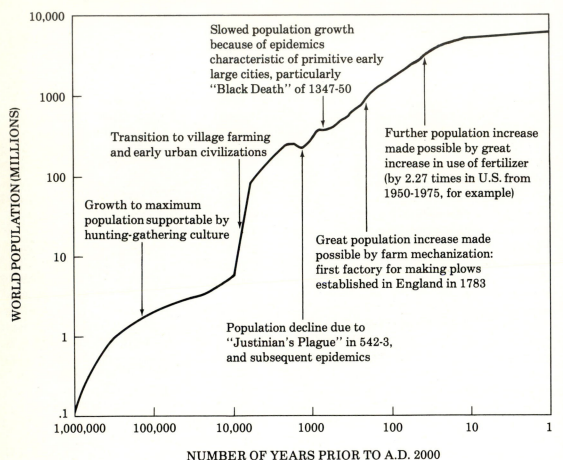

per year is allotted to the remote past, during slow growth, and a large amount of space is used per year for recent times, when growth was very rapid. As we can see from Figure 6.1, this approach to graphing human growth gives us far more insight into the determining forces. Now, growth history appears not as a long, smooth curve, but as a sequence of segments in which quite different situations prevailed.

The first humans were primitive hunters and gatherers of food. Two features of this situation kept human densities low. In the last chapter (Table 5.2) we saw that there is a tremendous loss of energy down through the levels of a trophic pyramid, resulting in much lower availability of food per acre, if the food eaten is meat rather than plants. Thus, early human populations were small, because so much of the food was meat rather than plants. Because food plants grew wild, rather than being cultivated, they would be interspersed with other plants, and a lot of energy would go into not only hunting, but searching for edible nuts, berries, roots, and seeds or stems to be eaten.

Over a long period, from the beginnings of human history to about 10,000 years ago, populations grew and spread from their origins in Africa, to new lands in Europe and Asia. A major change for humanity came with the shift to cultivation and permanent farming villages instead of a nomadic existence. With the switch to heavy dependence on cultivated crops, populations could rise rapidly, because now the trophic pyramids were being utilized primarily near their bases (the sun), so that much more energy and biomass could be obtained per acre (Chapter 5). However, about 2000 years ago, growth slowed almost to a standstill for a thousand years, for two reasons. First, there were no significant improvements in agricultural technology so as to increase yields per acre significantly. Second, people lived under appalling conditions of sanitation and sewage. Food was stored in houses in sacks or bins, making it accessible to rats and other small animals that carried fleas or lice that in turn carried plague organisms. Human excreta was often simply thrown out of bedroom windows in the morning, so that streets were less clean than the barnyard of a well-kept modern farm. There was little concern with sanitation or sewage disposal.

Some of the disease organisms brought into primitive towns by small animals were particularly infective and virulent; perhaps the worst of all was bubonic plague, produced by the bacterium *Pasteurella pestis*.

This had a terrible effect on early towns twice. The first time was in 542 to 543 A.D., when the population was knocked down by "Justinian's plague," which was probably carried in from Africa. The second time was in 1347 to 1350, when the "Black Death" was brought in from the Crimea by Genoese merchants. In this case, between a quarter and a half of the population of Europe died in four years. These two epidemics had a clear impact on human population growth, as we see in Figure 6.1. Not only did this disease spread rapidly because of the low level of public hygiene, but also, densities in the towns were high, making possible rapid spread of highly contagious diseases from one person to another. During epidemics the plague converted from a flea-borne to a pneumonic form in which coughing of the victims would fill the air with fine vapor droplets carrying the bacterium, spreading plague very rapidly in the towns. No one at the time had any idea where the disease came from or what to do about it.

However, by about 1500, the world human population began a period of growth that has been essentially unbroken since. Sanitation in cities began to improve, and farming was making steady progress, so that a unit of land could support more people. One milepost of importance was establishment of the first factory for making plows in England, in 1783. Now farm machinery could be manufactured in the cities, under assembly-line conditions, and the farmers were free to farm, rather than having to make their equipment also. Since then, there has been a continuous revolution in agricultural technology, with a gradual evolution to mechanized combines, threshing machines, fertilizers, and progressively larger tractors. This revolution continues to the present, with more and more intensive use of fertilizers and farm machinery, and scientific selection of most productive strains of livestock and crop plants.

Technology and Carrying Capacity

Looking at the overall pattern in Figure 6.1, we now see, not a long continuous process, but rather three distinct periods. In each of these, the world had a carrying capacity for people, set by the technique of obtaining food.

In the first period, humans were limited because they gathered rather than cultivating food. If we had never broken out of this period, the carrying capacity of the planet for people would have been about 20 million, and would have been reached when primitive humans gradually spread to all continents and habitats.

In the second period, humans were limited by agricultural technology. In this period, population would probably have levelled off at a billion people, or less.

The key to the great new increase in the number of people on earth in the last two centuries has been the industrial revolution and access to coal, oil, and gas. Up to two centuries ago, people largely lived off the energy from the sun, which was converted to human and animal muscle power and water and wind power. In the last two centuries, we have tapped an enormous new source of power for farming in the form of the fossil fuels, created by the entire history of arrival of solar energy on the planet.

Thus, the planetary carrying capacity for people depends on the ability of our food production to support population. That, in turn, depends on the nature of the food production system in a great many different ways, as we shall shortly see.

Figure 6.1 gave us an inadequate view of population growth in a number of senses. Where is it occurring? In all countries, population growth is only found in certain places. The United States probably provides a foretaste of the pattern that will appear everywhere, later. Initially, population growth was almost entirely in big cities; population in small towns and in rural areas grew slightly, if at all. That is the present pattern in most of the world: tremendous growth in a few very large cities in each country, with much slower growth rates in small cities and rural areas. However, this is evolving into a new pattern, in which there is still no growth in places of under a population of 1000, but there is little further growth in very large places, and the new centers of high growth rates are of intermediate size: places of 10,000 to 25,000. Presumably this happens because people come to dislike big cities, but because of their urban background, would have difficulty adjusting to farm or village life. Hence, as a compromise, they select the town.

Also, there are tremendous differences in the population growth patterns between countries. This will shortly lead to some surprising changes in the relative population sizes of different countries and regions of the world. Less developed countries are growing much more rapidly than more developed countries, so that in about 2010 A.D. the ldc's will go from having about twice as many people as the mdc's to four times as many.

Turning to specific countries, we discover that India, which has always had a much smaller population than China, will probably surpass China in population by 2010, and become the most populous nation on earth. The reason is that the Chinese have been relatively successful in widespread application of birth control; the Indians have not. The populations of Africa and Mexico are increasing very rapidly; the populations of North America, Japan, and Europe are not. This type of relative change will have a large array of surprising geopolitical consequences. Thus we discover that Mexico, which has always been a relatively small nation, by 2010 will have a considerably higher population than either Germany or Japan. There are two important differences:

Mexico is not industrialized to the degree the others are, and industrialization, after a lag of several years, leads to sharp decreases in the birth rate. But also, Mexico is Catholic, whereas the other two are not, and the official posture of the Catholic Church is inimical to birth control.

World population will continue to grow fast for some time. Industrialization is not yet sufficiently widespread to slow population growth significantly in poor countries, and methods of birth control are not yet widely understood or available. There is a deeper reason for prolonged high birth rates: a high proportion of the population of the world is in age groups that will shortly be in the most reproductively active years of life. The reciprocal relationships between population growth rates and population age structures will be a principal theme of this chapter.

However, there are grounds for hope about the population problem. The United States Bureau of the Census now projects that from 1976 to 2000, the annual rate of world population increase will drop from 1.9 to 1.6 percent.

There are two organizations that feel (correctly, in my view) that these present and future rates of population increase are much too high. Zero Population Growth would like the increase rate to drop to zero percent per year. Negative Population Growth would like the rates to be negative. That is, they would like to see a world population decline. While these goals will not be attained in the near future, it is inevitable that some time in the next century, world population will begin to decline, and will continue to do so for perhaps a thousand years. The driving force behind this decline will be the spreading realization that high populations imply a low standard of living. Many young couples in the United States have already figured this out. The figuring is even easier if you are unemployed.

THE CARRYING CAPACITY OF THE PLANET FOR PEOPLE

Figure 6.1 revealed that the human population of the planet has changed greatly. This leads us to inquire as to what might determine the steady-state carrying capacity of the planet for human beings. In fact, a large number of different factors affect the number of people supportable by this planet. Figure 6.2 analyzes this system of factors into three groups. The first group affects A_T, the total land area in the world suitable for farming. The second affects A_F, the amount of land required to feed one person. The third affects A_U, the amount of agricultural land converted to urban use per person added to the urban population. The figure shows how each of these three groups of variables affecting total world farm production can be further decomposed into constituent factors. Clearly, a surprising array of factors affects how many people can live on the planet, some obvious, others not. Thus, for example, if the cultural belief system changed suddenly so that everyone in the entire world became a vegetarian, the world would be able to support three to five times as many people as at present (because of the trophic pyramid argument).

Calculating the Carrying Capacity

To determine the relative importance of these factors in setting the carrying capacity of the planet for people, it is necessary to digress somewhat, and assemble reasonable values for each of the three groups of factors. In order not to break up the main flow of the argument, these sets of values are derived in Boxes 6.1 through 6.4.

Having obtained the reasonable ranges of value for A_T, A_F, and A_U, we can estimate the number of people that the world could support at equilibrium. Estimates for the

FIGURE 6.2

The causal system determining the carrying capacity of this planet for people. Note that flow charts such as this have two purposes. They demonstrate the system of relationships, but also can be used as the basis for programming a simulation model for a computer. Experimentation with this model would show how much the carrying capacity would change in response to changes in the various determining factors.

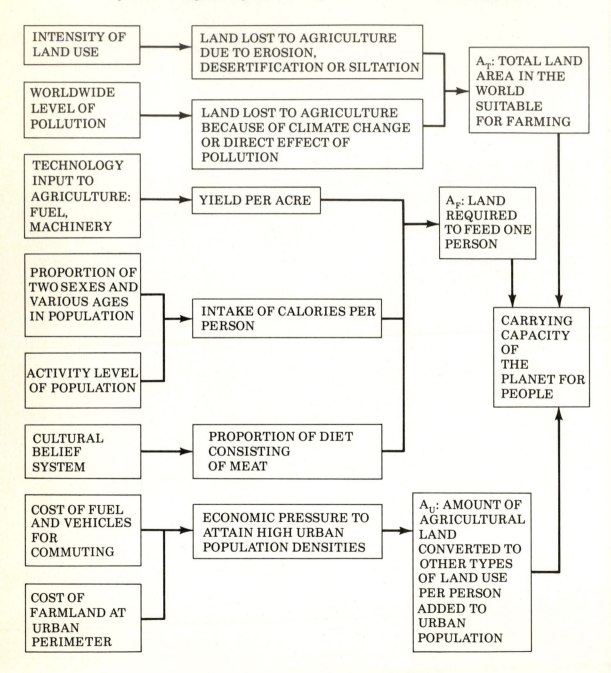

BOX 6.1
Overall approach to the problem of computing the carrying capacity of the planet for people

Suppose we want to find out the total number of people the world will be able to support in the future, under various sets of assumptions about future conditions. Let us designate the unknown number of people by N (the carrying capacity of the planet for people). Now we know that when equilibrium conditions are finally reached, so that the number of people can be supported indefinitely, the following relationship will apply:

$$N = \frac{\text{the total amount of land on which food can be grown, under equilibrium}}{\text{the amount of land required to produce the food for one person, at equilibrium}}$$

Now suppose that A_T represents the total amount of land suitable for agriculture before the development of civilization; and A_F represents the land required to produce the food for one person. Then, at first glance, it would appear that under equilibrium conditions:

$$N = \frac{A_T}{A_F}$$

However, there is a complication. We must subtract from the world total amount of land suitable for agriculture at the outset of civilization, that land which will have been converted to all nonagricultural uses by the time equilibrium is achieved. This difference will include all land covered by houses, freeways, railways, shopping centers, lakes behind hydroelectric dams, and the like. Now suppose that A_U (for A urban) represents the total amount of all this land lost to agriculture, per person in the world population at equilibrium. Now our equation is modified to

$$N = \frac{A_T - NA_U}{A_F}$$

or

$$NA_F = A_T - NA_U$$

so that

$$N = \frac{A_T}{A_F + A_U}$$

Now all we have to do is find out how N is affected by various combinations of these three variables. Specifically, for each of the three we determine plausible estimates of the lowest and highest values that variable could take at equilibrium conditions. Then we explore the sensitivity of N to variations in each of these three variables from the low to the high estimate, in all eight possible combinations (2^3).

eight possible combinations of the three A values are gathered together in Table 6.1.

Three very important conclusions follow from this table.

BOX 6.2
Deriving high and low estimates for carrying capacity factors of land for agriculture

Several people have made estimates in the last few years of the total amount of land in the world suitable in principle for producing food. Four of these, from the lowest to the highest, are:

deWit (1967)	2.29×10^9 hectares
Hendricks (1969)	3.25×10^9 hectares
Revelle (1976)	4.23×10^9 hectares
Borgstrom (1969)	(see below)

World total land availability for agriculture		
	$10^9 \ ha$	$10^9 \ ha$ *(cumulative)*
Presently tilled	1.408	1.408
Not utilized	.379	1.787
Pastures	2.568	4.355
Accessible forest	1.844	6.199

However, most and perhaps all forests should be left as is for four reasons. They are required to control water movement. That is, the absorption of rain water by forests is important in preventing too much runoff just after a rainfall. This means that forests act to prevent flooding downstream in the rainy season and drought in the dry season. Trees are necessary for lumber and pulpwood. The world will shortly be running short of these commodities, as well as agricultural land. Trees and forests are necessary to maintain soil structure. For example, keeping land under forest in the hot, wet tropics prevent the conversion of soil, under intense sunlight to cement-like laterite. Finally, forests are necessary to maintain the gas balance of the biosphere. Since people, other animals, and industry all consume oxygen and produce carbon dioxide, vast areas of plants are required to produce the reverse reaction by means of photosynthesis.

Thus, the maximum estimate we will take of A_T is 4.36 billion ha. The minimum estimate will be that of de Wit: 2.29 billion ha.

One further complication is introduced by erosion. Pimentel has pointed out that of 470 million acres of arable land in the United States, 200 million acres had already been ruined or seriously impoverished by erosion by 1940. Suppose we apply this proportion to the total of 4.355 billion ha. If only 270 to 470 acres were still useful under equilibrium conditions, this would drop the total to 2.5 billion hectares. However, since this figure is above the minimum estimate of 2.29 billion ha, it will not influence our calculations.

TABLE 6.1
The effect of various factors on the carrying capacity of the planet for people.

A_T: world total land area suitable for agriculture (billions of ha)	A_F: land needed to feed one person (hectares)	A_U: land lost to agriculture per person in population (ha)	N: the number of people the plant can feed (billions)
	2.12 {	1.73	.59
		.075	1.04
2.29	.045 {	1.73	1.29
		.075	19.08
	2.12 {	1.73	1.13
		.075	1.99
4.36	.045 {	1.73	2.46
		.075	36.33

BOX 6.3
Diet and agricultural production

First we need to know the nutritional requirements for the average member of the world population under equilibrium conditions. We will assume, for the sake of keeping the calculation simple, that the diet is balanced with respect to all constituents, so that we can do the calculations in terms of only one constituent: energy. The energy requirements of average people are as follows:

	kilocalories per day
15- to 18-year-old boy	3000
15- to 18-year-old girl	2300
moderately active man, 18 to 35	3000
women in most occupations, 18 to 55	2200

The equilibrium population would include children, whose needs are lower. I am assuming an age and sex composition for the equilibrium population in which the requirement of the average person will be for 2406 kilocalories per day, or .8782 million kilocalories per person per year. Knowing this number and the kilocalories produced per hectare per year under different types of agriculture, we can calculate the number of hectares required to feed one person for a year from the relationship:

$$\text{hectares required per person} = \frac{\text{kilocalories required per person}}{\text{kilocalories produced per hectare}}$$

BOX 6.3 (Cont.)

There are various ways we can estimate the kilocalories of food produced per hectare per year. One approach is to argue from the theoretical production capacity of plants grown under optimal conditions. All such estimates are many times higher than any nationwide average yields produced yet, even in countries that use a tremendous amount of fertilizer. Another approach is to use national data to discover the kilocalories of food produced on average, per hectare, for different mixes of food, and different levels of fertilizer application. The following table groups seven different estimates of A_F.

We will use 2.12 and .045 as high and low estimates of A_F.

Type of agriculture and diet	Kilograms of fertilizer applied per hectare	Kilocalories of food produced per hectare per year	A_F: hectares required to produce the food for one person per year, assuming a requirement of $.8782 \times 10^6$ kilocalories per year
Estimates of theoretical upper limit to crop production:			
Kleiber (1961)		2×10^8	.0044
Odum (1971)		1×10^8	.0088
de Wit (1967)		6.4×10^7	.014
1963 Japanese cereal production and diet consisting entirely of cereals	280	19.73×10^6	.045
1963 U.S. cereal production and diet consisting entirely of cereals	47	9.36×10^6	.094
1963 Indian cereal production and diet consisting entirely of cereals	2.6	2.95×10^6	.30
1975 U.S. agriculture and 1975 U.S. diet			2.12*

*This number assumes 1.06 acres for plant food, and an additional 4.17 acres for grazing. In 1975 there were 890 million acres of land in all categories used for grazing, or 4.17 acres per person in the population.

BOX 6.4
Land use

One source of an estimate for A_U, and indeed the highest such estimate we can obtain, is from recent U.S. history. The required data are grouped in the following table.

Year	Land in urban, industrial, and residential areas; rural parks; wildlife refuges; highway, road, and railway rights-of-way; ungrazed desert, rocky, barren land, swamp, tundra, and other land not otherwise counted in millions of acres	Total U.S. population, millions	Land used in these categories per person in the population, acres
1969	437	202.7	2.16
1940	137	132.6	1.03
increase 1940 to 1969	300	70.1	4.28

Thus in the U.S. during this interval, A_U, the rate at which land was lost to agriculture per person added to the population was 4.28 acres per person, or 1.73 hectares per person.

De Wit has used an estimate of .075 ha per person. This is much closer to the situation for countries older than the United States, with much less urban sprawl. We see from Figure 10.6 that in cities alone, land use per person is from .002 to 8.0 ha. However, to this we must add the land use for freeways, railways, and towns, so that .075 appears more reasonable for a high-density society. Thus, for A_U our maximum and minimum estimates will be 1.73 and .075.

Carrying Capacity, Diet, and Agriculture

If the whole world population had the diet we have in the United States, used the level of fertilizer that we do, and used as much land per person as we do, then this planet could support between .59 billion and 1.13 billion people, or between 12 and 23 percent of the likely 1985 world population of 4.816 billion people. Other countries have much higher population densities than the United States because they use far more fertilizer per acre than we do (Europe, Japan), eat far less meat (Asia), or both. In 1978, the average American ate 194 pounds of meat whereas the average Indian ate 3 pounds of meat.

Carrying Capacity and Land Use

The carrying capacity of the planet for people is strongly affected by A_U. If people all over the world were prepared to live at densities like those found in Calcutta or Beirut, this would free up a great deal of farmland, and the world population density could rise to almost ten times the present level. Of course, one might ask the question why anyone would want to live like that. It is curious that colleges of agriculture put an enormous amount of effort into research on how to decrease A_F, yet very little effort into research on A_U, which is obviously just as important.

Carrying Capacity and Life Style

There is no simple answer to the question of how many people the world can support. It depends entirely on the quality of life people want, and the extent to which they want to pay for and become dependent on an enormous energy subsidy to agriculture in the form of fertilizer and other components of agricultural technology. Indeed, farm production is like any other resource: how much there is depends strongly on the availability of cheap energy with which to produce the resource.

If people are willing to live packed into large, dense cities with poor diets and no land for recreation, then the world could support 36 billion people, about seven and a half times the likely 1985 population. But if people want a very high standard of living, then the world will only support about 600 million people, the population of the world in about 1675.

Thus, we are introduced to the important concept of "tradeoff." Whenever you get anything, it comes at some cost. In this case, the tradeoff is between high populations and a low standard of living, or low populations and a high standard of living. Each person has to decide which is more important: increasing the number of inhabitants of the planet or increasing one's standard of living by reducing birthrates to below the replacement level. If every couple in the world were to have one child, then within two generations the planet would be a vastly better place.

The tradeoff concept introduces another main theme of this book: the resolution of conflicts. People argue about the necessity for population limitation. Presumably, the people who argue for increased population see it as implying pure gain. However, if they saw all the implications of population increase, and understood the nature of the tradeoffs, they might change their minds. Perhaps they view the population controversy from only one level of perspective: that of immediate, personal economic gain. But when we expand our horizons to look at the worldwide balance of population and resources, the controversy may evaporate, since everyone would then see the problem the same way. The deep message in this is that resolution of conflicts of interest are critically dependent on choosing the correct hierarchical level from which to analyze the issue.

We are already pressing hard on resources worldwide. Further large increases in population will only be attained by a shift away from meat and by increased urban densities. These two processes are already observable, even in the richest countries. Further, given the extreme pressure humans are now exerting on resources worldwide, our situation could deteriorate with surprising suddenness unless we manage our resources with great care. Indeed, a model of such a collapse is well-known: Peruvian anchovy fishing. From 1938 to 1970, Peruvian fish catches increased amazingly, from 23 thousand metric tons to 12.6 million metric tons. But at that level, the anchovy was being overfished, and in 1976 catches were a third those in 1970.

Why has there been so little allusion to the oceans as an important source of food in this book? Simply because the oceans are an unimportant source of food. In recent years, five other important world food sources have collectively represented twenty times as much food by weight each year as all fish catches: corn, potatoes, rice, wheat, and meat. Also, fish catches have not increased much recently: they were the same in 1974 as in 1970, for example. Food from the sea also has about one-third the caloric content per 100 grams of edible portion relative to food from land, however, aquatic food is an important supplemental source of protein and minerals.

The importance of fish to humanity may rise in the future, not because of innovations in fishing, but because of innovations in ocean fish culture, or by stimulating fish population growth by means of thermal upwellings near atolls.

One further point needs to be made about the carrying capacity of the planet for people: population size enters into every calculation of environmental impact. If there are ten times as many people, then the impact will be at least ten times as great. This applies to pollution as well as resource depletion. The amount of environmental degradation is equal to the degradation per person multiplied by the number of people. Clearly, all our problems would be easier to solve if there were fewer people.

THE DETERMINANTS OF POPULATION GROWTH

The rate of population increase in any country is determined by a simple equation:

$$\text{rate of population increase}$$
$$= \text{birth rate} - \text{death rate}$$
$$+ \text{immigration rate} - \text{emigration rate}$$

In a primitive society, the birth rates and death rates are both very high. If the birth rate is slightly higher than the death rate, the population has a positive growth rate and the population increases. As a country becomes developed, sanitation, the level of public health and diet improve, and the death rate drops, often very rapidly. The result is a very high rate of population increase, until the birth rate also drops, under the influence of education and industrialization. While the country is converting from a high death rate and high birth rate state to a low death rate and low birth rate state, it is said to be undergoing a "demographic transition." A well-studied example of a nation passing through the demographic transition in recent years has been the island of Taiwan (Figure 6.3). The death rate had dropped tremendously by 1956, at which time the birth rate also began a spectacular drop. By 1975 the birth rate had dropped to about half the 1955 level, so that the rate of population growth also took a great drop. The speed with which this transition can occur, once a nation becomes convinced of the need for population planning, gives us hope for the future. The problem is to convince other lesser developed nations to emulate Taiwan, a country highly atypical because of its rapid industrialization and high level of literacy.

Until recently, birth and death rates had been viewed by most people as of far more significance for population growth rates than migration rates. But recently, very large rates of international migration have changed the situation markedly. One of the most interesting and important instances in the world is the vast immigration from Mexico to the United States, much of it illegal (6). A few numbers bring out the essential facts. The United States has a very low birth rate (14 per 1000) and a death rate of 9 per 1000. Thus, rate of natural population increase is $14 - 9$ per thousand, or 5 per thousand, or .5 percent. If the United States had sealed borders, then, the rate of population increase would be equal to the rate of natural population increase, or .5 percent. In fact, the rate of population increase in the United States is 1.3 percent. The difference, .8 percent, is due to immigration. Much of

FIGURE 6.3

The demographic transition in Taiwan. The solid lines are from measurements; the dotted lines are reasonable extrapolations, based on measurements from similar countries. Reprinted from World Population, *by N. Keyfitz and W. Flieger, by permission of the University of Chicago Press. Copyright 1968 by the University of Chicago.*

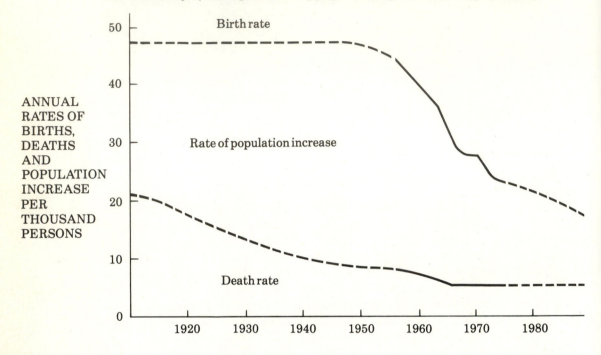

that immigration comes from Mexico. In Mexico, the birth and death rates per thousand are 42.0 and 6.5, respectively, which would give a rate of natural population increase of 3.55 percent if the rates hold constant. The actual rate of population increase from 1970 to 1977 was 4.26 percent. Hence, in this case, it would appear that migration across an international boundary will have a very large impact on the rates of population growth in both countries.

THE TREMENDOUS SIGNIFICANCE OF POPULATION AGE STRUCTURE

Population age structure has a very large impact on our environment, independently of the effect of population size, because the environmental impact of each human depends on his or her age: thirty-year-olds drive more than twelve- or seventy-year-olds, for example.

Population age structure differs greatly from country to country, and also undergoes large changes from time to time in each country. The determinant of age structure is the rate of population increase. If a population has been growing rapidly recently, there will have been a large number of young children born relative to the number of older people in the population; this fact can be expressed by drawing a population pyramid, as in Figure 6.4, in which the numbers in each age and sex are expressed as a percentage of the total population.. The charts are

FIGURE 6.4

Population pyramid charts. Data reprinted from World Population, *by N. Keyfitz and W. Flieger, by permission of the University of Chicago Press. Copyright 1968 by the University of Chicago.*

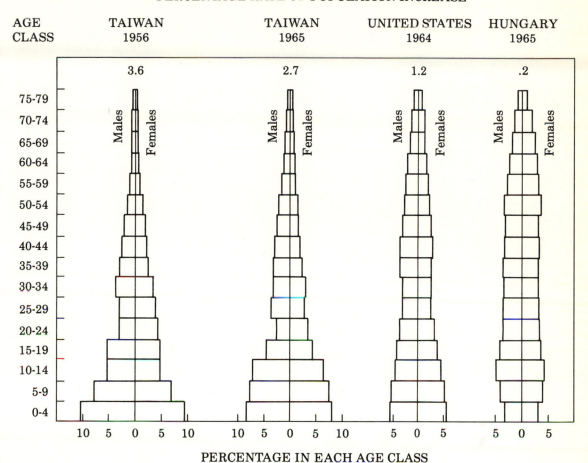

PERCENTAGE RATE OF POPULATION INCREASE

PERCENTAGE IN EACH AGE CLASS

arranged with equal age classes one on top of the other, the oldest at the top, with males on the left, females on the right. The pyramid looks like an Egyptian pyramid if the population has been growing extremely rapidly, and like a straight stick if the population has been growing extremely slowly. Four different situations are depicted in the figure, representing a gradient from rapid to slow growth. The two pyramids for Taiwan indicate the speed with which the shape of the chart can change.

Why are these pyramids important? Quite literally everything that goes on in a country depends on the shape of these pyramids. A few examples will make the point.

For a long time, it proved difficult to understand trends in birth rates in women.

FIGURE 6.5

Trends in gross national product per capita, and birth rate for fifteen- to-forty-four-year-old women, from 1929 to 1973. Data from Historical Statistics of the United States *and* Statistical Abstracts of the United States. *Copyright, United Nations. Reproduced by permission.*

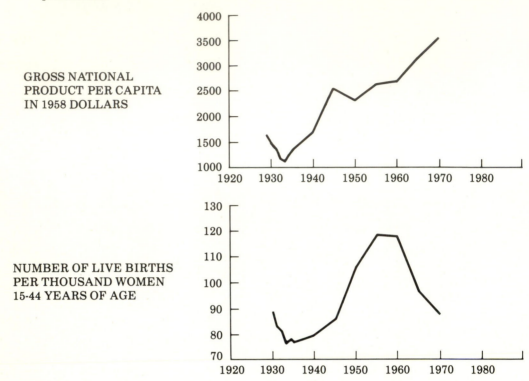

GROSS NATIONAL
PRODUCT PER CAPITA
IN 1958 DOLLARS

NUMBER OF LIVE BIRTHS
PER THOUSAND WOMEN
15-44 YEARS OF AGE

Birth rates were expected to drop when the economy declined, and rise when the economy grew rapidly again. As Figure 6.5 indicates, up to 1957 in the United States, this appears to have been the case. Gross national product per capita dropped precipitously from 1929 to 1934, and so did birth rates. The economy then improved almost without interruption to 1974. As we would have expected, birth rates also increased, apart from aberration produced by World War II, up to 1957. After that, something odd happened. While the economy continued to improve, birth rates for women of each age dropped, and have dropped ever since. Why? The conventional wisdom about how

birth rates are determined overlooks the role of population age distribution. Birth rates in particular age groups of people are not determined by the population-wide average level of affluence, but the level of affluence in the age group. In Chapter 5, particularly in connection with Figure 5.6, a theory was presented that the output from any system depends on the input to that system. What is the resource input for an age group of people? For young people, the most important resource available to them is the number of older people. For people twenty to twenty-four, for example, the important resource is the number of people who were twenty-four to forty-four years of age five years pre-

FIGURE 6.6

Testing the hypothesis that the number of people twenty-five to forty-four years of age are a resource for the people fifteen to twenty-four years of age, with the resource output being the number of births five years later. Each point represents one year. The dates identifying selected points are the years in which the births occurred. Data from Historical Statistics of the United States, *and reprinted from* World Population, *by N. Keyfitz and W. Flieger, by permission of the University of Chicago Press. Copyright 1968 by the University of Chicago.*

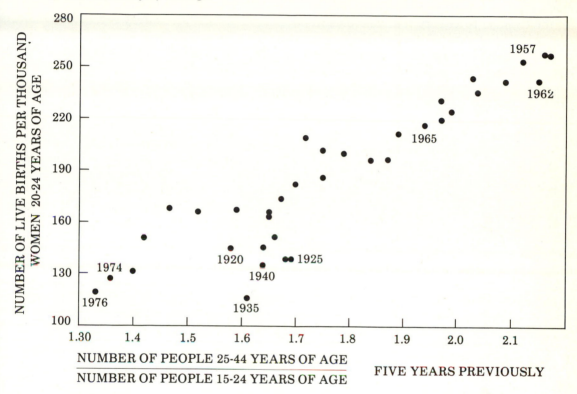

viously, because those were the people primarily responsible for generating the taxes that provided a good education, and the capital that provided new jobs in the labor force. If this argument is correct, we would expect to find that birth rates of twenty- to twenty-four-year-olds were higher following years in which there had been a high ratio of twenty-five- to forty-four-year-olds to fifteen- to twenty-four-year-olds, and lower when there were fewer twenty-five- to forty-four-year-olds, relative to the number of fifteen- to twenty-four-year-olds (5). This is

what we find (Figure 6.6). However, this figure has an additional significance: it not only explains trends in birth rates in the United States, it also exposes a mechanism that will produce very strong cycles in the society. Following a complete cycle through, we see that in 1925, there were few people twenty-five to forty-four years of age relative to the number fifteen to twenty-four years of age. Thus, five years later, in 1930, there were inadequate jobs for twenty- to twenty-four-year-olds, and their economic prospects looked bleak. Therefore, they had an unusually low birth rate. As a result, in the period 1954 to 1962, when the children born in the mid-1930s were at an age where they were trying to break into the labor force for the first time, there were few of them relative to the number of people in the labor force generating the capital to provide them with new jobs. Thus, the employment rate for twenty- to twenty-four-year-olds in this period was very high, and their economic prospects looked good, so they had high birth rates. But this meant that when their children, the grandchildren of the low-birth-rate group of the 1930s, attained adulthood in the late 1970s, they were super-abundant relative to the number of twenty-five- to forty-four-year-olds at that time, so the twenty- to twenty-four-year-old group in the late 1970s had the lowest birth rates in U.S. history. In short, we are describing a cycle-creating mechanism with a wave length twice the time from the time a person is born to the time they are trying to break into the labor force for the first time. This mechanism would tend to produce major forty-five to fifty year cycles in the economy, in culture, in resource demand, in political tastes and attitudes, and in everything else. (The cycles are called Kondratief Waves, after a Russian economist who first discovered them).

Would we expect to find a similar cycle in all countries? No, because children have a different meaning in different countries. In developed countries, children are correctly perceived as a significant financial responsibility. Thus, when economic prospects for young people look bleak, they would have a sharp decrease in birth rates. However, in developing nations, where little money is spent on young people, but they soon contribute to the farm labor force and are expected to provide for their parents in their old age, children are a significant financial asset. Thus, we would not expect the relationship of Figure 6.6 to apply in developing countries. In those cases, we would ex-

pect very high birth rates, even where the age ratio of Figure 6.6 was very low. This is indeed what we find. Further, we can postulate an intermediate condition for countries in transition, in which children are gradually becoming a financial responsibility rather than a pure financial asset.

Unemployment Rate as an Effect of Birth Rate

To this point, to maintain the flow of the argument, an important intermediate step has been assumed, rather than being demonstrated. It has been implied that unemployment rates of young people are strongly influenced by the birth rates which prevailed at the time when they were being born. In fact, 34 percent of the year-to-year variation in unemployment rates among sixteen- to nineteen-year-olds is accounted for by the birth rates nineteen years previously. This is a most curious result. Unemployment rates among a particular age group not only imply economic misery for that age group: they also imply an increased welfare burden on all age groups. This burden, in turn, implies increased government expenditures, which in turn imply less capital available for investment in new plant and equipment that would promote economic growth. Thus we see a direct link between excessive rates of population growth and a lowered rate of economic growth. This is opposite to the way that link is usually postulated to work (high rates of population growth imply higher rates of economic growth).

Other Consequences of Rapid Population Growth

Unemployment is only one of the causal pathways by which excessive rates of population growth can affect a society. Another causal pathway is via the costs per taxpayer of education (15). As the rate of population growth in a particular year increases, the number of students enrolled in elementary schools ten years later increases proportionately. Increased numbers of students, of course, translate directly into an increased tax burden per taxpayer. Specifically, increasing the population growth rate from .6 percent a year to 2.2 percent a year increases the number of students in elementary school from 240 per thousand people aged 25–64 to 400.

Excessive population growth rate not only implies an increased tax burden due to education, but also an increased likelihood that the taxpayers will simply be unwilling to meet the cost; the consequence is inferior education ten years after excessive population growth rate.

Another phenomenon that affects the economy under the influence of population growth rate is crime (7) and the cost of police protection. Criminal activity is highly sensitive to the age structure of the population, because crime rates are fourteen times higher among teenagers than among people over fifty-four. Consequently, high population growth rates imply a distorted age pyramid and unusually high crime rates relative to historic averages. When the population average age increases, crime rates decline a few years afterwards.

To this point, we have been discussing the effects of unusually high numbers of young people on a society. However, there can also be surprising effects of unusually high numbers of older people. The number of people over sixty-four years of age implies an economic cost with respect to retirement benefits. This burden is not significant if a society is growing rapidly. However, if the population growth rate declines sharply, as it did in the United States after 1957, this means that from then on, there will be a gradual increase in the number of people of retirement age relative to the number of

working ages. In fact, one can even develop a mathematical relationship between the proportion of the population over sixty-four and the proportion of gross national product that will have to be allocated to social security benefit payments. By the year 2000, the withdrawal of these payments from the economy will be twenty-three times as large a proportion of gross national product as in 1950, and will constitute a very significant brake on economic growth.

Clearly, there are great economic costs if a society undergoes violent oscillations in birth rate in a country where all people are well cared for and represent a significant financial responsibility for the family or the state. However, the consequences of changes in population age structure go far beyond the economy (5). The fashions, tastes, and culture of people is dependent on their age. People of different ages have different tastes in toys, baby food, sports, hobbies, clothing, leisure, music, art, entertainment, politics, and indeed everything else. Thus, a sufficiently large change in the average age of a population literally transforms it from one kind of a society into another kind of a society. A glance at the population on the street in two contrasting countries makes the point (Figures 6.7 and 6.8). Also, the extent to which a society uses resources is age-dependent. Babies and ninety-year-olds do not travel much in jets. Manufacturers, political parties, governments, educational institutions, and hospitals ignore changes in population age distribution at their peril.

Certain age distributions are sufficiently important to demographers (scientists who study human population dynamics) to be given special names. The stable age distribution occurs when the age distribution reproduces itself exactly from generation to generation. The population total size may change, but each age class remains a constant proportion of the entire population. If the population not only maintains a con-

FIGURE 6.7

A street scene from a country in which the population is growing very rapidly. Notice the large number of young people on the street. Photograph by Cary Wolinsky. Courtesy of Stock, Boston, Inc.

stant age distribution, but also its total size, it is called a stationary population. Clearly, stable age distributions and stationary populations are most uncommon in human experience. Indeed, many countries now have such distorted age structures that age distributions will undergo long-term fluctuations for centuries (8).

POPULATION CONTROL AND FAMILY PLANNING

Population control implies that a nation has decided to control its population size. Where this happens, as in China or Singapore, some type of widespread method will be used to bring the birth rate down. There may be social conventions that keep young men and women separate or deemphasize sexuality, or there may be tax incentives for having one or two children. Incentives may be very tough, as when obtaining or holding a job depends on the number of children one has.

Family planning is a quite different concept. This refers to the situation in which a husband and wife decide how many children they want, and when they wish to have them. They may wish to have twenty children. Clearly there is a profound difference between these two concepts. Under family planning, the concern is of, by, and for the family, without regard for the interests of the society at large. If the effect is beneficial for the society at large, it is a happy acci-

FIGURE 6.8

A street scene from a country in which the population is growing very slowly. Notice that almost everyone in the picture appears middle-aged. How do you think the tastes and character of a society like this would differ from that depicted in the previous figure? Photograph by Cary Wolinsky. Courtesy of Stock, Boston, Inc.

dent. Population planning, control, or policy are all concepts applied to the level of the nation, not the family. Application of these concepts, if successful, is highly likely to produce a fast decline in the rate of population growth. Family planning may or may not have an impact on the rate of population growth: it depends on the wishes of the average couple.

SUMMARY

The number of people the world can support at any time is dependent on three groups of factors:

1. The total amount of land available for food production.
2. The amount of food produced per unit of agricultural land and the food eaten per person.
3. The amount of land that could otherwise be used for agriculture taken up per person for city and other uses.

Population growth rate is determined by the difference between birth and death rates. The demographic transition occurs when first death rates and then birth rates drop.

Population age structure determines birth rates, unemployment rates, educational expenditures, and crime rates. The proportion of the population over retirement age determines the proportion of the wealth of a society going into retirement payments.

Thus, high rates of population growth have a variety of subsequent deleterious economic effects, which operate through population age structure.

INDIVIDUAL AND GROUP PROJECTS

Pick some environmental problem and analyze all available information to demonstrate how excessive population size and growth rate make that problem worse.

Use a calculator to conduct experiments on the effect of various changes in birth rates on future population size and age distribution in the United States or some developing nation.

When your local newspaper has news articles or editorials about local problems, look for the possibility that overpopulation is making the problem more serious than it otherwise would have been. Then write a letter to the editor pointing this out.

REFERENCES

1. Borgstrom, G., *Too Many*. London: Macmillan, 1969.
2. Clark, C., *Population Growth and Land Use*. London: Macmillan, 1967.
3. Deevey, E. S., "The human population," *Scientific American* 203, 9 (1960), pp. 195–204.
4. de Wit, C. T., "Photosynthesis: Its relationship to overpopulation," in A. San Pietro, F. Greer, and T. J. Army, eds., *Harvesting the Sun*. New York: Academic, 1967.
5. Easterlin, R., "What will 1984 be like? Socioeconomic implications of recent twists in age structure," *Demography*, 15 (1978), p. 397.
6. Ehrlich, P. R., L. Bilderback, and A. H. Ehrlich, *The Golden Door. International Migration, Mexico, and the United States*. New York: Ballantine, 1979.
7. Foin, T. C. Jr., "Systems ecology and the future of human society," in *Systems Analysis and Simulation in Ecology*, Vol. 2. New York: Academic, 1972.
8. Frejka, T., "Reflections on the demographic conditions needed to establish a U.S. stationary population growth," *Population Studies*, 22 (1968), p 379.
9. Hendricks, S. B., "Food from the land," in *Resources and Man*, Committee on Resources and Man, National Academy of Sciences. San Francisco: Freeman, 1969.
10. Keyfitz, N., and W. Flieger. *World Population*. Chicago: University of Chicago Press, 1968.
11. Kleiber, M., *The Fire of Life*. New York: Wiley, 1961.
12. Odum, H. T., *Environment, Power, and Society*. New York: Wiley, 1971.
13. Pimentel, D., "Land degradation: Effects on food and energy resources," *Science*, 194 (1976), pp. 149–155.
14. Revelle, R., "The resources available to agriculture," *Scientific American* 235, 3 (1976), pp. 165–178.
15. Singer, S. F., ed., *Is There an Optimal Level of Population?* New York: McGraw-Hill, 1971.

7

ECONOMIC
FACTORS AND
ENVIRONMENTAL PROBLEMS

The market price of every particular commodity is regulated by the proportion between the quantity which is actually brought to market, and the demand of those who are willing to pay the natural price of the commodity, or the whole value of the rent, labour, and profit, which must be paid in order to bring it thither.

Adam Smith, An Inquiry into the Nature and Causes of the Wealth of Nations, *Chapter VII, 1776.*

Neither a borrower nor a lender be:
For loan oft loses both itself and friend,
And borrowing dulls the edge of husbandry.

William Shakespeare, Hamlet *I. iii.*

MAIN THEMES OF THIS CHAPTER

Typically, supply and demand are in balance, because decrease in supply results in an increasing price, which reduces demand to match supply. However, this usually self-regulating and stabilizing mechanism often fails as a conserver of resources.

In the case of energy, consumer purchasing power in the United States rose more rapidly than energy prices for a long time, canceling out the usefulness of rising energy prices as depressants of demand. In other cases, such as lobsters and other shellfish, there are enough wealthy people that rising prices fail to dampen demand enough to ensure survival of the resource.

An issue that exposes the linkage between ecology and economics is the "windfall profits tax" on oil, which purports to prevent unfair profit-making by the oil companies. However, this tax ignores the enormously increased cost to drill for oil in the future resulting from the depletion described in Chapter 4.

Insufficient attention has been paid to the social consequences of substituting cheap energy for expensive labor, which include higher unemployment rates resulting from the displaced labor. Energy has been kept cheap in the United States to promote use of energy at a high and increasing rate and thereby stimulate economic growth. This argument is incorrect, because cheap energy produces economically destructive side effects.

A nation has a limited amount of capital to invest; the way in which that capital is invested determines the fate of the nation. Unwise patterns of capital allocation not only are environmentally destructive, they also dampen the rate of economic growth.

PRICE, SUPPLY, AND DEMAND

All environmental problems share a certain basic structure: the demand for some resource, commodity, service, or opportunity has risen to a level at which it can no longer be satisfied by supply. Some examples will demonstrate the various guises in which this problem structure can appear.

Suppose you go to a "wilderness" area that has logging or mining operations, and you find it swarming with people driving around in power boats, towing their friends on water skis, or taking photographs of bears. This simply means that demand for "wilderness" is no longer being met by the supply of land that is genuine wilderness. Suppose you try to drive your car out of a city at 5:10 P.M. on a Friday night, and discover that you are immobilized in a traffic jam that lasts for an hour. This means that demand for land for freeway right-of-way exceeds the supply of land that can be purchased for freeways with the tax money society is willing to spend for this purpose. Intolerable air pollution means that demand for clean air to dilute the pollutants a city or factory is emitting into the air cannot be met by supply, given the rate at which prevailing winds are bringing fresh air into the city. Rapidly escalating retail prices for lobsters, clams, steak, bread, clothing, housing, or gasoline means that demand for all these commodities is growing faster than supply. Increasing unemployment and crime rates means that the demand for job opportunities is growing faster than the supply of new jobs. If the countryside where you go for holidays is littered with rusting food cans and old cars, clearly, the demand for unlittered countryside is growing faster than supply.

Given the widespread occurrence of problems with this common structure, it is clearly worthwhile to ask some questions about the fundamental relationships between supply, demand, and price. It is simplest to begin by explaining how they would relate in an ideal situation: this is sketched in a flow chart in Figure 7.1. Causal pathways in this chart are referred to by numbers in parentheses. A set of factors regulate (1) size of total population, and another set of factors regulate (2) the per capita demand for any particular resource, commodity, service, or opportunity. Population (3) and per capita demand (4) multiplied together produce total demand (5). The resultant demand (6), together with total supply available to the entire population (7), produces a ratio of demand to supply, and as this ratio rises, so too does the resultant price (8). This price, with a lag, produces three effects: if price increases sharply, it can lead to an increase in supply (10), simply because it becomes very profitable for anyone to search for more of

FIGURE 7.1
The ideal relation between population, demand, supply, and price.

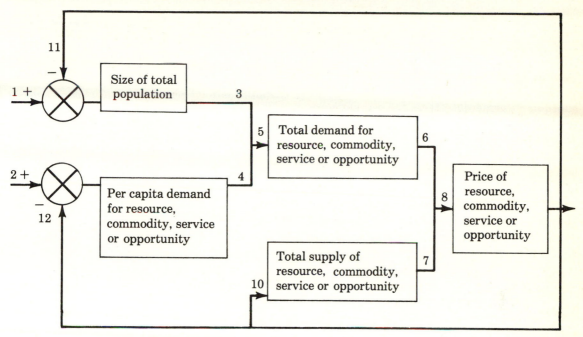

traditional resources, or invest in new ones; but price increase will also tend to reduce demand (12). The circle with a cross in it is a symbol for summation, referring to summation of the positive effect on demand coming from 2, and the negative "feedback" effect coming from 12; the third effect of increasing price (9) is to produce negative feedback (11) operating on population size, if the price increase lasts long enough. So we see that price is an effect responding to the joint operation of three causes: population size, per capita demand, and total available supply. In the ideal situation just sketched, the relationships are being regulated through the operation of the price mechanism. In this ideal situation, economic systems are self-regulating or homeostatic systems with the price mechanism being the counterpart of the density-dependent control systems

operating in renewable resource (biological) and demographic systems, as explained in the last two chapters.

Economics and the Environment

Now why do we get environmental problems? In each case, something has happened to prevent ideal operation of the price mechanism. In some cases, some institutional or governmental mechanism (or lack of an appropriate mechanism) has resulted in a failure of price to rise appropriately or has produced a dangerous delay in the price rise. Another type of breakdown occurs in the price mechanism when a few people are wealthy enough to afford the price for some commodity, without regard to the consequences. This is the situation when a few people are willing to pay higher and higher prices for some gourmet food item, such as lobster, oysters, clams, or crab, even when the overfishing made possible by such higher prices ultimately wipes out the resource.

If the price mechanism fails over the short or intermediate term for a great variety of resources simultaneously, but then after a long delay the prices of many commodities start shooting up together, this results in inflation. Inflation results when the government responds to excessive demand relative to supply by increasing the amount of money in circulation, so as to create the short-term appearance of a compensatory increase in consumer buying power. The result is a decrease in the value of money per unit, or inflation.

A revealing example commodity for illustrating the mechanism sketched in Figure 7.1. is gasoline. This is a particularly important commodity to analyze in terms of the price mechanism, because it is responsible for such a wide variety of environmental problems, from traffic congestion, urban sprawl, and air pollution to oil spills on beaches and poor city design in urban centers.

Figure 7.2 is a graph of the relationship between the price of 100 litres of gasoline and the gasoline consumption per capita for thirty-six countries in 1970. The straight line was fitted statistically to the data for all thirty-six countries and the data for eleven sample countries are plotted as individual data points. The slight slope of the line, and the great scatter of the individual data points about the line indicate that price alone has an insignificant effect on demand. The reason for this weak relationship is that price by itself is a rather poor indication of demand: it is also necessary to know the buying power of potential customers. Thus,

FIGURE 7.2

The relation between gasoline use per capita and price of 100 litres of gasoline. Gasoline prices include taxes and are the minimum prices for 100 litres of ordinary grade gasoline converted to U.S. dollars. These figures and the data on total national gasoline consumption are from World Road Statistics 1968–1972, *published by the International Road Federation. Statistics on population are from the Statistical Office of the United Nations. Copyright, United Nations (1972). Reproduced by permission,* Statistical Yearbook of the United Nations, *1971, pp. 67–73. The fitted relation was in the form* $\ln C = .298 - .466 \ln P$, *and the square of the correlation coefficient was .020.*

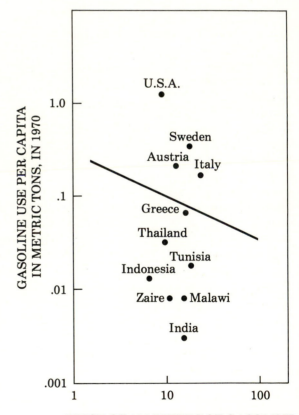

PRICE OF 100 LITRES OF GASOLINE IN U.S. DOLLARS, IN 1970

the president or another politician who argues that he or she will promote conservation of energy by ONLY raising its price is expecting us to believe that the relation in Figure 7.2 has a significant effect, when obviously it does not. In other words, whenever we try to find the relationship between price and demand, we must divide the price by some measure of the purchasing power of consumers.

One measure of the differences in purchasing power of average consumers between nations is the gross national product per capita. When we divide gasoline prices by this measure as in Figure 7.3, we now find a striking relationship between price and average per capita gasoline use. Indeed, we have a pattern close to what economists call unitary elasticity of demand, the situation in which doubling price halves consumption. Figure 7.3 has revealed a very important principle: use of any commodity depends on the ratio of price to average consumer buying power. Thus, for example, if a president announces an energy "conservation" program in which the price of energy will be allowed to rise more slowly than average consumer buying power, then we know that the president is in fact announcing a plan to stimulate the use of energy, not conserve it.

The other important point made by Figure 7.3 is that contrary to what some people in the consumer movement assert, U.S. energy prices are not terribly high; by international standards they are terribly low. Also, it is simply not true that much higher energy prices relative to buying power harm an economy: the economies of Switzerland, Denmark, Sweden, West Germany, Belgium, and Norway are growing faster and are already at a higher per capita level than that of the United States, even though their energy prices relative to buying power are more than twice as high as in this country.

Comparison across countries for a particular year showing that doubling gasoline price halves per capita use does not mean that if gasoline prices relative to wages were doubled in the United States, per capita gasoline use would quickly halve. The data points in the figure represent equilibrium conditions that have been reached in each country over a long period of time. If gasoline prices in the United States relative to wages were increased, even by as much as four times, it would take perhaps twenty years for per capita use to drop to about a quarter the present level. Time would be taken installing more public transportation, new energy generating systems, making cars more efficient, and in contraction of cities, so that average commute distances were smaller. This type of example brings out the great importance of time as a critical limiting resource. It also demonstrates the need for planning to look long into the future, if it is to be most socially useful.

Given that the determinant of energy consumption per capita is price relative to buying power, it is interesting to ask what has happened to this ratio in U.S. history. It is possible to explore an issue such as this by performing simple calculations using readily available government statistics. First, we need some measure of the buying power of a typical consumer. For this purpose, we use the average net spendable weekly earnings of a worker in manufacturing industry with three dependents, after federal income taxes and social security contributions have been deducted from gross earnings. As a measure of energy cost, we use the average value at the well of a barrel of crude oil. This statistic eliminates the necessity of having to correct for state-to-state differences in gasoline taxes and a host of other regional differences. Now the value of crude oil relative to average consumer buying power can be calculated by division. Average gasoline con-

FIGURE 7.3

The relation between gasoline use per capita and price, when price is corrected for gross national product per capita. Gasoline prices and statistics on total national gasoline consumption from the International Road Federation. Statistics on population and gross product per capita are from the Statistical Office of the United Nations. Copyright, United Nations (1972). Reproduced by permission. Statistical Yearbook of the United Nations, *1971, pp. 67-73. The fitted relation was in the form ln C = .000784 − 1.144 ln P, and the square of the correlation coefficient was .936.*

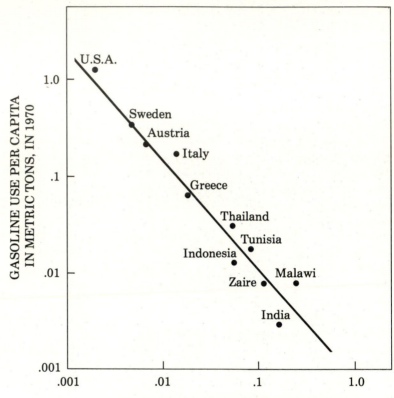

PRICE OF 100 LITRES OF GASOLINE
AS A PROPORTION OF GROSS NATIONAL
PRODUCT PER CAPITA, 1970

sumption per person is obtained by dividing U.S. total gasoline consumption in cars, taxis, and motorcycles by the U.S. resident population. Using these statistics, we discover that the driving force behind the increase in gasoline consumption per capita from 1955 to 1978 was the great decrease in cost of crude oil relative to buying power.

However, there is a long lag (five years) in this relationship, as previously noted.

The explanation is that between 1955 and 1978, a new life style evolved in the United States, with more cars being purchased, people moving to ranch bungalows great distances from the places where they worked, freeway systems being constructed, and the national public transportation system being virtually abandoned, except for airlines. It will take time for higher energy prices to deflect those processes. However, after crude oil prices relative to average consumer spendable earnings have risen for several years, there will be a gradual return to more compact cities and more use of public transportation.

If all commodities became scarce simultaneously, the prices of all of them would rise together and this would provide a powerful stimulus to runaway inflation. As Figure 7.1 indicated, one driving force behind such scarcity and resultant inflation is population. Thus, all other things being equal, we would expect further increases in world population to make inflation a serious problem, until large numbers of people come to realize the connection between inflation and world population, and help to deal with the population problem in a very personal, direct way (limiting the number of children they have).

Price as a Stabilizing Mechanism

It has already been noted, in Figure 7.1, that price operates as a regulatory or stabilizing mechanism in society. It is the equivalent in the social and economic arena, of homeostatic mechanisms that operate in biology, such as body temperature regulation, or the density-dependent mechanisms which regulate population sizes. The implications of this point are far-reaching. When anyone argues that high prices are "cruel," and anticonsumer or antilaborer, this is like arguing that it is cruel to have a mechanism that regulates the temperature of our bodies, and hence that mechanism should be removed surgically. If a commodity is becoming scarce and government or some other institution prevents prices from rising, the consequences can be totally unexpected, be-

cause of the complexity of the causal pathways operating in modern society (Chapter 11).

It is impossible to stop prices from rising; whenever this is attempted, the consumer merely pays the higher price in some roundabout way, and the ultimate price is higher than it would have been if there had been no attempt to tamper with the price mechanism. The classic case occurred in the mid-1970s, when Congress kept energy prices down, and the public paid higher prices for food, clothing, housing, and everything else, because of the depletion of U.S. domestic stocks of commodities, due to the vast scale on which they were exported to pay for imported crude oil.

PRICE AND RESOURCE DEPLETION

A most controversial topic in environmental economics concerns the relation between supply, demand, and price. There are three different ways of thinking about the problem, each illustrated by a diagram in Figure 7.4. In the traditional view of economics (top panel of figure), an increase in price for any commodity results in a decline in demand, and an increase in supply. The equilibrium price at any time is that price for which supply and demand are equal. The "fixed inventory" view results if we decide that the world has some fixed stock of a natural resource (the view adopted in Chapter 4) that cannot be increased by increasing price (second panel of figure). In this view, at an early stage in exploitation of a resource, supply exceeds demand, and the difference is a surplus. Later, when demand exceeds supply, there is a shortage. The first of these two views is incorrect, in that it does not accept the existence of physical limits to supply; the second is deficient, in that it does not include the role of price. A third view, result-

FIGURE 7.4

Three conceptual models of the relationships among supply, demand, and price for a natural resource.

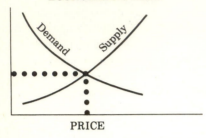

THE TRADITIONAL
ECONOMIST'S VIEW

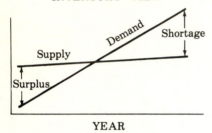

THE "FIXED
INVENTORY" VIEW

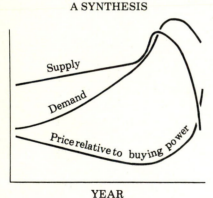

A SYNTHESIS

time. However, when demand finally surpasses supply, price rises very rapidly, and there is no accompanying resultant increase in supply.

Which of these three views is correct? Useful data for exploring this matter arise when demand finally becomes very great relative to productive capacity of the resource. Many fish and shellfish are already in this situation. Consider U.S. northern lobsters. This does not conform to the classical economic view, because a great increase in the value of the catch per pound did not result in constant increase in supply. Rather, there was some increase in supply in response to rising price, but then supply actually fell in response to further price increase. Thus, the actual situation corresponds to the bottom panel of Figure 7.4 in this instance. Even after correcting for increased consumer buying power, the price of lobsters is still rising rapidly. Consequently, lobsters are now one of a large number of driving forces behind inflation. When enough resources show this pattern, inflation will be very serious indeed, and at that time, inflation will only be reduced by lower human populations, or by increased frugality per person.

Price Must Rise Promptly to Promote Conservation

The timing of price increases for any resource is critical. If price does not begin to rise rapidly until a resource is almost depleted, then how useful is the price mechanism as a stabilizing or regulatory device? There are possible institutional devices that could be used to make the price of a commodity rise sooner, relative to the time at which it was going to be totally depleted. In the case of a nonrenewable resource, such as crude oil or natural gas, we could arrange to get an earlier warning of impending deple-

ing from a synthesis of the two preceding views, is represented in the third panel. Here, demand gradually increases relative to supply and passes it, as in the second view. As in the first view, price increase can stimulate production of supply for some

tion, if government would legislate sale of the resource, not at the price that would be reasonable on the basis of the cost to extract the resource being sold, but on the basis of the cost to replace it in the national inventory. A variety of techniques for driving up the price so as to delay depletion have been advocated by Herman E. Daly (3), Bruce Hannon (5), and others. Daly has suggested auctioning off the right to exploit portions of the remaining energy. Hannon has suggested an energy resource tax, geared to the wage level of the person being taxed. Both these devices would discourage the use of energy, and encourage the increased efficiency of society with respect to resource use.

Whether or not resources will be overexploited depends on whether they are common property or private property resources. That is, since some resources, such as the whale and fish stocks of the high seas, belong to no one, no one has an interest in conserving them, and this is a principal reason for their depletion. The same argument would be applied to the 80 million buffalo in the United States that were reduced to about thirty animals by 1888. Ownership of a high proportion of the world's remaining crude oil by the countries of the O.P.E.C. oil cartel may result in oil being used more slowly than if it were a common property.

The particular view we take of the extent to which resources are being depleted has enormous implications for our views on a wide variety of other, often politically explosive issues, such as the "windfall profits tax" (Box. 7.1).

BOX 7.1
An example of the link between ecology and economics: The "windfall profits tax"

Ecology and economics are merely different components of a single, larger subject, resources, in which resource availability (nonrenewable and renewable resources) is the essential link between them. Ecology deals with the factors that determine the productivity of resources; economics deals, in part, with the impact of resource availability on the price of resources. Given this linkage, one would expect to find that any phenomenon affecting a critical resource would impact both ecological and economic variables; also, one would expect to find that any error in thinking by most people about a critical resource would reveal itself as both an error in ecological thinking, and an error in economic thinking. An excellent recent example is public perceptions of the need for a "windfall profits tax."

To explain the defect in popular perception of the problem, it is necessary to introduce some economic terms. The concepts needed for the explanation are collated in the following paragraph (these definitions were kindly supplied to me by Dr. George David).

Money is not wealth, but rather, a medium of exchange and a store of value.
Inflation is an increase in the supply of money.
Prices rises are not inflation, but only one of its consequences.
Prices may rise either because of inflation, or because of scarcity (price rises in a besieged city are not inflation).

BOX 7.1 (Cont.)

Inflation causes scarcity by causing misallocation of resources: consumption
   of capital, overstatement of income, and understatement of depreciation.
Capital is the means to achieve a value; a value is the goal of an action; income
   is benefit; and depreciation is the recovery of cost over the useful life of a
   capital asset.
Cost is an opportunity foregone in the achievement of value.
Profit is an increase in capital.

As the O.P.E.C. (Organization of Petroleum Exporting Countries) have introduced one crude oil price rise after another, this has increased the amount of
money represented by the crude oil that major oil companies have in storage
(their inventory). Government and some constituencies have argued that this
increase in money represented by inventory represents an "unfair" profit by
oil companies, since they did no extra work to obtain it, but merely were pas-
sive beneficiaries of the "greed" of O.P.E.C.

The economic error in this line of argument follows from the same root cause
as the ecologically erroneous argument that there is no "real" energy shortage.
The root cause of both misperceptions is the failure to recognize that every
year, wells must be drilled deeper to find crude oil, a lower percentage of the exploratory wells will find any oil at all, and when found, the average reserve is
smaller than the average reserve the preceding year. In other words, there is a
genuine, rapidly developing, geologically real scarcity of crude oil (Chapter 4).

Now we turn to an analysis of the economic fallacy. The increase in monetary equivalents of the crude oil in inventory represents an increase in the
medium of exchange, and a store of value, but not an increase in capital: the
crude oil is the capital asset. The increasing amount of money represented by
the crude oil in inventory gives a misleading picture of the real situation of the
oil companies for two reasons. First, the money is dropping in value constantly, because of inflation. Thus, in 1980, if the dollar cost of anything increased by 13 percent, the real purchasing power received by the seller did not
increase at all. But this is by far the lesser of two problems with the so-called
"inventory profits." The major problem is that since there is a rapidly developing scarcity of crude oil, the real dollar cost of finding new crude oil is rising
rapidly (Figure 4.4). That is, the amount of money, corrected for inflation, or
decrease in the value of money required to replace crude oil in inventory is rising rapidly. If "windfall profits" are taxed as if they are real, this ignores the
impact of the increasing cost of getting oil on depreciation. In fact, oil companies should be constantly setting aside larger and larger amounts of money in
a depreciation fund, to compensate them for the constantly increasing future
costs involved in replacing crude oil in inventory that has been processed in refineries. In short, a "crude oil windfall profits tax" is simply catering to a distorted, erroneous public perception of the resource situation, and transferring
to government the money that oil companies will need desperately for exploratory drilling in the years ahead. The "staggering profits" of oil companies

BOX 7.1   (Cont.)

don't seem quite so staggering when we notice that they spent 3.1 billion dollars for drilling in 1973, but 7.5 billion dollars for drilling in 1976, a 145 percent increase over just three years.

The phenomenon we have been describing is the "money illusion," which occurs when people incorrectly decide that "making money" is an important goal of action at a time when money is dropping in value rapidly relative to capital assets, such as crude oil. This economic illusion is a particularly distorted perception of reality when it is coincident with the ecological-geological phenomenon of rapidly depleting cheap fossil resources, such as crude oil.

RELATIVE PRICE OF DIFFERENT RESOURCES, AND SUBSTITUTION BETWEEN RESOURCES

There are many different kinds of resource inputs to any activity; land, energy, labor, and capital are important examples. It seems reasonable to expect that if the prices of these different resources were to change relative to each other, productive activities would gradually respond by substituting the resource becoming cheaper for the resource becoming more expensive. If this process of substitution occurs, the implications could be very far-reaching. For example, if the cost of energy were to drop relative to the cost of labor, not only would this lead to greater mechanization and automation, with resultant increased rates of resource depletion and pollution, but also it would displace labor, thus leading to increased rates of unemployment and crime. Putting the matter differently, we would expect to find that cheaper energy accompanied by more expensive labor leads to increase in labor productivity (by having each laborer use more units of energy, capital, and other resources) but decrease in energy productivity.

This is what we find in the real world. The average effect of increasing wages in manufacturing faster than energy prices was to gradually replace employees by energy. In other words, cheap energy and expensive labor in U.S. manufacturing industries simply induced those industries to become more energy-intensive and more labor-extensive, or to increase the productivity of labor and decrease the productivity of energy. However, the process of change is gradual and occurs with a lag. Consequently the great increase in energy prices that occurred between 1971 and 1981 came as a shock to the system, which has not yet adjusted. However, after the system has had a chance to adjust, it will respond in the direction of more use of labor relative to energy (if energy prices keep rising more rapidly than wages).

If the argument about substitution between resources in response to price is correct, then there should be a number of sets of evidence for this in the real world. For example, if cheap energy coupled with expensive labor does result in a replacement of labor by energy, then we should expect to find a number of patterns in comparisons of different economies. Cheap energy relative to expensive labor should be found together with high rates of energy use per capita, and high unemployment and crime rates; expensive energy relative to average wages should be found along with low unemployment rates and low levels of energy use per capita. In fact, when we examine the data on the most developed economies we find the expected pattern: countries with a high level of energy consumption per capita have high unemployment rates; countries with lower levels of energy consumption per capita have lower unemployment rates. Consequently, cheap resources come at a price: high unemployment rates are an unsuspected part of that price, as are higher crime rates.

ECONOMIC GROWTH, GROWTH IN USE OF RESOURCES, AND POPULATION GROWTH

One of the most contentious issues related to the environment concerns the desirability of "growth." Statements on both sides of the debate may be very strong. For example, pro-growth proponents argue that high and rising levels of energy consumption per capita are necessary for growth in the economy; further, they argue that any decrease in our energy consumption will result in a return to the caves or cruel removal of electrification from the farmers of America. Developers, of course, argue for the value of population growth as an economic stimulus. Such comments are self-serving to some interest group; they do not reflect the facts.

A principal reason for the continued debate about growth is confusion surrounding three different measures of growth: economic growth, growth in resource consumption, and population growth. Many people believe that the three are necessarily linked, so that population growth and growth in resource use is required for economic growth.

In fact, for developed societies such as the United States, the way to increase economic growth per person is to decrease both resource use and the rate of population growth. We can argue this issue either from

first principles, or by examining the data on all countries (10).

We consider first the link between growth in use of resources and economic growth. A fundamental theme was introduced in Figure 5.6: as the resource input to any system is increased, system output first increases to an optimal level, then decreases. The decrease in output at high levels of resource input results from some type of toxic effect, suffocation, or supersaturation of the system by the resource. It is reasonable to expect, therefore, that as we increase the input of energy per person to any nation, this would have a beneficial impact on economic growth up to some optimal level, but beyond this level would have a negative impact. That is what we find when we analyze the data for all countries (Figure 7.5). This graph suggests that the United States would actually increase the rate of growth in the economy, per person, if there was a great decrease in the use of energy per person. The result would not be a lowered standard of living, but a higher standard of living achieved through efficient use of resources, as we find in Sweden, Switzerland, and a number of other countries.

Turning to the link between economic growth and population growth, the discussion on page 148 provides the essential scientific principle. In developed societies, where children are an economic responsibility, periods with high birth rates impose a subsequent strain on the economy, because of educational costs and costs of creating new work places in the labor force. In underdeveloped countries, where children are an economic asset, periods with high birth rates do not impose such a high economic strain. In other words, we would expect high birth rates, which occur at times of high population growth, to be more of an impediment to high rates of economic growth in developed nations than in underdeveloped

FIGURE 7.5

The relationship between energy consumption per capita and the rate of economic growth per capita. The numbers underneath each point represent the number of countries for which the point represents an average. The countries identified are typical of those represented by the point and represent a stage in development. Copyright, United Nations (1973, 1978). Reproduced by permission. Data sources: Statistical Yearbook of the United Nations, *1972, pp. 353–356;* Statistical Yearbook of the United Nations, *1977, pp. 732–735 (Table 190).*

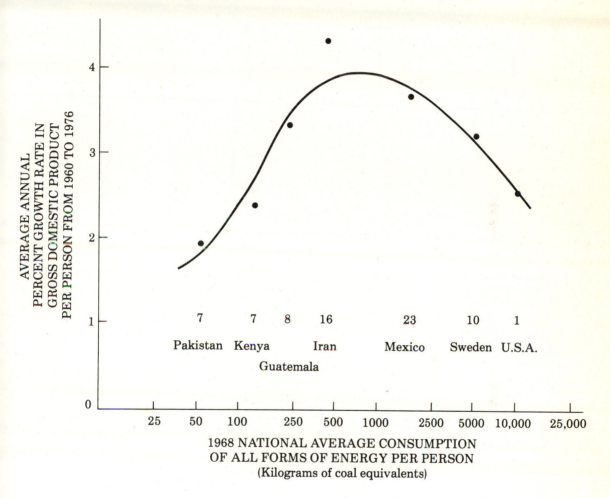

nations. This is the pattern revealed in Figure 7.6. We see that in developed countries, as the rate of population growth rises, economic growth per person decreases. In a less developed country, the impact of population growth rate on rate of economic growth is much less striking.

This is not to say that population has no impact on the economy in less developed countries. Rather, in such countries the prin-

FIGURE 7.6
The relationship between rate of population growth and rate of economic growth for high and low energy consumption countries. The numbers above the points indicate the number of countries for which data were averaged. Copyright, United Nations (1973, 1978). Reproduced by permission. Data sources: Statistical Yearbook of the United Nations, *1972, pp. 80–87;* Statistical Yearbook of the United Nations, *1977, pp. 732–735.*

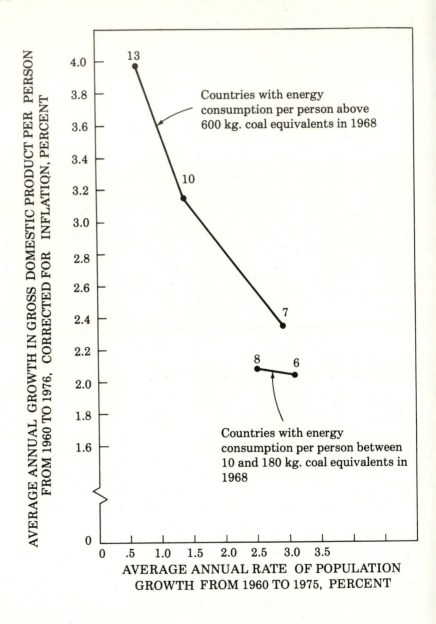

cipal impact on the economy is through population size and density, not growth rate by itself. In the simplest terms, poor countries are poor because there are not enough resources per capita, not because of the economic burden young people put on older people: the older people have virtually nothing to give the younger people.

In short, population growth, growth in resource use, and economic growth do not all increase together. The highest rate of economic growth would be expected in a country with a small population and use of resources per person.

It is not clear that economic growth need ever come to an end. The fuel behind economic growth is increase in efficiency of resource use and increase in the sophistication of information use by a society. As a society develops more and more, the basic character of economic growth will change. Up to recently, the driving force behind economic growth in the world has been use of fossil fuel energy. In the future, the new driving force will increasingly be information processing so as to increase efficiency in the use of other resources. It should come as no surprise, therefore, to discover that this will be a major new area of job opportunities.

CAPITAL REQUIREMENTS, CAPITAL ALLOCATION, AND GROWTH

Recently, Amory Lovins (7) and others have begun to point out how capital availability is related to environmental concerns. Energy technologies that will have very destructive environmental impacts, such as oil and gas from remote areas or deep oceanic wells, or synthetic fuels from strip-mined coal, will cost ten times as much as present energy; nuclear-electric systems will cost about a hundred times as much as present energy sources (when all costs are internalized). In-

creasingly, some planners are concluding that most countries will not be able to afford such technologies and will have to depend, rather, on improved efficiency of energy use and solar energy for long-term survival. This argument raises a more interesting general notion: different countries, just as different families, can see fit to allocate their capital resources in very different ways. When we examine the data, it is not only interesting to discover just how different these capital allocation strategies are, but it is also quite startling to see some of the apparently related effects. For example, among the developed countries there have been very different patterns of capital allocation to different modes of passenger transportation. The United States has allocated a very large amount of capital to the car-freeway mode, so has a low number of passenger-kilometers traveled in trains per car in use. In the other developed countries, particularly Japan, there has been a much larger investment in the train-rail system, so that there is one hundred twenty times the ratio of passenger-kilometers traveled in trains to the number of cars in use to that in the United States. These differences in allocation of capital to trains versus cars of course are associated with very different national philosophies of industrial development and resource use: Japan is more oriented to manufacturing for export and to satisfaction of communal consumer wants as opposed to individual consumer wants. As we might expect, these different national strategies show some relationship with the rate of economic growth. There is a startling relation between high use of trains relative to cars, and high rate of economic growth. This is presumably because train use implies high efficiency in energy use. Environmentally destructive national economic strategies may also produce low economic growth rates. In short, economic policies and environmental policies are related. The causal pathways explaining such a relationship will be discussed in Chapter 11.

National patterns of capital allocation become habit-forming. A nation, like a family, may fall into a pattern of allocating its resources over various activities that are completely irrational; the nation may be merely following, mindlessly, a trend it has followed for years or decades. In recent testimony before Congress, Amory Lovins has presented an argument concerning trends in patterns of allocating capital within the United States that is of the utmost importance. He argued that because the United States has made a commitment to a "hard" energy path, involving large coal- and nuclear-powered electricity generation, rather than a "soft" energy path involving much greater reliance in the future on conservation and solar heating, the energy sector of the U.S. economy would increase its capital demand from one quarter of all new private investment to three quarters. Following such a policy, the United States would not then have enough capital left over to build the things that would use all the energy generated. If that is true, then it would be an amazing instance of mindless capital allocation policies being pursued to the bitter end.

To illustrate how such a policy could get the United States into trouble: Chapters 10 and 11 will present data and theory, respectively, to support the notion that the United States is now critically dependent on production of agricultural products for export, in order to pay for imported crude oil. This assumes that there will always be adequate capital for the farm sector to buy machinery and supplies to maintain production at very high levels. If the energy-production sector of the economy becomes so capital-hungry that there is inadequate capital for the farm sector, then we would have spent money on energy-production so excessively that the

society ran short of liquid fuels to power our vehicles. Further, the farm exports are absolutely necessary to maintenance of a high rate of U.S. economic growth. (Exports are an important source of economic vitality for any nation.)

THE ECONOMIC THEORY OF POLLUTION ABATEMENT

An example of the way in which cheap energy prices lead to bad economic strategies is pollution abatement. There are two different economic theories as to how society can regulate pollution: output-oriented and input-oriented. The output-oriented approach argues that the basic driving force behind pollution is a failure equitably to internalize social costs and benefits: polluters have inadequate motives to cut down on emission of pollutants from their operations because they make money out of the pollution-generating activities, and someone else absorbs the costs.

A typical example occurs when a factory situated beside an orange grove generates air pollutants that decrease production of oranges. The factory has no motive to stop destroying oranges if the owner of the grove absorbs all the costs caused by the pollution. The usual approach to correcting the situation is to invent some institutional mechanism that shifts the costs of destroying oranges onto the polluter. This is an output-oriented approach, because it focuses on the minimization of pollution output from the industrial activity. An input-oriented approach to control of pollution would question why the factory could afford to use its inputs of material and energy so wastefully that a lot of them would be discharged as useless (and destructive) pollutant "residuals." Presence of the pollution evidently means that the price of the inputs to the factory is so low, that the factory is given no motive to use the inputs so efficiently that there will be only negligible residuals to be discharged into the environment. The output- and input-oriented approaches to pollution abatement offer two different economic levers for regulating the operations of the factory: increasing cost of the output from the factory, and the input, respectively.

BUSINESS CYCLES AND THE ENVIRONMENT

Everyone knows that the economy exhibits cycles of "boom" or "bust." Much less well-known is the notion that these cycles are related to the quality of the environment. Recessions or depressions result whenever misallocation of capital in a country results in there being too much of certain goods and services relative to demand. The result is run-down of the excessive inventory which has been "overhanging the market" and depressing prices. But inventory reduction is achieved by sharp decreases in manufacturing rates, and layoff of workers (8). The result is a decrease in national consumer buying power, and a recession, or a depression. A major contributor to the Great Depression of 1929–1934 was excessive home-building in the United States between 1920 and 1928 (9, 11). But clearly, excessive manufacturing rates not only depress the economy subsequently but also create excessive rates of resource depletion and pollution. Thus, economic health and environmental quality are linked. Policies creating a healthy environment over an extended period of time will also create a healthy economy, and vice versa. In general, healthy economies and environments result from pursuing national policies that emphasize

efficiency in the use of materials and energy; unhealthy economies and environments result from trying to use matter and energy as rapidly as possible.

THE SIGNIFICANCE OF THE TIME HORIZON AND THE DISCOUNT RATE

Private individuals, families, corporations, and governments are constantly confronted with alternative opportunities for investing their money. Should we buy more whaling vessels or invest our money in some other business? Should we buy another nuclear reactor, or spend that capital in retrofitting old houses with solar energy? Typically, of course, there are not two options, but many. Economic theory enters into the way the relative attractiveness of the different options is computed, and the choice finally selected will often have large environmental implications. Therefore, the precise way in which investment attractiveness is computed has enormous impact on our lives and the future of the world. At present, the interest rate on borrowed capital is a central ingredient in the formula for computing investment attractiveness. Since different investments will have different time schedules of financial return, there has to be some means of correcting for this when comparing investment options. Therefore, the net return for any future year in the life of an investment is expressed in terms of its present value, using the interest rate as in the simple formula:

$$\begin{gathered} \text{present value of net return,} \\ n \text{ years from now} \\ = \frac{\text{net return } n \text{ years from now}}{(1 + \text{interest rate})^n} \end{gathered}$$

The total present value of any investment is computed by adding up the present value for each year into the future. There are two very important tricks in this computation.

The first is that a dollar of return next year will always be more valuable than a dollar of return further into the future, if there is any interest rate (or "discount" rate) at all. Few people seem to have noticed that if this argument is taken to its extreme, then the optimal strategy is to pick the investment that returns all it is going to, immediately. That point has typically been overlooked because it was rarely technologically feasible or economically desirable to wipe out a resource instantaneously. But as world demand becomes larger and larger relative to the supply of various resources, we run into more and more cases where application of this "discounting to the present value" leads us to wipe out resources remarkably fast, including whales, petroleum, tuna, and anchovies. The argument in essence is that the sooner we recover our capital and get our profit out, the sooner we can invest it somewhere else and go on pyramiding our wealth. At its roots, this is the philosophy of rape, not the philosophy of being a guardian of the planet so that future generations will have something to inherit.

This approach to choosing investment strategies appears even more bankrupt when we explore the matter of the time horizon. A particularly useful example is that of the hydroelectric dam. Clearly, after some length of time, the dam will silt up and be useless. Therefore, one can manipulate the apparent investment attractiveness of the dam, simply by determining the time horizon over which one will compute net economic return. If the dam silts up in 200 years, then it looks like a great investment if we do the computation for a 100-year period; if we extend the time horizon to 500 years, it looks like a rather poor investment. In short, selection of short time horizons makes fast-deteriorating strategies appear more attractive relative to strategies that

will be profitable over the long haul. Clearly, it pays to be very curious and alert whenever anyone is presenting statistics on the relative economic attractiveness of various investment proposals, particularly in the political arena.

THE STEADY STATE ECONOMY

In order to explain this concept, it is necessary to distinguish between three notions: zero economic growth, zero population growth, and zero energy growth. The economy can grow, simply through an increase in the number of people. To eliminate this type of growth from further consideration, we will define economic growth as growth in disposable income per capita in constant dollars. Thus "growth" due to inflation, increase in social security payments, or increased police expenditures to combat rising crime are identified for what they are: nongrowth. Only growth in real (uninflated) dollars, per person, in spendable money, as opposed to taxed money represents growth that improves the quality of life of the individual. Zero economic growth means that growth that benefits the individual has ended. Zero population growth is a separate concept: population growth may have stopped, and may even be negative, long before the economy stops growing. Indeed, a declining population would lead to an increase in economic growth, as I have defined it, perhaps continuing for centuries. Likewise, zero energy growth or negative energy growth is also distinct from zero economic growth: less use of energy would imply higher energy prices relative to the cost of labor, and this would make for a healthier economy. Lower use of energy would imply a massive stimulus to technological innovation to find new sources of energy and make more efficient use of all forms of energy. Both of these activities would be important stimuli to job creation.

In short, future policies that lead to negative population growth and negative energy growth will not produce zero economic growth, but positive economic growth. However, some time in the distant future, long after the human population of the planet has fallen to its long-term equilibrium level of perhaps one-tenth the present population, the economy will stop growing. At that time, humanity will be in a long-term economic steady state, or state of zero economic growth. Later chapters of the book will explain policies for making an orderly transition to that state.

THE ENVIRONMENT AND FUTURE PATTERNS OF ECONOMIC ORGANIZATION

Many people express concern about a slowdown in growth of energy use per capita on the grounds that this will lead to less equitable income distribution in society. They are expressing a variant of the "trickle down" theory of economic growth, that argues that continuous economic growth is necessary, in order to improve the lot of the poor. The real point, of course, is that if growth continues, enough may trickle down to the poor so that they will be less likely to become militant about inequitable distribution of the resources of society. Consequently, an end to economic growth or growth in consumption of energy is to be feared, because then the real roots of poverty would be exposed: inequity. In fact, reduced growth in energy consumption per capita or even a decline in total energy consumption per capita is much more likely to affect the rich differentially rather than the poor. Ivan Illich has analyzed this matter carefully (6). The profligately wasteful consumption of energy in

very rapid and frequent long-distance travel, for example, allows the rich to engage in the activities that allow them to increase the income differential between themselves and the poor. The real impact of energy use on economic equity is exposed when we convert the measure of economic assets from money to time. When we make this transformation, suggested by Illich (6), we discover that the poor spend so much time working to pay for a vehicle or a ticket to travel at very high speeds, that they might as well have walked the distance. The rich, on the other hand, have made their time so valuable, that in some cases it would be an economy for them to travel in something faster than a supersonic transport, in order to make more efficient use of their time. So increasing average national energy consumption per capita does not increase equity. The facts bear out this argument. From 1950 to 1977 in the United States, while total energy consumption per capita increased by 57 percent, the percentage of aggregate U.S. income received by the 40 percent of all families with the lowest incomes only increased from 16.5 percent to 16.8 percent. Evidently, the motive or the knowledge of people who argue for higher energy consumption on the grounds of equity is suspect. Contrariwise, an increase in the equity of income distribution is entirely compatible with a decrease in energy consumption per capita.

SUMMARY

This chapter has argued that price relative to consumer buying power is an important stabilizing force in society. Unfortunately, prices for fossil fuel energy that were unreasonably low relative to the long-term situation of humanity on this planet have prevailed for several decades. Because of these low prices, human populations have risen to very high levels, such that the total buying power of the population is now sufficient to wipe out many resources. From now on, increases in energy consumption per capita will not be economically possible, because of the side-effects caused by substitution of cheap energy for more expensive labor, because of capital limitations, and because of deleterious effects on the rate of economic growth. Also, increased energy consumption per capita has not increased the equity of income distribution.

For all these reasons, before long we shall likely see a decrease in U.S. energy consumption per capita, and a new national pattern of capital allocation, with an increased proportion going to public transportation, less to the car-freeway system, and more going into technological innovation to find new sources of energy and make more efficient use of energy.

SUGGESTIONS FOR INDIVIDUAL AND GROUP PROJECTS

Calculate data for and make new figures to replace those in this chapter, only using different resources. Do calculations to find out how resource prices and consumption per capita affect the equity of income distribution. Compare, for example, the relation between equity of income distribution from country to country with resource consumption per capita from country to country. Analyze data on lobsters and other shellfish to test theories about the relations between supply, demand, and price. Plot, for example, lobster catch and value per pound of lobster against time. Did higher price lead to a higher catch? How do you account for similarities and differences in the resulting graphs?

Explore the cost of travel as affected by the speed of travel, where cost is expressed in hours, rather than dollars. Show how the relationship between this measure of cost and velocity is different, depending on income level. Page 165 in reference (12) shows how to display the information. Include the number of hours that must be worked to pay for the ticket or the vehicle as part of the cost of travel (besides the actual travel time). Work up budgets for travel by walking, bicycle, car, train, and commercial jet transport.

A number of people might work together as a team, to collect data on the comparative cost of pollution abatement from a local factory using an input approach or an output approach. Try to enlist the help of the factory manager, and offer to make the results of the investigation available to him or her.

REFERENCES

1. Clark, C. W., *Mathematical Bioeconomics.* New York: Wiley-Interscience, 1976.
2. Commoner, B., *The Poverty of Power.* New York: Alfred A. Knopf, 1976.
3. Daly, H. E., ed., *Towards a Steady-State Economy.* San Francisco: W. H. Freeman, 1973.
4. Dorfman, R., and N. S. Dorfman, eds., *Economics of the Environment.* New York: W. W. Norton, 1972.
5. Hannon, B., "Energy conservation and the consumer," *Science* 189 (1975), pp. 95–102.
6. Illich, I. D., *Energy and Equity.* New York: Harper and Row, 1974.
7. Lovins, A. B., *Soft Energy Paths.* Cambridge, Mass.: Ballinger, 1977.
8. Mass, N. J., *Economic Cycles: An Analysis of Underlying Causes.* Cambridge, Mass.: Wright-Allen Press, 1975.
9. Temin, P., *Did Monetary Forces Cause the Great Depression?* New York: W. W. Norton, 1976.
10. Watt, K. E. F., *The Titanic Effect.* Sunderland, Mass.: Sinauer Associates, 1974.

11. Watt, K. E. F., "The structure of post-industrial economies," *Human Social Biology,* 1 (1978), pp. 53–70.
12. Watt, K. E. F., L. F. Molloy, G. K. Varshney, D. Weeks, and S. Wirosardjono, *The Unsteady State: Environmental Problems, Growth and Culture.* Honolulu: U. of Hawaii Press, 1977.

8 POLITICS, GOVERNMENT, AND THE ENVIRONMENT

Therefore, one who becomes a prince through the favor of the people ought to keep them friendly, and this he can easily do seeing they only ask not to be oppressed by him.

Nicolò Machiavelli, The Prince, *Chapter IX, 1513.*

MAIN THEMES OF THIS CHAPTER

The previous chapter has shown various deleterious effects of cheap energy. Energy prices in the United States have been kept down as a matter of government policy. Why should government adopt an inappropriate energy policy, and why, more generally, should government be inefficient on environmental matters?

Government policies are at least partly responsive to popular perceptions; government has had inappropriate energy policies because the public has been ill-informed on this issue.

Government is inefficient in dealing with the environment for several reasons. There are conflicts of interest between different constituencies that influence government policy. The vast stream of data flowing to government and the large number of people trying to influence government make it very difficult to communicate with politicians, because of competing demands for their time. Government may not always represent the interests of other interest groups, because government itself has become a powerful interest group with its own unique goals.

HOW THE IDEAL GOVERNMENT WOULD WORK

Chapter 1 pointed out that government involvement is a characteristic of environmental problems. Is this a coincidence, or does government involvement somehow contribute to the severity and persistence of environmental problems? A revealing way of analyzing the performance of government is comparison to an ideal model. Appearance of the problem would result in the public perceiving it, in turn generating debate as to what ought to be done. The debate would be led by the heads of the political parties and by those speaking for various constituencies and interest groups. Gradually, this debate would lead to a clearer popular perception of the nature and seriousness of the problem, its causes, and the indicated strategies for dealing with it. A consensus would develop as to what ought to be done. Either the positions of all the parties to the debate would move together, or in the course of the debate it would become clear to a majority of the electorate that one of the existing positions was preferable.

After the consensus was formed, this view of the situation would be communicated to Congress and the president. On state and local issues, the consensus viewpoint would be communicated to state and local legislators. Congress would then enact appropriate legislation to deal with the environmental problem, either on its own initiative or in response to a proposal from the president. Finally, after the legislation was enacted, the government bureaucracy would administer it effectively.

Now how do events in the real world conform to this ideal view?

PUBLIC PERCEPTIONS OF ENVIRONMENTAL PROBLEMS

In a democracy, a legislative body is only likely to enact legislation in the public interest in response to pressure from an informed and aroused electorate. However, in the United States in the late 1970s the lack of information, the misinformation, and the confusion among the public on environmental issues was startling, to say the least. By 1977, the United States was importing $44 billion worth of crude oil a year. This trade was probably the biggest single influence on the behavior of the economy in the late 1970s. It created an enormous trade deficit; U.S. dollars accumulated in other countries faster than they could be spent; and consequently the value of those dollars dropped with respect to other currencies. (The value of anything decreases when supply exceeds demand.) The result was a sustained weak economy: inflation with recession, or "stagflation." We would have expected everyone to have been aware of such a massive rate of importation of crude oil into the country. Yet during 1977, various polls showed that between 38 and 48 percent of the U.S. public was unaware that the United States was importing any energy at all! Pollsters discovered that the public was very unclear in its thinking about the energy problem. When interviewed, many people said that they wanted a low price for energy, and unlimited gasoline and natural gas, and did not want to use coal because it was "dirty."

Cultural Effects on Information Processing

This ignorance about the problem is more amazing as we learn more about the channels by which most people acquire their information. Surveys conducted for the Federal Energy Administration showed that 45 percent of consumers get their information about energy from the newspapers, and 42 percent get it from television. There is a constant reference to the energy problem in these media. Television networks have presented news analyses and documentaries about the energy issue that were accurate, informative, and reasonably comprehensive. This suggests that the problem lies deeper: there may be real cultural blocks to receiving information about resource shortages. Many writers have provided clues about the origin of such cultural blocks. Spengler, Ortega y Gasset, and Deutsch (3, 11, 14) have all noted that as a nation or civilization matures, the population moves off the farms into nonagricultural occupations and cities. This erodes the constituency that understands the need for wise resource management. Further, Spengler has pointed out that in this civilization, very great importance is attached to personal freedom. There can be no real constituency for conservation of natural resources if this interferes in any way with personal freedom. Higher gasoline prices would certainly lead to conservation of energy, but to most people, higher gasoline prices imply a curtailment of personal freedom, because they do not understand the extent to which the economic system could adjust by more energy-efficient cars, sophisticated mass transit, and the like. If several different constituencies each think that their freedom is of paramount importance, and if different groups have different perceptions of the meaning of freedom, then if there is no willingness to compromise, no consensus perception can develop.

Another cultural block comes about because conservation is only achievable with higher unit prices for resources, and this seems in opposition to the dominant political paradigm of "egalitarian redistributionism," which seeks to transfer wealth from the rich to the poor (but in fact transfers it to certain elements of the middle classes). It is widely assumed that higher unit prices for resources would differentially penalize the poor. Of course, this assumption ignores both the fact that the rich use far more energy than the poor, and the impact that higher energy prices would have on the increased efficiency of cars, houses, appliances, and the like.

An example shows the effectiveness of this cultural blocking out of information about the environment and the need to conserve. After the revolution in Iran, for all of January, February, and March 1979, the media were filled with information about the impact of the Iranian situation on U.S. oil and gasoline stocks. Information freely available in newspapers that could be purchased anywhere in the country showed that U.S. crude oil stocks each week were between 88 and 94 percent of their level the corresponding week the previous year, and that U.S. use of gasoline was running 5 to 6 percent higher each week than in the corresponding week of 1978. Responsible government leaders were seen virtually daily on the evening network television news programs, making statements such as "Western civilization as we have known it since the end of the Second World War could shortly come to an end." Despite all of this, a Gallup Poll published on March 26, 1979, showed that only 40 percent of the public favored a gasoline rationing law that would require the public to drive one fourth less, only 34 percent favored prohibition of gasoline selling on Sunday, and only 43 percent thought that the U.S. energy situation was very serious.

Effects of Advertising

Quite apart from cultural blocks, rational response to the conservation issue may have been systematically eroded over a long period by skillfully designed propaganda and advertising that has habituated people to a high rate of resource consumption. Much of this material has contained extremely sophisticated subliminal messages that have shifted the U.S. public from a production ethic to a consumption ethic. Certainly, advertising campaigns for automobiles and other elements of the consumption society are increasingly based on extremely subtle and refined techniques of persuasion (Chapter 2). To illustrate the amount of advertising on environmental issues by vested interest groups, Common Cause, a citizens' organization for improvement of the political and governmental systems, found that between January 1 and May 31, 1977, industry and trade groups placed energy advocacy ads costing $1,131,588 in just four major newspapers (*Washington Post, New York Times, Wall Street Journal,* and *Washington Star*). To counteract vast expenditures for information dissemination on behalf of special interests, very little is spent on behalf of the public interest. Why would anyone be motivated to pay for such public interest advertising? A few people would be carrying the costs of improving the lot of everyone. This is a variant of the tragedy of the commons, a concept popularized by Garrett Hardin (6). No one has a motive to take care of that which belongs to everyone jointly and to which no one has sole ownership rights.

While the difficulty in educating the public about immediate environmental problems is very great, the difficulty in communicating more complex and long-range environmental problems is vastly greater. Authoritative books on supply-demand trends for energy and minerals, for example, may be extremely long and complex, because they must analyze the situation separately for each country to be credible to experts. Further, estimates of reserves still in the ground may be based on highly technical geological information, subjected to so-

phisticated computer analysis techniques. Such books and documents are often costly and are therefore relatively inaccessible.

In short, a democracy can be expected to work well when it is confronted by relatively simple, easy-to-understand problems, on which information is readily available and well-circulated. However, now humanity is faced with new problems of a much more complex nature than ever before, on which complete and accurate information may be very hard to get, and the public is not well aware of the simple information that is widely available. Clearly, the democratic system is being confronted with a novel kind of situation, not contemplated by the founders of the system.

POTENTIAL BLOCKS TO DEVELOPMENT OF A CONSENSUS

Quite apart from the information problem, there may be difficulties in forming an effective political consensus because several constituencies may each have a view of the world which is produced by ideology, not reality.

To illustrate, some religious organizations are opposed to birth control. However, if parents do not consciously practice birth control, the world population would ultimately become so large relative to the capacity of the planet to support life, that living standards for all people would sink to a very low level. It is difficult to see, therefore, how unlimited procreation would further the goals of humanitarianism, which surely must be a goal of religious groups.

Very large multinational corporations typically have continued economic growth as a stated or implied goal. The problem is that this growth would ultimately so deplete the world of resources that these corporations would no longer have the very input (readily accessible resources) that has made possible their growth to this point. They must shift their goals, either to base growth in profits on provision of services rather than goods, or to maintain stability, rather than grow. The goals of multinational corporations are important, because they and their employees are such large and powerful constituencies.

In fact, multinational corporations are already reaching the point at which economic growth of the corporation is being slowed because the corporate strategy is based on out-of-date ideology, rather than wise, realistic use of resources. Oil companies are an example of a business that in many geological areas has reached the law of diminishing returns, and further exploitation is no longer profitable. They could make better use of their capital assets by shifting to new ways of obtaining energy. Alexander Stuart has pointed out that offshore oil and gas drilling by industry has been remarkably futile. Over a twenty-four-year period, industry paid the U.S. government $26.5 billion in bonuses, royalties, and leases for the right to drill offshore. In exchange for this investment, the industry did not even recover that cost, let alone exploration or development costs, or profit (15). Industry has learned from this experience, and more recently has bid far lower amounts for lease rights.

Liberal politicians and their constituencies are an extremely powerful political force. However, a view of many in this constituency is that the world in general and the oceans in particular are inexhaustible sources of resources. Therefore, it is believed, no matter how much the national or world population grows, all people should be guaranteed a minimum wage that keeps rising along with resource costs. Unfortunately, this view guarantees that the world's resources will be quickly depleted, because it does nothing to inhibit either population size or resource consumption per capita.

The "technological optimists" are a constituency united by two sets of beliefs. The first is that humanity does not face any limits to growth, because human ingenuity in the form of modern technology can surmount any problem. The second is that there is no limit to the availability of resources, because "proved reserves" will increase indefinitely, as the price for resources goes up. This belief holds that if you double the price of a resource, you can afford to exploit lower-grade ores or more inaccessible oil, gas, or coal deposits, so that these become added to "reserve" totals. This belief ignores the net energy problem. Ultimately a point is reached at which the ore grade is so low or the oil, gas, or coal so inaccessible that the energy cost of getting the resource is in excess of the worth of the resource when it is obtained and refined.

Curiously, Marxists share with many capitalists and the "technological optimists" the notion that resources are limitless and the ingenuity of humanity will always triumph, although by "humanity" Marxists mean "the state."

The consumer movement believes that you improve the relative economic position of consumers by pushing down energy prices. The problem with this view, as we shall see in Chapters 10 and 11, is that it drives up the prices for everything else, and hence is anticonsumer.

Utilities pushing for nuclear power may be financially destroyed by it because of the low net energy (Chapter 4).

The labor movement believes that you improve the prosperity of the working class by increasing wages. In fact, you improve the lot of working people by increasing their buying power, which may often be impaired by excessive increases in wages. Too rapid wage increases only encourage all organizations to displace labor by automation and mechanization. This increases the unemployment rate, so that the laborers still employed must pay higher taxes to pay for unemployment compensation. But this only exacerbates the increased tax rate caused by moving into a higher income bracket. Thus, the beneficial impact of higher wages on buying power turns out to be totally illusory on closer inspection. This line of argument is not a theory, but a description of recent American experience. To illustrate, from 1972 to 1978, for an average worker in private non-agricultural industries with three dependents, gross weekly earnings in current dollars increased from $121.10 to $176.00 (45 percent). During the same period, income in constant (1967) dollars corrected for social security payments and federal income taxes declined from $96.6 to $93.0 (4 percent). If the costs of state and local taxes, and insurance, all caused by increased population, were included in the calculation of net buying power, the decline would be much greater. Clearly, the labor movement has a self-defeating goal in pushing for higher and higher gross wages, just as management can defeat itself with higher prices that suppress demand. The lot of the working classes would be better if they and every other constituency banded together to attain the political goal of higher buying power, not higher gross wages.

Sheepranchers are a constituency with a self-defeating goal, pushing for the extermination of the coyote. In the course of attaining this goal, very large numbers of other species of avian and mammalian predators of small herbivores would be exterminated. The result would be release of controls on field mice, hares, grasshoppers, and other herbivores that compete with sheep for range vegetation. Sheep would very soon be outcompeted by these species, which can exploit very close-cropped plants and low grade food.

In short, many political constituencies actively pursue goals that are based on ideology or limited short-term self-interest, rather than understanding.

Stalemated Conflicts of Interest

Formation of a consensus to push for useful political goals is blocked because constituencies may be in conflict with other constituencies, thus producing a stalemate in which no constituency wins (16).

One example concerns the issue of growth. One constituency argues that indefinitely continued growth in the world economy and in the world average per capita rate of resource consumption is necessary in order to raise the living standards of the poor of the world. Another constituency argues that if such growth were to continue, the world's resources would be depleted before the poor of the world could become rich. This constituency argues that the way to improve the lot of the poor is not by further growth, but by transfer of assets from rich countries and individuals to poor countries and individuals. A problem with this issue is the scale of world total resource consumption implied: if the resource consumption rates of the rest of the world were to be brought level with those in the United States, then all the resources of the world would be used up surprisingly rapidly. Indeed, because of the extremely high level of U.S. use of resources, we are in fact cutting off any opportunity for most of the rest of the people in the world ever to live as we have lived. To illustrate, in 1977, the average American used about 25 barrels of crude oil. As of 1977, there were about 1668 billion barrels of crude oil left in the world to be produced. If 5 billion people used crude oil at the same rate as people in the United States, the world supply would last thirteen years.

The numbers of all other resources yield the same message: people in this country are using resources at a per capita rate that would simply not be sustainable for more than a few years if the entire world were to share these use rates. In addition, the citizens of the United States, used to a higher living standard, will face a more severe collapse in their life styles by continued overuse of resources, than if the citizenry were to curtail their use and prolong the life of the resources.

As we shall see in subsequent chapters, conflicts between constituencies often occur because neither side has complete or accurate information, or a full understanding of the implications of their position. If a well-informed arbitrating or negotiating group can bring the necessary information and understanding to each constituency party to a conflict, the stalemate can often be resolved.

Deutsch has pointed out the critical balance between mobilization of interest groups (development of awareness of their unique rights and needs), and their integration into a national community of interest groups (3). Federal government cannot afford to antagonize one or more constituencies too much, or gradually the centrifugal force of mobilization will exceed the centripetal force of integration, and the nation will fly apart, as in a revolution.

The formation of a consensus may be blocked because the geographical boundaries of a jurisdiction do not coincide with the extent of a problem. The result is that the constituency that has a motive to deal with a problem may live elsewhere than the constituency that has the political power to deal with it. The root problem in such cases is that government is inappropriately organized to deal with real-world problems. An important example is large metropolitan regions, wherein power is divided between several counties, and a very large number of municipalities or towns. Such division of power is too fragmented to deal with many air or water pollution problems or the attainment of regional energy conservation through regional public transportation systems. The appropriate constituency to solve such problems would be regionally based, rather than a large and disorganized set of small constituencies representing cities and towns. The difficulties are illustrated by the Los Angeles area. Here, the prevailing winds (from the west) blow the air pollution from Los Angeles to the east, where it affects Riverside and San Bernardino counties. However, these counties are powerless to deal with the problem, because it originates in Los Angeles County.

An analogous problem arises in the case of water pollution. The boundary line between California and Nevada divides Lake Tahoe. Consequently management of the lake and the surrounding basin is a jurisdictional nightmare: seventy different agencies are involved. The Great Lakes are polluted by Canada and the United States, the Baltic is polluted by eight countries, and the Mediterranean by a large group of countries. In any of these cases, effective remedial action is only possible through some type of intergovernmental organization that matches an appropriately sized and spatially distributed constituency to the size and distribution of the problem (4). An example is a United Nations commission working with several nations to end pollution in the Mediterranean.

The fisheries and whale stocks of the open ocean beyond the 200-mile jurisdiction of nation states are an international concern and necessitate an international planning and management commission or organization.

One way of forming effective constituencies with a consensus on environmental problems would be through a massive program to educate the electorate. In theory, the best agency to undertake such a task would be the executive branch of government in any country, such as the president in the United States. But could the president actually undertake the task of forming a consensus to deal with an environmental problem? Clearly no head of state in this country or elsewhere has ever made a major, sustained effort at public education on this theme. Why not? To achieve the presidency requires a staggering organizational effort and financial outlay (9). A candidate cannot muster the support for an activity on the required scale unless he or she has a good chance of winning. But, the chance of winning drops if the candidate gambles. Trying to educate the electorate on complex, unpleasant environmental truths would definitely constitute a gamble, even for a candidate who began the effort with polls showing 75 percent popular support. The old adage that people dislike the bearer of bad news is a correct perception. Therefore, few presidents or presidential candidates, or indeed other politicians have dared to tell the public the truth about resource depletion, pollution, or other environmental problems in any detail or on a sustained basis. Indeed, most politicians have every reason to be vague, and to become skilled at appearing to be saying something meaningful, when in fact they are saying nothing with any semantic content at all.

COMMUNICATION WITH PUBLIC OFFICIALS

It is enormously difficult to communicate a lengthy, complex message to most elected officials. The pressure on their time is incredible. While the public demands the right to communicate by means of personal letters or telegrams with elected officials, they would never approve the necessary budget for adequate machinery to analyze such messages. The president gets about 30,000 letters a week, and a senator may receive 20,000 letters on a single issue. Consequently, most of the important communication to politicians is on a face-to-face basis from highly paid and lavishly budgeted lobbyists who can afford to make a full-time chore out of finding a politician and making sure he or she listens to them, no matter how long they have to wait for an appointment. Unfortunately, there is far more money available for lobbying on behalf of special interests than for lobbying on behalf of the general public (20). However, the degree of organization can substitute, to some extent, for a huge budget. A small minority of dedicated people can have a large impact on government if sufficiently well-organized.

A consensus can be communicated to Congress through presentation before Congressional committees. Unfortunately, the sheer chaos often surrounding this activity has to be seen to be believed. For example, in testifying before a committee of fourteen, on highly technical issues for which testimony by scientific witnesses requires two or more days, there would rarely be more than five of the fourteen committee members present at once, and often only one or two members are present. The problem is that the particular members present change from time to time, so that the members hearing testimony late on the second day are not those who heard it early on the first day. This is much like trying to present a novel or play to a constantly changing audience, none of whom have any knowledge of the parts that came before or will come after they leave.

Given that legislators may not have the time to attain technical competence in areas in which they make multimillion or multibillion dollar decisions, what are the implications? They, like appointed officials, may make decisions on the basis of preconceptions based more on ideology than fact, on political pressure from interest groups or as a consequence of their character (1). But interest groups may themselves be uninformed or biased for other reasons (1). If legislators and heads of the executive branches of government do not have an objective technical knowledge of highly technical fields, the consequences may radiate downwards into the entire organizations that they lead. The result may be inappropriate decisions, or failure to make any decisions at all for fear of being wrong or antagonizing one or more constituencies.

Two Legislative Case Studies

Two most interesting case studies bring out the problems of communicating with legislators. One concerns the solar energy industry in California. In the interests of getting new legislation and tax advantages for customers to benefit this new industry, leaders of the industry testified up to forty times a year before California State legislative committees at their own expense. The result was counterproductive: legislation and tax incentives to install solar energy systems in houses that the industry labelled as "disasters." Here, in the name of promoting an environmentally useful new industry, government actually impeded it. However, what industry called a disaster might be a long-range benefit to them.

To indicate that this was not an isolated instance, a revealing book by William Simon, Secretary of the Treasury under Presidents Nixon and Ford and head of the Federal Energy Office is most instructive (13). Simon testified before congressional committees about 400 times on the economy, energy, and their interrelationships, so if he alone had testified on these subjects Congress would have little excuse for ignorance about them. Of course, a large number of other experts on these themes also testified a great many times. In spite of this, at the time this book was written, Congress had still not taken any meaningful action on the energy issue. They had indeed passed a number of highly complex and lengthy pieces of energy legislation, but these were both ineffective and incomprehensible.

Former Secretary Simon believes that the real roots of the energy problem are in the failure of Congress to deregulate the price of energy, which would stimulate both conservation and the development of new sources of energy; further, he notes that energy production in the U.S. is strangled by fifty-five federal and hundreds of state and local regulatory agencies. Thus we see that politicians themselves have cultural blocks that make it virtually impossible to communicate with them.

THE DESIGN AND ENACTMENT OF ENVIRONMENTAL LEGISLATION

There has been some effort in the last few years to develop a comprehensive systems analysis capability in government by combining the resources of several departments, but the effort has not yet succeeded. The reason is that authority and responsibility for national problems is thoroughly fragmented among departments and sections of departments (a contention documented in the White House "Global 2000" study). When an outside consultant points out how a particular government department could better deal with a problem by cooperating with one or more other departments, there is terrific resistance. This involves abdication of "territorial rights," which departments do not want to do, even in the interests of the country. Consequently, government departments and agencies often compete rather than cooperate, so each department or agency is only able to look at a part of a larger problem, rather than the whole problem. The point of view and method of Chapter 11 in this book (also found in many other books) is simply not available to government, amazingly. While there have been vigorous and well-thought-out schemes for an overview in government (17), von Mises explained in 1944, that government could tolerate no such overview because it would reveal the deleterious role of government itself (18).

Not only is government not organized to take the overview and the long view, but it dare not, even if it were so organized. The reason stems from the shortness of terms in office. The politician who wishes to be re-elected cannot afford to support policies that require the electorate to make a short-term sacrifice in the interests of a compensatory long-term gain. To illustrate, it would be useful over the long term to make the short-term sacrifice of increased energy prices, in order to stimulate energy conservation and the development of new sources of energy, such as solar energy. It is clear from Chapter 4 that it is necessary for society to develop a new energy source and start building up the national population of energy generating systems of a new type long before they are critically necessary, because of the net energy problem. But politicians would be defeated at the polls if they voted for deregulation of energy prices to attain the clearly necessary result. While small, well-informed groups understand what needs to be done, it has been understood since Machiavelli that political power is based on the masses (8). We are approaching a novel situation for humanity in which continued social survival may depend on preparing long in advance for problems that might not become disastrous for forty years (Chapter 4 showed it could take that long to get new energy-generating systems in place). We have a mismatch in the design of our political system, between the short time frame forced on the politician, and the long time span required for planning to survive. The political system as presently designed

and functioning is based on the assumption that we could run out of one type of energy, then immediately, with almost no notice, get another type of energy generating system in place to replace it.

Government may err in the design of legislation, because it operates on the basis of some ideology that is totally or partially at odds with the facts. For example, government may believe that it is immoral to promote conservation of natural resources, on the grounds that high and rising per capita rates of resource consumption are a prerequisite to improving income distribution within the population. Indeed, designing legislation based on this perception may be seen by politicians as a particularly effective way of gaining the support of low-income constituencies. To determine if the perception is realistic, we compare energy consumption per capita across countries, and the percentage of national income received by the poorest 20 percent of the population as a proportion of the same percentage received by the richest 5 percent of the population. This relation is plotted in Figure 8.1. The straight line was fitted statistically to the data points. The large amount of scatter about the line reflects that only 14 percent of the country-to-country difference in income distribution is accounted for by energy consumption per capita. The graph suggests why energy consumption has such a weak effect on income distribution: Venezuela and Romania, for example, have very similar levels of energy consumption per capita, yet income distribution is very even in Romania, and very uneven in Venezuela. The political system far outweighs the impact of resource consumption on income distribution. Thus a reasonable inference is that there are far better ways of improving income distribution than by increasing the rate of resource consumption. Indeed, we achieve higher rates of resource consumption per capita by keeping resource costs down relative to wages, but that in turn pro-

FIGURE 8.1

The relation between per capita energy consumption and the equitability of income distribution in a country. Data on income distribution from World Bank, World Tables 1976 *(Baltimore and London: Johns Hopkins University Press, 1976);* Statistical Yearbook of the United Nations, *1972, pp. 353–356. Copyright, United Nations (1973). Reproduced by permission.*

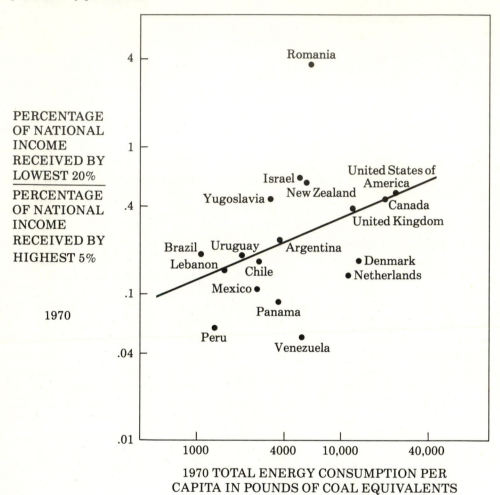

PERCENTAGE OF NATIONAL INCOME RECEIVED BY LOWEST 20%

PERCENTAGE OF NATIONAL INCOME RECEIVED BY HIGHEST 5%

1970

1970 TOTAL ENERGY CONSUMPTION PER CAPITA IN POUNDS OF COAL EQUIVALENTS

motes unemployment, which decreases the equitability of income distribution.

While government may be regarded as a regulatory agency, in some cases it may operate as a destabilizing social force in the environmental area. The misperception about government probably arises because people in any organization tend to see that organization as being socially useful and effective. Therefore, they would be biased in favor of perceiving government as the logical source for a solution of environmental problems. Could we realistically assume that government would decide that a nongovernmental solution was preferable? No organization operates with vigor to put itself out of business. Therefore it is reasonable to assume that government would not only be unconsciously biased to see itself as the solution to problems, but would also be unconsciously biased to seek solutions that tend to make the problem persist, so that government always has lots of work for its staff. In effect, we are questioning the deeper motivations of people interested in power.

Legislation that Works Against the Public Interest

This line of argument, of course, is becoming very common (10). It has not passed unnoticed that government has seen, in the energy and environmental crises, the opportunity to create bureaucracies on a scale and with a cost never before seen. The Department of Energy spent $7.8 billion in 1978. To put this amount of money in perspective, only $7.5 billion was spent drilling for oil and gas in the United States in 1976. Now what does the United States get for the $7.8 billion spent on the Department of Energy? A vigorous program of development of new energy sources? No; that must come from the private sector. A vigorous program of conservation? No; that would be politically unacceptable. Amazingly, we come to wonder if government really is the appropriate place to look for solutions to environmental problems.

Once we perceive the significance of government itself being an interest group of great size and power, with a large and growing control over gross national product, some surprising insights are revealed. Suppose, for example, that the government puts its own short-term interest ahead of the long-term interest of the nation, what type of phenomena would that produce? Figure 8.2 depicts one curious possibility: by trying to win favor with the electorate, so as to

stay in power, elected officials keep the retail price of energy down. This, in turn, conceals from the public that the real cost of extracting energy is rising sharply, so that the public has no direct evidence of an energy shortage. Therefore, there is no constituency to raise retail energy prices so as to promote conservation, and the search for new energy sources. This erodes the constituency of anyone inside or outside government trying to justify higher energy prices (deregulation). Consequently, the public is reinforced in its belief that anyone arguing for low, or lowered retail energy prices was acting in the best interests of the public. In short, public perception of the energy situation and the government posture on energy have become part of a positive feedback loop, each reinforcing the other, and spinning out of control.

This lack of control in turn has interesting consequences. The top panel of Figure 8.3 indicates the likely retail price of regular gasoline in uninflated (1967) cents each year since 1970, in the absence of attempts by the government to regulate the price of energy. This trend in increasing prices would have given a clear signal to automobile manufacturers to produce more energy-efficient cars, for example. The bottom panel shows the national average trend that in fact occurred. Clearly, such a trend sends out very confusing signals to the market place. Viewed this way, it seems plausible that the bewildering trend in retail energy prices, engineered by government regulation, had a great deal to do with the confusion in the mind of the public as to whether there is or is not an energy shortage.

Another problem in the design of energy legislation relates to the way in which different variables get coupled in legislation. Sometimes new legislation links items that should not be linked, thus creating a blunt, ineffective policy lever for dealing with either problem. Thus, energy legislation

FIGURE 8.2

Postulated circular causal pathway connecting government behavior on retail energy prices, with public perceptions of the energy situation. This constitutes an uncontrolled, positive feedback loop, in which each element tends to increase the others.

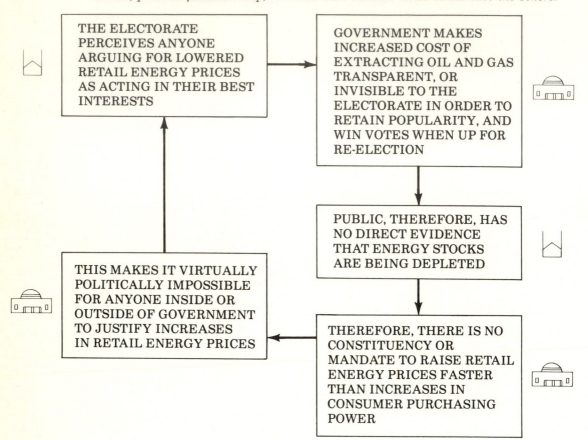

may be conceived as a means of attaining conservation, promoting development of new energy sources and achieving equitable income distribution by ensuring that the poor do not pay too much for energy. This is like trying to design a jet plane that swims well. The simplest, most efficient solution is to avoid use of legislation to solve either problem.

An opposite type of error in the design of legislation is failure to link variables that must be linked if the legislation is to be effective. Thus, since the consumption of energy depends on the retail energy price rela-

tive to consumer average net spendable earnings, energy prices and consumer earnings must both be specified in any legislation that purports to stimulate conservation. It makes no sense to increase the price of energy 5 percent a year in the interests of conservation, if consumer purchasing power (average net spendable earnings) is simultaneously allowed to increase 10 percent a year. This situation leads to constant increase in per capita use of energy, all in the name of energy conservation. The complexity required in good energy legislation, and the political difficulty of producing such

FIGURE 8.3

Trends in constant-dollar prices for one gallon of regular grade gasoline in the United States. The top panel suggests the national average price trend that would have occurred in the absence of government efforts to regulate energy prices. The bottom panel is the price trend that actually occurred (national average).

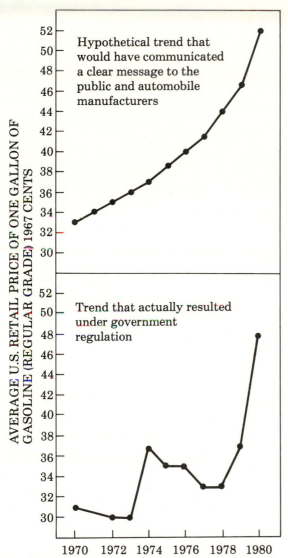

Hypothetical trend that would have communicated a clear message to the public and automobile manufacturers

Trend that actually resulted under government regulation

AVERAGE U.S. RETAIL PRICE OF ONE GALLON OF GASOLINE (REGULAR GRADE) 1967 CENTS

market place, which would presumably be much less baffling to interpret than the fruits of regulation by government.

THE ADMINISTRATION OF LEGISLATION BY BUREAUCRACIES

One of the most important points to be made about government bureaucracies is that they increasingly have the political power to thwart the will of other constituencies, even the executive and legislative branches of government. Further, a bureaucracy has goals different than those of any other constituency in a country (10, 18). An example is the energy bureaucracy in the federal government, a large number of whose members have a strong bias in favor of atomic energy, because so many of them began their careers in the Atomic Energy Commission. It is no secret, for example, that the federal government has spent far less money on solar energy development than on nuclear power development. For each bureaucrat, the way to a quieter life is to keep his or her own bureaucracy growing (10, 18). The systemic consequences of this phenomenon are revealed when we consider the growth in the number of people working for state, federal, and local governments, expressed as a percentage of the entire U.S. labor force (from 10 percent in 1950 to 16 percent in 1975). The significance of this vast growth in government staff, and the associated budget, is that each 1 percent increase in relative tax burden depresses income growth of a state by .5 percent (5). Why has this happened?

There are various means by which a society can seek to regulate itself. Two common methods are the price mechanism and government regulation. Within the last few years, the United States has evolved in the direction of dealing with environmental problems through government regulation rather than the price mechanizm. The result

without angering constituencies, suggest that no energy legislation at all might be the best solution. This would leave the energy sector of the economy to the free play of the

has been the development of vast bureaucracies that deal with environmental impact statements, energy regulations, the monitoring of air and water pollution, and so on.

Managing Bureaucracies

We need to analyze what goes on in these bureaucracies. Can they be managed? What are their real goals? And how do they respond to perceptions of the nature of environmental problems?

Gigantic bureaucracies cannot be managed. There is no way that the president of the United States and the two hundred senior government staff members whom he appoints can impose a philosophy, a management style, a set of goals, or working methods on a federal government staff of three million people. Messages from the president downward through the bureaucracy are subject to "interpretation" or modification on the way down through administrative levels, and messages from the working level upward to the president may be modified beyond recognition by the time they reach the president (2). In effect, what the president is told will be determined by what senior bureaucrats want him to hear, and what the working level hears about the president's intentions will be determined by what several layers of bosses want them to hear. Thus, the bureaucracy is largely self-directed.

Decision-making in Bureaucracies

That being the case, it is of great interest to determine what the real goals of such an administrative structure might be (10, 18). Two important characteristics of bureaucracies determine the behavior of decisionmakers within them. First, how large are the rewards for outstanding performance relative to the punishment for poor performance? If an organization has relatively low rewards and relatively large punishments, executives will not take risks. Few managers will be daring, and innovation will be stifled. On the other hand, where there is extremely rapid upward promotion for excellent performance, and minimal punishment for failure, executives will be very daring, and the entire organization will be highly innovative. Thus, we see that the reward and punishment weighting can be used as a lever for determining the characteristics of an organization. Second, do executives get paid and promoted on the basis of the quality of their work, and the speed with which they solve problems, or rather on the basis of the size of the staffs that work for them? If pay and promotion are determined by speedy solution of problems, then problems will tend to be solved more speedily. If, rather, pay and promotion are on the basis of staff size, then problems, strangely, will not be solved, but will persist, and indeed get larger, so that larger and larger staffs are required to "solve" them. Clearly, by manipulating the criteria for paying and promoting government executives, we can have an effect on the probability of solution of environmental problems.

Given this background, suppose we consider the decision-making behavior of a government executive responding to perceptions concerning an environmental problem. An interesting example concerns the decision to raise the price of energy. Suppose the government awards a grant or contract to a consulting organization outside the government to study energy policy. Suppose that organization produces a report which states (a) that the price of energy should increase, (b) that the government should take major steps to discourage the use of cars and encourage the use of public transportation, and (c) that the government should provide major stimulus to a new industry to develop solar energy for heating and cooling houses and heating water. What are the options available to the government bureaucrat who receives such a report? There are at least four (19).

If the bureaucrat accepts the report results and acts on them right away, there will be a major political risk, because all these policies will be unattractive over the short term. On the other hand, if the executive does not act on the report immediately, and subsequently it turns out that the report was correct, then if the electorate knows the executive saw the report, he or she is politically vulnerable later. In short, the executive is damned now through taking action, but damned later if he or she does not. This suggests the third option. If a research activity outside the government but funded by government grants or contracts is producing policy recommendations that are politically unpleasant no matter what is done, an indicated option is to stop awarding grants or contracts to the organization producing that material. The fourth option, and the one chosen by sophisticated executives, gives one the best of all possible worlds. The executive closes down the research activity outside the government, but starts one up inside, under his or her personal control. The staff in that activity is made to conduct research in such a way that in effect they work backwards from the politically most acceptable answer, over the short term, to the research that will yield that answer. Now the executive can say that he or she has the benefit of the most sophisticated modern research techniques, but does not have to face the possibility of receiving politically unacceptable findings from that activity. This suggests that it is in the public interest to have completely uncontrolled research conducted in the private sector to serve as a check on the research done in the public sector (government). With the advent of extraordinarily cheap new computers, this research can now be done at very modest cost.

It is important to note that the great growth of the government bureaucracy is just one of the many reflections of environmental problems. As we shall see in Chapter 11, excessive pollution, resource depletion, unemployment, crime, government bureaucracy to deal with all these problems, taxation, and inflation all have certain common origins in the relative prices for various resources, including labor.

SUMMARY

This chapter has shown that one of the origins of environmental problems lies in the nature of our style of government. This system works fine in a society with relatively simple, clearly bounded problems. However, where a problem is very large, fuzzily bounded, complex, contains many different kinds of components and hierarchical levels, and is systemic in character, it defies solution by our existing political and governmental systems and institutions. Significant modification of those institutions is required, so that they constitute a more appropriate match to the nature of the problems.

Also, culture affects government, and then the behavior of government reinforces cultural perceptions of environmental matters, such as the availability of energy. Government policy, as determined by culture, affects retail prices, and prices, in turn, affect resource use and pollution. Using the code employed earlier in this book, we have:

| Culture | Government | Prices | Resource use | The physical environment (pollution) |

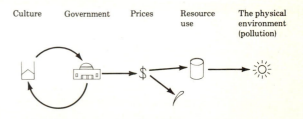

SUGGESTIONS FOR INDIVIDUAL AND GROUP PROJECTS

Select an environmental problem that has received considerable attention from local, state, or federal government, and analyze the way in which it has been dealt with against a background of the notions presented in this chapter.

Split up into teams representing the different political actors in an environmental controversy. Act out the behavior of each of the parties, trying to understand their motivations, and act out their decision-making as realistically as possible. One of the best such controversies concerns the sheeprancher-conservationist controversy over coyotes.

Invent a design for an organization to send letters and telegrams to federal legislators urging them to vote for effective environmental legislation. Invent a way to make the most rapid, efficient use of telephones so you can mobilize support rapidly.

REFERENCES

1. Barber, J. D., *The Presidential Character*. Englewood Cliffs, N.J.: Prentice-Hall, 1972.
2. Beer, S., *Platform for Change*. London: Wiley, 1975.
3. Deutsch, K. W., *Nationalism and Its Alternatives*. New York: Knopf, 1969.
4. Falk, R. A., *A Study of Future Worlds*. New York: The Free Press, 1975.
5. Genetski, R. J., and Y. D. Chin, "Study on the effect of tax burdens on economic growth rates of states for the Harris Bank of Chicago," as summarized in the *Wall Street Journal*, Sept. 21, 1979, p. 16.
6. Hardin, G., and J. Baden, eds., *Managing the Commons*. San Francisco: W. H. Freeman, 1977.
7. Laszlo, E., ed., *Goals for Mankind*. New York: E. P. Dutton, 1977.
8. Machiavelli, N., *The Prince*. Chicago: Encyclopaedia Britannica (Great Books of the Western World), 1952. (First published in 1513.)
9. McGinnis, J., *The Selling of the President 1968*. New York: Trident Press, 1969.
10. Macrae, N., "The brusque recessional," *The Economist* (London), December 23, 1978, pp. 45–62.
11. Ortega y Gasset, J., *The Revolt of the Masses*. New York: W. W. Norton, 1932.
12. Pirages, D. G., and P. R. Ehrlich, *Ark II. Social Responses to Environmental Imperatives*. San Francisco: W. H. Freeman, 1974.
13. Simon, W. E., *A Time for Truth*. New York: Reader's Digest Press, 1978.
14. Spengler, O., *The Decline of the West*, vol. I and II. New York: Knopf, 1926 and 1928.
15. Stuart, A., "That very interesting dance in the Baltimore Canyon," *Fortune*, Sept. 11, 1978, pp. 66–70.
16. Thurow, L., *The Zero-Sum Society*. New York: Basic Books, 1980.
17. Tugwell, R. G., *A Model Constitution for a United Republics of America*. Palo Alto, Calif.: James E. Freel, 1970.
18. von Mises, L., *Bureaucracy*. New Haven, Conn.: Yale University Press, 1944.
19. Watt, K. E. F., "Why won't anyone believe us?" *Simulation*, 28 (1977), pp. 1–3.
20. Wertheimer, F., ed., *How Money Talks in Congress*. Washington, D.C.: Common Cause, 1979.

9 CULTURE AS THE ROOT CAUSE OF ENVIRONMENTAL PROBLEMS

If the Early period is characterized by the birth of the City out of the country, and the Late by the battle between city and country, the period of Civilization is that of the victory of city over country, whereby it frees itself from the grip of the ground, but to its own ultimate ruin.

Oswald Spengler, Perspectives of World History, *Chapter IV, 1928.*

MAIN THEMES OF THIS CHAPTER

Culture exerts subtle but powerful and all-pervasive influences on all beliefs concerning the environment. Thus we have a quite different set of beliefs than would have resulted from observation and logic alone. According to the prominent cultural historian Oswald Spengler, part of our present belief system results from the rather late stage we are at in the cycle of growth and decline of this civilization; other parts are unique to this particular civilization. Two clusters of beliefs are of primary importance as origins of our attitudes toward the environment: de-

nial of the idea that there are limits to resources and the notion that we must master nature, rather than working in harmony with it.

However, it appears that we are in the midst of a cultural revolution. As the innovative potential of our old cultural belief system is more completely exploited, it becomes sterile and senile. But a new belief system is gaining momentum worldwide. Unlike the old system, it is holistic, not dualistic; has a systemic, not fragmented world view; and is interested in tapping nature's energy flows, rather than in finding fossil fuel energy stocks.

The old culture has driven us to keep increasing energy use, whereas nature and the new culture systems use energy as efficiently as possible.

THE ROLE OF CULTURE IN THE FORMULATION OF BELIEF SYSTEMS

In the previous chapter we saw that the constituency for politicians to vote rationally on environmental issues is small, because many people hold inaccurate beliefs about the state of the environment. Where do these inaccurate beliefs come from?

Three sets of factors operate to produce the beliefs held by a person. One component of the belief-producing system is purely rational: the higher levels of the brain-mind system (the neocortex) attempt a purely logical analysis of information from the external world reaching the brain from the sense organs. A second influence is the personal feelings of the individual, which originate in our biological makeup (the structure of lower levels of the nervous system) and the individual's life history. A third source of beliefs is the culture that surrounds us. Since each of us is totally bathed in influences from the culture, which are often subtle and veiled or diguised, and since we rarely have complete enough knowledge of another culture to perceive the unique characteristics of our own, its effects often escape our notice.

However, there is a simple way to make the point that each of us is strongly affected by our culture without being aware of it. We will consider a pure abstract problem, from which all details have been eliminated that would elicit a culturally determined response. Then, we will clothe the problem in enough detail so we can see how it relates to our daily lives. We will discover that our so-

ciety consistently approaches complex problems in a stereotyped fashion that is only one of many possible approaches. The fact that our society consistently selects a particular type of solution to complex problems, whereas many types of solutions are available, is evidence of the subtle impact of culture in shaping our thought processes, and contributing to environmental problems.

Consider the situation in which we have had a problem to which we applied a particular type of solution. The problem has not been solved, and may now appear to be even worse than it was before we tried to solve it. Applying nothing but logic to such a situation, there are clearly a large number of options available for future action:

1. We might try to increase the intensity of application of the solution we have already been using.
2. We might stop using the particular solution we have been using, and do nothing until we see what happens.
3. We might replace the "solution" we have already been using with some different type of remedy.
4. We might use the solution we have already been using in combination with a new type of solution.
5. We might use the existing solution with a variety of different types of solution used in combination, or consecutively.

In short, logic alone suggests that there are a remarkable variety of approaches that might be used in the situation where a problem has not been solved by an existing solution.

However, what does our culture actually do in this archetypal problem situation? Suppose a city has had a developing problem of traffic congestion, which it has tried to solve by building more freeways. If, as invariably happens, the result of building more freeways is to make traffic congestion worse, not better, our instinctive response is to build still more freeways (9). If spraying insecticide to kill an insect pest results in still more insect pests, our typical reaction is to increase the number of spray applications (15). A failure of "more government" to solve social problems typically results in a call for "still more government" in the hope that that will finally solve the problems. Indeed, a failure of bombing in Vietnam to "solve" the Vietnam war often resulted in the suggestion that the indicated solution was to bomb still more. All at once, a pattern becomes clear. The belief system of this culture typically leads people, including institutional decision-makers, to invariably gravitate to a particular option (number 1 in the preceding list) when in fact logic would suggest that a multiplicity of options is actually available (6, 10). This cultural influence has widespread effect in modern civilization: we have developed a style and philosophy of planning that is bankrupt, preoccupied with the extrapolation of existing trends rather than trying to make alert responses to changing conditions.

Given that we have now established that culture has an effect on our thinking, we turn to analysis of the particular types of effects, especially as they relate to environmental problems.

OSWALD SPENGLER'S PHILOSOPHY OF CULTURE

The particular beliefs of our culture that affect environmental decision-making fall into two classes. Some of these beliefs are associated with the stage of development of our culture and would be found in any higher civilization at this stage. But some of our other cultural beliefs are peculiar to this culture. The writings of Arnold Toynbee (14) have popularized two notions: that our civilization is only one of many that have existed on earth, the rest being long since gone, and that civilizations have had a typical pattern of birth, growth, decline, and death.

Oswald Spengler, a German writer on the history and philosophy of culture and civilization (11, 12), is not as well known to English-language readers as is Toynbee, but has developed a more penetrating analysis of the reasons for the rise and fall of civilizations, together with an elaborate picture of the attributes that civilizations assume as a consequence of their stage of development. In his world view, each of the high civilizations grows out of a culture originating in an undeveloped area, where almost the entire population lives on the farm or in small towns and villages. In this situation, the primitive economy is totally tied to resources. The dominant mode of life is that of the peasant: pure production is the main concern, and people think about life in terms of goods and possessions. Everyone understands that the standard of living is utterly dependent on farming, fishing, hunting, forestry, and mineral production.

A successful culture gradually becomes transformed into a civilization. The key to this transformation, according to Spengler, is intense urbanization. Gradually, almost all life and activity becomes concentrated in very large cities. The population that inhabits the cities undergoes a profound shift in thinking, away from the values of the rural peasants among whom the culture parent to the civilization began. Among the city population, production of resources assumes a lower and lower importance, whereas trade and the money that facilitates trade become of dominant importance. Gradually, the vast mass of people who occupy the city become uncompromisingly hostile to all the traditions of the culture, including the traditional belief that there are limits to the knowledge humanity can acquire, even through science. People in the city come to believe that humanity has no limits, and look down with steady contempt on the land-economy all around the city. A great faith and confidence in the ability of the state to solve all problems develops. Finally, the death-knell of a civilization is sounded when (and if) most of the people come to expect solutions that cannot be provided by the resources to which the state has access. To an ecologist, it would appear that the end of a civilization has arrived when the population has become too large to be supported by the resource base, but has developed a set of attitudes that make it absolutely impossible for them to recognize this simple truth.

It should be noted that while Spengler has presented a very thoroughly elaborated and documented statement of the theory just given, many other scholars agree on parts of it. The Spaniard Ortega y Gasset (8) was also aware of the central role of urbanization in producing unrealistic beliefs about resource capability in the great mass of the population, and many writers have discussed the unrealistic attitudes of the present culture.

However, a cavalier attitude toward the resource base is only one of the destructive features of the belief system of a senile civilization. The other problem is that civilizations finally exhaust the innovative possibilities inherent in their original cultural belief systems. That is, Spengler argues, the belief systems that produce civilizations have a time course. When a belief system is young, it has immense potential to suggest all kinds of ideas and theories that could be developed or exploited. After the process of exploiting new ideas inherent in a new belief system is well under way, the tempo of idea generation picks up, and the power and usefulness of the ideas also increases. After many centuries, there is a virtual explosion of really basic innovations that are derived as remote corollaries of the original basic belief system. Now we have a culture of great vigor. At this stage, there are many towering intellects on the scene, such as Bach, Beethoven, Kant, Newton, Liebnitz, Euler, and Gauss. But some time after intense urbanization has converted the culture to a civilization, most of the really profound implications of the basic belief system have already been discovered. Increasingly, it becomes difficult to make new major profound discoveries; increasingly, innovations are merely refinements of earlier discoveries. By now, a civilization has become old, tired, and sterile. What passes for innovation is largely merely the extension of existing theories and technologies.

Spengler thought this entire life cycle, from the inception of a new culture to the death of the resultant civilization, typically lasted about a thousand years, and that our cycle began about 1000 A.D. Spengler's other important idea is that each culture and the civilization that springs from it are totally different from all previous ones. Or, each culture and civilization has a uniquely characteristic soul. This soul has a profound shaping effect on the way the people in a civilization perceive the world and on everything they do. The unique soul of each culture expresses itself in art, architecture, music, city design, technology, science, exploration, commerce, and all other aspects of life. Thus, the Graeco-Roman (classical) civilization was preoccupied with the here and now; the present civilization is preoccupied with the infinite. Euclidean geometry describes only shapes without regard to time; Cartesian geometry can be used to describe functions of time.

Figure 9.1 illustrates the way in which different civilizations have expressed their belief systems through their architecture.

THE BASIC BELIEFS OF OUR CIVILIZATION AT PRESENT

Against a background of Spengler's views, we can see more clearly how certain of the basic beliefs of this civilization follow from our stage of development, while others are peculiar to this particular civilization (as opposed to other civilizations, such as the Romans, Egyptians, Aztecs, Persians, and Incas).

The Fixation on Money

One cluster of beliefs held by our civilization at present has been characteristic of all previous civilizations at the same late stage of development we are at now. This set of beliefs attaches great importance to money and has absolute contempt for resources and the industries that produce them. We routinely accept monetary measures of the performance and value of people and systems to the exclusion of all other measures; we accept monetary efficiency as the appropriate measure of efficiency, and "productivity" almost always means "economic productivity" or "profit." When we hear or read about "productivity," it never occurs to us that the reference might be to the productivity of land, of energy, or of minerals. Rather, we always try to make the most efficient possible use of people and capital by making more and more intensive use of land, energy, and minerals. Few people spot the pattern that there can be simultaneously strikes or economic tension in agriculture,

mining, fishing, and the oil and gas industries. An outside observer would rightly think that we mistreated all these industries because we did not believe they were important to us. Further, measuring individuals in terms of wealth results in immense value being attached to apparent "private property" with a corresponding low value being attached to public property, which is routinely littered, vandalized, and despoiled. To see that these are not the only values possible, it is only necessary to look at the native American culture we displaced, in which bravery and esteem of the group were the desiderata, and land was not thought of as "owned."

We show amazing contempt for nonmonetary features of our lives. The amazing destruction of the shallow-bottom ocean surrounding continents and islands and the shore-to-shore litter of discarded beer cans on river bottoms are just two examples.

However, three other clusters of beliefs important now are not a characteristic feature of this stage in the decline of a civilization, but are unique to this civilization (4, 7, 11, 12, 17). It is noteworthy that since the present technological civilization has spread everywhere (this is the international technoculture), these beliefs are just as important in Nigeria, Brazil, or Fiji as in Russia, Japan or the United States.

The Belief in Omnipotent Technology

The first belief peculiar to this civilization is the notion that technology can and indeed ought to be used to solve any problem. Associated with this idea is optimism: this civilization has no sense of tragedy or of impending possible doom. Some earlier civilizations believed that their existence might terminate at the end of a time cycle

A-1 EWING GALLOWAY. COURTESY OF E. P. JONES.

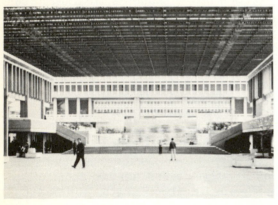

A-2

A-3 WALTER S. SILVER/THE PICTURE CUBE.

A-4 EWING GALLOWAY. COURTESY OF E. P. JONES.

FIGURE 9.1

This figure is designed to point out the unique attributes of our civilization by contrasting four representative works of architecture (column A) with four representative scenes from other civilizations or cultures (column B). Two interesting points are made by column A. First, our civilization, which originated in the time of gothic cathedrals in Europe, progressed to the Industrial Revolution, and has culminated in the international technoculture, is a completely international phenomenon. These four pictures are from Honolulu; Vancouver, Canada; Atlanta, Georgia; and Paris, France, but similar examples could have been photographed in a very large number of countries. Second, wherever it is found, a characteristic

B-1 H. ARMSTRONG ROBERTS. COURTESY OF E. P. JONES.

B-2 CHRISTOPHER K. WALTER/THE PICTURE CUBE.

B-3

B-4

of our civilization is a fascination and preoccupation with the infinite, which reveals itself in architecture as the attempt to create a sense of vast space, in which the individual person feels insignificant by comparison. Also notice that in our architecture, as in everything else we do, there is a sense of the abstract, of being cut off from the real world of plants, animals, and landscape. The architecture of colonial Spain (the ultimate culmination of a Moorish, or Middle-Eastern influence) creates, by contrast, a cosy, natural, down-to-earth feeling. It is particularly noteworthy that examples A1 and B3 are both in Honolulu. Notice how different the feeling is that these two structures evoke, even though they are in almost exactly the same geographic setting.

if their prayers were inadequate to appease the gods. However, while we have great faith in technology, it is in a particular kind of technology: the simple technological "fix." Thus, this civilization is very skilled at dealing with gigantic problems of the type that can be dealt with by a device: the space shot, the nuclear reactor. Our world abounds with problems that could be dealt with easily by the application of a mix of technologies applied in combination, yet it has not occurred to us to take this step. The energy problem requires a great mix of devices and systems, and we have great difficulty organizing this. Meetings and conferences could often be dealt with far better by linking telephone, television, and computer technologies, rather than by having many people travel great distances to a meeting site, yet we have not taken that step. It has somehow seemed easier and cheaper to fly large numbers of people on 4000-mile round trips within forty-eight or fewer hours. Our belief in technology has had two odd side-effects. First, rather than solving certain problems, it has seemed easier to use the technology of propaganda in a highly sophisticated fashion to make people think about the problem differently (3). Second, we have often transferred a technology from one country to another when the particular technology was quite inappropriate for the country to which it was being transferred. Perhaps the most striking example is modern agriculture: a very capital- and energy-intensive technology requiring little labor has often been transferred to countries that were desperately short of capital and energy and had massive unemployment problems. Associated with our faith in technology is the belief that because of the omnipotence of our technology, modern humanity is not limited in any way. This notion has a complex origin, however, in part tracing to the notion that we should and can dominate nature, so that no limits imposed by nature are relevant for us.

The Belief in Management through Fragmentation

A second belief peculiar to this civilization now is the notion that the appropriate way to view and manage the world is to fragment everything. This view has probably grown out of our history in applying technology. As the types of problems we solved became bigger and bigger, it became necessary to organize larger and larger numbers of people to manage the problem solution. This was achieved by "division of labor" and through immense specialization, at the expense of maintaining a generalist, or "holistic" worldview. The notion is clarified by considering how a government, a large corporation, or a university organizes itself. When such an organization has a very large problem to solve, the person or team responsible for solving it splits the problem into pieces, and a subteam is assigned to work on each piece. Similarly, the subteams split their problems into pieces, which are worked on by subsubteams, and so on. Gradually, there develops in association with this style of management, a way of perceiving reality as existing in discrete fragments. This comes to be institutionalized in administrative structures, so that there are departments of commerce, interior, agriculture, energy, and state. Universities have their many separate departments, also. Then who has responsibility for dealing with fundamentally systemic problems that involve all departments? Unfortunately, no one. As Stafford Beer (2) and many others have pointed out, our institutions are therefore ideally suited to the management of things, but not to the management of systems. But increasingly, the problems of the modern world are problems of systems.

The Belief in Force

Spengler has pointed out that this civilization is oriented toward the use of force to master history, events, situations, and resources. This implies that we will work against nature, not with it. Further, we are so committed to concepts such as "the will-to-power" and the "will-to-infinity," whether that means infinite material power, intellectual power, or creative power, that we unwittingly stumble into several traps. These notions lead to a hidden assumption that this civilization is so powerful that it is immortal. This makes it difficult for any of us to accept that through our own actions, we might create hazards to the life spans of our civilization or even our species (11, 12, 17).

The concern with great personal achievement has had a curious side-effect. In this civilization as in no other, the human beings of towering achievement have been concerned primarily with extending the limits of human accomplishment to the ultimate possible limit, rather than with making their creations accessible to a mass audience. Often, therefore, this work has been produced for an elite and typically for a tiny elite. This has been true for much of our best art and music, science, engineering, and philosophy, along with scholarship in all other areas. The result is that our leaders in these areas are not really an integral component of the social fabric in which they live. Indeed, the recent drive to make the products of culture popular is so much out of character with the last 1000 years that it can therefore be taken as evidence of the impending decline of this civilization. (Bach was for an elite; rock is for everyone.)

It is noteworthy that the systems point of view (as illustrated by the research conducted for the Club of Rome) has much to offer humanity. However, it is not really being accepted by or incorporated into this civilization. Why not? The problem is that our will to master nature is basically a dualistic posture (humanity against nature). A systems point of view is based on a philosophy of humanity with nature as part of an integrated system; therefore trying to graft such a view onto this civilization is like trying to graft an apple on to an orange tree.

Implications of our Beliefs

Some of the implications and consequences of these four beliefs, separately and in combination, are obvious. Others are very subtle.

Our preoccupation with money and monetary measures blinds us to the fact that there are many possible ways of measuring the efficiency of any system. Money output/money input is only one way. Two of the many other possibilities are energy output/energy input and distance traveled per unit time spent traveling. There are many different types of resources besides money (capital), and any of these could be used in the numerator or the denominator of measures of the efficiency of social systems. Further, the strategies selected to optimize the behavior of any type of system will depend on the particular measure of system efficiency that was selected. Two examples suffice to show the profound impact that preoccupation with money output/money input has had on the selection and design of social systems. Consider urban transportation systems. If money output/money input is the sole criterion of efficiency, and if you do not figure in the cost of peoples' time before and after working hours, then decision-making tends to overlook the mass transportation option, and concentrates on building more and more freeways to accommodate cars. However, if we consider other criteria of social systems efficiency, such as efficiency in the use of energy, and more efficient use of peoples' time in traveling certain distances, then freeways look less attractive relative to buses and urban railways. The second basic belief of our culture (the importance of a fragmented, as opposed to a systemic overview) also affects urban transportation systems planning and design. The problem of congestion can be dealt with in part by sophisticated rail systems with high density bus feeder lines. Also, congestion can be ameliorated by staggering working hours, and a variety of toll and parking fee devices. (For example, toll fees can be inversely proportional to the number of passengers in a vehicle.) However, these are "systems" solutions, and this culture is oriented to the technological "fix."

In Chapter 4 it was noted that historically in the United States it has taken between sixty-nine and seventy-eight years for a new energy source to supply 30 percent of national energy needs. Also, it was shown that because of the net energy of a national population of energy-generating systems, that interval could not be reduced by much without producing an energy deficit for the entire population. Thus, if either solar or nuclear energy were to be able to produce 30 percent of national energy needs by the year 2010, the process should have been started about seventy years previously, or about 1940. Of course, this did not happen, and consequently, the energy crisis will probably have to be dealt with by a sharp cutback in use. Yet despite these considerations, the

country is making no plans for such an eventuality, supremely confident that some type of technological solution will be found. It is interesting to examine the source for this level of confidence in technology. Given that this is the most scientifically oriented civilization that has ever lived, it would be reasonable to expect that our confidence in technology was the product of historical evidence or experimental test. Surprisingly, neither is true. Eugene Schwartz (10) has pointed out that much of our faith in technology is based on illusion and delusion. Technology not only may not solve problems, but on the contrary, the simple, technological-fix solutions to existing problems typically generate new problems, exponentially. There is a surprisingly vast but little-known literature on this theme.

Further, our faith in technology is not based on experimental tests and proofs, because there are immense institutional and cultural pressures against such tests. How often do we hear about an experiment to close a freeway to see if that helps deal with traffic congestion (6, 9), or an experiment to stop the use of pesticides to see if that deals with an insect pest problem? Surprisingly, in the few cases where experiments of this type are attempted, they yield the opposite answer to that expected: the problem mysteriously evaporates when the "solution" is removed (6, 9).

In fact, our faith in technology is the product of immensely sophisticated, widespread, and sustained intensive information management. To indicate the extent to which culture can condition us to see a phenomenon in an unrealistic fashion, our belief in the inevitability of economic growth is so strong that it is scarcely ever noticed that the stock market indices, in constant dollars (corrected for inflation) have all dropped enormously in the last decade. The notion that "growth is desirable, inevitable, and necessary" is so often taken to be true that it is rarely examined. Only recently have some economists begun to point out that the attractions of growth even violate common logic: for example, Fred Hirsch (5). That "growth is good" is an important cultural belief with immense and pervasive impact can be made clear by pointing out how different the world would be if we all believed that growth is unimportant, but variety was very important. A world that stressed the importance of variety would be a stable world (Chapter 5). "Time-space efficiency is better" would imply more efficient use of human time. But at present constant growth in material possessions, population, gross national product, airplane size, and everything else is accepted by almost everyone as being a step in the right direction. How often do we hear a president of the United States say, "The Gross National Product increased by 10 percent over last year, but real buying power of the average citizen decreased by 3 percent, so we will readjust our policies to increase buying power, even if it means a decrease in gross national product"?

It is noteworthy that as we stress world systems more and more, the links between subsystems become more tightly coupled (Chapter 11). As we run out of crude oil, our links to Arab nations become stronger, and as Russia runs out of wheat, its links to the West get stronger. Therefore, it is necessary that our present fragmented way of looking at complexity be replaced by an appropriate evolution towards a systemic view that matches the real nature of present-day reality (2).

Otherwise, we can perceive only bits of the "big picture" or true system, lifted out of context. Further, as Stafford Beer (2) has noted, our fragmented misperception leads to strongly fragmented organizations, with layer upon layer of organizational hierarchies and no capability of responding to systemic problems.

Our strong belief in our ability to master and manage everything around us has some most curious consequences. If we believe that humans have mastery over their total surroundings, then a corollary of this notion is that humans can control the economy through such policy tools as "fine-tuning" the rate of increase of the money supply. This is clearly a culture-dependent belief; if, contrariwise, we believed in the importance of natural flows as influences over our environment, we would perceive that weather and climatic fluctuations could have large impacts on the monetary system (Chapter 11). Confusion about the roles of weather and climate runs through our belief systems, because we are so committed to the notion of our own omnipotence as managers of all around us. Thus, on the one hand we invoke climatic change for the disappearance of the dinosaurs, "the year without a summer," "1800 and froze to death," but on the other hand, we assume that such phenomena are peculiar to the past, and could not occur again.

Our commitment to belief in our own power as masters and managers of the world around us leads us subtly in two other important directions. Because our belief system involves commitment to the value of force and will-to-power, we are constantly drawn in the direction of the big activity rather than the little activity. This means that we perceive as being most appropriate to our needs energy-generating systems releasing massive amounts of energy at a point source, rather than lots of little energy-generating systems producing energy where it is needed: we have become a civilization of refineries, coal mines, hydroelectric dams, and giant gas and gasoline storage farms, rather than backyard windmills or rooftop solar collectors. In other words, our cultural belief system has been a driving force in the direction of centralization rather than decentralization, because centralization comes with the big system.

Additionally, because we believe in our own force over nature and deny the existence of limits, we are failing to take action in time to redesign our society so it will be able to survive when fossil fuels run out.

THE CULTURAL REVOLUTION TAKING PLACE AMONG US

To this point, the analysis of our culture and its effects on our environment has gloomy implications. However, it appears that something historically novel could be our salvation. Always before, when a dying civilization was revitalized, the new creative impulses immigrated from a new civilization developing elsewhere. However, our civilization is international. There is no geographical location from which important new ideas could come, outside the sphere of influence of this civilization. However, since about 1970, some very new ideas have begun to win converts rapidly within this civilization, and thus, for the first time, the rejuvenating process of a new culture could come from within a dying old civilization. Once we know what to look for, the evidence of this phenomenon is rather striking. The great new interest in use of solar and wind energy is one bit of evidence.

In short, culture is dynamic: it can change and it does change. Further, given the right circumstances, change is very rapid. Thus, while we are living in the midst of an old civilization that has exhausted the creative potential in its basic beliefs, a new set of basic beliefs is springing up around us that has immense potential to rejuvenate the civilization, or form a new one in the ashes of the old (4). Table 9.1 compares the central

beliefs of the old belief system with the central beliefs of the new one.

Spengler argued that after about a thousand years, the creative potential of an old belief system is played out. But the early days of a new belief system would offer great potential for stimulating new ideas. In other words, we would expect to find that people, institutions, and governments committed to the old beliefs were, on average, rather unsuccessful, whereas those committed to the new beliefs should be highly successful. Indeed, it is an interesting exercise to classify all the corporations listed on the New York and American Stock exchanges on the basis of which belief system they fit best, then ascertain the average growth rate in profits of the two groups. This exercise has had a devastating effect (the "shock of recognition" phenomenon) on groups with which it has been demonstrated.

A few examples illustrate the effect of following the two paradigms. Imagine two people sitting on a rock at the edge of the ocean, trying to figure out how to get energy from it. The person committed to the old belief system would see nothing odd about drilling for oil eighty-five miles east of Atlantic City in 400 feet of water, fighting the wind and the waves every inch of the way. All such offshore oil and gas drilling, up to March 1978, yielded all industries involved $98 for every $100 they spent on bonuses, royalties, and rentals to the Federal Government for the permission to lease drilling sites offshore. The total return to the government from these sources was $26.5 billion (13). Industry not only hasn't made enough from offshore drilling to cover the cost of this payment; industry didn't even recover exploration and drilling costs. This is a typical example of the sterility of the old belief system (see Figures 9.2 and 9.3).

Now consider a person sitting on the rock, thinking about the ocean in terms of the new paradigm. Such a person would speculate as

TABLE 9.1
The nature of the cultural revolution in our civilization

The central beliefs of the old civilization	*The central beliefs of the new culture*
Technology is not limited by human ingenuity, thermodynamic constraints (the net energy problem of Chapter 4), or limitations of the resource base. Therefore, we should plan on using technological innovations ("technological fixes") to recover more and more of the stock of nonrenewable resources on the planet. The basic driving force behind civilization will be the consumption of fixed stocks (that is, the principal accumulated through past energy production by the sun: coal, oil, and gas).	Technology is limited by thermodynamic constraints; human ingenuity can only function at a limited speed; and the resource base is limited. Therefore, we must switch from a society run off a dwindling stock of nonrenewable resources to a society run off constant flows of renewable resources (that is, the interest resulting each day from the energy production by the sun: solar, wind, biomass, waves, and ocean thermal gradients).
The appropriate way to manage systems problems is by fragmenting problems into components (the "reductionist" approach). Humanity and nature are separate (the "dualistic" belief system).	The appropriate way to manage systems problems is by using methods based on a holistic perspective of the entire system. Humanity and nature are interacting components of an integrated system (the "monistic" belief system).
Humans can and should use their own will and force to master nature and triumph over competitors: this is the essence of life. The way to achieve mastery is to be the competitor exploiting the largest share of the available material and energy resource base. Since other competitors will have the same strategy, this means that being the winning competitor will require using a constantly increasing volume of resources.	The way to be a winning competitor and a survivor in the struggle to succeed within environmental limits is to maximize efficiency in the use of resources, not production. Further, this implies that the efficient processing of information will be used as a substitute for the production of matter and energy (the "information society").
Since the essence of life is maximizing production, the way to do this is through use of the largest possible systems. This implies very large refineries, coal-mining operations, ocean-going tankships, liquid natural gas port facilities, and the like. In general, that in turn implies great centralization of energy, economic, and political systems so as to maximize economics of scale.	Since the essence of life is maximizing efficiency, the way to do this is through small, decentralized systems that produce energy where it is to be used, and therefore avoid the hidden overhead energy cost of transmission and distribution, and also are dispersed efficiently enough to capture energy from dispersed sources as the sun, wind, and waves, with a resultant savings in fossil fuel.
Since humans can and do manage the system, then it follows that they, not natural forces, are the dominant factor in determining system behavior. Therefore, in trying to manage the economy, we overlook the role of natural forces as causes of inflation or recession (such as crop-growing weather fluctuations, or real increases in the cost of obtaining fossil energy), but instead try to manage economic cycles by "fine-tuning" the rate of increase in the money supply, and adjusting interest rates on borrowed capital.	Since natural forces and flows and available stocks of resources are important determinants of economic fluctuations, we try to maintain a stable economy by adjusting to changes in those forces, flows, and stocks. Thus, we would try to adjust to increased real cost of extracting U.S. crude oil by changing our social patterns so as to use energy more efficiently, rather than by importing more and trying to compensate for the consequences by printing money faster (inflating the currency).

FIGURE 9.2
An outer continental shelf oil-drilling rig. Given the obviously vast capital investment represented by these structures, it would be reasonable to assume that they constitute a highly profitable activity. But they do not, as a great many articles in business magazines and newspapers have pointed out (see, for example, article by Stuart (13)). Rather, they are a symbol of irrational commitment to an obsolete cultural paradigm. Continuation of this activity is mute testament to the enormous inertia in cultural belief systems. Photography by Eric A. Roth/The Picture Cube.

to why energy could not be obtained from the ocean itself, so obviously rich in kinetic energy. The problem is an information problem: waves vary in size unpredictably from wave to wave, throughout the tide cycle, and according to the time of year. But in an age of cheap, miniaturized computer circuits and electronic sensing devices, an indicated strategy would be to mount a floating but anchored energy-tapping device in the ocean with a sensor connected to a small computer a few score yards out to sea to adjust the height of the system so as to make most efficient use of the energy in each wave. Clearly, in this instance, information is being used to

make more efficient use of energy. Such substitutions are typical of the new paradigm. They are starting to show up in the form of novel types of windmills to pump irrigation water on farms, motels with solar energy packages to heat water, and highly efficient distributed information-processing systems with computer terminals in each office of a large organization. It takes little study of the corporate statements on a wide variety of corporations to expose the immense impact on profits of the new paradigm. Therefore, it will spread fast.

An interesting way to bring out the way in which culture affects decision-making in

FIGURE 9.3
Solar rooftop energy collectors. These small, unostentatious devices are symbols of a new cultural paradigm based on flow, as opposed to stock resources, and decentralization, rather than centralization of economic, political, and energy power. This is a solar-heated home in a low-income area. Project initiated and completed by ABCD (Action for Boston Community Development). Funded by the Department of Energy. Photograph by Read D. Brugger/The Picture Cube.

society is to read essays or letters to the editors of technical journals concerning the advisability of undertaking new ventures, such as ocean energy technologies based on wave energy or thermal gradients from top to bottom. One group of letters on this theme appeared in *Science* (198 [Dec. 9, 1977], pp. 989–992). The three letters plus a rejoinder from the writer being quoted represent remarkably different positions on an issue about which all four writers are obviously very well-informed. The positions range from extremely enthusiastic and positive, to extremely dubious and negative.

It is most revealing to notice, however, that a principal objection raised by critics against novel ocean energy technologies is the initial capital cost of the systems. This is most curious, because no advocates of nuclear power ever pointed out in the early days how steep the capital costs would be for that. Thus, there is a danger that development of novel ocean energy technologies could be blocked now by use of arguments that would have stopped nuclear power development dead in its tracks decades ago. At that point, it becomes very clear that the real issue being debated about energy systems is validity of different cultural belief systems, rather than the efficiencies of different technologies.

OVERVIEW OF THE FIRST NINE CHAPTERS

From the material covered in the first nine chapters, we can begin to discern certain basic themes explaining why our present civilization has environmental problems. These patterns are brought out in Figure 9.4, which summarizes the themes of these chapters and shows why our civilization has developed a high productivity/biomass ratio, whereas the natural world has evolved to a low productivity/biomass ratio.

At the root of our environmental problems is a basic question of extreme importance: what is the most efficient, effective means to alter human behavior? The available tools are economic (the price mechanism), legislation and the legal system, and modification of the cultural belief system. To this point, the economic tool has been rendered ineffective through government regulation. In other words, the present approach to managing the environment is based on the hidden assumption that legislation is a more effective, efficient means of altering human behavior so as to improve the environment than the free play of the market. In short, we are acting as if we believe that the best way to correct defective behavior is to make it illegal, not to make it too expensive. Historical experience should lead us to question this belief. For example, the Volstead Act illustrates the uselessness of legislation that only has partial support of the population. This act provided for Federal enforcement of the eighteenth amendment to the Constitution, which prohibited the manufacture, sale, or transportation of intoxicating liquor. Millions of people drank liquor while the law was in effect, and this massive violation of the law provided an enormous source of revenue for organized crime. Finally, the twenty-first amendment to the Constitution in 1933 repealed prohibition.

In fact, legislative codes are replete with laws that represent attempts by one group of people to alter behavior of another; many are laxly administered, and none are really effective unless the entire population accepts their value and legitimacy. One can only conclude that the price mechanism would probably be a more effective means of regulating excessive rates of resource depletion and pollution.

SUGGESTIONS FOR INDIVIDUAL AND GROUP PROJECTS

This chapter began by arguing that three sets of factors influence the response of a person to any problem of decision: logic, feelings, and the culture. Train yourself to analyze your responses to various situations, to find out the relative role of each of these three. Now apply your insights gained from this self-analysis to interpretation of conflicts over environmental issues you see in your locality and in the nation. Would you expect that a person in a position of great power and authority would have exactly the same feelings that you do? How would you expect such a person to respond to a challenge to his or her authority, even if it was justified?

A group might work together to analyze a complex local environmental conflict from this point of view. To gain insight into the feelings of each of the political actors and explore the role of culture on each of them, it can be helpful to play a group game, in

FIGURE 9.4

The relationships between the basic themes brought out in the first nine chapters.

THE PRESENT CIVILIZATION

CHAPTER 9

Dualistic, power-oriented belief system produces excessive commitment to growth in resource use.

CHAPTER 6

Excessive birth rates in human population.

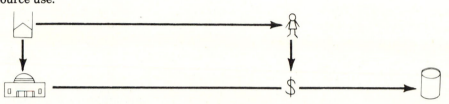

CHAPTER 8

Politicians fear that they will not be re-elected unless they spend more than they raise in taxes and tolerate high rates of resource consumption; thus government stimulates growth in the money supply (inflation), keeps energy prices down, and keeps raising minimum wage and tolerating large union settlements.

CHAPTER 7

The economy is characterized by a high inflation rate, a low real growth rate, high rates of resource depletion, pollution, unemployment and crime. High productivity/capital stock ratio.

CHAPTER 4

Excessive rate of energy consumption stimulated by high inflation rate and high wage/energy cost ratio which produced unrealistic view of real purchasing power in the population.

THE NATURAL WORLD

CHAPTER 3

The natural world of plants and animals is bound by limits set on all rates of production by natural rates of energy input and mineral cycling.

CHAPTER 5

Natural communities of plants and animals undergo succession which results in making the most efficient possible use of incident solar radiation. High biomass/productivity ratio.

which each player takes the role of one of the actors in the real-life conflict. Afterward, you can all pool notes on how you thought cultural factors influenced your decision-making behavior. (This technique is sometimes used in conflict resolution and analysis.)

REFERENCES

1. Anderson, W., *A Place of Power. The American Episode in Human Evolution.* Santa Monica, Calif.: Goodyear Publishing Co., 1976.
2. Beer, S., *Platform for Change.* London: John Wiley and sons, 1975.
3. Ellul, J., *The Technological Society.* New York: Alfred Knopf, 1964.
4. Harman, W. W., *An Incomplete Guide to the Future.* New York: W. W. Norton, 1979.
5. Hirsch, F., *Social Limits to Growth.* Cambridge, Mass.: Harvard University Press, 1976.
6. Leavitt, H., *Superhighway—Superhoax.* Garden City, N.Y.: Doubleday & Co., 1970.
7. Moncrief, L. W., "The cultural basis for our environmental crisis," *Science,* 170 (1970), pp. 508–512.
8. Ortega y Gasset, J., *The Revolt of the Masses.* New York: W. W. Norton, 1932.
9. Schneider, K. R., *Autokind vs. Mankind.* New York: W. W. Norton, 1971.
10. Schwartz, E. S., *Overskill. The Decline of Technology in Modern Civilization.* New York: Quadrangle Books, 1971.
11. Spengler, O., *The Decline of the West: Volume 1, Form and Actuality.* New York: Alfred Knopf, 1926.
12. Spengler, O., *The Decline of the West: Volume 2, Perspectives of World History.* New York: Alfred Knopf, 1928.
13. Stuart, A., "The Very Interesting Dance in the Baltimore Canyon," *Fortune,* Sept. 11, 1978, pp. 66–68.
14. Toynbee, A., *A Study of History* (new edition, revised and abridged). New York: Oxford University Press, 1972.
15. van den Bosch, R., *The Pesticide Conspiracy.* Garden City, N.Y.: Doubleday & Co., 1978.
16. Watt, K. E. F., L. F. Molloy, C. K. Varshney, D. Weeks, and S. Wirosardjono, *The Unsteady State. Environmental Problems, Growth and Culture.* Honolulu: The University Press of Hawaii, 1977.
17. White, L. Jr., "The historical roots of our ecologic crisis," *Science,* 155 (1967), pp. 1203–1207.

III

The Dynamics of Multilevel Hierarchical Environmental Systems with Many Types of Components

To this point, each chapter has dealt with one type of component in environmental systems. However, Chapter 1 pointed out that in order to understand and deal with environmental problems, we must examine the way in which many different types of components affect each other.

Chapter 10 introduces data showing how different kinds of components interact in complex environmental systems, and develops the notion of a hierarchy of levels of organization, with causal pathways running up and down through several levels.

By the end of Chapter 10, some readers will feel the need for a more organized view of the interrelationships between types of components and hierarchical levels. Chapter 11 introduces such a scheme, which clarifies the way in which causal pathways move between levels, and also between types of components. This scheme is useful as a way of thinking about problems and clarifying ways of dealing with them. Such a scheme is also a first step on the road to construction of a computer systems model that could be used to conduct policy games, in which the best way to solve environmental problems is decided by trial and error, repeated a great number of times.

10 SYSTEMS AT DIFFERENT LEVELS

Man is a prisoner of his own way of thinking
and of his own stereotypes of himself.

His machine for thinking
the brain
has been programmed to deal with a vanished world.

This old world was characterized by the need
to manage *things*—
stone, wood, iron.

The new world is characterized by the need
to manage
complexity.

Sir Stafford Beer, *Platform for change,* 1975.

MAIN THEMES OF THIS CHAPTER

Up to this point, the various components of environmental problems have been considered largely in isolation from each other. This chapter introduces data showing how causal pathways move between different kinds of components, so that weather, resources, demographic factors, and economic, political, and cultural variables can be considered as constituents of integrated systems, with components interacting so as to determine the character of the environment as a totality.

Also, this chapter focuses on the concept of hierarchical levels, and demonstrates how causal pathways move between hierarchical levels (city, nation, the international trading system of nations). The chapter provides the background data required to justify the conceptual systems models and flow charts of Chapter 11. Also, the chapter encourages the student to develop a style of reasoning that draws inferences from comparison of different cities and different nations and from international trade patterns.

REVIEWING THE HIERARCHICAL SYSTEM

Chapters 1 and 5 introduced the concept of hierarchical system, in which we can think of reality as being organized into levels, from subatomic particles up to the ecosystem, and ultimately, the entire cosmos. This chapter focuses on three levels of reality: the city, the nation, and the international trading system made up of all nations. To illustrate the significance of hierarchical levels for environmental systems, we now consider a particular example.

We can consider phenomena at any of these levels as being the effects of causes operating at the same level. Thus, for example, we can think of the volume of traffic flow down a main street in a city as being dependent on the area and population density of the city. However, we can also think of effects at any level as having ultimate causes at different levels. Thus, while it is true that the volume of traffic flow down the main street of a city depends on the area and density of a city, those two variables in turn depend on the rate at which the country is converting farmland or forest land to urban use. That rate will be high if the country has a lot of farmland (or forest land) per capita,

but low if the country is short of farmland (or forest land) per capita. Also, the area of cities will tend to be regulated by the cost of fuel for transportation: cheap national fuel prices tend to encourage urban sprawl; expensive energy tends to produce compact cities. Thus, city-level phenomena, such as the volume of traffic flow down main arteries, can be thought of as originating at the national level, in national supply/demand ratios for basic resources, such as farm and forest land and energy. But further, national supply/demand ratios of such resources will also be affected by worldwide demand/supply ratios for those resources. Thus while the United States has a superabundance of agricultural land, and Canada has a superabundance of forest land, demand will begin to outstrip supplies if Canada exports wood on a massive scale, and the United States exports food on a massive scale in order to pay for imports of other commodities for which either country has a shortage.

In fact, as we shall see in this chapter, causal pathways flow up and down through all levels. Thus a cause may originate at the national level, have an effect on the international level that loops back on the national level, and finally affects the city level. Events at the city level may then trigger a causal pathway that acts on the national level, thus closing the entire causal pathway connecting the three levels.

THE CITY LEVEL

Land is an important resource for cities, its availability and the way it is used determines their character. The amount of farm land converted to city use for each person added to the city population varies from region to region in a large country. Such a pattern is revealed when we consider the data for all large metropolitan areas in the United States. Where farm property at the metropolitan area edge is very valuable, as for San Francisco or New York City, as little as .02 hectares is converted to urban use for each person added to the metropolitan area population. Where the land surrounding cities is of low value, as in some cities in Oklahoma, Arizona, or Nevada, there is a high land conversion rate per person (up to .32 hectares). In general, when we analyze all the data for all metropolitan areas in a country, we find that the rate of conversion of land to urban use is described by a straight line function of land value at the urban edge (when we plot the data on log-log graph paper). As land value increases at the urban edge, the rate of conversion per person added to the city population drops. Further, land values at the edge of cities vary astoundingly from city to city, they are thirty-two times as high at the edge of some as at the edge of others. However, the particular straight line that best describes this relationship depends on whether we are considering conversion rates during recent decades, or over the entire life of the city. To explain why this is so, consider the decade 1960 to 1970. By this time farmland was being conserved somewhat more than in the early days of city expansion, and therefore the land conversion rates were lower. Further, a growing city may sprawl fast, but later develop by filling in empty space within the city boundary. Because the intrinsic value of farmland at the edge of the city is an important determinant of the rate of conversion of land to city use, it follows that this intrinsic farmland value is an important determinant of city density.

Now what are the consequences of city density? A city with a dense urban core, with a high volume of traffic flowing to and from that core, has a greater need for public transportation. This, in turn, has an effect on the efficiency of energy use in the city, because energy consumption per person per mile depends on the rate of traffic flow, and the type of transportation system being used (Figure 10.1). For each mode, at very low rates of traffic flow, energy consumption per passenger-mile is high because the vehicles are underloaded. Increase in traffic flow implies that the vehicles have a higher proportion of their seats filled, and that the vehicles make more efficient use of their energy consumption. For each type of vehicle, for this reason, increasing the traffic flow rate decreases the fuel consumption per passenger mile. However, fuel consumption per passenger mile does not drop indefinitely as traffic volume rises. Beyond an optimal rate of traffic flow, further increase saturates the right-of-way space with vehicles, so that congestion delays occur. These delays make the vehicles shift from continuous energy operation to stop-and-start driving, which uses more fuel per passenger mile. There is a tradeoff between space for right-of-way and energy use: more space means less congestion and more efficient use of energy.

The level of traffic flow at which stop-and-start driving occurs is different for each type of vehicle. Buses are less affected by high traffic flow rates than cars, because they fit more people into a square foot of vehicle (or imaginary moving right of way) than a car. Trains fit still more people into a unit of space than a bus. Therefore, as city densities increase and the density of activity in the downtown area increases, cities must move along a sequence of transportation modes from cars, to buses, to trains in order to alleviate insufferable congestion delays. Indeed, very large cities with an immense amount of activity at the urban core could scarcely function without subway trains. London, Tokyo, and New York are examples.

FIGURE 10.1

The effect of traffic flow rate, traffic congestion, and choice of transportation mode (cars, buses, or rail) on transportation fuel efficiency.

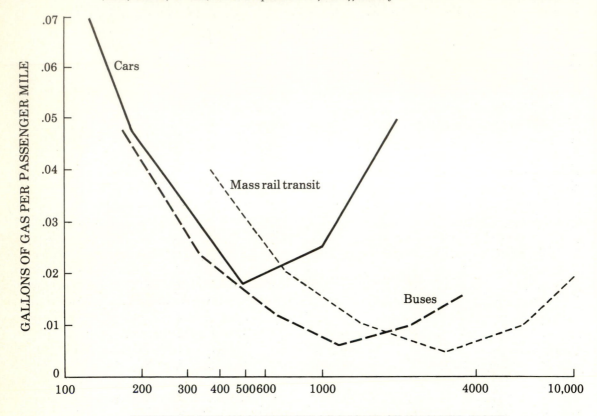

Transportation systems analysts can work out the relationship between the millions of square feet of nonresidential floorspace in the downtown area and the best type of transportation system for a city. The planners for a city can look at a chart, as in Figure 10.2 and determine when their city has become large enough to justify a new type of transportation system.

There is a relationship between the land used per person in a city and the proportion of the population that travels to work in public transportation. Denser cities have less urban land per person and a higher proportion of the city labor force commuting to and from work in public transportation instead of cars. Figure 10.3 shows the relation between the population density of metropolitan areas and the proportion of the commuting population using transit. Transit, in turn, makes more efficient use of energy per passenger mile than cars (see Table 4.6). Consequently, as we would expect, we find that as the proportion of the

FIGURE 10.2

The relation between the size of the downtown area, in millions of square feet of non-residential floor space and the most suitable type of transit mode. From Transportation Research News, *The Transportation Research Board, No. 67, Nov.–Dec. 1976, p. 9.*

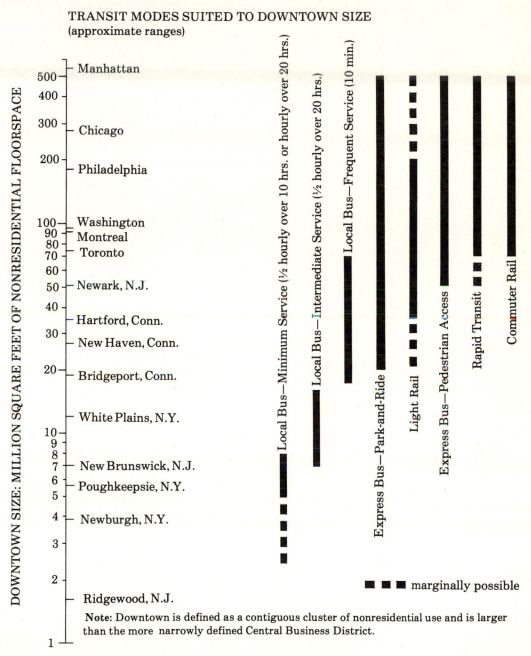

TRANSIT MODES SUITED TO DOWNTOWN SIZE
(approximate ranges)

DOWNTOWN SIZE: MILLION SQUARE FEET OF NONRESIDENTIAL FLOORSPACE

■ ■ ■ marginally possible

Note: Downtown is defined as a contiguous cluster of nonresidential use and is larger than the more narrowly defined Central Business District.

FIGURE 10.3

The relation between the population density of standard metropolitan statistical areas and the percentage of workers using public transportation to commute to work. Data from Section 33, Statistical Abstracts of the United States for 1972, *U.S. Department of Commerce. The straight line was fitted to the data for fifteen of the largest metropolitan areas; data points for twelve cities are identified, to suggest the appearance of cities represented by different positions along the line.*

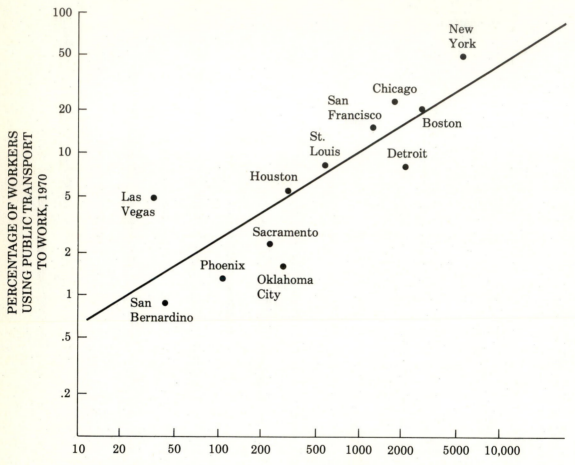

POPULATION DENSITY OF STANDARD METROPOLITAN STATISTICAL AREA
(Numbers of People Per Square Mile, 1970)

labor force of a city commuting to work by public transit increases the fuel consumption per person per year in the city decreases.

A second factor also affects energy consumption per person per year in city transportation: the availability of freeways. Cities with less than .070 miles of freeway per 1000 people use less energy for transportation than cities with more than .074 miles of freeway per 1000 people. Evidently freeways encourage energy consumption in transportation. This fact brings out a fundamental principle of human behavior: people will do what it is easy to do. If we fill a city with freeways, thereby facilitating a lot of long-distance automobile travel at high speeds, the city will have a higher level of energy use in transportation than would otherwise have been the case. Similarly, if a city is filled with transit, this will lower energy consumption.

The Argument to This Point

Let us review the argument to this point. The value of agricultural land depends on its intrinsic soil fertililty and on demand relative to supply for agricultural commodities, which in turn determines the rate at which land is converted to urban use per person added to the urban population. Population also enters as a driving factor: the rate at which agricultural land is converted to urban use is determined by the number of people added to the urban population per year, multiplied by the land transfer rate (agricultural to urban) per person. Small agricultural to urban land conversion rates make small-area, high-density cities. High agricultural to urban land conversion rates make for large, low-density cities. City densities in turn determine the type of transportation system used in the city, and this in turn determines the energy consumption per person in the city, because mass transit makes more efficient use of energy than cars. Viewing the entire argument, it appears that there is a relationship between the demand for agricultural land at the edge of the city, and the amount of energy people use in transportation in the city: more valuable farmland leads to more efficient energy use.

One way to examine this proposition directly is to examine the energy consumption per capita, county by county, in all U.S. counties. This is a different way of viewing the data than previously, because examining only counties, we look at each part of a metropolitan area separately. Some urban counties will have much higher population densities than the average density for the entire metropolitan area of which they are a part. This relation between hectares of land per person in a county and energy consumption per person in the county in transportation is graphed in Figure 10.4. The long, essentially flat part of the line in the center of the graph describes urban counties where there is little public transportation, and car-driving per person is relatively constant over a wide range of urban densities. The sharp drop at the lower left corner of the graph describes a few very dense urban counties in the United States, where land in and around the urban area is very valuable. The sharply rising part of the curve at the upper right hand corner describes remote mountain and desert counties, where the land has low value, and a great deal of driving is required for survival. Note that the availability and hence the price of energy will determine whether a society can afford to operate cities in remote areas, as well as the choice of transportation mode and the use of energy in each mode.

Now that we have established a relation between land value, county densities, and their energy use in transportation, an interesting question arises. Could some outside factor operating on either energy prices or agricultural land prices have a sufficient impact on city densities to significantly alter their energy use? The answer to this question will be found at the international level, later in this chapter.

In summary, land, population density, and energy are three basic, interacting determinants of the character of cities.

FIGURE 10.4

The relation between the hectares of land per person in a county and the gallons of gasoline sold per person at retail outlets in the county. Data sources: County and City Data Book, *U.S. Department of Commerce, Bureau of the Census, 1972, and the* Census of Business for 1967 Retail Trade, *Publication BC67-R57, 1971.*

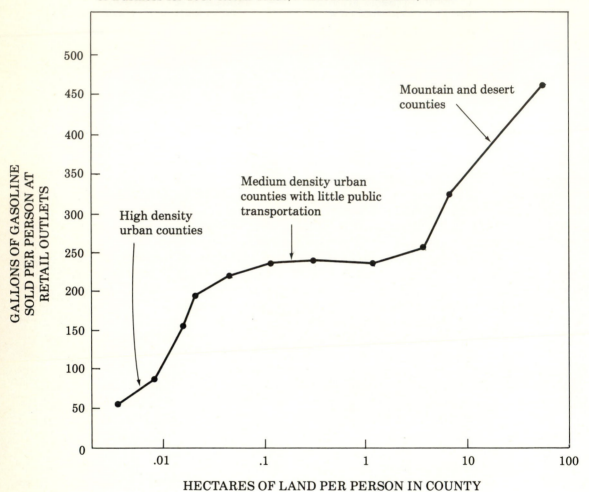

THE NATIONAL LEVEL

Some people might like to think that differences between the wealth of nations are almost entirely due to variations in the intelligence, industriousness, talent, or capacity for technological innovation of their populations. However, in addition, much of the difference between the wealth of nations can be explained in terms of resource availability per capita, statistics on which can be found in many compendia (1, 2, 4, 5, 6, 9, 10), or in terms of the stage in the life cycle of resource development (7).

A simple demonstration of the striking relation between wealth and resources is given in Figure 10.5, which shows the relationship between gross national product (GNP) per capita and energy consumption per capita, which holds over a remarkably

FIGURE 10.5

The relationship between gross national product per capita (a measure of the wealth of a nation) and consumption per capita of all forms of energy (a measure of resource availability per capita). Copyright, United Nations (1977). Reproduced by permission. Data sources: Statistical Yearbook of the United Nations, 1976, *pp. 372-375, 686-688.*

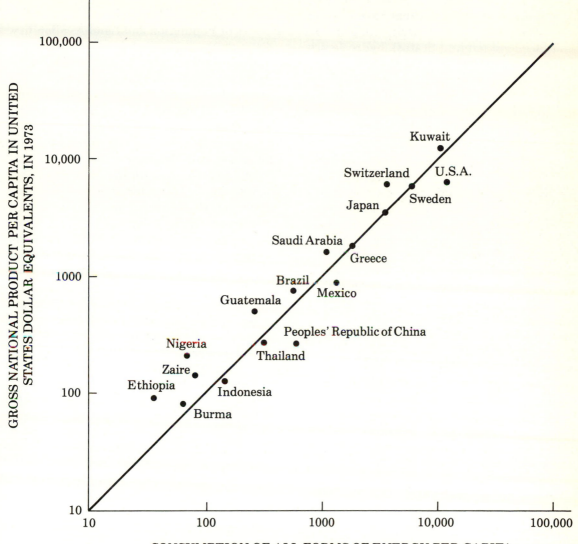

CONSUMPTION OF ALL FORMS OF ENERGY PER CAPITA
IN 1973 IN KILOGRAMS OF COAL EQUIVALENTS

wide range of values for both variables. However, it will be noticed that the nations plotted do not all fall exactly on the line. Thus, for example, the United States falls well below the line and Switzerland falls well above it. This means that the United States gets little GNP per capita per unit of energy (is inefficient) whereas Switzerland gets a large GNP per unit of energy (is efficient in use of energy). Even so, resource availability per capita is clearly much more important than efficiency in resource use, in determining national standard of living.

But just what do we mean by "resource"? Some of the wealthy nations have obvious sources of wealth: oil (Kuwait); oil, gas, coal and farmland (United States); hydroelectric power (Switzerland and Sweden); very high yields per hectare resulting from high technological inputs to agriculture (Japan). If a country lacks certain basic resources, then there are two ways to compensate for this. One is to pay for imports of the commodities in short supply through exports of some other commodities (as when the United States sells agricultural commodities to buy crude oil, or Japan sells manufactured goods to pay for imported oil). The other is to use some important natural asset as a source of income to compensate for shortage of agricultural produce, forests, and minerals: Singapore, Hong Kong, and Malta have important assets in their natural harbors, Panama and Egypt have important assets in their canals, and Switzerland and Japan have enormous assets in the quality of their educational systems.

Thus, the position of each of the 175 countries when plotted on a figure such as 10.5 does not just express its energy resources: rather, the energy consumption per capita is a composite measure of a country's energy stocks or hydroelectric capacity, together with its ability to trade some other resource to purchase energy that it does not have itself. But should anything happen to the energy resources of a nation, or the abundance of the other resources being sold to pay for energy, the standard of living would go down. This remark has to be interpreted very broadly, however. A nation may have major resources and not realize it, as in the case of Peru, which as recently as 1947 did not realize it had the world's largest fishery resource off its coast (the anchovies), or oceanside desert countries, which could couple solar energy and desalinization technologies to get fresh water and increased agricultural production, as well as energy.

Effects of Population and Land Availability

Two factors that have an overwhelming effect on the environment in every country are the population size, and the amount of land available for agriculture, including grazing land. When population size is divided into the amount of available agricultural land, giving the area of agricultural land per person, we have an index of the state of a country with implications for almost everything happening there. One important effect of agricultural land availability is on the character of cities. As shown in Figure 10.6, as the number of hectares of agricultural land per person in the country increases, more land will be available for city use. Thus, in general, very compact cities with an average building height of four to ten stories occur in countries where agricultural land is so precious that cities must accommodate population increase by becoming taller, rather than by increasing in area. As we might expect therefore, cities of Asia and Europe tend to use a small amount of land per resident and have high population densities. Urban sprawl is great in cities surrounded by large quantities of agricultural land per capita. However, in very large countries, such as the United States, Canada, and Australia, the availability of agricultural land per capita varies from region to region, and the value of agricultural land also varies from region to region. Thus, where a city is surrounded by very high quality soil (such as Chicago in Figure 10.6), it tends to use less city land per city resident than where a city is surrounded by land of little value for agriculture (for example, Las Vegas).

FIGURE 10.6

The effect of the number of hectares of agricultural land per person in a country on the number of hectares of metropolitan area land used per person in metropolitan areas of that country. Agricultural land data from sum of columns 3, 4, and 5 in Table 1, 1974 Production Yearbook, Food and Agriculture Organization of the United Nations. Population data from the Statistical Yearbook, Statistical Office of the United Nations. Copyright, The United Nations 1975. Used by permission. U.S. metropolitan area statistics from the bureau of the Census.

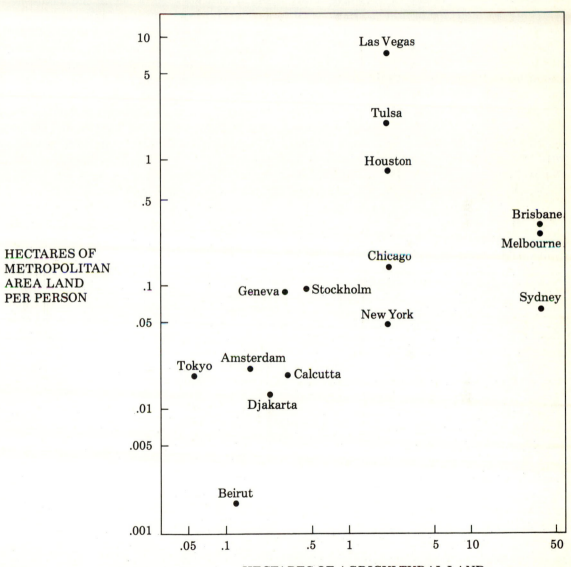

Characteristics of Countries

Table 10.1 compares twelve of the most developed countries with respect to six important characteristics. The first column measures the total amount of energy used per person in each country, all converted to pounds of coal equivalents. The twelve countries are ranked from first to last with respect to this variable. The second column measures the rate of production of all goods and services in each country: the gross national product per capita, all converted to a common base, 1975 U.S. dollars. The most striking feature of the first and second columns is how little they are related to each other: Switzerland was the last of the twelve with respect to energy use per capita, but the first with respect to GNP per capita. Six of the countries had GNP per capita approximately equal to or considerably higher than the United States; all of these six used significantly less energy than the United States. A level of energy use as high as that in the United States is not necessary for a very high level of economic activity. This observation is specifically contradictory to much that we read or see in the media.

The third column compares the electrical energy production of the twelve countries. Again, we see that electrical energy and total energy are not closely related. Norway, for example, produces over twice as much electrical energy per capita as the United States, but half as much total energy. This brings out a very important point: the patterns of social-economic organization among these twelve countries are surprisingly different. Each has found itself in a somewhat different situation, and has worked out an

TABLE 10.1

Relations between various measures of national socio-economic organization[1]

Country	1974 use of all forms of energy per person, in kilograms of coal equivalents	1975 gross national product per person, in 1975 United States dollars	1974 production of electrical energy per person, in kilowatt hours	Expectation of life, at birth, for males, in years	Number of new book titles published per million people per year	Kilometers traveled per person in trains, 1973
United States	11485	7099	9283	67.4	388	71
Canada	9816	6935	12410	69.3	307	116
Belgium	6637	6474	4376	67.8	519	829
Netherlands	6191	5886	4088	71.2	885	608
Australia	5997	6168	5229	67.6	356	—
Sweden	5804	8450	9205	72.1	958	602
West Germany	5689	6842	5023	67.6	654	642
Denmark	5114	7106	3498	70.8	1311	637
Norway	4925	6944	19234	71.3	1129	414
Finland	4505	5600	5593	66.6	1407	596
Japan	3839	4425	4201	70.5	290	2870
Switzerland	3608	8754	5847	70.2	1316	1478

[1]Copyright, United Nations (1977). Reproduced by permission. *Statistical Yearbook of the United Nations, 1976*, pp. 372–375, 686–693, 386–395, 79–83, 872–877, 482–484.

adjustment to that situation. Norway, as with several countries in the list, has many high mountains covered with snow much of the year, and many fast, deep rivers suitable for generation of hydroelectric power. This contrasts with the United States, which discovered petroleum in great quantities at an early stage in its development. This difference explains a number of things about the countries.

Column four gives the life expectancy, at birth, in males for the twelve countries. We notice that high life expectancy is not well correlated with energy consumption per capita, but shows a stronger relation to gross national product per capita. Presumably this is because high energy consumption per capita implies a high rate of pollution production per capita, and this implies a higher level of environmental health hazard.

Column five gives the number of new book titles published per year per million people. This statistic measures a cultural attribute. This attribute, surprisingly, may be strongly related to city density, because high city density promotes a high concentration of cultural activity in the urban core. The only high-city-density country with a low number of book titles published per year per person is Japan, in which the level of affluence is significantly lower than for other members of the group.

The sixth column indicates the number of kilometers traveled per person per year in trains. Again, these numbers reflect very different patterns of social organization in the different countries: the train replaces a great deal of car use in Japan and Switzerland.

THE INTERNATIONAL LEVEL

Countries, just like families, should balance their books. To some extent, a country, like a family, can go in debt, by buying more than it can pay for through sale of goods or service. However, this national indebtedness to other countries is limited: if it goes too far, the money of the excessive spender piles up in other countries where it comes to lose its value, contributing to decreased buying power at home in the over-spending country. (Devaluation of U.S. money in West Germany creates inflation here by making us pay more for a German car.) Thus, the books of any country are approximately in balance.

Examination of the books of any country is enormously revealing. By seeing what a country has been selling in great quantities, we learn about the productive capacity and resource potential of the country. By discovering what a country is buying, we learn about the commodities in which it is undersupplied domestically. But more than this, we learn about how a country fares with respect to each of the factors discussed in this book to date. If a country is importing vast quantities of one commodity, not only do we know that the country is running out of that commodity, but also, we know that the economic, political, and cultural systems in that country are inadequately effective in discouraging use of the commodity. Also, if a country is selling a great deal of some other commodity, we know that the country not only has the potential to produce the commodity and that the climate allowed it to be produced in quantities above those needed domestically, but that the political, cultural, and economic systems allowed the production of the exported commodity in amounts in excess of national needs. We would expect the international trade pattern of the United States in recent years to be of great interest, because we learned in Chapter 4 that crude oil in the United States was running out (Figure 4.3) and it was consequently becoming much more expensive to find and produce (Figure 4.4).

What happens to a country when it is subjected to a major perturbation of this type? One way to explore this issue is to

TABLE 10.2
The eroding position of the United States in world trade

Category	Value of U.S. exports less value of U.S. imports (in billions of current dollars)				
	1970	*1976*	*1977*	*1978*	*1979*
Mineral fuels and related materials	−1.5	−29.8	−40.1	−38.2	−54.5
Machinery and transportation equipment	6.7	19.7	15.5	11.6	16.8
Other manufactured goods	−5.7	−12.4	−17.7	−23.6	−22.2
Chemicals	2.4	5.2	5.4	6.2	9.8
Subtotal, manufactured goods and chemicals	3.4	12.5	3.2	−5.8	−5.4
Wheat and flour	1.1	4.0	2.9	4.5	5.5
Corn	.8	5.2	4.1	5.3	7.0
Soybeans	1.2	3.3	4.4	5.2	5.7
Subtotal, major agricultural commodities	3.1	12.5	11.4	15.0	18.2

break out the U.S. trade statistics by category, and for each of these compute the net change in sales over the period 1970 to 1978. For each category in each year of interest we compute the following quantity:

(exports − imports)

All these quantities are expressed in a common unit: billions of dollars. The results are gathered in Table 10.2, which allows us to see how the United States paid for the greatly increased cost of imported energy (mostly crude oil). First, we see that the magnitude of the increase in cost of crude oil is startling: from a net deficit of $1.5 billion in 1970 to $38.2 billion in 1978. Next we see that it was not possible to cover all of this cost by an increase in sales of manufactured products. The net total U.S. sales of all manufactured products actually declined from 1970 to 1978. This is startling, given that we usually think of the United States as a major manufacturing nation. The problem is, however, that our labor is very expensive compared to labor in many other countries; thus, it becomes increasingly difficult

for us to sell many kinds of manufactured products to other countries. The result is that when the U.S. sharply increases its purchases of any commodity or product from other countries, this must be paid for by a sharp increase in U.S. sales of raw materials, but principally agricultural commodities. This we did, by $11.9 billion worth, from 1970 to 1978. It is noteworthy that the forest resources of the United States have been sufficiently depleted that they can no longer be a major help in counteracting a deteriorating international trade position in fuel.

To dramatize this last point, Table 10.3 is the analogue of Table 10.2, only for Canada instead of the United States. It is revealing to compare the similarities and contrast the differences in the trade situations of the two countries. Both countries are confronted with a growing trade deficit for mineral fuels, although the magnitude of imports is only 11 percent as great for Canada as for the United States, because the Canadian population is only about 10 percent as large. Both countries are unable to balance their fuel import cost increases by increases in

TABLE 10.3

The relative importance of manufactured products and raw materials in maintaining the Canadian balance of trade in the face of increases in imports of crude oil[1]

Item	Value of exports from Canada, billions of dollars, 1974	Value of imports to Canada, billions of dollars, 1974	Value of exports from Canada, billions of dollars, 1977	Value of imports to Canada, billions of dollars, 1977	Increase (+) or decrease (−) in net trade balance for Canada from 1974 to 1977, in billions of current dollars
	A	B	C	D	(C − D) − (A − B)
Coal, gas, and crude petroleum	3.9	2.9	3.8	3.9	−1.1
All manufactured goods	9.2	18.4	14.9	26.0	−1.9
Food, feed, beverages, and tobacco	3.8	2.4	4.4	3.3	− .3
Wood, and all wood products	4.9	.6	7.0	.7	+2.0

[1]Import statistics from Table 18.30 and export statistics from Table 18.31 in *Canada Year Book 1978–79*. Statistics Canada: Ottawa, 1978. Reproduced by permission of the Minister of Supply and Services, Canada.

exports of manufactured goods, and must resort to increases in exports of renewable natural resources to balance their merchandise trade accounts with other countries. However, there is a major difference between the two countries: the United States is able sharply to increase exports of agricultural produce, but not forest produce; Canada, on the other hand, has not been able to sharply increase agricultural exports, but has been able to sharply increase forest produce exports. This should not be surprising: when we fly over the two countries, it is plain that the major asset Canada has is forest land; the major asset the United States has is agricultural land.

In both countries, these massive increases in exports of raw materials will have a variety of surprising side-effects. In both countries, cities have increased in area enormously in the last thirty-five years. Much of

that increase has been at the expense of agricultural and forest land. It is clear that now that same land is desperately necessary for producing raw materials that the United States and Canada must export to pay for imported crude oil. Consequently, from now on in both countries, we can expect to see intense competition between agricultural and urban uses of the same land at the city fringe in the United States, and between agricultural and forest use, versus urban land use in Canada.

Causal Pathways Between Hierarchical Levels

Now we begin to see how all types of system elements and all hierarchical levels are involved in certain causal pathways. In Chapter 3 we saw that crop production could decrease sharply under the influence of weather fluctuations due to geophysical accidents, such as volcanic eruptions, comparable to those which occurred in the nineteenth century. Further, other countries must be able to pay for our surplus food and wood products, but must also have sufficient production shortfalls in their own countries that they need to buy the quantities that we need to sell, in order to pay for our imports of crude oil. What would happen to the United States and Canada if the crop-growing weather in countries such as Russia and China was so good that they did not need our excess food? (What would happen to us if they sharply increased food production by increasing fertilizer application?) These are only two obvious questions raised by our export of vast quantities of food, but there are many other kinds of effects on our own country.

Weather, mineral fuels, and renewable natural resources are all linked through the system of international trade. Human population sizes are also part of the causal pathway, because demand for resources per capita must be multiplied by population size to show the magnitude of total national demand for any particular resource. Economic factors are also involved, because the price of each of the commodities involved in international trade determine the demand for and supplies of that commodity. Governmental factors are involved, since government determines the actual retail price of energy in each country, and hence the demand for it. Thus, in the 1970s governments in North America kept retail energy prices down through regulation, whereas in Europe governments kept energy prices up through taxation. Thus the United States and Canadian governments stimulated gasoline use; European governments discouraged gasoline use. Finally, the cultural belief systems of nations are basic to the systems we are considering, because this factor determines the voting patterns of legislative bodies. Thus we see that seven different types of elements are all involved in complex environmental problems.

IMPACTS OF THE INTERNATIONAL LEVEL ON THE NATIONAL LEVEL

We have seen that the characteristics of cities are affected by the demand for agricultural land at the city edge. Therefore, we are curious as to whether the huge foreign purchases of U.S. agricultural commodities have had a significant impact on the demand for U.S. agricultural land. After 1972, when energy imports began to increase very sharply, there was a great increase in the acreage of crop land harvested. The phenomenon is particularly striking because while there were changes from 1950 to 1972 in the amount of land planted out to any given crop, the total amount of land planted out to the three major crops stayed remarkably constant at about 140 to 155 million acres over that period. But from 1972 to 1977, after we began importing vast quantities of crude oil, the acreage planted out to these three crops (wheat, corn, and soybeans) quickly jumped to over 194 million acres. This jump is highly significant, because the maximum number of acres with appropriate soil to be planted out to these three crops is only 288 million. Thus, after a long period in which only 50 to 54 percent of the available land was used for these three crops each year, use suddenly jumped to using 67 percent of the land. Also, of course, the best land would come into production first, and the poorest land last. Therefore, the production per acre would drop as more land was added to production. As we would expect, therefore, we find that U.S. energy imports affected the price of U.S. agricultural land relative to the price of urban land. U.S. agricultural land increased in price relative to urban land by 14 percent from 1970 to 1975. This implies a lower rate of conversion of agricultural to urban land, less land for houses, and a higher price for house sites. Thus energy imports are now affecting U.S. land use policy, and this will increasingly affect our ability to afford houses.

In Chapter 1, we only considered the impact on the U.S. economy of the projected *average* increase in amounts of agricultural exports in order to pay for imported energy: higher retail food prices, higher housing costs, and higher agricultural land prices at the city edge, with the expected impact on land conversion rates at the city edge, from rural to urban land use.

However, there is another significance of making the U.S. dependent on its ability to pay for imported energy with exported food. Fluctuations about the trend in food exports have effects on the stability of the U.S. economy. To illustrate this point, Table 10.4 computes the expected annual foreign de-

mand for U.S. wheat, on the assumption that this results from multiplying world population outside the United States, by the demand per capita of that population for wheat less foreign wheat production. That demand per capita, in turn, is assumed to increase gradually as world economic activity increases. Then, the expected demand for U.S. wheat is subtracted from actual exports of wheat from the United States each year. Clearly, actual exports of wheat fluctuate violently around the trend line (trajectory) of expected exports of wheat. Why? The explanation is to be found in fluctuations in crop-growing weather in nations that import great quantities of U.S. wheat.

The violence of the fluctuations since 1970 has been particularly striking. Actual wheat exports were much lower than expected in 1971, much higher than expected in 1972 and 1973, then much lower than expected in 1976 and 1977. How can we explain these patterns? The answer can be

TABLE 10.4

Computation of likely trend in foreign demand for U.S. wheat and difference between this trend and actual U.S. wheat exports

Year	Non-U.S. world population (millions)	Per capita non-U.S. world wheat expected demand (bu)	Per capita non-U.S. world wheat actual production (bu)	Expected total foreign demand for U.S. wheat (millions of bu)	Actual U.S. wheat exports (millions of bu)	Actual U.S. wheat exports less expected foreign demand (millions of bu)
1969	3362	3.26	3.06	672	606	−66
1970	3430	3.31	3.09	755	741	−14
1971	3502	3.36	3.13	805	610	−195
1972	3576	3.41	3.16	894	1135	241
1973	3648	3.46	3.19	985	1217	232
1974	3720	3.51	3.23	1042	1019	−23
1975	3795	3.56	3.27	1101	1173	72
1976	3871	3.61	3.30	1200	950	−250
1977	3948	3.66	3.33	1303	1145	−158

found in fluctuations in crop-growing weather, and hence in crop production, as brought out in Table 10.5. We notice, first, that there is great variation in crop production for all the major crops. Thus, for wheat produced in the United States, the difference in production between the least productive year of the period (1970) and the most productive year (1976) was 20.8 million metric tons, or 36 percent of the production in the most productive years. We also notice that some of the other crops have even more variable production: the difference in production between the most and least productive years for Russian wheat was 40 percent of the amount produced in the most productive year. However, because average wheat production in Russia is so much greater than average wheat production in America, the difference in production between the most and least productive years in Russia, for wheat, was equal to 75 percent of entire production for the best wheat-growing year the U.S. ever had. A shortfall in Russian wheat production, as in 1972, becomes a

huge surge in demand for exported U.S. wheat in 1972 and 1973, above what we expected. Russian shortages again generated huge demand for wheat and corn in the United States in 1979 and 1980.

This brings out some of the new types of phenomena that we see when we explore the impact of the international level on the national level.

The point is that if resource pricing policies by the U.S. president and Congress should promote a dependence of the U.S. economy on the ability of the United States to sell food to other countries in order to pay for imported crude oil, then some most curious phenomena could result. In effect, this establishes very tight coupling between Russian crop-growing weather and U.S. economic stability.

The fluctuations in foreign crop growth (as in Table 10.5) can be used to account for fluctuations in U.S. crop exports (as in Table 10.4). One complication is that a foreign shortfall in crop growth will not show up immediately in increased demand for U.S.

TABLE 10.5
Variability in production of some major world crops[1] (in millions of metric tons)

Year	U.S.S.R. wheat	China rice	India rice	U.S.A. wheat	U.S.A. corn
1978	121	132	79	49	180
1977	92	130	79	55	163
1976	97	129	63	58	159
1975	66	128	73	58	148
1974	84	126	60	48	119
1973	110	121	66	47	144
1972	86	114	59	42	142
1971	99	118	65	44	143
1970	100	113	63	37	105
Difference between most and least productive years	55	19	20	21	75

[1]Copyright, United Nations (1979). Reproduced by permission. Data source: *Statistical Yearbook of the United States, 1978*, pp. 130–149.

crops, because the other country will normally have a large carryover on hand from previous years. A shortfall in one growing season will often only be revealed by a surge of demand on foreign markets the following year, or two years later. Russia had good crop-growing years in 1970 and 1971; U.S. exports of wheat were low in those years. But then Russia had a small wheat crop in 1972, so that U.S. wheat exports were higher than expected in 1973. In 1973, Russia had a very large wheat crop, so that U.S. wheat exports were lower than expected in 1974.

Consequences of Fluctuations in Foreign Production

What are the consequences of these big fluctuations in crop production in Russia and other foreign countries that are major importers of U.S. agricultural produce? Table 10.6 presents the possible combinations of crop-growing weather conditions in this and other countries and the resulting economic scenarios, as they might be portrayed and considered in a U.S. cabinet meeting, for example.

If crop-growing weather is good in the United States and in other countries that typically import U.S. agricultural commodities, then while U.S. crop exports are high, they are not high enough to prevent domestic stocks from becoming very high. In this instance, there is little agricultural commodity price inflation, because domestic supplies are very large relative to domestic demand for agricultural commodities. But the United States cannot sell enough commodities to pay for crude oil imports. Since the United States is buying foreign crude oil at a faster rate than other countries buy commodities from the United States, our currency accumulates in the banks of other countries (because they can't spend it as fast as it arrives). This leads to decline in the value of the U.S. dollar relative to the value of other currencies (such as the Japanese yen, the Swiss franc, and the German mark). This happened in 1977 and 1978, for example. The other rows of Table 10.6 outline the consequences for the U.S. economy of other combinations of crop-growing weather conditions. The table makes one point very clear: by keeping the price of energy low, Congress inadvertently arranges to have violent fluctuations of alternating inflation

TABLE 10.6
Impact of weather on economic scenarios for the United States

Crop-growing weather in United States	Crop-growing weather in countries importing U.S. crops	U.S. crop exports	U.S. domestic commodity stocks	U.S. commodity price inflation	Value of U.S. dollar relative to other currencies	Tendency to depression radiating outward from agriculture	Approximate probability of this scenario
Good	Good	High	Very high	Little	Dropping	High	.55
Good	Bad	Very high	Very low	Serious	Stabilizing	None	.36
Bad	Good	Very low	Low	Serious	Dropping	Moderate	.01
Bad	Bad	Low	Extremely low	Very serious	Stabilizing	Moderate	.08

Conclusion: Congress, by keeping energy prices so low as to encourage massive importation of crude oil, makes the U.S. economy very sensitive to violent economic fluctuations between inflation and depression.

and depression originate in the farm sector of the United States. In years when crop growth in other countries is good, U.S. farmers produce far more than they can sell, and the prices for their produce drops, even though the costs to them for their inputs are constantly rising (tractor fuel, fertilizer, pesticides, farm machinery). In years when crop growth elsewhere is bad, the farmers enjoy enormous if short-lived, prosperity, but everyone else pays exorbitant prices for food.

In short, by failing to take a sufficiently systemic view of the impact of environmental factors on the world economy, the U.S. government creates unnecessary hardship for the population. In effect, the government adopts as its basic policy keeping energy prices low and having all other national policies follow from that: economic policy, land use policy, foreign policy, and so on. It would make far more sense for the government to settle on a reasonable price to the consumers for food, and a reasonable price to the farmers for their effort, and let all other national policies, including energy policy, flow out from those two basic decisions.

RECIPROCAL RELATIONSHIPS BETWEEN THE CITY LEVEL AND THE OTHER TWO LEVELS

From discussion to this point, it should be clear that there are continuous loops of causal pathways running up and down through the three levels: city, national, and international economic-environmental system. Year-to-year changes in worldwide food demand affect year-to-year changes in demand for U.S. agricultural land at the city edge. These fluctuations occur about a gradually rising trend in demand for land, as the world economy is currently constituted (with low U.S. energy prices). Thus, world demand for

food will regulate the rate at which land is converted to urban use at the city edge, and hence, in turn, city density and the volume of traffic flow down main city arteries. Also, this implies decreased consumption of gasoline by the people in cities as they travel in less energy-consumptive modes of transportation than the family car. This, in turn, results in less need for the nation to export food.

However, the preceding discussion only brings out a partial aspect of the implications of U.S. energy policy. It also has implications for the rate of growth of the world economy. If U.S. cities use too much energy, but the U.S. cannot export enough food to pay for it, then our dollars pile up in other countries. That not only means that our currency cheapens relative to foreign currencies: it also means that foreign currencies become more expensive relative to ours. That means, ultimately, that it becomes more difficult for West Germany to sell cars in the United States, or for Japan to sell cars, color televisions, or high-fidelity equipment in the U.S. That means, in turn, that there are layoffs in German and Japanese factories, and their economies cannot grow so fast. The ultimate consequence would be that German and Japanese people were less able to buy U.S. commodities and manufactured products, and our economy would grow more slowly.

In short, because of the interrelationships between components and levels, causes and effects become linked together in a great variety of ways. The resultant complex interactions imply that we are all involved with systems that constantly generate completely unforeseen or counterintuitive consequences, given conventional methods of thinking about reality. For this reason, we require a completely unconventional method for viewing reality that matches the character of the systems around us; such a method is presented in the next chapter.

Can National Energy Policy Affect Mortgages?

One of the most convincing, yet widely unnoticed examples of causal pathways flowing between hierarchical levels concerns the impact of national energy policy on the interest rate on home mortgages, and hence the cost of housing. If the U.S. energy price is too low, because of government policy, thus stimulating domestic consumption and discouraging domestic energy production, the result is a net out-flow of U.S. money to other countries to pay for imported crude oil. As this U.S. money accumulates, unwanted, in the banks of other countries (because they do not buy so much from us as we buy from them), the value of our money drops relative to the value of foreign currencies.

At any time, a great deal of the investment in the United States is by people from other countries; for them to continue to invest here, they must receive an interest rate equal to the rate they receive at home, plus a premium to compensate them for the fact that our money is dropping in value relative to theirs. For this reason, the interest rate on borrowed money in the United States, which is in effect set by the Federal Reserve Board, must rise whenever the U.S. trade deficit becomes worse, so as to encourage foreign investors to leave their money in this country despite its drop in value relative to their own currency. In short, as our crude oil imports rise relative to our exports, the interest rate on borrowed money in the United States must rise to keep foreign money here. Thus, there is a direct connection between U.S. national energy policy and the interest rate that U.S. citizens must pay when they borrow money to buy a house (or anything else). The national level cause (defective energy policy) has an effect on an international phenomenon (international trade and money flows), which in turn affects a national variable (Federal Funds interest rate), which ultimately affected the local level variable: cost of a house. The same international trade and money system has produced a surge in demand for U.S. agricultural produce and U.S. crop-growing land. This increased the competition for land for houses, so that the cost of land has risen from 11 percent of house cost in 1949 to 25 percent now (3).

Thus we see that the two most rapidly rising components of the cost of new houses are affected by our national energy policy, yet few people perceive this as one of the many costs of the defective energy policy. The reason, of course, is that few people think in terms of causal pathways that move between hierarchical levels.

SUMMARY

This chapter has shown that there are various cause-effect pathways that operate amongst all seven types of components but also between the three hierarchical levels. Thus, something as basic as national energy pricing policy has a wide variety of systemic effects that would be unexpected by most people, on land use, the character of cities, and the rates of growth of the U.S. and world economies.

SUGGESTIONS FOR INDIVIDUAL AND GROUP PROJECTS

Using *The Statistical Abstracts of the United States,* update Tables 10.4 and 10.5. Can you see a continuing pattern in the relation between foreign crop production and U.S. crop exports?

How close is our total use of agricultural land getting to the maximum amount of land available for crop agriculture?

Using Table 10.6 as a guide, try to trace through the effects of crop-growing weather in the United States and other countries on year-to-year fluctuations in the state of the U.S. economy. Now write a flow chart to express your ideas.

Update Figure 1.5, using *The Statistical Abstracts of the United States,* and see how energy policy and crop production have affected consumer purchasing power.

REFERENCES

1. Borgstrom, G., *The Hungry Planet.* New York: Macmillan, 1965.
2. Borgstrom, G., *Too Many.* London: Macmillan, 1969.
3. Carberry, J., "Land plays rising role, labor a reduced one in the long, steep climb in cost of new homes," *The Wall Street Journal,* Oct. 11, 1978.
4. Darmstadter, J.; J. Dunkerley; and J. Alterman, *How Industrial Societies Use Energy.* Baltimore: The Johns Hopkins University Press, 1977.
5. *The Economist,* "The World in Figures" 1976.
6. Eyre, S. R., *The Real Wealth of Nations.* New York: St. Martin's Press, 1978.
7. Forrester, N. B., *The Life Cycle of Economic Development.* Cambridge, Mass.: Wright-Allen Press, 1973.
8. Watt, K. E. F.; J. W. Young; J. L. Mitchiner; and J. W. Brewer, "A simulation of the use of energy and land at the national level," *Simulation* 24 (1975), pp. 129–153.
9. The Workshop on Alternate Energy Strategies (WAES), *Third Technical Report: Energy Supply-Demand Integrations to the Year 2000. Global and National Studies.* Cambridge, Mass.: The MIT Press, 1977.
10. The World Bank, *World Tables 1976.* Baltimore: The Johns Hopkins University Press, 1976.
11. Zeimetz, K. A.; E. Dillon; E. E. Hardy; and R. C. Otte, *Dynamics of Land Use in Fast Growth Areas.* Economic Research Service, U.S. Department of Agriculture, Agricultural Economic Report No. 325. Washington: U.S. Department of Agriculture, 1976.

11 HOW THE WHOLE SYSTEM WORKS

Constantly regard the universe as one living being, having one substance and one soul; and observe how all things have reference to one perception, the perception of this one living being; and how all things act with one movement; and how all things are the cooperating causes of all things which exist; observe too the continuous spinning of the thread and the contexture of the web.

Emperor Marcus Aurelius (121–180 A.D.), The Meditations, *Book IV.*

MAIN THEMES OF THIS CHAPTER

Previous chapters have examined a number of individual causal pathways. However, understanding each of these is not equivalent to understanding the implications of the system that results when all these causal pathways function together. The features of the systems we have been considering are particularly difficult to comprehend.

In the first place, a cause operating at one hierarchical level can trigger an effect at another level. To illustrate, defective national energy policy that depresses retail energy prices produces pollution at the local level. National energy policy also has international effects, such as the increased volume of world trade resulting when energy-short countries with a superabundance of food trade the food to buy energy. Another example is very high wages in one country (a national-level cause) stimulating massive immigration into that country from low-wage countries (an international-level effect). So cause-effect pathways may have surprising ultimate effects when they cross hierarchical levels.

In the real world, cause-effect pathways can also cross between types of factors. A political cause can have an economic effect,

235

which in turn has an effect on a nonrenewable resource, which in turn has an economic
effect, and so on. This type of causal pathway keeps cutting across barriers (which
exist only in our heads and the structure of
our institutions) and hence may have ultimate consequences very difficult for us to
perceive. Indeed, it will be clear from this
chapter that a variety of political constituencies are vigorously pushing for policies
that would ruin them if put into effect: the
constituency simply hasn't traced the consequences of their proposed policies through
all the relevent causal pathways so as to discern the ultimate effects.

A SIMPLE EXAMPLE OF A
SYSTEM: INTERNATIONAL TRADE
AND LAND USE

Few people understand the counterintuitive
(surprising) behavior of complex systems
(Figure 11.1). An excellent example, discussed in previous chapters, is the large
number of causal pathways relating to international trade and land use (16). The collective, systemic properties of all these causal
pathways can be expressed in a single flow
chart such as Figure 11.2.

1. The first step is low-priced gasoline in
   combination with high national average
   disposable personal income.
2. This produces high gasoline consumption, as we have seen in the United
   States in recent years.
3. This, in turn contributes to high U.S. oil
   consumption.
4. The low U.S. national oil price has depressed oil production.
5. High demand in combination with low
   supply leads to high U.S. oil imports.
6. This in turn produces the high wheat exports we have experienced since 1973.

7. Those high wheat exports have lowered
   wheat reserves.
8. These lower U.S. stocks of wheat have
   produced the inflation in wholesale
   wheat prices, and also in the prices of all
   foods, which we have recently experienced in the supermarket.
9. The higher wheat wholesale prices have
   also made farming seem more financially attractive, and therefore have
   driven up the price of farmland.
10. This has decreased the rate at which
    farmland is converted to urban use at
    the edge of cities.
11. The result has been a decrease in the
    rate of urban sprawl.
12. That will shortly lead to higher urban
    densities.
13. The result will be increased availability
    of public transport, to avoid the traffic
    congestion that would be created by
    cars at very high passenger flow rates
    down main streets.
14. When more public transportation be-
    comes available, people will shift to use
    of public transportation instead of cars,
    and a higher percentage of the commut-
    ing labor force will travel by public
    transportation. That is, there will be a
    change in the relative use of different
    modes of transportation (the "modal
    split").
15. Because of the increased use of public
    transportation, the overall efficiency of
    energy use in the transportation system
    will increase (because public transporta-
    tion delivers more passenger-miles of
    transportation per gallon of fuel).
16. That implies a lower national require-
    ment for transportation fuel consump-
    tion per person.

Since total U.S. transportation fuel consumption is consumption per capita multiplied by population size, pathway (16) im-

FIGURE 11.1

The reason why systems have counterintuitive (surprising) features. "Counterintuitive" describes systems so complex that their responses to "remedial" policies are opposite to those most people would expect (3).

Many people might understand that

Factor A affects factor B, or	A ⟶ B
and that A affects C, or	A ⟶ C
and that B affects D, or	B ⟶ D
and that C affects D, or	C ⟶ D
and that D affects F, or	D ⟶ F
and that F affects G, or	F ⟶ G
and that E affects G, or	E ⟶ G
and that G affects H, or	G ⟶ H
and that H affects E, or	H ⟶ E
and that H affects A, or	H ⟶ A.

But how many people would, therefore, perceive that this was a self-regulatory system, in which A was affected by every other system component, as in the following diagram?

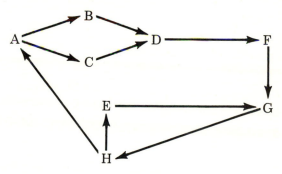

plies a reduction in the future need for national fuel consumption (3).

Thus, we have closure of a very long causal loop. If national oil consumption rises to very high levels, as it has done, this sets in motion a sequence of cause-effect pathways, which after a long lag produce lowered national oil consumption. Such loop closure is characteristic of highly complex systems (4, 8, 10, 11). When their structure is exam-

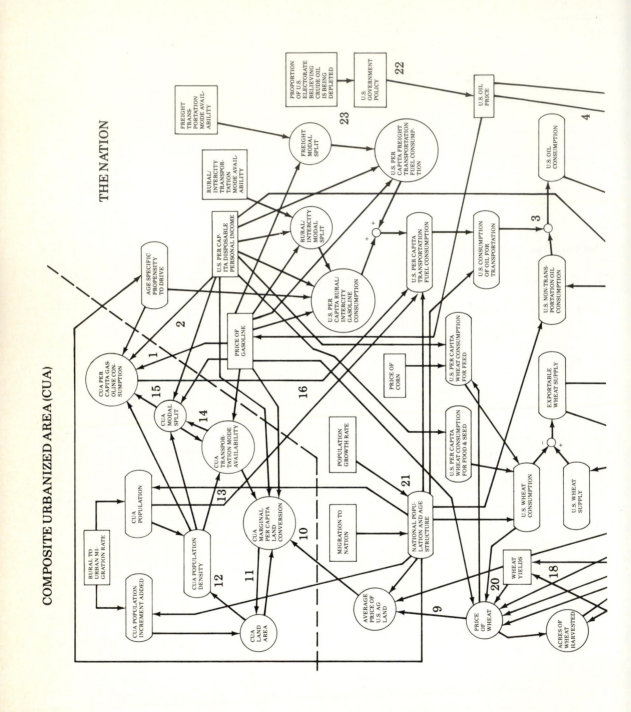

COMPOSITE URBANIZED AREA (CUA)

THE NATION

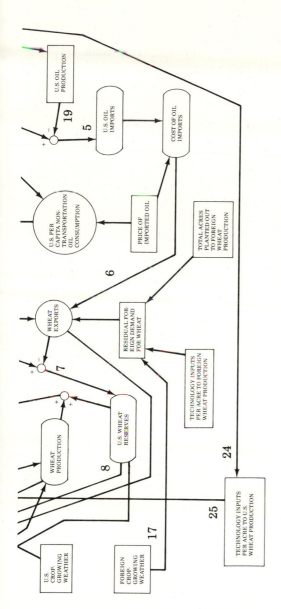

The diagram contains the following labeled elements:

U.S. OIL PRODUCTION

19

U.S. OIL IMPORTS

5

COST OF OIL IMPORTS

U.S. PER CAPITA NON-TRANSPORTATION OIL CONSUMPTION

PRICE OF IMPORTED OIL

6

TOTAL ACRES PLANTED OUT TO FOREIGN WHEAT PRODUCTION

WHEAT EXPORTS

RESIDUAL FOREIGN DEMAND FOR WHEAT

7

TECHNOLOGY INPUTS PER ACRE TO FOREIGN WHEAT PRODUCTION

WHEAT PRODUCTION

U.S. WHEAT RESERVES

8

24

U.S. CROP-GROWING WEATHER

FOREIGN CROP-GROWING WEATHER

17

25

TECHNOLOGY INPUTS PER ACRE TO U.S. WHEAT PRODUCTION

STATE VARIABLE. A state variable takes more than one time unit to return to its steady state, or equilibrium value after a perturbation alters it. Because of this inertia, or stiffness, causing state variables to tend to maintain an equilibrium value, these are the variables which tend to maintain the character of any system.

STATE DEPENDENT VARIABLE. These variables respond within one time interval to any change in one or more state variables that affect them. This means that state dependent variables have no inertia or stiffness: they are extremely sensitive to (respond rapidly to) change in the state variables operating on them.

INPUT VARIABLES, or EXOGENOUS VARIABLES. These variables are thought of as external to the system described by the flow chart. Changes in these variables, due either to natural causes or policy decisions alters state, and state dependent variables.

FIGURE 11.2

The system of cause-effect relationships connecting energy use, transportation, oil and gasoline prices, international trade, agriculture, land use, and city characteristics. This figure introduces the notion that system variables are of different types. Three different types are distinguished in this figure, using the code for shapes. Reprinted with the permission of the copyright holder, Simulation Councils, Inc. (adapted from 16).

ined, they turn out to be negative feedback control loops, but with such long time lags that the entire system can depart a long way from its equilibrium state before equilibrating forces can begin to pull it back to a stable state. By that time it may have found a new equilibrium.

Figure 11.2 brings out a point mentioned previously in this book: complex systems involve causal pathways flowing between very different kinds of components and between different hierarchical levels. Thus, in this figure we find causal pathways flowing from the physical environment (17, 18) in the form of crop-growing weather; a nonrenewable resource, oil (19); a renewable resource, wheat (20); a demographic factor, population growth rate (21); and various prices (economic factors, such as 1 and 4). Federal government policy regulates the U.S. crude oil price (22), and culture, in turn (the beliefs of the electorate concerning energy), is a driving force operating on that government policy (23). Also, we note that national level factors affect the international economic system, as at pathway 5, where a shortfall in U.S. oil production triggers importation; the national system affects the typical city through the land conversion rate (10), as well as through the price of gasoline (1). An economic variable, the U.S. oil price, affects a cultural variable, the type and amount of technology inputs per acre to U.S. wheat production (24). Thus, if oil is cheap, agricultural pests will tend to be controlled with chemical pesticides; if oil becomes expensive, pests will tend to be controlled by biological control agents (insect parasites and predators), which are selected by means of a highly labor-intensive research effort. Similarly, if oil is cheap, fertilization will be by chemical fertilizers; if it is expensive, horses will be more important on farms and a higher proportion of fertilizer applied will be manure.

The type and amount of technology inputs to agriculture, in turn, will operate on a renewable natural resource variable: wheat yields (25).

The U.S. oil price, as determined by government policy, will not only determine domestic oil production; it will also determine domestic demand for gasoline (1).

The lags associated with a system of this type might be two decades or more in length because of the great time required to get new types of transportation systems in place. (Thirty-two years elapsed from the initiation of planning to project completion of the San Francisco Bay Rapid Transit system; METRO in Washington, D.C., and the Metropolitan Atlanta system [MARTA] were also very lengthy projects.)

Merely inspecting this chart, we can see the reasons for many of the striking differences between countries, or the historical changes within any country. To illustrate, the "composite urbanized area marginal per capita land conversion rate" measures the rate at which land is converted from agricultural to urban use at the outskirts of the typical urban area, per person added to the urban population. If this rate is very high, we have a great deal of urban sprawl, as in the United States, Canada, and Australia. If the rate is very low, cities have high densities and sharply defined boundaries with the surrounding area, as in Holland, Switzerland, and other European countries. What determines if this land transfer rate is high or low? Either a country may have an absolute shortage of farmland per capita as in Europe, or there may be a shortage of farmland, after subtracting the very high proportion of all farmland that must be set aside to grow food for export to buy imported crude oil, as in the United States.

Similarly, changes in this rate of land transfer through time have altered the rate of change in city density. Within the last few years, the rate has declined in the United States, and cities will now become more compact.

THREE-DIMENSIONAL MODELS OF ENVIRONMENTAL PROBLEMS

A problem with flow charts such as Figure 11.2 is that we can never be sure that we have included all the factors that are important in the dynamics of the system. It would be preferable to design some systematic template for displaying the important cause-effect pathways operating in any system that ensures that we don't leave out any of the pathways. To this end, we introduce the notion of three-dimensional flow charts that include boxes for all possible types of factors. Initially, these charts are explained in terms of a plane projection of a solid; then we will use perspective drawings of the solid.

Figure 11.3 is one view of the solid: it imbeds the subsystem of Figure 11.2 within a more comprehensive conceptual model. Figure 11.3 is designed to ensure that all possible systemic impacts of various factors are included in any analysis of an environmental problem, by expressing the causal system in the form of a two-dimensional grid. In this grid, or matrix, the seven rows represent the seven sets of factors introduced in Chapters 3 to 9. The five columns represent positions along a five-step causal sequence, from ultimate causes, to key driving factors, then key driving processes, immediate effects, then finally ultimate effects.

The ultimate causes are basic to everything else in the system. They are either exogenous variables, totally beyond human control, such as volcanic eruptions or variations in solar radiation intensity, or they are state variables, such as cultural values, with

a great deal of inertia (resistance to change). Typically, all these variables interact to produce key driving factors.

Charts with these seven rows and five columns of boxes can be used as templates on which to enter the causal pathways describing any complex environmental phenomenon. (In using computer modeling for environmental policy analysis, the next step would be to write a computer program with one equation representing each arrow in the chart. The contents of the boxes would be represented by the values stored in blocks of "memory" locations in the core of the computer.)

To illustrate the character of environmental systems, arrows have been entered on the Figure 11.3 flow chart representing many of the causal pathways discussed in this book.

Generalizations Revealed by the Flow Chart

A number of interesting generalizations follow from inspection of such a chart.

There are two ways one can look at any problem. One way is to analyze the problem insofar as possible, working within the confines of a particular academic discipline, such as geology, biology, economics, or sociology. If one does this, then the result is a mental model of the problem largely enclosed by one of the rows in this chart, or by a row and the two adjacent rows. The second way of looking at a problem is to use any disciplines one must in order to understand all the causal pathways involved in the problem. This is an interdisciplinary perspective, and leads to a mental model characterized by a lot of arrows connecting all seven rows. It leads to a quite different perspective than the intradisciplinary perspective.

To illustrate, suppose we consider the impact of climate on trade and the economy. A

FIGURE 11.3

Flow chart of a conceptual model of the United States, with some of the arrows for a national model included. This chart represents only the national level of the full model, which includes also the city and international levels. Further, conceptual models in this form are very highly aggregated: in more detailed charts from which computer code is written, the boxes would be broken down into component boxes, between which there were arrows, as well as arrows between clusters of boxes.

CAUSAL SYSTEM GOVERNING RATE OF ECONOMIC GROWTH IN ADVANCED ECONOMIES

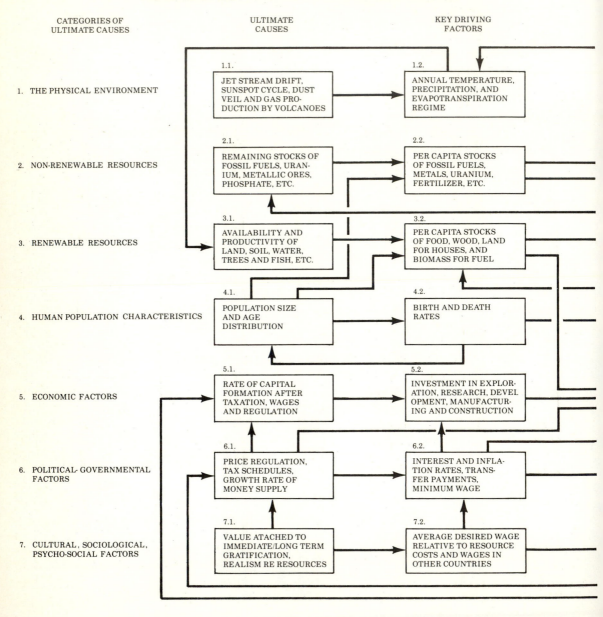

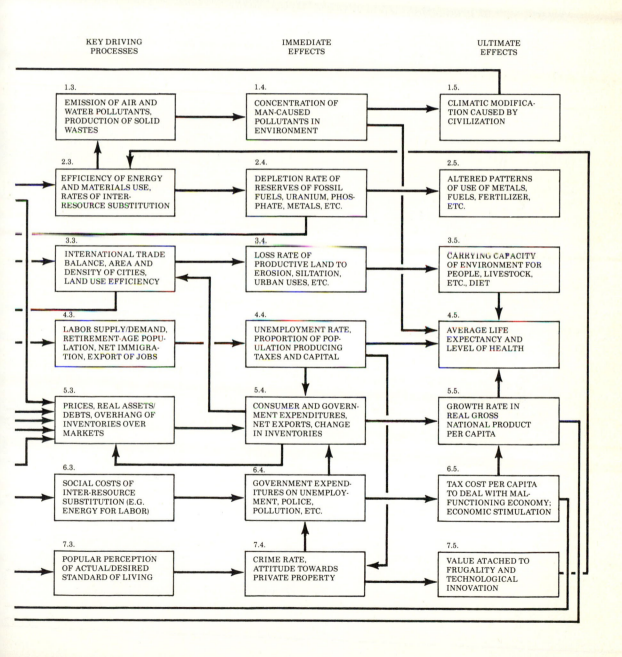

KEY DRIVING
PROCESSES

IMMEDIATE
EFFECTS

ULTIMATE
EFFECTS

1.3.
EMISSION OF AIR AND
WATER POLLUTANTS,
PRODUCTION OF SOLID
WASTES

1.4.
CONCENTRATION OF
MAN-CAUSED
POLLUTANTS IN
ENVIRONMENT

1.5.
CLIMATIC MODIFICA-
TION CAUSED BY
CIVILIZATION

2.3.
EFFICIENCY OF ENERGY
AND MATERIALS USE,
RATES OF INTER-
RESOURCE SUBSTITUTION

2.4.
DEPLETION RATE OF
RESERVES OF FOSSIL
FUELS, URANIUM, PHOS-
PHATE, METALS, ETC.

2.5.
ALTERED PATTERNS
OF USE OF METALS,
FUELS, FERTILIZER,
ETC.

3.3.
INTERNATIONAL TRADE
BALANCE, AREA AND
DENSITY OF CITIES,
LAND USE EFFICIENCY

3.4.
LOSS RATE OF
PRODUCTIVE LAND TO
EROSION, SILTATION,
URBAN USES, ETC.

3.5.
CARRYING CAPACITY
OF ENVIRONMENT FOR
PEOPLE, LIVESTOCK,
ETC., DIET

4.3.
LABOR SUPPLY/DEMAND,
RETIREMENT-AGE POPU-
LATION, NET IMMIGRA-
TION, EXPORT OF JOBS

4.4.
UNEMPLOYMENT RATE,
PROPORTION OF POP-
ULATION PRODUCING
TAXES AND CAPITAL

4.5.
AVERAGE LIFE
EXPECTANCY AND
LEVEL OF HEALTH

5.3.
PRICES, REAL ASSETS/
DEBTS, OVERHANG OF
INVENTORIES OVER
MARKETS

5.4.
CONSUMER AND GOVERN-
MENT EXPENDITURES,
NET EXPORTS, CHANGE
IN INVENTORIES

5.5.
GROWTH RATE IN
REAL GROSS
NATIONAL PRODUCT
PER CAPITA

6.3.
SOCIAL COSTS OF
INTER-RESOURCE
SUBSTITUTION (E.G.
ENERGY FOR LABOR)

6.4.
GOVERNMENT EXPEND-
ITURES ON UNEMPLOY-
MENT, POLICE,
POLLUTION, ETC.

6.5.
TAX COST PER CAPITA
TO DEAL WITH MAL-
FUNCTIONING ECONOMY;
ECONOMIC STIMULATION

7.3.
POPULAR PERCEPTION
OF ACTUAL/DESIRED
STANDARD OF LIVING

7.4.
CRIME RATE,
ATTITUDE TOWARDS
PRIVATE PROPERTY

7.5.
VALUE ATACHED TO
FRUGALITY AND
TECHNOLOGICAL
INNOVATION

volcanic eruption would spew vast quantities of gas and fine dust into the upper atmosphere, decreasing penetration of the earth's gaseous cover by solar radiation. This cause (1.1) would lead to a global temperature depression (1.2), which in turn would lead to decreased production of agricultural commodities in the United States (3.1). Decrease in production would lead to decreased per capita stocks of wheat, corn, and soybeans in the United States (3.2), and this would drive up prices (5.3). There would be less money available to spend on houses and durable goods, after paying for food, so consumer expenditures for those items would decrease (5.4), leading to a decrease in the growth rate in real gross national product per capita (5.5).

The Seven Types of System Components

This chart exposes the seven key driving processes that explain both differences between nations, and historical changes in a nation. Each of these driving processes is associated primarily with one of the categories of ultimate causes. Humanity operates on the fate of a nation by:

1. Polluting the physical environment.
2. Making inefficient use of nonrenewable resources and making unwise substitutions of rare resources for abundant resources (as when we substitute too much energy for labor).
3. Imposing excessive strain on the long-term productive capacity of agricultural and forest soil, by excessive deforestation and exporting too much agricultural and forest commodities; and by making inefficient use of productive land (as when we cover it up with cities).
4. Creating imbalances in the population subsystem, by excessive immigration, excessive emigration of jobs, or age-specific birth rates based on no thought of the future, which set up subsequent imbalances between population age groups.
5. By unwise management of the economy, running down stocks of resources so as to drive up prices, or by using up resources too fast by means of purchases based on debt rather than assets, or by short-term excessive rates of use of resources only creating excessive inventories of houses or manufactured goods which subsequently saturate demand and lead to recession or depression.
6. By unwise substitution of resources for one another. To illustrate, when we allow cities to sprawl too much, too much driving is required to get around in the city. This means that intensive use of energy is being used to compensate for extensive use of land. In effect, there is unwise substitution of energy for land: it would have been better to have more compact cities, and increase the productivity of land so as to allow an associated more productive use of energy.
7. By a popular perception that the standard of living depends on a high rate of resource consumption, rather than efficiency in resource use. This happens when the public has an unrealistic perception about the availability of all kinds of resources and therefore sees no point in using them as productively as possible.

Figure 11.3 brings out the pervasive effects of the ultimate causes. For example, population size operates on the whole system, because prices are affected by stocks *per capita*. Culture operates on every aspect of the system: the crime rate, the value attached to technological innovation and hence on the efficiency with which resources are used, the rate at which government is expected to change the amount of money in circulation (the inflation rate), and government expenditures, which determine the amount of capital available to the private sector for investment in further economic growth (15). Climate, energy and mineral stocks, soil quality, and the tax schedule have similar effects that permeate the whole system.

Also, the system is replete with closed, homeostatic (self-regulatory, negative-feedback) loops. Unfortunately, a chart of this type is difficult to read when all the arrows are entered. However, when they are entered, it appears that any box trips causal pathways that ultimately loop back and operate on that box. Even in this chart, in which many of the causal pathways operating in the real system are not represented by arrows, many examples of closed loops can be found (5.1 to 5.5 to 5.1; 6.1 to 6.5 to 6.1; 4.1 to 4.2 to 4.1).

Many causal pathways are implied by this chart. To illustrate, land availability (3.1) is a determinant of the energy price within a country. If a nation has a small amount of agricultural land per capita, as in the case of Japan or Northwest Europe, this is compensated for by boosting the productivity of the land per hectare. This is achieved by increasing the inputs of agricultural technology per hectare (such as fertilizer or tractor use), all of which require crude oil or natural gas. Such countries run down their domestic supplies of energy more rapidly than they would if they had more land. In other words, land and energy are resources that can be substituted for each other on the farm, just as they can in the city. A country can achieve high agricultural production with either vast acreages under cultivation with low fertilizer input and production per acre (the United States or Russia), or small acreages under cultivation with very high fertilizer input and productivity per acre (Japan or Holland).

The point of this book is to show how environmental problems can be traced back to their ultimate causes or to show how ultimate causes can be followed out to their ultimate effects.

Immediate effects exhibit rapid response to alteration of a key driving process. To illustrate, if domestic food stocks drop rapidly because of higher rates of food export, and food prices consequently increase (5.3), this means that people have a lower percentage of their spendable earnings available for nonfood items (5.4).

Note that all the "ultimate effects" in this chart could in turn become causes for the "ultimate causes," because of the closed-loop character of these systems. To illustrate, following a long period with a high rate of economic growth (as in 1919–1929), there can be a sharp decrease in the level of economic activity (as in 1930–1939). This, in turn, has pronounced effects on the psychological state of the population, reflected in the way they invest money more cautiously and much less speculatively than spending patterns in an economic boom. The system is a closed loop with the mood of the population (from unrealistic overoptimism in a boom to unrealistic pessimism in a bust) ultimately affecting economic growth rate, which in turn then feeds back on the collective mood. Of course, many scholars have been aware of this particular loop for a long time. It is widely believed that such loops are the driving forces behind business cycles of various lengths, from the four- or five-year "business cycle" to the much longer, forty- to sixty-year "Kondratieff Wave," named after the Russian economist who first noticed it. These cycles and waves are intimately interlinked with environmental issues: people overexploit the environment in a boom and are more frugal, cautious, and conservative in a bust.

HIERARCHICAL MODELS OF ENVIRONMENTAL PROBLEMS

Figure 11.3 does not capture the complete system of cause-effect pathways operating in complex environmental phenomena, because it omits the role of multiple hierarchical levels (10, 11). To illustrate, low national average energy prices create excessive pollution in metropolitan regions, but have very little impact on the pollution level in the wilderness of Nevada, Utah, New Mexico, or Arizona. Also, we will overlook the significance of such phenomena as immigration, differences between nations in crop-growing weather, or inability of the United States to pay for foreign raw materials in adequate quantities if we only look at the national level.

Therefore, we introduce a third axis into our conceptual model: hierarchical level (6, 10, 11). For the purposes of the rest of this book, it will suffice to consider just three hierarchical levels: the international level, the national level, and the metropolitan region (or city).

Now we can imagine a three-dimensional system of environmental cause-effect relationships, in which one axis represents a sequence of types of factors (from physical environment to cultural factors), one represents a sequence from ultimate causes to ultimate effects, and a third represents the hierarchical level (international, national, or metropolitan region). Figure 11.3 can be thought of as a central upright plane in this box; Figure 11.4 displays the twenty-one elements representing all possible categories of ultimate causes for this conceptual model: it

represents the floor of the box. The central column in Figure 11.4 is the first column in Figure 11.3.

The first column of Figure 11.4 exposes causes that arise either because of average worldwide conditions, or differences between nations. The third column of Figure 11.4 highlights causes that are peculiar to metropolitan regions (or other urban centers) but would not be found in other locations within nations.

Now we see how certain phenomena arising at each of the three levels can only be understood in terms of causes at one of the other two levels. For example, migration of people into the United States makes no sense if we only look at the U.S. national level; the phenomenon can only be understood in terms of differences in the population density and age distribution between the United States and other countries and differences in the capital assets per person and the way they are distributed throughout the population. International trade can only be understood in terms of differences in the supply relative to demand for food, minerals, and other resources between nations (6, 10).

Many people have difficulty in visualizing a three-dimensional object in terms of plane projections, as in the last two figures. This is particularly true if we are trying to think through the consequences of causal pathways that not only move upward or downward in such a structure, but also horizontally or vertically *and* horizontally. Plane projections of lines and arrows in a solid are simply incomprehensible. Accordingly, the device used for communicating the structure of such systems to students is three-dimensional flow charts superimposed on a perspective drawing, as in Figure 11.5. This chart consists of three rows, seven columns, and five levels of elements, each of which corresponds to a subsystem in complex envi-

ULTIMATE CAUSES OPERATING AT THREE DIFFERENT HIERARCHICAL LEVELS

	INTERNATIONAL	NATIONAL	METROPOLITAN REGION
1. THE PHYSICAL ENVIRONMENT	AVERAGE GLOBAL CLIMATIC CONDITIONS; BETWEEN-NATION DIFFERENCES IN SUITABILITY OF WEATHER FOR CROP GROWTH	JET STREAM DRIFT, SUNSPOT CYCLE, DUST VEIL AND GAS PRODUCTION BY VOLCANOES	BETWEEN-REGION DIFFERENCES IN CLIMATE, AND PHYSICAL AND CHEMICAL CHARACTERISTICS OF AIR, SOIL AND WATER
2. NON-RENEWABLE RESOURCES	DIFFERENCES BETWEEN NATIONS IN REMAINING STOCKS OF FOSSIL FUELS AND METALLIC ORES, ETC.	REMAINING STOCKS OF FOSSIL FUELS, URANIUM, METALLIC ORES, PHOSPHATE, ETC.	BETWEEN-REGION DIFFERENCES IN REMAINING OIL AND GAS RESERVES, ETC.
3. RENEWABLE RESOURCES	DIFFERENCES BETWEEN NATIONS IN AVAILABILITY AND PRODUCTIVITY OF SOIL AND FORESTS, ETC.	AVAILABILITY AND PRODUCTIVITY OF LAND, SOIL, WATER, TREES AND FISH, ETC.	BETWEEN-REGION DIFFERENCES IN SOIL FERTILITY AND PRODUCTIVITY OF LAKES, ETC., LOCAL SOIL EROSION
4. HUMAN POPULATION CHARACTERISTICS	DIFFERENCES BETWEEN NATIONS IN POPULATION SIZE AND AGE DISTRIBUTION	POPULATION SIZE AND AGE DISTRIBUTION	LOCAL POPULATION AGE DISTRIBUTION LOCAL POPULATION DENSITY
5. ECONOMIC FACTORS	DIFFERENCES BETWEEN NATIONS IN RATE OF CAPITAL FORMATION	RATE OF CAPITAL FORMATION AFTER TAXATION, WAGES AND REGULATION	VALUE OF LOCAL CAPITAL ASSETS: LOCAL CAPITAL STOCK
6. POLITICAL-GOVERNMENTAL FACTORS	DIFFERENCES BETWEEN NATIONS IN PRICE REGULATION, TAX SCHEDULES, AND GROWTH IN MONEY SUPPLY	PRICE REGULATION, TAX SCHEDULES, GROWTH RATE OF MONEY SUPPLY	LOCAL PROPERTY TAX SCHEDULES, LOCAL POLICY ON LAND ZONING, SUPPORT FOR MASS TRANSIT
7. CULTURAL, SOCIOLOGICAL, PSYCHO-SOCIAL FACTORS	DIFFERENCES BETWEEN NATIONS IN VALUE ATTACHED TO IMMEDIATE/LONG TERM GRATIFICATION, RESOURCES	VALUE ATTACHED TO IMMEDIATE/LONG TERM GRATIFICATION, REALISM ABOUT RESOURCES	LOCAL ATTITUDES CONCERNING PUBLIC TRANSPORTATION, ZONING, POLLUTION, ETC.

FIGURE 11.4

The ultimate causes operating at three different hierarchical levels.

FIGURE 11.5

Three-dimensional flow chart of the whole system, with lines (representing causal pathways) between symbols omitted for clarity at this stage. The symbols represent the seven different types of factors introduced in Chapters 3 to 9. This object can be visualized as seven layers, from left to right, each layer being distinguished by a different symbol, for one of the types of factors. Alternatively, the object can be viewed as five floors, from top to bottom, each representing a step in a causal pathway. Finally, the object can be perceived as three faces, from front to back, representing different hierarchical levels, from the international, global level, to the regional, metropolitan level.

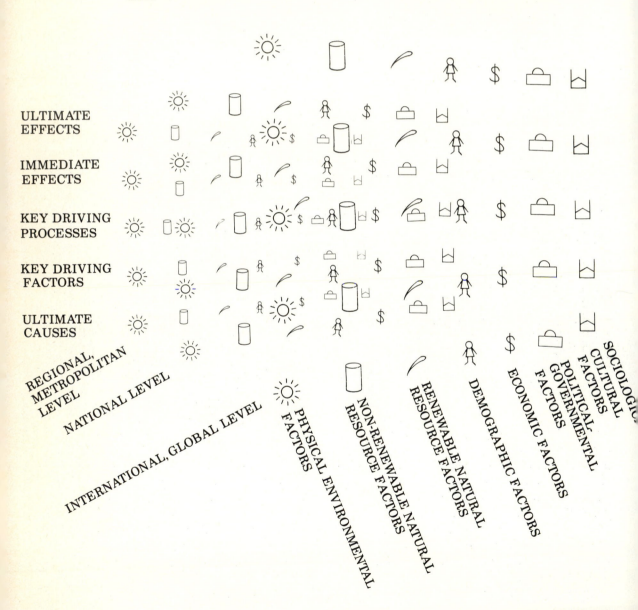

ronmental problems. All environmental problems of modern societies can be understood at an aggregated level in terms of causal pathways connecting various combinations of the 105 elements in this chart. By "aggregated level" we mean that relationships between subelements *within* any one of the boxes are ignored at this overall perspective. (Disaggregation of the subelements within boxes may be a necessary second stage of analysis, prior to writing computer code.)

COUNTERINTUITIVE FEATURES OF COMPLEX ENVIRONMENTAL SYSTEMS

Professor Jay Forrester of M.I.T. has used the term "counterintuitive" to describe systems so complex that their responses to "remedial" policies are opposite to those most people would expect. We will now show how flow charts can be used to clarify situations in which political constituencies operate on the basis of certain assumptions about systems behavior that are intuitively plausible but wrong, because the systems are counterintuitive.

One of the most important beliefs in this country at present is that low energy prices and high energy consumption per capita are prerequisites for a high rate of economic growth. Therefore, it follows, raising energy prices so as to promote conservation and ameliorate pollution would be a bad policy, because it would come at a price of lowered economic growth. Yet Figure 7.5 showed that among developed countries, higher per capita rates of energy consumption are correlated with lower rates of real economic growth per capita. Further, Table 1.2 showed that countries with much lower rates of energy consumption per capita than the United States now have higher levels of

G.N.P. per capita, as well as higher growth rates.

We can use flow charts to explain these paradoxical observations. There are two important causal pathways by which the price of energy affects the economy: one is by means of resource substitution within the United States (Figure 11.6); the other is by means of trade with other countries (Figure 11.7).

In Figure 11.6 downward regulation of energy prices by the federal government leads to low retail energy prices relative to the cost of labor (1). This, in turn, leads to substitution of cheap energy for expensive labor (2). This in turn has five effects: increase in pollution in metropolitan regions (3), increased rate of depletion of domestic fossil fuels (4), increased unemployment rates (5), increased investment in energy generating and using systems (6), and increased crime rates because of the increased unemployment rates (7). These five effects, in turn, all lead to increased tax costs to deal with various types of social dysfunction (police, for example). The increased tax costs (8) lead to a decrease in capital available to promote economic growth (9), and the lowered economic growth, after a delay alters cultural values concerning the optimal strategy for promoting economic growth (10). Altered cultural values and perceptions would ultimately impact on government policy (11), which in turn would affect retail energy prices at the national level (1), and thus the loop is closed.

Keeping energy prices down to combat a general price increase for consumers ignores all these consequences of substitution between resources. Consequently, most people have difficulty perceiving any relationship between irrationally low energy prices, and the fact that their after-tax income available for purchase of durable goods and leisure has dropped, in constant dollars, over the last twelve years.

FIGURE 11.6
The consequences for the United States of retail energy prices rising more slowly than wages (resource substitution loop only).

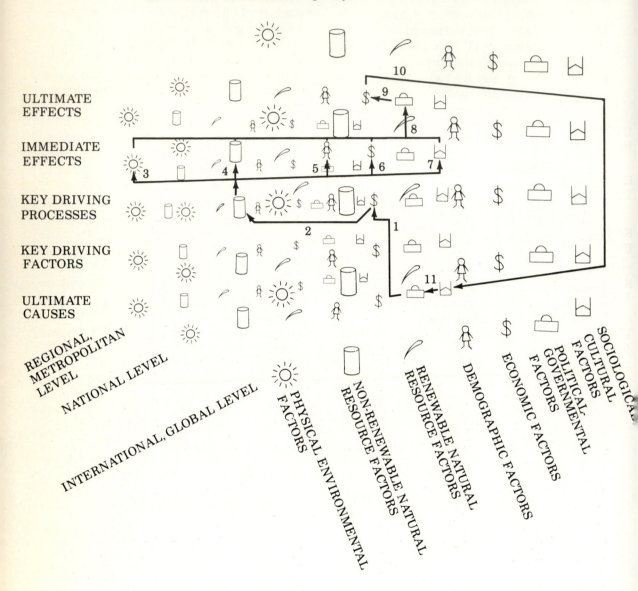

FIGURE 11.7

The effects of attempts by Congress to combat increases in the general price level for consumers by holding down the price of energy (international trade and monetary consequences).

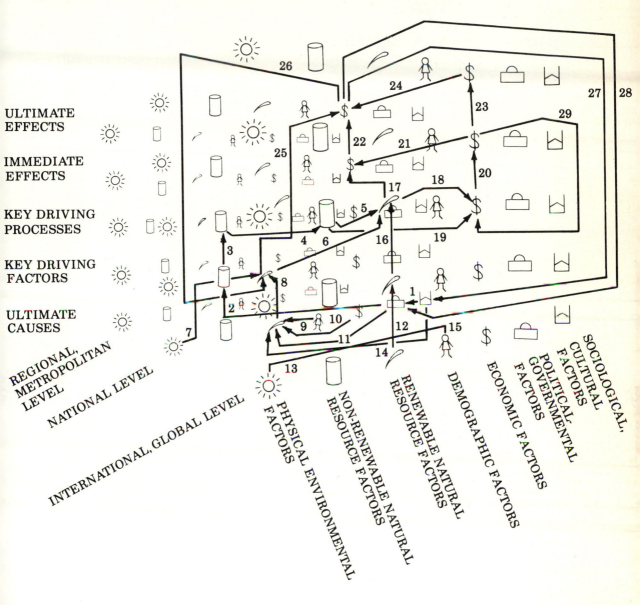

Cheap Energy and International Trade

A general increase in prices is an extraordinarily complex, counterintuitive phenomenon, with many different root causes. (Note that a general increase in prices is not synonymous with an increase in the inflation rate: the former means an increase in the average of all retail prices whereas the latter means an increase in the rate of increase in the money supply.) Efforts to deal with a general price increase elicit a remarkable variety of often surprising responses, because the system being affected consists of many different types of elements and hierarchical levels. Figure 11.7 is designed to reveal the counterintuitive results of Congress keeping U.S. retail energy prices down, supposedly in the interests of combatting a general increase in prices and maintaining the purchasing power of consumers. The figure tracks causal pathways through the international flows of trade and money.

Because of a defective cultural belief system operating on government policy (1), government keeps energy prices down. This depresses U.S. domestic energy production and elevates consumption, thus producing a shortfall in domestic energy supplies (2). This necessitates increased energy imports (3), which implies increased international trade in energy (4), which the U.S. must balance by increased international trade in agricultural commodities (5).

Two groups of causal pathways govern the extent to which the United States is able to pay for imported crude oil by exporting agricultural commodities: our ability to export and demand from other countries for our commodities.

One determinant of the volume of U.S. crops exported is the size of our stocks of agricultural commodities available for export (6). This, in turn, is controlled by six causal pathways. The first influence is from U.S. crop-growing weather (7). The second is from the acreage of crops planted in the United States (8). That, in turn is determined by U.S. population size (9), the price for agricultural commodities (10), government agricultural policy (11), and technological inputs to agriculture (12). These include the state of our knowledge, research and development with respect to fertilizers, pesticides, techniques of cultivation and soil preparation, irrigation, crop plant breeding, and techniques of protection against plant diseases and various species of pests. Acreage planted out is ultimately limited by the amount of land with suitable soil and climate.

The volume of crops we can export is also determined by foreign demand. The forces governing the magnitude of this demand (16) include their crop-growing weather (13), the amount of productive land they have under cultivation (14), and their population size (15); foreign commodity prices, government agricultural policy, and technology inputs to agriculture have been left off the diagram, to facilitate comprehension of the basic loops.

The international trade between the United States and other countries affects our balance of payments with them. The size of our trade deficit is determined by the extent to which our exports (18) can pay for our imports (19). If we export at a lower rate than the rate at which we import, our money will tend to accumulate in the banks in other countries. This, in turn, results in a drop in the value of U.S. currency relative to the Japanese yen, the German mark, and the Swiss franc (20). The consequence is that foreign goods, such as the Volkswagen, Toyota, Volvo, or Swiss watches cost more in the United States, adding to consumer expenditures and decreasing savings (21). If the United States exports a lot of agricultural commodities, this decreases domestic stocks of those commodities; that, in turn increases U.S. retail food prices, which implies less consumer expenditures on other items (17).

We have arrived at a most curious finding: attempts by Congress to hold down the U.S. general retail price level by keeping energy prices down in fact elevates the general price level through two different causal pathways: one through food prices (17) and one through the prices of foreign manufactured goods (21), which experience has shown, then tend to drive up the price of domestic competing manufactured goods. Further, one of these two pathways is always operating. If the U.S. is able to export enough agricultural commodities to pay for imported crude oil, then domestic stocks of those commodities are drawn down far enough to increase retail food prices. If, on the other hand, we are not able to export commodities fast enough to pay for imported energy, then the result is increases in the prices of manufactured goods. In either case, an increase in consumer prices results from an effort by government to prevent an increase in consumer prices by keeping energy prices down. This is a clear instance of Forrester's counterintuitive property of large, complex systems.

There are other consequences for the United States and world economies of applying various policies to this system. If food prices are high, an excessive proportion of peoples' purchasing power is thus absorbed, so that less is available to be spent on durable goods, such as cars, consumer electronics, and appliances; the rate of growth of the economy suffers (22). If the value of U.S. money drops relative to the value of foreign currencies, then ultimately sales of foreign goods in the United States will decline, because high prices would discourage purchase. This decreases the rate of growth of foreign economies because foreign manufacturers would have to lay off workers (23); that would lead to lowered purchases of U.S. goods by those people, lowering the growth

rate of the U.S. economy (24). The growth rate of the U.S. economy is also affected by profitability within the agricultural sector (25). If farmers produce too much relative to demand, food prices drop, and farmers are caught in a squeeze between high prices for tractors, other farm machinery, fertilizers, and pesticides, and low prices for the commodities they sell. They must respond by buying less, and the "ripple effects" from these lower purchases of farm machinery and so on radiate through the economy, decreasing its growth rate.

Slow growth rate of the U.S. economy trips three other causal pathways. People buy less food (26), the cultural belief system changes gradually, losing faith in the effectiveness of low energy prices (27); this affects government policy (1), but also, there are immediate, direct effects on government (28). Government responds by regulating the amount of land on which farmers grow food (11) and by regulating the price of energy and hence its availability (2).

As with all other large, complex systems, this one is self-regulatory, or homeostatic. Feedback loop 29 compensates for low value of the dollar by decreasing purchases of foreign goods, causing less accumulation of unwanted dollars abroad, which tends to equalize the value of U.S. and foreign currencies. Loops 26, 27, and 28 all tend to restore balance. Government effects adjustments through loops 11 (amount of agricultural land used) and 2 (stocks of energy).

The problem is that several of the regulatory loops tend to be slow-acting. There is a lag before they restore the system to equilibrium. On the other hand, the instability introduced by short-term fluctuations in crop-growing weather (loops 7 and 13) is very fast-acting. In short, by keeping energy prices down, government unwittingly designs the U.S. economic system so as to be extraordinarily sensitive to perturbations introduced by crop-growing weather in the

U.S., and to much greater extent, crop-growing weather abroad. Crop growth fluctuates more rapidly than the control or feedback loops can respond. Since there aren't any feedback control loops in the system that can adjust fast enough to respond to fluctuations in foreign crop-growing weather, low U.S. energy prices in combination with that weather jointly produce a system that is out of control. The U.S. economy is alternately buffeted by a tendency to depression radiating outwards from the farm sector and high prices radiating outwards from manufactured goods (when crop exports are low), or high prices radiating outwards from the farm sector (when crop exports are high).

Also, government masks the impact of low energy prices on decreased consumer purchasing power by increasing the amount of money in circulation (inflation). However, because this decreases the purchasing power of each unit of money, it merely delays the arrival of the ultimate consequence of excessively cheap energy: at some time in the future, people will discover that their rapidly rising gross incomes are accompanied by an even more rapidly dropping real purchasing power.

Which Should Be Top Priority: Energy or Agricultural Policy?

Viewed from this overview perspective, a most curious feature of present U.S. government policy is revealed. Congress and the White House have made low U.S. energy prices the basis for many other aspects of U.S. policy. Having decided to keep energy prices low, then all other national policies follow from this: land use policy, agricultural policy, policy on international trade, the value of the dollar relative to other currencies, economic stability, inflation, and U.S. rate of economic growth. Indeed, the government has worked itself into a curious position in which the president urges the heads of state of other countries, such as West Germany and Japan, to help stimulate the rate of growth of the world economy, when U.S. energy price policy makes it impossible for them to do that. This is because our low energy price increases the value of their currency relative to ours, making it more difficult for them to sell their manufactured goods in the United States. Thus, our energy price policies make their economies grow slower, not faster, while we are telling them to grow faster.

It would make far more sense for the U.S. government to decide that the most basic aims were to ensure that consumers paid a fair price for food, and that farmers received a fair price for their commodities, and then have all other national policies be determined by that, including energy policy.

Another popular myth is that higher energy prices, in the interests of energy conservation, would wipe out jobs. On the face of it, this seems odd, because the unemployment rate in the United States has been higher than in any other developed country, on average, over the last three decades, and this country has had by far the lowest energy prices and highest per capita use of energy. Indeed, unemployment rates among the developed countries tend to be inversely proportional to energy use per capita, the opposite to what the "conventional wisdom" would have us believe. Figure 11.6 explained the causal pathway (resource substitution) that leads to the opposite effect than that generally expected.

Some people are afraid that increased energy prices would lead to excessive centralization of economic and political power in the United States and less equitable income distribution. The former is not true, because higher energy prices would be an enormous stimulus to the development of solar and wind power, both of which can be done competitively at the local level by small companies. This industry would not be highly capital-intensive and does not depend on economies of scale, as found in automobile or television manufacturing. Solar and wind energy systems are inherently simple and do not require massive assembly lines for their production. Expensive energy would not lead to inequitable income distribution; that has certainly not happened in many countries that have much more expensive energy than in the United States but more equitable income distribution (New Zealand, for example).

To this point, we have considered only the qualitative characteristics of complex environmental systems models. Of course, in actual policy analysis, one wants to know not only that a certain causal pathway exists, but also the magnitude of the effects it is likely to generate. To this end, the conceptual models are converted into quantitative form by using equations to express the magnitude of the effect represented by each arrow, and numbers to represent the current values of the variables represented by each symbol. Quantitative parameter values for each equation are obtained by using statistical procedures to describe actual historical data. The starting values for the variables corresponding to each symbol are obtained from statistical records of the actual phenomenon being described mathematically. The equations used in computer simulation modeling update the values of the variables each time step being simulated in a computer game. Thus, for example, a computer simulation of the United States energy situation might begin with all the values representing the state of the situation in 1970. During the first "year" simulated in the course of the computer program, the values for the variables in 1971 would be computed; then from these, the values for 1972 would be simulated, and so on. In effect, the computer simulation exercise is merely a fast, automatic way to play a more complex variant of a game such as monopoly or chess.

The object of the exercise is to discover the sequence of policies for "playing the game" that produces the desired environmental outcome at the end of a predetermined sequence of years.

THE NOTION OF BASIC POLICY LEVERS FOR A NATION

One way of visualizing environmental systems is to think of each nation as having a set of policy levers that can be adjusted so as to have desired effects on key driving processes that affect the fate of the nation. These "levers" are such variables as the prices of resources, the minimum wage, the quotas on immigrants, the interest rate on loans, and the rate of growth in the money supply.

Each nation can be thought of as playing a game against nature, so as to try to maximize the chance of long-term survival of the nation with the best possible quality of life for the citizens. What is the optimal strategy for the nation? Each country begins the game blessed with certain resources, such as harbors, fresh water in lakes and rivers, potential hydroelectric power, forests, sunshine, wind, and agricultural land. These are all flow resources: carefully husbanded, they should last for a very long time. But also, most nations start their game with certain stock resources, such as diamonds, coal, oil, gas, gold, nickel, iron, and uranium ores.

The long-term survival of each nation depends on selecting the strategy that husbands flow resources so that they last indefinitely, and uses stock resources to create permanent assets for the society. These permanent assets would include such capital investments as desalinization plants to convert sea water to fresh water, solar and wind energy systems, and systems to derive energy from ocean tides and thermal gradients, manufacturing plants, public transportation systems, port facilities, and so on. Stock and flow resources should also be used to build up the cultural assets of the society, such as the educational system and the manufacturing and business skill of the citizens.

Optimal National Strategy

Now how can each nation pursue an optimal national strategy, given these goals? A nation has the best possible chance of long-term survival with a high quality of life if it stretches out its initial supplies of stock resources as long as possible. This maximizes the time for the nation to build up the technological sophistication required to make the transition to dependence on flow resources (that is, from dependence on fossil fuels to dependence on sun, wind, and ocean energy sources). The ways to do this are to minimize the immigration and birth rates, so as to minimize population pressure on resources. The successful society would also keep the price of labor low relative to the cost of resources, to encourage efficient use of resources and stimulate the rapid development of sophisticated engineering knowledge. The price of land should be kept high to encourage soil conservation and discourage urban sprawl, which wastes energy.

Also, capital lending policies by banks and other financial institutions should be designed so as to encourage investments that guarantee long-term survival rather than maximizing short-term profit.

Differences between nations with respect to production of both renewable and nonrenewable resources affect the economic growth rate and the capital assets of a nation. This simple truism is most starkly revealed in the relation between exports of a nation and its rate of economic growth. The most economically vigorous nations are those that have the most to export, whether that be oil, diamonds, copper, transistor radios, or jet transports. The rate of growth of gross national product per capita in a nation is strongly influenced by the per capita dollar value of exports. Thus, differences between nations at any time or changes in the fate of a nation from time to time are strongly influenced by the resource base of that nation. Indeed, human history is largely a history of the care with which various nations have tended their resources. Those that mismanaged and depleted or destroyed nonrenewable or renewable resources suffered major declines in their status as world powers.

Government policies have a large effect on the economy and capital assets of a nation. Government may see fit to have a slow growth rate in the money supply, producing little inflation, or a high growth rate, producing destructive inflation. Inflation implies artificial stimulation of consumer buying power, and resource use. Similarly, the way in which the government sets prices of various resources determines the rapidity of the substitution of energy for labor, and hence the pollution rate, the resource depletion rate, the unemployment rate, and the crime rate. Government can adopt pricing policies for a resource that gradually drain all the capital out of a society, as at present, when scores of billions of dollars a year leave the United States permanently because we buy more crude oil than we can pay for by all the goods we can export. This phenomenon is entirely attributable to the setting of a price for crude oil by the government, which excessively stimulated importation of foreign crude oil.

However, the capital assets of a society also have an effect on government policy. The government of a poor country is sharply limited in the extent to which it can be foolish, spendthrift, or unrealistically optimistic. On the other hand, in a country temporarily very rich in raw materials, incredibly stupid and short-sighted government policies will be masked temporarily by the great real wealth of the country. In a nutshell, a rich nation can afford to be tolerant of mistakes; a poor nation can not.

Finally, culture affects government, and government affects the cultural value system of a nation. If the people of a nation are unrealistically over-optimistic about their situation, they will elect representatives who share that value system. On the other hand, an unduly pessimistic society would not tolerate a spendthrift legislator or prime minister. But wise, articulate leaders can also mold the belief systems of their people. To illustrate how this works out in practice, the U.S. public is currently very concerned about air pollution, but also has a very deep emotional and cultural commitment to the life style and value system associated with cheap gasoline. Most legislators feel, therefore, that it would be difficult for them to get reelected if they strongly supported sharply higher energy prices. As a result, energy prices stay low, and the causal pathways that produce higher pollution levels are difficult to deal with.

ADDITIONAL FEATURES AND PROBLEMS OF ENVIRONMENTAL SYSTEMS

As our society becomes more complex, a number of kinds of issues concerning the environment come up that have been of little if any concern before. For students who wish to pursue such extensions of systems considerations, examples are covered in supplementary, boxed illustrative discussions.

Box 11.1 points out some costs of centralization: transmission and distribution overhead and vulnerability in case of terrorism or war. Box 11.2 considers time lags, cumulative effects, and thresholds (all of which make it more difficult for most people to discern the relation between cause and effect in complex environmental systems).

These boxed examples, together with the preceding material in this chapter, are intended to interest the student in a style of thinking required in environmental policy analysis. In this activity, the object is to decide which of a number of available policies is optimal, through evaluation of all the systemic consequences of each. The intent is to set the stage for analysis of the way in which systems generate conflicts (Chapter 14), and the means by which systems approaches resolve conflicts (Chapter 18).

BOX 11.1
Centralization versus decentralization as a major systems dichotomy

Only recently have a few analysts begun to point out that there are two very different paths along which modern societies could evolve: toward great centralization or great decentralization. Until recently, it has been widely assumed, when people thought about the matter at all, that obviously the best way to organize complex societies was by means of great centralization of economic and industrial activity. The argument for centralization was that by this means, such a large volume of output could be produced at a site that the cost per unit volume produced could be kept very low. The argument for decen-

BOX 11.1 (Cont.)

tralization is that when production is centralized, there are significant costs of distributing or transmitting the items produced. However, until recently, it has always been assumed that the costs of transmitting and distributing production to retail consumers would be much smaller than the gains due to centralization. The implications of this argument for environmental issues are enormous: if the costs of transmitting or distributing energy from generating plants or refineries are larger than had been hitherto suspected, then highly decentralized energy production systems, such as solar and wind generation systems at each house, make a lot of sense. Some recent calculations show that for the smaller customers of electric utilities, only about 29 percent of their electricity bill actually went into electricity, the rest going into construction and maintenance of transmission and distribution equipment (7). This suggests that decentralized systems, such as solar and wind-electric systems, might be more economically competitive than anyone had thought. This will be particularly true as fossil fuel energy prices rise and technological innovation reveals cheaper ways of manufacturing solar and wind energy systems components.

There is another reason for decentralization being more attractive than centralization. As world population densities rise, there will be progressively more intense competition between different groups of people for the same land and resources. Unfortunately, humanity to this point has not taken the rational response to this situation: sharply lowered birth rates so as to produce a net decline in population in both competing groups, thus lessening the motive for conflict. On the contrary, humans have dealt with excessive competition for limited resources by increasing the death rate through war or more local violence. Indeed, a compelling argument has been put forth that warfare is the most likely explanation for the very rapid evolution in size of the human brain over the last million years (12).

Because of the long record of violence being used by human beings as the principal means of dealing with competition for limited resources, it is reasonable to believe that with the sharply intensified competition of the next few decades, there will be an increase in violence, particularly local violence or terrorism. Terrorists have already shown that they well understand the high political leverage they get in attacking very capital-intensive targets, such as jumbo jets and airbuses. Some incidents have already indicated that terrorists understand how politically vulnerable a modern society is because of its dependence on centralized energy-generating systems, such as nuclear reactors, dams, and refineries. Also, of course, power-generating plants and hydroelectric dams were recognized as high-leverage targets in the Second World War. Obviously, in any future conflicts, a society largely dependent on highly decentralized energy-generating systems will be far less vulnerable to being incapacitated by destruction of energy-generating systems, than a society based on extreme centralization of such systems.

Some students may find it callous to plan to minimize risks in a future war. However, the critical military vulnerability of highly centralized power-gen-

BOX 11.1 (Cont.)

erating systems has been well understood for a long time. For example, consider the following from a June 16, 1940, memorandum from Prime Minister Winston Churchill to the prime minister of four British Commonwealth countries: "Meanwhile, of course, our bomber force will be striking continually at their key points, especially oil refineries . . ." (1). The most dramatic instance of the vulnerability of modern societies because of centralized energy generating systems occurred on the evening of May 16–17, 1943. The situation is well explained by Albert Speer, of Hitler's cabinet (13):

> Four weeks later, however, the first attempt was made—not by us but by the British air force—to influence the course of the war by destroying a single nerve center of the war economy. The principle followed was to paralyze a cross section, as it were—just as a motor can be made useless by the removal of the ignition. On May 17, 1943, a mere nineteen bombers of the RAF tried to strike at our entire armaments industry by destroying the hydroelectric plants of the Ruhr. . . . That night, employing just a few bombers, the British came close to a success which would have been greater than anything they had achieved hitherto with a commitment of thousands of bombers.

Clearly, a realistic assessment of the future prospects for humanity suggests that excessive dependence on highly centralized energy generating systems would be foolhardy. On the other hand, converting a nation to dependence on energy-generating systems using wind and sun adjacent to each building would give a nation maximum invulnerability to attack by terrorists or another nation.

BOX 11.2
The significance of temporal and spatial features of systems

A complication in many of the causal systems dealt with in this chapter is that they exhibit time lags, cumulative effects, and thresholds. That is, an effect may appear some time after the cause that gave rise to it was operating, but also, an effect now may be produced not just by a cause five years ago, but by the sum of all the causes operating between five and ten years ago. One of the most clear-cut examples of such cumulative effects occurs when the cumulative assault of environmental pollutants on the human organism finally triggers cancer.

Development of the cancer tissue now is the result of cumulative exposure to pollution over a period of years, probably many years ago. The policy implication of cumulative effects and lags is that it may be difficult to mobilize a political constituency to deal with an environmental problem of this lagged and cumulative type, because it is not clear in the minds of the affected people that there is a connection between a cause operating long ago and an effect now. It takes sophisticated statistical analysis of data and marshalling of evidence to struc-

BOX 11.2 (Cont.)

ture an argument, to make the case really convincing. Threshold effects are the same type of phenomenon: they make it more difficult to demonstrate to a constituency that there is a clear-cut relation between cause and effect, and therefore make it more difficult to mobilize political action to deal with a problem.

A clear-cut instance of a threshold effect is congestion delays on freeways. There is some rate at which vehicles attempt to move down a freeway per hour at which the freeway is totally congested, so that no motion occurs at all: the ultimate traffic jam. Clearly, at five percent of this rate, there is no congestion delay at all; nor is there at 25 percent of total saturation. But at some very high rate of vehicle flow on the freeway, congestion delays first start to show up: obviously, a threshold that just triggers congestion delays. The political problem created by thresholds is that if one had been arguing for public transportation to be constructed to relieve future congestion, prior to the density at which congestion delay occurs an opposing political constituency could always argue that there was no evident need for the massive capital investment in public transportation. There never will be, until it is too late. But when it is too late, it will probably take at least ten years to plan and build a public transportation system.

The same type of phenomenon occurs in many areas, including energy: the problem does not become acute and unarguably evident to everyone until it is long past the time at which it was necessary to begin building a solution to the problem. Obviously, society needs some new mechanisms that allow an objective "look-ahead" to provide early warning of problems whose impending arrival is being veiled by the operation of a threshold.

Time and space are both important resources, yet often this simple point is missed, because it is so easy to confuse both with the resources they contain. As pointed out in the chapter on energy, time itself is a resource, because there are certain times that provide a unique opportunity to take a critically important action. Space itself is a resource, without regard to the contents of that space. Decreased space availability per person, as population density rises, can have negative but also positive effects. Increased density in a country means less agricultural land, less forest land, and less urban land per person. After some threshold is surpassed, the society will no longer have the necessary land to grow food to feed the population, or to grow trees to house it and provide newsprint and paper for books and magazines. But on the other hand, increased density in a country means that the average distance between the origin and destination of trips will be shorter. If you live in midtown Manhattan, there are many things missing, but on the other hand a very wide variety of commodities can be purchased within a few blocks. Thus increased densities decrease the transportation energy overhead on all activities. The joint operation of these positive effects with increasing density, but negative effects that become intense at very high densities imply that there will be some optimal density for human activities. That is, for us as for all other species, there are optimal patterns of spatial organization.

SUMMARY AND CONCLUSIONS

This chapter has argued that modern postindustrial societies have reached a degree of systems complexity such that it is often difficult to perceive the ultimate consequences of any particular cause. Therefore, there is often great confusion and controversy within the electorate as to the best strategy for attaining particular goals. One group of people think that the best way to combat inflation and increase consumer buying power is to keep energy prices down relative to wages; another group argues that such low energy prices will increase inflation, and will lead to a variety of environmental problems, including pollution, resource depletion, and excessive urban crime rates. Hopefully, the reader will have been convinced that it is necessary to try and think through to the ultimate effects, the consequences of alternative strategies. Also, there are other properties of such societal systems that add confusion to political dialog: lag effects, cumulative effects, and thresholds. If complex modern environmental problems are to be solved, it will be necessary for the electorate to examine such problems with a fresh, systemic style of thinking, instead of traditional styles of thought that tend to view subsystems components lifted out of context.

SUGGESTIONS FOR INDIVIDUAL AND GROUP PROJECTS

Take any three important environmental problems where you live and develop flow charts for them superimposed on a copy of Figure 11.3 or 11.5.

Develop an argument showing how environmental controversies stem from the operation of lags, cumulative effects, or thresholds, using for examples problems where you now live.

Pick an important national environmental problem different than those discussed in this chapter. Now develop a systems-level hypothesis about how that problem arises and show how it might be dealt with, using a flow chart. Now test your hypothesis by making graphs of data from some statistical compendium, such as the *Statistical Abstract of the United States* (sold all over the country on newsstands as "The American Almanac" in soft cover by Grosset and Dunlap, for about four dollars). To test the hypothesis that one variable, X, affects another variable, Y, plot Y against X and see if the plotted points form a line that slopes upward or downward. If all the points constitute a circular area or a line parallel to the X-axis, then X has no discernible effect on Y. If, on the other hand, there is a line of points, sloping upward or downward to the left of the graph paper, then at the least, Y is "correlated with" X, and there may be a causal relationship that could be brought out by further investigation. The case for a relationship between X and Y becomes stronger when there have been natural or contrived experiments, such that a decline in X caused a significant increase or decrease in Y.

Read newspapers for 1816–1818, 1836–1838, or 1883–1885 to discover all the effects of very cold weather.

Assume that we are in fact exporting wheat, corn, and soybeans to pay for imported crude oil. There are four possible types of situations that could produce large-scale effects.

Case 1. Crop-growing weather in this country is excellent, but it is also excellent in all those countries that normally buy our grain, thus allowing us to purchase crude oil. Which of the following best describes the consequences?

1. The price of wheat increases in the United States.
2. The price of crude oil in other countries increases.

3. The United States suffers a massive trade deficit, and the value of the dollar drops with respect to other currencies.
4. The price of wheat increases in Russia.
5. The United States has a massive trade surplus, and the cost of the dollar rises so much with respect to other currencies that we cannot compete in the international market for manufactured goods.

Case 2. Crop-growing weather in this country is excellent, but it is terrible in Russia, China, and Europe. Which of the following best describes the consequences?

1. The price of wheat alone increases in the United States.
2. There is an increase in the price of many kinds of food in the United States.
3. The United States suffers a massive trade deficit, and there is a drop in the value of the dollar with respect to other currencies.
4. The price of wheat in Russia decreases.
5. The United States has a massive trade surplus.

Case 3. Crop-growing weather is terrible in this country, but terrific elsewhere. Which of the following best describes the consequences?

1. There is a world-wide inflation (increase in all prices and decrease in the value of money per unit) outside the United States.
2. The price of energy declines in the United States.
3. There is inflation in the United States.
4. Energy use increases in the United States.
5. There is a great increase in the amount of oil imported into the United States.

Case 4. Crop-growing weather is terrible world-wide. The most likely consequence is:

1. The price of energy declines in the United States.
2. The price of food and energy increase in the United States.
3. Use of energy increases in the United States.
4. The United States has a massive trade surplus.
5. The value of the dollar rises with respect to other currencies.

Now given your answers to the preceding questions, what is the best indicated strategy from now on?

1. Raise the price of energy, and import only as much energy as we can pay for with the amount of food we can export without driving up domestic food prices.
2. Keep the price of energy down with government regulations, as at present.
3. Increase taxes on energy.
4. Increase sales of food to other countries.
5. Plant less wheat, corn, and soybeans.

Imagine the following situation. You live in a small town in an agricultural valley. Life is slow and pleasant; the air is clean and you can catch trout in the streams. You don't make a great deal of money, but life is satisfying. Without warning, something happens that promises to alter the lives of everyone in the area drastically and permanently: a geological exploration crew discovers that under the entire area there is a gigantic coal bed. The people in the town have a town meeting to decide what to do about this, since feelings are rather mixed.

The meeting is held, with almost everyone in the community in attendance. Gradually, two patterns appear. First, almost everyone in the town can think of immediate and direct ways in which they will benefit economically from rapid exploitation of the coal. But finally, it appears that there is another, deeper pattern. The reason almost everyone is for development of the coal now is that the prodevelopment arguments are simple and obvious to everyone and relate to the here and now, which everyone at the meeting can understand. The arguments are also very "event-oriented," a way of viewing the world that everyone is thoroughly programmed to grasp easily, because that has been the orientation of television, radio, and newspaper reporting of the news. Any anti-coal-development arguments are more subtle, and "process-oriented." They require a way of looking at the world that is basically inhuman. That is, people must look beyond events, the here-and-now, to processes over extended time spans. Also, they must extend their horizons to include not just this place, but the ensemble or population of all places. How does it change the way we examine our future when we have to consider the futures of a great many places?

Invent five arguments to present to the town meeting explaining why development of the coal now may not be the best strategy for the community. Your argument may include proposals for alternate strategies. Whatever your arguments, they must be logical, and rooted in scientific fact.

It is worthwhile to ask if there are *any* valid arguments for refusing to develop a resource at the rate at which people would like to buy it from you. There may be, because the Saudis and other O.P.E.C. countries, on a grand scale and for the first time in history, may collectively decide to produce a resource at a much lower rate than the rate at which prospective customers would like to buy it. (See "World oil production," by Andrew R. Flower, *Scientific American*, March 1978, pp. 42–49.) Thus we are alerted to the possible existence of entirely valid arguments for stalling on production.

To illustrate the possible form of arguments you might use, consider the law of diminishing returns. For any resource, the unit production drops per unit effort at production, as the cumulative production effort increases. This means that as the population of all places producing coal produce more and more of what they have, it will cost more and more to produce additional increments of coal, and the price will rise. Suppose the coal price is rising at 3 percent a year. If one produced all the coal now, and invested the resulting money in the bank at a 6 percent interest rate, one would be ahead, ten years into the future. But suppose coal has become so scarce that the price is rising at 20 percent a year. Is it still worthwhile to produce it now? That would only be true if you could invest the money you made from selling your coal at a compound interest rate of 20 percent a year. Where would you find a "safe" investment to absorb a large amount of capital at this interest rate? Indeed, it is precisely the difficulty in finding such investments which has major banks scrambling all over the world looking for ventures to invest in, no matter how shaky. (See, for example, "Must lend, will travel," an eighty-four-page article on major banks in the *London Economist* of March 4, 1978.) This problem of reinvesting money you have earned by producing a resource becomes larger, the larger the resource. The ultimate solution, if your resource in the ground is appreciating very rapidly (if the value is rising by over 12 percent a year) is to leave it in the ground and use it as collateral for loans you take from banks.

In dealing with this question, you may wish to explore the following avenues of inquiry:

1. The effect on purchasing power of money in a town with rapid development.
2. The effect on housing, education, sanitation, taxes, police requirements, and the like.

3. The effect on the carrying capacity of the town for people, and the consequence of that carrying capacity being dropped unceremoniously some time in the future (the "boom-town–ghost-town" phenomenon).
4. The effect on the political power of the town relative to the political power of the region and the country, over a 100-year cycle of resource depletion.
5. Equity of income distribution. Who exactly will benefit from a big coal mine in this town: the people already here?

You may find it helpful to reason by analogy or homology. For example, you may want to think through the history of the political power of Appalachia relative to the rest of the United States, and attempt to discern why Appalachia has had this "vast" power.

Try to make your arguments brief, compelling, logical, realistic, and original.

REFERENCES

1. Churchill, W. S., *Their Finest Hour*. Boston: Houghton Mifflin, 1949.
2. Commoner, B., *The Poverty of Power*. New York: Knopf, 1976.
3. Forrester, J. W., "Counterintuitive behavior of social systems," in *Toward Global Equilibrium: Collected Papers,* edited by D. L. Meadows and D. H. Meadows. Cambridge, Mass.: Wright-Allen Press, 1973.
4. Forrester, J. W., *World Dynamics,* 2d ed. Cambridge, Mass.: Wright-Allen Press, 1974.
5. Forrester, N. B., *The Life Cycle of Economic Development*. Cambridge, Mass.: Wright-Allen Press, 1973.
6. Hughes, B. B., *World Modeling*. Lexington, Mass: Lexington Books, 1980.
7. Lovins, A. B., *Soft Energy Paths*. Cambridge, Mass.: Ballinger, 1977.
8. Meadows, D. H.; D. L. Meadows; J. Randers; and W. W. Behrens III, *The Limits to Growth*. New York: Universe Books, 1972.
9. Meadows, D. L.; W. W. Behrens III; D. H. Meadows; R. F. Naill; J. Randers; and E. K. O. Zahn, *Dynamics of Growth in a Finite World*. Cambridge, Mass.: Wright-Allen Press, 1974.
10. Mesarovic, M., and E. Pestel, *Mankind at the Turning Point*. New York: E. P. Dutton, 1974.
11. Miller, J. G., *Living Systems*. New York: McGraw-Hill, 1978.
12. Pitt, R., "Warfare and Hominid brain evolution," *Journal of Theoretical Biology* 72 (1978), p. 551.
13. Speer, A., *Inside the Third Reich*. New York: Macmillan, 1970.
14. Watt, K. E. F., *The Titanic Effect*. Sunderland, Mass.: Sinauer Associates, 1974.
15. Watt, K. E. F.; L. F. Molloy; C. K. Varshney; D. Weeks; and S. Wirosardjono, *The Unsteady State*. Honolulu: The University of Hawaii Press, 1977.
16. Watt, K. E. F.; J. W. Young; J. L. Mitchiner; and J. W. Brewer, "A Simulation of the Use of Energy and Land at the National Level," *Simulation* 24 (1975), p. 129.

IV The Consequences of Environmental Systems Dysfunction

To this point we have examined the types of components in environmental systems, how they all work together, and how our perceptions and activities with respect to the environment are shaped.

Now we examine what happens when the system isn't working. The basic argument advanced in Chapters 12, 13, and 15 is that destruction of the environment is the consequence of an unrealistic desire for a high rate of resource consumption per capita, a defective cultural belief system (Chapter 9). Pollution and environmental degradation result from the mindless sacrificing of the long-term health and survival of a nation for short-term gratification. Politicians, bureaucrats, and national leaders cater to this desire to maintain their popularity and power (Chapter 8). Since a very high rate of resource consumption per capita cannot be maintained indefinitely in a normally functioning economy (consumers could not earn enough to buy such high quantities of resources), government artificially elevates consumer purchasing power over the short term by increasing the amount of money in circulation (inflation).

Thus pollution, environmental degradation, a lowered standard of living, inflation, and eventually, a decline in national power are interlinked phenomena with a common root cause: an unrealistic cultural belief system concerning the availability per person of resources.

12 POLLUTION

> . . . an impure and thick mist, accompanied by a fuliginous and filthy vapor, corrupting the lungs, so that catarrhs, coughs and consumptions rage more in this one city, than in the whole Earth.
>
> *John Evelyn,* Fumifugium, or, the Inconvenience of the Air, and Smoke of London Dissipated. Together with some Remedies humbly proposed by J. E. Esq., to his Sacred Majesty, and to the Parliament now Assembled, *1661.*

MAIN THEMES OF THIS CHAPTER

This chapter examines the meaning of pollution in a broader context: pollution indicates that some input to a process was wasted by being released, unused, into the environment. If the price of that input had been higher, it would have been used more efficiently, and would not have turned up as a waste item in the environment.

Pollution also means that human activities are being concentrated, or centralized. More decentralized activities would result in lower concentrations of pollution at any one place.

Ultimately, pollution depends on the price of resources relative to average wages: as this ratio rises, there will be less pollution.

Pollutants are not only poisons; they may also be nutrients released in such large concentrations that they have a harmful effect on the environment, or substances that may suddenly appear in the environment in quantities that overwhelm natural recycling processes. Crude oil is such a substance.

Mobilizing political constituencies for strict pollution control is difficult, because of the technical complexity of the arguments required to establish proof that an alleged cause of an apparently pollution-caused disease *was* in fact the cause, beyond reasonable doubt. This has been particularly difficult in the case of photochemical smog, herbicides, and nuclear fallout or radiation.

INTRODUCTION: THE MEANING OF ENVIRONMENTAL SYSTEMS DYSFUNCTION

Chapters 1, 7, and 11 argued that there is a relation between various environmental problems and defective resource pricing policies. That is, if resource costs are too low relative to consumer purchasing power, resource consumption per capita is artificially stimulated, so that waste and inefficiency are encouraged. Pollution, being the unused proportion of the inputs to any activity, is simply evidence of waste and inefficiency. In this chapter and the next, we explore the implications of malfunctioning resource pricing for pollution and environmental degradation.

Pollution means either that a poison or destructive agent (such as crude oil) has been added to the environment, or that a nutrient or waste product has been added in concentrations at which the impact is destructive. Environmental degradation, on the other hand, means that something useful has been taken away from the environment, or destroyed. Erosion of top quality agricultural soil, deforestation on a watershed, or reduction in the species diversity in a community are examples. Excessive use and waste of resources is sustained by inflated consumer purchasing power. The critical role of inflation as an ultimate cause through which the defective, unrealistic cultural belief system has impact on the destiny of a nation has been clear throughout history. Inflation was the critical element in the decline of Spain under Philip II (10), the Germany of Hitler (2), and for all ancient civilizations, as well as modern America. In any society sufficiently developed to have a money economy, the critical causal link that must be understood for pollution and environmental degradation to be comprehensible is the effect of inflation (increase in the money supply) on consumer purchasing power.

Thus we see that the presence of pollution has a hidden meaning that is rarely pointed out. When we see pollution, this means that the cost of mineral and fuel inputs to the economy is so low relative to the average cost of labor that it is not economic to use energy or materials wisely. Pollution is simply matter of energy being wasted. If there had been an adequate economic incentive to use it efficiently, waste would have been very carefully minimized.

How Resource Prices Affect Pollution

This bald statement of the situation does not explain the pathways by which the relative prices of matter and energy, on the one hand, and wages, on the other, operate on pollution. In fact there are three distinct pathways, as outlined in the systems flow diagram of Figure 12.1. The circle encloses the decision variable, or variable over which there is human control, allowing manipulation through economic or political mechanisms (taxes, for example). If this variable, the ratio of resource costs to labor costs, is low, then resources will be cheap for people to buy, and they will waste them. Also, there will be no incentive to conserve resources in manufacturing. Cars will be much heavier then they need to be, for example. Since the second law of thermodynamics states that all other things being equal, waste will increase in proportion to consumption, more use of metal per car will imply more pollution from various stages of the car manufacturing process, from extraction of ore in the

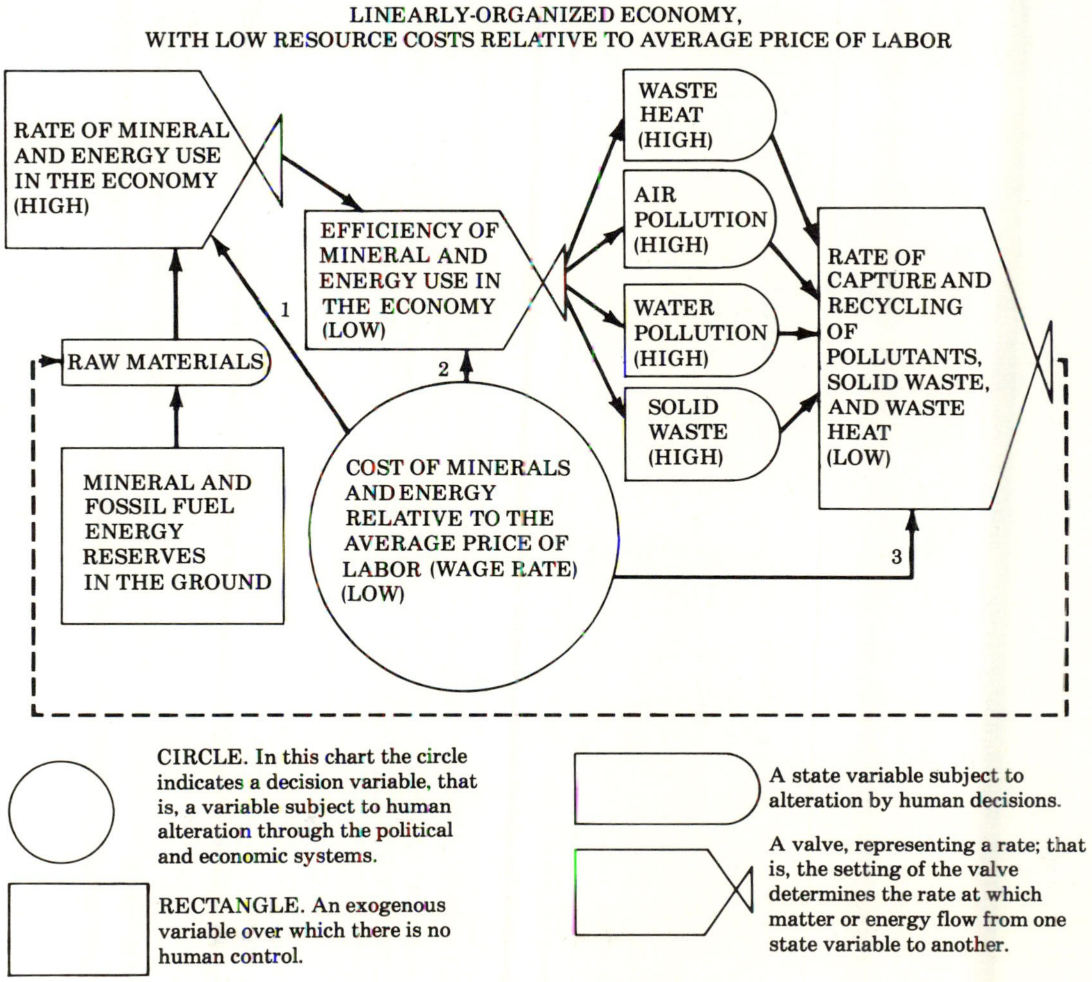
LINEARLY-ORGANIZED ECONOMY,
WITH LOW RESOURCE COSTS RELATIVE TO AVERAGE PRICE OF LABOR
RATE OF MINERAL AND ENERGY USE IN THE ECONOMY (HIGH)
EFFICIENCY OF MINERAL AND ENERGY USE IN THE ECONOMY (LOW)
WASTE HEAT (HIGH)
AIR POLLUTION (HIGH)
WATER POLLUTION (HIGH)
SOLID WASTE (HIGH)
RATE OF CAPTURE AND RECYCLING OF POLLUTANTS, SOLID WASTE, AND WASTE HEAT (LOW)
1
2
3
RAW MATERIALS
MINERAL AND FOSSIL FUEL ENERGY RESERVES IN THE GROUND
COST OF MINERALS AND ENERGY RELATIVE TO THE AVERAGE PRICE OF LABOR (WAGE RATE) (LOW)
CIRCLE. In this chart the circle indicates a decision variable, that is, a variable subject to human alteration through the political and economic systems.
RECTANGLE. An exogenous variable over which there is no human control.
A state variable subject to alteration by human decisions.
A valve, representing a rate; that is, the setting of the valve determines the rate at which matter or energy flow from one state variable to another.

FIGURE 12.1
Systems flow diagram to reveal the basic forces determining the amount of environmental pollution occurring in a society. Four different symbols are used in this diagram, in accord with the code.

ground through manufacture of steel to manufacture of the finished car. If resource costs are low relative to wages, not only will there be more use of resources and energy than there otherwise would have been (pathway 1 in the figure), but also, the resources used will be used less efficiently (pathway 2). That is, the manufacturing process will not be designed to minimize wastage of energy and materials in the manufacturing process. Finally, if resource costs are low relative to wages, any wastes that do occur will be allowed to escape into the environment, rather than being captured and recycled in the plant (pathway 3). All three of these pathways occur because low resource costs relative to wages imply that waste of resources can easily be passed on to the consumer and absorbed in the purchase price; everyone is being paid so well relative to the cost of resources that this hidden passthrough of the cost of wasted energy and resources goes unnoticed. The dashed line, indicating recycling in the figure, is largely absent from the system. Thus we say the system is linear: energy and materials enter as inputs, and all escape as output, either in the form of the intended products, or as wastes (pollution).

However, if the cost of resources were to rise significantly relative to wages, the situation would change dramatically. Since people would not be able to afford so much matter and energy, they would have to make much more economical use of them. The absolute minimum amount of matter and energy required to make a car, for example, would be used. Economies would be in effect along all three of the pathways in Figure 12.1. Less matter and energy would be used (1); it would be used more efficiently, with an absolute minimum of waste in the manufacturing process (2); and what little waste there was would be recycled back into the plant to be used in the manufacturing process (3). In short, pollution is simply a

signal from the economic system that there is an inappropriate perceived relative price for resources relative to labor rates. Pollution is just one of many such signals, along with unemployment, crime, inflation, and a low rate of economic growth as we have seen in Chapter 11.

Pollution also means that the whole human socioeconomic system is not in balance: an output (waste, or pollution) is being produced faster than it is being consumed, removed, or broken down by the system. By contrast, the principal characteristic of natural biogeochemical cycles, as in Figure 5.11, is that they are maintained in balance, through stabilizing or equilibrating mechanisms.

Pollution, Centralization, and Economies of Scale

Pollution has a second significance, besides the absence of recycling and waste due to inappropriate prices. Pollution occurs because there is tremendous spatial concentration of manufacturing effort. If a nation had a large number of small electrical generating plants, rather than a small number of large plants, for example, natural circulation processes in the atmosphere would be better able to dissipate gaseous wastes. Spatial concentration of manufacturing, in turn, implies that there are "economies of scale," or an economic advantage to mass production. This occurs where matter and energy are cheap relative to labor, so that very large and heavy pieces of equipment to replace labor are economically attractive. If labor was much cheaper relative to resource costs, so that we could afford to have more person-hours of labor in a typical car, then it would not be so necessary for car plants to be so large. Manufacturing would be less dependent on very large, expensive pieces of equipment, and more dependent on skilled labor, which could work just as well in groups of a few hundred as in groups of many thousand.

Thus, curiously, the cost of resources relative to the cost of labor is central to the pollution production phenomenon, no matter which point of view we use to explore the issue.

POLLUTION AND THE RELATIVE COSTS OF LABOR AND RESOURCES

If the argument of the previous section is correct, then it should be possible to demonstrate that the rate at which pollutants are produced increases when wages increase relative to resource costs. Demonstration of this cause-effect pathway is important, not only to help us understand the fundamental nature of pollution, but also to confirm the indicated strategy for dealing with the problem: adjust upwards the ratio of resource costs to the price of labor. This could be done by government deregulation of resource costs, by taxation, by wage and price controls, or other means. Any of these approaches might be called a front-end solution to the problem of managing the pollution-generating system, management is at the input, or resource-consuming end of the system. The other possible type of pollution management is what we have now: back-end management. That is, given that a certain amount of pollution has been generated, what do we do to get rid of it, or prevent it from entering the environment?

Fertilizers and Pesticides as Pollutants

Pesticides, being poisons, can obviously pollute. Fertilizers can cause excessive, and environmentally destructive growth of algae in fresh water, and thus are also pollutants. Accordingly, they are both appropriate examples for use in demonstrating the existence of the causal pathway just mentioned. Table 12.1 demonstrates how the relevant statistics are derived for fertilizers, so students can see how to derive the variables of interest from raw government statistics. From population size and total national fertilizer consumption (columns two and three), we compute fertilizer consumption per capita (column six); from average cost per ton of fertilizer (column 4) and an index of average wages (column 5), we obtain the ratio of unit fertilizer cost to the index of wages (column 7). Fertilizer use per capita has risen continuously, except for a slight decline in 1975. The ratio of fertilizer cost to wages dropped from 1960 to 1972, rose sharply to 1975, and now is dropping very rapidly. The fact that fertilizer use per capita only dropped in 1975, the year when the ratio of fertilizer cost to wages was highest, strongly suggests that this ratio is a controlling variable for fertilizer use. When fertilizer cost relative to wages dropped sharply after 1975, fertilizer use rose to a historical peak.

Table 12.2 summarizes similar computations for synthetic organic pesticides. In this case, unlike that of the fertilizers, cost relative to average wage did not drop after 1975. The large increase in pesticide cost relative to wages reversed the rising trend in pesticide use per capita that had been in effect since at least 1960. Evidently, price of a potentially polluting resource relative to wages is an effective policy lever for controlling use, and hence, pollution.

Table 12.3 collates data on the time trends in the value of shipments for both industrial organic chemicals and organic non-cellulose fibers, in both cases with the dollar amounts corrected for inflation. The value of industrial organic chemical shipments grew more slowly from 1974 to 1975 than in other

TABLE 12.1
Demonstration that fertilizer use per capita is determined by ratio of fertilizer cost to average spendable earnings.

Year	Population[1] (millions)	Consumption of all commercial fertilizer[2] (millions of tons)	Average cost per ton of fertilizer[3] (dollars)	Average spendable weekly earning of worker with three dependents[4] (dollars)	Consumption of all commercial fertilizers per person in United States (tons)	Ratio of cost of fertilizer per ton to average spendable weekly earnings
1960	180.0	24.9	53.98	73.0	.14	.74
1965	193.5	31.8	62.70	86.3	.16	.73
1970	203.8	39.6	60.35	104.6	.19	.58
1972	208.2	41.2	65.29	121.1	.20	.54
1973	209.9	43.3	77.46	127.4	.21	.92
1974	211.4	47.1	123.31	134.4	.22	.92
1975	213.1	42.5	150.19	145.9	.20	1.03
1976	214.7	49.2	122.60	156.5	.23	.78
1977	216.3	51.6	118.00	170.3	.24	.69

[1]From Table 2, *Statistical Abstract of the United States, 1978.*
[2]From Table 1189, *Statistical Abstract of the United States, 1978.*
[3]Obtained by dividing total cost of fertilizer in Table 1193 by volume used in Table 1189.
[4]From line 5, Table 682, *Statistical Abstract of the United States, 1978.*

TABLE 12.2
Demonstration that per capita use of synthetic organic pesticides is determined by ratio of pesticide cost to average spendable earnings.

Year	Consumption of all synthetic organic pesticides per capita[1] (lb)	Ratio of cost of synthetic organic pesticides per pound to average spendable weekly earnings[2]
1960	3.17	.0063
1965	3.95	.0075
1970	4.32	.0095
1972	4.91	.0088
1973	5.11	.0088
1974	6.46	.0099
1975	6.18	.0123
1976	5.56	.0129

[1]Obtained by dividing number of pounds of pesticides produced by U.S. population. (Data from Tables 363 and 2, *Statistical Abstract of the United States, 1978.*)
[2]Data from Tables 363 and 682, *Statistical Abstract of the United States, 1978.*

TABLE 12.3
Trends in value of shipments, industrial organic chemicals, and organic noncellulose fibers.

Year	Value of shipments, industrial organic chemicals, in billions of 1972 dollars[1]	Value of shipments, organic noncellulose fibers, in billions of 1972 dollars[1]
1965	6.76	2.47
1970	7.08	2.70
1972	7.47	2.95
1973	8.08	3.74
1974	10.99	3.33
1975	11.08	3.17
1976	12.54	3.30

[1]Table 1438, *Statistical Abstract of the United States, 1978.*

years, and the value of organic noncellulose fibers shipped actually declined in 1975. In both cases, the 1975 values are attributable to sharp increases in the price of petrochemicals derived from crude oil in 1974.

Evidently, an effective means of controlling use of substances that are pollutants themselves, or that are produced in manufacturing processes that generate pollution, is to let the price of the input materials rise.

Perhaps the most compelling argument for preventing pollution from being generated, rather than dealing with it at the output end of a process, is the expense of the latter. To illustrate, the cost of pollution abatement and control outlays by the U.S. government, per resident, increased from $9.20 to $28.2, just over the period 1974 to 1979. Clearly, we need a better fundamental approach to dealing with this problem.

THE SOURCES AND TYPES OF POLLUTION

Table 12.4 assembles information on various types of pollutants and points out important examples within each type. There are three broad classes of pollutants: poisons, nutrients, and substances, such as crude oil, that are important largely because of a physical impact on the living organism by immobilizing it or impairing normal functioning.

Nutrients

The notion that a nutrient can function as a pollutant appears paradoxical. However, if a nutrient enters the environment in excessive concentrations, as when rain washes chemical fertilizers off farm fields into nearby waters, we have a harmful superabundant resource availability, as noted in Chapter 5. The ultimate effect is to overstimulate biological wastes. This creates such a demand for oxygen to react with the waste that the water is depleted of oxygen for use by other living organisms. Some species with a very high requirement for dissolved oxygen, such as trout and salmon, will be sensitive even to low levels of oxygen depletion. Many species will be affected if the process is sufficiently extreme.

TABLE 12.4
The types, sources, and effects of pollution.

Type	Sources	Effects
A. POISONS		
1. Metals		
Vanadium	Production of steel alloys designed to withstand high temperatures.	Compounds of vanadium are extremely corrosive. Variations in incidence of mortality from city to city in the United States are more strongly statistically associated with vanadium concentrations than with concentrations of any other metal in air.
Nickel carbonyl	Results from reaction of carbon monoxide and finely divided nickel, as from metallurgy or combustion.	Incidence of cancer, leukemia, and heart disease in U.S. cities strongly associated with incidence of nickel compounds in air.
Mercury	Used in electrical switches, agricultural and industrial fungicide, thermometers, special metallurgical applications (nuclear reactors).	Concentrates in top predators in aquatic food chains, such as swordfish; when eaten by humans causes destruction of nervous system.
Lead	Petroleum industry; gasoline combustion, mining; smelting; manufacture of paint, pigment, cutlery and storage batteries; insecticides.	Poisons nervous system, gastrointestinal tract, and blood-forming tissues. Incidence of lead in air statistically associated with incidence of cancer and leukemia in U.S. cities. Symptoms include abdominal pain, poor appetitie, anemia, gradually developing paralysis.
Cadmium	Electroplating.	Inhalation of vapor or dust is poisonous.

TABLE 12.4
(Cont.)

Type	Sources	Effects
Beryllium	Specialized high-precision metallurgy (including gyroscopes and computer components); brake drums.	Soluble compounds are acute poisons.
Chromium	Steel alloys, pigments, tanning.	Chromium compounds cause skin ulcers and cancers of the respiratory tract. Strong statistical association with respiratory cancer, diabetes, and heart disease.
2. Radioactive Isotopes		
Strontium-90 and Cesium-137	Nuclear reactors; nuclear accidents.	Collect in bone; concentrate in food chains. Accumulate in aquatic trophic pyramids and concentrate in top predators, such as pike.
Iodine-131	Nuclear reactors.	Collects in thyroid.
Plutonium-239	Nuclear reactors.	Intensely toxic in air or water.
3. Pesticides		
D.D.T. and P.C.B.'s (polychlorinated biphenyls)	Accumulations in soil, water, animals, or human fat resulting from spraying of farms, forests, or gardens.	Probable health effects in humans resulting from long-term exposure. Magnitude and nature of effects controversial.
4. Herbicides		
TCDD (impurity occurring as contaminant in 2,4,5-T)	Accidental constituent of "Agent Orange," a weed-killer used to cause defoliation in Vietnamese war and in United States.	Extremely toxic substance; causes birth defects, leukemia, and diseases in laboratory animals; may also represent threat to humans.

TABLE 12.4
(Cont.)

Type	Sources	Effects
5. Organic		
Chemicals	Water-borne wastes from plants making plastics, synthetic fibers, or other organic chemicals.	Massive fish kills (as in Escambia Bay in Florida).
6. Gases		
Nitrogen oxides and photochemical smog (PAN)	Automobile exhausts; reaction product from action of sunlight on mixture of air pollutants.	City-to-city differences in incidence of various cancers and heart diseases are strongly statistically associated with city-to-city differences in concentration of nitrogen oxides and smog in air.
Sulfur oxides	Combustion of coal.	Acid rain; city-to-city differences in incidence of digestive system cancer are more strongly associated with differences in concentration of sulfur oxides in air than with any other environmental chemical. Implicated in diabetes and heart disease.
B. NUTRIENTS		
Phosphates and nitrates	Fertilizer; detergent (phosphate).	Stimulate eutrophication, producing an unusually large volume of biological waste, which creates high levels of B.O.D. (biological oxygen demand), lowering oxygen concentration in water. Eutrophication eliminates species requiring high oxygen levels from the aquatic community, and they are replaced by other species requiring less oxygen.

TABLE 12.4
(Cont.)

Type	Sources	Effects
C. VISCOUS MATERIALS, CRUDE OIL	Tanker and oil rig accidents at sea.	Immensely controversial topic, probably because severity of effects varies from case to case, depending on two factors: (1) cold temperatures increase viscosity of crude oil, and may make it more difficult for birds to remove; (2) the effect will probably be greater if oil is washed ashore and trapped in a bay.

Poisons

Metals enter the environment from iron and steel mills, smelters, inorganic chemical manufacturers such as fertilizer producers, and organic chemical manufacturers such as synthetic rubber manufacturers. Chromium, lead, nickel, vanadium, mercury, cadmium, and beryllium all are poisons. Chromium, nickel, and vanadium are all used in certain alloys of steel, so all are present in the environment. These metallic poisons enter the air in very small concentrations via the smokestacks of plants. The clearest evidence of the impact of such concentrations on living tissue is the almost total absence of growing plants for great distances around certain smelters, a phenomenon particularly visible from an aircraft.

Ionized particles from nuclear explosions or various steps in the nuclear fuel industry are dangerous poisons. These substances include the noble gases krypton and xenon and a wide variety of alkaline and alkaline earth metals that are an unfamiliar part of the environment to our bodies and those of other living species. Further, the nuclear industry not only produces metals so rare that living tissue has no evolved protection against them, but produces radioactive isotopes of these elements that are not even known to occur naturally and may be very biologically active.

People cannot possibly be aware of the radioactive gases produced by nuclear explosions, or nuclear plants, because these gases, such as xenon and krypton, are colorless, odorless, and tasteless. However, certain radioactive isotopes, such as xenon-138 and krypton-89, give rise to very biologically active radioactive isotopes, such as cesium-138 and strontium-89, respectively. Strontium-89 is an ephemeral substance, having a half-life of only fifty-two days. However, it can do much harm in this period, because it is deposited in bone, where it replaces calcium; its radiation then damages bone marrow, and impairs the formation of new blood cells. Also, it may induce cancer. The real significance of these exotic by-products of nuclear explosions and reactions is that there are brief periods in fetal and newborn human development that are very susceptible to interference from radioactive materials. A possible result of this interference is a variety of unusual congential malformations in the newborn infant. These include Down's syndrome, microcephaly, congenital heart defects, fetal death, stillbirth, and leukemia.

A source of poisonous chemicals is the agricultural chemicals industry. Pesticides such as DDT (dichlorodiphenyltrichloroethane) are complex organic molecules designed to kill various types of organisms. Often these chemicals can cause damage to organisms other than the target organisms if they are present at low concentrations in the environment for long periods of time.

Insecticides, herbicides, and rodenticides can enter the environment by a number of pathways. Rain may wash them off the agricultural land into streams and rivers, so that they gradually accumulate in lakes or the ocean. Alternatively, they may be ingested by insects, which are ingested by small mammals or birds, which are finally ingested by larger carnivores such as the birds of prey. At each step in this process of transfer through the trophic pyramid, such agricultural chemicals become concentrated. Finally, by the time they enter the highest carnivore levels, they may become so concentrated as to be a threat to the continued survival of the carnivore level.

The herbicide 2,4,5-T is used to kill unwanted vegetation on powerlines, grazing lands, and forest lands. It is also used by the National Forest Service to kill hardwoods in order to encourage the growth of softwoods. Near forests where spraying with 2,4,5-T occurs, there was an unusual incidence of dead, deformed, and miscarried human babies between 1976 and 1978. In one small northern California town, sixteen out of thirty pregnancies resulted in dead, de-

formed, or miscarried babies in that period. The problem appears to be an ingredient, dioxin, which can kill a guinea pig at concentrations of one part per billion.

One group of pollutants is produced by the internal combustion engine. Incomplete combustion of carbonaceous fuels, such as gasoline, produces carbon monoxide. When combustion takes place at high pressure, as in automobile cylinders, nitric oxide is produced. Under the influence of photochemical processes (influenced by light energy), some of this nitric oxide is converted to nitrogen dioxide, a toxic and colored gas. The chemistry of air pollution is quite complex and results in a set of end products including various organic compounds cotaining nitrogen. Photochemical "smog" is a complex mixture of organic chemicals, ozone, and other constituents, which altogether function as "oxidant." This means that this group of chemicals operates all together to combine with other chemical substances, including those within our bodies, as oxidizing agents. The full significance of this becomes clear when we realize that modern research on the aging process suggests that antioxidants may be able to slow aging. Thus, it is reasonable to expect that oxidants would hasten aging. If this is true, then we would expect to see evidence in the form of higher death rates in the presence of oxidant pollutants, not just due to certain classes of diseases, but due to all classes of degenerative disease involving cell decay and malfunction, such as all types of cancer and cardiovascular system breakdown for example.

There are large differences in the relative importance of various sources of the commoner constituents of air pollution. Road vehicles are important sources of carbon monoxide, hydrocarbons, and nitrogen oxides, but not of sulfur oxides or particulates. Electric utilities, on the other hand, are important sources of sulfur oxides, but not of carbon monoxide or hydrocarbons. Industrial processes are not important sources of nitrogen oxides. These differences between sources with respect to their pollutant emissions imply that different cities will have different mixes of pollution, depending on what goes on there. Cities such as Los Angeles, with a tremendous amount of automobile driving, will have an atmosphere with a considerable load of nitrogen oxides. An area with little driving but close to electric utilities will have a heavy load of sulfur oxides but few nitrogen oxides.

Viscous Waste: Crude Oil

All of us are aware of exhaust fumes from cars, trucks, and buses, and the plumes of smoke streaming out of the smokestacks of factories, refineries, electrical generating plants, and smelters. There are other kinds of pollution that the typical person is less likely to experience, but that are also important. Tankships must periodically flush out the large tanks in which they transport crude oil. This is done by pumping the tanks full of sea water, and flushing the sea water out at sea. This is usually done considerable distance out in the ocean, perhaps to avoid political repercussions when people saw what the flushings looked like in the ocean. Sometimes the tanks are flushed out in cold parts of the ocean, as off the southeast coast of Newfoundland. The problem, then, is that the viscosity of the crude oil becomes even greater than it usually is inside the ship, because of the cold ocean water. This sticky, almost tar-like material gets into the feathers of large numbers of marine birds, so they are incapacitated and ultimately die. Their bodies wash up in large numbers on certain coasts, such as those of Newfoundland. For example, the murre is the most abundant northern hemisphere sea bird. A minimum of 400,000 murres a year are known to be destroyed on the coast of Newfoundland by this sticky oil flushing, and the total figure may be as high as several million birds a year. This is a significant number, because the entire world population of murres is only about 50 million birds, and the reproductive rate is low, as in penguins, for which the murres are the northern hemisphere counterpart. Further, while few people would ever have reason to know of the existence of murres, they are important to the recycling of minerals in the ocean, because they eat about 100 million pounds of plankton and fish weekly. This is important because the productivity of the entire ocean system is critically dependent on recycling nitrates and phosphates, which would otherwise drift in dead fish to the bottom of the sea. Murres are heavy feeders on bottom fish in the summer, so clearly make a significant contribution to this recycling process. The point is that while there are many forms of pollution we all know about, there are other forms we do not know about that may be equally important to our well-being. The ocean pollution by crude oil from tankships and from offshore oil well spills or wastes has another significance. Heat exchange between the ocean and the atmosphere is an important process in regulation of world weather systems. Much of the ocean is now in the process of being covered with a thin film of crude oil, if indeed the process is not already complete.

Other pollutants

The rock, asbestos, used in insulation, is implicated as a cancer-causing agent. Small particles of asbestos in the air are dangerous, which is why workers installing insulation wear protective masks.

Jet contrails are another source of environmental alteration rarely noticed. A remarkably high proportion of all the cloud cover near large airports with a great deal of jet activity may be due to the coalescence of jet contrails, particularly if the atmospheric conditions are such that cloud cover is slight, but contrails can promote cloud formation. Few people have any reason to observe a particular patch of sky continuously for many hours; consequently, they have no reason to realize that much of the cloud they see has been produced by gradual expansion and coalescence of contrails. Sequences of photographs or time-lapse photography would be required to understand the origin of the clouds. However, despite a great deal of research on the possible environmental significance of these clouds, it seems fair to say that the case has not yet been resolved. The impact of supersonic jet contrails on the very high altitude environment in which they fly is still a subject of great controversy. Some scientists believe that a great deal of such contrail formation would lead to modification of the ozone layer, and consequently increased incidence of skin cancer due to increased penetration of the atmosphere by ultraviolet radiation normally shielded out by the ozone layer. Other pollutants, such as aerosol sprays and nitrogenous fertilizer may also destroy or diminish the ozone layer, thereby also increasing atmospheric penetration by the dangerous ultraviolet radiation from the sun.

Another type of pollutant is heat. The heat released from all combustion and air conditioning in a city may raise the temperature of the city relative to that of the surrounding countryside; this is called the "urban heat island effect." That effect is merely uncomfortable, and can be dealt with by fountains, which cool the air by means of latent heat used up in the process of conversion of water to water vapour. However, many kinds of plants, such as nuclear plants, use water from a river to cool equipment in the plant. If the equipment is hot enough, the river temperature may be raised significantly when the "coolant" water is returned to it. This, of course, has implications for the survival or health of any fish or other organisms living in the river.

SPREAD, ACCUMULATION, AND CONCENTRATION OF POLLUTANTS

One aspect of pollution that makes it very difficult to deal with politically is the surprising way in which it spreads. It is probably well-known that pesticides such as D.D.T. are now spread all over the planet: in the ocean, near the poles, and in all living things. It is not as well-known, perhaps, that radioactivity from nuclear tests or nuclear reactors has effects on human beings far away, in the opinion of many scientists. This phenomenon has gradually been revealed through a series of accidental discoveries, such as an increase in the incidence of leukemia in children in the Albany-Troy area of New York, following a nuclear bomb test in Nevada.

There are several complications in this phenomenon. In the first place, pollutants may have biological effects that do not reveal themselves until long after operation of the cause. After the nuclear bomb explosions in Hiroshima and Nagasaki, the peak incidence of leukemia did not occur for six to eight years. Similarly, peak incidence of leukemia in the New York state children did not occur until six to eight years after the Nevada blast. Since there is a long lag from the time a cause occurs to the time its effect appears, few people would notice the relation between cause and effect; this is one of the principal problems in getting an effective political constituency organized to put pressure on government to tighten up pollution controls.

Another complication appeared in the New York state childhood leukemia: the unusual number of cases included many children who were not even conceived until a year or more after the arrival of the fallout. This suggested that there might be some effect on neonatal children carried over from the parents.

To illustrate the way pollutants can have an effect far away from their origin, incidence of mortality amongst infants in their first year of life in the United States in the period 1949 to 1952 appears to be related to Soviet atom-bomb tests.

The distribution of air pollutants can be affected by temperature inversions. This occurs when cool air near the surface of a city is trapped by warmer air above it. Since cool air cannot rise through warm air, the cool air will hover over a city until blown away by winds. This trapped cool air will steadily increase in air pollutant concentration. Incidents in which air is trapped for an extended period in an area with high rate of production of pollutants may result in sharp increase in the mortality rate. This occurred in London in December 1952, when 3000 people died because of smog trapped by a temperature inversion (16).

Pollutants are concentrated up through food chains, as are radionuclides. Thus, while the concentration of pollutant in air or water may not be serious by itself, once this material has passed from herbivores to carnivores, or plants to herbivores to carnivores, the concentrations may be great enough to exterminate a species. A well-known example is the thin-shelled egg phenomenon in various predatory bird species, such as falcons and brown pelicans. In these species, increased concentration of pesticides in the body causes thinner eggshells. When the eggshells are too thin, they crack before the young bird can hatch. When this phenomenon occurs in the entire population, it goes extinct.

An interesting example of concentration of a pollutant in a food chain was found after a nuclear disaster in the Soviet Union, in which radioactive isotopes were accidentally released from a waste disposal site (9). One unit used to measure the amount of radioactivity in tissue is the microcurie per kilogram of tissue. This represents 37 million nuclear transformations per second per kilogram of tissue. Because living organisms are constantly processing chemicals from the surrounding environment, they tend to accumulate radioactive isotopes in the medium surrounding them. The magnitude of this concentration is illustrated by the following table of measurements from a lake following the Soviet accident. Thus pike muscle, a food of humans, contains about 240 times the concentration of cesium-137 as in the lake water.

	Concentration of Cesium-137 (microcuries per kilogram)
Lake water	.029
Algae and plankton (the food of the roach)	38.0
Muscles of the roach (the food of the large pike)	4.0
Muscles of large pike	7.0

The same type of concentration occurs in terrestrial communities.

Pollutants of certain types accumulate in particular parts of the body. Thus, pesticides such as D.D.T. accumulate in fat, liver, and brain. People with unusual accumulations of pesticides in the organs tend to have made unusually heavy use of pesticides in home gardens, where pesticides are sometimes used at far higher concentrations than on farms or anywhere else. Consistently high levels of pesticides have been found in the tissues of people who died of cirrhosis of the liver, cancer, and hypertension, compared to average people in the population (11). However, a great deal of research would be required to determine whether this correlation is accidental, or implies that the pesticides were somehow implicated in the deaths of these people. Radioactive iodine accumulates in the thyroid gland, and radioactive strontium accumulates in bone.

THE EFFECT OF POLLUTION ON HUMANS

The preceding parts of this chapter are merely background for the really essential question concerning pollution: does pollution have any demonstrable impact on humans, how much impact does it have, and what exactly is the evidence? Clearly, one cannot put human beings in cells, pollute them to various degrees, then conduct tests to find out how sick the experimental subjects are, or why they died. Consequently, all our knowledge of direct effects of pollution on human beings comes from natural experiments, in which we observe statistical association (correlation) between incidence of environmental pollution and sickness in the populations of people exposed to that pollution. Thus most of our insight into the nature of the link between pollution and human beings is statistical.

Types of Statistical Evidence

The statistical evidence is of two types: cross-sectional and longitudinal. By cross-sectional evidence we mean that differences between places with respect to the incidence of various diseases is associated with differences between those same places with respect to the incidence of various pollutants. By longitudinal evidence, we mean that changes through time in the incidence of pollutants is associated with corresponding changes in the incidence of disease. For example, the Arab oil embargo constituted a major natural experiment, producing data that could be subjected to longitudinal analysis. S. M. Brown and his co-workers studied the impact of the embargo on San Francisco and Alameda counties in California (1). Gasoline sales in the first three months of 1974 were 9.5 percent lower in the two countries than they had been in the four previous years. Associated with this drop in gasoline sales, and hence a drop in air pollution, there was a striking drop in several measures of mortality rate, compared with the corresponding three-month period in the four previous years. As we would expect, the drops in mortality rate were largest for those diseases we normally think of as being most associated with air pollution: chronic lung disease (about a 35 percent decline).

However, this result could be most deceiving. It measures the impact of a reduction in air pollution on the level of acute air-pollution induced mortality. It does not necessarily follow that the pattern would be the same for chronic, long-term, low-level exposure to air pollution.

That is, it is reasonable to think of air-pollution-induced mortality as being of two types. On the one hand, we would expect to find in each urban area a long-term average level of mortality produced by the long-term average level and mixture of air pollutants characteristic of that area. This type of pollution-caused mortality would probably be cumulative: the impact of pollution in any time period would be greater for a person who had already been subjected to that level of pollution for a greater length of time. Further, we would expect the effect of this type of pollution to reveal itself after a long time lag, of the type associated with long-term exposure to smoking. Finally, the long-term, chronic effect of air pollution might be quite surprising: rather than having the primary impact on the lungs, the target organ system we would expect to be most susceptible, it would not be surprising to discover more systemic effects on the entire body due to prolonged exposure to smog.

On the other hand, in contradiction to chronic air-pollution induced mortality, we would expect to find acute air-pollution induced mortality. During short periods of unusually high air-pollution concentrations, associated with temperature inversions, we would expect to find that people chronically ill from air pollution would die prematurely because of unusual stresses placed on the body by the pollution. However, these deaths would not be due to immediate systemic causes. The immediate cause of death would be respiratory failure or heart failure. In a short period of very intense air pollution, such as in London in 1952, the large number of sudden deaths are due to acute air-pollution induced mortality. Similarly, the reduction of deaths in the San Francisco Bay area in 1974 would be partly due to a lowered rate of acute air-pollution induced mortality (there would have been no days of unusual smog concentration in the interval), but partly due to a lowered rate of chronic air-pollution induced mortality.

Separating the Effects of Chronic and Acute Mortality

The question we now ask is, "How large a mortality rate is being caused by chronic, as opposed to acute air-pollution induced mortality?"

The difficulty in assessing the severity of the chronic air pollution effect is that we must compare mortality rates between different cities in which there are different air pollution concentrations. But this makes us vulnerable to the statistical problem of confounding: cities differ from one to the other in many other respects besides air pollution concentration and mixture. Many of these other factors will also have an effect on mortality rates. Therefore, we run the risk of attributing an increased death rate to increased pollution concentration, when it is in fact due to something else. The problem is to demonstrate that an increased death rate allegedly due to high pollution concentration is *in fact* due to pollution, rather than some other factor. Since two urban areas might differ in many ways, this can be a very difficult problem. Given the great controversy surrounding efforts to clean up pollution, however, and the great cost, it is important to be able to demonstrate as precisely as possible the exact mortality due to pollution, and consequently, the cost of the premature deaths due to pollution.

To illustrate the significance of confounding, suppose we collected statistics on the death rates of all the large metropolitan areas in the United States, and tried to relate them to air pollution concentrations, ignoring the effect of all other factors. We would quickly conclude that El Paso is a very healthy place, and Scranton a very unhealthy place. But the median age (age that bisects the youngest and oldest halves of the population) in El Paso is under twenty-three; in Scranton it is over thirty-five. Therefore, our view of El Paso as healthy and Scranton as unhealthy may be almost entirely due to a difference in the ages of the people in the two cities. To illustrate some of the other factors of this type, smoking history, race, sex, income, educational level, and character of the house are all strongly related to the level of health. Further, the occupation and local weather may have an effect on the probability of death. In some cases, quite different types of local factors, such as the presence of organisms carrying infectious diseases, may be important determinants of probability of death.

There are two ways of dealing with all these confounding influences. The first approach is not to correct for any of these confounding influences. Our aim is to work with such a large number of different cities or sections of cities, for each of which we attempt to explain death rates in terms of pollutant concentrations only, that the confounding influences will tend to cancel each other. The second approach is to correct for as many of the confounding influences as we can, given the available data.

The problem with the first approach is that the confounding influences may not cancel out. The problem with the second approach is that we may simply lack data on all the possible confounding influences, or it may be too expensive to obtain it. Indeed, some of the information may be unobtainable in principle: people may consider it an infringement of their privacy to reveal certain data of medical importance. But there is also a statistical problem when we try to correct for all the confounding influences. The data in each category become smaller and smaller as a scheme for classifying data becomes more complex. So if we classify death rates on the basis of age, race, sex, and ten other characteristics, the data in each category may finally be so scarce that it is impossible to prove anything. That is, normal "sampling error" or statistical variation veils the truth. To illustrate, if the number in a certain classification is so small that on average only five deaths a year would be expected, normal variation could lead that number to vary from none to ten over a sequence of years. (The exact range would depend on the inherent year-to-year variability

in the death rate.) Thus, an increase of two deaths a year, on average, would be very difficult to detect. Consequently, we initially adopt a course between the two approaches mentioned above: we correct only for age. That is, we try to interpret differences in death rates between urban areas in terms of departures from the rates we would have expected, given the age in each area.

Pollution and the Rate of Aging

When this is done, we make a most curious discovery. Comparing people of the same age in different urban areas, we find much larger differences between polluted and unpolluted areas with respect to the total death rate, than with respect to death rates we would have expected to be affected by pollution. This suggests that pollution is not just operating on suspected target organs, but on all parts of the body. For example, we would expect air pollution to affect death rates due to lung and heart diseases. But if the differences between polluted areas and unpolluted areas in the number of total deaths is much greater than the difference in number of deaths due to heart and lung diseases, then clearly many diseases are being affected by air pollution. This is a most curious and important conclusion if true. How would we test this idea?

One way is to correct the death rates due to each type of disease for the effect of age, then see if the resultant death rates are related to each other. In other words, if air pollution is increasing the incidence of all types of disease, then we should expect to find that cities high in one type of disease tend to be high in all the others also, and that these are particularly polluted cities. This is what we find. For example, when the death rates due to all forms of cancer and the death rates due to heart disease are plotted against each other, both being adjusted for median age, we find that cities high in one tend to be high in the other. If we perform a statistical analysis of the data for thirty-eight metropolitan areas, we find that 27 percent of the city-to-city variation in total cancer death rate is accounted for by heart disease death rate. On the face of it, this makes no sense: cancer and heart disease are apparently totally unrelated phenomena. But perhaps this common-sense understanding is incorrect: perhaps both causes of death are produced by some underlying factors (3, 4).

We get a clue as to what these factors might be when we examine the situation for specific cities. Las Vegas has only one major industry, which does not produce air pollution. It has by far the lowest concentration of nitrogen dioxide in the air of any of the thirty-eight cities. This makes sense, because it is in a windy desert, where automobile smog is unlikely to be trapped or accumulate. Further, it is very spread out, so that main traffic arteries that would be likely to accumulate pollution are far from each other. Sulphur dioxide concentrations are much lower than in many other cities. No known pollutant for which measurements have been made is present in high concentrations in Las Vegas, and most are present in very low concentrations. Boston has about four times the concentration of nitrogen dioxide as Las Vegas. Among large American cities, Washington is unusually free of polluting industries. As one might expect, it has much lower concentrations of many air pollutants. To illustrate, it has about a third the nickel, a quarter the zinc, and 80 percent as much nitrogen dioxide per unit of air as Boston. Thus there is some plausible basis for believing that there might be some complex of factors and some reasonable causal pathway leading to simultaneous elevation of the death rates due to many different diseases in certain cities.

The Theory

But exactly what is that causal pathway? R. J. Hickey (3) has advanced a theory in which air pollution is perceived as inducing chronic disease and the chemicals in pollution speed up the mutation rate in all living cells and lead to premature human senescence. Since all people are genetically different, this premature senescence will first reveal itself in each individual by breakdown of the organ system or tissue that is most congenitally predisposed to succumb to the mutagenic effects of the pollution. This notion that different people will succumb to the same stress in different ways should not be surprising. Most people will have noticed that in certain families, there is a tendency, generation after generation, to die of respiratory disease, or stomach cancer, or heart failure, for example. This reflects a congenital weakness in the organ system in question, and those congenital weaknesses are being stressed and exposed by air pollution through its mutagenic effect.

Specifically, Hickey argues that nonradioactive pollutants in air can act as mutagens, so as to cause mutation of the genetic material in all cells. If ambient air pollution concentrations are characteristically sufficiently high, this leads to an accumulation of mutations. This imples gradual decrease in the degree to which the intracellular genetic material has the appropriate pattern of molecular organization, and this, in turn, implies a gradual increase in the likelihood of chronic disease, particularly in those tissues or organs most susceptible to breakdown in any case because of inherited weakness.

Now if this theory is correct, we would expect to find that in polluted environments, many different kinds of diseases increase in incidence simultaneously, and also that the death rates of just those diseases believed to be the prime targets of air pollution give us a serious underestimate of the overall impact on death rate of chronic air-pollution induced mortality. When we compare death rates for polluted and unpolluted counties in Southern California, we find that the increased death rate per 100,000 due to lung disease is only seven in the polluted counties. But when we look at all diseases, the corresponding increase is sixty-seven. Thus, by only looking at the impact of pollution or mortality due to the expected target diseases and the expected target organ system, we underestimate the overall impact of mortality due to air pollution by a factor of over nine times.

This suggests, in turn, that instead of exploring the relation between pollution concentration differences and death rates due to particular diseases, it would be more revealing to explore the relation between these concentration gradients and the total death rate.

The test areas, eight southern California counties, were selected because the climates in all eight are naturally conducive to good health and the standard of living in general is high. The one obvious respect in which these counties differ markedly is in the concentration of air pollution. Further, to elimi-

nate possible effects on mortality rate of age, sex, and race, the data selected were only for forty-five- to forty-nine-year-old white men. The index of pollution chosen, oxidant concentration, accounts for 62 percent of the variation in death rate between counties. Great care was taken in this analysis to avoid various types of error. The population base was obtained from the 1970 census, so is as accurate as can be obtained. The mortality statistics were obtained by averaging the deaths for the years 1969 to 1973, inclusive, to obtain a number of deaths for 1971 that would be relatively free from the effect of any short-term environmental fluctuations. Further, by averaging deaths over five years, we minimize the effect of normal statistical sampling error due to chance fluctuations or variations. On the face of it, it would appear that a variation in pollution concentration through the range of conditions actually encountered in southern California can alter the mortality rate 40 percent.

Clearly, if this is true, it is a rather important conclusion. Obviously, many people would raise a variety of objections: the people in the "polluted counties" are all poor, or

TABLE 12.5

The relation between average annual death rates from all causes per 1000 population according to economic and air pollution levels of the census tract of residence, for white men fifty to sixty-nine years of age in Buffalo, New York, and environs, 1959 to 1961.

Economic level of census tract of residence	Air pollution level of census tract of resident				
	1 (low)	2	3	4 (high)	Total
1 (low)		36	41	52	43
2	24	27	30	36	29
3		24	26	33	25
4	20	22	27		22
5 (high)	17	21	20		19
Total	20	24	31	40	26

Data from W. Winkelstein, Jr., et al., "The relationship of air pollution and economic status to total mortality and selected respiratory system mortality in men. I. Suspended particulates," *Arch. Environ. Health,* 14 (1967), pp. 162–171.

smoke more, or live in more crowded, unsanitary conditions, or the like. Given that the polluted counties include such places as Palm Springs, these objections may not be that damaging to the argument.

However, scientists who have studied the public health effects of air pollution carefully are always sensitive to this type of criticism about confounding of other effects with effects due to air pollution. Accordingly, in a few studies, pollution and public health effects have been assessed at the level of individual census tracts, and individuals have been kept separate on the basis of sex, age, race and economic level of the census tract. When all these variables have been controlled, as in Table 12.5, it appears that air pollution increases the death rate by approximately 50 percent.

The Economic Significance of Pollution

Now what is the economic significance of such results? Lave and Seskin (5, 6) have asked what we could afford to spend to deal with this problem. A 10 percent decline in air pollution would extend the average U.S. life expectancy by seventeen weeks. Translating that into dollars by using insurance company tables, we find that air pollution reduction by 10 percent could cost $1.222 billion a year and we would break even. For example, if there are 115 million cars in the country, we could therefore afford $11 per car per year, or $55 per car every five years. It is amazing, in view of these numbers, how little support there has been for vigorous enforcement of air pollution legislation, and more effective legislation. Arguments by manufacturers that the necessary changes are impossible seem odd in view of the rapid innovation in cars in Japan, for example.

For all the other forms of pollution we could have discussed in this chapter, the ultimate conclusion would have been the same: the cost to effect a major reduction in pollution concentration would easily be justified by savings resulting from the lowered pollution concentration. Thus the fact that these things do not happen once again is a commentary on our culture, our perceptions, and our economic and political systems, rather than on the logistical difficulty or cost of attaining the desired effect.

FALLOUT FROM NUCLEAR TESTING

Fallout from nuclear testing is a particularly useful example pollutant for illustrating the problems involved in resolving controversies surrounding environmental contamination. Some analysts, such as E. J. Sternglass (7) have argued for years that the fallout from nuclear bomb tests and low-level radiation from reactors affects mortality in infants. Nuclear advocates argue that this position is nonsense, of course.

There were twenty-six periods from 1951 to 1958 when some residents of Utah were exposed to fallout from nuclear bomb tests, mostly over certain rural counties. Previous research has suggested that sensitivity to radiation carcinogenesis is greatest in children under fifteen years of age. Accordingly, a study was conducted to see if there was any association between the incidence of leukemia in Utah children under fifteen, and fallout from bomb tests (8). This research was carefully done: it separated the data on the basis of type of cancer or leukemia, location relative to fallout concentration, age of child, time of appearance of cancer or leukemia, and corrected the mortality rates for age and sex. In the published paper, leukemia incidence in all of Utah and in the United States was also plotted. Figure 12.2 shows one way of displaying the results of the analysis. Clearly, there was an increase, by a factor of three, in the incidence of leukemia in high fallout counties in the eight

FIGURE 12.2

Leukemia mortality rates, adjusted for age, per 100,000 Utah residents between 1944 and 1975. The rates are plotted against year of occurrence and are separated into high fallout counties, which received a lot of fallout from bomb tests, and low fallout Utah counties. Reprinted, by permission, from Figure 2 in "Childhood leukemias associated with fallout from nuclear testing," by J. L. Lyon, M. R. Klauber, J. W. Gardner, and K. S. Udall, New England Journal of Medicine, *300:397, 1979. Lines for the entire state and the United States have been omitted: they were virtually identical to the line for low fallout counties in Utah.*

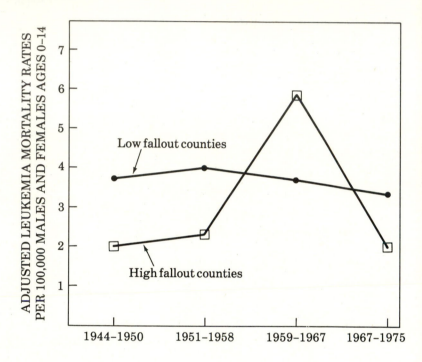

years after the termination of bomb tests, above the incidence normally encountered in the rural, high fallout counties. This result is certainly highly suggestive, but as the authors were careful to point out, they could have been due to fallout or to some other unexplained factor. However, if a series of analyses of this type, for different times, different places, and different bomb tests all showed the same pattern, the possibility that some other factor was implicated would become vanishingly small.

POLLUTION: THE BIG PICTURE

For years, the American population has been bombarded with information of the type presented in this chapter. One result has been creation of the Environmental Protection Agency, the President's Council on Environmental Quality, and a mass of legislation to achieve pollution abatement. The results have sometimes been discouraging, as when one California newspaper had a front-page headline suggesting that the war with pollution was not being won. One can only conclude that there is some basic error in the approach of our society to pollution control.

Students may want to give some thought to this basic question: what is the best way for society to discourage and punish asocial or dangerous behavior? Laws may have some effect, but in the long run, wouldn't price have an even greater effect? Students may also want to consider if laws can be effective without each individual realizing the seriousness of the pollution problem and taking personal action.

My own students find that determination of the most appropriate role for government is the most difficult issue raised by environmental problems. One surprising conclusion they arrive at is that perhaps the degree of public intervention should most appropriately be inconsistent from one problem to another, as when government has minimal involvement with energy pricing, but a great deal of involvement with disposal of toxic chemicals and nuclear waste. In these last instances, the perils to society may be so great that there is an intolerable level of risk. In such instances, satisfactory reduction of all risks can only be achieved through legislation accompanied by strict administration of the law.

SUMMARY

There are two fundamentally different approaches available for dealing with pollution. One can either dispose of or recycle the output from a process, or make the input to the process so expensive that it will be used more efficiently in the process, thus decreasing the output. Viewed this way, one of the underlying causes of pollution is unrealistically low prices for resources, which result in inadequate incentive to use them efficiently.

Pollutants are not only poisons, but may also be nutrients or other naturally occurring substances that people introduce into the environment faster than they can be removed by natural processes.

One rarely recognized cause of pollution is centralization; a process which would not produce a dangerous concentration of pollutants if dispersed is dangerous when the activity is concentrated.

The political process does not respond appropriately to pollution because many hazardous substances only have their ultimate medical effect after a very long time lag following the time of their first introduction into the environment. Also, the technical problems involved in providing a legally convincing proof that pollution has increased the death rate make it difficult to explain the argument to a mass public.

Despite major governmental and legal innovations to deal with pollution, the results have left much to be desired. There is still a great deal of thinking to be done about the best way to deal with this difficult and baffling problem.

SUGGESTIONS FOR INDIVIDUAL AND GROUP PROJECTS

Select some instance of pollution in your community, and try to assess as accurately as possible the cost of the damage resulting from it and what it would cost to clean it up. If lost life is involved, use actuarial tables to compute the dollar cost of premature human death.

REFERENCES

1. Brown, S. M., M. G. Marmot, S. T. Sacks, and L. W. Kwok, "Effect on mortality of the 1974 fuel crisis," *Nature* 257 (1975), pp. 306–307.

2. Craig, G. A., *"Germany 1866–1945."* New York: Oxford University Press, 1978.

3. Hickey, R. J., "Air pollution," in *Environment,* W. W. Murdoch, ed. Sunderland, Mass.: Sinauer Associates, 1971.

4. Hickey, R. J., D. E. Boyce, E. B. Harner, and R. C. Clelland, *Exploratory Ecological Studies of Variables Related to Chronic Disease Mortality Rates.* Philadelphia: University of Pennsylvania, 1971.

5. Lave, L. B., and E. P. Seskin, "Air pollution and human health," *Science* 169 (1970), pp. 723–733.

6. Lave, L. B., and E. P. Seskin, *Air Pollution and Human Health.* Baltimore: John Hopkins University Press, 1977.

7. Le Cam, L. M., J. Neyman, and E. L. Scott, eds., *Proceedings of the Sixth Berkeley Symposium on Mathematical Statistics and Probability. Volume VI. Effects of pollution on health.* Berkeley: University of California Press, 1972.

8. Lyon, J. L., M. L. Klauber, J. W. Gardner, and K. S. Udall, "Childhood leukemias associated with fallout from nuclear testing," *New England Journal of Medicine,* 300 (1979), p. 397.

9. Medvedev, Z. A., *Nuclear disaster in the Urals.* New York: W. W. Norton, 1979.

10. Parker, G. *Philip II.* Boston: Little, Brown and Co. 1978.

11. Radomski, J. L., W. B. Deichmann, and E. E. Clizer, "Pesticide concentrations in the liver, brain and adipose tissue of terminal hospital patients," *Food and Cosmetics Toxicology* 6 (1968), pp. 209–220.

12. *The San Francisco Examiner and Chronicle,* "The tragedy of 2, 4, 5,-T," April 22, 1979.

13. Singer, S. F., ed., *Global Effects on Environmental Pollution.* Dordrecht, Holland: D. Reidel, 1970.

14. Tuck, L. M., *The Murres.* Ottawa: Canadian Department of Northern Affairs and National Resources, Canadian Wildlife Series 1, 1960.

15. Watt, K. E. F., "The Titanic effect," Chapter 4 of *Environmental Pollution.* Sunderland, Mass.: Sinauer Associates, 1974.

16. Wise, W. *Killer Smog.* New York: Rand, McNally: 1968.

13 ENVIRONMENTAL DEGRADATION

Now therefore command thou that they hew me cedar trees out of Lebanon . . .
And he sent them to Lebanon, ten thousand a month by courses: a month they
were in Lebanon, and two months at home . . . And Solomon had three score and
ten thousand that bare burdens, and fourscore thousand hewers in the mountains.
1 Kings 5:6–15 *(describing events of midtenth century B.C.).*

. . . but Lebanon has been kept down mainly by man and his goats. Much of the
former forest land, now reduced to four small groves, is so severely eroded that
only geologic weathering can build a new soil, a process that will require
thousands of years and no goats.
Vernon Gill Carter and Tom Dale, Topsoil and Civilization, *Chapter 5 rev. ed., 1974.*

MAIN THEMES OF THIS CHAPTER

Chapter 5 pointed out that natural systems maintain a degree of stability, because they have a variety of stabilizing mechanisms that tend to prevent components from departing too far above or below their long-term average (equilibrium) values. Environmental degradation results when people ignore the value of maintaining stability in natural ecosystems. Instability results when we take actions that result in great increase or decrease in the level of material or energy flow into or out of ecosystems.

Deforestation, excessive grazing, salinization, waterlogging, and destruction of the shallow ocean bottom all affect the rate at which materials and energy enter or leave ecosystems.

An important form of environmental degradation is covering up productive land with buildings, asphalt, or cement. High-density

291

housing developments and more efficient urban land use work against this process.

One of the most important causes of environmental degradation is excessive cropping in arid or semiarid lands. This process produced the "dust bowl" in Kansas and Oklahoma in the 1930s.

Deforestation of hillsides leaves the soil exposed to violent rainfalls that wash minerals off hillsides into streams at the bottom of the watershed. This process disturbs all the living organisms in the water.

BALANCED AND UNBALANCED ECOSYSTEMS: AN OVERVIEW

As civilization develops in any part of the earth, three things can happen that singly or in combination can degrade the environment. Even if demand per capita for a particular resource, such as meat, wheat, or firewood is low, if population becomes excessive, the total population-wide demand for these rudimentary resources will overwhelm the capacity of the environment to supply them, and environmental degradation will result. On the other hand, even if population size is small relative to the carrying capacity of the environment for people, if demand per capita rises to very high levels, as in affluent America, environmental degradation may become serious. Thirdly, long before population becomes too large for an environment, or demand per capita becomes very high, humanity may destroy the productive capacity of an environment simply through thoughtless mismanagement. Many of the problems covered in this chapter can only be alleviated through lowered populations, or lowered resource demand per capita; however, environmental degradation can be lessened by wiser management in many cases.

Because of the great variety of ways in which humanity can degrade the environment, a discussion of this topic is in danger of disintegrating into a lengthy catalogue of examples and remedies, which altogether become difficult to remember. A more modern way of looking at this subject is to deepen our insight by imbedding the topic of environmental degradation into the conceptual framework of the ecosystem, introduced in Chapter 5. This means that we now try to understand the effect of various management practices on agricultural, forest, and ocean systems in terms of their effects on energy and materials flows into and out of the system. Bormann and Likens (1) have been particularly influential in developing this point of view, as a consequence of their research on the Hubbard Brook watershed in New Hampshire.

Categories of Inputs and Outputs

The point of view is illustrated by Figure 13.1, which depicts the matter and energy flows into and out of a typical terrestrial ecosystem. We see that there are six categories of flows into and out of the system: energy, water, minerals, soil, plants, and animals. The terrestrial system is made up of water, minerals, soil, plants, herbivores, carnivores, and saprophytes (organisms that live off dead material and facilitate decomposition and recycling of nutrients). In addition to flows into and out of the system, there is constant recycling within the ecosystem: minerals, for example, are returned to the soil when a plant or animal dies and decomposes, then get reincorporated into the system via the roots of plants. Water may run out of a watershed via small streams into a pond; that water may reenter the system via the roots of plants or by being drunk by animals.

In a healthy, productive ecosystem, the various pairs of flows, on average, are in balance through time. That is, water does

FIGURE 13.1
Energy and materials flow into and out of terrestrial ecosystems.

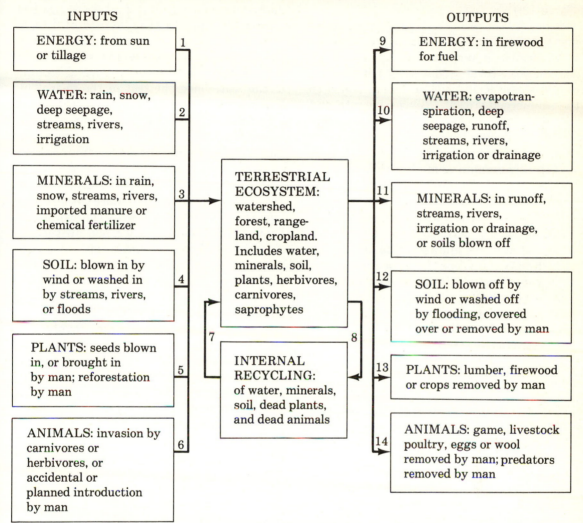

not leave the system faster than it enters, nor does potassium, nitrates, topsoil, or anything else. Similarly, nothing enters faster than it leaves, for any extended period of time, without environmental degradation. If too much heat, water, potassium, silt, dust, or rock, or too many rabbits, grasshoppers, or goats enter an ecosystem for any length of time, the result can be degradation of the productive capacity of the environment. Thus, wise management implies monitoring

ecosystems being used by humans to ensure that inputs are in balance with their corresponding outputs, and taking remedial action when the system is not in balance.

Eight Types of Environmental Degradation

To illustrate this concept further, we now examine eight different types of environmental degradation to see how they can be understood in terms of inbalances in addition to, or subtraction from an ecosystem (Table 13.1).

Excessive covering over of arable land, as under cities, airport runways, freeways, or hydroelectric impoundments, all lower national agricultural productivity. In the case of dams, water and soil are being added to the submerged area at an excessive rate, and where we asphalt or concrete over areas, topsoil is withdrawn from production at an excessive rate (pathway 12).

Excessive cropping implies that too high a percentage of the country is planted out to a crop such as corn. This occurs not only where the total area under cultivation is too great, but where, within the area under cultivation, land is not allowed to lie fallow long enough between crops. Both of these situations imply that too high a proportion of all land is exposed to the sun, rain, and wind, because there is a lot of uncovered soil between rows of a row crop. This exposure in turn means that the action of rain or wind can wash away or blow away the exposed soil. Also, in tropical countries, exposure to the sun for extended periods turns the bare soil into laterite, a rock-like earth covering that is useless to agriculture. Excessive cropping leads to excessive rates for flows 10, 11, 12, and 13 because too much water, minerals, soil, and plant material are carried or blown out of the ecosystem by water or wind erosion.

Deforestation has two kinds of principal effects on a watershed. The bare surface of the soil is vulnerable to erosion by rainfall, because there is no plant cover to break the full force of the raindrops when they hit the soil surface. But also, when trees are felled and their roots are dead, the tremendous sponge-like function of the living roots in absorbing water into the watershed is lost. The bare surface in combination with the loss of subsurface absorbing roots imply that a much higher than normal proportion of incident rain will run off the surface immediately instead of being absorbed and retained. This means that instead of a fairly even flow of water out of the watershed all through the year, there will be violent flooding and runoff after heavy rains and drought in the watershed the rest of the year. This flooding, in turn, has several consequences. The force of the water rushing off hilly slopes carries off topsoil, but also scours out gullys, so that the surface becomes too uneven for cultivation. The soil washed off the surface contains nutrients essential to plant growth on the slopes, and more essential nutrients are washed off with the rainwater. Downstream, the water washed off the hillsides causes flooding, and creates waterlogging and swamps. The silt and plant debris carried along by the floodwaters fills up irrigation pipes and ditches, so that they become useless unless cleaned out, at great effort. Deforestation often also involves an excessive denudation of trees for firewood from hilly parts of a watershed (pathway 9), and this has the same set of consequences as clear-cutting lumber. In summary, deforestation of hills or mountains to get lumber or firewood ultimately results in a massive transport of minerals and soil from the highlands of a country to the lowlands, with tragic lowering of productivity in both sites. This phenomenon has occurred in Lebanon, Greece, Turkey, and Syria, and is presently occurring in Nepal, Pakistan, Bangladesh, and India.

Excessive grazing by sheep and goats crops plants so close to the surface of the ground that many plants will die, and the ground surface will be too exposed to the action of wind and rain. Denuded, heavily trampled topsoil can be blown away by wind, to make massive dust storms. Alternatively, the top layers of the soil may be washed off in rainstorms. In either case, the

TABLE 13.1

Environmental degradation in terms of altered energy and materials flows into and out of ecosystems.

Type of ecosystem mismanagement	Immediate consequences	Ultimate consequences	Flows with excessive rates	Flows with inadequate rates
1. Excessive covering over of productive land	Arable land covered by water, silt, asphalt, concrete, or houses	Lowered national agricultural productivity	2 and 4, or 12.	
2. Excessive cropping	Too large a proportion of soil exposed between rows of row crops	Lowered national agricultural productivity due to wind or rain-caused erosion	10, 11, 12, 13	
3. Deforestation	Soil surface unprotected and absorption by living tree roots lost in watersheds; runoff after rainfall increases	Soil erosion off hills; flooding, siltation, swamp formation downstream; nation becomes dependent on imported energy and wood	9, 10, 11, 12, and 13	
4. Excessive grazing	Soil surface unprotected and young trees and shrubs eaten off	Erosion due to wind and rain; dust storms; no forest regeneration; lowered national agricultural and forest productivity	6 (herbivores); 11, 12, 13; 14 (carnivores)	6 (carnivores); 14 (herbivores)
5. Salinization	Mineral content of soil too high for best plant growth	Lowered national agricultural productivity	3	2, 10, 11
6. Waterlogging	Soil too wet to grow crops	Towns and cities submerged	2, 3, 4	10, 11, 12
7. Pollution of rivers and estuaries	Nursery beds of fish and shellfish poisoned	Destruction of fishing and shellfish industries	1, 3, 4	
8. Destruction of coastal ocean bottom	Nursery sites and food for fish and shellfish eliminated	Destruction of fishing and shellfish industries	12, 13, 14	

consequence is sharply lowered agricultural productivity in the areas from which the soil has been blown or washed off. But also, if the population of sheep or goats is too high for the carrying capacity of the environment, shoots of young trees and shrubs are likely to be all clipped off before the perennials can become high enough for their green tissues to be out of the reach of herbivores. When forest land or savannah is so overgrazed, there is no regeneration of the trees, and desertification results. There is another mechanism that can produce this situation besides accidental or deliberate human overstocking of herbivores (pathway 6). If carnivores are hunted so hard that their populations are reduced or eliminated (pathway 6 is too low for carnivores or pathway 14 is too large for carnivores), then unless we compensate for this loss by increasing hunting or cropping of herbivores, the plant level of the trophic pyramid will suffer. A problem repeated throughout human history has been our lack of sensitivity to the ecosystem consequences of hunting off the carnivores for sport, on the grounds that they are dangerous predators of humans or livestock. Precisely because carnivores are the enemies of herbivores, they are, in effect, the defenders of vegetation. If we remove carnivores, we must compensate for their absence by having the same impact on herbivores that they would have had, or the herbivores will overgraze the landscape. Overgrazing has been destructive to the nations bordering the Sahara desert on the north and the south, and to northern India, among many others.

Salinization occurs when the movement of dissolved minerals into a region is too great (pathway 3), or the flushing action of water into (2) or out of (10) a region is inadequate, or the flushing out of minerals is not fast enough (11). Two types of situations lead to this difficulty. In the first case, there is inadequate maintenance of an irrigation system in an arid or semiarid agricultural region. Dissolved minerals are not flushed out fast enough, and as the water in which they are dissolved evaporates from the soil surface in the hot sun, the topsoil becomes too salty to support crop growth. In the second case, there is excessive pumping of fresh water out of wells near the coastline of an ocean. The result is that the strata of rock that held the water (aquifers) become depleted, salt water from the ocean intrudes to replace the empty spaces in the aquifers. Finally, this salt water is pumped to the surface, and the wells are useless. Indeed, in any major projects to divert fresh water away from coastal areas, there is a risk of intrusion of salt water if ever the rate of diversion becomes excessive.

Waterlogging results when water, minerals, and soil are washing into an area (pathways 2, 3, 4) faster than they are being flushed out (10, 11, 12). This situation typically occurs in lowlands being fed by streams and rivers flowing out of a watershed in which logging, firewood gathering, or grazing have been excessive. Flash flooding swamps an irrigation system, if it exists, and dumps vast quantities of silt into all waterways. Waterways become shallow and are likely to overflow their banks at flood peaks. The result is the creation of a vast area of swamp. Indeed, this massive deposition of silt originating in headwaters of a river system created the world's great delta areas off the mouths of the Nile, Amazon, and Mississippi rivers, for examples. If waterlogging, swamp formation, and silt deposition become serious enough under flash flooding, gradually hundreds of cities, towns, and villages will be buried under the silt, as on the Plain of Antioch at the Syrian-Turkish border.

Pollution of rivers and estuaries occurs when runoff of agricultural chemicals from farmland is excessive during heavy rains. Accumulation of these pesticides or fertilizers in water either poisons fish and shellfish or their food organisms (pesticides) or in the case of fertilizers, produces excessive blooms of algae that cut off the oxygen supply under the surface of the water. This buildup of nutrients (called eutrophication) and algae is inimical to the survival of fish or shellfish populations, which cannot tolerate low levels of oxygen. Alternatively, pollution comes about because chemical plants discharge massive quantities of waste chemicals into the water of rivers or estuaries. Indeed, coastlines are a preferred site for chemical plants, because of their great need for both intake water supply, and a cheap place to dump their wastes. The particular significance of eutrophication or poisoning of coastal waters is that while these represent a small proportion of the total world area of oceans, they have an importance as nursery grounds for young oceanic fish out of all proportion to their area. Thus, destruction of a tiny proportion of the world's ocean area as a habitat for fish may render sterile a large proportion of the high seas.

Few people who live inland have any reason to be aware of the vast destruction of the shallow coastal ocean bottom. As a snorkeler, I have been horrified to discover that the shallow waters of the coasts of tropical islands may be vast aquatic deserts. The reason is that generation after generation of divers have torn the ocean bottom (coral reefs) apart with crowbars, searching for food (such as octopi) or coral fragments or shellfish that could be sold to tourists. The result is that the shallow ocean bottom is turned into a lifeless expanse of rock and sand that is useless to support the young fish and shellfish so essential to create the foodstocks of such regions.

All of the preceding problems come about because people allow flows into or out of eco-systems to depart from equilibrium rates, resulting in unbalanced and unproductive crop or grazing lands, forests and oceans. But just as surely as we can unbalance a system, we can reestablish the balance if we understand the mechanisms producing the undesired effects. Consequently, we now turn to a series of case studies that give more understanding of these mechanisms and therefore suggest wise management practices.

EXCESSIVE COVERING OVER OF PRODUCTIVE LAND

Pimentel et al. (11) have assembled statistics on the rate at which land is being lost to agriculture in the United States by being covered over. There is a surprising net loss of 1.25 million acres of arable cropland from the national agricultural stock per year, or about 3.3 percent of the current total every ten years. To determine why this loss is so large, we break out the amount per person by categories. The loss is .93 acres per person per year due to erosion, .30 acres due to highways, roads, and the entire passenger car system, .09 due to urban uses, and .21 acres due to all other uses. Why are these rates as large as they are, and how could they be made smaller? This question in turn relates back to the analysis of land transfer rates introduced in Chapter 10. Conversion of U.S. agricultural land to other types of land use results from our history of attaching a low value to agricultural commodities and agricultural land, relative to the value we attached to automobile transportation, the single-family ranch bungalow, and massive urban freeway systems that generate urban sprawl. In turn, these phenomena follow from a cultural value system that assigns a low value to resources rela-

FIGURE 13.2

Relative widths of rights-of-way required for transportation corridors to move 50,000 people per hour (one direction). Figures calculated from analyses by R. J. Smeed, 1961, The Traffic Problem in Towns, Manchester Statistical Society, pp. 1–59.

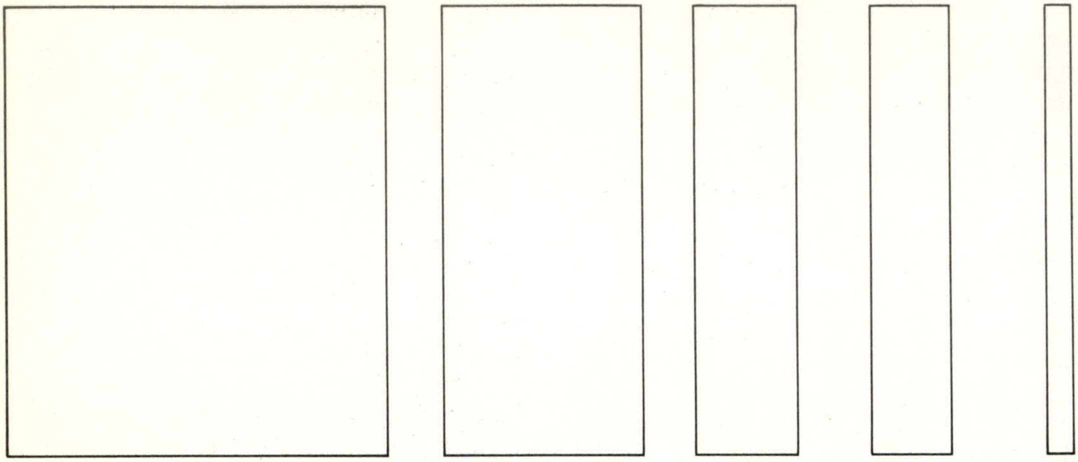

Corridor required to move 50,000 people per hour, in cars each with driver only

(407 feet wide)

Corridor required to move 50,000 people per hour, in cars with average of 1.5 occupants

(267 feet wide)

Corridor required to move 50,000 people per hour, in cars with average of 4 occupants

(100 feet wide)

Corridor required to move 50,000 people per hour in buses with average of 32 occupants

(74 feet wide)

Corridor required to move 50,000 people per hour in urban railway line

(17 feet wide)

tive to the value assigned to high wages (Chapter 9). Inefficient, thoughtless resource use is the inevitable result.

Particularly, it is noteworthy that the passenger car system uses half of the total loss of cropland to highways, urbanization, and all other special uses. Why is this value so high? The explanation is that cars are a means of passenger transportation that makes remarkably inefficient use of land. To make the point, Figure 13.2 shows the relative widths of the rights-of-way required for a transportation corridor to move 50,000 people per hour. Common sense indicates that these figures are reasonable: two cars, one after the other, each with one person, take up roughly the same highway space as one bus, at low speeds. This gives the rule of thumb that buses move sixteen times as many people per unit area (with thirty-two

FIGURE 13.3
A pyramid-shaped multifamily residential unit in Lucerne, Switzerland. Note the proximity to a landscaped park.

passengers) as two cars with one person each. The figure suggests that the actual ratio is eleven times, not sixteen.

Clearly, one way to reduce the rate at which land is being transferred from crop use to other uses, per person added to the population, is to switch from ranch bungalows on large lots to multiple-family dwellings, and from cars to buses or rapid transit trains.

American readers will object to this conclusion on the grounds that multiple-family dwellings constitute an unpleasant life style. Apartments and townhouses can be designed to be unpleasant; they can also be designed very differently. One of the principal reasons why apartment living can be unpleasant is that any sense of privacy is lost because the thickness of walls between units is such that noise moves freely between units. In many new multiple-family dwell-

ings in Europe, on the other hand, there is concrete block, or other sound-impermeable wall structure between units, so that no sound whatsoever travels from unit to unit.

Because wise use of urban land is so important in high-density, therefore land-poor Europe, and because there is a tradition of great concern with the quality of urban life, there are many interesting European experiments with new designs for high-density urban living. One approach, as in Figures 13.3 and 13.4 is to design a pyramid-shaped multifamily structure, so that on each floor, each unit has a large balcony that can be used for growing plants. Consequently, the entire unit comes to resemble a vertical garden. Particularly when the building is adjacent to a large park anyway, as in these figures, we see that high-density living can coexist with a feeling of being close to nature. Indeed, all over Europe, there has

FIGURE 13.4
A closeup view of the pyramid structure in the previous figure.

FIGURE 13.5
A panoramic view of the "city in one building" residential structure at Lignon, at the edge of Geneva, in Switzerland. This structure is so immense that its size could only be grasped in a photograph taken from a balloon or helicopter. This photograph was taken from the top of one of the towers. The grassy area in the immediate rear of the building contains shops, restaurants, schools, churches, recreation areas, and a small zoo. The automobile parking is under the ground. Further to the rear is a forest for hiking.

FIGURE 13.6
Services in the rear of the "city in one building" structure at Lignon. This photograph gives some idea of the scale of the entire complex in the preceding picture: it is an interior shot of one half of the restaurant-shopping center complex in the rear of the main building, and appeared as the tiny one-story building in the immediate center of Figure 13.5.

clearly been a conscious design effort to bring the population into proximity to forests, parks, and gardens.

One of the most striking experiments in very high-density urban living is at Lignon, on the Swiss-French border at the edge of Geneva. This is an example of the city-in-a-building experiment. Here, very large numbers of people live in one gigantic residential structure. Public transportation comes directly to the front of the building; there is a forest in the rear. Figure 13.5 is a panoramic view of the structure. The small buildings to the rear of the structure include shops, restaurants, schools, churches, and all other services, including a small zoo where the children living in the structure may keep more exotic pets. Figure 13.6 gives an idea of the multiplicity of services in the rear of

the residence, and Figure 13.7 indicates the proximity to woodlands.

This structure represents a substitute for the U.S. life style of life in vast tracts of single-family ranch bungalows, with no parks, public gardens, or forests anywhere near most houses, and the nearest stores perhaps miles away.

Vast amounts of farmland have been converted to these enormous expanses of tract housing in the United States. Since an option was the pleasant multifamily structures in the figures, the loss of farmland due to the single-family ranch bungalow has been unnecessary.

Associated with the differences in housing have been profound differences between nations in land use and the spatial layout of cities. In most ancient cities, and in modern cities where land and gasoline are expensive relative to the cost of labor, land use is intense throughout the downtown area. Buildings are three to seven stories in height, vehicle use is minimal or nonexistent in the heart of the shopping area, and pedestrian use is very great. Figure 13.8 is of the main street in Northwich, a very old English city in which the urban core has been renovated to resemble the way it looked many centuries ago. By contrast, in a city surrounded by an enormous expanse of land, and where gasoline is very cheap, we may find a great deal of underutilized land immediately adjacent to the skyscrapers in the urban core, as in Houston (Figure 13.9).

In nations with a small amount of agricultural land per capita, little of it can be transferred to urban use per person added to the urban population. Under those circumstances, high-rise structures extend right out to the edge of town, where they form a line separating city and countryside, as in Amsterdam (Figure 13.10).

These examples suggest that we can create a sharply reduced rate of land degradation due to urbanization by use of wise housing and urban land use policies.

FIGURE 13.7
The area to the immediate rear of the shops and restaurants behind the residential structure at Lignon. Thus, high-density living can be enjoyed in immediate proximity to natural forests and hiking country. Note the striking contrast to the life style depicted in the next figure.

FIGURE 13.8
Main Street in Northwich, renovated to resemble appearance in sixteenth century. Notice that the street is designed for pedestrian activity and excludes vehicles.

FIGURE 13.9
One aspect of the downtown area in Houston. The picture is designed to reveal the surprisingly low density land use very close to the skyscrapers at the heart of the downtown area.

A CASE STUDY IN EXCESSIVE CROPPING: THE DUST BOWL OF THE 1930s

As the settlers moved west in the United States, they opened up farmland which received 10 to 30 inches of rainfall a year, or even less, rather than the 30 to 60 inches a year characteristic of the eastern states. Thus, attempting to grow crops, or raise livestock in Nebraska, Kansas, Colorado, Oklahoma, or Texas as if they were states further to the east can lead to serious problems of desertification, particularly in extraordinarily dry years. The years 1931 to 1937 were extraordinarily dry in many western states. Two strategic errors in utilization of these naturally dry states created the dust bowl and dust storm conditions of the 1930s. The first strategic error was overgrazing. Much of the American West is so arid that twenty or more acres may be required to support a cow for a month. In-

stead, stockowners attempted to graze at twice that stocking density. The result was that most of the principal range plants were depleted by half or more (8). The second strategic error was that after cropping, vegetative cover was not left on the denuded fields while they were lying fallow. Ideally, such cover would be left on the soil until soil moisture was sufficient to ensure the successful start of the next crop (8). These two strategic errors lead to the same result. The soil lies bare under the hot sun, and the surface becomes very dry. Since there is insufficient plant cover for the soil surface to lock it down, winds can produce drifting of the loose soil surface, and rain storms wash the soil off. Much of Texas, Oklahoma, Kansas, and Colorado is so dry that the semiarid grasslands should never have been ploughed in the first place. But because they were, a dust bowl of blowing sand was created in the 1930s that blew Great Plains topsoil all over eastern America and clouded the skies time

FIGURE 13.10

Zürich, Switzerland. In contrast to the Houston area, there is such an acute shortage of agricultural land in Switzerland that all land must be used very carefully. Therefore, there is no waste land within cities, and high-rise structures come right to the edge of the city, forming a line just inside the farmland that borders the city. Photograph courtesy of the Swiss National Tourist Center, New York.

after time, year after year. The result was fifty million acres of land largely denuded of their topsoil, with the land crossed by gullies gouged out of fields by flooding after rainstorms (4). In terms of Figure 13.1, there was excessive loss from the ecosystem of water, soil, minerals, and plants, all of which imply permanent decrease in productive potential.

Figures 13.11 and 13.12 convey some idea of the enormous impact of the dustbowl on western states.

The Potential for a Modern Dustbowl

A recent study by Brink, Densmore, and Hill (3) indicates the extent to which we might be running the risk of a repetition of the 1930s situation and explains why this has come about and what remedial actions can be taken. The pressure on U.S. agricultural soils has increased enormously since 1970, because of the massive amounts of food that must be exported to pay for imported crude oil (Chapters 10 and 11). To in-

FIGURE 13.11
Soil drifts on farmstead near Guymon, Oklahoma. United States Department of Agriculture, Soil Conservation Service photograph by G. L. Beene.

dicate the enormity of this increase in pressure, U.S. corn exports were only 517 million bushels in 1970, but had risen to 1750 million bushels just seven years later. As a consequence, several major changes have occurred in U.S. farm counties where the soil and climate are suitable for growing corn. These changes are exemplified by Dane County, Wisconsin, which was studied intensively by these three scientists.

They discovered that there had been a 57 percent increase in corn acreage in just ten years. The significance of this is that corn fields are unusually vulnerable to erosion, as mentioned earlier. They also found a 26 percent decrease in dairy cows. The number of farms had declined, and the farming was being done by less people. Finally, they discovered a great increase in the amount and size of power equipment being used for farming. In short, they found a shift from decentralized, labor-intensive farming to centralized, energy-intensive farming. (By centralization we mean a tendency to shift from a large number of small operations to a small number of large operations, with fewer owners: in other words a trend towards centralization of control by a progressively

FIGURE 13.12

Two examples of the impact of erosion when farming is attempted on very arid land. In both cases, cultivation removes the natural plant cover, and leaves the exposed, dry soil vulnerable to wind or water erosion. (A) a badly eroded farmyard in the Stillwater district of Oklahoma, 1936. (B) crop land that was in cultivation in 1935 showing removal of soil by wind erosion as deep as cultivated, and also showing accumulation of blow dirt around Russian thistles, Seward County, Kansas. Both pictures from United States Department of Agriculture, Soil Conservation Service.

A

B

smaller number of farmers.) Typically, associated with a trend to more energy-intensive farming is rougher, more routined management of the soil. As we might expect, therefore, Brink, Densmore, and Hill found that in each of five different intensively farmed watersheds in Dane County, the recent annual rates of soil loss due to erosion were in excess of those that the soil could tolerate and still remain productive.

What might be done to stop this ultimately destructive rate of soil erosion? One important tool is strip-cropping; growing alternate strips of hay and cultivated crops. In the Dane county case, examination of aerial photographs showed that strip-cropping had been dropped from 2000 acres since 1967. This change could more than double the soil loss. On sloping cropland, contour farming is an important measure to prevent soil erosion. Under contour farming, furrows are ploughed in concentric circles around a hill, rather than straight rows. The reason for using contour patterns for growing strip crops in hilly country is to avoid having the furrows between rows of crops turn into little rivers in which soil is washed off hillsides after heavy rainstorms. Other means of minimizing erosion are terracing (step-like terraces of soil follow the contours of the hills), use of sod waterways to control the patterns of runoff of rainwater, and conservation tillage. The basic idea underlying conservation tillage is to keep some kind of cover on the ground between rows of crop plants for as much of the time as possible. This is to prevent violent rainstorms or windstorms from washing or blowing the soil off the bare surface.

To show how important it is to follow these sound conservation practices, we consider the difference between the runoff of rainwater from farmland at Hastings, Nebraska, after a 2.75-inch rain storm under straight row cereal cultivation, and an area 65 percent of which was being farmed using sound conservation practices. The run off was twice as great under straight row cultivation (10).

THE EFFECTS OF FOREST CUTTING ON WATER AND MINERAL FLOWS

For a long time, foresters and soil scientists have been alert to the effects on ecosystem balances produced by clear-cutting forests on watersheds. Accordingly, there have been many studies to measure the flows itemized in Table 13.1. Typically, this type of research compares the streamflows out of a control forest, where there has been no cutting, and a cut forest. Prior to the experiment, flows for both control and experimental forests are measured for a few years. The data thus produced are used to develop statistical relationships between the flows for control and experimental forests; these relationships are then used to project for each year, the amount of runoff from the experimental forest that would have been expected had there been no cutting at all. Figure 13.13 is typical of the results from this type of study. Immediately after the forest is cut, there is a great increase in the amount of water running off the watershed after rainfalls compared to what we would have expected had there been no logging. Over a twenty-four-year period, in this instance, there was a gradual decline in runoff until the next time the forest was cut.

What is the significance of cutting forests and the resultant great increase in runoff on the mineral balance of the watershed? This question has been considered exhaustively in a major research project on the Hubbard Brook watershed in New Hampshire (1, 2, 9). Clear-cutting a forest not only sharply increases the runoff from the watershed, but also sharply increases the mineral outflow. In an experiment conducted at Hubbard Brook in the winter of 1965–1966, the forest

FIGURE 13.13

The increase in water yield from a watershed after clear-felling a forest. Notice that the runoff increased almost exactly the same amount after two successive clear-cuttings of the forest, twenty-three years apart. From A. R. Hibbert, 1967, Forest treatment effects on water yield, *Proc. Int. Symp. For. Hydrol. 527-543. Penn. State University, Pergamon Press.*

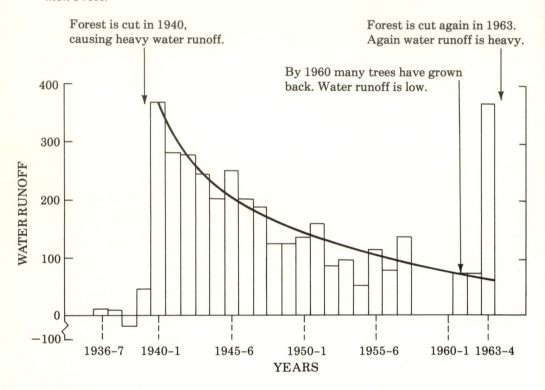

biomass of an experimental watershed was completely leveled. All trees, saplings, and shrubs were cut, dropped in place, and limbed. None of this cut vegetation was removed from the forest, and great care was taken to prevent disturbance of the soil surface, which could facilitate erosion. In the summer of 1966, regrowth of the vegetation was inhibited by application of a herbicide. The concentration of minerals in the stream water flowing out of the watershed was profoundly affected by the cutting and herbicide application. Four minerals drained out of the watershed at markedly higher rates than would otherwise have been the case,

while sulfate left at a lower rate than normal. Apparently, the ability of the ecosystem to retain nutrients is strongly dependent on the presence of living trees and other plants. These results not only have implications for the productivity of the forest itself, but also for the streams running out of the watershed. On the one hand, the forest is depleted of minerals, but on the other hand, the streams may get an overload of minerals. This increase in mineral concentration can lead to a great bloom of algal growth, which cuts off the penetration of light to lower levels of the streams. Further, the accumulation of biological debris in such streams from dead algae can deplete the oxygen supply in the water. This means that streams that had been oxygen-rich habitats suitable for trout and salmon become suitable only for fish species that can tolerate lower levels of oxygen concentration in the water. These processes related to increase in mineral concentration are collectively called eutrophication (or food enrichment). While the total amount of biological production in the streams increases, the type of activity may be less desirable than what had been there prior to the eutrophication.

Minimizing Environmental Degradation from Forest Cutting

How can environmental degradation due to forest cutting be minimized? There are two methods. On the one hand, large tracts of forest should not all be clear-felled simultaneously. It is better to cut selectively, so that some trees are always left standing, to keep some living roots in place to absorb water and mineral nutrients. The other means is to plant new tree seedlings as soon as possible after the old trees are cut. This way the time the watershed is without living tree roots in place is kept as short as possible.

In the developing world, forests are not simply cut for lumber, but also for firewood. The unfortunate problem with forest conservation in very poor countries is that it always seems possible to cut the last living tree on the grounds that the welfare of a human being now is more important than the welfare of the forest in the future. The problem with this argument is that the welfare of the forest in the future may well determine the welfare of the nation in the future. Unfortunately, political priorities are misranked; as Eckholm (5) notes, tree-planting programs do not win elections in poor countries.

ENVIRONMENTAL DEGRADATION: THE ROOT CAUSES

Two causes of environmental degradation are apparent; overpopulation and a cultural belief system that puts great value on present benefits relative to future costs. However, in the case of a developed country such as the United States, another cause is more subtle and difficult to discern. This is excessive centralization and highly energy-intensive agriculture and forestry. This leads to a substitution of brute force for skill and finesse or sophistication in managing resources. The role of these factors, which stem from a low energy cost relative to the cost of labor, are apparent when we compare agriculture and forestry between the United States on the one hand, and Switzerland on the other. Switzerland is currently a richer country than the United States, and for a long time its rate of growth in the economy has been higher than that of the United States. Thus the greater labor-intensivity of resource management in agriculture and forestry in Switzerland than in the United States is not the product of a poor society. Rather, it is the product of much higher energy prices relative to labor costs than in the United States. Therefore, energy is not being used as a substitute for labor in Switzerland to the extent found in the United States. The consequences of this show up in many differences between agriculture and forestry. For example, U.S. forests are clearly mined; Swiss forests are farmed. A U.S. forest after a logging operation is often a shocking mess, with parts of trees spread all over the landscape, streams often blocked by debris from the cutting operation. A Swiss forest, by contrast, looks like an army standing at attention on drill parade. All the trees are in regular rows and columns, and have obviously been planted. The forest is in immaculate condition; as soon as a tree is damaged by insect pests or plant diseases, it is cut down, taken out of the forest, cut up, and removed. Swiss farms have smaller average field sizes than U.S. farms, and a great variety of different crops are interspersed. This means that entire farm districts are less likely to be simultaneously affected by one insect pest species or plant disease species, such as corn blight or wheat rust, which could destroy whole regions of the U.S. planted out largely to the same crop plant species. Management of these small Swiss fields is made possible because farm crews are more labor-intensive; it is typical to see three people with one tractor, two with hand tools. In the United States, all three people would be driving large tractors.

Thus, the ratio of the cost of energy to the cost of wages, pointed out as a fundamental determinant of the character of society in previous chapters, also has implications for the approach a society takes to agriculture and forestry. Parenthetically, it also has implications for fishing. The switch from longline clipper ships for catching Pacific tuna, with many workers manning the lines, to the large purse-seine vessels that catch dolphins as well as tuna, is also the product of cheap energy replacing expensive labor. If energy had been priced more realistically in the United States relative to its long-run value, the slaughter of dolphins by tuna clippers would not have occurred.

REVERSING ENVIRONMENTAL DEGRADATION: THE EXPERIENCE IN ISRAEL

One of the most alarming types of environmental degradation in the world today is desertification (7). Estimates from various sources differ by a few percentage points, but there is a consensus that roughly a third of all land on earth is desert. Other land types are being converted to desert at up to .052 percent of all land on earth, every year. The land at risk of conversion to desert is about 28 percent of the total land on earth. This would all be converted to desert in 538 years, if present trends were to continue. Clearly, that cannot be allowed to happen.

Perhaps the most revealing case study indicating how land can be prevented from becoming desert, how it becomes desert, and how desert can subsequently be reclaimed is Israel (6). The Negev desert only receives annual rainfall of three to four inches. We know from ancient papyri that around the year 569 A.D., the Negev produced barley and wheat, and supported vineyards and orchards. We know that this required careful attention to water management, because water conduits are also mentioned in these papyri. Ruins of six ancient cities confirm the notion that the Negev highlands were once a rich farming area.

The secret of farming in the Negev desert is the collection of rainfall in catchment areas thirty times larger than the area used for cultivation. Thus, if four inches of rain fall, and one quarter of this runs out of a catchment area to a cultivation area a thirtieth as great, the cultivation area receives the equivalent of a thirty-four-inch rainfall. In short, a fraction of the desert has been converted to an area with rainfall equal to the average in Washington D.C., Buffalo, Chicago, or Seattle. It is now known that the secret of ancient agriculture in the Negev was the sophisticated use of catchment agriculture, not higher rainfall than at present. Modern experiments to reconstruct the catchment system of agriculture in the Negev have shown that after about 1400 years of neglect, it is once again possible to grow a variety of fruit trees and other crops. Certain plants that make particularly good use of scarce water do very well under this catchment system of agriculture: almonds, pistachios, asparagus, alfalfa, and wild oats.

Thus desertification is not the product of a climatic change: it is caused by people, and can be reversed by people.

SUMMARY

The wise management of natural resources, and the avoidance of environmental degradation can be thought of as the problem of maintaining balanced flows of energy and materials into and out of ecosystems. We have seen that with some understanding of the balancing mechanisms within ecosystems these balances can be maintained. However, a number of forces are now operating in the world which make wise management unlikely, unless the root problems are dealt with. These problems are overpopulation, a cultural belief system that puts too much value on present benefits relative to future costs, and an excessive wage rate/energy cost ratio in a few countries, principally the United States.

SUGGESTIONS FOR INDIVIDUAL AND GROUP ACTIVITIES

Identify a situation in the area where you live where your observations suggest that environmental degradation is occurring. This may be a stream, pond, or lake where you see few living fish or frogs or the only thing you see is a dense mat of algae; a hillside with apparent erosion; or fields with evidence that soil blows loose in high winds.

Now do some detective work to find out what causes this situation, and evaluate the effects. Interview people in the area to see if they can offer explanations for the phenomena you see. Try to find out about the history of the area from people who have lived there a long time.

Do chemical measurements of the water or the soil to find out how it compares with water or soil from other locations that appear more normal.

Write a report on your findings, in which you explain what aroused your curiosity in the first place, the methods and materials or equipment you used for your research, what your results were, and the significance of your results.

At the end of your report, give a list of references to documents you used, including those that explain the chemical or other measuring techniques you used, and documents on the history of the area you studied.

REFERENCES

1. Bormann, F. H., and G. E. Likens, "The watershed-ecosystem concept and studies of nutrient cycles," pp. 49–76 in *The Ecosystem Concept in Natural Resource Management*, G. M. Van Dyne, ed. New York: Academic Press, 1969.
2. Bormann, F. H., G. E. Likens, D. W. Fisher, and R. S. Pierce, "Nutrient loss accelerated by clear-cutting of a forest ecosystem," *Science*, 159 (1968), p. 882.
3. Brink, R. A., J. W. Densmore, and G. A. Hill, "Soil deterioration and the growing world demand for food," *Science* 197 (1977), pp. 625–630.
4. Carter, V. G., and T. Dale, *Topsoil and Civilization*, rev. ed. Norman: University of Oklahoma Press, 1974.
5. Eckholm, E. P., *Losing Ground. Environmental Stress and World Food Prospects*. New York: W. W. Norton, 1976.
6. Evenari, M., "Desert Farmers: ancient and modern," *Natural History*, 83 (1974), p. 43.
7. Gore, R., and G. Gerster, "The desert: an age-old challenge," *National Geographic* 156 (1979), p. 586.
8. Jacks, G. V., and R. O. Whyte, *Vanishing Lands. A Survey of Soil Erosion*. New York: Arno Press, 1972.

9. Likens, G. E., F. H. Bormann, R. S. Pierce, J. S. Eaton, and N. M. Johnson. *Biogeochemistry of a Forested Ecosystem*. New York: Springer-Verlag, 1977.

10. Pereira, H. C., *Land Use and Water Resources in Temperate and Tropical Climates*. London: Cambridge University Press, 1973.

11. Pimentel, D., et al., "Land degradation: effects on food and energy resources," *Science*, 194 (1976), pp. 149–155.

12. Van Dyne, G., ed., *The Ecosystem Concept in Natural Resource Management*. New York: Academic Press, 1969.

14 SOCIAL, ECONOMIC, AND POLITICAL PROBLEMS

> The sailors are quarrelling with one another about the steering—every one is of opinion that he has a right to steer, though he has never learned the art of navigation and cannot tell who taught him or when he learned, and will further assert that it cannot be taught, and they are ready to cut in pieces any one who says the contrary. They throng about the captain, begging and praying him to commit the helm to them; and if at any time they do not prevail, but others are preferred to them, they kill the others or throw them overboard, and having first chained up the noble captain's senses with drink or some narcotic drug, they mutiny and take possession of the ship and make free with the stores; thus, eating and drinking, they proceed on their voyage in such a manner as might be expected of them.
>
> *Plato (c. 428–348 B.C.),* The Republic, *Book VI.*

MAIN THEMES OF THIS CHAPTER

Social, economic, and political problems may be the effects of or may cause environmental problems. Additionally, social, economic, and political problems may have causes in common with environmental problems: unemployment, crime, political conflict, and war are examples.

Previous chapters have demonstrated some of these links. In this chapter, we have a different goal: to find some of the basic characteristics of all of these problems, in order to see if a set of institutional reforms and policy innovations might help deal with all of them. In general, political conflict arises over competition for resources, pest management failures, and impediments to technology development that would provide new resources or promote conservation. This chapter demonstrates the need for reforms in government operations, techniques for conflict resolution, and future planning, all of which will be addressed in Chapter 18.

INTRODUCTION AND OVERVIEW

Some social, economic, and political problems may be caused by environmental problems. Intense political conflicts between constituencies result from ineffective pest management strategies or strategies with unwanted side-effects. The conflicts concerning coyotes and their control, the fire ant, spruce budworm, and D.D.T. are illustrative. Intense political controversies, sometimes leading to civil war or war between nations have environmental root causes. The "cod war" of the North Atlantic has come about because too many people are trying to exploit too few cod, so conflict has developed between Great Britain and Iceland. At their roots, the conflicts of the Middle East, Northern Ireland, and Quebec have come about because rate of human population growth has been too rapid given the limited resource base. As a result, the poorest (typically the most rapidly reproducing) become progressively more militant in seeking their fair share of the resource supply. Obviously, there are long histories of genuine injustice and deprivation in all these cases. But how often is it mentioned that overpopulation and resource depletion is the root problem?

Social, economic and political problems may be the causes of as well as the effects of environmental problems. Government malfunctioning may lead to continual raising of the minimum wage, and continuous depression of the retail energy price.

Some social, economic, and political problems share common root causes with environmental problems; unemployment, crime, and war have some of the same causes as pollution and resource depletion. For example, excessive substitution of cheap resources for expensive labor contributes to unemployment and crime, resource depletion, and pollution. Also, if population growth is too fast, this not only depletes resources too fast, but also produces a distorted age distribution that results in a variety of political and economic and social problems.

Table 14.1 seeks to get at the fundamental nature of the social, economic, and political problems related to the environment. One feature is common to the five different types of environmentally related conflicts in the table: lack of information and lack of understanding on the part of some or all parties to the conflict is an essential ingredient in the mix of factors fomenting the conflict. We conclude from this that there is a mismatch between the complexity of these problems and the simplicity of the institutional tools typically used for dealing with them. Further, not only are the tools simple, but their design renders them particularly vulnerable to outside influences that interfere with their effective functioning.

This chapter explores a series of case studies in the interests of discovering exactly how problems arise and persist that involve environmental, social, economic, and political elements.

PEST-MANAGEMENT FAILURES

Ineffective, unwise large-scale pest-management campaigns with unwanted side-effects cause much political controversy in modern societies. We will examine two such cases: the coyote–sheep-rancher problem and the problem of chemical pesticides.

The Coyote-control Program

Sheep ranching is a major industry in the western United States. However, the profit margin in the industry is only about 2 to 4

TABLE 14.1

The role of environment in causing conflict between people.

Nature of conflict	Role of environment in causing conflict	Examples
Competition for scarce resources	Overpopulation; resource cost too low relative to wages, promoting excessive resource demand per capita	Conflicts over land, water and grazing rights; international conflict over offshore fishing and mineral rights; Middle East conflicts over territory; terrorism
Tension between constituencies because one or both sides has inadequate information, or inadequate understanding of system	Complexity of food web makes comprehension difficult; complexity of large-scale socioeconomic-environmental systems impedes attempts at comprehension or rational management; complexity puts extraordinary demands on efforts at research or communication	The whaling controversy; long-term inadequacy of many pest-management campaigns (such as coyotes, spruce budworm, fire ants, pests of oil palms and cotton); conflict between U.S. and European governments over U.S. energy and economic policies
Conflict between two interest groups being sustained or fomented by misinformation or management failure by third party with vested interest in maintaining conflict	Complexity of environmental systems creates potential for obfuscation	Politicians presenting high incidence of crime as simple "law and order" issue; solar energy development impeded because many corporate and government interests committed to nuclear development; pest management problems sustained by corporate interests or government agencies supported by particular strategy of pest management
Genuine ideological conflict or apparent ideological conflict caused by ideological confusion	Environmental systems often have consequences remote in time and space, impeding efforts to correct ideological confusion	Conflicts within the United States about extent to which immigration should be restricted
Criminal activity	Distorted population age distribution because of excessive growth rate; high unemployment because of cheap energy; too much population concentration in very large cities	High homicide rates in United States and Kuwait; high robbery and burglary rates in United States in late 1960s and 1970s

percent. Given that the industry suffers an annual loss to predators of about 3 percent (28) it should come as no surprise that sheep ranchers have intense feelings about predators. Consequently, killing coyotes has been widely practiced for many years, and tremendous amounts of money have been spent to kill coyotes by various means. To give some indication of the costs associated with predation on sheep, one recent survey for California indicated an annual loss of 40,400 sheep, with a direct value of about $1.7 million. Including the cost of predator control by all levels of government (about a million dollars in 1974), and estimating the economic "multiplier effects" due to the rippling impact of sheep predation effects through the economy, the entire annual impact of sheep predation on the California economy alone is about $5 million (22).

However, despite a history of killing several hundred thousand coyotes a year throughout the Western States (about 80,000 a year by government trappers; the rest by private hunters), an estimated million coyotes live there (28). If anything, the coyote population is increasing, not decreasing (8). Understandably, sheep ranchers are tense and frustrated about their inability to deal with a problem that has such a large impact on the profitability of their business.

Other Constituencies with a Stake in Coyotes

To make matters worse, however, four other constituencies have a political stake in the coyote-control program. Further baffling attempts at resolution, three of the constituencies are not typically recognized as having an interest in the issue.

Besides sheep ranchers, the other constituency clearly recognizable is conservationists and animal lovers. A number of recent books and articles (23, 32) from this constituency have made the following points.

Coyotes are attractive, appealing, highly intelligent, and interesting animals. The techniques used for killing them (trapping, poisoning) are brutal and inhumane. People do not have a moral right to annihilate other species of living organisms, particularly an obviously higher organism such as the coyote. Besides, only a small part of the coyote diet consists of sheep.

A third constituency consists of professional wildlife scientists, university scientists (ecologists), and others who are concerned with the dynamics of the entire species community in range country used for sheep. This group argues that at the rate at which coyotes are now being killed, the control program is increasing, not decreasing the number of coyotes, if indeed it is having any significant impact at all. Also, most coyote control programs using traps or poisoning are in fact area-wide programs to control all large mammal and bird predators. As such, if the coyote control program were successful, it would, as a side-effect, eliminate the predator species that control all the small rabbit, hare, rodent, and insect herbivores that compete with sheep for range plants.

Eliminating all those predators would quickly result in the elimination of the sheep by those small herbivores. Against them, there could be no control. They are so numerous and breed so fast (for example, mice and grasshoppers) that the only control against them would be to poison the range. Unfortunately, the constituency with this ecosystem-oriented or community-oriented view of the coyote–sheep-rancher controversy seems to have had precious little impact on the coyote control program for most of its history.

A fourth constituency involved with the coyotes is the staffs in the various levels of government who earn a living in whole or in part from the control program. There are 420 predator-control agents (28), and when all office staff and managers are included, this entire constituency might number several thousand people. However, it is important to note that in this conflict, as in many others, the relevant government authorities do not constitute a neutral party, motivated purely by the desire to solve a problem by negotiating a conflict resolution settlement for the other constituencies. Rather than being such an outside "deal-maker," the government staffs have a very large stake in the problem themselves. In this case, if they solve the problem, they will need new employment. Indeed, since salary in the government is often tied to rank, which is in part determined by the number of employees one has, and number of employees is determined by the size of the problem, the government bodies involved in coyote control have a stake in keeping the problem at a constant size, or even enlarging it.

The fifth constituency involved in the coyote control problem is the taxpayers who must pay for it. If this constituency gave any thought to their stake in the problem, they would wonder why they were paying to support an industry, through pest control, that was so marginal in the first place. The United States is not short of meat and wool does have substitutes. Also, it could be argued that the industry does receive a form of hidden public subsidy in the form of widespread grazing on public lands.

Conceptual Model of the Coyote Problem

The major contribution science can make to problems of this type is to provide information and conceptual models that give a clearer notion of the effect of various control policies on each of the five constituencies. If this can be done successfully, and if government managers involved in control can be given a motive to be truly objective, then a rational solution is attainable. The models also clarify the way in which the nature of the problem generates political conflict.

On the basis of all the available information about coyotes, a computer simulation model was developed to indicate the consequences of coyote control programs (8). Figure 14.1 shows the structure of the computer model used to simulate the effect of different degrees of kill or of control by birth suppression. The technique used for birth suppression is to distribute meat covered with a chemosterilant in coyote range.

The computer model was developed by creating equations to describe the various steps in the life cycle. Thus, for example, it was necessary to have an equation showing the effect of coyote population density on the proportion of female coyotes with litters. Since yearling female coyotes have a much lower probability of having a litter than adult coyotes, two different equations were needed, one for the adult females, and one for the yearlings. The equations used are depicted in Figure 14.2. Equations were also used to describe the effect of density on the number of coyote pups per litter, and the proportion of the coyote population dying of natural causes. In all cases, "coyote density" is expressed, not in terms of numbers of animals per unit area, but numbers of coyotes as a proportion of the average numbers under natural conditions, in the absence of control. Thus, a density of .6 implies that the coyote population is at 60 percent the average natural density in the absence of control.

How are these graphs developed? We know from Chapter 5 that the birth and survival rates of populations decline when resource availability per capita declines. This means that when population densities drop, there is an increase in resource availability per capita for the surviving individuals; consequently, their birth and survival rates rise. From this notion, we know the basic shape that must be taken by the relationships in Figure 14.2 and all the other relationships in the computer model. While not enough field data are available to know

FIGURE 14.1

Diagram of coyote population dynamics model, used as the basis for constructing a computer simulation model to mimic the response of a typical coyote population to control by artificial birth suppression or killing. The items in boxes represent state variables, describing the current state of the coyote population. The items in ellipses represent control variables that man can use to affect coyote population dynamics. From reference (8). Reproduced by permission of the Division of Agricultural Sciences, University of California.

DIAGRAM OF COYOTE POPULATION DYNAMICS MODEL

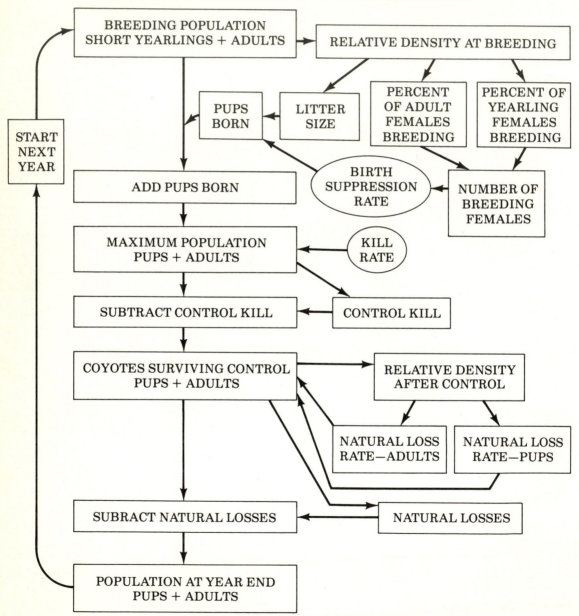

FIGURE 14.2

Proportions of female coyotes breeding in relation to density. From reference (8). Reproduced by permission of the Division of Agricultural Sciences, University of California.

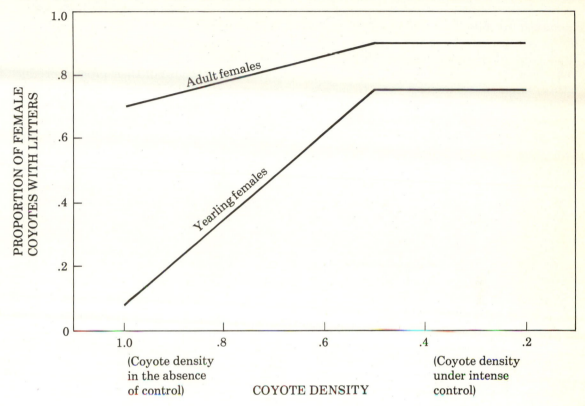

the exact form of these equations, each was based on the best data available (8). However, the results of this study inspire considerable confidence because many slight alterations to these relations tested during the course of developing the model did not alter the conclusions significantly.

Use of the Model to Test Control Strategies

The model was used to test various coyote control strategies by simulating the long-term consequences of each strategy for enough "years" of the simulation to produce an equilibrium state in the population as represented in the computer. The object was to determine the long-run consequences of various percentages of pups plus adults being killed annually. The results are astounding. They show that the population adjusts to increasing kill rates so that up to 60 percent kill, the effect of "control" is actually counterproductive. One must kill over 70 percent of the pups and adults each year to achieve significant reduction in coyotes. That is, at kill rates up to 60 percent, the result of control is to raise the coyote population to a higher level than it would have attained in the absence of control. One of the most important mechanisms for producing this surprising result is that increasing kill rates result in a compensatory sharp increase in the proportion of yearling coyote females with litters. This illustrates the fundamental dilemma encountered in all pest management programs. Pest populations, like all populations of living organisms, have evolved homeostatic, or self-regulatory, mechanisms to allow them to survive in the face of catastrophic mortality that occasionally occurs in the wild state. When humans attempt control by killing the pests, they merely elicit a response by these mechanisms. The only solution is to develop some method of pest management that thwarts those responses.

Another possibility for controlling coyote populations is to interfere with their reproduction, by means of chemosterilants distributed in bait. The simulation showed that this method of control would be much more effective than killing. Unfortunately, while this method of control holds great promise in principle, there are some practical difficulties. Many coyotes are not exposed to the baits, and the chemosterilant drug is only effective in the female coyote for a limited period (8).

Implications for Sheep Ranchers

Consider the implications of this simulation study for the economic position of sheep ranchers. If they attempt to control coyote populations by paying hunters or trappers or by distributing poisoned bait on sheep range, the effort is doomed to be counterproductive unless very high percentages of the coyote population are killed. However, if on the other hand the percentages of coyotes killed are very high, then a new type of risk is encountered. A high enough percentage of other species of mammal and bird predators are likely to be killed by the poisoned baits to risk eradicating all such predators from the sheep range. If that happened, there would be an explosion in the populations of all herbivores on the range, including mice, voles, gophers, rabbits, hares, and grasshoppers. Sheep could not compete with those herbivores, because of their great reproductive capacity. In summary, on the face of it, the sheep ranchers are confronted with a frustrating and baffling situation: they are damned to be ineffective if they kill small percentages of coyotes, and they are damned to competition from small herbivores if they kill very large percentages of coyotes. And of course, all the while they are killing a visibly high proportion of the coyote population, they are subjected to criticism by the conservationist constituency (23, 32), which only adds to the irritation of the sheep ranchers.

Happily, there is a solution to the coyote problem. All research done to date indicates that for the typical coyote, sheep only constitute a small proportion of the diet, about 10 percent (11). The reason why some coyotes attack an unusually large number of sheep is that something has happened to the coyote to alter its normal behavior. One important cause of such altered behavior is the loss of a part of a leg in a trap: the coyote is no longer nimble enough to survive on fast-moving foods such as rabbits and rodents, and must shift to slow-moving prey such as sheep. Sheep make up 56 percent more of the diet of such "peg-leg" coyotes than for average coyotes (36). In view of this phenomenon, a major study of the coyote problem concluded that the most effective solution was removal of specific sheep-killing individual coyotes (4). This can be done by skilled hunters who identify those individuals. This approach is not only the most efficient means of contending with sheep predation; it also minimizes losses to nontarget species.

Conflicts over the Environment and Information

This example illustrates a general principle common to environmental problems that generate political conflict: the constituencies affected are penalized by inadequate knowledge and understanding of the phenomenon. This suggests the opportunity available to a "deal-maker" or negotiator who enters the situation to effect a political settlement: additional information and understanding is an important tool for mediation.

Insect Pest Management

Insect pest management has become a major source of social, economic, political, and legal problems. Pests and/or the programs for managing them can create unbearable economic burdens for farmers. Also, because different constituencies have very different stakes with respect to insect pest control, management programs can generate sufficiently intense conflict to terminate in court.

At least six different interest groups can be recognized in the insect pest management political arena.

Farmers and foresters want to maximize their profit. This means that they seek the pest management strategy that maximizes the difference between gross profit and overhead. Thus farmers would be willing to increase expenditures on pest management wherever it resulted in an even greater increase in harvest. However, it is not in the interest of farmers to increase their expenditures on pest control unless there is a corresponding greater increase in yield. It makes no economic sense, for example, for a farmer to spend money on pest control following a

winter that has been so severe that all the pests have been killed in the region. Also, it is questionable business strategy to keep spending money on a method of eliminating pests that invariably results in there being more pests next year than there would have been in the absence of control. Unfortunately, the weight of evidence suggests that this is just what has happened. The total weight of synthetic organic pesticides produced in the United States increased by a factor of two and a half from 1960 to 1975, yet in the face of this control effort, many well-known pests have spread into more areas than ever before and are creating at least as much damage as ever before. The cotton bollworm and budworm, the spruce budworm, the fire ant, and the onion maggot are examples. Occasionally farmers, in desperation, spray up to seventy times a year to control these pests. Clearly, there is no possible way to grow enough to support this level of economic overhead, and many farmers have been forced to close down their farms.

The agricultural chemicals industry also needs to operate at a profit. But in years when no pests of a particular type are present, the industry and the farmers have opposing interests: the industry needs to sell the pesticide but the farmers have no need to buy it. However, farmers are often not sensitive to this difference in interest and buy the pesticides anyway.

The consumers of agricultural and forest products represent another constituency. They want safe, attractive consumer goods at the lowest possible price. Thus this constituency has a conflict with both the producers and the suppliers of agricultural chemicals. The consumer constituency also has an internal conflict: the most attractive possible consumer goods, such as apples, are completely free of any pests. But this comes at a steep price, since there is a law of diminishing returns operating on the effect of pesticides: greater intensity of pesticide application, or frequency of application, lowers the incremental benefit of an additional increment of pest control. Therefore, the cost to get from a crop 95 percent free of pests to a crop 100 percent free of pests is tremendous. In short, consumers are faced with a tradeoff between produce so free of pests and pest damage as to be cosmetically attractive, or produce with a small amount of pest damage at a significantly lower cost.

A fourth constituency involved in pest management is the conservation or nature-loving constituency. This constituency has been well aware of the devastating effects of pesticides on wildlife since 1962 (5, 19, 31). It is no exaggeration to say that many species would go extinct if we were to continue with heavy use of pesticides. However, this constituency, at least on first thought, appears to be in conflict with the first three constituencies. How can we grow food without pesticides? If we are to avoid driving wildlife into extinction by avoiding the use of pesticides, doesn't that mean that we must therefore starve ourselves?

A constituency affected by insect pest control is other industries that may be deleteriously affected as an unintended side-effect of a control campaign. To illustrate, the blueberry industry is critically dependent on the insects that pollinate the blueberry plants. If these pollinating insects are killed in large numbers by drift of insecticidal spray from nearby forest stands that have been sprayed by aircraft to control the spruce budworm, the blueberry industry could be driven close to bankruptcy. There is no doubt that pesticides used to control insect pests can have dramatic side-effects on a wide range of terrestrial and aquatic organisms. In some cases, the species populations recover quickly when spraying stops, but in other cases they do not (20).

The final constituency affected by pesticide use is all of us. There is now considerable evidence that pesticides may accumulate in the environment for a long time after they were applied. Computer simulation studies suggest that it is likely that D.D.T. concentrations in fish, for example, could actually increase for about ten years after a decline in D.D.T. use began (30). Since D.D.T. also accumulates in the fat tissue of human beings, and since there is some evidence that pesticides are implicated in higher human death rates (29), it is in the interests of all of us to lessen use of pesticides. However, there is clearly a tradeoff here. We would then need some means of controlling the pests.

The Effects of Pesticides

To gain more insight into how pesticide use generates controversy within and between these various constituencies, we now need to consider the evidence on what actually happens when chemical pesticides are used.

Use of chemical pesticides constitutes an enormously powerful type of natural selection operating on pest populations: 90 percent or more of the individuals least able to withstand the pesticide are killed. A reasonable assumption is that the survivors happened to have genes that conferred some biochemical or physiological property preventing action of the pesticide; alternatively, the surviving pests may carry a genetic factor that leads the bearer to avoid contact with the lethal pesticide. In either of these cases, the offspring of the survivors are likely to carry genes that confer on the carrier a strongly reduced propensity to succumb to the pesticide. By 1961 at least 137 species of pest showed evidence of such inherited resistance to pesticides (20).

Sublethal doses of pesticide may actually stimulate the reproductive rate in the surviving pests; this mechanism by itself can partially compensate for the high pest mortality rate (13).

In Chapter 5 we saw how populations compensate for a drop in their numbers through an increase in birth and survival rates; in the case of insect pests, as with the coyote, this means that when we control pests, we stimulate increased birth and survival rates, merely for this reason, In other words, spraying elicits not only genetic and physiological homeostatic responses, but also an ecological homeostatic response.

Spraying pests elicits a homeostatic response at the community level of organization, as well as the population level. Because of the inefficiency of energy flow down through trophic pyramids (Chapter 4) predators and parasites of pests always occur at lower densities than the pests. This means that if we kill an equal percentage of the pest species populations and the predator and parasite populations that normally control them, the predator and parasite populations may be reduced to such low densities that the population cannot maintain themselves until there is immigration from unsprayed areas.

The preceding is only a partial sample of the complications surrounding insect pest control. A number of books and monographs give a more complete treatment of the subject (3, 9, 12, 14, 43).

For all of these reasons, the farmer attempting to deal with insect pests lives in a world of continuous irritation, as with the sheep ranchers attempting to deal with the coyote. A central characteristic of the situation is its counterintuitive nature: common sense suggests methods of dealing with the pests that often only make matters worse. Box 14.1 is illustrative.

BOX 14.1
Case study: Pests of Malaysian oil palms

One such case has been documented rather completely (41, 42). Oil palms were introduced into West Malaysia in 1917, and until recently, pest attack by leaf-eating caterpillars had been insignificant at worst. However, recently broad-spectrum insecticides were used on oil palms to combat minor pests of other kinds, or limited infestations of two leaf-eating species of caterpillars. Subsequently, there were major outbreaks of the caterpillars. Spraying was repeated until it was realized that this was not controlling the caterpillars, but rather, was the cause of the outbreaks. Since this conclusion is in such blatant defiance of common sense, experiments were conducted to test it. The broad-spectrum insecticide dieldrin was sprayed recurrently in a small experimental check plot of two acres of oil palms. Before this treatment, and for four generations of caterpillars afterwards, pest caterpillar densities were measured at the edge of the experimentally sprayed plot, and various distances outwards from it. The distances were measured in terms of numbers of oil palm trees outwards from the plot, because the trees are planted equidistantly apart, in rows. As we see in Figure 14.3., the pest gradually increased in and spread outward from the sprayed plot, forming an infestation gradient.

FIGURE 14.3 (Box 14.1 cont.)
The effect of spraying with the insecticide dieldrin on population densities of the bag-worm in oil palm plantations in West Malaysia. Data computed from (41).

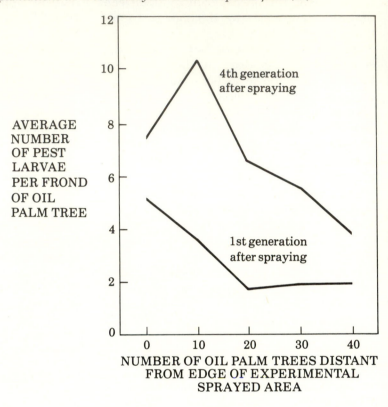

It is no wonder that farmers become irritated and frustrated in their efforts to cope with insect pests. The control methods are an important cause of pest outbreaks in many cases. In effect, they are trying to combat fires by hosing them with gasoline, instead of water. This irritation may be directed against other constituencies, such as the conservation and consumer constituencies, which are innocent bystanders in this situation. The underlying political problem is that none of the constituencies have sufficient understanding of the homeostatic properties of pest populations. Further, a variety of institutional pressures make it very difficult to conduct objective research of the type described in Box 14.1. It is noteworthy that the research was conducted in West Malaysia, remote from the political influence of pesticide companies that would be threatened by demonstration that pesticides can be counterproductive. One author has described some of the political influences at work in determining how strategies of insect pest control would be selected (1).

Happily, there is a solution: a broad strategy for control has been developed, called integrated pest management. This approch controls pests with a mix of strategies selected because they work well together. One component of the mix involves use of biological control agents. This means that parasites, predators, or diseases are released to control the pests. Pesticides can also be used, but the pesticides are selected because they have minimal destructive effects on the biological control agents. As in the case of coyote control, solution of the political, social, and economic problems associated with an environmental problem requires more understanding of the biological aspects of the problem than we find in some of the constituencies. Thus, the key to conflict resolution is an educational program by a "dealmaker" with no stake in advancing one particular point of view at the expense of others.

RESOURCE MANAGEMENT FAILURES

The fate of the great whales is a topic that can generate intense controversy. There are three distinct important constituencies in this conflict, although many others could be recognized. Remarkably, only the viewpoint of the first of these constituencies is at all well known or understood in the United States.

The Great Whales

The first constituency is the conservationists. They are deeply sensitive to two sets of facts: whales are the largest animals on earth, are enormously appealing and fascinating, and all evidence indicates that they have great intelligence and a complex social existence. They have very large brains, create complex and interesting music, and exhibit elaborate family or tribal life that appears to us as evidence of a high level of understanding, and even of altruism (18, 27). Well-publicized incidents in which wild whales or their smaller relatives, the

dolphins, show extraordinary regard for each other or for other animals, together with their amazing tricks in marine parks or oceanaria help create sympathy or sentimental attachment to them. Whales are hunted with methods that appear incredibly brutal. Also, it is well known that overharvesting has driven the largest species down to very low levels compared to their original population sizes (Table 14.2). To this point, the case seems completely cut-and-dried: whaling is cruel and inhuman treatment of another large mammal of great intelligence, and should be stopped.

However, there is a remarkably different viewpoint: whaling is a small part of certain nations' strategy for providing a meat diet to their population (21). Then we ask, "What is a fair share of planetary meat production for each person, and what are the most feasible means for that meat to be provided?"

Meat Requirements for Good Health

One way of answering that question is to discover the minimum amount of meat that seems to be necessary for good health. Figure 1.5 depicted the relation between expectation of life at birth and the average number of pounds of meat eaten per person per year. The line was based on data from 36 countries, and all the data are for 1970, or a year close to 1970. As we would expect from the theory advanced in Chapter 5, life expectancy increases with increasing meat consumption, because meat is a resource. However, the curve for increasing life expectancy clearly reaches a peak at annual personal consumption of about 60 kilograms of meat a year. Indeed, beyond that level of meat consumption, there is a clear drop in life expectancy with increasing meat consumption per capita. This should come as no surprise: there is an extensive literature establishing causal pathways between meat consumption and a variety of human dis-

TABLE 14.2
Original and present sizes of Antarctic whale stocks, and largest harvests relative to the harvests that could have been sustained over a long period without depleting the stocks (maximum sustainable yield). Clearly, the stocks have not been harvested with the intent of preventing extinction. All stock sizes and harvests are given in thousands of animals.

Species	Maximum length of whales (feet)[1]	Original size of Antarctic stock[2]	Present size of Antarctic stock[2]	Maximum sustainable yield[2]	Largest harvest taken in any year[3]	Year in which largest harvest was taken[3]
Blue	100	150	5–10	3–4	29.4	1931
Fin	85	350–400	70–80	8–12	28.76	1961
Sei	50	150	70–80	5	20.38	1965
Humpback	50	90–100	1.7–2.8	2–4	4.5	1937

[1]From N. A. Mackintosh, *The Stocks of Whales,* a Buckland Foundation Book. London: Fishing News (Books), 1965, p. 25.

[2]From D. G. Chapman, "Status of antarctic rorqual stocks," in *The Whale Problem,* W. E. Schevill, ed. Cambridge, Mass.: Harvard University Press, 1974, p. 236.

[3]From J. L. McHugh, "The role and history of the international whaling commission, in *The Whale Problem,* W. E. Schevill, ed. Cambridge, Mass.: Harvard University Press, 1974, pp. 306–307.

eases (10,15,16). Indeed, cardiovascular disease total death rate in the United States is about 2.65 times the total death rate for the second most important mortality category (malignancies), and there is little doubt that excessive consumption of heavily marbled (fatty or "prime") meat is implicated in cardiovascular disease. Therefore, it is not scandalous, but rather entirely reasonable for a country where meat consumption is well below 60 kilograms a year per person to argue that countries eating a lot more meat could share some of theirs without undue sacrifice or hardship.

Against this argument, it is interesting to inspect the meat consumption of various countries with respect to their position in the whaling debate. In Figure 1.5 we see that the United States has an extremely high level of meat consumption, whereas the only two countries that still have a major whaling industry, Japan and Russia, have per capita meat consumption about 1/6 and 1/3 that of the United States, respectively.

Therefore, they can both view us as a country that eats a lot of meat, telling them who eat much less that they cannot supplement their meat diets with whale meat from the ocean. Further, they find it entirely remarkable that we argue against whale catching on the grounds that it is unreasonable slaughter of other large animals; we kill about 130 million head of livestock a year.

A third important constituency in the whaling controversy is the whaling industry. Their point of view must be quite different than that of the conservationist or meat-eater. They must seek to maximize their total discounted net revenue from exploiting the resource (7). Under this point of view, we imagine that over the future, for each year, there will be a price we get for selling whales and a cost we bear for catching them. Our object is to maximize the present value of the sum of future prices less costs.

Clearly, on the face of it there seems to be an irresolvable conflict between the U.S. conservationists, meat-eaters in other countries, and the Japanese and Russian whaling industries. Two essential stumbling blocks impede resolution of the conflict. None of the three constituencies has any real sympathy for the positions of the other two. Thus, for example, few Americans have any sensitivity to the small amount of meat eaten in Japan and Russia, and the consequent importance of whale meat as a supplement to the meat diet. But also, there is no person or institution in existence who has the interest, the resources, or the mandate to act as an objective resolver of this conflict.

Resolution of the Whaling Conflict

Suppose there were such an institution. What possibilities for conflict resolution are open and perhaps negotiable? One possibility is for the Japanese and Russian whale industries to agree to a complete moratorium on whaling in exchange for certain concessions or payments from the United States. The most interesting way to placate both Japanese and Russian meat-eaters, on the one hand, and American conservationists on the other, would be to negotiate an arrangement in which the United States agreed to sell some very large amounts of meat to those countries every year, in exchange for an agreement to stop use of whale meat. To balance up the merchandise trade accounts, the United States would have to agree to increase purchases of Japanese and Russian exports, up to a certain level, in exchange for the meat sold to them. Of course it would take great diplomatic skill and patience to settle the conflict this way, but it is possible. The major problem at the moment is the lack of any institution that would perceive this type of negotiation as its responsibility. Certainly, neither the International Whaling Commission nor the Food and Agriculture Organization of the United Nations have this type of negotiation as part of their domain of responsibility. Perhaps some new international organization could take this on as a chore.

An essential feature of the whale dilemma is that whales of the open ocean are an international common property resource. Thus, since no nation owns them, no nation has a motive to conserve them. Only an international institution and agreement can resolve the problem. However, similar problems can occur when the resource is essentially the property of only one country.

Problems of managing an oceanic resource largely under control of one nation can create tremendous political problems within that nation (Box 14.2).

BOX 14.2
Case study: The Peruvian anchovetta fishery

One of the most famous recent examples of an intranational resource management failure is that of Peruvian anchovetta. Traditionally, Peru had not been a major fishing nation. As recently as 1947, Peru only caught 2.5 percent the weight of fish as the United Kingdom, or 1.4 percent as much as Japan. But from 1947 to 1960, Peruvian fish catches increased by a factor of 118, and from 1960 to 1970 they quadrupled. By 1970, Peru, with .37 percent of the world population, was catching 18.2 percent of the entire world fish catch. Almost all of this catch was the tiny anchovetta. This one fish had become of extraordinary importance to the Peruvian and the world economy. In 1970, the weight of fish caught in Peru was 2.1 times the weight of all other food produced in

BOX 14.2 (Cont.)

TABLE 14.3
The history of the Peruvian anchovetta fishery at its peak (7).

Year	Number of fishing boats	Number of fishing days	Number of boat-days of fishing effort (millions)	Total catch (millions of tons)
1959	414	294	.12	1.91
1962	1069	294	.31	6.27
1964	1744	297	.52	8.86
1966	1650	190	.31	8.53
1968	1490	167	.25	10.26
1970	1499	180	.27	12.27
1971	1473	89	.13	10.28
1972	1399	89	.12	4.45
1973	1256	27	.034	1.78

Peru, including meat, milk, fruit, vegetables, and grains. If ever a nation had stumbled on a bonanza, this was it. Unlike coal, oil, gas, diamonds, or gold, properly managed, the resource would have lasted forever. What happened to this bonanza is an extraordinarily important object lesson. The mismanagement had implications not just for Peru, but for the world, because Peruvian fish meal was an important item in the international protein trade.

Table 14.3 exposes the essential features of the anchovetta fishery during its most active years. The number of vessels increased very rapidly from the beginning of the fishery to 1964. The number of days a year that the fishery operated was reduced steadily after 1964, from 297 in 1964 to 27 in 1973. In short, the fishing fleet built up so rapidly that the inertia and overoptimism in the shipbuilding program produced a terrible problem of overcapacity. By 1973, only 72 percent of the number of vessels of 1964 could fish at all, and they could only fish for 9 percent of a normal fishing season. The fishing industry had developed 15 times the capacity it needed. This overcapacity creates several types of social, political, and economic problems. Most obvious is the personal hardship to people who have invested their life savings in equipment for which there is no use. From the standpoint of the entire Peruvian nation, a vast amount of capital that might have been more wisely invested has been diverted to overcapacity in the fishing and fish meal processing industries. This is a particularly serious problem, since Peru is a nation of capital shortage, not surplus. But more insidious is the political problem. When a natural resource industry develops overcapacity, there are tremendous political pressures to use that capacity. The argument directed against the government would take the form, "I have already invested my life savings in fishing gear. Why don't you let me use it? My family needs to eat now, and even if we fish the anchovy population too hard, perhaps they will come back next year." In short, even wise politicians, well aware of the way this argument has ruined

BOX 14.2   (Cont.)

fishery resources in other countries, might feel that their reelection was at stake if they tried to block use of all existing gear, even if it meant total and permanent destruction of the resource. (For example, the California sardine fishery has permanently disappeared, and overfishing is certainly implicated.) Indeed, fisheries raise basic dilemmas for a democratic society. On the one hand, the democratic ideal suggests that the right to fish a common property resource, such as oceanic anchovettas (that is, the right of entry to the fishery) ought to be constitutionally guaranteed. On the other hand, if the government allows unlimited right of entry to the fishery, it shortly discovers that the number of people geared up to exploit the resource is more than enough to wipe it out. In this case, after all the capital has been misinvested, the government is face to face with the unpleasant policy option of having to restrict entry to the fishery (25). A more rational course of action is to restrict entry to the fishery before all the capital is misinvested in overcapacity. This way the government avoids all the tremendous political pressures for overexploitation of the resource that follow the development of overcapacity.

At what point would a government know that overcapacity is imminent? The problem is that for oceanic fisheries based on very short-lived species such as the anchovetta, which rarely lives more than two years, there is little warning of imminent collapse. Much of the dynamic behavior of the population is dependent on oceanographic conditions, such as currents and upwelling systems, which are as unpredictable as the weather. The only way to manage such a fishery rationally is to allow the fishing fleet to increase only very slowly. In effect, one tests the fish stock to see if it can withstand one level of fishing, before a further slight increase in the level of fishing. Note in Table 14.3 that the Peruvian fishing fleet increased an average of 33 percent a year from 1959 to 1964. At this great rate of growth, an industry is vulnerable to discovering that the fleet was large enough two years ago, only by now the fleet is 77 percent larger than it was two years ago. The problem is that it will not be instantaneously evident that the fleet is too large: the fact will only become apparent from the impact on catches over the next two years. The only insurance against this situation is to hold the growth rate of the fleet down to a much lower level, such as five percent a year. While the industry will bring great pressure against the government to increase this rate of growth, the problems for the government will be less than they would have been, given a situation such as that which occurred in Peru.

UNITED STATES ENERGY POLICY AS A SOURCE OF INTERNATIONAL TENSION

Environmental policies adopted by the government of one nation may have side-effects that create economic tensions and misunderstandings between nations: the international repercussions of U.S. energy policy are illustrative. In 1977 and 1978, it was U.S. national policy to keep energy prices down. We have already seen, in Chapters 10 and 11, how this creates the need for the United States to export massive quantities of agricultural commodities to balance up the trade accounts between nations. However, we also saw in those chapters that in many years, the shortfall of crop production in Russia, China, and other importers of U.S. food will not be great enough for the United States to raise the money it needs to pay O.P.E.C. countries for their crude oil. What happens then?

The period 1977–1978 illustrated the consequences. If the United States cannot sell as much to other countries as it buys, all other countries collectively will have accumulated more dollars by selling to the United States than they can spend by buying from the United States. These unwanted dollars accumulate in the banks of other countries.

However, money obeys the laws of supply and demand, like all other commodities. If a country such as West Germany, Switzerland, or Japan has a surplus of U.S. dollars, at first, the central bank of that country attempts to buy enough dollars to inflate demand artificially relative to supply, but if accumulation continues, that finally becomes impossible.

Finally, because the supply of dollars in the other country overwhelms demand, the price of the U.S. dollar drops. Late in 1977 and early in 1978, this drop in value of the U.S. dollar relative to other currencies was happening simultaneously in several countries. This in turn means that those countries must raise the price of their products, in dollars, when they sell them in the United States. That means, in turn, that when the price increases become sufficiently large, they discourage Americans from buying the foreign merchandise.

For most other countries, exports are relatively more important to the health of the economy than they are to the United States. Consequently, if there is a significant decline in sales to the United States by Germany, Japan, Switzerland, and several other countries, all at once, this could throw the world into a depression. In short, domestic U.S. energy policy has implications that go far outside our own borders.

During the period from December 1977 to February 1978, European business and government leaders became bitter about the way in which U.S. policy of keeping energy prices down lead to a weak U.S. dollar, and hence trouble for European and Japanese economies. One example will illustrate the severity of the impact. The West German machine tool industry exports 70 percent of its total sales. It estimated in 1976 that the dollar would lose 3 percent of its value every year for the next three years. In fact the dollar sank 20 percent in 1976 and 1977, and the results were devastating to the German machine tool industry. The results of a big decline in sales to the United States had a series of unfortunate impacts on West Germany. In late 1977, German leaders were worried that these would include more terrorist attacks, rising unemployment, rising labor costs. As one article said, "But the Carter administration's lack of concern about the dollar is viewed by the Germans not only with fear but with sadness; they feel they are watching a friend blindly persist in a disastrous blunder. I believe in the good will of the Americans, but they have been operating on a false theory, Wilfred Guth, a top executive of the Deutsche Bank, said at a recent news conference in Dusseldorf" (24).

Not many Americans were well informed about the severity of the international currency crisis in late February of 1978. A few quotations from European currency dealers make the point. "Nobody wants to buy dollars because of American policy." "Washington is doing nothing more than paying lip service to the idea of stopping the collapse of the dollar. All we hear is talk, we never see any action." In an interview, the French Socialist leader Mitterand said that the United States was responsible for the monetary upheaval of late February 1978, because since the 1960s it had pursued a policy of "brutal financial expansionism" reflecting the dollar's privileged position as a currency used in international transactions (40). In fact, the monetary turbulence was an accidental byproduct of a short sighted U.S. policy of keeping energy prices down. M. Mitterand was trying to exploit U.S. energy policy to get the French government defeated in an election.

In short, the world is now one interlinked environmental-social-economic-political system. A U.S. energy policy adopted in the interests of winning short-term favor from an uninformed electorate can have all kinds of unexpected side-effects, not only in this country but also in all other countries.

TECHNOLOGY DEVELOPMENT FAILURES

During the 1950s, 1960s, and 1970s in the United States, there were three conspicuous technology development failures related to the environment, and energy conservation, that would have large subsequent social and economic implications. These failures were in transportation, energy generation, and housing. All were the result of institutional dysfunction.

In transportation, cities made a commitment to almost total reliance on the car-freeway system for moving people. Many books were written pointing out the strategic error being committed, but these books had very little impact on public policy (17, 35). Only after great political difficulty was it possible to divert some of the tax moneys for transportation to mass transit. Consequently, when energy prices started to rise sharply in the 1980s, cheap public transportation, which makes much more efficient use of energy than the car, was not available as an alternative means of travel in most cities.

For several decades after the Second World War, most branches of government and business organizations concerned with energy in the future conceived nuclear power as the major new energy source, not solar power. Again, this was because of an institutional breakdown. The scientists who advised the president and Congress did not represent a random sample of U.S. opinion. Rather, they were a small, self-selected group who on balance were strongly committed to the nuclear option (37). They repeatedly cultivated the notion that nuclear power was the one important new energy source when testifying before Congress and advising the White House, until this notion became the dominant paradigm in government, to the exclusion of all other paradigms.

The point of this history is that the highest levels of government are vulnerable to influence by a small, but highly energetic, bright, and apparently objective group with superior academic qualifications. The effects of this indoctrination lasted and spread, because when the new Department of Energy was formed in 1978, many of the senior staff came from the old Atomic Energy Commission, bringing with them their myopic fixation on nuclear energy as the one and only solution to the national energy problem. Thus, atomic energy, terribly expensive and also dangerous, for a long time held the place that would not be occupied by solar energy until much later. The necessary move to solar energy was probably stalled by forty years because of the influence nuclear "fans" had on national government policy on energy. As we have seen in Chapters 1 and 2, the impact of this myopia so spread within government that all branches in effect conspired to promulgate all possible good news about nuclear energy, which was often propaganda, rather than objective information, and all agencies, including the Central Intelligence Agency, withheld any information about nuclear dangers that would impede public acceptance of the reactor and waste disposal programs.

In the case of housing, the principal institutional problems were the tremendous social inertia created by the systems of building codes and practices of the construction unions. For both these reasons, a style of house construction and window design evolved over many decades that resulted in houses with excessive heat exchange between the interior and exterior. In Sweden where all institutions were concerned about efficiency of energy use, houses lost far less heat to the exterior in winter, and gained far less heat from the exterior in summer (34).

WHAT IS THE FUNDAMENTAL REASON FOR THESE PROBLEMS?

What do the problems of pest management, whaling, Peruvian anchovies, energy policy, transportation, and housing all have in common? In each case, society had a desperate need for two functions: planning and conflict resolution. In each case, the planning would have had to be objective, and the planners required the authority and the budget to develop a constituency for a rational plan, through use of the media. Also, there is a need for a conflict resolution agency with no committment to any of the points of view represented, but rather committed to resolving the conflict in a manner that will be fair and just to all the parties under the best compromise that can be worked out.

It is no secret that a major problem with the United States is the lack of a major governmental capacity for planning. In the most carefully designed new model constitution for the United States, one of the most conspicuous additions to the present system is a planning branch (39). Planning should be recognized as an extremely important institutionalized activity at the highest level of government. Planning should be conducted as an activity independent of the president and Congress, just as the Supreme Court and the Federal Reserve Board are politically independent. The Planning Branch should not invent more regulations to be enforced by government; in most cases, the result of good planning would be to remove many of the existing regulations. The point of a planning branch would be to give the nation a look-ahead capability that was completely interdisciplinary, cut across all departmental boundaries, and was completely uninfluenced by any political constituencies. The terms of reference of the branch would be to ensure the survival of the nation, and the future high-quality life of its citizens.

Since conflict resolution would use much of the same information base as planning, it would make administrative good sense to have conflict resolution made part of the administrative responsibility of the same organization that did the planning.

Why a New Organization is Needed

Two arguments make it clear why government must have a separate organization responsible for planning and conflict resolution. The technical and professional requirements for competence in planning in a complex modern society are enormous; also, we don't want resolution by vested interests with a "stake" in the consequences of policy selection.

Therefore, since planning is in fact always done anyway, if properly trained and organized planning staffs are not available, the planning will be done on an *ad hoc* basis by someone who is not able to do the job properly. In this type of situation, as in the instances discussed in this chapter, all the parties to the conflict will probably remain uninformed and plagued by misunderstandings as to how to attain their goals. If the various parties to a conflict are not aided by modern methods of planning, it will be difficult for each of the parties to foresee how policy changes taken now will affect the system in the future. Therefore, the lobbyists for the constituencies may be pushing for goals that are counter to the long-term interests of the constituency. At present, this is often the case. The basic reason we need professional planning agencies equipped to use the new methods of Chapter 18 is the sheer complexity of modern environmental problems.

An aim of this chapter has been to demonstrate that at present, the people and institutions supposedly solving problems are in fact an important independent constituency. Pest control agencies either have a vested interest in a particular form of pest control, without regard to its real effectiveness, or worse yet, have a stake in not controlling the pest. The archetypical example is the bounty hunter: what does the professional bounty hunter do for a living when every individual on which there is a bounty has been caught? The International Whaling Commission and the Peruvian government authorities regulating the anchovetta fishery both have their primary allegiance to the industry they are regulating. The Atomic Energy Commission had a responsibility to promote the use of atomic energy, as well as a mandate to regulate the use of atomic energy. Highway Departments were not designed to divert highway construction funds to the construction of mass transit, a competitor of highways.

In short, a democratic society can get confused about the identity of an agency that at first glance appears to have the responsibility and authority to solve a problem that lies within its jurisdictional domain. A conflict cannot be resolved, a deal cannot be worked out, a problem cannot be solved by a party primarily concerned with its own stake in the situation, whether it be whaling, fisheries, pest management, transportation, housing, or energy planning. The only body we can expect to be an objective planner or conflict resolver is a body for which that is the sole responsibility, and which is completely free of political influence by any of the parties to a conflict.

Reviewing all the information, it seems mandatory that there be new institutions created in government for the express purpose of planning and resolving conflicts. Such institutions need not add further to an already overswollen bureaucracy, because a stated goal of the planners would be to see how to eliminate socioeconomic-environmental-political problems by eliminating government regulations, thus allowing the free play of the market to restore homeostasis to subsystems.

ENVIRONMENTAL POLICY, UNEMPLOYMENT, AND CRIME

One of the most important and least recognized relationships between environmental factors and socioeconomic factors operates through the impact of the environment on crime.

We will expose the nature of the relationship by testing four hypotheses. First, since this is a widely held notion, we will examine the relationship between the degree of inequity of income distribution and crime rate. The theory being tested is that crime is likely in proportion to the gulf between the status of the rich and the poor. The second hypothesis we will examine is that crime rates are affected by population age distribution and hence population growth rates. The argument here is that young people are less likely to have acquired traditional cultural values, and hence are more likely to behave in a manner not in conformity with traditional cultural values. Then, we will explore the notion, presented in Chapters 10 and 11, that cheap energy in combination with high wages results in replacement of labor by energy, implying higher unemployment rates and consequently higher crime rates. Finally, we will test the hypothesis that crime is somehow affected either by city density or by the extent to which people live in large cities. There is considerable evidence that crowding results in various types of social disintegration, in humans as well as in other animals (38).

Is There a Relationship between Income Inequity and the Crime Rate?

One statistic which measures the equity of income distribution is the percentage of all the income in a nation received by the richest 5 percent of the population divided by the percentage received by the poorest 20 percent. The higher the ratio, the more inequitable is the income distribution. If the conventional wisdom is correct, then we would expect to find that as the inequity of income distribution increases, the incidence of crime increases. We know that there are problems about measuring and defining a crime, even between cities in the United States (26). Accordingly, in making cross-country comparisons, it is safest to take murder as the type of crime to be compared, because there is less ambiguity about the definition than for "felony," "misdemeanor," "grand theft," or other types of crime. For the few countries for which we have the data to test the hypothesis, the result is not clearcut. The United States has much more equitable income distribution than some other countries, which, however, have homicide rates about a tenth as great. One could rationalize this on the theory that the tension in a society between rich and poor becomes greatest as the poor approach their goals for equity sufficiently closely to

be intensely frustrated by their inability to completely close the gap. However, exceptions to that hypothesis are the low homicide rates in Israel, Canada, and the United Kingdom, all of which have about the same degree of equitable income distribution as the United States.

Are Crime Rates Affected by Population Growth Rate?

Table 14.4 displays the relation between age and arrest rate for the United States population in 1968 and 1976. We seek an answer to the question, "Why did the total number of people arrested in the United States increase from 5.349 million in 1968 to 7.384 million in 1976, an increase of 38 percent?" Clearly, part of the explanation lies in the increased incidence of 18–24 year olds associated with rapid population growth. But there is another question. Did the population become inherently more criminal in this period? Table 14.4 shows that while the incidence of crime in the under-twenty-four age groups increased by about 44 percent over the eight years, there was essentially no change in the incidence of crime amongst people thirty-five years of age and older. This suggests a hypothesis. Perhaps it is more difficult to transmit traditional cultural values to young people when the population is growing very rapidly, because the number of young people relative to the number of older people is simply too large for adequate contact and communication between the two age groups. At any rate, there was no change in the cultural value system as a whole, because there was no significant change in the arrest rate of people old enough to have acquired a cultural value system when the population was growing slowly. Thirty-five-year-olds in 1976 would have been born in 1941 and probably would

TABLE 14.4

The relation between age and the arrest rate in the United States. The arrest rate is the number of persons arrested per capita.

	Arrest rate	
Age Group	1968	1976
Under 18	.021	.030
18–24	.062	.089
25–34	.039	.050
35–44	.035	.037
45–54	.027	.026
55 and over	.011	.009

Data on arrests from the Federal Bureau of Investigation, Uniform Crime Reports for the United States; data on population from the Bureau of the Census.

have developed a basic value system by 1951. From these data it would appear that high rates of population growth come at a steep price. This notion is supported by statistics showing that there can be very high crime rates in developing countries with very high rates of population growth (for example, Kuwait).

Does Cheap Energy Lead to High Crime Rates?

Now we test the hypothesis that cheap energy, leading to high energy consumption, replacement of labor by energy, and high unemployment causes a high crime rate. Consider the relationship between homicide rates and energy consumption for twenty-one countries. There is a slight tendency for homicide rates to rise with increasing energy consumption, and the United States, with very high energy consumption, has a very high homicide rate. However, Canada has per capita energy consumption almost equal to that of the United States, yet its homicide rate is much lower. This suggests that some other factor is having a large

effect on crime rate differences between nations, and this factor is not operative in Canada to anything like the extent to which it operates in the United States. But is it correct that low energy prices coupled with high wages lead to high unemployment rates, thus setting the stage for high crime rates? Consider the relation between average unemployment rate from 1972 to 1976, and per capita energy consumption (a measure of wages/energy prices). In country-to-country comparisons, there is such a relation, and this supports the hypothesis that cheap energy tends to be substituted for expensive labor, thus increasing the unemployment rate. Thus it appears that national policy on energy pricing not only has implications for conservation and pollution, but also some generally unrecognized implications for social problems.

Does City Density Affect Crime Rates?

Finally, we turn to the residual factor that accounts for a lot of the variation in crime rates place to place not accounted for by the other factors: city size and crowding. There

TABLE 14.5

The relation between size of urban area, and the incidence of crime.

Degree of urbanization	Number of violent and property crimes known to the police per 100,000 population, 1976.
Rural areas	2215
Cities under 10,000	3988
Cities of 10,000–24,999	4676
Cities of 25,000–49,999	5537
Cities of 50,000–99,999	6243
Cities of 100,000–249,999	7558
Cities of more than 250,000	8263

Data from U.S. Federal Bureau of Investigation, Uniform Crime Reports for the United States. (Table 277, Statistical Abstracts of the United States for 1977.)

is evidently a striking relation between crime rates and the number of people living together in a city, within the United States (Table 14.5). This would lead us to expect that when making comparisons across countries, there would be a relation between the crime rate, and the proportion of the population living in large cities. We find such a relationship. Further, a very high degree of urbanization in the United States helps explain why the data for the United States is so aberrant relative to crime in other countries with roughly equal equity of income distribution depicting the effect on crime of energy consumption. Thus, we conclude that the unusually high crime rate in the United States results from the interacting effect of two environmental variables: energy price and the distribution of the population in space, with excessive aggregation in large cities leading to excessive crime rates.

Thus we see that there are several largely unrecognized relationships between environmental, and social problems. All other things being equal, it is unwise for a nation to have a high rate of population growth, ex-cessively cheap energy, or excessive urbanization of the population into gigantic metropolitan centers.

SUMMARY

This chapter has argued that social, economic, and political problems may be the effects of inappropriate policies of environmental management. The tensions associated with shortsighted pest management policies, whale and fisheries management, and crime and unemployment are examples. Social, economic, and political problems may cause environmental problems. The dysfunction of many large institutions with respect to planning objectively and sophisticated strategies of conflict resolution are examples. Further, the low standard of living of many people leads them to overexploit resources, thus taking the crucial gamble that they will not destroy their source of livelihood in the process.

This chapter demonstrates that environmental, social, economic, and political problems are all interconnected and need to be treated as such. Thus, the chapter sets the stage for later chapters on methods of dealing with environmental problems through legal, economic, and institutional reforms.

SUGGESTIONS FOR INDIVIDUAL AND GROUP PROJECTS

Pick an example of an environmental problem that has resulted in social, economic, or political problems, other than the examples in this chapter. Now try to identify the issues that create conflict. Try to identify the different constituencies who constitute parties to the conflict. What are the positions of each of these constituencies, and how do the differences between the positions foment the conflict?

Now pick an example of an environmental problem that results from defective planning or a lack of skilled conflict resolution. What has gone wrong in the management of this problem? How would you trace that problem back to inadequate planning? How could improved planning or conflict resolution aid in dealing with the problem? Can you discover specific ways in which present planning misses some aspects of the problem, or is too shortsighted? How would the approach to problem management change if planning took a longer look into the future? Can you detect ways in which the approach to the problem is counterproductive? Does the problem have some counterintuitive feature that is baffling planners and managers attempting to deal with it?

Can you think of any environmental problems that defy solution because all the constituencies affected have not been brought into the conflict resolution process?

Using standard bibliographic aids in the library (such as *Biological Abstracts, The Zoological Record, Environmental Informa-* tion ACCESS), write a history of one of the following: the fire ant control program; the gypsy moth control program; the spruce budworm control program; the collapse of the California sardine industry; the tuna-dolphin controversy; the controversy about sea otters and abalone; the "cod war" between the United Kingdom and Iceland; pollution in the Mediterranean or the Baltic Sea; controversy surrounding the use of nuclear power. In each case, try to identify the various parties to the controversy, and determine what their position was. Can you think of ways an outside, independent arbitration body would attempt to deal with any of these problems?

Gather crime statistics on the state where you live, and conduct a program of examination of those data to test the hypothesis that crime is basically an ecological phenomenon. Reference (6) is a useful source of ideas about information sources and data-processing methodology for such an examination.

REFERENCES

1. Alexander, R. D., "Natural Enemies in Place of Poisons," *Natural History,* April 1975, p. 92.
2. Bekoff, M., and M. C. Wells, "The social ecology of coyotes," *Scientific American* 242 (April, 1980), p. 130.
3. Bottrell, D. G., and P. L. Adkisson, "Cotton insect pest management," *Annual Review of Entomology* 22 (1977), p. 451.
4. Cain, S. A.; J. A. Kadlec; D. L. Allen; R. A. Cooley; M. G. Hornocker; A. S. Leopold; and F. H. Wagner, *Predator Control—1971.* Report, Institute for Environmental Quality: University of Michigan, Ann Arbor, 1971.
5. Carson, R., *Silent Spring.* Boston: Houghton-Mifflin, 1962.
6. Cho, Y. H., *Public policy and urban crime.* Cambridge, Mass.: Ballinger, 1974.

7. Clark, C. W., *Mathematical Bioeconomics: The Optimal Management of Renewable Resources.* New York: Wiley, 1976.

8. Connolly, G. E., and W. M. Longhurst, "The Effects of Control on Coyote Populations," *Bulletin 1872.* Division of Agricultural Sciences: University of California, Berkeley, 1975.

9. DeBach, P., ed., *Biological Control of Insect Pests and Weeds.* New York: Reinhold, 1964.

10. Enselme, J., *Unsaturated Fatty Acids in Atherosclerosis,* 2d ed. Oxford, England: Pergamon, 1969.

11. Ferrel, C. M.; H. R. Leach; and D. F. Tillotson, "Food habits of the coyote in California." California Fish and Game 39 (1953): 301.

12. Geier, P. W.; L. R. Clark; D. J. Anderson; and H. A. Nix, *Insects: Studies in Population Management.* Ecological Society of Australia Memoirs No. 1: Canberra, 1973.

13. Hueck, H. J.; D. J. Kuenen; P. J. Den Boer; and E. Jaeger, "The increase of egg production of the fruit tree red spider mite (Metatetranychus ulmi) (Koch) under the influence of DDT," *Physiol. Comparata et Oecol.* 2 (1952), p. 371.

14. Huffaker, C. B., ed., *Biological Control.* New York: Plenum, 1971.

15. Jerushalmy, J., and H. E. Hilleboe, "Fat in the diet and mortality from heart disease—a methodological note," *New York State J. Med* 57 (1957), p. 2343.

16. Katz, L. N.; J. Stamler; and R. Pick. *Nutrition and Atherosclerosis.* Philadelphia: Lea and Febiger, 1958.

17. Leavitt, H., Superhighway-Superhoax. Garden City, N.Y.: Doubleday, 1970.

18. McIntyre, J., ed. *Mind in the Waters.* New York: Charles Scribner's Sons, 1974.

19. Moore, N. W., ed., "Pesticides in the Environment and their Effects on Wildlife," *J. Appl. Ecol. 3* (Supplement), 1966.

20. Moore, N. W., "A Synopsis of the Pesticide Problem," in *Advances in Ecological Research,* Volume 4, J. B. Cragg, ed., pp. 75–129. London: Academic Press, 1967.

21. Myers, N., "The whaling controversy," *American Scientist* 63 (1975), p. 448.

22. Nesse, G. E.; W. M. Longhurst; and W. E. Howard, "Predation and the Sheep Industry in California," *Bulletin 1878.* Division of Agricultural Sciences: University of California, Berkeley, 1976.

23. Olsen, J., *Slaughter the Animals, Poison the Earth.* New York: Simon and Schuster, 1971.

24. Paul, B., "Fearful foreigners: Many in Europe think U.S. vastly underrates dangers in dollar's fall," *The Wall Street Journal,* December 19, 1977, p. 1.

25. Paulik, G. J., "Anchovies, birds and fishermen in the Peru current," in *Environment, Resources, Pollution and Society,* W. W. Murdoch, ed. Sunderland, Mass.: Sinauer, 1971.

26. Penick, B. K. E., and M. E. B. Owens II, eds., *Surveying Crime.* Washington, D.C.: National Academy of Sciences, 1976.

27. Porter J. W., "Pseudorca stranding." *Oceans* 10, 4 (1977), 8.

28. Pringle, L., "Each Antagonist in Coyote Debate is Partly Correct," *Smithsonian,* April, 1974.

29. Radomski, J. L.; W. B. Deichmann; E. E. Clizer; and A. Rey, "Pesticide concentrations in the liver, brain and adipose tissue of terminal hospital patients," *Food and Cosmetics Toxicology* 6 (1968): p. 209.

30. Randers, J., "DDT Movement in the Global Environment," in *Toward Global Equilibrium: Collected papers,* D. L. Meadows and D. H. Meadows, eds., pp. 49–83. Cambridge, Mass.: Wright-Allen Press, 1973.

31. Rudd, R. L., *Pesticides and the Living Landscape.* Madison: University of Wisconsin Press, 1964.

32. Ryden, H., *God's Dog.* New York: Coward, McCann, Geohagen, 1979.

33. *San Francisco Chronicle,* "Devastating blasts at Soviet A-plant told," November 26, 1977, p. 10.

34. Schipper, L., and A. J. Lichtenberg, "Efficient energy use and well-being: The Swedish example," *Science* 194 (1976), p. 1001.

35. Schneider, K. R., *Autokind vs. Mankind* New York: W. W. Norton, 1971.

36. Sperry, C. C., "Food habits of peg-leg coyotes," *Jour. Mamm.* 20:190 (1939).

37. Steinhart, J. S., "The impact of technical advice on the choice for nuclear power," in *Perspectives on Energy*, L. C. Ruedisili and M. W. Firebaugh, eds. New York: Oxford University Press, 1975, pp. 504–513.

38. Trotter, R. J., "Cities, crowding and crime," *Science News* 106 (Nov. 2, 1974), p. 282.

39. Tugwell, R. G., *Model for a New Constitution* Palo Alto: James E. Freel, 1970.

40. *The Wall Street Journal*, "U.S. dollar plunges on overseas markets as gold reaches highest level in three years." February 21, 1978, p. 16.

41. Wood, B. J., "Integrated control: Critical assessment of case histories in developing countries," in *Insects: Studies in Population Management*, P. W. Geier, L. R. Clark, D. J. Anderson and H. A. Nix, eds., pp. 196–220. Canberra: Ecological Society of Australia Memoirs No. 1, 1973.

42. Wood, B. J., "Development of integrated control programmes for pests of tropical perennial crops in Malaysia," in *Biological Control*, C. B. Huffaker, ed., pp. 422–457. New York: Plenum Press, 1971.

43. Woods, A., *Pest Control: A Survey*. London: McGraw-Hill, 1974.

15
ENVIRONMENT AND THE DECLINE OF CITIES, NATIONS, AND CIVILIZATIONS

From the time the first person said and proved that the number of births or of crimes is subject to mathematical laws, and that this or that mode of government is determined by certain geographic and economic conditions, and that certain relations of population to soil produce migrations of peoples, the foundations on which history had been built were destroyed in their essence.

By refuting these new laws the former view of history might have been retained; but without refuting them it would seem impossible to continue studying historic events as the results of man's free will.

Leo Tolstoy, War and Peace, *Chapter XII, Second Epilogue, 1869.*

MAIN THEMES OF THIS CHAPTER

To this point, we have been considering rather rapid, short-term effects of environmental mismanagement. What if there are subtle, very long-term effects that occur so slowly relative to one human lifetime that they would scarcely be detected? One way of compensating for the shortness of a lifetime is to increase enormously the time span over which we consider environmental change: we can examine the record of history.

In this chapter we examine the record of a number of vital, energetic cities, countries, and civilizations that died or suffered great decline in power. Only environmental explanations satisfactorily explain the facts, and modern research is accumulating much evidence to support such a view.

This chapter also illustrates how systems methods of the type proposed in Chapter 11 have been applied to the retrospective analysis of historical, anthropological, and archaeological information.

MAIN ARGUMENT OF
THIS CHAPTER

Chapter 1 contended that one of the root causes of environmental problems was a mismatch between their slow but ultimately explosive development and the mechanisms by which the conscious mind develops a mental model of how the world works. Since the amount of information streaming into the sense organs from the environment is so voluminous that it would simply baffle any person, thus reducing the capacity to function, a principal role of the nervous system must be the filtering out of unnecessary data. Clearly, one means of filtering is to exclude from the conscious worldview data on phenomena that are very similar from place to place or that change almost imperceptibly through time.

Such filtering will increase the probability of survival in an environment undergoing only trivial fluctuations about long-term average conditions. But this usually beneficial filtration can render the organism vulnerable to catastrophe when the environment is undergoing slow but consistent deterioration away from average and beneficial conditions.

The Irish potato famine and the energy crisis of the 1980s have already been offered as examples of such slow, but ultimately calamitous changes. Another was the gradual destruction of much of the Middle East by soil erosion, silting, or salinization following destruction of irrigation systems.

In this chapter we suggest a strategy: since the human mind has difficulty perceiving patterns in slowly deteriorating environments, we will compensate for this by enormously increasing the time span over which we search for the patterns. It is as if we were searching for slowly unfolding patterns in plant growth by time-lapse motion pictures, which we then view enormously speeded up. Accordingly, we now turn to a more histori-cal perspective on environmental problems. Through case studies we will be seeking parallel patterns in superficially dissimilar situations.

The Role of Elites

The evidence of history, vast ruins, and other artifacts proves that repeatedly, previous nations and civilizations have declined and sometimes totally disintegrated. This phenomenon can be explained in terms of a conceptual model that combines two ideas introduced in previous chapters. Chapter 6 showed that human populations could become large enough to overwhelm the carrying capacity of the resource base on which they depend for survival. Chapters 8 and 14 argued that governments or ruling elites act so as to ensure their short term political power; the long-term survival of the environment and the society it supports is a secondary consideration.

Thus when the human population of a nation or civilization first begins to exceed the carrying capacity of the environment, the ruling elite does not respond by encouraging lower birth rates and a shift of the labor force into the basic resource-producing industries, particularly agriculture. Both of these measures would be unpopular and would tend to decrease the prestige and hence the power of the elite. Accordingly, when overpopulation begins to decrease the food intake and the standard of living of a society, the ruling elite does not respond by dealing with the problem, but rather shifts the labor force away from agricultural production into activities that will increase the short-term prestige of the elite. These prestige-building activities, such as monument-building or military adventures, further aggravate the imbalance between low supply and high demand for resources. The result is a rapid decline in the standard of living and the survival rate, disintegration of social organization, and finally a decline in population size.

High population densities not only destroy a society by depletion of the food, wood, and mineral supply; they may also be destructive by allowing for rapid spread of infectious diseases among people living in excessive proximity, given a low standard of living.

The ultimate consequence of unwise use of the environment is sharply lower human populations living in a ruined landscape. The world offers many examples: Chan Chan in Peru, Palmyra in Syria, Babylon in Iraq, and Antioch in Turkey.

In short, the basic reason for maintaining the environment of a nation lies deeper than avoiding pollution or excessive resource depletion. The basic reason is holding on to national power, and ultimately, surviving.

HISTORY, AS VIEWED BY DIFFERENT DISCIPLINES

Until recently, the notion that environmental factors played a central role in the rise and fall of civilizations has not been widely accepted. Indeed, if one looks up the index of many of the most respected history books, one will find no listing of words such as soil, forest, trees, watersheds, irrigation systems, or erosion. Until recently, the prevailing of history was that the rise and fall of civilizations was caused by fluctuations in national will, or vitality, fortunes in war, and in the quality of leadership.

This special view of history is not surprising: it comes to us from historians. And who are historians? In a very important passage, Carter and Dale (4) pointed out that historians are people who "usually write about the relations of human beings

with each other and seldom about the relations of people to the land." They go on to say that historians are typically people who live in cities and obtain their food from the market place. By the time the food supply of a civilization has begun to run out, a city is either importing food from afar, or its civilization has so declined that few historians are leaving records. By that time, everyone in a society is preoccupied with the difficult task of simple survival; there is little pay for documenting the collapse. Thus, until recently, we have had a very one-sided view of the process of decline and disintegration of civilizations.

What has brought about a change in our view of the relation of environmental factors to the fate of cultures and civilizations? Several different kinds of people have contributed to a new view of history. One important group of contributors has been the geographers, agricultural scientists, and soil conservation experts. One of the most important early members of this group was G. P. Marsh (22), followed by Jacks and Whyte (20), Hyams (17, 18), and Carter and Dale (4). Some great interdisciplinary scholars saw patterns on the large scale: Oswald Spengler (27, 28), student of culture, but also a scientist sensitive to the significance of resources; Braudel (2), a geographer who became a historian; Zinsser (34), a bacteriologist who became interested in history; and McNeill (21), a historian who became interested in epidemiology. Useful insights came from people who allowed their curiosity to roam far outside their usual fields. Millia Davenport (6) became curious about shifts in clothing styles over large areas that occurred at the same time, and gradually discovered that climate was a key to trends in fashions; John Hale presents a picture of the relationship between styles in painting and the optimism of a culture, as determined by the seriousness of the problems with plagues (8). When the Black Death was most destructive, people needed the emotional support that can come from a belief in the miraculous. Consequently, religious paintings show the Virgin Mary hovering supernaturally in the air when plague is worst; at plague-free and optimistic periods, she sits down, solidly anchored to the ground, like any other mother.

The point of this catalogue is that our perception of reality is determined by our interests: if we have no interest in soils, agriculture, resources, or the environment, we will develop a view of history in which these factors do not figure. Historians and soil scientists live in two separate cultures.

THE SURPRISING FACTS ABOUT THE DECLINE OF CULTURES AND CIVILIZATIONS

Each of us lives in a civilization so apparently healthy, vigorous, capable, and widespread that the notion of an entire civilization disintegrating and vanishing seems almost unthinkable. However, we are able to contemplate the possibility of death of our own civilization more realistically, and get more motivated to work against that possibility, if we take a close look at the surprising facts about decline of other civilizations. One of the first big surprises is the number of civilizations no longer extant: of the thirty-four distinct civilizations Toynbee (30, 31, 32) considers to have existed at some time, eighteen have vanished. When we explore the details of these vanished civilizations, many kinds of evidence impress us with the staggering vitality they must have had. This makes the fact of their departure more mystifying. Three examples from different times and parts of the world illustrate the scale of what has been lost.

From about 600 B.C. to 900 A.D., Tikal in the jungle of Guatemala was a great center of civilization. The city occupied 25 square miles, and had at least 50,000 inhabitants. There are 3000 known constructions of up to 224 feet in height. Only recently was this great collection of abandoned architecture discovered in the jungle, overgrown with vegetation.

Chan Chan in Peru has 14 square miles of ruins. In the fourteenth and fifteenth centuries it probably had 100,000 inhabitants, and was a center of pre-Inca civilization.

At the time of Nebuchadnezzar (605-562 B.C.), the outer walls of Babylon enclosed a city of 2.2 square miles. The center of an extraordinarily vital culture and extraordinarily productive agricultural region, this city, like Chan Chan, is a ruin in the center of desert wasteland.

Not only did many vanished or presently weakened nations and civilizations have impressive imperial cities; the magnitude of the area they controlled or influenced is often staggering. For example, while Spain has not vanished, the magnitude of its decline in power and influence is staggering; in the three centuries following 1492 Spain was a particularly compelling example of a society that had achieved immense influence over an awesome area, in a short time, with a handful of people. Ferdinand and Isabella reconquered Granada from the Islamic Moors in 1492; having thus made Spain whole, they financed Columbus. Spain in quick succession conquered Cuba and Puerto Rico (1511); Ponce de Leon discovered Florida and Balboa the Pacific Ocean in 1513; Cortez conquered Mexico in 1521; Guatemala and El Salvador were conquered in 1523-1524; Pizarro conquered Peru in 1531-1535; De Soto explored what is now the southeastern United States to the Mississippi River in 1540-1542; and Coronado explored the southwest to Kansas in the same period.

However, not only did Spain accomplish the amazing feat of all this exploration and conquest with a few hundred men, but followed it up with a sustained program of institution creation: major universities were started in Mexico and Peru in 1551, and government and church systems were imposed throughout the conquered territory. The period 1556 to 1598 under Philip II was the zenith of power and culture for Spain: it gave the world a Golden Age of art and literature including *Don Quixote*, the paintings of El Greco, and Spanish Gothic architecture. By 1580 Buenos Aires was founded, but then in 1588 the "invincible" Spanish Armada was defeated by Sir Francis Drake. After that, a phenomenon occurred that has been observed repeatedly throughout history: there was a rollover of power in Europe from Spain to the nations of northern Europe. A tiny, extraordinarily vital nation which had left its mark over an immense tract from San Francisco to St. Louis quickly subsided to being a minor actor on the world scene. Can a decline of that magnitude be explained simply by appeal to poor leadership or military defeat? In short, can we explain all such declines, from Babylon to the present simply in terms of military defeat, decline of cultural vitality, or some other such explanation?

We note that many phenomena accompany these declines. In all these cases, there is a great loss in population. Babylon under Hammurabi reached a pitch of civilization that some experts say has never since been surpassed in Asia. Fifteen to twenty million people lived in 10,000 square miles under intensive irrigated cropping. In 1968, only 7.6 million people were living in all of Iraq, an area of 168,000 square miles. Thus the average density had dropped from 1500 to 2000 per square mile under Hammurabi, a density now found in only one large country, Bangladesh, to 60 per square mile, about the same as in the United States at present.

What happened to Babylon? Why this great decline in population? We also know, on the basis of recent discoveries, that some ancient civilizations had made a variety of advances in map-making and observational astronomy that were simply lost for thousands of years (9, 12, 13). Finally, an important clue is provided by the general appearance of the environment at many of the sites of important ancient civilizations. Chan Chan in Peru, Palmyra in Syria, and Babylon, like many other great ruins, obviously once were the sites of very large-population cities where now the desert would be hard pressed to support a small town. Arid or semi-arid treeless wastes now occur worldwide in many places that were once famous for vast forests, the cedars of Lebanon being an obvious example.

CONVENTIONAL THEORIES FOR THE DECLINE OF CIVILIZATIONS

Several explanations have been put forth by historians to account for the decline and disintegration of civilizations in the past. Perhaps the most comprehensive theory is that of Toynbee (30, 31, 32), who perceives the fates of civilizations as explicable through a theory of challenge-and-response. Under this theory, the decline of a civilization occurs because the various elements in society are no longer meeting the challenges they confront. The quality of the leadership in the civilization declines, and a schism develops between the leaders and the citizenry. Where previously the masses had supported their leaders voluntarily because the obvious merit of the leaders made clear their value, in a disintegrating civilization the poor leaders must maintain their power by suppression. A disintegrating civilization finally exhausts itself because lack of any moral cohesion between social classes or geographically separated subunits leads to local wars and insurrections as parts of the civilization try to throw off the yoke of a ruling class no longer perceived as desirable.

One might also argue that war or invasion can destroy a civilization. In an analysis by Barzun (1), it is noteworthy that the disintegration of eight civilizations coincided with military defeat at the hands of an invader (as when Spain conquered Mexico and Peru, the Persians conquered Babylon, or Alexander the Great conquered Persia and Egypt). It might be argued that a civilization dies because of the death of a great leader, or a fire or natural disaster, or a change of climate.

However, all these explanations seem inadequate on closer inspection. Why should a civilization decline because of bad leadership? History shows that civilizations have repeatedly bounced back from terrible leadership, provided the basic assets of the society were still intact. France survived Napoleon's terrible defeat in Russia, and Germany, China, and Japan recovered from terrible wars. Calamities obviously cannot destroy a civilization if the resource base is still adequate: many of the world's leading cities have been largely destroyed once, and in some cases, many times: Moscow, San Francisco, London, Berlin, Chicago, Rotterdam, Hamburg, Warsaw, Stalingrad, Leningrad, Nagasaki, and Hiroshima have all recovered from fearful destruction. Ancient Troy was rebuilt eight times.

In short, we have a real puzzle. Some cities and civilizations have bounced back from terrible leadership, terrible military defeats, total destruction by warfare or natural disasters, changes in climate, death of very high proportions of the entire population by plagues (between a quarter and a half of all Europe died between 1345 and 1350 in the Black Death), and a variety of other mishaps. Yet they are still with us, perhaps healthier than ever. Other civilizations and cities are now with us only in the form of enormous tracts of rubble decaying in desert or jungle. How can we explain the baffling difference between these two fates?

AN ENVIRONMENTAL THEORY OF THE COLLAPSE OF CIVILIZATIONS

A new theory of the rise and fall of civilizations comes to us from two sources: geographers and soil scientists, who have realized that the detailed picture of the environment they see about ruined civilizations corresponds to an end point in a process they see around them in the modern world; and students of the history of culture, such as Spengler (27, 28) and Ortega y Gasset (23), who have perceived a long cycle among people's attitudes toward the resource base. A brief summary of a theory that can be compiled from these two sources follows.

The rise and fall of civilizations is largely explicable in terms of the intensity of pressure by the civilization on the resource base that supports it, and the attitude among the population concerning the importance of wise management of the resource base, so as to make it last over the long term. Civilizations have their origins in a rural agricultural population that can produce enough surplus food per average farmer to support a town population. This only happens where the soil is naturally good and the climate conducive to high yields per acre. In some cases the soil is too waterlogged, and the road to civilization begins with the introduction of drainage technology (Mesopotamia); in other cases, the region is too arid, and civilization begins with the introduction of an irrigation system to bring in fresh water from elsewhere (the pre-Inca and Inca civilizations in Peru). After the lands of Mesopotamia were sufficiently drained for intensive agriculture to be sustained, the drainage system was converted to an irrigation system.

Environmental Consequences
of Civilization

As civilization develops and urbanization increases, three great resource problems have developed for all civilizations. Forests are cut further and further uphill on the watersheds from which the agricultural waters flow. This happens because the trees are needed for fuel or lumber, but also because the agricultural land in the valleys is inadequate to grow food for the constantly increasing population. This removal of trees means that the watersheds are no longer occupied by sponge-like living tree roots, which absorb most of the water when it rains and prevent a high proportion of rainfall from immediately running off the surface. When the roots are gone, torrential downpours result in large sudden movements of water off the hillsides into streams and then rivers, with resultant flash-flooding. This runoff and flooding sequence washes the surface soil off the hillsides, covering the lowlying areas with silt and water. Flash-flooding also gouges great quantities of soil out of the stream and river valleys, thus decreasing the area useful for crop or livestock production.

The second problem for a developing civilization is sheet erosion. As the population grows and the need for food increases, cropping and grazing extend into lands that are so arid as to be fragile, and if the cropland is not allowed to lie fallow frequently enough, or if there is too much grazing, vegetation is inadequate to protect the surface of the soil from wind storms. Consequently, over-used marginal lands can simply blow away under high winds. Perhaps the instance most memorable to Americans occurred in the great dust storms of Kansas and Oklahoma in the 1930s.

The third problem for a developing civilization is maintenance of the irrigation system. If the uplands have been overgrazed or overforested and a great deal of silt has washed down into the irrigation system, the pipes and ditches may become clogged. If this silt is not removed from the irrigation system, the irrigation waters cannot flow out freely enough. In a hot climate, the moisture always quickly evaporating from the land causes a gradual increase in the salinity of the soil moisture and finally the surface soil. When this becomes too great, the agricultural land is no longer an optimal environment for crop plants, and there is a tremendous decline in crop productivity.

In short, when a population becomes too large for the resource base to support it, water and wind erosion and salinization of the soil reduce the carrying capacity of the environment for people. Since the critical factor in the growth and maintenance of a civilization is the ability of farmers to produce enough food over and above their own needs to support a large urban population, this drop in carrying capacity wipes out the civilization. This theory argues that whenever a civilization succumbed in the face of invasion, that civilization was in fact on the wane prior to the invasion because of a decline in the carrying capacity of the resource base.

The student will realize that this theory shows a number of fascinating parallels with the theories of regulation of biological populations and communities presented in Chapter 5. A key concept in Chapter 5 is the notion that a curve for the rate of population increase first rises then falls with increasing resource availability per capita. A population that is too small makes inadequate use of the resource base; one that is too large decreases the productivity of the resource base. A population that tries to make excessive use of a resource base runs into the law of diminishing returns. Clearly, a civilization is comparable to a population. Interestingly, some historians even mention this concept of the law of diminishing returns. Civilizations also illustrate the principle of the optimum availability of a resource. Ellsworth Huntington (16) has shown that the development of high civilization is dependent on an optimal climate, and it is clear that there must also be an optimal concentration of various chemicals, such as mineral salts, in the soil. Lester Holdridge's work (14) suggests that civilizations begin in climatic zones that are optimal for steppe-type plant formations: annual temperatures from 6 to 12°C, and annual precipitation of 250 to 500 mm.

It was also argued in Chapter 5 that where stability of the physical environment over a long time has allowed for the accumulation of a great diversity of species, the resultant community of species itself shows a great deal of stability. In countries, economic activities correspond to species populations in biological systems. Countries with the greatest diversity of activities show the greatest stability over extended periods. Countries with a more restricted array of activities are more vulnerable to perturbations. This idea even permeates the language of common sense: we all feel that there is something vulnerable about a "banana republic" that is largely dependent on one crop, whether it be sugar cane, pineapple, coffee, gold, bananas, wheat, beef, or wool.

Ruling Elites and Decline

To this point, we have considered only the resource base component of the causal system that governs the health of a nation or civilization. For a complete understanding of the processes that trigger decline and disintegration, we must consider also the way in which ruling elites or governments respond to crisis, and the way this behavior interacts with other components of the soci-oeconomic-political-cultural-environmental system.

One case for which the properties of this system have been most thoroughly studied is the collapse of the classic Mayan civilization in what is now the Yucatan of Mexico, Guatemala, and Belize. Scores of experts have contributed to a comprehensive picture of what actually happened (5), a great deal of quantitative information is available (26) and a computer simulation model of the society has been built and used to mimic the actual collapse (15).

A flow chart of the causal system producing the decline is sketched in Figure 15.1. In this flow chart, a positive sign beside the arrow connecting two variables indicates that when the cause at the origin of the arrow increases, the effect at the end of the arrow also increases. A negative sign beside the arrow means that when the cause increases, the effect decreases. To illustrate, when trade with other countries increases, the prestige of the elite increases; when elite prestige increases, there is less prestige-building activity (such as monuments); when elite prestige declines, there is an increase in the amount of activity that builds prestige for the elites.

According to this flow chart, there are two ultimate causes that can operate separately or in combination to start a nation or civilization down the road to decline. Both of these affect the rest of the system by producing a decline in the level of prestige of the elite that rules the nation. An increase in external pressure from neighboring countries decreases the volume of international trade; this will intensify domestic shortages that were being made up by trade. The result will be to increase the ratio of population to resource availability. The population senses an increased resource scarcity, and the inability to deal with this problem decreases the prestige of the ruling elite class in the eyes of the commoners. Alternatively,

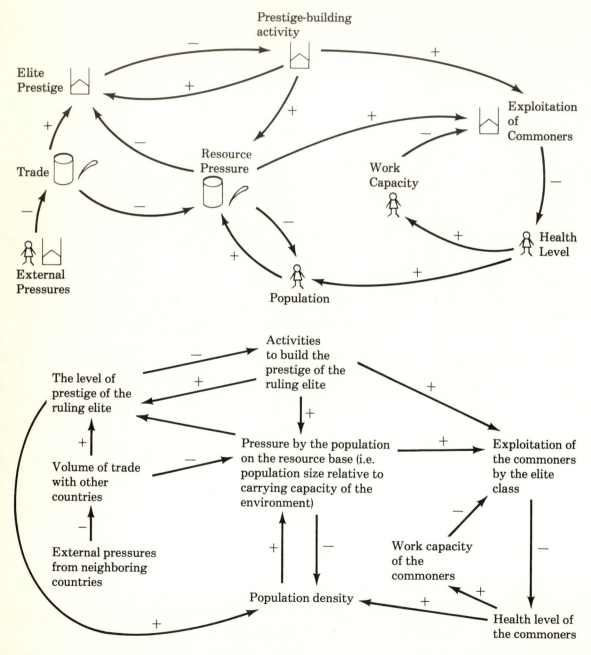

the pressure by the population on resources may have increased simply by an excessive level of population. The result is the same, whether imbalance between population and environment originated from reduced inflow of goods and materials from other countries or excess population: in either case there is a reduction in the prestige of the elite. As explained in Chapter 8, elites typically operate to enhance their own short-term self-interest, not the long-term interest of the society they lead. Consequently, elites do not respond appropriately to a decline in their prestige, that is, by discouraging the population from having children or shifting capital investment and labor to basic resource industries, so as to increase the availability of resources.

Rather, elites typically respond to a decline in their prestige by promoting activities that will restore their prestige over the short term. These activities include building monuments, large, impressive buildings, or immense numbers of large, impressive warships, tanks, guns or missiles to impress the population of commoners. However, vast expenditures on such activities shunts the labor force away from food production, and consequently intensifies the pressure of population on resources; this causes further decrease in the prestige of the elite, if food had already been in short supply. The level of prestige of the elite, the prestige-building activity, and the pressure on resources come to form a vicious circle (positive feedback loop) that spins out of control. Declining prestige causes more prestige-building activity that causes more pressure on resources, making the prestige of the elite decline even further.

The flow chart reveals other important and related side-effects of this cycle spinning out of control. The exploitation of commoners by the elite class increases. This decreases the health level, and hence the work capacity of the commoners, which

means that there must be progressively more intense exploitation of the commoners to get the desired work output.

Finally, the health level of the commoners sinks so low that the mortality rate increases. This produces a drop in the population size. Further, because of the intense pressure by the population on the resource base, it will have deteriorated significantly. This will be revealed in the form of exhausted mines, eroded and unproductive soil, silted-up irrigation systems, a nationwide shortage of trees for building houses, ships, or firewood, or in the most extreme case, outright desertification, with almost nothing growing.

Butzer (3), reasoning from his studies of ancient Egypt, has developed a theory of the interplay between environment, the ruling elite, and the commoners, which is very similar to the theories devised to account for the collapse of the Mayans. He perceived that the organizational pyramid of a nation is the analogue of the trophic pyramids mentioned in Chapter 5: the ruling elite feeds off the commoners as top predators such as tuna, salmon, and sharks prey on smaller creatures in the oceans.

EXAMPLES OF DECLINE OF CULTURES AND CIVILIZATIONS

To illustrate the theory presented in the previous section, we consider three examples: the Middle East, Spain, and Tikal (part of the classic Mayan civilization) (4, 20).

The Middle East

The irrigation canals of Babylon silted up and were abandoned, the Euphrates became clogged with silt from the deforested uplands, and the area became a salty desert about the time of the breakup of Alexander the Great's empire in 323 B.C. The Mongol hordes under Genghis Khan wrecked a major canal and its dam in the thirteenth century. Flood erosion thereafter cut the land to pieces. By 1405, the time of the invader Tamerlane, mud and silt had so ruined the irrigation works that agricultural yields were only about a fifth what they had been under Hammurabi, 3155 years earlier. Nowadays, Babylon lies in an arid plain where the dusty soil tastes salty when the wind blows it up.

The cedars of Lebanon (formerly called Phoenicia) were once a forest of 2000 square miles (somewhat more than a million acres). Now they are only four tiny protected groves. Bronze axes were used to lumber off the slopes in ancient times. Now, farms have replaced forests on 34° slopes, whereas anything over a 25° slope is unfit for cultivation because of the potential for erosion. Goats have overgrazed the herbs that replaced the forests. (Natural control on overgrazing by goats was removed when all large predators were annhilated at the beginning of Phoenician history.) Seedling trees are eaten off by goats as soon as they start to sprout. Erosion and flooding lead to soil destruction, so that modern Lebanon is a remarkably barren and eroded country, given the glory that was once Phoenicia.

Syria and Turkey represent two of the most spectacular examples of the results of centuries of bad management. Antioch, just north of the Syrian-Turkish border, is now buried under 28 feet of water-borne silt that erosion carried off the cultivated and deforested highlands in the watershed above. The plain of Antioch is covered by the ruins of 175 towns and villages, but only seven towns are inhabited now. Nearly a quarter of the plain is covered by marshy swamp created by silt that blocked the flow of streams, and the remains of twenty-five towns are submerged in this swamp. The remainder of the plain is covered by leached out erosion debris from the highlands. The silt deposi-

tion has been so great that the floors in some of the earliest towns are below the ground water table. The ruins of most of these towns are covered by mounds of dust and sand—mainly products of wind erosion from formerly cultivated fields.

Perhaps one of the most imposing and obvious examples of resource mismanagement in the entire world is Palmyra in Syria. In the third century B.C. this was probably one of the three greatest cities in the world. It was able to wage war against Rome and Persia and was the center of a country of 9 million people; spectacular columns of rosy-white limestone lined its avenues. Now Palmyra is a large expanse of ruins and rubble, but more remarkably, lies in the heart of a barren, unproductive desert wasteland that can scarcely support a small, poor village (Fig. 15.2). In 1963 there were only 4.8 million people in Syria. The entire Palmyra area either is high and dry on a desert, or lies below shifting sands. The small, impoverished village occupies a small fraction of the site that used to be occupied by one of the richest cities that has ever existed. It is

FIGURE 15.2 (opposite)

A panoramic view of the ruins of Palmyra, in Syria. These spectacular ruins cover two square miles, and are among the most startling evidence of environmental mismanagement on earth. In A.D. 270, under Queen Zenobia, Palmyra was one of the three major centers of power in Europe and Western Asia (with Rome and Persia), and had conquered Syria, Persia, Arabia and Egypt. Palmyra also illustrates the difference in interpretation of the same evidence by different disciplines. Historians attribute its decline to shift in trade routes away from Palmyra, and hostility from other empires (Rome, then in succession Turkish, Arabian, Mongol, Ottoman). Ecologically sensitive soil scientists such as Carter and Dale (4) attribute the decline to overly intense dry-land farming, and grazing, which exposed the soil surface to erosion and subsequent soil depletion. Photograph by George Rodger/Magnum Photos.

remarkable that this large area of ruins is all that is left of a city once considered such a rich prize that every empire of Europe and Asia fought for it up to 1300 A.D.

Spain

Spain suffered a remarkable transfer of its power to North Europe around 1600. Thanks to a massive amount of research by Fernand Braudel (2) and Geoffrey Parker (24) we now have about as complete a set of data on this particular decline in power as on any in history.

Spain is a hot dry country. In over half of Spain, the rainfall is under 500 mm per year. Given that the annual temperature is about 14°C, we can determine from the bioclimatic studies of Holdridge (14) that over half of Spain is a grassland with thorny shrubs and trees. Only in the extreme northwest of Spain and in two small strips on the Spanish side of the Pyrenees mountains does the rainfall exceed 1000 mm per year, creating the necessary conditions for moist forest. Consequently, forests are a limiting resource for Spain. From modern atlases we can discover that forests of all types only cover about 29 percent of the land area of Spain, or about 145,900 square km. Assuming that all of this could be used for construction, and assuming that on average, the growth of the forest each year would only be 1.36 percent of the stock of trees, then only 1984 square km of trees would be available for construction each year. A reasonable assumption is that climate in the fifteenth and sixteenth centuries was not sufficiently different from the present to change this number by more than a factor of two. In fact, while that period was colder, which would have decreased tree growth rate, it was wetter, which would have increased it, and these two changes would therefore tend to cancel each other.

By the sixteenth century, Spain was so desperately short of wood for ship-building that Philip II was trying to buy timber from as far away as Poland. Now we have the essential clue as to the decline of Spain as a world power. All we need is the equation between volume of shipping and area of forest required to build the shipping. We know that when Spain was a major world power, power of a nation was very dependent on sea-power, which in turn depended on oak for planking and pine for masts, together with other woods for a variety of specialized purposes. This equation is unfortunately available from only one source. In 1604 a traveller in the Lisbon harbor, where ship-building techniques were similar to those in Spain at the time, mentioned that an incredible amount of wood went into the building of ships: a forest of many leagues would not suffice for the building of two ships of 1500 tons (2). The old Spanish league was 4.23 km. Suppose we assume that the remark of this traveller meant that it took a forest five leagues by five leagues to build 3000 tons of shipping, or $(5 \times 4.23)^2 = 447$ square km of forest. The entire Spanish fleet at the time, including both merchant and military ships, was about 188,000 tons of ships. From old records cited in Braudel (2) it appears that the average life of a vessel was only twenty years, so on average, one-twentieth of the fleet, or 9400 tons, would have had to be built every year. This would represent 9400/3000 times 447, or 1400 square km of forest. But we have previously calculated that only 1984 square km of trees grew in Spain each year, and this would also have been needed for fuel and building construction. Clearly, when the Armada was destroyed in 1588, the 130 ships that had to be replaced, together with those that had to be replaced from other military losses about the same period and losses to pirates and storms, overtaxed the ability of Spain to grow wood. This wood shortage was a widespread problem for the countries and states bordering the Mediterranean at that time. It is significant that up to about 1600 A.D., for about five thousand years the center of world political and economic power had been on or close to the Mediterranean for much of the time. By 1600, power shifted from the Mediterranean to northern Europe and elsewhere, and was never to return. Deforestation of the entire basin is one of the central explanations for this phenomenon. The whole Mediterranean basin was still fairly well forested as late as 1500 A.D., but in the following century, most of this forest was cut for timber. Not only did this mean that this area was henceforth dependent on foreign powers for timber, but the deforestation also lead to erosion, flooding, and desertification, all of which lower the food-producing capability (carrying capacity) of the area.

Not only did Spain and the Mediterranean in general exceed the carrying capacity of the basin in 1600 with respect to oak, pine, and other trees; they also exceeded it with respect to wheat. The population of the Mediterranean countries doubled from 1500 to 1600, from about 32 million people to about 64 million. By 1600 population pressure was beginning to overwhelm the ability of the basin to produce wheat. Famines increased toward the end of the century; this was not as a result of poor harvests. The entire Mediterranean region became dependent on imported food. In Spain, for example, self-sufficiency in wheat lasted until about 1560. By 1583 the shortage of flour spread through all of Spain and disrupted the entire economy. (Much the same phenomenon had occurred in Italy in the period 1548 to 1564.)

The critical nature of the food shortage is indicated by records of the numbers of people trampled to death at church-operated food giveaways. Until 1550 to 1560, the more people there were, the more food was produced. Thereafter, the law of diminishing returns began to operate. Once again, the level of resource availability per capita had sunk below the optimal level, and the power base of a nation was gone. Nowadays, while Spain is able to export fish and fruit, it imports other foods, with the staple maize accounting for 4 percent of the financial cost of all imports. This figure would be higher, but for the extraordinary dependence of modern Spain on imported crude oil, which accounts for 22 percent of the value of all imports. Spain absolutely conformed to the pattern of a ruler creating images of power and running down the resources of society, instead of focusing on husbanding, conserving, and managing resources wisely. Parker (24) discovered that the national debt of Spain increased three and a third times from 1560 to 1598.

The Mayans

A third example of collapse of civilization is that of the Mayans. Modern color atlases of the scale and artistry of the Mayan ruins (19) can only leave us amazed. Particularly stunning is Tikal. Just the central area of architectural ruins occupies a square mile, yet the entire city was essentially forgotten for centuries and, when rediscovered about 1830, had been largely overgrown with vegetation for about 900 years. The explanation for the collapse of this civilization about 900 A.D. has been worked on by Sabloff (25) and others. In dense tropical jungle, such as surrounds Tikal, much of the nutrient in the ecosystem is in the trees, not the soil. If the jungle is cut or burned, and the area converted to permanent maize cultivation, productivity stays high only for one or two years following the clearing of the forest. After that, the soil loses minerals to the growing crops, and now, being directly exposed to the tropical sunshine, can become converted to a brick-like form (laterite), free of the humus that supported the luxuriant growth of the forest.

By trial and error, all civilizations living in jungle learn to adapt to this situation by slash-and-burn agricultural practice, in which crop-growing areas are abandoned after one or two plantings, and a new crop growing area is wrested from the jungle by cutting down and burning the trees in a new area. This shifting form of agriculture, in which each formerly cropped area must lie fallow for eight or more years after cropping, will only support low population densities. In Mayan lands today, this type of agriculture will support about 150 people per square mile. At the height of urbanization in Tikal, there were approximately 1600 people per square mile in the central area of 25 square miles, and 250 people per square mile in the surrounding 40 square miles. Apparently, excessive demands on the soil around Tikal depleted the soil fertility, yields dropped, the carrying capacity of the region for people dropped, the large urban civilization could no longer be supported, and the site was simply abandoned. Once again, it appears that for any civilization, there is an optimum population density that must not be exceeded.

THE KEY TO ARRESTING DECLINE OF A CIVILIZATION

The type of resource destruction illustrated by these three examples can be found in Oklahoma, the Hawaiian island of Molokai, Iran, Pakistan, Northern India, Afghanistan, Nepal, Mexico, Guatemala, and indeed, much of the world. The root cause is ultimately overpopulation. The fact that humanity is gradually destroying the planet has been obscured because the central activity sites for civilization keep shifting. That

is, the fundamental character of civilization up to now has been nomadic: ruin a site and move on. Thus, for example, power passed from Spain to northern Europe, but when the latter finally exceeded the carrying capacity of its resource base, power shifted again, to the United States and Russia. People tend not to see this pattern, because those who ruin one site are typically not those who ruined the previous sites; that happened long ago and far way. The times and spaces involved in this process have been too great for people to spot the pattern until very recently. Jet travel exposes the pattern, because viewed from about 40,000 feet, the world reveals an obvious correlation between the color of countries and the length of time civilization has occupied them: the older countries are brown or grey, the newer ones are green. The only exceptions are very well managed countries (as in Europe), and very wet ones (as in southeast Asia).

The key to arresting and reversing this process is to breed an immense respect for the importance of the resource base amongst the entire population, including those people who live out their lives in large cities. Chapter 8 showed how intense urbanization can destroy peoples' comprehension of the critical importance of the resource base for the life of a civilization. Novel educational experiences, which bring young urban dwellers into contact with farming, forestry, fishing, and soil conservation can be the means to the survival of a society.

A SPECIAL PROBLEM: THE ROLE OF DISEASE IN THE FATE OF CIVILIZATIONS

The discussion of the rise and fall of civilizations up to now in this chapter has been overly simplistic, concentrating only on one phenomenon: the effect of population density on the carrying capacity of the site for people. However, while this phenomenon was of overriding importance, history has also been affected by another environmental phenomenon: epidemic disease.

Four preconditions for wildfire-like spread of a disease like Black Death (bubonic plague) were found in most cities until about 1700. Rats were everywhere, and there was virtually no awareness of their significance as intermediate hosts of the plague bacterium, or of rat fleas as its vector. Consequently, grain was stored in sacks everywhere, supporting the rat population. The same was true of mosquitoes. Antibiotics and vaccines were unknown and nobody had any idea where diseases came from.

Population densities in all older cities were very high. Thus, once an epidemic disease had been transmitted from an animal vector or intermediate host to one or a few people, there was a very high probability that the disease would be transmitted to other people. This could either occur through the bacterium or virus being ejected into the air in a fine water vapor, through the coughing of infected people, or by an infected person being bitten by a flea, mosquito, or other vector that would then transmit the pathogen to the next person or persons bitten.

Finally, there was so little travel that populations might be largely isolated from the outside world for long periods of time. Thus, while one group of people might gradually develop natural immunity to an infectious disease, other populations not exposed to that disease would not. Consequently, when the two groups of people did make contact through warfare, invasion, or exploration, the group with immunity might spread a new disease to a group that did not have immunity, never having experienced the disease before, and the results would be calamitous.

Epidemic Disease and History

Two particularly important examples illustrate how these factors affected history.

In 1259 the Khan's Mongol empire included more territory than had ever before been held as a uniform, homogeneous entity. Thus was created a very far-flung system of communication, which from 1279 to 1350 was connected by horseback messengers. They were trained to ride one hundred miles a day for weeks on end. For the first time, there was constant human contact between western Europe and the foothills of the Himalayas of Burma, India, and China. These foothills had been one of the ancestral reservoirs of the plague bacterium. Perhaps because of the Mongol messengers, a new reservoir for plague became important around Lake Issyk Kul in south central Siberia. From there plague was carried to Caffa in the Crimea, where it spread to Genoese merchants. They carried it back to Genoa, and during 1346 and the three following years it spread through most of Europe killing at least 25 million people, a quarter of the entire population of the continent. Survival rate from the plague was only 0 to 10 percent without antibiotics. Catastrophes of this order have a profound impact on culture and civilization, particularly when the cause is a total mystery. Today, our lives appear rational, with a widespread belief in a logical system of cause-effect relationships as the basis for the functioning of the world around us. However, in a time and place where 90 percent of the people in a city can die suddenly and horribly for no apparent reason, their view of the universe will be one of confusion and mystery, in all probability. This may explain why European civilization seemed to stand still during the fourteenth century. The art of the times tends to support this impression of a confused, brooding, pessimistic state of mind. Paintings were designed to generate feelings of awe and promote a mystical as opposed to a rational point of view.

How did a tiny number of Spanish conquerors take over the gigantic Aztec and Inca empires? Cortes conquered a city of a million inhabitants with 400 Spaniards, and Pizarro conquered an Inca army of 50,000 with 180 Spaniards. McNeill (21) has presented an epidemiological theory of this historical mystery. For a very long period, Europeans and Eurasians had been developing immunity to a variety of childhood diseases, such as smallpox. The Western Hemisphere Aztec and Inca empires had had no previous contact with these diseases. Consequently, the invaders of Cortes and Pizarro introduced diseases to which the new empires were completely vulnerable, but to which the invaders were immune. The very night when the Aztecs repulsed the initial onslaught of Cortes on what is now Mexico City, an epidemic of smallpox was raging in the city. There were 30 million people in the Aztec-controlled area at this time, but fifty years after the landing of Cortes, there were only 3 million, and 79 years after the conquest, there were only 1.6 million. Not only would the great losses of the Aztecs to smallpox have had an immediate and direct effect, the effects on morals and organization would have been important also. The immunity of the Spaniards to disease would have been interpreted to mean that the Gods were on the side of the invader. As Aztec leaders died and, subsequently, their replacements died, there would have been confusion about the succession to power. This would have lead to civil war, and made the natives even more vulnerable to the Spaniards who were quick to exploit such situations. Certainly by 1523 smallpox was raging throughout the Inca empire also, and it appears to have been brought in by a few Spanish adventurers who preceded Pizarro. The Inca ruler and the successor he designated when he was dying of smallpox both succumbed to the disease (18).

SUMMARY

Modern science suggests a new view of history that tends to support Tolstoy's position: history results from the working out of natural laws on a grand scale, not the exercise of free will by a handful of powerful decision-makers.

Cities, nations, and civilizations that have kept their populations in balance with their resource supplies, and managed soil, forests, and water carefully have survived indefinitely. Where nations have become overpopulated, allowed agricultural land to deteriorate, and slash-cut forests without replanting, decline in power and population followed.

A key to understanding the environmental fate of nations is the wisdom and altruism of ruling elites. If they are more concerned about their own prestige than the survival of their nations, they will shunt national resources to prestige-building but useless activities, rather than careful husbandry of resources. A most revealing index of the survivability of a society is the attention it pays to agriculture, forestry, soil, and water.

Disease has also played an important role in determining the relative power of various civilizations. Particularly when two nations meet in war, there is grave danger to the one that lacks immunity to the infectious diseases of the other.

INDIVIDUAL AND GROUP PROJECTS

Take some time and place in history that interests you, and on the basis of books, articles, or raw data that you can gather, reinterpret history in terms of environmental factors such as overpopulation, deforestation, or epidemic disease.

Develop a very brief educational package that could be used to explain to audiences or classes how to prevent this civilization from going the way of its predecessors.

REFERENCES

1. Barzun, J., *What Man Has Built.* New York: Time-Life Books, 1965.
2. Braudel, F., *The Mediterranean and the Mediterranean world in the time of Philip II.* New York: Harper and Row, 1972 (vol. 1) and 1973 (vol. 2).
3. Butzer, K. W., "Civilizations: Organisms or systems?" *American Scientist 68* (1980), pp. 517–522.
4. Carter, V. G., and T. Dale, *Topsoil and civilization,* rev. ed. Norman: University of Oklahoma Press, 1974.
5. Culbert, T. P., ed., *The Classic Maya Collapse.* Albuquerque: University of New Mexico Press, 1973.
6. Davenport, M., *The Book of Costume,* Vol. 1, New York: Crown, 1948.
7. Engel, F. A., *An Ancient World Preserved.* New York: Crown, 1976.
8. Hale, J. R., *Renaissance.* New York: Time Inc., 1965.
9. Hapgood, C. H., *Maps of the Ancient Sea Kings.* Philadelphia: Chilton, 1966.
10. Hardoy, J. E., *Pre-Columbian Cities.* New York: Walker, 1973.
11. Hawkes, J., ed., *Atlas of Ancient Archaeology.* New York: McGraw-Hill, 1974.
12. Hawkins, G. S., *Stonehenge Decoded.* Garden City, New York: Doubleday, 1965.
13. Hawkins, G. S., *Beyond Stonehenge.* New York: Harper and Row, 1973.
14. Holdridge, L. R., *Life Zone Ecology.* San Jose, Costa Rica: Tropical Science Center, 1967.
15. Hosler, D., J. A. Sabloff, and D. Runge, "Simulation model development: A case study of the classic Maya collapse." Chapter 25 in *Social Process in Maya Prehistory,* N. Hammond, ed. New York: Academic Press, 1977.
16. Huntington, E., *Civilization and Climate.* New Haven: Yale University Press, 1922.
17. Hyams, E., *Soil and Civilization.* London: Thames and Hudson, 1952.
18. Hyams, E., and G. Ordish, *The Last of the Incas.* New York: Simon and Schuster, 1963.
19. Ivanoff, P., *Monuments of Civilization: Maya.* New York: Grosset and Dunlap, 1973.
20. Jacks, G. V., and R. O. Whyte, *Vanishing Lands. A World Survey of Soil Erosion.* New York: Arno Press, 1972.
21. McNeill, W. H., *Plagues and Peoples.* Garden City, New York: Anchor Press/Doubleday, 1976.
22. Marsh, G. P., *Man and Nature, or Physical Geography as Modified by Human Action.* Cambridge, Mass.: Belknap Press, 1864.
23. Ortega y Gasset, J. *The Revolt of the Masses.* New York: W. W. Norton, 1932.
24. Parker, G. *Philip II.* Boston: Little, Brown, 1979.
25. Sabloff, J. A., "The collapse of classic Maya civilization," in *Patient Earth,* J. Harte and R. H. Socolow, eds. New York: Holt, Rinehart and Winston, 1971.
26. Sidrys, R., and R. Berger, "Lowland Maya radiocarbon dates and the classic Maya collapse," *Nature* 277 (1979), pp. 269–274.
27. Spengler, O., *The Decline of the West,* Vol. 1. New York: Knopf, 1926.
28. Spengler, O., *The Decline of the West,* Vol. 2. New York: Knopf, 1928.
29. Tompkins, P., *Mysteries of the Mexican Pyramids.* New York: Harper and Row, 1976.
30. Toynbee, A., ed., *Cities of Destiny.* London: Thames and Hudson, 1967.
31. Toynbee, A., *A Study of History,* rev. ed. Oxford: Oxford University Press, 1972.
32. Toynbee, A., *Mankind and Mother Earth.* New York: Oxford University Press, 1976.
33. Turner, B. L. II, "Prehistoric intensive agriculture in the Mayan lowlands," *Science* 185 (1974), p. 118.
34. Zinsser, H., *Rats, lice, and history.* New York: Bantam Books, 1960.

V Solving Environmental Problems

Previous chapters have pointed out many environmental problems, and in passing, have hinted at reforms that would rectify these problems. We now turn to four specific types of solutions. Innovations in the economic system can encourage conservation and stimulate the search for new resources and new techniques for fostering efficiency. The law offers a variety of means for dealing with environmental problems. Some of these means are traditional; others involve newer types of legal maneuvers. Various types of innovations in institutions, both government and private, will help, as will a change in the design of cities. Finally, educational innovations will gradually result in a more realistic cultural belief system. This last change is basic to and a prerequisite for major change in the other approaches.

Throughout this section, there will be an emphasis on planning and working through options on a systems basis. Also, our point of view shifts from consideration of the past and the present to examination of future options and scenarios.

16 ECONOMIC SOLUTIONS TO ENVIRONMENTAL PROBLEMS

That part of the annual produce, therefore, which, as soon as it comes either from the ground or from the hands of the productive labourers, is destined for replacing a capital, is not only much greater in rich than in poor countries, but bears a much greater proportion to that which is immediately destined for constituting a revenue either as rent or as profit.

Adam Smith, An Inquiry into the Nature and Causes of the Wealth of Nations, *Chapter III, 1776.*

MAIN THEMES OF THIS CHAPTER

The economic system offers a wide variety of tools for dealing with environmental problems; taxes, quotas, the price system, rents, and fees are just a few examples.

In fact, there are so many available economic tools, that we need some systematic procedure for picking the best. Accordingly, this chapter begins by examining the criteria that good economic management schemes ought to meet. Then available tools are considered in light of those criteria.

Alternative approaches to pollution abatement are considered. Again, the basis for selection is the systems consequences of the different options.

THE GOALS OF ECONOMIC SOLUTIONS TO THE ENERGY CONSERVATION PROBLEM

The surprising thing about solutions to environmental problems is not how few there are but rather how many there are. However, these solutions raise a new type of problem for us. There is no solution possible in principle that is completely satisfactory in every possible way. A moment's thought will show that this must be true. For example, there are "lazy man's" solutions, and there are very democratic, but time-consuming solutions. Under a "lazy man's" solution, the average person pays no attention to how the problem of energy conservation is solved, but is perfectly content to have it solved, and to have the process of solution require no personal effort. The problem is that this lack of effort would come at a price: some other people or some institutions would be solving the conservation problem for us, and the price they would extract would be a transfer of economic and political power from us to them. Under very democratic solutions to the energy conservation problem, there would be a minimization of transfer of economic and political power to certain individuals or institutions, but the price to all of us would be the time it took for us to get involved in decision-making and other work.

Clearly, more is at stake in any energy conservation scheme than the success of the scheme in conservation. Any such scheme also has the potential for major transfers of wealth and power between groups in society. Thus, when we examine environmental problems carefully, we discover that they also involve the problem of social equity. This suggests that in evaluating various proposed schemes for conserving energy or other resources, we need to examine the scheme from a variety of points of view. Indeed, at least the following nine questions appear to apply about any such scheme.

1. *Stimulus to conservation.* Ideally, we want to provide the maximum possible stimulus for conservation. Further, we not only want to maximize the population-wide average level of energy conservation; we also want to ensure that each individual is given the maximum possible incentive to conserve, without regard to his ability to pay for a lot of a scarce resource. This means that ideally, the economic penalty for using twenty units of energy per month should be greater than twice the penalty for using ten units per month. That is, we want a penalty for excessive consumption that becomes increasingly punitive for each additional unit of energy used, as the number used becomes greater per month. This is to prevent very wealthy people from using as much of a resource as they want, without regard to increasing price, while simultaneously ensuring that poor people get enough to meet their needs.

2. *Search for traditional energy sources.* We want to provide the maximum necessary economic stimulus for exploration and development of conventional fossil fuel energy resources (coal, oil, and gas). Given the sharply increasing cost of this search, it will terminate unless financial rewards are adequate.

3. *Search for novel energy sources.* We want to ensure that there is the maximum possible stimulus for development of unconventional energy sources: wind, solar, tidal, and geothermal energy, and energy from exploiting temperature gradients down through the depths of the oceans.

4. *Removing the roadblocks.* We want to reduce or remove institutional impediments to conservation. For example, if building codes, construction union rules, or savings and loan institution lending policies tend to inhibit design of residential structures that minimize heat loss in winter, we want to get rid of those im-

pediments through new legislation or other means.

5. *Financial stimulants.* We also want to reduce or remove institutional impediments to search for or development of novel energy sources. For example, if banks are reluctant to loan money for development or installation of solar energy systems, the government should guarantee such loans. This is not a novel role for government. The 1957 Price-Anderson Act limits the liability for any single nuclear accident to 500 million dollars, and specifies that only 82 million maximum would be paid by private insurance companies, the remainder being borne by the federal government. This act, in effect using tax money to underwrite risk on the nuclear industry, made possible the development of that industry. Thus, the precedent has been established under which the government could guarantee loans for other, safer types of energy.

6. *Environmental safeguards.* Any scheme of energy conservation would ideally also safeguard the environment and minimize environmental degradation in the course of producing the energy. Thus, for example, after strip-mining, there should be a major effort to rehabilitate the landscape by planting forests over the wasteland, using plants that can tolerate the inhospitable soil and acid water.

7. *Equitable income distribution.* Minimization of inequitable distribution of wealth is an important goal if we are to conserve energy. Why? Any scheme for conserving any resource can be undercut if in the course of applying the scheme, there is a resultant transfer of wealth so that some people become very rich. The reason is that consumption of any resource is determined by the ratio of prices to incomes. Consequently, if prices for a resource rise rapidly, but the incomes of certain individuals rise even more rapidly because of a transfer of wealth, those individuals might be able to afford enough of the resource to deplete it. We have already seen this example in the case of shellfish, in which consumption of lobsters, shrimp, and crabs continued to rise even after great increases in the prices of those resources. The same phenomenon could happen in the case of oil, gas, and coal, if a conservation scheme unwittingly transferred vast wealth to certain individuals.

An extension of this idea is the notion that where a few people benefit handsomely from resource depletion, they may be able to afford the vast cost of advertising or propagandizing to extoll the merits of growth. Where there has been a great concentration and transfer of wealth, no other group will have the resources required to do research on and propagandize for a "no-growth" or "conservationist" philosophy towards resources. There is always more money available to promote an idea that helps a few than an idea that helps the majority. An example is advertising and propaganda to allow building of more tract subdivisions. This propaganda argues, "Increase the population and broaden the tax base so as to lower taxes." Of course, as so many people have discovered to their dismay after the fact, population growth and broadening the tax base increases, rather than decreases, taxes. But did the public ever have the same resources to propagandize for the beneficial effects of no growth on tax reduction, that vested interests had to propagandize for the opposite argument? By the same token, concentration of economic power allows for promulgation of the message that "faster energy consumption leads to a healthier economy." The message is incorrect, but that doesn't matter if no one has the financial resources required to advertise the facts supporting the counter-message.

8. *Political power concentration.* We also require a policy of energy conservation that minimizes dangerous, undue concentration of political power. A policy that concentrates such power in a government bureaucracy is just as dangerous as one that concentrates it in a few large corporations.

9. *Efficient, fast-responding markets.* A final goal is to minimize problems due to imperfect functioning of markets. Ideally, the market should flash a signal that a resource shortage is developing early enough so that a replacement resource will be available before the first resource is dangerously depleted. The market has malfunctioned if the price of a resource being depleted spurts upward just before the resource is all gone; here the signal of impending depletion occurs too late to be socially useful. Could that happen? Yes; one mechanism that can keep prices down too long for a resource dangerously close to depletion is government regulation.

Classical economic theory holds that prices are set by free market forces, in which equilibrium price is set by interaction between demand and supply. But this will not work out in the appropriate fashion if there is in effect a third party to the bargaining, the government, which is acting neither as an agent for the seller or the buyer, nor a simple negotiator. The government may represent a third constituency (itself) that decides for its own reasons, such

as the desire to be reelected or reappointed, to keep prices down. Examples of this are the relation of the Federal Power Commission to natural gas prices and the attitude of Congress towards gasoline prices.

There are other ways in which the market system may malfunction. For example, if an energy supplier offers a lower price per unit of energy consumed to a large customer than a small customer, then in effect it encourages everyone to be a large customer rather than a small customer (that is, to use more).

Also, energy-consumption systems may be designed so as to have positive, rather than negative, feedback loops. An example is the highway system, which derives income from gasoline taxes. Thus, as more highways are built, more money is spent on gasoline, and more highways are built. Such a system grows exponentially unless a brake is imposed from outside.

In the case of fossil fuels, where the cheapest-to-extract resources are exploited first, by design, the retail cost of each unit sold is an inaccurate index of the cost to replace that unit in inventory.

Some institutional mechanism is needed to offset all these market imperfections.

FIVE SAMPLE SOLUTIONS TO THE ENERGY CONSERVATION PROBLEM

Having considered the kinds of goals that should be attained by any ideal scheme for energy conservation, we now examine five such schemes. There is a very large number of schemes we might consider and these five are simply a sample; however, they do bring out the lines of argument involved in evaluation of any such scheme.

Raw Materials Taxes

A number of books, such as *The Unfinished Agenda* (1) and *Blueprint for Survival* (5), have suggested the idea of a raw materials tax, in which the tax rate increased annually as the remaining stock of the resource dropped. If the price rose faster than the average wage, this scheme would provide some stimulus for conservation. It would increase the incentive to explore for and develop new conventional fuels. A deliberate intention of this type of tax would be to raise the price of energy sufficiently to stimulate the development of solar and wind energy, and other "flow" as opposed to "stock" energy sources. Indeed, the authors of *The Unfinished Agenda* intended that this scheme would make the price of natural gas equal to the price of income energy (flow) sources after just five years. A problem with this type of scheme is that it would concentrate economic and political power in central government, although to some extent this could be compensated for if large numbers of small solar and wind energy companies became economically viable. The government could stimulate such companies through legislation to ensure minimum impediments to such little companies getting loans from lending institutions.

Depletion Quota Rights

A second scheme for resource conservation has been proposed by the economist Herman E. Daly (2). The government would determine for each year a quota for the amount of each basic resource that could be depleted. The legal rights to deplete up to the amount of the quota would be split up into convenient units, and these rights would be auctioned off by the government at the beginning of each year. The rights would be purchased by private firms, individuals, and public enterprises. After purchase from the government, the quota rights could be transferred by sale or they could be handed over as gifts. Clearly, as population and economic growth pressed harder against resources, the bidding for these quota rights would become more competitive, and prices of the depletion quotas would be driven higher and higher. The government could further induce conservation by reducing the quotas to lower and lower levels each year. This would drive up the price of the quotas still further. The government could spend the money derived from auctioning off the quota rights by paying a social dividend, or in other ways. For example, the government might underwrite the cost of development of solar energy systems of novel design. This scheme would have numerous side-effects. Most of these are positive, but economic and political power would be enormously concentrated in government, which could then be corrupted. Proceeds from the auctions could be used simply to enlarge the federal bureaucracy. Also, rich people would still be able to afford the now very expensive energy, but it could be priced totally out of reach of a large proportion of the population.

Ownership Rights Coupons

A third scheme for conserving energy has been proposed by Bruce Hannon (6). Energy would be rationed by the government through the use of coupons. A store of energy would be guaranteed to each consumer, who would be given coupons that could be used for different types of energy at different exchange rates. In effect, each person would be guaranteed ownership of some small fraction of each type of fuel. The consumer would have a number of options as to how to treat this owned energy. It could be used now. Or, the owner could decide to save it for use later. This scheme breaks up the "Tragedy of the Commons" phenomenon publicized by Hardin (7). This tragedy occurs when a resource is a common property resource (like a common pasture for a community's livestock) that does not belong to anyone, so is taken care of by no one. Many resources are common property resources, and their history is one of overexploitation. The reason is that when a resource is a common property, each exploiter of the resource has a motive to use it up before someone else gets to use it up. Thus, no one has a motive for conservation, because the conserver merely gets beaten out in economic competition with the nonconserver. However, under the Hannon scheme, each unit of a resource is owned by someone. Or, the owner might decide to enter a market with his or her ownership coupons, and sell them for the best price he or she could get. Obviously, the market price for these coupons would rise very rapidly. Again, the government could manipulate this process, by making the coupons represent smaller and smaller amounts of the resource, year after year. Under this scheme, the poorest people would have just as many coupons to begin with as the richest people. Instead, if the rich decided to buy up the coupons of the poor, and the poor agreed to sell them, there would indeed be a transfer of wealth, from the rich to the poor. Again, this scheme transfers enormous political power to government, and the scheme is corruptible. But energy prices would quickly become so high that there would be enormous stimulus to conserve and to develop technologically novel sources.

Penalties for Excessive Use

Under a fourth scheme, the government distributes coupons to be handed over when resources are being purchased. The consumer who wishes to buy ten units of one type of energy a month would get ten units of one color. But if the consumer wished to buy twenty units of that type of energy, the second ten coupons would be in a different color. If he or she wished to buy thirty units of energy, the coupons for the last ten units would be a third color. The coupons would be obtained free from the government, but handed over to the retailer when gasoline, for example, was purchased. The price paid would depend on the color of the coupon handed over. Thus, if the consumer used only ten units of gasoline a month, there would be one price. But for the second ten gallons, the price would rise, and for the third ten gallons it would rise still more. The government could determine the shape of the curve for price per gallon as a function of a number of gallons consumed per month. Under this scheme, the coupons would be printed at taxpayer expense, but the various prices would go entirely to the retailer. His or her wholesale price, in turn, would be a weighted average based on the distribution of different colored coupons collected.

This scheme does impose a penalty for using a lot of energy, and does not price the poor out of the energy market. It does not make the government the recipient of enormous economic and political power, because the money goes into the energy industry, not government. No one, including the rich, could argue that their behavior was being limited; people would simply pay a premium to have any amount of freedom they wanted. On the other hand, people could feel free to do whatever they could afford, but on the other hand, they would pay a constantly increasing premium for the right to raise their personal rate of resource exploitation. Note that at the present, you get a lower price by buying in quantity.

Clearly, both the coupon schemes are vulnerable to black marketing and counterfeiting of coupons.

Deregulation

The fifth scheme for energy conservation is that suggested by some people in the energy industry, some political conservatives, and some people interested in conservation. This scheme is very appealing, because it is simple, it eliminates the need for a lot of bureaucracy and paperwork, and it does not lead to concentration of a great deal of power in government. This scheme is simply to deregulate the price of all forms of energy. The government would repeal all energy legislation and disband all bureaucracies that had anything to do with energy regulation. While this method appears to have limitations at first glance, these limitations can be overcome. For example, government could prevent excessive accumulation of assets in the energy industry by excess profits taxes. However, as explained in Chapter 4, the accumulation of capital in the energy industry will not be that great in any case, because their costs for new exploration and development, as in offshore oil wells, are going to be tremendous.

One of the most serious potential weaknesses with this policy is not that energy prices would rise too rapidly, but rather that they would rise too slowly. Competition between suppliers might conspire to keep the retail price moving up too slowly to provide an adequate incentive for development of new energy sources (such as solar). It is curious that while government in the United States has thought the market price of energy was too high, government in other countries has thought the market price of energy was too low, and increased the retail price sharply with taxes. For example, in 1972, taxation was 70 percent of the gasoline price in Sweden, 66 percent in Switzerland, 82 percent in Turkey, 70 percent in West Germany and 80 percent in India. In the same year, it was only 31 percent in the United States. Thus other governments have already recognized that energy retail prices might rise so slowly as to have a socially undesirable effect unless made to rise more rapidly through taxation.

COMPARATIVE EVALUATION OF THE FIVE SAMPLE SCHEMES

Each of the five schemes has certain strengths and certain weaknesses: in a democracy, it is the task of the political system to seek some compromise solution that is most satisfactory to the largest number of people. Table 16.1 assembles the facts we need to evaluate these schemes. Which one we decide is best depends in turn on the relative importance we attach to each of the nine goals. From the table, we see that if equity is a primary consideration, then the third and fourth schemes seem best. The second would probably raise the energy price and promote conservation as rapidly as any. The fifth is best if we are primarily nervous about concentration of power in the federal energy bureaucracy.

A final possibility remains: we might combine these policies in some way to make use of the attractive features in several of the schemes, while trying to avoid their unattractive features. One way to do this is through a combination of the fourth and fifth schemes. The energy industry would be allowed to deregulate prices, with government serving only as a watchdog to tax excessive profits by means of a windfall profits tax scheme. Under this scheme, government would tax the energy industries only if their profits were rising at a rate faster than that required by their need for capital for future exploration, drilling, production, and transportation (Chapter 7). The profit rate at which these taxes were required could be arrived at in federal bargaining, involving representatives from the energy industry, government, and independent mediators and experts from universities, foundations,

TABLE 16.1.
The relative impacts of five different schemes for energy conservation.

Category of impact	Escalating raw materials tax	Depletion quota auctions	Consumers granted ownership rights	Price increases with use	Deregulation
Stimulus for conservation	waste not penalized	waste not penalized	waste penalized	waste penalized	waste not penalized
Stimulus to develop conventional sources	large	large	large	large	very large
Stimulus to develop unconventional sources	very large	very large	very large	very large	very large
Reduced institutional impediments to conservation	probably	probably	probably	probably	probably
Reduced institutional impediments to search for new energy sources	probably	probably	probably	probably	probably
Minimization of environmental degradation	probably	probably	probably	probably	probably
Minimization of inequitable income distribution	not much	not much	a lot	a lot	not at all
Minimization of dangerous concentration of political power	too much in government	too much in government	too much in government	too much in energy industry	too much in energy industry, but can be limited by tax
Minimization of problem of imperfect functioning of government regulation or markets	depends on accuracy of government assessment of need for higher taxes	likely	likely	depends on accuracy of government assessment of need to have energy price escalate	market forces may not drive up prices fast enough

independent research and consulting corporations, or citizens' actions organizations. However, in addition to deregulation, the government would issue coupons of various colors, which would represent, not different prices, but different multiples of the base retail price set by the energy industry. Here are the details on such a scheme.

In 1974, the average gasoline consumption among all Americans was 350 gallons (in cars only). The government might first compute a gasoline consumption that would be allowed to each person at the base rate for gasoline being charged by industry. It might argue, for example, that any person should be allowed sufficient gas for 260 round trips per year of ten miles each, in a vehicle averaging 20 miles per gallon. Thus the "base allotment" for each person would be (260 working days per year × 10 miles per round trip to work)/20 miles per gallon, or 130 gallons. Each person would then be allowed 130 coupons, one per gallon, to buy gas at the base price per gallon. These coupons might be green, for example. Any person who wished to use up an additional 130 gallons could then request from the government an additional 130 coupons, this time yellow. Gasoline sold at the pump island in exchange for these coupons would cost twice the base price. Finally, anyone wishing to use more than 260 gallons of gasoline a year could request any additional number of coupons, only these would be red. Gasoline sold at any pump island in exchange for these coupons would cost five times the base price. The effect of this system would be to discourage wasteful use of gasoline, and to encourage living close to the place of work and driving an energy-efficient car.

Obviously, this system is corruptible, as is any scheme involving coupons. The U.S. Treasury Department would need an increase in staff to guard against and seek out counterfeiting operations making bogus coupons, and the Internal Revenue Service would need to do computer checks of gasoline sales against coupon receipts. However, with adequate safeguards of this type, the scheme seems workable. The windfall profits feature would avoid excessive concentration of economic or political power in energy companies. The price of energy would go up enough to encourage exploration, research,

drilling, and production of conventional energy sources, and also would stimulate the development and installation of new energy systems. The system is also reasonably equitable. Poor people who had to drive to work would pay the base price for energy, and would have access to a reasonable amount at that base price. Rich people would have to pay a punitive premium for being wasteful. There would be no need for a great increase in the federal government energy bureaucracy. All the new positions required could be filled by transfers from old agencies that would no longer be necessary, such as the Department of Energy. The scheme would rely on the leverage of a dollar to stimulate initiative in the private sector, which is greater than the leverage of that same dollar in the public sector.

However, this scheme, like the other five, has a major weakness. It does not address the problem of the environmental impacts of energy development, or of energy generation and use. We now turn to the separate issue of economic solutions to the pollution problem, therefore.

ECONOMIC SCHEMES FOR REDUCING THE LEVEL OF POLLUTION

Four simple ideas are basic to an economic analysis of pollution abatement:

1. Costs of control,
2. Costs versus benefits,
3. Equity,
4. Effectiveness of control.

The first of these concerns an objective technique for estimating how much we can spend to control pollution. Unfortunately, we can not spend an unlimited amount of money to obtain a perfectly clean environment: we could not afford that, and no one would be interested in paying the price in any case. In other words, we seek some reasonable balance between the cost of minimizing pollution and the benefits derived from achieving a given level of pollution control. These benefits include not only lower levels of damage to paint, clothing hung out to dry, and cement or brick buildings, but longer life expectancies for the entire population, because of lower mortality rates due to pollution (Chapter 12).

We would decide the amount of money we could spend on pollution control by developing two curves from data we could collect: one showing how cost of additional pollution control changes as a function of the level of

pollution control, and another showing how the benefits from pollution control change as a function of the level of control.

As we see in Figure 16.1, as we strive for a greater level of pollution control, each additional increment in reduction of pollution level will be more expensive. This merely expresses the law of diminishing returns: it will cost far more to reduce the level of pollution from 20 percent of the present level to 10 percent, than to reduce it from 100 percent of the present level to 90 percent. Similarly, we face a law of diminishing returns operating on the benefits: the cleaner the air (or water) becomes, the less

FIGURE 16.1

Curves for marginal costs and benefits associated with increased levels of pollution control.

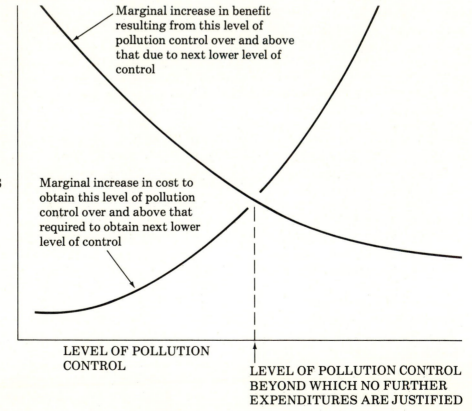

benefit will be derived from making it still cleaner. Consequently, as in the figure, the curves for incremental cost and incremental benefit (marginal cost and marginal benefit) will cross at some point. At that point, the further improvement in reduction of damage (increase in benefits) due to pollution will be less than the additional cost to achieve the reduction. That is the point beyond which pollution control makes no sense.

The second notion basic to pollution control is that of equitable internalization of costs and benefits. In many types of economic activity, the producer reaps all the benefits from the activity, and pays all the costs. However, in some activities (those that produce pollution) the producer reaps all the benefits, but pays only some of the costs. There is a private cost from running a chemical-manufacturing plant but there is in addition a social cost (created by the damage due to the pollutant effluents from the plant). Since the public is bearing some of the costs of running the plant, which is dumping wastes into communally owned air and water, we say that there is inequitable internalization of costs and benefits. Under equitable internalization, the plant owners would not only reap all the benefits from their operations, but they would also pay all of their costs. All pollution abatement schemes are designed to achieve some measure of equitable internalization.

The third notion basic to pollution abatement policy is that of equity, but attaining equity is not straightforward or simple. Suppose two families drive identical cars, but one of these families lives in a smog-filled city, and the other lives in a remote desert or mountain village. Should each family pay the same penalty for polluting? Is it equally necessary that each family stop polluting? Many people would feel that pollution control is unimportant in the remote area, but important in the city. Thus, true equity in pollution control should be based on circum-

stances where one lives. In other words, penalties for polluting should be determined by how necessary it is not to pollute.

Finally, pollution abatement legislation must take into consideration the most effective and efficient way to attain a given effect. For example, how should we minimize pollution from automobiles: by regulating the design of the engines, or by regulating the amount of pollution? A little thought shows that these similar-sounding ideas work out rather differently in practice. If we regulate the design of the engines so that they produce minimum pollution, a minimum amount of government inspection is required by the scheme, because very large numbers of people will be buying identical engines. Once the government has approved a particular engine design as producing no more than the maximum allowable pollution, the manufacturer simply mass-produces the approved design.

There are two weaknesses with this scheme. The first is that failure to maintain the engine in good working order may lead to a significant increase in pollution. But because some people will be maintaining the engine and others will not, some engines will continue to meet specifications and others will not. This suggests a different type of scheme, in which government regulation is not focused on the design of the engine, but rather on the way each engine works in each inspection year. This scheme has the disadvantage of requiring a vast inspection effort. This could be reduced by instituting a system of spot checks, so that no individual car-owner would know when he or she was going to be checked. But this approach based on performance rather then engine design has a major advantage: it stimulates individual initiative to discover novel ways of reducing pollution. Thus, small companies are encouraged to seek innovative additions to or modifications of existing engines which can be sold at a profit. In short, pollution regulation based on design is cheap to enforce, but produces a variable response and does not stimulate individual initiative. On the other hand, regulation based on performance is expensive to enforce, but produces a more uniform response, and does encourage individual initiative and technological innovation. With regulation based on engine design, the incentive for initiative or innovation has evaporated as soon as the car is sold.

Of course, similar arguments apply to all types of pollution sources, from factories to refineries, smelting plants, airplanes, and ships.

SUMMARY

The theme running through this chapter is that while there are many economic techniques available for environmental management, all of these can have a great variety of effects, some of which might not have been expected. Therefore, the way to pick the most appropriate technique is to think carefully through all of our objectives, then evaluate each proposed solution against each of them. Our ultimate concern is with day-to-day performance of vehicles, power generating systems, and factories, not with their design, so regulating schemes should be designed to affect performance, not design.

An ideal scheme for allocating scarce resources, such as gasoline after 1984, would involve careful balancing of power between government and energy corporations. Government would issue rationing coupons in several colors, the particular color indicating if a penalty should be imposed for excessive use. However, the oil companies would collect the penalty, not government. Government would only impose a windfall profits

tax, if energy companies collected more money than that required to maintain a program of exploratory drilling.

SUGGESTIONS FOR INDIVIDUAL AND GROUP PROJECTS

Stage a mock debate on the five different ways of stimulating energy conservation, in which five different teams act out the roles of various constituencies: refineries, gas station owners, motorists, government bureaucrats, and independent solar energy installation companies, for example.

Try to invent new, better schemes for conserving energy, or reducing pollution.

Try to interest your local congressional representative in introducing legislation to enact your scheme into new federal law.

Which type of scheme would work best to reduce water pollution in the city where you live?

REFERENCES

1. Barney, G. O., ed., *The Unfinished Agenda. The Citizen's Policy Guide to Environmental Issues.* New York: Thomas Crowell, 1977.
2. Daly, H. E., ed., *Toward a Steady-State Economy.* San Francisco: W. H. Freeman, 1973.
3. Dorfman, R., and N. S. Dorfman, eds., *Economics of the Environment.* New York: W. W. Norton, 1972.
4. Goldman, M. I., ed., *Ecology and Economics: Controlling Pollution in the 70's.* Englewood Cliffs, N.J.: Prentice-Hall, 1972.
5. Goldsmith, E.; R. Allen; M. Allaby; J. Davoll; and S. Lawrence, *Blueprint for Survival.* New York: New American Library, 1972.
6. Hannon, B., "Energy conservation and the consumer," *Science,* 189 (1975), pp. 95–102.

7. Hardin, G., "The tragedy of the commons," *Science,* 162 (1968), pp. 1243–1248.

8. Krier, J. E., "Environmental law and its administration," pp. 413–436 in *Environment* (2d ed.), W. W. Murdoch, ed. Sunderland, Mass: Sinauer Associates, 1975.

9. Ruff, L. E. "Environment and economics," pp. 399–411 in *Environment* (2d ed.), W. W. Murdoch, ed. Sunderland, Mass.: Sinauer Associates, 1975.

17 LEGAL SOLUTIONS TO ENVIRONMENTAL PROBLEMS

We have said that the laws were the particular and precise institutions of a legislator, and manners and customs the institutions of a nation in general. Hence it follows that when these manners and customs are to be changed, it ought not to be done by laws; this would have too much the air of tyranny: it would be better to change them by introducing other manners and other customs.

Charles de Montesquieu, The Spirit of Laws, *Book XIX, Chapter 14, 1748.*

MAIN THEMES OF THIS CHAPTER

This chapter suggests the various types of legal procedures available for dealing with different types of environmental problems. Traditional civil law provides a number of avenues by which to seek redress of environmental wrongs. However, these can be expensive and time-consuming, and the courts will seek a solution in terms of the community as a whole. This means that the individual or group who initiates the action may not feel that their cause has been fairly served.

Another possibility is to use imaginative, novel possibilities within the law. Organizing a group of people to seek collective action under a class action suit, working through one of the new organizations specializing in environmental law, arguing about violations of the constitution of the United States, and use of the Freedom of Information Act may be more successful in the long run than the traditional civil law.

AN OVERVIEW OF THE LEGAL SITUATION

There are two broad types of approach to obtaining correction of environmental injustices in the courts. The first is the traditional approach, using the law of torts, or civil wrongs. The second involves collective action based on shared goals among a group of people.

Under the law of torts, an individual, group of individuals, or corporation seeks to correct a perceived environmental injustice by bringing a civil suit against the offending party or parties. In theory, this sounds great, but in practice, there are four very large problems. It might take the court years to arrive at a decision, because of the extremely technical nature of the evidence and arguments. (The chapter on pollution gives the merest hint of the complexity of environmental cases.) The plaintiff might literally go bankrupt while waiting for the court to order the offending party to stop doing whatever is causing the plaintiff to lose money. Secondly, the cost of waging a successful court battle to prevent a defendent from committing an environmental wrong might be astronomical. To illustrate, the plaintiff might spend ten thousand dollars on each of ten technical witnesses, including the cost of their time to prepare testimony, the cost of transcontinental air fares, hotel bills, and the like. Legal fees could easily bring the total cost to $200,000 or more. The total cost might be much higher, because the plaintiff might have to fund an expensive research program to prove every step of the chain of evidence implicating the defendant. (The author has been involved in one case with precisely this pattern of expenses.) The third problem is that there may be inherent inequity in the court action, with the plaintiff shouldering a gigantic financial burden that should rightly be shared by many plaintiffs. That is, a defendant might be wrecking the environment for tens of thousands of people. However, perhaps only a handful of these might want to pay for a court action. This may be the only option open for the plaintiff, because of the prohibitive amount of time, effort, and money that might be required to organize a class action, one of the second type of approaches we will discuss. The largest problem in an environmental civil suit is that the burden of establishing proof of guilt falls on the plaintiff. Two examples illustrate the difficulties in establishing such proof. Suppose a plaintiff in the Los Angeles Basin wished to assign guilt proportionately to the polluters in the Basin. The problem is that there are so many polluters, it would be essentially impossible to do this equitably. The other type of difficulty occurs when there is a long-chain causal pathway, each step of which must be proven. For example, suppose it is being alleged by a plaintiff that aerial spraying of spruce budworm in forests leads to poison drifting out of the forest onto adjacent blueberry patches, where it kills pollinating bees, thus lowering blueberry production. It must be proven in court that the spray causes the reduction in blueberry production, with a resultant economic impact that is attributable to the spray and no other cause. Further, to obtain an injunction against further forest spraying in the vicinity of the blueberry patches, in addition to damages for losses due to past spraying, it would be necessary to prove that spraying has no beneficial effect on the forest under attack by the spruce budworm. Clearly, to establish all the steps in this argument involves private underwriting of a type of research effort that would normally only be undertaken by government.

All these difficulties with appeal to the law of torts suggest a different approach. In this approach either an organization is formed for the purpose of conducting a suit of interest to many people, or the suit is undertaken by an organization already in existence that specializes in this type of environmental law action. The advantages of forming an organization or using an existing organization are several. Where many people can organize to spread the load of effort in organizing for and preparing a case, there is clearly much more chance of success. A large group of people have access to more money, are more likely to have useful technical contacts or to have access to a variety of scientific and legal skills, and can sustain an activity for several years with less sacrifice than a few individuals. The ultimate extension of this notion is the permanent organization with a large national following that exists for the express purpose of conducting major environmental law battles: the Environmental Defense Fund is the best-known example. In this case, the organization has sufficient staff to be able to identify major environmental legal problems on its own. The organization then initiates actions, which may even include suits against government agencies. The Environmental Defense Fund not only has great in-house legal and scientific expertise, but can draw on volunteer help from an international circle of scientific and legal colleagues the collective competence of whom would intimidate any prospective adversary, including the largest corporations or the federal government. Clearly, in this situation, the adversaries are much more evenly matched than in some civil suits to right environmental wrongs.

ENVIRONMENTAL INJUSTICE AND THE LAW OF TORTS

In general, the court will seek equitable justice for all parties to an action. This means that the court is unlikely to rule in favor of the plaintiff if the cost to deal with the environmental problem is clearly in excess of the benefits that would result from the solution. Thus, the logical structure of the argument by the plaintiff's attorney must be that the damage to the plaintiff is in excess of what it would cost the defendant to redress the problem.

If this is the case, then there are four possible approaches to arguing the case in court.

Negligence

The first is to demonstrate negligence on the part of the defendant. Thus, if the plaintiff is a citrus grower or a company harvesting shrimp, there would be an attempt to show that a chemical plant, through negligence, was causing excessive damage to the citrus trees or shrimp. Negligence can be demonstrated if it can be shown that the defendant has failed to conform to a reasonable standard of conduct. However, since the court does seek equitable justice in the sense of the community, it will balance the social usefulness of the offending activity (chemical pollution, in this case) against the probability of risk to citrus or shrimp, the degree of risk, and perhaps the frequency of risk. This means that if the chemical plant is by far the most economically important employer in the region, and the citrus and shrimp are relatively unimportant economically to the region, the defendant (the chemical plant) might not be punished. As in the Los Angeles air pollution or blueberry cases, it might be almost prohibitively expensive to obtain the technical information necessary to establish the argument. In any case, the court would seek to balance the cost of a marginal improvement in the pollution damage against the cost to the polluter of controlling the pollution. If it takes $5 million in extra pollution control equipment or retrofitting to produce $250,000 less damage, the plaintiffs might well lose.

Strict Liability

The second approach to arguing an environmental civil suit is to prove strict liability. For example, it might be argued that some industrial chemical leaked into the environment, as through plant effluent from the smokestack, was so transparently lethal that its release was a dangerous and abnormal activity. A central issue in such a case would be the extent to which reasonable care had been taken to avoid activities dangerous to the plaintiff.

Trespass and Nuisance

A plaintiff might argue trespass and nuisance. For example, if a group of people or a corporation came on to private land and destroyed its productivity because of excessive use of off-road vehicles, then a case for trespass and nuisance would be reasonable.

Public Nuisance

A fourth line of argument is to demonstrate public nuisance. Curiously, to obtain damages, the plaintiff must be able to show that he or she suffered not the average amount of damage being borne by all aggrieved parties, but rather a greater amount of damage than the general public.

There are two motives for taking an environmental case to court. The first is to obtain damages. Here, the argument is that because of something the defendant was doing to me, I lost X dollars, or it cost me X dollars to clean up the mess, and I want to be compensated for that cost or those losses. A much more valuable objective is to seek a permanent injunction from the court to prevent the defendant from repeating the offending activity. Again, the problem is that the court will decide the ultimate costs to the community of any decision. Thus, for example, a court is unlikely to award an injunction that has the effect of saving the plaintiff a million dollars a year, but as a side-effect results in the loss to the community of one thousand jobs, which carried average salaries of fifteen thousand dollars per year.

NOVEL MEANS OF SEEKING ENVIRONMENTAL JUSTICE

Four techniques that have just recently come into heavy use seem to offer far more high-leverage means of obtaining environmental justice. All of these are tricky and require special knowledge or technical information, intelligence obtained through some type of private intelligence activity, and some planning.

The first is the class action suit. The second is the suit brought against one or more government agencies, making use of technical arguments to demonstrate that they are not enforcing existing laws. The third approach makes imaginative use of the Fifth Amendment. The fourth makes very clever use of the new Freedom of Information Act.

Class Action Suits

The class action suit brings a civil action against a defendant on behalf of all the members of a class of people who allegedly were in common the victims of an environmental wrong. The members of the class might all have become sick, lost their jobs, or had their business or homes ruined or decreased in value because of a chemical pollutant, noise adjacent to an airfield, or some other environmental problem. The class of plaintiffs is organized, in effect, by the court, which publishes a notice in a local newspaper announcing the class action. This notice is called a notice of pendency of a class action. The notice states the identities of the plaintiffs who have initiated the case and the defendants, gives the address of the office of the clerk in which the suit will be conducted, and gives the number of the civil action. The notice explains the nature of the suit, and contains also, the following.

> The purpose of this Notice is to inform those persons who might be a member of such class of the pendency of this lawsuit so that they may decide what steps they wish to take in relation to it. . . . This Notice is not to be understood as an expression of any opinion by this Court as to the merits of any of the claims or defenses asserted by either side in this litigation. The Court has not yet made its ruling in this case.

Such notices then explain very carefully how membership in the class is defined. It might consist of all people who were employees of a certain corporation between certain dates, worked in certain buildings on certain operations between those dates, or were shrimp fishers in a specified bay between certain dates.

The notice will then explain the rules under which people are included in or excluded from the class:

If you believe that you are a member of the class and do not wish to be involved in this lawsuit, you may write the Court to exclude you from the class, provided that your request is in writing and postmarked not later than. . . . If you request to be excluded from the class, you will not be bound by any judgement entered in this lawsuit. You will be free to pursue whatever legal rights you may have at your own expense. IF YOU DO NOT NOTIFY THIS COURT OF YOUR DESIRE TO BE EXCLUDED FROM THIS CLASS AND THIS LAWSUIT, YOU WILL AUTOMATICALLY BE INCLUDED IN THE CLASS AND THE LAWSUIT. . . . If you are a member of this class and do not request exclusion, you will be included in and bound by the judgement in this litigation. You will be bound by any judgement favorable to the Defendants and adverse to the class. Conversely, you will be entitled to share in the benefits of any judgement which is favorable to the class and will hereafter be required to submit to the Court proof of your membership in the class and a statement of the extent of your damages.

Notices of pendency are typically very lengthy, and explain all the details of the case and provide detailed instructions for possible plaintiffs who want into or out of the class. Clearly, there are potential benefits from being a member of a class if the plaintiff wins, but there are also benefits from being excluded from the class if the plaintiff loses. A strategy option open if you did not initiate the suit but agree with it and think the plaintiffs can win if they have enough money and legal and technical support is to contact them and arrange to help provide one or more of those types of support. Given that the Court is in the curious position of announcing all this publicly, thus aiding in the formation of the class, and given that the class action opens up the possibility of several or a large number of plaintiffs pooling resources, this type of action has the potential for being more effective than the individual suit. The big problem is that of getting enough people to join the action. Clearly, undertaking a class action would offer no benefits over a private action unless it were clear in advance that many people would agree that they had been done an environmental injustice, in common.

Actions Against Government

A second novel legal approach, against government agencies for not enforcing the law, is illustrated by a very ingenious case brought against the U.S. Environmental Protection Agency, the Department of the Interior, and the Bureau of Reclamation by the Environmental Defense Fund. The suit charged that as of 1977, when the suit was filed, there had been federal laws in existence for ten years requiring enforcement of water quality standards to control salinity pollution. Instead of issuing federal water quality standards, the Environmental Protection Agency allowed the seven basin states on the Colorado River Basin to set their own salinity standards, which were "illegal and ineffective" according to the Fund. The result was that ever-increasing salt concentrations from natural sources and spiraling human-caused growth were causing $50 million worth of damages every year, with the cost doubling in twenty years if the salinity were not controlled. The costs are borne by agricultural, domestic, and industrial water users. They occur because salinity pollution reduces or eliminates crop production, destroys soil, decreases drinking water potability, corrodes plumbing systems and appliances, increases treatment costs, and at extreme levels can pose human health hazards. The significance of this problem is indicated by the importance of the Colorado

River: it is the only significant source of surface water in the arid Southwest, and it is the chief source of water for millions of acres of irrigated agriculture, millions of homes, and industries. Clearly, the Environmental Defense Fund is performing a tremendous public service in taking on this case. Unfortunately, public support for such activities is inadequate. During the three years 1973 to 1975, the organization suffered deficits of $426,000. Accordingly, there were budget cutbacks in 1976. To indicate the cost of running such an organization, for the year ended December 31, 1976, the expenses were $1.45 million. What the public gets from such an organization is a somewhat more evenly matched legal contest against large institutions. The Fund has a staff with very impressive collective scientific and legal expertise, who can draw on help from many other people with similar technical ability. One strategic option for a person or group considering being a plaintiff would be to interest such an organization in the case and provide them with some of the help required to conduct it. This would probably give one a higher probability of ultimate success than going to a law firm that did not have an equivalent background in this highly technical legal area.

Use of the Due Process Provision

A third novel development in environmental law is the use of the Fifth Amendment as a basis for argument. The Fifth Amendment to the U.S. Constitution is popularly known for its guarantee of the rights of the accused. However, it also speaks to the due process of law. This aspect of the Amendment has been used in environmental law in a most ingenious way. Environmental groups and thirty-seven individuals who live near the site of two nuclear plants planned by the

Duke Power Company near Charlotte, North Carolina, brought suit in a lower court, challenging the constitutionality of the Price-Anderson Act of 1957. This act was designed to encourage the development of the nuclear power industry by private corporations. It limits the total recovery by all those injured in any one nuclear accident to $560 million. This would come from a combination of private insurance, a $5 million assessment on each new licensed nuclear power plant, and government funds. The notion underlying the act was that as more plants were built, the insurance provided by industry would grow to the point at which the government contribution would no longer be needed, and the total fund could eventually exceed $560 million. Obviously, without this act there was the possibility that a nuclear accident could bring such massive suits against the power company that its insurers would be bankrupted. This in turn implied that prior to the Price-Anderson Act, the risk to even the largest insurance companies in giving policies to nuclear power plant corporations could not be contemplated, and the fledgling nuclear power industry could not get started.

However, the lower court held that the limitation on liability violated the due process clause in the Fifth Amendment "because it allows the destruction of the property or the lives of those affected by nuclear catastrophe without reasonable certainty that they will be justly compensated." The court also found that the Price-Anderson Act violated the Constitution's equal protection guarantee because it "provides for what Congress deemed to be a benefit to the whole society (the encouragement of the generation of nuclear power), but places the cost of that benefit on an arbitrarily chosen segment of society, those injured by nuclear catastrophe." The Supreme Court decided to review the judgement by the lower court.

On June 26, 1978 the Court decided that the Act did not violate the due process clause either on the grounds that the amount of recovery was not rationally related to potential losses, or that the Act tended to encourage irresponsibility in matters of safety and environmental protection.

This case illustrates the way in which the courts function. The underlying goal of the legal system is to try and balance the net sum of social costs and benefits. The way to use the legal system to obtain correction of environmental injustices is to try and develop arguments that can be documented showing that some environmental act constitutes an unjust transfer of wealth from the defendant to the plaintiff. This happens wherever one party derives a financial benefit which in whole or part is also a cost borne by another party who does not share in the benefit.

The Freedom of Information Act

The final novel approach under the law makes use of a new law in a most ingenious fashion. The Freedom of Information Act allows citizens or institutions to obtain from the government information that had previously been classified as secret or confidential. This act has environmental significance if the public has an incorrect understanding of some matter and where release of the documents would change that understanding so as to diminish political support for an action of probable or possible environmental impact. The public understanding for a long time was that the probability of nuclear catastrophe due to nuclear power plant operations or nuclear waste storage was remote. Certainly, many prominent figures have repeatedly so assured the public.

Thus it was of considerable interest when an exiled Soviet scientist reported in 1976 that thousands of persons were killed or suffered radiation sickness when buried nuclear waste at a site in the Ural Mountains overheated and exploded in 1958 (Chapter 2). A reasonable assumption was that the Central Intelligence Agency would have a great deal of information on such an incident. In fact, as of November 1977, it had twenty-nine documents on it. Thus, it seemed worthwhile to use the Freedom of Information Act to request from the agency release of this information. Accordingly, Ralph Nader's Critical Mass Energy Project and the *Washington Post* so used the Act, and on November 26, 1977, contents of fourteen of the documents were made public, in part. Unfortunately, the released files were heavily censored, and the Agency argued that some of the fifteen files not released were so sensitive that they could not be made available even with deletions.

The material that was released was most revealing (Chapter 2). One C.I.A. informant traveling in the area three years after the explosion described the scene:

> We crossed a strange, uninhabited and unfarmed area. Highway signs along the way warned drivers not to stop for the next 20 to 30 kilometers because of radiation. The land was empty. There were no villages, no towns, no people, no cultivated land; only the chimneys of destroyed houses remained. I asked the driver to stop because I wanted to drink water. The driver refused. "One doesn't stop here. You drive quickly and cross the area without any stops," he said.

Clearly, use of the Freedom of Information Act to obtain release of documents classified by the government can bring a lot more information into political discussion of sensitive environmental issues, and lead to more balanced consideration of both sides of a controversy. In this instance, use of the act has initiated a sequence of events, each of which has created the stimulus for an-

other event. Finally, on Sunday, November 9, 1980, the network television program "Sixty Minutes" devoted a segment to the Kyshtym disaster, and this information will now become an important part of the public debate about nuclear safety.

EXAMPLES OF SUCCESSFUL ENVIRONMENTAL LEGAL ACTIONS

On May 4, 1979, the Environmental Defense Fund won a major legal battle to preserve a 20,000 acre wetland hardwood forest in the Red River region of Louisiana. A U.S. District Court found that clearing, draining, and converting such land to another use are prohibited under the Clean Water Act in the absence of appropriate permits.

This decision was important for two reasons. First, wetlands are an important natural resource that is rapidly being destroyed by conversion to other types of land use. To illustrate, more than three-fourths of the forested wetlands in the Mississippi River floodplain have been destroyed by conversion, primarily for agricultural use. We need wetlands: they serve as a natural filtration system to help purify polluted waters, and they are a spawning ground and nursery for fish and a habitat for many kinds of wildlife.

The case is important, additionally, because of the legal precedent that has been established. This precedent can be used in many other cases, in almost all of which alternative ways of providing land for housing, industry, and agriculture are available.

In 1973, 300,000 porpoises were killed by becoming entrapped in nets set in the Pacific by yellowfin tuna fishers. In 1972, the Marine Mammal Protection Act was enacted, with the support of the Environmental Defense Fund. Late in 1977, eleven organizations won a Federal ruling reducing the dolphin kill quota by 50 percent by 1980, and requiring the tuna industry to use improved equipment and fishing techniques. This was the first major reduction ordered under the 1972 act; by 1978 porpoise kills were only 15,000.

One of the most interesting environmental legal actions concerned the pesticide D.D.T. The legal program began in 1967 when a scientifically minded attorney in Long Island, Victor Yannacone Jr., filed a suit in state court to stop a county agency from spraying marshes with D.D.T. In the course of this action, Yannacone met Charles Wurster, a biology professor. Out of their joint activity the idea of cooperative efforts by teams of attorneys and scientists was born. The team grew, and by 1973 the ultimate result of meticulously prepared arguments on the effects of D.D.T. was a Federal ban on use of the substance in the United States.

The Environmental Defense Fund initiated a lawsuit that led the Environmental Protection Agency to issue national air emission standards for asbestos, mercury, and beryllium.

An even more sophisticated type of activity occurs when a legal and scientific approach is coupled to economic analysis. Dr. Wayne Willey of the Environmental Defense Fund used financial analysis to demonstrate that the Pacific Gas and Electric Company could cut 90 percent of its planned new nuclear and coal plants by shifting investments to presently available alternate energy sources. This would meet all the projected energy needs of the ratepayers, and amazingly, at lower cost to them and the company.

The Center for Law in the Public Interest, Los Angeles, has goals similar to those of the Environmental Defense Fund.

SUMMARY

There is now precedent for a wide variety of types of uses of the legal system to deal with environmental problems. Given all these options, it seems only common sense to seek the technique that allows one to make the highest leverage use of limited resources in righting a perceived injustice. Recent experience suggests that traditional use of the law of torts, arguing negligence, liability, trespass, or nuisance, may not give one as high leverage as some more novel, ingenious methods. These newer approaches require guidance from one of the several firms or organizations specializing in the interface between environmental science and environmental law because of the highly technical character of arguments that are likely to succeed.

SUGGESTIONS FOR INDIVIDUAL AND GROUP EXERCISES

Identify an environmental problem in your area that appears as if it might be amenable to correction by use of the law. Now try to invent a legal procedure by which the problem could be corrected. Examine publications on environmental law (see "References") to see if the experts have thought of a more effective way of proceeding with a legal action in cases like this. Rewrite your proposed legal procedure, making use of these new ideas. If any are available, check your approach with an environmental law professor.

An excellent means of staying abreast of developments in environmental law, and also helping in this activity, is to join an organization that takes on environmental law cases in the public interest. Two such organizations are: The Environmental Defense Fund, 475 Park Avenue South, New York,

NY 10016; and Center for Law in the Public Interest, 10203 Santa Monica Boulevard, Los Angeles, CA 90067.

REFERENCES

1. Butler, W., "Law and science team up to preserve environmental quality," *Environmental Science and Technology,* 7 (1973), p. 30.

2. *The Environmental Law Quarterly.*
3. *Environmental Law Reporter.*
4. Henkin, H.; M. Merta; and J. Staples, *The Environment, the Establishment, and the Law.* Boston: Houghton Mifflin, 1971.
5. *The Natural Resources Lawyer.*

18 LEGISLATIVE AND INSTITUTIONAL SOLUTIONS TO ENVIRONMENTAL PROBLEMS

> The worst of all abuses is to pay an apparent obedience to the laws, only in order actually to break them with security. For in this case the best laws soon become the most pernicious; and it would be a hundred times better that they should not exist. In such a situation, it is vain to add edicts to edicts and regulations to regulations. Everything serves only to introduce new abuses, without correcting the old. The more laws are multiplied, the more they are despised, and all the new officials appointed to supervise them are only so many more people to break them . . .
>
> *Jean-Jacques Rousseau,* A Discourse on Political Economy, *1755.*

MAIN THEMES OF THIS CHAPTER

This chapter outlines three kinds of legislative and institutional adjustments that will allow society to maintain a high quality of life for people in a future world of lower resource availability per capita. The first innovation makes use of new methods in planning, decision-making, conflict resolution and regulation to improve the performance of existing institutions. The second innovation gradually changes the spatial design of society and methods of housing and transportation so as to make much more efficient use of resources. The third innovation involves a number of basic changes in the attitudes of people that can be instilled through education, so as to make society and its institutions function better in the face of the new circumstances we will encounter. All of these changes will occur because they will be necessary for the continuance of organized society as we know it. Their combined impact will be to produce patterns of social existence remarkably different than those in which we now live.

INTRODUCTION AND OVERVIEW

Students who have learned the material in the rest of this book become convinced that if society as we know it is to survive, legislative and institutional reforms will be required. However, they split into three schools of thought as to which particular types of reforms are most essential.

One school holds that the basic structure of our institutions is appropriate for the demands that will be placed on government in the future, but that novel, powerful methods for planning, decision-making, reacting to new information and developments, conflict resolution, and regulation need to be built into government to make it more effective.

A second point of view might be characterized as the "Small is Beautiful" school (11). The basic target of this point of view is bigness, wherever and however it occurs. It is argued that the very design of our society has a variety of basic defects, all due to bigness.

The enormous size of the population means that politicians have to gain the support of masses in order to get elected; the electoral process disintegrates into a popularity contest, enormously vulnerable to expensive, sophisticated media manipulation of the public image of political candidates. Campaigning on the basis of a frank, honest statement of planned programs risks losing the support of constituencies, more than offsetting potential gain of the support of other constituencies. Since the truth about overpopulation, resource depletion, pollution, and environmental degradation is simply unacceptable to most people, honesty about these matters appears to be the very worst policy for a politician. So sheer bigness of the electorate encourages the legislative and executive branches of government into a pattern of trying to be popular, rather than undertaking a desperately necessary program of education. Gradually, the sheer size of government insulates government from the public; important decision-making processes are cloaked in secrecy, and government becomes self-serving.

The size and complexity of modern socio-political-economic-environmental systems is beyond the comprehension of most people, particularly when big institutions manipulate information. Thus, few in the electorate can vote wisely on particularly complex issues, such as energy policy.

For these kinds of reasons, the second point of view holds that the enormous difficulty of managing large systems provides a rationale for returning to a simpler life style built around smaller, more managable systems. This point of view puts great stress on local initiative, intermediate technology, and the "decoupling" of subsystems from systems. Thus, small regions of the United States would attempt to be as locally self-sufficient as they could in every respect.

Giant areas of suburban sprawl, giant corporations and farms, and giant central government have all been products of cheap energy, which facilitates economies of scale (lowering the cost of handling one unit of anything by making the number of units handled very large through cheap mechanization and automation). If energy prices rise significantly, it is argued, all of these examples of gigantism will go the way of the dinosaur.

So the second group of students argue that the future will be a world of small cities, small corporations, small farms, and small governments. Indeed, if much of our energy is to come from solar power, the diffuse origins and low concentration of this power as well as its higher price will lead us to decentralization and smallness. Gigantism will die because we will not be able to afford the large hidden subsidies that make it workable, as in the long daily commute from home to work. This vision of the future is replete with solar and wind energy collectors, energy from biomass (alcohol and methane from agricultural and forest wastes, and garbage). It is a future of compactness and highly efficient use of everything. Cars will be small and efficient, and technologically innovative mass transport will be everywhere. The conference call system and the use of phones for transmitting data between computers (the dataphone system) will substitute for sending large numbers of people by jet to attend a three-day meeting. Since this vision of the future involves heavy use of home computers, telephones, television, and high-fidelity sets, all linked to provide complex new home technologies, it does not represent a revolt against technology. Rather, it represents an evolution to genuinely sophisticated technology, rather than the use of technology to be profligately wasteful with energy, minerals, and land. It is a future of intermediate technology and small-is-beautiful, built around the efficient use of information rather than the inefficient use of other resources.

Some students gravitate to a third viewpoint. They argue that neither modernization of techniques by existing institutions nor decentralization and intermediate technology are by themselves adequate to allow for a smooth transition to a future of resource shortages. They argue that the basic problem underlying our difficulties with institutional malfunction is a cultural belief system inappropriate for our present situation. They argue that we are too materialistic and selfish, too lacking in resourcefulness and a holistic outlook, and not altruistic enough. Without a change in our cultural belief system new solar energy industries will quickly become gigantic, and any effort at decentralization will quickly be thwarted unless people become genuinely different.

The problem with each of these three proposals for changes is the time they require to effect sufficient change in existing systems. Because it is unlikely that any of the three approaches to change could work fast enough by itself to change the system in time to avoid a traumatic transition to the future, I assume that all of them will have to function together.

REFORMING THE PLANNING FUNCTION

Two types of information are necessary to the politician or planner selecting from among a set of available policies that policy deemed to be most effective for attaining socially desirable goals. On the one hand, one needs a grasp of the way in which systems external to human beings behave. For example, if the price of energy increases, what happens? On the other hand, one needs an understanding of judgement and decision processes. Neither of these kinds of understanding by itself is adequate for effective planning, but if both types of understanding are used together, they give us a new planning tool of extraordinary power. Such a tool has now been developed independently in two different branches of science. One source of the tool has been operations research and applied statistics, in which fields the tool is called "decision analysis" (9). A remarkably similar tool, "strategic judgement theory," has evolved within psychology (2, 3, 4, 5). Both tools can be defined as computer-assisted quantitative aids to decision-making. A single simplified and condensed explanation follows, showing the elements found in either method when they are applied in their most elaborate form. To illustrate the application of the methodology, we will use as an example the control of air pollution in Denver.

Denver has a problem shared by a number of cities, including Phoenix and San Diego. People migrated to these cities to get away from the filth, polluted air, and congestion of older cities. But very large numbers of people migrated to these cities, and they all wanted single-family ranch bungalows in the suburbs, and no controls over the use of land, immigration, or the number of automobiles. In short, the inhabitants of these cities wanted unlimited growth in the area of the city, in population size, and in the size of the city automobile fleet, but they wanted none of the congestion, pollution, or other problems that come with this growth. The result has been a considerable degree of frustration in such places. How can a politician, legislative body, or planner make the population as happy as possible?

Decision analysis and strategic judgement theory offer us an elaborate methodology for dealing with such problems. Both of these methodologies have been elaborated over a rather long time and have been applied to a large number and variety of important practical problems. Each of these methodologies recognizes certain basic elements in complex decision-making problems where there are multiple conflicting objectives.

Measuring Performance of the Managed System

What concerns us in a system we are trying to manage? Clearly, for any complex system we are trying to manage, there is a set of *indicators of interest*, or performance measures, that tell us what we most want to know about the system. Thus, for air pollution in Denver, we want the following bits of information:

Economic information: what did it cost to deal with air pollution, and what did the effects of air pollution cost us? Clearly, such a measure would need to include the cost of building destruction, lost days or years at work, the cost of crop destruction, and so on.

Travel information: what was the average time to travel from the door of one's house to the door of one's office (called the "portal-to-portal trip time")? Since any concerted attempt to deal with air pollution might well involve major alterations in the transportation system, we would want to know about the effects on travel time.

Health information: several measures of sickness and premature mortality would be useful; average decrease in life expectancy can be calculated and dramatizes the seriousness of the problem to a decision-maker.

Life style: a significant attack on air pollution would involve an effort to reduce average trip lengths by trying to move some of the population into high-density living quarters downtown from their ranch bungalows thirty to forty miles from city center (the average radius of the Denver metropolitan area in 1970 was thirty-eight miles). Thus, a policy-maker would need to know how committed the population was to the single-family ranch bungalow life style.

Metropolitan land area: legislators and planners analyzing air pollution decisions would quickly come to see that the total amount of land taken up by the metropolitan area was an important factor. All other things being equal, the total amount of driving and hence the total amount of pollution generated in the transportation sector tend to increase with city area.

The car: obviously, Americans are very attached to their cars. Cars do not just represent a means of transportation to many Americans: they are a source of freedom and privacy, security, and a symbol of social position and other themes not suitable for an environment textbook. Clearly, a politician wades into this quicksand with fear and care. Thus, comprehensive decision-making about pollution would include information about the local attachment to the car.

Note that this collection of disparate types of information has a number of important implications. Clearly, tradeoffs are involved. Reduction in pollution must be balanced off against the reduction in car use people are prepared to accept. Also, the various measures are of quite different kinds of things, and hence are in different units. We need some means of comparing and combining these different kinds of information.

We now have two problems to deal with. First, we want some common yardstick for dealing with measures of very different kinds of variables. But secondly, we need some precise way of expressing preferences, values, and judgements as to the appropriate values that should be taken by these various indices. In other words, when we manage the system to make it turn out a certain way in the year 2000, precisely what would be that preferred outcome, for each of the six indicators of interest? This is indicated by using *utility functions* that express the way each decision-maker feels about the relative attractiveness of various values of the indicator of interest, on a scale of 0.0 to 1.0.

Figure 18.1 illustrates how a particular politician might express his or her judgements about the state of Denver in the year 2000. While the numbers in this chart are hypothetical, they have been selected to be as realistic as possible. The first panel suggests that while we want to keep the cost of air pollution control as small as possible, our concern about increasing cost increases more rapidly at beyond $2 billion. The second panel indicates that the typical person is most reluctant to have the work-to-home trip take over 40 minutes. The third panel suggests that a decreased life expectancy of a few weeks might not mean much to most people, a decreased life expectancy of over 30 weeks would be regarded as very worth avoiding. The fourth panel expresses the fact that most people prefer a lot (house plus garden) of about 2000 square feet per family member (8000 square feet for a typical family). Less than this would be regarded as too confining, and more would be regarded as too much trouble to keep up. The fifth panel expresses the judgement that beyond 4000 square miles, increased size of the metropolitan area creates more problems than it solves. The sixth panel expresses the judgement that most people would want to have about 50 percent of all their intracity tripmiles occur in a private car. Below this implies too much sacrifice of privacy and convenience; above this, excessive use of the car creates excessive congestion and pollution problems.

Note that Figure 18.1 only describes how one decision-maker feels about the optimal set of characteristics for the city in the year 2000. Further, that person's full judgement is only expressed by the set of these curves, together with a set of weights that describe the relative importance the decision-maker attaches to each of these six indicators. The curve shapes together with the weights are referred to as a *value function* in decision analysis, or a *subsequent condition policy* in strategic judgement theory.

In the most elaborate applications, each of these types of decision theory can deal with a trajectory of indicators into the

FIGURE 18.1

Hypothetical utility functions for indicators of interest describing Denver (or Phoenix, San Diego, or another city) in the year 2000.

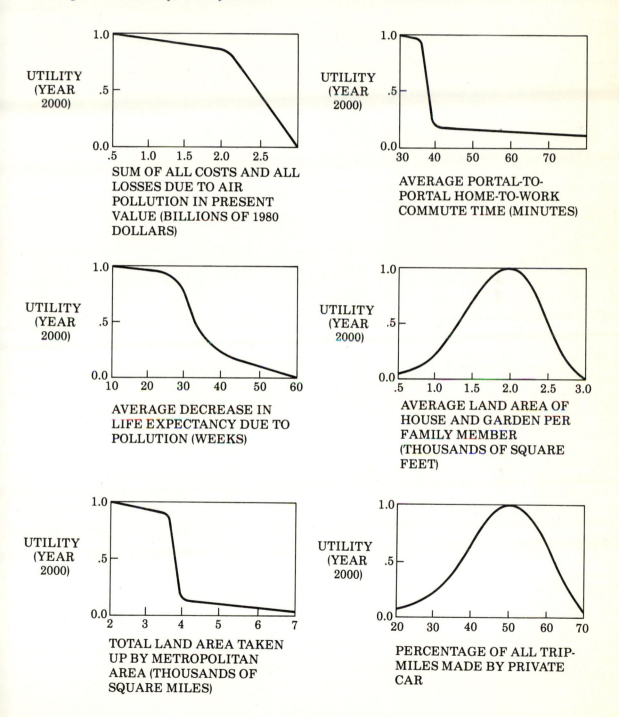

SUM OF ALL COSTS AND ALL LOSSES DUE TO AIR POLLUTION IN PRESENT VALUE (BILLIONS OF 1980 DOLLARS)

AVERAGE PORTAL-TO-PORTAL HOME-TO-WORK COMMUTE TIME (MINUTES)

AVERAGE DECREASE IN LIFE EXPECTANCY DUE TO POLLUTION (WEEKS)

AVERAGE LAND AREA OF HOUSE AND GARDEN PER FAMILY MEMBER (THOUSANDS OF SQUARE FEET)

TOTAL LAND AREA TAKEN UP BY METROPOLITAN AREA (THOUSANDS OF SQUARE MILES)

PERCENTAGE OF ALL TRIP-MILES MADE BY PRIVATE CAR

future. That is, the politician may want to decrease the percentage of all trip-miles made by car gradually, over a twenty-year period.

The goal of our analysis is to discover how to attain a state for Denver in 2000 that best matches the wishes of the electorate, as expressed in such sets of charts and weights developed by their representatives. To do this, we use an elaborate computer model to mimic the way Denver will change in response to various actions that might be taken to affect air pollution. The computer matches the responses against the desired response, and ranks sets of actions in order of their effectiveness in producing the desired response.

Describing What Actions We Can Take

However, just as we needed some objective quantitative means of expressing the desired state of Denver, we need an objective, quantitative means of expressing the sets of actions we might take. One term used to describe the mix of actions we might take (from strategic judgement theory) is *policy intervention package*. To illustrate the types of actions that might be included in such a package, consider the following partial list:

Expenditures on mass rail transit and buses.
Expenditures on freeways.
Restriction of the use of cars, by any or all of the following: state gasoline taxes, gas rationing, a limitation on the number of cars per family, heavy downtown parking fees, limitation on the area available for parking downtown.
Restriction of urban sprawl by down-zoning land at the urban periphery from urban classification to farm use classification.
Penalties and fines for polluting from either a moving or stationary source.

Discourage the use of single-family ranch bungalows, by restricting sales of land to developers, and the like.
Encourage construction and use of apartments and townhouses in the city center, for example, through tax breaks.

Just as the *value function* was created out of a set of utility functions and weights, so the *policy intervention package* would be defined in terms of a set of curve shapes for each of the separate actions and a set of weights.

Also, the sequence of decisions might extend through time, making a *decision tree* (decision analysis). Figure 18.2 illustrates the possible form of a decision tree. Three different options were available in 1980. For each of these selected, there are two options available in 1985. But after that, the tree is no longer symmetrical. Why? Selecting certain options in 1980 would make certain others unnecessary in 1990. For example, sharply increased gasoline prices in 1980 would make stringent land use controls against urban sprawl unnecessary in 1990: the double-edged sword of pollution control through regulation of gasoline and land would be excessive to obtain the desired reduction in pollution concentration.

The development of Denver with respect to pollution generation, as with the development of any large, complex system will be affected by three categories of factors: the policy intervention package; ever-present cause-effect relationships, such as in the free play of the market place with price determining use; and chance. Chance introduces uncertainty in the performance of Denver (or any other system), and that must be dealt with by *uncertainty analysis*. Figure 18.3 illustrates how we can deal with uncertainty. In this figure, the square denotes a decision node, as in the previous figure, but the circles denote chance nodes. This means that for given inputs, it is not certain what

FIGURE 18.2

Example of a decision tree, which comes about when the states created by prior decisions open up new subsequent alternative options, and further decisions, which lead to new states, and so on.

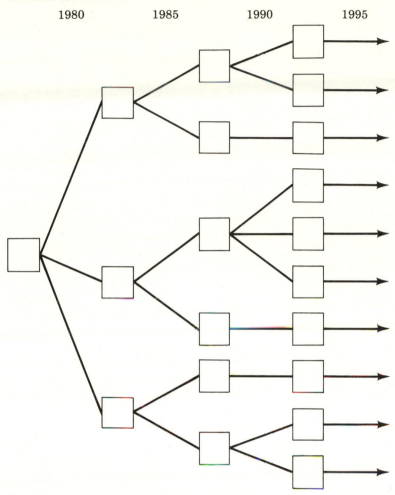

the outputs will be; several are possible. For example, for given sets of government regulations on gasoline use, parking, and land use, it is not certain how the population will respond. We can express this by trying to guess all possible outcomes and the probability of each. This "guessing" can be made quite scientific, either through statistical analysis of historical data, or by consulting with panels of experts for their judgements

as to what will happen and the probability of each possible outcome.

The major task in either decision analysis or strategic judgement theory is to develop a complex computer model that can be used to generate scenarios (detailed histories) of how a system develops into the future in response to policy intervention packages, cause-effect relationships, and chance. The cause-effect relationships incorporated into

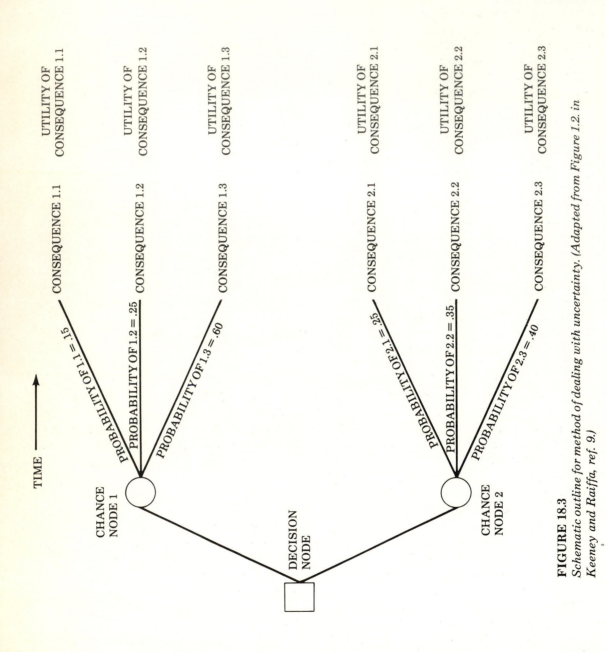

FIGURE 18.3
Schematic outline for method of dealing with uncertainty. (Adapted from Figure 1.2. in Keeney and Raiffa, ref. 9.)

the computer model comprise a set of equations that produce the state of the system in the second of a pair of years, given the state of the system in the first of the pair. Using such sets of equations, the model can generate the state of the system in the second year, from the state of the system in the first year, then the state of the system in the third year from the state of the system in the second year, and so on, stepping up the state of the system by one year each iteration (repetition) of the computation.

The policy intervention packages are evaluated by generating a complete scenario through to the year 2000 (or other terminating year) for each package. Then the packages are evaluated by ranking them with respect to the value function of the decision-maker (or legislature, or constituency, or electorate). The package producing the final state of the system closest to that desired is clearly the policy intervention package to choose.

Clearly, methods of this type constitute a powerful tool for finding the set of actions that will yield a future most like the future some person or group desires. However, what happens if several different groups want different futures? At that point we introduce a new problem, that of conflict resolution, to be dealt with later in this chapter.

BUILDING NOVEL POLICY-MAKING CAPABILITIES INTO INSTITUTIONS

Uncertainty was mentioned in the previous section. In fact, uncertainty will increasingly become a dominant characteristic of the environment in which all governments and corporations find themselves. This uncertainty results in a variety of ways from the increased pressure humanity is putting on the planet. If a country has used up all its cheap resources of a particular type (crude oil or bauxite, for example), then it must import these from other countries. But now the importing country is confronted with a novel source of uncertainty: the imports might cease without warning, for reasons of political or economic tension, weather, war, or terrorism. Indeed, there are many new sources of environmental uncertainty: we are becoming increasingly dependent on obtaining raw materials from deep ocean-bottom sources far out on the continental shelf, where the geology is insufficiently known for us to have an accurate idea of the probability of finding oil; the enormously complex systems of international trade and money flow are highly vulnerable to disruption because of weather and inflation (Chapters 9 and 10).

The intensity and variety of competing and conflicting demands for the same land or resources (water in the western states, for example) pose a new type of problem for government.

Building Resiliency into Organizations

How can our corporations and governmental agencies develop a rational response to all these sources of uncertainty? One research team has evolved a system for dealing with this problem, out of several years of experience with many different environmental planning tasks in several countries (6). The central concept of this team is that in order to cope effectively with uncertainty, organizations must take on the characteristic that allows natural systems to survive in the face of uncertainty: resilience. An organism or an organization has resilience when it is able to absorb, recuperate from, and bounce back to normal functioning after being subjected to an environmental perturbation. This perturbation might be anything from a sudden severe drop in temperature to a sudden large increase in the price of energy. The means of maintaining resilience seems to have at least two components: maintaining a quick-response adaptive capability, and making sure that future options are not being fore-closed.

The quick-response capacity is built into organizations by means of a series of work-shops, attended by a mix of analysts, admin-istrators, and field staff of the client organi-zation. These workshops last a week, in which the members of the client organiza-tion build a model containing all the ele-ments discussed in the previous section. Working with the model gives a preliminary notion of the way the system being managed by the organization will respond to various management strategies. It also suggests types of data that might usefully be gath-ered to make the model more realistic. After six months, the team is reassembled for another of these workshops at which the management model is refined and the conse-quences of additional management policies are discovered through simulation. The aim of such workshops is to build into the client organization the ability to develop an on-going program of model-building and simu-lation that affects policy, generates new data, and, finally, after several months, leads to a new round of modeling. In other words, the real-world management, the data resulting from monitoring the effects of management, and the modeling that takes the data as input and then suggests new management innovations, all enter into an operations loop. This continuous loop of activities is designed to ensure that the organization keeps very careful track of de-velopments in the most important indicator variables and responds quickly and appro-priately with management innovations to cope with any new circumstances in the managed system.

Avoiding foreclosure of options takes a great deal of thought about the future. One important strategy is to avoid spending so much of the capital and other resources of an organization on one particular way of deal-ing with future events, that there are inade-quate resources for development of other options, if the first option should fail for some reason. Thus, for example, a difficulty with the nuclear energy option is that it absorbs so much of the money in society that there is scarcely any left over for any other options. Thus, if the nuclear option should fail, no other options will be available on an adequate scale (10).

Other Strategies for Improving Organizations

Of course, many other things can be done to improve the capacity of governments to respond appropriately to new circum-stances. Common Cause, among other orga-nizations, has pointed out some of these. The performance of individual legislators and government bodies should be monitored closely, and "performance scorecards" on key votes should be made available to the electorate. There should be restrictions on lobbying and campaign contributions, to ensure that legislators are working for the public and not special interests. There should be much stricter regulation of the use of "security" and "secrecy" to withhold in-formation from the public. It is clear that in the past, the motive for keeping information secret has often been to serve the interests of particular individuals or groups in the government, rather than to serve the inter-ests of the public.

A most important innovation for dealing with complex environmental problems would be for governments at all levels to employ interdepartmental, interdisciplinary integrated systems modeling to evaluate alternate environmental management poli-cies. The precedent for such modeling was established in the federal government with the Global 2000 Study of 1977–1978. This was coordinated and managed by a team in the White House, but data and parts of models were supplied by thirteen different agencies.

Government has to increase the rewards for being successful at obtaining the final solution to a problem, relative to the risk for failure. Up to recently, the punishment for failure was so large relative to the reward for success, that daring innovation was actively suppressed.

REFORMING THE CONFLICT-RESOLUTION FUNCTION OF GOVERNMENT

In the discussion of strategic judgement theory and decision analysis, we did not deal with those instances where different constituencies are absolutely opposed to each other with respect to how some situation should be managed.

Simulation modeling refers to the use of computer games to mimic the behavior of a real world phenomenon. It can be used as a tool for turning stalemated controversies into consensus as to what ought to be done (1). Suppose nine different constituencies have an attitude toward the way in which their town is going to develop if there is no use of innovative policies to direct events. Each of these constituencies is asked to express its attitude toward the expected future situation in the form of a numerical rating, from −14 (most opposed) to +14 (most in favor). On the first vote, we find that constituencies 1, 5, and 9 are in favor of the likely future; the other six are opposed (Figure 18.4). Computer simulation modeling is then used to simulate what the town will be like in the future, in response to four different policies designed to have a favorable impact on the situation and turn stalemate into consensus. Then each of the nine

constituencies is asked to rate the attractiveness of each of the four sets of outcomes. Charts such as Figure 18.4 are used to record all the responses. Clearly, policy number 4 creates a consensus, none of the others do. Thus, policy number 4 would be adopted. This computer tool could be exploited by people specially trained to be "deal-makers" or arbitrators, as in the case of the great whales (Chapter 14).

Clearly, this discussion assumes that information is the appropriate tool to use in conflict resolution. Therefore, it is important that propaganda (biased information) by vested interests is not allowed to fill a void created by a lack of objective information coming from prospective "deal-makers."

Reforming the Regulatory Function of Government

The environmental movement of the late 1960s and the early 1970s made Americans concerned about the environment, at least temporarily. The ultimate outcome of this concern was the notion that government should protect the environment by means of environmental impact statements and regulations. But are impact statements and regulation by government the most appropriate way to safeguard the environment? Impact statements rarely address the real systemic implications of a new development. Thus, an impact statement will deal with the possible dangers of a new gasoline storage tank, when the most important issues concern the collective national implications of all such storage tanks. Also, few people are aware of the tremendous social cost of regulation: government attempts to regulate an activity may cost a significant percentage of the entire cost of the activity. The budget for the Federal Department of Energy was about 7 percent of the total amount received

FIGURE 18.4

Evaluations by a panel representing nine different consituencies of the state of a town in the future with no policy assistance, and under four different policies (adapted from reference 1). Reprinted with the permission of the copyright holder, Simulation Councils, Inc.

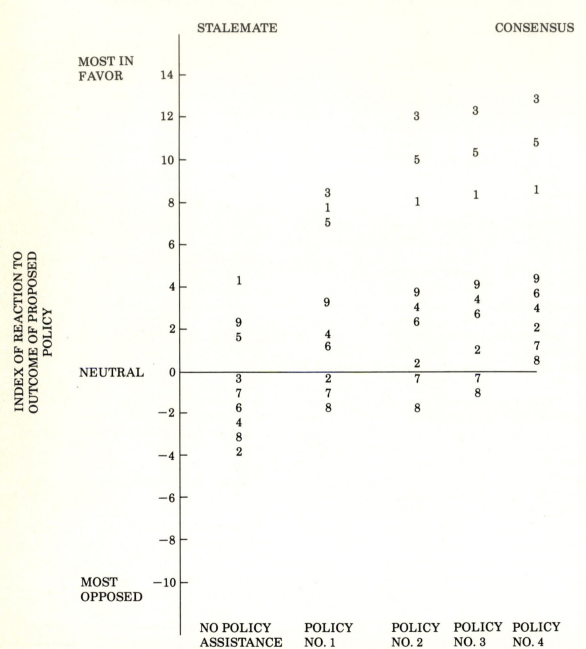

in the United States from the sale of all coal and oil products combined. But to this bill must be added the prorated costs of the amount of time spent by the White House staff, the Senate, and the House of Representatives on energy and the budgets for all state and local governments' efforts concerning energy.

Given that regulation is enormously costly, is it worth it? Indeed, is regulation by government the best way to achieve socially desirable effects? One part of the answer deals with the impacts of government regulation on technological innovation. Government in the United States virtually regulated the solar and wind energy businesses out of existence, by keeping energy prices down during the 1970s through regulation. It is noteworthy that governments in many other countries tried to elevate the retail price of gasoline while the U.S. government was trying to keep it down. Government not only provided a disincentive to the solar and wind energy industries by keeping energy prices down, it also discouraged the search for oil and gas in the United States and discouraged technological innovation in new materials and techniques of insulation and building design to conserve energy. Higher energy prices would have stimulated the conversion to a more efficient manufacturing plant in the United States. One of the reasons that nations such as Japan and West Germany provide such formidable competition to the United States in world markets for manufactured goods is that their national manufacturing plant is more modern, and energy efficient.

Obviously, an alternate approach to government regulation is to deregulate all energy and resource prices and allow the system to regulate itself through the free play of the market. The counterargument to this is that inequitable income distribution would result: the rich would get richer and the poor would get poorer. The answer to this is that regulation of energy prices is a very ineffective tool for ensuring equitable income distribution. Further, high energy prices are not so inequitable as they appear, if they are at all. In the first place, higher energy prices would discourage the replacement of expensive labor by cheap energy; more of the unskilled and semiskilled would be able to compete for jobs against mechanization and automation. Also, as indicated in Chapter 14, income distribution can be equitable where energy prices are much higher relative to labor costs than in the United States.

A NEW DESIGN FOR SOCIETY

Many students, perhaps a majority, decide that no amount of modification of existing institutions will solve the problems faced by modern society in coping with the environment. Their argument is that our farm operations, cities, governments, and corporations are all too big. They want to see decentralization instead of centralization, intermediate technology instead of large-scale, centralized technology (such as windmills instead of nuclear reactors), more compact, efficient cities, and in general, small-is-beautiful (11).

There are several ways of considering this issue. One way is to explore the implications of the price of energy for the spatial design of society. The specific hypothesis we pose is that more expensive energy will stimulate more compact cities. Accordingly, we consider a theory of the relationships between city area and density, average income, average cost of living, maximum possible city size, and the price of energy (Figure 18.5). The validity of this theory can be tested by examining data on U.S. metropolitan areas.

FIGURE 18.5

Graphic representation of a theory of the relationships between average income, aver-age cost of living, city density, city area, maximum possible city area, and the price of energy.

BEFORE INCREASE IN PRICE OF ENERGY

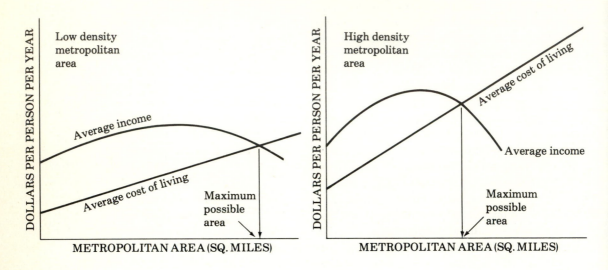

AFTER INCREASE IN PRICE OF ENERGY

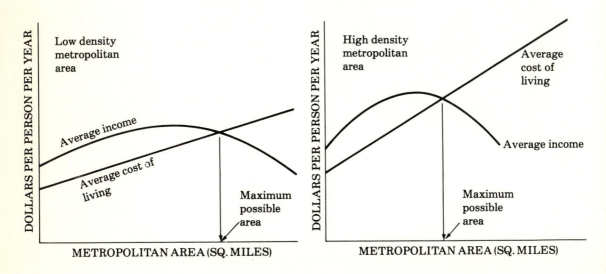

In Figure 18.5, we see that for any city density or energy price, average cost of living rises steadily with increasing city area. The reason for this, we postulate, is that larger city areas imply a greater average distance between randomly selected pairs of points (such as home and place of work), and this in turn implies a larger hidden energy cost overhead on transportation of all people and goods within the city. On the other hand, larger cities imply more opportunities for ways to derive income, up to some optimal area. Beyond this optimal area, incomes drop with increasing area because of the hidden social costs of integrating such a widespread system. Thus, the curves for average income as a function of area rise and then fall with increasing area.

The area at which the income and cost of living curves cross is the maximum possible metropolitan area that is economically viable. At any larger area, average income becomes lower than average cost of living. The figure displays low density graphs on the left side; high density city graphs are on the right. At high densities, incomes are higher for a given area, because there are more economic opportunities for the derivation of personal income per square mile. However, the cost of living curve rises more steeply, and the income curve peaks at a lower area than for low-density metropolitan areas. The reason is that because of the higher densities, decreased incomes, and increased costs occur at relatively low areas because of the great problems with congestion due to high traffic flow densities at high population densities.

Now what happens to either low or high density cities if the price of energy rises? Since this price is a component of the cost of living, the cost of living rises for all areas (the line shifts upwards in the two bottom graphs). Thus, the area at which the cost of living lines and the income lines cross shifts downward, and metropolitan areas must become more compact.

But what happens to the United States when the energy price goes up? Clearly, as this process continues, which it must because energy price increases are inevitable, we will discover that many American cities have areas too large and densities too low to be economically viable. The likely consequence is for densities to increase around centers of activity, which then will gradually become discrete towns as the intervening very low density areas gradually revert back to farmland or rural use. In other words, if this theory is correct, higher energy prices by themselves will produce decentralization, and smaller, more compact cities. But is there any evidence in support of the theory?

We conduct the test of this hypothesis in two parts. In the first part, we examine the relation between city areas and densities, and average income. As postulated in Figure 18.5, we discover that average incomes are in fact higher at higher densities. Also, at the highest and lowest densities we discover that income drops at the highest areas. Given the striking patterns revealed by such research, it is surprising that more people are not concerned about living in high density, compact cities!

Second, we can test the notion that the cost of living is affected by city densities and areas. We discover that based on the statistics for U.S. metropolitan areas, gasoline costs per person are lower in more dense cities; they rise as a function of area for high and low density cities; but they rise more steeply in high density cities as area increases. The one discrepancy between the data and Figure 18.5 is that gasoline costs are much lower for high density cities than low density cities. However, Figure 18.5 graphed the average cost of living due to all categories of costs, not just gasoline. Increases in other components of the cost of living in high density cities over low density cities would tend to cancel out the lowered gasoline cost.

At any rate, there does seem to be a basis in fact for Figure 18.5, and hence the notion that higher energy prices will imply a decrease in the economically viable maximum city areas. Decentralization seems inevitable.

However, apart from energy prices encouraging decentralization, there are a number of other forces at work in society that will encourage it and could be used to encourage it. As the use of income energies increases (solar and wind energy, or energy from new ocean technologies), it will be much cheaper for people to live close to the energy source, rather than far from it. Since these energy sources are diffuse, not concentrated, they will tend to produce a society with a diffuse, not concentrated pattern of spatial distribution. That is, of course, very different than the pattern of spatial distribution in the United States now.

Other factors that will have a bearing on centralization versus decentralization are utility rate structures and the design of taxation schemes. If the charge per unit of energy decreases as more units are used, then clearly there is a tremendous driving force behind centralization. This economy of scale will encourage big cities, big corporations, and big farms. On the other hand, if the costs of energy and water were to be higher per unit as more units were used, this would be a tremendous force for decentralization. As energy and water become scarcer relative to demand, such rate structure changes may occur, and the net effect will be to encourage decentralization.

Federal or state government can produce a tendency to either centralization or decentralization at will through taxation, zoning, and other means. For example, a very fast move towards smaller towns could be stimulated through lower federal and state taxes on people living in small towns.

Many students also feel that society should change in the direction of more local self-reliance and less coupling between the economic systems of different regions. This line of reasoning can lead to some surprising conclusions. For example, why should we export grains to pay for imported energy, then use some of the imported energy for tractor fuel to produce grain? Clearly all this international trade occurs because the United States is short of tractor fuel, but long on horse fuel (grains). Wouldn't it make sense, then, to farm with horses and avoid some of this international trade? Certainly, at least for small, hilly farms, it would have a dramatic impact on the economics of farming (8). One reason farmers are in such financial trouble is that their inputs, including fuel, are more expensive than their outputs (food) in some years. By farming with horses, farmers would have more control over the cost of their inputs. But even more important, they would surmount the problem of uncertain supply of the inputs. Another O.P.E.C. embargo would not cut off farmers' supplies of tractor fuel.

In short, quite apart from the fact that all our large institutions are becoming unwieldy and inefficient, there are many reasons why decentralization is both desirable and likely for the future.

A variety of institutional changes would promote a new, decentralized pattern of city location and land use for America. One set of proposals include legislation that would permit individuals to lease, at no cost, tracts of publicly held land provided they would make their home on it. The leases would be renewed indefinitely if some part of the land were cultivated. Up to two million people could be accommodated this way, simply in unused and abandoned military bases (12).

Another proposal in this same set is to sell publicly owned, abandoned city dwellings to families for a low price, in exchange for the new owner's agreement to bring the building up to city codes within 18 months and occupy it for at least five years (12). To illustrate the potential for such an idea, in 1975 about 30,000 buildings were abandoned in New York City alone. Many of our old cities contain large tracts of unused buildings that are still structurally sound. A National Conurbation Act could develop a regional pattern of distinct cities and towns; designed as no-growth entities, they would include farms and open space (12).

Another idea for altering land use patterns is for a group of like-minded people to buy up parcels of land they want to keep in perpetuity for particular types of land use. We already have precedent for this in the retirement village, condominiums, private holiday resorts, and so on. Thus, if a group of people wishes to preserve a natural area for hiking, they could buy it collectively.

An idea that has appeared recently is for the federal government to stop the ruin of areas such as Lake Tahoe by buying up land on the Nevada side of the lake, which is planned for more casinos, among other uses, using money obtained by selling federal land around Las Vegas (7). The suggested strategy is for the federal government to sell to private buyers land throughout the United States that is not particularly scenic, then use the money to preserve land that is particularly scenic, buying it back from private owners.

AN INSTITUTIONAL INNOVATION TO ENCOURAGE WISE USE OF THE ENVIRONMENT

At present, the principal means of dealing with large-scale problems in America is through federal government agencies. However, more and more writers are pointing out that such Departments as Energy, Housing and Urban Development, and Transport among many others have four problems: they are very large and expensive; they are very inefficient; they impose an immense regulatory burden on society that stifles innovation and individual initiative; and they do not seem to show rapid progress in ameliorating the problems they are designed to solve. They also have a pronounced tendency to be vulnerable to capture by special interests that thwart their realization of their supposed goals.

It is surprising that it has not been widely noticed that there is another institutional mechanism for dealing with social problems. There is a group of private organizations in the United States that publish magazines offering advice to consumers, and operate independent product testing laboratories —Consumers Union and a number of organizations that publish magazines evaluating photographic equipment, high-fidelity equipment, records, tapes, and books are examples. These organizations give excellent value for the money, do not impose any regulatory burden on society (one is free to buy or not buy the magazines, accept or reject the advice), and are absolutely invulnerable to seizure by special interests, because the only thing they have to sell is credibility, which they protect with extreme care.

This institutional model could be extended considerably. For example, private magazines linked with testing laboratories and field crews could ask places of work for permission to measure or continuously monitor places of work, nuclear plants, waste disposal sites, wilderness camp grounds, and the like. They could also monitor air and water pollution; waste disposal; building safety; and vulnerability to risk at airports, in airlines and particular models of planes, and in ships. If permission to make the measurements or do the monitoring was denied, that fact would simply be published. The results of all such testing and monitoring would routinely be published in magazines. No one would be forced to buy the magazines. People who wished to avoid danger or risk could do so by operating on the basis of the advice in the magazines. There would be no regulatory burden, and all compliance would be optional. This mechanism does not discriminate against the poor, because all such magazines are found in all large libraries.

This approach seems to make more sense as a means of improving the environment than the present approach, which is extremely costly, burdensome, and ineffective. The proposed approach makes more sense in terms of human nature, as noted at the end of Chapter 12.

SUMMARY

Changes in the environment will necessitate three types of responses from people and their institutions. First, existing institutions will have to make use of new techniques for planning and resolving conflicts. Secondly, society will have to decentralize government, corporations, cities, and farms. Finally, all institutions will work better if the belief systems of the culture change, but circumstances are likely to bring about the required change, in any case.

SUGGESTIONS FOR INDIVIDUAL AND GROUP PROJECTS

Complete the example on page 391. Develop utility functions for each of the constituents of the policy intervention package. These functions should be based on the same type of reasoning that went into the utility functions of Figure 18.1. Now how would you attach weights to each of these actions expressing their relative attractiveness to you? How would you expect trajectories of these actions to be expressed by changes in the shape of the utility functions through the next fifty years?

Develop an analysis of this type for an environmental problem of concern in the city or state where you live.

REFERENCES

1. Ford, A., "Policy simulation for boom towns," in *Simulation of energy systems,* Part 1, ed. K. E. F. Watt, pp. 87–94. Simulation Councils Proc. Series Vol. 8, No. 1., 1978.

2. Hammond, K. R., "Toward increasing competence of thought in public policy formation," in *Judgment and Decision in Public Policy Formation,* K. R. Hammond, ed., pp. 11–32. Boulder, Colorado: Westview Press, 1978.

3. Hammond, K. R.; J. K. Klitz; and R. L. Cook, *How Systems Analysts Can Provide More Effective Assistance to the Policy Maker.* Laxenburg, Austria: International Institute for Applied Systems Analysis, Research Memorandum RM-77-50, 1977.

4. Hammond, K. R.; J. Rohrbaugh; J. Mumpower; and L. Adelman, "Social judgment theory: applications in policy formation," in *Human Judgment and Decision Processes in Applied Settings,* M. F. Kaplan and S. Schwartz, eds., pp. 1–27. New York: Academic Press, 1975.

5. Hammond, K. R.; T. R. Stewart; B. Brehmer; and D. O. Steinmann, "Social judgment theory," in *Human Judgment and Decision Processes,* M. F. Kaplan and S. Schwartz, eds., pp. 271–312. New York: Academic Press, 1975.

6. Holling, C. S., ed., *Adaptive Environmental Assessment and Management.* New York: Wiley, 1978.

7. Irving, C., "A plan to sell Las Vegas land and use money to save Tahoe," *San Francisco Sunday Examiner and Chronicle,* p. 10, Section A, Sept. 30, 1979.

8. Johnson, W. A.; V. Stoltzfus; and P. Craumer, "Energy conservation in Amish agriculture," *Science,* 198 (1977), p. 373.

9. Keeney, R. L., and H. Raiffa, *Decisions with Multiple Objectives: Preferences and Value Tradeoffs*. New York: Wiley, 1976.

10. Lovins, A. B., *Soft Energy Paths*. Cambridge, Mass.: Ballinger, 1977.

11. Schumacher, E. F., *Small is Beautiful*. New York: Harper and Row, 1973.

12. Steinhart, J. S., and six others. *Pathway to Energy Sufficiency: The 2050 Study*. San Francisco: Friends of the Earth, 1979.

VI The Future
And What the Individual
Can Do About It

We have now examined how the environmental system works, why it can work badly, and what could be done to effect improvement.

Now what about the future? Chapter 19 explains that in order to understand how the future could turn out, we have to identify and measure trends in the principal driving forces that have determined the past. Then by extrapolating trends in those forces, we can see how they must affect the future.

No amount of science can predict the future with precision. However, science can be used to show how present decisions will influence the future. Therefore, the value in scientific study of the future is that it shows us how to work backward from a future we would like to the present decisions that are most likely to produce that desired state.

This chapter introduces the notion that the world is not like a game or team sport in which all the players operate under the same rules. Different nations can have different goals and rules, and this will be increasingly important in shaping each country's destiny, as more and more countries deplete their resources and become dependent on international trade with other countries.

19 THE ENVIRONMENT IN THE FUTURE

Although I have often foretold long before what hath afterwards come to pass, and in particular regions, acknowledging all to have been done by divine virtue and inspiration, I was willing to hold my peace by reason of the injury—not only of the present time, but also of the future—because to put them in writing, the Kingdoms, Sects, and Regions shall be so diametrically opposed, that if I should relate what will happen hereafter, those of the present Reign, Sect, Religion and Faith, would find it so disagreeing with their fancies, that they would condemn that which future ages shall find and know to be true.

Michael Nostradamus, preface to the first edition of The True Prophecies *or* Prognostications, *March 1, 1555.*

MAIN THEMES OF THIS CHAPTER

While the future cannot be predicted in detail, it is possible to identify and project certain basic driving forces that will have a powerful and pervasive impact on the socio-economic-environmental system in the future. Trends in population size and availability and price of energy, minerals, land, and wood will have a profound shaping effect on all aspects of social existence, including city design, the economy, government, and culture.

It is inevitable that America will be very different by the beginning of the next century, with a cultural commitment to efficiency as a primary characteristic, as opposed to the present commitment to intense resource exploitation. However, there are two different tracks by which we could get there. One trajectory is through a trauma-free, gradual transition resulting from timely planning and preparation. The other path leads through an abrupt, painful discontinuity resulting from procrastination in making necessary and comprehensive adjustments to resource scarcity.

Increasingly, the fate of people in all countries will result from the interplay between the strategies of different nations and groups of nations. This introduces a major complication into projections of the future, because not all nations have similar goals. Increasingly, one nation, such as the United States, will find that another nation operates in a fashion that makes no sense in terms of our world view, just as our world view makes no sense to certain other nations.

A more and more common feature of life in the future will be that other nations will not wish to sell us raw materials in the quantities that we would like to purchase. This will be one of the most important single constraints on our national destiny.

INTRODUCTION AND OVERVIEW: THE LIMITS TO KNOWLEDGE OF THE FUTURE

Three types of forces will operate to shape our future environment.

The first type includes powerful, underlying driving forces that shape the fundamental character of socioeconomic-environmental life in any country at any time; population size and the availability and price of critical resources are of paramount importance (2, 10, 20, 21, 22, 23). These forces tend to increase or decrease in a continuous fashion over very long periods of time. Breaks or discontinuities involving sudden changes in direction of these forces are of critical importance, but often can be predicted rather accurately. Thus, for example, M. King Hubbert predicted in 1962 that U.S. domestic crude oil production would

peak about 1967; it peaked in 1970 and many discontinuities resulted from this (12).

The second type of determinant of the future consists of chance events (statistical "Acts of God") that cannot be predicted or managed, and that can modify the operation of the driving forces. Examples are major volcanic eruption that alters world climate, an unexpected outbreak of an extremely virulent infectious disease, or a completely unexpected technological breakthrough.

The third type of force shaping the future will be changes in the cultural belief system and government policy changes resulting from the beliefs (8). This type of shaping force may have limited impact on the end result of societal adjustment, but can have a major impact on the timing of events prior to that result. For example, the shift to a more energy-efficient society is inevitable, because of higher prices for energy from any presently imaginable source. However, culture and resultant government policy will determine if the shift comes earlier in a gradual smooth transition or if procrastination in making necessary social adjustments will result in a tardy, abrupt, and traumatic transition.

We are limited in the extent to which we can predict the future because of our inability to predict the second and third types of driving forces. However, by doing research on the forces shaping the future and publicizing the findings, we can influence the cultural belief system and deal with the third type of force to some extent. Suppose we could build complex and realistic computer or other types of models showing how future consequences were causally produced by various alternative present policies (21, 23, 24, 27). Such research could be introduced into the political and policy-making arena and used as a guide to selection of policies that produced the most attractive future. If this attempt were successful, research on the future would have become a driving force for shaping the future.

LOOKING AT THE DRIVING FORCES

Some examples will clarify the preceding generalizations.

The four panels of Figure 19.1 illustrate the types of trends characteristic of the first type of driving forces that shape society: smooth, gradual trends over long periods of time, with sudden major discontinuities signifying a major change in the behavior of the social system. Panels 1 and 2 show a large part of the explanation for increasing affluence in the United States up to 1972: the value of labor increased steadily relative to the wholesale prices of energy and metals, meaning that the average person could buy more energy or metals with an hour of labor. However, after 1972, the wholesale prices of fuels and metals began to increase much more rapidly than labor. This happened because the wholesale price of these commodities began to reflect the sharply increased cost of extracting geological materials in the United States, as revealed in Figure 4.4, only with a lag of seven years (extraction costs for energy began to rise sharply after 1965).

The sharp increase in farmland value relative to labor costs that began in 1956 reflects two phenomena: after 1955 it was no longer possible to compensate for population increase in the United States by increasing the acreage of prime farmland under cultivation; and a tremendous increase in exports of agricultural commodities from the United States began in 1972, associated with the need to balance our international trade accounts, particularly because of massive importation of foreign crude oil. The surprising cyclical pattern of wood costs relative to labor costs revealed by Panel 4 is associated with a long cycle in supply/demand trends in residential housing construction. Overbuilding of houses in the 1920s raised wood prices; underbuilding in the 1930s and 1940s depressed wood prices.

In summary, the overall character of the economy and the environment in the United States up to 1955 was determined by superabundance of energy, minerals, farmland, and wood relative to population, which translated into a tidal wave of rising affluence. Since then, our lucky self-sufficiency in one resource after another has come to an end. As we move into the next two decades, the character of life will increasingly be determined by a decrease in resource availability relative to population and consequently, an increase in the general level of resource prices (17). This situation offers us some important and very clear-cut choices.

Figure 19.2 is one means of depicting simply and forcefully the consequences of taking two different options. In this figure, which is based on the first panel of Figure 19.1, the solid lines express the trend in actual and projected likely ratios of wholesale energy prices to labor costs. The dotted lines indicate popular perceptions of the situation.

In the top panel, the United States continues along the track begun around 1974, in which the country pretends that cheap domestic energy is still available in the quantities necessary to meet domestic demand. Instead of responding to domestic energy shortages by becoming more energy-efficient, the country pretends that there is no need for that, keeps retail prices of energy down by government regulation, imports energy on a massive scale, and maintains the appearance of economic health in the face of this by compensating for money outflows by increasing the supply of United States money (inflation). For a long time, there is a serious discrepancy between the popular image of reality and the actuality, resulting in enormous financial and, hence, psychological stress on people as they borrow more and more money to maintain the standard of living that the popular perception holds to be appropriate and realistic.

FIGURE 19.1

Examples of long-term trends in underlying driving forces shaping socioeconomic-environmental systems in the United States. Panel 1: Trend in U.S. average compensation for one hour of labor relative to wholesale fuel price index. Panel 2: Trend in U.S. average compensation for one hour of labor relative to wholesale metal price index. Panel 3: Trend in U.S. average compensation for one hour of labor relative to cost of farmland.

1
LABOR COST RELATIVE TO
WHOLESALE FUEL PRICE
(UNITED STATES AVERAGES)

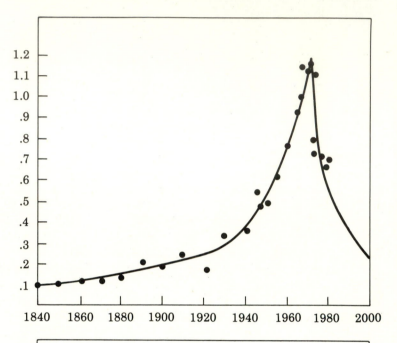

2
LABOR COST RELATIVE TO
WHOLESALE METAL PRICE
(UNITED STATES AVERAGES)

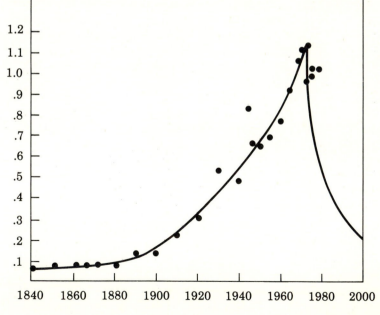

FIGURE 19.1 (cont.)

Panel 4: Trend in U.S. average compensation for one hour of labor relative to wholesale lumber and wood products price index. The trends in these ratios are significant because they determine the rate at which the cheaper of two resources will be substituted for the more expensive. In each case, the numerators and denominators in the ratios were indices (usually compiled by the government) expressing national average value for the variable, relative to its value in a base year (1967).

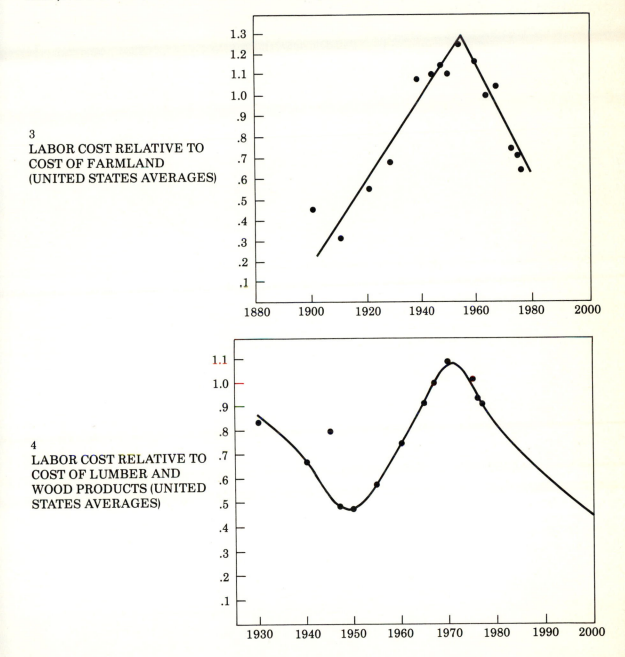

3
LABOR COST RELATIVE TO
COST OF FARMLAND
(UNITED STATES AVERAGES)

4
LABOR COST RELATIVE TO
COST OF LUMBER AND
WOOD PRODUCTS (UNITED
STATES AVERAGES)

FIGURE 19.2
Two scenarios of the future, defined in terms of the realism of popular perceptions of the value of labor relative to the wholesale price of energy. The dotted lines reflect perceptions of the trend in relative prices or values, the solid lines reflect the actuality. The top panel describes an unrealistic popular perception, in which people try to compensate for inflation by borrowing. In the bottom panel, people are depicted as realistic, and hence frugal, technologically innovative in the interests of efficiency, and more mentally healthy, because of absence of stress due to image being separated from reality.

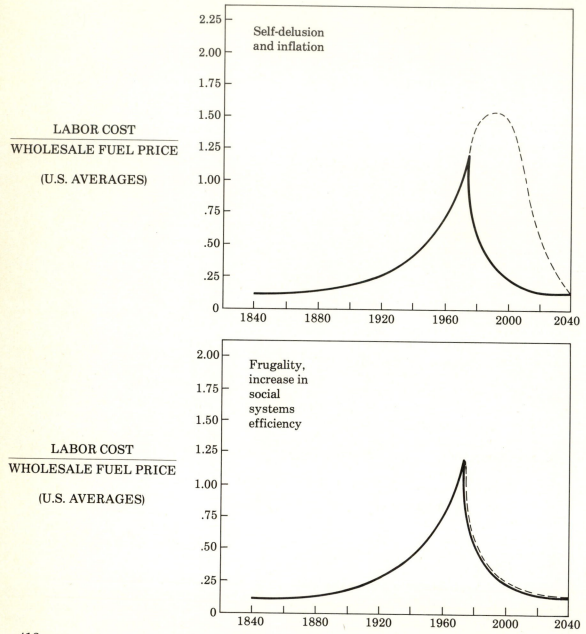

In the bottom panel, there is a rapid shift to a more energy-efficient society, with more efficient cars, more public transportation, more compact city design, better insulation, solar heating of homes, and living closer to work. This scenario differs significantly from the preceding one in that the popular image of reality tracks reality exactly. One would expect the mental health of the average person to be much higher in the second scenario. Indeed, one way of defining the level of mental health is "the degree to which the perception of reality accurately reflects reality."

THE IMPACT OF GEOPOLITICAL COMPETITION BETWEEN GROUPS OF NATIONS ON THE FUTURE

This book has already pointed out the central importance of crude oil importation into the United States from other countries. In order to make realistic projections of the amount of crude oil the country will be able to import in the future, it is now necessary to consider the decision rules about exporting crude oil that would likely be of paramount importance to the oil-exporting nations. What kinds of considerations would appear to be most important to these nations, in determining how much crude oil they export each year? Six factors seem of most importance; the strategic goal should be to select the optimal rate of export that best satisfies all six.

1. Oil-exporting nations clearly wish to maximize the present value of all future income obtained from selling the crude oil they own. This rather simple-sounding concept is in fact quite complex. We can explain the various complexities in terms of a simple formula:

Present value of all crude oil ever sold, from 1979 to the last year it lasts =

$$\sum_{t=1979}^{t=t_{last}} \left[\frac{\left(\begin{array}{c}\text{price per}\\\text{barrel in}\\\text{year } t\end{array}\right)\left(\begin{array}{c}\text{number of}\\\text{barrels sold}\\\text{in } t\end{array}\right)}{(1+r)^t} \right]$$

The Greek capital sigma means "the sum of all such terms as the following." The r in the denominator is the interest rate on borrowed capital. The significance of the denominator term is that all things being equal, we would always like to sell a barrel of crude oil sooner rather than later. The reason is that if we sell a barrel now instead of five years from now, we have five years in which to invest and draw interest on the proceeds from the sale that we otherwise would not have. The higher the interest rate, the more valuable it is to sell now rather than later. Putting it differently, high inflation rates, which result in high interest rates, tend to encourage high rates of resource depletion. Another complication is that the currency of a nation buying crude oil (such as the United States) may be dropping in value more rapidly than other measures of value (such as gold, Swiss francs, German marks, or Japanese yen). This problem can be dealt with as illustrated in Table 19.1. The nation selling crude oil will simply raise the price to compensate for the drop in the value of the currency of the purchasing nation. The selling nation could compute how much to charge by ensuring that the oil is being sold for a constant amount of gold (13). Thus, as the dollar is worth less gold, it takes more dollars to buy the barrel of crude oil. Notice that for the last eleven years, a barrel of crude oil has tended to be priced at about 6 or 7 percent of an ounce of gold.

Another complication implied by the present value formula is that there are two alternate strategies a selling nation can use to increase the present value.

TABLE 19.1

Adjustments in the price of crude oil sold by foreign nations to the United States to compensate for decrease in the value of the dollar relative to an ounce of gold.

Year	Price of one ounce of gold, in U.S. dollars	Price of one barrel of crude petroleum imported into the United States, in U.S. dollars	The cost of one barrel of crude petroleum, in ounces of gold
1970	36.37	2.30	.063
1973	97.79	3.41	.035
1974	159.72	11.11	.070
1980	606.00	28.00	.046
1981	462.00	35.00	.076

One approach is to sell all the barrels as quickly as possible, thus minimizing the effect of the denominator term $(1 + r)^t$, which obviously increases in value rapidly with increasing t. A quite different approach is to hold barrels of crude oil off the market, thus creating a shortage of supply relative to demand and driving up the price. This can be an effective strategy, if there is a tightly organized cartel of selling nations, as in the case of O.P.E.C.

2. The O.P.E.C. nations could also recognize that time is a resource and try to make their crude oil last as long as possible in order to buy the time necessary to convert totally to a post-fossil-fuel economy (solar, wind, or fusion nuclear power; the time required for this conversion would be between thirty and fifty years).

3. O.P.E.C. nations don't want to increase oil income so rapidly as to subject their nations to the type of socio-political-economic upheaval that follows from excessive rates of modernization (as in Iran in 1978–1979).

4. O.P.E.C. nations would also want to avoid increasing oil prices so fast as to either destroy the economies that buy the oil from them or to invite a military response from those countries.

5. O.P.E.C. nations would also wish to avoid increasing their prices so slowly as to provoke hostility from other O.P.E.C. nations or internal rebellion.

6. Recognizing that culturally and politically healthy societies are most likely to evolve in a stable economic environment, O.P.E.C. nations are likely to want to avoid violent increases or decreases in the amount of money they receive from the sale of crude oil. This could result from either violent price per unit fluctuations or abrupt increases or decreases in the amount sold.

Given the complexity of the problem of picking the best strategy for arriving at the trajectory of sales volumes, year by year, it is reasonable to assume that the O.P.E.C. countries would use computers to simulate the consequences of various decision rules. The objective would be to pick the strategy that gave the highest present value from the complete sequence of sales years, consistent with the other strategic objectives.

When they assessed their situation, the O.P.E.C. countries would discover that by cutting back on production some time after 1982, they would create a world shortage of crude oil supply relative to demand, and this would drive the price up enough to compensate for the smaller amount sold. It is known now that some time between 1982 and 1990, world demand for crude oil will probably not be met by supply (9). This will happen either because the O.P.E.C. countries decide voluntarily to cut back on production, or alternatively, because limitation of their reserves forces them to cut back on pumping rate. A rule of thumb in petroleum production is that no more than 10 percent of reserves should be pumped in a year. If more is pumped, this can decrease the ultimate amount recovered from the oilfield.

Further, it is realistic to project that if there is no further increase in collective O.P.E.C. crude oil production after 1982, the price per barrel will rise by at least 2.8 percent per year in constant dollars (which implies a far faster rise in inflated, or current, dollars). This rate of rise would just compensate O.P.E.C. for the sales lost through curtailment of pumping. In other words, increased price per unit would be used to compensate for decreased growth in number of units sold. Indeed, a 2.8 percent annual real increase is a very conservative assumption. To illustrate the magnitude of price rises that are possible now in physical commodities, farm real estate in the United States rose by 13.5 percent a year, a much higher rate of increase than the overall inflation rate. This suggests that we are now in a period when we can expect to see rapid price increases in raw commodities for which demand constantly increases relative to supply, on average, year after year.

This is a most significant finding. If it is true that the response to limitation in O.P.E.C. production will be a compensatory price increase per barrel, then after 1980, O.P.E.C. countries will have no motive to increase production. They will make just as much money selling a smaller amount of crude oil as they would make selling a larger amount. Indeed, given that after 1980, non-O.P.E.C. countries will collectively find it virtually impossible to meet their own increase in demand for crude oil by increasing their own production, it would be in the interests of O.P.E.C. to limit production to the lowest possible level consistent with objectives 4 (provoking attack) and 5 (hostility from other nations or internal rebellion) in their list of presumed goals. As production decreases, the price per unit is likely to increase.

Clearly, in trying to project the future, a different light is shed on a situation involving various political interest groups, if we try to understand the decision processes of the other political actors, as well as our own (16). In this instance, if we think about world trade in crude oil strictly from the point of view of a nation that is a net importer, it seems true that the exporter would want to sell us the oil as fast as we wanted to buy it. However, from the standpoint of an oil-exporting nation, the optimal strategy is to limit production whenever we are incapable of providing an equally cheap substitute.

SUMMARY

The shape of the future will be determined by the operation of certain basic driving forces, just as the past has been. The underlying principle is that society will always use the cheapest means available to achieve any given objective. That means that among broad categories of inputs, such as labor, energy, minerals, land, wood, and capital, there will be substitutions of one for the other, with the cheapest replacing the most expensive. Further, within any category, such as energy, the cheapest form will replace the most expensive.

Imported crude oil is still the cheapest source of energy, and that is why we still use it so much. However, with closer and closer approach to depletion, the character of society will change radically as new forms of energy come on stream. All of these will be much more expensive, so there will be tremendous economic pressure to conserve.

The most recent available evidence suggests that nuclear power will not spread as predicted; it is simply too expensive. Solar energy (solar to thermal heating, and solar to electric) will become widespread, because they are cheap relative to the options. With increasing frequency, major technical advances and cost decreases in solar technology will be announced.

Perhaps the most basic message in this chapter is that the future will be very surprising. Events have been following a variety of trends for several centuries; around 1973, we reached a major historical discontinuity, although still, few people really grasp that. We are moving into a new world with respect not only to resource availability, technology, and prices, but also to the relative power of nations. The old, comfortable assumption that the United States could have anything in the world it wanted is no longer true. Not only can we no longer afford all that we would like; some nations would not see fit to sell us certain commodities even if we could afford them. They simply have different attitudes than we do about the relative value of present and future benefits.

For all these reasons, we can no longer afford to follow one foot after the other, blindly, into tomorrow. Hopefully, readers of this book will have come to perceive the need for present decisions based on careful evaluation of their future consequences.

SUGGESTIONS FOR INDIVIDUAL AND GROUP PROJECTS

Invent your own list of the fundamental driving forces operating to shape the character of nations and civilizations in the past, at the present, and in the future. Did you discover any not mentioned in this chapter?

Take one important decision for modern America, and develop scenarios to explore all the consequences of each of the various policy options that might be selected.

Can you think of a new way to improve the technique by which society makes policy selections on important matters?

Figure out what type of environment you would like to have when you are fifty years old, and work backwards to determine the policies that must be selected now to get that type of environment.

REFERENCES

1. Boughey, A. S., Strategy for survival. Menlo Park, Calif.: W. A. Benjamin, 1976.
2. Brewer, J. W.; K. E. F. Watt; J. W. Young; J. L. Mitchiner; C. Ayers; and Y. L. Hunter, "Simulation of energy flow and land use: Speculater 1975," *Simulation Today*, 40 (1976), pp. 157–160.
3. Clark, J., and S. Cole, *Global Simulation Models: A Comparative Survey*. London: Wiley, 1975.
4. Cornish, E., *The Study of the Future*. Washington, D.C.: World Future Society, 1977.
5. Cundiff, W., *Modeled World Futures: Aspects of a Cybernetic Approach to World Order*. Ontario, Canada: York University, 1977.
6. Daly, H. E., *Toward a Steady-State Economy*. San Francisco: W. H. Freeman, 1973.
7. Dix, S. M., *Energy: A Critical Decision for the United States Economy*. Grand Rapids, Michigan: Energy Education Publishers, 1977.
8. Elgin, D. S.; D. C. MacMichael; and P. Schwartz, *Alternative Futures for Environmental Policy Planning: 1975-2000*. Washington D.C.: U.S. Government Printing Office, 1975.
9. Flower, A. R., "World oil production," Scientific American, March, 1978, pp. 42–49.
10. Forrester, J. W., *World Dynamics*. Cambridge, Mass.: Wright-Allen Press, 1971.
11. Greenberger, M.; M. A. Crenson; and B. L. Crissey, *Models in the Policy Process*. New York: Russell Sage Foundation, 1976.

12. Hubbert, M. K., *Energy Resources: A Report to the Committee on Natural Resources.* Washington, D. C.: National Academy of Science—National Research Council Publ. 1000-D, 1962.

13. Jastram, R. W., *Golden Constant: The English and American Experience, 1560–1976.* New York: Wiley-Interscience, 1977.

14. Kahn, H., and B. Bruce-Briggs, *Things to Come. Thinking about the 70's and 80's.* New York: Macmillan, 1972.

15. Klein, L. R., and E. Burmeister, *Econometric Model Performance. Comparative Simulation Studies of the U.S. Economy.* Philadelphia: University of Pennsylvania Press, 1975.

16. Laszlo, E., *Goals for Mankind.* New York: E.P. Dutton, 1977.

17. Lovins, A. B., *Soft Energy Paths.* San Francisco: Friends of the Earth International, 1977.

18. Macrae, N. "The coming entrepreneurial revolution: a survey," *The Economist,* December 25, 1976, pp. 41–65.

19. Mar, B., *Environmental Modelling and Decision Making. The United States Experience.* New York: Praeger, 1976.

20. Mass, N. J., *Economic Cycles: An Analysis of Underlying Causes.* Cambridge, Mass.: Wright-Allen Press, 1975.

21. Meadows, D. L.; W. W. Behrens III; D. H. Meadows; R. F. Naill; J. Randers; and E. K. O. Zahn, *Dynamics of Growth in a Finite World.* Cambridge, Mass.: Wright-Allen Press, 1974.

22. Meadows, D. H.; D. L. Meadows; J. Randers; and W. W. Behrens III, *Limits to Growth.* New York: Universe Books, 1972.

23. Mesarovic, M., and E. Pestel, *Mankind at the Turning Point.* New York: E. P. Dutton, 1974.

24. Naill, R. F., *Managing the Energy Transition.* Cambridge, Mass.: Ballinger, 1977.

25. Warfield, J. N., *Societal Systems: Planning, Policy, and Complexity.* New York: Wiley-Interscience, 1976.

26. Watt, K. E. F., *The Titanic Effect. Planning for the Unthinkable.* Sunderland, Mass.: Sinauer Associates, 1974.

27. Watt, K. E. F.; J. W. Young; J. L. Mitchiner; and J. W. Brewer, "A simulation of the use of energy and land at the national level," *Simulation,* 1975, pp. 129–153.

GLOSSARY

Biomass: the total mass of living tissue in a population or a community.

Birth rate: the number of offspring born per female per unit time. In human beings, typically expressed as the number of births per thousand women per year.

Carrying capacity: the number of organisms of a particular species that can be supported in a particular habitat under average conditions there. Thus, the carrying capacity of this planet for people is the number of people earth can support under average climatic conditions.

Class action: a civil legal action against a defendant on behalf of all the members of a class of people who are allegedly wronged.

Common property resource: a resource of which no one has legal ownership.

Community: a set of species that interact with each other.

Competition: diminution of birth, survival, or growth rates because two or more individuals or populations in the same locality have a common need for a resource in limited supply, and insufficient for the needs of all competitors.

Counterintuitive behavior: the type of behavior in any system that violates our common-sense expectations of how the system ought to behave.

Cumulative discoveries: cumulative production plus proved reserves of any non-renewable resource, such as crude oil.

Death rate: in humans, usually expressed as number of deaths per 1000 people per year.

418

Demographic transition: a conversion from high birth and death rates to low birth and death rates; death rates drop first.

Economic growth rate: various definitions are used. The least revealing, "annual rate of growth in gross national product in current dollars," adjusts for neither decreased purchasing power of money nor population increase. Therefore, a more revealing definition is "annual rate of growth in gross national product per person, in constant (deflated) dollars."

Economies of scale: lowered cost of producing an average unit obtained by spreading production costs over a large number of units.

Ecosystem: a community, together with the energy that cascades through it, the matter that cycles through it, and all associated storages of matter and energy (such as leaf litter on the forest floor).

Emergent properties: characteristics of higher levels of organization that are not simply the sum of characteristics in lower levels.

Eutrophication: nutrient enrichment of natural waters, typically followed by a dense growth of algae.

Exponential growth: a rate of growth per unit time that is always proportional to the mass or number of the growing individual or population.

Homeostasis: self-regulation.

Inflation: an increase in the money supply. Excessive inflation becomes a problem when the money supply increases faster than the sum of all the real assets of a society (such as land, buildings, and equipment). Thus, inflation implies a drop in the purchasing power of money.

K-strategy: a strategy of surviving by maintaining stability.

Law of diminishing returns: as the cumulative production of a resource increases, the average production cost will rise, because the most cheaply accessible proportion of the resource has already been produced.

Modal split: the proportion of all traffic carried by each mode of transportation.

Model: a mental image of how the real world functions. Most models only deal with some very small component of the real world, by intent.

Monoculture: the agricultural practice of planting out large tracts of land to one crop (such as corn).

Negative feedback loop: a control mechanism that operates by decreasing a growth rate if a system is too large, or increasing a growth rate if a system is too small.

Net energy principle: the net energy we get from any energy extraction or generation program is the gross energy obtained, less the energy spent to get this gross output.

O.P.E.C.: the Organization of Petroleum Exporting Countries.

Policy intervention package: the mix of actions we might take to deal with an environmental problem.

Population density: the number of individuals per unit area.

Population pyramid: a chart giving the number of people of each age within each sex in a population, arranged in the form of a pyramid, with infants at the bottom level.

Positive feedback loop: a closed, cause-effect pathway in a system in which increasing output leads to increased input; commonly referred to as a "vicious circle."

Price mechanism: the effects of increased price: increased supply and decreased demand.

Productivity: the rate of energy flow through a living system; typically measured as units of energy per unit area per unit time.

Proved reserves: the volume of a resource remaining to be produced, which can be recovered in the future under existing economic and operating conditions. Thus, an increase in the price of a resource will increase proved reserves, up to the point at which cost of extraction per unit equals the value of the unit extracted.

R-strategy: a strategy of success through high growth rate.

Scenario: a detailed account of one way in which the future might unfold.

Second law of thermodynamics: all energy conversion processes are inefficient.

Species: a population within which all individuals are free to interbreed; alternatively, a population of functionally homogeneous individuals.

Stagflation: inflation with recession.

Succession: a process in which groups of species replace each other through time because of changes in the environment resulting from the activities of earlier groups of species invaders into the environment.

Survival: the percentage, or proportion of a population surviving from one time to the next. Thus "egg survival" is the proportion of all just-laid eggs surviving to time of hatching.

System: the structure of the set of cause-effect pathways in a mental model of the real world.

System component: a single variable in a real world system; alternatively, a single variable enclosed by the boundary enclosing our mental model of the system.

Torts: the law of civil wrongs.

Tragedy of the commons: the situation in which a resource is not legally owned by anyone, so no one has a motive to take care of it.

Trophic level: a level within a trophic (feeding) pyramid, such as green plant, or producer level, herbivore, or carnivore level.

Trophic pyramid: a feeding pyramid, supported by a broad base of food producers or green plants, with a second level of herbivores, a third level of primary carnivores, a fourth level of secondary carnivores, and so on; rarely more than six levels high.

Utility functions: graphs representing the relative attractiveness of various values of some desired state.

Windfall profits tax: tax on added value of oil in inventory which has come about because of increase in the world price of oil.

INDEX